The Zohar

by
Rav Shimon bar Yochai
From The Book of Avraham

with
The Sulam Commentary

by
Rav Yehuda Ashlag

The First Ever Unabridged
English Translation with Commentary

Published by
The Kabbalah Centre International Inc.
Dean Rav S. P. Berg Shlita

Edited and Compiled by
Rabbi Michael Berg

Published by
The Kabbalah Centre International Inc.

155 E. 48th St., New York, NY 10017
1062 S. Robertson Blvd., Los Angeles, CA 90035

Director Rav Berg

First Printing 2001
Revised Edition 2008

Printed in USA

ISBN: 1-57189-162-5

In Loving Memory of my
father Anatoliy ben Avraham,
grandmother Esther bat Eliyahu,
grandfather Israel ben Joseph,
and all my family who's not with us.
May the Light of the Zohar elevate their Souls.

I pray for myself and the entire world,
may we connect to the Zohar's full energy and achieve
true spiritual transformation and fulfillment in this lifetime:
To my son Daniel ben Esther,
My mother Rachel bat Esther,
My brothers Iliyahu & David ben Rachel.
With so much love
to my Kabbalah family and friends.
Rav, Karen, Yehuda, Michael, and their families.
To my teacher and all the Chevre.

"It's all about the Zohar"

Esther

בזכרון אוהב
אבא שלי אנטולי בן אברהם
סבתא שלי אסתר בת אליהו
סבא שלי ישראל בן יוסף
וכל מי ממשפחתי שלא נמצא איתנו.

APPLYING THE POWER OF THE ZOHAR

The Zohar is a book of great mystical power and wisdom. It is Universally recognized as the definitive work on the Kabbalah – and it is also so Much more.

The Zohar is a wellspring of spiritual energy, a fountainhead of metaphysical power that not only reveals and explains, but literally brings blessing, protection, and well-being into the lives of all those who read or peruse its sacred texts. All that is required is worthy desire, the certainty of a trusting heart, and an open and receptive mind. Unlike other books, including the great spiritual texts of other traditions, The Zohar is written in a kind of code, through which metaphors, parables, and cryptic language at first conceal but ultimately reveal the forces of creation.

As electrical current is concealed in wire and cable before disclosing itself as an illuminated light bulb, the spiritual Light of the Creator is wrapped in allegory and symbolism throughout the Aramaic text of the Zohar. And while many books contain information and knowledge, the Zohar both expresses and embodies spiritual Light. The very letters on its pages have the power to bring spiritual wisdom and positive energy into every area of our lives.

As we visually scan the Aramaic texts and study the accompanying insights that appear in English, spiritual power is summoned from above – and worlds tremble as Light is sent forth in response.

It's primary purpose is not only to help us acquire wisdom, but to draw Light from the Upper Worlds and to bring sanctification into our lives. Indeed, the book itself is the most powerful of all tools for cleansing the soul and connecting to the Light of the Creator. As you open these pages, therefore, do not make understanding in the conventional sense your primary goal.

Although you may not have a knowledge of Aramaic, look first at the Aramaic text before reading the English. Do not be discouraged by difficulties with comprehension. Instead, open your heart to the spiritual transformation the Zohar is offering you.

Ultimately, the Zohar is an instrument for refining the individual soul – for removing darkness from the earth – and for bringing well being and blessing to our fellow man.

Its purpose is not only to make us intellectually wise, but to make us spiritually pure.

Torah

Also known as the Five Books of Moses, the Torah is considered to be the physical body of learning, whereas the Zohar is the internal soul. The literal stories of the Torah conceal countless hidden secrets.` The Zohar is the Light that illuminates all of the Torah's sublime mysteries.

Beresheet	Genesis
Shemot	Exodus
Vayikra	Leviticus
Bemidbar	Numbers
Devarim	Deuteronomy

Prophets

Amos	Amos
Chagai	Haggai
Chavakuk	Habakkuk
Hoshea	Hosea
Malachi	Malachi
Melachim	Kings
Michah	Micah
Nachum	Nahum
Ovadyah	Obadiah
Shmuel	Samuel
Shoftim	Judges
Tzefanyah	Zephaniah
Yechezkel	Ezekiel
Yehoshua	Joshua
Yeshayah	Isaiah
Yirmeyah	Jeremiah
Yoel	Joel
Yonah	Jonah
Zecharyah	Zechariah

Writings

Daniel	Daniel
Divrei Hayamim	Chronicles
Eicha	Lamentations
Ester	Esther
Ezra	Ezra
Nechemiah	Nehemiah
Iyov	Job
Kohelet	Ecclesiastes
Mishlei	Proverbs
Rut	Ruth

Sir Hashirim	Songs of Songs
Tehilim	Psalms

The Ten Sfirot – Emanations

To conceal the blinding *Light* of the Upper World, and thus create a tiny point into which our universe would be born, ten *curtains* were fabricated. These ten *curtains* are called Ten Sfirot. Each successive Sfirah further reduces the emanation of *Light*, gradually dimming its brilliance to a level almost devoid of *Light* – our physical world known as *Malchut*. The only remnant of Light remaining in this darkened universe is a *pilot light* which sustains our existence. This Light is the life force of a human being and the force that gives birth to stars, sustains suns and sets everything from swirling galaxies to busy ant hills in motion. Moreover, the Ten Sfirot act like a prism, refracting the Light into many *colors* giving rise to the diversity of life and matter in our world.

The Ten Sfirot are as follows:

Keter	Crown
Chochmah	Wisdom
Binah	Understanding
Da'at	Knowledge
Zeir Anpin	Small Face,
	(includes the next six Sfirot):
Chesed	Mercy (Chassadim - plural)
Gvurah	Judgment (Gvurot - Plural)
Tiferet	Splendor
Netzach	Victory (Eternity)
Hod	Glory
Yesod	Foundation
Malchut	Kingdom

The Partzufim - Spiritual forms

One complete structure of the Ten Sfirot creates a *Partzuf* or Spiritual Form. Together, these forces are the building blocks of all reality. As water and sand combine to create cement, the Ten Sfirot combine to produce a Spiritual Form *[Partzuf]*. Each of the Spiritual Forms below are therefore composed of one set of Ten Sfirot.

These Spiritual Forms are called:

Atik	Ancient
Atik Yomin	Ancient of Days
Atika Kadisha	Holy Ancient
Atik of Atikin	Anceint of Ancients
Aba	Father
Arich Anpin	Long Face
Ima	Mother
Nukva	Female
Tevunah	Intelligence
Yisrael Saba	Israel Grandfather
Zachar	Male

These names are not meant to be understood literally. Each represents a unique spiritual force and building block, producing a substructure and foundation for all the worlds make up reality.

The Five Worlds

All of the above Spiritual Forms *[Partzufim]* create one spiritual world. There are Five Worlds in total that compose all reality, therefore, five sets of the above Spiritual Forms are required.

Our physical world corresponds to the world of: Asiyah – Action

Adam Kadmon	Primordial Man
Atzilut	Emanation
Briyah	Creation
Yetzirah	Formation
Asiyah	Action

The Five Levels of the soul

Nefesh	First, Lowest level of Soul
Ruach	Second level of Soul
Neshamah	Third level of Soul
Chayah	Fourth level of Soul
Yechidah	Highest, fifth level of Soul

Names of God

As a single ray of white sunlight contains the seven colors of the spectrum, the one Light of the Creator embodies many diverse spiritual forces. These different forces are called *Names of God*. Each Name denotes a specific attribute and spiritual power. The Hebrew letters that compose these Names are the interface by which these varied Forces act upon our physical world. The most common Name of God is the Tetragrammaton (the four letters, *Yud Hei Vav Hei* יהוה.) Because of the enormous power that the Tetragrammaton transmits, we do not utter it aloud. When speaking of the Tetragrammaton, we use the term *Hashem* which means, *The Name*.

Adonai, El, Elohim, Hashem, Shadai, Eheyeh, Tzevaot, Yud Hei Vav Hei

People

Er	The son of Noach
Rabbi Elazar	The son of Rabbi Shimon bar Yochai
Rabbi Shimon bar Yochai	Author of the Zohar
Shem, Cham, Yefet	Noach's children
Shet	Seth
Ya'akov	Jacob
Yishai	Jesse (King David's father)
Yitzchak	Isaac
Yosef	Joseph
Yitro	Jethro
Yehuda	Judah

Angels

Angels are distinct energy components, part of a vast communication network running through the upper worlds. Each unique Angel is responsible for transmitting various forces of influence into our physical universe.

Adriel, Ahinael, Dumah (name of Angel in charge of the dead), Gabriel, Kadshiel, Kedumiel, Metatron, Michael, Rachmiel,

Raphael, Tahariel, Uriel

Nations

Nations actually represent the inner attributes and character traits of our individual self. The nation of Amalek refers to the doubt and uncertainty that dwells within us when we face hardship and obstacles. Moab represents the dual nature of man. Nefilim refers to the sparks of Light that we have defiled through our impure actions, and to the negative forces that lurk within the human soul as a result of our own wrongful deeds.

Amalek, Moab, Nefilim

General

Aba	Father
	Refers to the male principle and positive force in our universe. Correlates to the proton in an atom.
Arvit	The Evening prayer
Chayot	Animals
Chupah	Canopy (wedding ceremony)
Et	The
Avadon	Hell
Gehenom	Hell
Sheol	Hell
	The place a soul goes for purification upon leaving this world.
Ima	Mother
	The female principle and minus force in our universe. Correlates to the electron in an atom.
Kiddush	Blessing over the wine
Klipah	Shell (negativity)
Klipot	Shells (Plural)
Kriat Sh'ma	The Reading of the Sh'ma
Mashiach	Messiah
Minchah	The Afternoon prayer
Mishnah	Study
Mochin	Brain, Spiritual levels of Light
Moed	A designated time or holiday
Negev	The south of Israel
Nukva	Female

Partzuf	Face
Shacharit	The Morning prayer
Shamayim	Heavens (sky)
Shechinah	The Divine presence, The female aspect of the Creator
Tefilin	Phylacteries
The Dinur river	The river of fire
Tzadik	Righteous person
Zion	Another name for Jerusalem
Yisrael	The land of Israel
	The nation of Israel or an individual Israelite
Zohar	Splendor

The Hebrew vowels

Chirik **א**, Cholam **יא א**, Kamatz **א**, Patach **א**, Segol **א**, Sh'va **א**, Shuruk **יא א**, Tzere **א**.

The Twelve Tribes

Asher, Dan, Ephraim, Gad, Issachar, Judah, Levi, Menasheh, Naphtali, Reuben, Shimon, Zebulun

Jewish Holidays

Rosh Hashanah	The Jewish New Year
Yom Kippur	Day of Atonement
Sukkot	Holiday of the Booths
Shmini Atzeret	The day of Convocation
Simchat Torah	Holiday on which we dance with the Torah
Pesach	Passover
Shavout	Holiday of the Weeks

כרך ח

פרשת שמות וארא

Vol. VIII

Shmot, Vaera

A Prayer from The Ari

To be recited before the study of the Zohar

Ruler of the universe, and Master of all masters, The Father of mercy and forgiveness, we thank You, our God and the God of our fathers, by bowing down and kneeling, that You brought us closer to Your Torah and Your holy work, and You enable us to take part in the secrets of Your holy Torah. How worthy are we that You grant us with such big favor, that is the reason we plead before You, that You will forgive and acquit all our sins, and that they should not bring separation between You and us.

And may it be your will before You, our God and the God of our fathers, that You will awaken and prepare our hearts to love and revere You, and may You listen to our utterances, and open our closed heart to the hidden studies of Your Torah, and may our study be pleasant before Your Place of Honor, as the aroma of sweet incense, and may You emanate to us Light from the source of our soul to all of our being. And, may the sparks of your holy servants, through which you revealed Your wisdom to the world, shine.

May their merit and the merit of their fathers, and the merit of their Torah, and holiness, support us so we shall not stumble through our study. And by their merit enlighten our eyes in our learning as it stated by King David, The Sweet Singer of Israel: "Open my eyes, so that I will see wonders from Your Torah" (Tehilim 119:18). Because from His mouth God gives wisdom and understanding.

"May the utterances of my mouth and the thoughts of my heart find favor before You, God, my Strength and my Redeemer" (Tehilim 19:15).

SHEMOT

Names of the articles

1. "And these are the names"

A Synopsis

An explanation of the title verse proceeds from a discussion of the meaning of the quotation, "And they who are wise…" This, we learn, contains the secret of the Firmament, which illuminates the Garden of Eden and the Tree of Life. Those imbued with supernal Wisdom – the internal and external angels, and the life giving souls born of the Tree of Life – inhabit the Tree, and these beings merit eternal life. The branches of the Tree spread over all forms and beings of Holiness, and the fruit of the Tree gives life to all. The side of Impurity, however, does not dwell in the Tree of Life, and derives no nourishment from it. There follows a description of the splendor of the Tree, which ascends to great heights, and the one radiation in the Tree, which contains the colors white, red and green. Rising in direct light and descending in returning light, these colors come to rest only in the Tree. From this Tree, the twelve Tribes of Israel went down into the exile of Egypt with the light that does not illuminate (Malchut), accompanied by multitudes of heavenly hosts.

The Relevance of the Passage

This passage explains that those of us who embrace the "secret of wisdom--which is the Holy Zohar – sparkle and shine with the Light of Chochmah. Chochmah is one of the highest spiritual dimensions of the Upper World. This is the flawless reality known by the code term "Tree of Life."

The Tree of Life is the source of our joy. It's the place where wisdom and pleasure come from. It is a realm of immortality and eternal peace. When we're connected to this divine dimension, we know only fulfillment, joy, and perfection. The turmoil of human existence occurs when we find our ourselves disconnected from the Tree of Life, languishing in our physical domain of darkness known as the Tree of Knowledge reality.

The opening verses of this powerful section of Zohar unite us with the Tree of Life. Immediately, order emerges from chaos. We are impervious to the negative influences of the twelve constellations.

The illumination we generate by virtue of these verses banishes darkness from our lives and from all existence. We ignite the forces of immortality, expelling death from human existence. We become wise in the ways of the Creator.

Upon the merit of this passage, our exile ends as we rise out of Egypt (the material world of pain and suffering) and experience the Garden of Eden forevermore.

1. וְאֵלֶּה שְׁמוֹת בְּנֵי יִשְׂרָאֵל הַבָּאִים מִצְרַיְמָה אֵת יַעֲקֹב אִישׁ וּבֵיתוֹ בָּאוּ, וְהַמַּשְׂכִּילִים יַזְהִירוּ כְּזֹהַר הָרָקִיעַ וּמַצְדִּיקֵי הָרַבִּים כַּכּוֹכָבִים לְעוֹלָם וָעֶד וְהַמַּשְׂכִּילִים: אִלֵּין אִינוּן דְּמִסְתַּכְּלֵי בְּרָזָא דְּחָכְמְתָא. יַזְהִירוּ: נַהֲרִין, וְנָצְצִין בְּזִיוָא דְּחָכְמְתָא עִלָּאָה. כְּזֹהַר: נְהִירוּ וּנְצִיצוּ דְּנַהֲרָא דְּנָפִיק מֵעֵדֶן. וְדָא אִיהוּ רָזָא סְתִימָא, דְּאִקְרֵי רָקִיעַ. בֵּיהּ קַיְימִין כּוֹכָבַיָּא וּמַזָּלֵי שִׁמְשָׁא וְסִיהֲרָא, וְכָל אִינוּן בּוּצִינִין דִּנְהוֹרָא.

1. "And these are the names of the children of Israel who came into Egypt with Jacob, every man came with his household" (Shemot 1:1). "And they who are wise shall shine as the brightness of the firmament; and they who turn many to righteousness like the stars for ever and ever" (Daniel 12:3). "And they who are wise," are those who observe the secret of wisdom; "shall shine," means they illuminate and sparkle with the shine of supernal Chochmah; and "as the brightness," MEANS the brightness and sparkle of the river that emanates from Eden. This is the concealed secret that is called 'firmament'" for in it are located the stars and the constellations, the sun, WHICH IS THE ZEIR ANPIN, and moon, WHICH IS THE NUKVA, and all the candles that give light, WHICH ARE ALL THE LIGHTS THAT ARE IN THE WORLDS BRIYAH, YETZIRAH AND ASIYAH.

2. זֹהַר דְּהַאי רָקִיעַ נָהִיר בִּנְהִירוּ עַל גִּנְתָּא. וְאִילָנָא דְּחַיֵּי קַיָּים בִּמְצִיעוּת גִּנְתָּא. דְּעַנְפּוֹי חַפְיָין עַל כָּל אִינוּן דְּיוֹקְנִין וְאִילָנִין וּבוּסְמִין דִּבְגִנְתָּא, בְּמָאנִין דְּכַשְׁרָן. וּתְטַלְּלִין תְּחוֹתֵיהּ כָּל חֵיוַת בָּרָא. וְכָל צִפֳּרֵי שְׁמַיָּא יְדוּרוּן תְּחוֹת אִינוּן עַנְפִין.

2. The brightness of this firmament illuminates the garden, WHICH IS MALCHUT, and the Tree of Life, WHICH IS TIFERET, stands in the center of the garden – THAT IS, IN THE CENTRAL COLUMN. Its branches, ITS SFIROT, cover all forms, NEFASHOT, trees, RUCHOT, and spices, NESHAMOT, in the garden that are in fitted vessels, MEANING THEY HAVE THREE COLUMNS, RIGHT, LEFT AND CENTRAL. And all the wild animals, WHO ARE THE EXTERNAL ANGELS, find shelter in its shadow. And all the birds of the sky, THE INTERNAL ANGELS, sit under its branches.

3. זֹהַר אִיבָּא דְּאִילָנָא, יָהִיב חַיִּין לְכֹלָּא. קִיּוּמֵיהּ לְעָלַם וּלְעָלְמֵי עָלְמִין

סְטְרָא אַחֲרָא לָא שַׁרְיָא בֵּיהּ, אֶלָּא סְטְרָא דִקְדוּשָׁה. זַכָּאָה חוּלְקֵיהוֹן אִינוּן דְּטַעֲמִין מִנֵּיה, אִינוּן קַיְימִין לְעָלַם וּלְעָלְמֵי עָלְמִין. אִלֵּין אִקְרוּן מַשְׂכִּילִים, וְזַכָּאָן חַיִּין בְּהַאי עָלְמָא, וְחַיִּין בְּעָלְמָא דְאָתֵי.

3. The splendor of the fruits of the tree, WHICH ARE THE SOULS THAT ARE BORN FROM IT, gives life to all. It exists forever. The Other Side OF IMPURITY does not dwell in it, MEANING THAT THE OTHER SIDE HAS NO NOURISHMENT FROM THE TREE OF LIFE, WHICH IS ZEIR ANPIN IN GREATNESS. Only the side of holiness is nourished. Fortunate are those who taste from it, for they live eternally, AS IS WRITTEN: "AND HE WILL TAKE ALSO FROM THE TREE OF LIFE AND EAT AND WILL LIVE FOREVER" (BERESHEET 3:22). They are called "they who are wise" and merit life in this world and in the World to Come.

4. זֹהַר אִילָנָא דָא, זַקְפָא לְעֵילָא לְעֵילָא. חֲמֵשׁ מְאָה פַּרְסֵי הֲלוּכֵיה, שִׁתִּין רִבּוֹא אִיהוּ, בִּפְשִׁיטוּתֵיה. בְּהַאי אִילָנָא, קַיְימָא חַד זֹהֲרָא, כָּל גַּוְונִין קַיְימִין בֵּיה אִינוּן גַּוְונִין סָלְקִין וְנַחְתִּין, לָא מִתְיַשְּׁבֵי בְּדוּכְתָּא אַחֲרָא בַּר בְּהַהוּא אִילָנָא.

4. The splendor of this tree, WHICH IS ZEIR ANPIN, rises higher, and higher. WHEN RISING it is a distance of 500 parasangs. WHEN RISING HIGHER, its spread is 600,000 parasangs. In this tree, there is one radiation, WHICH IS MALCHUT, in which body, all the colors – WHITE, RED AND GREEN, WHICH ARE THE SECRET OF THE LIGHTS OF CHESED, GVURAH AND TIFERET – exist. These colors rise IN OR YASHAR ('DIRECT LIGHT') and descend IN OR CHOZER ('RETURNING LIGHT'), and do not settle anywhere except in this tree BECAUSE IT IS THE SECRET OF THE CENTRAL COLUMN.

5. כַּד נָפְקֵי מִנֵּיה לְאִתְחֲזָאָה בְּגוֹ זֹהַר דְּלָא נַהֲרָא, מִתְיַשְּׁבָן וְלָא מִתְיַשְּׁבָן, קַיְימָן וְלָא קַיְימָן, בְּגִין דְּלָא מִתְיַשְּׁבָן בְּאֲתָר אַחֲרָא. מֵאִילָנָא דָא נָפְקֵי תְּרֵיסַר שְׁבָטִין. דְּמִתְחַמָּן בֵּיה, וְאִינוּן נַחְתּוּ בְּהַאי זֹהַר דְּלָא נַהֲרָא, לְגוֹ גָלוּתָא דְמִצְרַיִם, בְּכַמָּה מַשִׁירְיָין עִלָּאִין, הה"ד וְאֵלֶּה שְׁמוֹת בְּנֵי יִשְׂרָאֵל וְגוֹ'.

5. When THE LIGHTS emanate from it, FROM THE TREE, to appear in the glow that does not illuminate, THESE LIGHTS sometimes settle and SOMETIMES do not settle in it; they sometimes exist and sometimes do not exist, because they settle in no other place EXCEPT THIS TREE. From this tree emanated twelve tribes whose boundaries are therein contained. They descended in this splendor that does not illuminate, into the exile of Egypt with many supernal camps. This is the meaning of: "And these are the names of the children of Israel…"

2. "The word of Hashem was"

A Synopsis

From Rabbi Shimon's discourse on the title verse, we learn that the word *hayah* is repeated in the title quotation because the first refers to the exile in Egypt and the second to the Babylonian exile. Rabbi Shimon reinforces Ezekial's role as a faithful prophet in his comparison of the Babylonian and the Egyptian exiles. The Babylonian captivity, we learn, caused far more pain and suffering for the children of Israel than the Egyptian exile. The children of Israel were able to endure the exile in Egypt patiently because they were familiar with the suffering of their father, the righteous Jacob. However, the Babylonian exile brought suffering to the point of despair, and they came to believe that God had deserted them. As a result, they were pitied in heaven and on earth, and God called His entire celestial army together and sent them to be with the children of Yisrael in captivity. When they arrived, the spirit of Prophecy descended on Ezekial. He announced his vision to the children of Israel, but they did not believe him. Thus, he was compelled to reveal his entire celestial vision to them. At this, their joy and love for God returned. This is why Ezekial revealed the whole of his vision – and with the permission of God.

The Relevance of the Passage

When we choose to walk the spiritual path, our moments of hurting and sorrow are mercifully brief. If, however, one indulges his own self-seeking desires, then suffering is intensified and prolonged. The Light cast through this particular narrative ends our personal and global exile. The tears that have flowed throughout history, and those that flow today are dried up as the Heavens open to reveal the warming rays of the Creator. Upon the merit of Jacob, whose magnificent soul encompasses all humanity, we rejoice as our redemption is actualized through this awesome Book of Splendor.

6. רִבִּי שִׁמְעוֹן פָּתַח, הָיָה הָיָה דְּבַר ה', הָיָה הָיָה תְּרֵי זִמְנֵי אֲמַאי. וְתוּ אִית לִשְׁאֵלָה, אִי יְחֶזְקֵאל נְבִיאָה מְהֵימָנָא הֲוָה, אֲמַאי גַּלֵּי כָּל מַה דְּחָמָא, מַאן דְּמַלְכָּא אָעִיל לֵיה בְּהֵיכָלֵיה אִית לֵיה לְגַלָּאָה רָזִין דְּחָמֵי. אֶלָּא וַדַּאי יְחֶזְקֵאל נְבִיאָה מְהֵימָנָא הֲוָה, וְכָל מַה דְּחָמָא בִּמְהֵימָנוּתָא אִיהוּ, וּבִרְשׁוּתָא דְּקוּדְשָׁא בְּרִיךְ הוּא גַּלֵּי כָּל מַה דְּגַלֵּי, וְכֹלָּא אִצְטְרִיךְ.

6. Rabbi Shimon opened the discussion saying: "The word of Hashem was (Heb. *hayoh hayah*)..." (Yechezkel 1:1). HE ASKS: Why is the word *hayah* repeated twice? We should further ask why Ezekiel revealed all that he saw if he was a faithful prophet. Should one whom the King brought into His sanctuary reveal what he saw? HE ANSWERS: Certainly Ezekiel was a faithful prophet, and all that he saw was by Faith, and whatever he revealed was with the permission of the Holy One, blessed be He, and all was as it should have been.

7. אָמַר ר"ש, מַאן דְּרָגִיל לְמִסְבַּל צַעֲרָא אע"ג דְּאָתֵי לְפוּם שַׁעְתָּא צַעֲרָא, סָבִיל מַטְלָנוֹי, וְלָא חָיִישׁ, אֲבָל מַאן דְּלָא רָגִיל בְּצַעַר, וַהֲוָה כָּל יוֹמוֹי בְּתַפְנוּקִין וְעִידוּנִין, וְאָתֵי לֵיהּ צַעֲרָא, דָּא אִיהוּ צַעֲרָא שְׁלִים, וְעַל דָּא אִצְטְרִיךְ לְמִבְכֵּי.

7. Rabbi Shimon said: Even though pain comes to him temporarily, someone who is accustomed to suffer pain bears his yoke and does not worry. But when pain comes to one who has spent all his days in pleasures and luxuries and is not accustomed to pain, this is complete pain and deserves weeping.

8. כָּךְ יִשְׂרָאֵל, כַּד נַחְתּוּ לְמִצְרַיִם, רְגִילִין בְּצַעֲרָא הֲווֹ, דְּהָא כָּל יוֹמוֹי דְּהַהוּא זַכָּאָה אֲבוּהוֹן בְּצַעֲרָא הֲוָה, וְעַל דָּא סָבְלוּ גָּלוּתָא כַּדְקָא יָאוֹת. אֲבָל גָּלוּתָא דְּבָבֶל הַהוּא הֲוָה צַעֲרָא שְׁלִים, הַהוּא הֲוָה צַעֲרָא דְּעֶלָאִין וְתַתָּאִין בְּכָאן עֲלֵיהּ.

8. Yisrael was accustomed to pain when descending into Egypt, for all the days of that righteous man, their father, were spent in pain. Therefore, they endured the exile properly AND DID NOT WORRY GREATLY. But the exile of Babylon was in complete pain; it was a pain for which both those above and below wept.

9. עֶלָאִין: דִּכְתִּיב, הֵן אֶרְאֶלָּם צָעֲקוּ חוּצָה וְגוֹ'. תַּתָּאִין: דִּכְתִּיב: עַל נַהֲרוֹת בָּבֶל שָׁם יָשַׁבְנוּ וְגוֹ' כֻּלְּהוֹן בָּכוּ עַל גָּלוּתָא דְּבָבֶל. מ"ט. בְּגִין דַּהֲווֹ בְּתַפְנוּקֵי מַלְכִין דִּכְתִּיב בְּנֵי צִיּוֹן הַיְקָרִים וְגוֹ'.

9. Those above wept, as it is written: "Behold, the mighty ones shall cry outside" (Yeshayah 33:7). Those below cried, as it is written: "By the rivers

-9-

of Babylon, there we sat down..." (Tehilim 137:1). They all wept over the exile of Babylon. Why? Because previously they had the luxuries of kings, as is written: "The precious sons of Zion..." (Eichah 4:2).

10. דִּתְנַן אָמַר רִבִּי יִצְחָק, מַאי דִּכְתִּיב עַל הֶהָרִים אֶשָּׂא בְכִי וָנֶהִי. אֶלָּא, אִלֵּין אִינּוּן טוּרַיָּא רָמָיָא דְּעָלְמִין. וּמַאן אִינּוּן טוּרַיָּא רָמָיָא, אִינּוּן, בְּנֵי צִיּוֹן הַיְקָרִים הַמְסוּלָּאִים בַּפָּז וְהַשְׁתָּא הֲווֹ נַחְתִּין בְּגָלוּתָא, בְּרֵיחַיָּא עַל קַדְלֵיהוֹן וִידֵיהוֹן מְהַדְּקָן לַאֲחוֹרָא. וְכַד עָאלוּ בְּגָלוּתָא בְּבָבֶל, חָשִׁיבוּ דְּהָא לֵית לְהוּ קִיוּמָא לְעָלְמִין, דְּהָא קוּדְשָׁא בְּרִיךְ הוּא שָׁבִיק לוֹן, וְלָא יַשְׁגַּח בְּהוֹן לְעָלְמִין.

10. As we learned, Rabbi Yitzchak said: What is meant by the verse, "On the mountains I will take up a weeping and wailing" (Yirmeyah 9:9)? The mountains that are referred to are the loftiest in the world. And who are these lofty mountains? They are "the precious sons of Zion comparable to fine gold." And now they are descending into exile with grindstones on their necks and their hands tied behind. And when they arrived in the exile of Babylon, they thought that they would never have support because the Holy One, blessed be He, had forsaken them and would no longer watch over them.

11. וְתָנֵינָן, אָמַר רִבִּי שִׁמְעוֹן, בְּהַהִיא שַׁעֲתָא קָרָא קוּדְשָׁא בְּרִיךְ הוּא לְכָל פָּמַלְיָא דִּילֵיהּ, וְכָל רְתִיכִין קַדִּישִׁין, וְכָל חֵילֵיהּ וּמַשְׁרְיָּיתֵיהּ, וְרַבְרְבָנוֹי, וְכָל חֵילָא דִּשְׁמַיָּא, וְאָמַר לוֹן, מָה אַתּוּן עַבְדִּין הָכָא, וּמָה בְּנֵי רְחִימָאי בְּגָלוּתָא דְּבָבֶל, וְאַתּוּן הָכָא, קוּמוּ חוּתוּ כֻּלְּכוֹן לְבָבֶל, וַאֲנָא עִמְּכוֹן. הֲדָא הוּא דִּכְתִּיב, כֹּה אָמַר ה' לְמַעַנְכֶם שִׁלַּחְתִּי בָבֶלָה וְגוֹ'. לְמַעַנְכֶם שִׁלַּחְתִּי בָבֶלָה, דָּא קוּדְשָׁא בְּרִיךְ הוּא. וְהוֹרַדְתִּי בָרִיחִים כֻּלָּם, אִלֵּין כָּל רְתִיכִין וּמַשְׁרְיָּין עִלָּאִין.

11. We learned that Rabbi Shimon said: At that moment, the Holy One, blessed be He, summoned all His company, all the Chariots and camps and His officers and all the hosts of heaven. And he said to them: 'What are you doing here? My beloved children are in the exile of Babylon and you are here! Arise, all of you descend to Babylon and I with you.' This is the

meaning of: "Thus says Hashem, 'For your sake I have sent to Babylon'" (Yeshayah 43:14). This refers to the Holy One, blessed be He. "And will bring down all of them as fugitives..." (Ibid.). These are all the supernal Chariots and camps.

12. כַּד נַחֲתוּ לְבָבֶל, אִתְפַּתָּחוּ שְׁמַיָּא, וְשַׁרְאַת רוּחַ נְבוּאָה קַדִּישָׁא עַל יְחֶזְקֵאל, וְחָמָא כָּל מַה דְּחָמָא, וְאָמַר לוֹן לְיִשְׂרָאֵל, הָא מָארֵיכוֹן הָכָא, וְכָל חֵילֵי שְׁמַיָּא וּרְתִיכוּ, דְּאָתוּ לְמֵידָר בֵּינַיְכוּ. לָא הֵימְנוּהוּ, עַד דְּאִצְטְרִיךְ לְגַלָּאָה כָּל מַה דְּחָמָא, וָאֵרֶא כָּךְ, וָאֵרֶא כָּךְ. וְאִי גַּלֵּי יַתִּיר, מַה דְּגַלֵּי כֹּלָּא אִצְטְרִיךְ. כֵּיוָן דְּחָמוּ יִשְׂרָאֵל כָּךְ, חַדוּ. וְכַד שָׁמְעוּ מִלִּין מִפּוּמֵיהּ דִּיחֶזְקֵאל, לָא חַיְישׁוּ עַל גָּלוּתְהוֹן כְּלָל, דְּהָא יָדְעוּ דְקוּדְשָׁא בְּרִיךְ הוּא לָא שָׁבִיק לוֹן. וְכָל מַה דְּגַלֵּי בִּרְשׁוּתָא גַּלֵּי.

12. When they descended to Babylon, the heavens opened and the holy spirit of prophecy rested on Ezekiel. And he saw whatever he saw and said to Yisrael: 'Behold your Master is here and all the hosts of heaven and the Chariots that have come to dwell with you.' They did not believe him until he was obliged to reveal all that he saw – 'I saw thus, I saw thus...' and if he revealed more, whatever he revealed was altogether necessary. As soon as Yisrael saw this, they rejoiced. And when they heard the words from Ezekiel's mouth, they no longer feared their exile at all because they knew that the Holy One, blessed be He, would not leave them. And everything that he revealed, he revealed with permission.

13. וְתָנֵינָן בְּכָל אֲתַר דְּיִשְׂרָאֵל גָּלוּ, תַּמָּן שְׁכִינְתָּא גָּלְתָה עִמְּהוֹן, וְהָכָא בְּגָלוּתָא דְּמִצְרַיִם מַה כְּתִיב, וְאֵלֶּה שְׁמוֹת בְּנֵי יִשְׂרָאֵל וְגוֹ'. כֵּיוָן דִּכְתִיב בְּנֵי יִשְׂרָאֵל, מַהוּ אֶת יַעֲקֹב, הַבָּאִים אֹתוֹ אִצְטְרִיךְ לְמֵימַר. אֶלָּא, אֵלֶּה שְׁמוֹת בְּנֵי יִשְׂרָאֵל אִינוּן רְתִיכִין וּמַשִׁרְיָין עִלָּאִין, דְּנַחֲתוּ עִם יַעֲקֹב, בַּהֲדֵי שְׁכִינְתָּא, בְּגָלוּתָא דְּמִצְרַיִם.

13. We learned that in each and every place to which Yisrael was exiled, the Shechinah was exiled with them. And here by the exile of Egypt, it is written: "And these are the names of the children of Israel..." (Shemot 1:1). AND HE ASKS: Since it is written, "the children of Yisrael," why does it conclude: "with Jacob"? It should have said, 'Who came with him.' AND

HE ANSWERS: "These are the names of the children of Israel," refers to the supernal Chariots and camps that descended with Jacob together with the Shechinah into the exile of Egypt. THIS ALSO ANSWERS WHY "HAYOH-HAYAH" (YECHEZKEL 1:3) IS WRITTEN TWICE. THE FIRST HAYOH REFERS TO THE EXILE OF EGYPT, AND THE SECOND HAYAH REFERS TO THE EXILE OF BABYLON.

3. "Come with me from Lebanon, my bride"

A Synopsis

Rabbi Chiya opens a discussion of the meaning of the title verse with his interpretation. He explains that God spoke these words to the children of Israel upon the presenting them with the Torah on Mt. Sinai. Unlike the children of Seir and the children of Ishmael, who refused the Torah when it was offered to them, the children of Israel accepted the Torah, united in faith and Holiness. In answer to the question regarding the meaning of the verse, "He came in Holy multitudes," Rabbi Chiya refers to an ancient tradition that reveals how the heavenly multitudes protested at the moment when God was about to present the Torah to the children of Israel, since they desired it for themselves. God rebuked the angels, explaining that the laws contained therein are not designed for those unable to participate in such evils as murder, adultery, falsehoods, and so on. The angels then ended their protests and praised God for His wisdom, which was even too subtle for them to grasp fully.

This explanation of, "He came in Holy multitudes," leads Rabbi Yosi to offer an alternative interpretation, relating it to the descent of the Shechinah into the Egyptian captivity.

Finally, Rabbi Shimon provides his contrasting interpretation of the title verse. He explains that this verse contains allusions to the mystical union between Voice and Speech. The relationship between these forms is one of interdependence, as wisdom cannot be transmitted orally without the throat, breath, tongue and lips, all of which are referenced in the verse.

The Relevance of the Passage

Unification between the Upper World and our Lower World, between humans and the Light of the Creator, is the underlying theme woven throughout this passage.

For instance, the phrase "my bride" refers to the moon, which is made full and complete by the sun's light, which is represented here by "Lebanon." In the same way, our physical world is fulfilled by the Upper World.

Next, the Zohar speaks of the union voice and speech. The phrase "the voice of His word" (paragraph 15) alludes to Creator's profound unity as revealed by the Torah.

Human speech, we're told, equates to our physical world; and voice pertains to the realm of Zeir Anpin, the Upper World, our source of Light. Through the power of speech, we can unite the two worlds.

This profound unification is achieved through the vocalization of the Torah during the Sabbath (and the reading or scanning of Zohar at any time).

When our world is disconnected from the spiritual realm, there is darkness in our life. This simple truth is alluded to in the verse:

"Voice is not COMPLETE without speech and speech is not COMPLETE without voice" (Paragraph 19).

Often, our own words in fact disconnect us from the Source of all goodness. When we speak unkind words borne of anger, hostility, or envy, we sever our connection to the Creator. Moreover, our words are often weapons that cause spiritual murder. When we humiliate someone, thus causing blood to rush to his face from embarrassment, then we have committed the sin of *spilling blood.* Or if we utter words that slander and defame another person, we have destroyed her character.

This passage purifies us from previous sins committed through the words we have spoken. The impulse to speak *evil tongue* is eradicated from our nature.

The mystical vibrations that arise from the Torah readings resonate throughout existence. We now achieve unification with the Upper World by virtue of the Zohar verses that explicate upon these sublime mysteries.

14. וְאֵלֶּה שְׁמוֹת בְּנֵי יִשְׂרָאֵל הַבָּאִים מִצְרָיְמָה אֵת יַעֲקֹב אִישׁ וּבֵיתוֹ בָּאוּ. רִבִּי חִיָּיא פָּתַח אִתִּי מִלְּבָנוֹן כַּלָּה אִתִּי מִלְּבָנוֹן תָּבוֹאִי תָּשׁוּרִי מֵרֹאשׁ אֲמָנָה מֵרֹאשׁ שְׂנִיר וְחֶרְמוֹן מִמְּעוֹנוֹת אֲרָיוֹת מֵהַרְרֵי נְמֵרִים. הַאי קְרָא עַל כְּנֶסֶת יִשְׂרָאֵל אִתְּמַר, בְּשַׁעֲתָא דְּנַפְקוּ יִשְׂרָאֵל מִמִּצְרַיִם, וְקָרִיבוּ לְטוּרָא דְּסִינַי לְקַבְּלָא אוֹרַיְיתָא, אָמַר לָהּ קוּדְשָׁא בְּרִיךְ הוּא, אִתִּי מִלְּבָנוֹן: מִן הַהוּא עֲדוּנָא עִלָּאָה קָא אָתָאת. כַּלָּה: שְׁלֵימָתָא, כְּהַאי סִיהֲרָא דְּאִשְׁתְּלִימַת מִן שִׁמְשָׁא בְּכָל נְהוֹרָא וּנְצִיצוּ, אִתִּי מִלְּבָנוֹן תָּבוֹאִי, בְּגִין לְקַבְּלָא בָּנַיִךְ אוֹרַיְיתָא.

14. "And these are the names of the children of Israel who came into Egypt with Jacob; every man came with his household" (Shemot 1:1). Rabbi Chiya opened the discussion saying: "Come with me from Lebanon, my bride, with me from Lebanon: look from the top of Amanah, from the top of Senir and Chermon, from the lions' dens, from the mountains of the leopards"

(Shir Hashirm 4:8). This verse refers to the Congregation of Yisrael, WHICH IS MALCHUT. At the time that Yisrael left Egypt and approached Mt. Sinai to receive the Torah, the Holy One, blessed be He, said to her, "with me from Lebanon," MEANING that she comes from the supernal Eden, WHICH IS CHOCHMAH THAT IS CALLED 'LEBANON'. Bride MEANS 'whole', like the moon that is made whole by the sun with all the light and sparkle, WHICH ARE *OR YASHAR* ('DIRECT LIGHT') AND *OR CHOZER* ('RETURNING LIGHT'). "Come with me from Lebanon," in order that your children shall receive the Torah. UNTILL MALCHUT CAN RECEIVE CHOCHMAH, WHICH IS CALLED 'LEBANON', YISRAEL CAN NOT RECEIVE THE TORAH BECAUSE THEY LACK THE FIRST THREE SFIROT.

15. תָּשׁוּרִי מֵרֹאשׁ אֲמָנָה, תָּשׁוּרִי: כד"א וּתְשׁוּרָה אֵין לְהָבִיא. תְּקַבִּיל תַּקְרוּבְתָּא עַל בָּנַיִךְ. מֵרֹאשׁ אֲמָנָה: מֵרֵאשִׁיתָא דְּעָאֲלוּ בִּמְהֵימָנוּתָא עִלָּאָה, וְאָמְרוּ כָּל אֲשֶׁר דִּבֶּר ה' נַעֲשֶׂה וְנִשְׁמָע, וַהֲווֹ בְּמַתְקְלָא חֲדָא כְּמַלְאָכִין עִלָּאִין, דְּהָכִי כְּתִיב בְּהוּ, בָּרְכוּ ה' מַלְאָכָיו גִּבּוֹרֵי כֹחַ עוֹשֵׂי דְבָרוֹ לִשְׁמוֹעַ בְּקוֹל דְּבָרוֹ. כְּדֵין קַבִּילַת כְּנֶסֶת יִשְׂרָאֵל תְּשׁוּרָה.

15. "Look (Heb. *tashuri*) from the top of Amanah." "*Tashuri*" has the same meaning as in "There is not a present (Heb. *teshurah*) to bring" (I Shmuel 9:7). LIKEWISE, "*TASHURI*" MEANS accept a present for your children; "from the top of Amanah" – meaning when they came in the beginning with supernal Faith (Heb. *emunah*) and said: "All that Hashem has spoken we will do and obey" (Shemot 24:7). And they were equal to supernal angels, as is written about them: "Bless Hashem, you angels of His, you mighty ones who perform His bidding, hearkening to the voice of His word" (Tehilim 103:20). Then the Congregation of Yisrael received a present WHICH IS REFERRED TO IN: "*TASHURI* FROM THE TOP OF AMANAH," WHICH MEANS ADDITIONAL MOCHIN.

16. מֵרֹאשׁ שְׂנִיר וְחֶרְמוֹן: דָּא טוּרָא דְּסִינַי, דְּקָרִיבוּ לְגַבֵּיהּ, וְאִתְעֲתָּדוּ תְּחוֹתֵיהּ. דִּכְתִיב, וַיִּתְיַצְּבוּ בְּתַחְתִּית הָהָר. מִמְּעֹנוֹת אֲרָיוֹת: אִלֵּין בְּנֵי שֵׂעִיר דְּקוּדְשָׁא בְּרִיךְ הוּא זַמִּין לוֹן בְּאוֹרַיְיתָא, וְלָא בָּעוּ לְקַבְּלָהּ, מֵהַרְרֵי נְמֵרִים: אִלֵּין בְּנֵי יִשְׁמָעֵאל. דִּכְתִיב ה' מִסִּינַי בָּא וְזָרַח מִשֵּׂעִיר לָמוֹ הוֹפִיעַ מֵהַר פָּארָן וְאָתָא מֵרִבְבוֹת קֹדֶשׁ.

16. "From the top of Senir and Chermon" (Shir Hashirum 4:8). This was Mount Sinai that they approached and gathered under, as is written: "And they stood at the foot of the mountain" (Shemot 19:17). The lions' dens" (Shir Hashirm 4:8), are the children of Seir that the Holy One, blessed be He, invited to receive the Torah, but they did not want to accept it. "From the mountains of leopards" (Ibid.), are the children of Ishmael, as it is written: "Hashem came from Sinai, and rose from Seir to them; He shone forth from mount Paran, and He came from holy multitudes" (Devarim 33:2). PARAN IS THE CHILDREN OF ISHMAEL.

‏17. מַאי וְאָתָא מֵרִבְבוֹת קֹדֶשׁ. דְּתָנֵינָן, כַּד בָּעָא קוּדְשָׁא בְּרִיךְ הוּא לְמֵיהַב אוֹרַיְיתָא לְיִשְׂרָאֵל, אָתוּ מַשִׁרְיָין דְּמַלְאָכִין עִלָּאִין, פַּתְחוּ וְאָמְרוּ, ה׳ אֲדוֹנֵינוּ מָה אַדִּיר שִׁמְךָ בְּכָל הָאָרֶץ אֲשֶׁר תְּנָה הוֹדְךָ עַל הַשָּׁמָיִם, בָּעָאן דְּיִתְיְהִיב לוֹן אוֹרַיְיתָא.

17. What is the meaning of: "And he came from holy multitudes" (Ibid.)? We learned that when the Holy One, blessed be He, wanted to give the Torah to Yisrael, camps of supernal angels came and said: "Hashem our ruler, how majestic is Your name in all the earth; who have set Your glory above the heavens" (Tehilim 8:2). Then they asked that the Torah be given to them AND NOT TO YISRAEL.

‏18. אָמַר לוֹן קוּדְשָׁא בְּרִיךְ הוּא, וְכִי אִית בְּכוֹן מוֹתָא, דִּכְתִּיב, אָדָם כִּי יָמוּת בְּאֹהֶל. וְכִי יִהְיֶה בְאִישׁ חֵטְא מִשְׁפַּט מָוֶת וְהוּמָת. חֵטְא אִית בֵּינַיְיכוּ, וְכִי אַתּוּן בָּעָאן לְדִינִין. אִית בֵּנַיְיכוּ גֵּזֶל. אוֹ גְּנֵבָה, דִּכְתִּיב, לֹא תִגְנוֹב. אִית בֵּינַיְיכוּ נָשִׁין דִּכְתִּיב, לֹא תִּנְאָף. אִית בֵּינַיְיכוּ שְׁקָרָא, דִּכְתִּיב, לֹא תַעֲנֶה בְרֵעֲךָ עֵד שָׁקֶר. אִית בֵּינַיְיכוּ חֶמְדָּה, דִּכְתִּיב, לֹא תַחְמוֹד. מַה אַתּוּן בָּעָאן אוֹרַיְיתָא. מִיָּד פַּתְחוּ וְאָמְרוּ, ה׳ אֲדוֹנֵינוּ מָה אַדִּיר שִׁמְךָ בְּכָל הָאָרֶץ. וְאִלּוּ אֲשֶׁר תְּנָה הוֹדְךָ עַל הַשָּׁמַיִם לָא כְּתִיב. וְע״ד וְאָתָא מֵרִבְבוֹת קֹדֶשׁ, כְּדֵין מִימִינוֹ אֵשׁ דָּת לָמוֹ.

18. The Holy One, blessed be He, said to them: 'Are you mortal, as written, "When a man shall die in a tent" (Bemidbar 19:14), "And if a man have committed a sin worthy of death, and he is put to death" (Devarim 21:22)? Do you have sins that you need laws? Is there robbery or stealing among you, as written, "You shall not steal" (Shemot 20:13)? Have you women, as written: "You shall not commit adultery" (Ibid.)? Do you have falsehood that it says, "Do not bear false witness against your neighbor" (Ibid. 14)? Do you have coveting that it is written, "You shall not covet" (Ibid. 13)? Why are you requesting the Torah?' Immediately they said: "Hashem our ruler, how majestic is Your Name in all the earth." But, "who have set Your glory above the heavens" is not written. Therefore it says, "And He came from holy multitudes" (Devarim 33:2), MEANING THAT HE CAME FROM NEGOTIATING WITH THE ANGELS. Then it says: "From His right hand went a fiery law for them" (Ibid.), WHICH IS THE TORAH WHICH IS LIKENED TO FIRE BECAUSE OF THE JUDGMENT THAT IS IN IT. THUS, SEIR AND ISHMAEL DID NOT WANT TO ACCEPT IT UPON THEMSELVES, AND THE ANGELS COULD NOT ACCEPT BECAUSE THEY DO NOT HAVE THE QUALITY OF JUDGMENT.

19. ר' יוֹסֵי אוֹקִים לְהַאי קְרָא, כַּד נַחְתָּא שְׁכִינְתָּא בְּגָלוּתָא דְּמִצְרַיִם. ור"ש אָמַר, הַאי קְרָא, עַל רָזָא דְּיִחוּדָא דִּמְהֵימָנוּתָא אִתְּמַר, אָתִי מִלְּבָנוֹן כַּלָּה, קוֹל אָמַר לְדִבּוּר אָתִי, בְּגִין דְּהָא קוֹל אָתֵי לְדִבּוּר, וּמְדַבֵּר לָה בַּהֲדֵיהּ, לְמֶהֱוֵי כַּחֲדָא בְּלָא פֵּרוּדָא כְּלָל. בְּגִין דְּקוֹל אִיהוּ כְּלָל, דִּבּוּר אִיהוּ פְּרָט. וע"ד כְּלָל אִצְטְרִיךְ לִפְרָט, וּפְרָט אִצְטְרִיךְ לִכְלָל. דְּהָא לֵית קוֹל בְּלָא דִבּוּר, וְלֵית דִּבּוּר בְּלָא קוֹל. וע"ד אָתֵי מִלְּבָנוֹן כַּלָּה וְגוֹ', דְּעִקָּרָא דְּתַרְוַויְיהוּ מִלְּבָנוֹן קָא אַתְיָין.

19. Rabbi Yosi explains this verse as referring to when the Shechinah descended into exile in Egypt BECAUSE OF THE QUESTION OF RABBI ABA, WHO ASKS: DID SHE COME FROM LEBANON? INDEED, SHE ASCENDS TO LEBANON. IT SHOULD HAVE SAID, 'ASCEND WITH ME TO LEBANON!' HE EXPLAINS IT TO BE AT THE TIME THE SHECHINAH DESCENDED FROM THE PLACE LEBANON INTO EXILE IN EGYPT. THEREFORE IT SAYS, "COME WITH ME FROM LEBANON." And IN ORDER TO ANSWER THE PREVIOUS QUESTION OF WHY IT DOES NOT SAY 'ASCEND WITH ME TO LEBANON', Rabbi Shimon said: This verse is based upon the secret of the union of Faith, WHICH IS MALCHUT. It says, "Come with me from Lebanon, my bride" (Shir Hashirm 4:8). 'Voice', WHICH IS ZEIR ANPIN, said to 'Speech', WHICH IS MALCHUT, "with me," because voice comes to speech and leads it, so as to be one, without any separation, for the voice is general. BEING THE LIGHT OF CHASSADIM, WHICH IS PRESENT IN ALL

THE GRADES, speech is particular – BEING THE LIGHT OF CHOCHMAH, WHICH IS IN THE LEFT COLUMN OF BINAH, AND WHICH IS PRESENT ONLY IN MALCHUT. Therefore, the general needs the particular, AS ZEIR ANPIN DOES NOT HAVE THE THREE FIRST SFIROT, EXCEPT FOR THE LIGHT OF CHOCHMAH IN MALCHUT. And the particular needs the general, FOR THE LIGHT OF CHOCHMAH THAT IS IN MALCHUT ILLUMINATES ONLY WHEN IT IS CLOTHED IN THE LIGHT OF CHASSADIM THAT IT RECEIVES FROM ZEIR ANPIN, WHICH IS GENERAL. Voice is not COMPLETE without speech and speech is not COMPLETE without voice. Therefore, it is written: "With me from Lebanon, my bride," because the essence of both comes from Lebanon, WHICH IS BINAH.

20. תָּשׁוּרִי מֵרֹאשׁ אֲמָנָה: דָּא אִיהוּ גָּרוֹן, דְּמִתַּמָּן נַפְקָא רוּחָא לְאַשְׁלְמָא כֹּלָּא, מֵרָזָא דִלְבָנוֹן סָתִים וְגָנִיז. מֵרֹאשׁ שְׂנִיר וְחֶרְמוֹן: דָּא אִיהִי לִישָׁנָא רֵישָׁא וְאֶמְצָעִיתָא, דְּמִחַתְּכָא לַדְּבּוּר. מִמְּעוֹנוֹת אֲרָיוֹת: אִלֵּין אִינּוּן שִׁינַיִם. מֵהַרְרֵי נְמֵרִים: אִלֵּין אִינּוּן שִׂפְוָון, שְׁלִימוּ דְּאִשְׁתְּלִים בְּהוּ דִּבּוּר.

20. "Look from the top of Amanah," which is the throat, WHICH IS BINAH, WHICH RECEIVES FROM THE PALATE, WHICH IS THE SECRET OF CHOCHMAH, from which breath emanates, WHICH IS ZEIR ANPIN, to complete everything from the secret of concealed and hidden Lebanon – THAT ZEIR ANPIN OPENS WITH THE SECRET OF THE CENTRAL COLUMN. "From the top of Senir and Chermon," is the top and the middle of the tongue, WHICH IS THE SECRET OF TIFERET, AND ITS TIP IS THE SECRET OF DA'AT that articulates speech. "From the dens of lions," thereto are the teeth, WHICH ARE NETZACH AND HOD. "From the mountains of the leopards," refers to the lips, WHICH IS MALCHUT. AND ALL THESE SFIROT, WHICH ARE OF ZEIR ANPIN, ARE the completion through which speech is completed, WHICH IS MALCHUT, THE NUKVA OF ZEIR ANPIN.

4. "Do not eat the bread of one who has an evil eye"

A Synopsis

Rabbi Chiya explains that if the children of Yisrael in Egypt had not tasted the bread of the evil Egyptians, they would not have suffered the oppression of the Egyptians and they would not have remained in exile. When Rabbi Yitzchak points out that the exile was a fulfillment of a divine decree, Rabbi Chiya reminds him that the decree does not mention Egypt specifically. Thus, Rabbi Yitzchak understands and embraces the concept that one should not partake of the bread of an evil man.

The Relevance of the Passage

Our social and physical environment exerts profound influence upon us. If we consort with negative individuals, inevitably we will walk in their ways and emulate their self-destructive deeds.

This holds true for our own ego. When we indulge or yield to the cravings of our ego (eating the bread of an evil person), we eventually fall to the lowest depths (Egypt). We become prisoners to the dark side of our nature, oblivious and distant from the longings of our soul, our true self.

This passage banishes our reactive, egocentric impulses. Moreover, we attract kind, spiritual people into our life and infuse our environment with positive energy and Light.

21. וְאֵלֶּה שְׁמוֹת בְּנֵי יִשְׂרָאֵל. רַבִּי חִיָּיא פָּתַח, אַל תִּלְחַם אֶת לֶחֶם רַע עַיִן וְאַל תִּתְאָו לְמַטְעַמֹּתָיו. אַל תִּלְחַם אֶת לֶחֶם רַע עַיִן, בְּגִין דְּנַהֲמָא אוֹ הֲנָאָה דְּהַהוּא בַּר נָשׁ דְּהֲוֵי רַע עַיִן, לָאו אִיהוּ כְּדַאי לְמֵיכַל וּלְאִתְהֲנֵי מִנֵּיהּ. דְּאִי כַּד נַחְתּוּ יִשְׂרָאֵל לְמִצְרַיִם, לָא יִטְעֲמוּן נַהֲמָא דְּמִצְרָאֵי, לָא אִשְׁתְּבָקוּ בְּגָלוּתָא, וְלָא יְעִיקוּן לוֹן מִצְרָאֵי.

21. "And these are the names of the children of Israel..." (Shemot 1:1). Rabbi Chiya opened the discussion saying: "Do not eat the bread of him who has an evil eye, nor desire his dainties" (Mishlei 23:6). "Do not eat the bread of him who has an evil eye," because the bread or benefit from that person who has an evil eye is not worth eating or benefiting from. When Yisrael descended into Egypt, had they not tasted the bread of Egypt, they would not have been forsaken in exile IN EGYPT, and the Egyptians would not have been able to harm them.

22. אָמַר לֵיהּ רִבִּי יִצְחָק, וְהָא גְּזֵרָא אִתְגְּזַר. א"ל, כֹּלָּא אִיהוּ כַּדְקָא יָאוּת, דְּהָא לָא אִתְגְּזַר בְּמִצְרַיִם דַּוְוקָא, דְּהָא לָא כְּתִיב כִּי גֵר יִהְיֶה זַרְעֲךָ בְּאֶרֶץ מִצְרַיִם, אֶלָּא בְּאֶרֶץ לֹא לָהֶם, וַאֲפִילוּ בְּאַרְעָא אָחֳרָא.

22. Rabbi Yitzchak said to him: But it was decreed THAT YISRAEL SHOULD BE IN EXILE, AND IT WAS INCUMBENT THAT IT BE FULFILLED EVEN IF THEY DID NOT EAT THEIR BREAD. He said to him: All this is right. But it was not decreed that the exile be necessarily in Egypt, since it is not written: 'Your seed will be a stranger in the land of Egypt' but rather "in a land that is not theirs" (Beresheet 15:13). And it could even be in a different land.

23. אָמַר ר' יִצְחָק, מַאן דְּאִיהוּ בַּעַל נֶפֶשׁ, דְּמֵיכְלֵיהּ יַתִּיר מִשְׁאָר בְּנֵי נָשָׁא, אוֹ מַאן דְּהוּא אָזִיל בָּתַר מֵעוֹי, אִי אִיעָרַע בְּהַהוּא רַע עַיִן, יְכוּס גַּרְמֵיהּ וְלָא יֵיכוּל מִנַּהֲמָא דִּילֵיהּ, דְּלֵית נַהֲמָא בִּישָׁא בְּעָלְמָא, בַּר מֵהַהוּא לֶחֶם רַע עַיִן, מַה כְּתִיב כִּי לֹא יוּכְלוּן הַמִּצְרִים לֶאֱכֹל אֶת הָעִבְרִים לֶחֶם כִּי תוֹעֵבָה הִיא לְמִצְרָיִם, הָא לָךְ לֶחֶם רַע עַיִן.

23. Rabbi Yitzchak said: One with a Nefesh, who eats more than other people or one who follows his intestines, MEANING THAT HE IS ACCUSTOMED TO FILL HIS STOMACH WITH DAINTIES, should slaughter himself rather than eat his bread if he meets that evil-eyed one. For there is no worse bread in the world than the bread of an evil-eyed person. It is written: "Because the Egyptians could not eat bread with the Hebrews because it was an abomination to Egypt" (Beresheet 43:32), MEANING THEY COULD NOT LOOK UPON THE HEBREWS AS THEY ATE. Such is the bread of an evil-eyed!

5. Three who reject the Shechinah

A Synopsis
This section discusses the three types of people who drive the Shechinah from this world and make it impossible for God to fix His abode here, thereby causing prayers to go unanswered. These people are: those who cohabit with women during menstruation, those who lie with heathens, and those who intentionally abort the embryo, thereby preventing it from coming to fruition. The world is Judged for these sins, we're told, and meets with war, famine, and pestilence as a result. We learn that in exile, the children of Israel remained free of such sins and fulfilled the commandment to increase and multiply. Consequently, they were worthy of liberation. Indeed, Rabbi Chiya discusses the verse, "And he made the laver of brass…" as an indication of the purity of the Israelite women in Egypt, whose ritual ablutions and eagerness to obtain husbands made them worthy of great honor.

The Relevance of the Passage
Profound and penetrating forces of spiritual purification are ignited in this mystical passage. The darkness caused by the iniquities spoken of in this section of Zohar is expelled from the world. Negative desires are purged from our hearts. The truth of the Creator and an awareness of the spiritual laws governing our world propagate throughout humanity as our eyes gaze upon these sacred words.

24. תְּלָתָא אִינּוּן דְּדַחְיָין שְׁכִינְתָּא מֵעָלְמָא, וְגַרְמִין, דְּדִיּוּרֵיהּ דְּקוּדְשָׁא בְּרִיךְ הוּא לָא הֲוֵי בְּעָלְמָא, וּבְנֵי נָשָׁא צַוְוחִין וְלָא אִשְׁתְּמַע קַלֵּיהוֹן. וְאִלֵּין אִינּוּן מַאן דְּשָׁכִיב בַּנִּדָּה, בְּגִין דְּלֵית מְסָאֲבוּ תַּקִּיף בְּעָלְמָא בַּר מְסָאֲבוּ דְּנִדָּה. מְסָאֲבוּ דְּנִדָּה קַשְׁיָא מִכָּל מְסָאֲבוּ דְּעָלְמָא, אִסְתָּאַב אִיהוּ, וְכָל דְּמִתְקַרְבִין בַּהֲדֵיהּ יִסְתַּאֲבוּן עִמֵּיהּ, בְּכָל אֲתַר דְּאַזְלִין אִתְדַּחְיָיא שְׁכִינְתָּא מִן קַמַּיְיהוּ.

24. There are three kinds of people who reject the Shechinah away from the world and prevent the dwelling of the Holy One, Blessed be He, from inhabiting this world, and then people cry out IN PRAYER but their voices are not heard. They are: 1) One who lies with a menstruating woman, for there is no stronger impurity in the world like the impurity of the menstruation. The impurity of the menstruating woman is more severe than all the impurities of the world. He WHO DOES SO becomes impure and all

who are close to him become impure with him. Wherever they go, the Shechinah is repelled by them.

‎25. וְלֹא עוֹד, אֶלָּא דְּגָרִים מַרְעִין בִּישִׁין עַל גַּרְמֵיהּ, וְעַל הַהוּא זַרְעָא דְּיוֹלִיד, דְּכֵיוָן דְּיִקְרַב ב"נ לְגַבֵּי נִדָּה, הַהוּא מְסָאֲבוּ דָּלִיג עֲלוֹי, וְיִשְׁתָּאַר בְּכָל שַׁיְיפִין דִּילֵיהּ, זַרְעָא דְּיוֹלִיד בְּהַהוּא שַׁעֲתָא, מָשְׁכִין עֲלוֹי רוּחַ מְסָאֲבוּ. וְכָל יוֹמוֹי יְהֵא בִּמְסָאֲבוּ, דְּהָא בִּנְיָנָא וִיסוֹדָא דִּילֵיהּ אִיהוּ בִּמְסָאֲבוּ רַב וְתַקִּיף מִכָּל מְסָאֲבָא דְּעָלְמָא, דְּמִיָּד דְּקָרִיב ב"נ לְגַבֵּי נִדָּה, הַהוּא מְסָאֲבוּ דָּלִיג עֲלוֹי, דִּכְתִּיב, וּתְהִי נִדָּתָהּ עָלָיו.

25. And in addition, he brings bad sicknesses upon himself and on the children that he will beget. As soon as a person comes near to a menstruating woman, that impurity leaps onto him and remains STUCK in all his limbs. The children that he begets at that moment draw on the Spirit of Impurity. And all his days he will be in impurity, because the edifice and foundation of the baby is greater and stronger than all the impurities of the world. And as soon as a man comes near to a menstruating woman, her impurity leaps on him, as is written: "And her menstrual flow be upon him" (Vayikra 15:24).

‎26. מַאן דְּשָׁכִיב בְּבַת אֵל נֵכָר, דְּאָעִיל בְּרִית קוֹדֶשׁ וְאָת קַיָּימָא בִּרְשׁוּ אַחֲרָא, דִּכְתִּיב, וּבָעַל בַּת אֵל נֵכָר. וְתָנֵינָן, לֵית קַנְאָה קַמֵּי קוּדְשָׁא בְּרִיךְ הוּא, בַּר קַנְאָה דִּבְרִית קַדִּישָׁא, דְּאִיהוּ קַיָּימָא דִּשְׁמָא קַדִּישָׁא, וְרָזָא דִּמְהֵימְנוּתָא. מַה כְּתִיב וַיָּחֶל הָעָם לִזְנוֹת אֶל בְּנוֹת מוֹאָב מִיָּד וַיִּחַר אַף ה' בְּיִשְׂרָאֵל.

26. 2) One who lies with a daughter of a strange El, A GENTILE WOMAN, who inserts the sign of the holy Covenant into another domain, as written: "And has married the daughter of a strange El" (Malachi 2:11). We have learned that there is no jealousy before the Holy One, blessed be He, like the zeal for of the Covenant, which is the Covenant of the Holy Name and the secret of the Faith. It is written: "And the people began to commit harlotry with the daughters of Moab" (Bemidbar 25:1), and immediately, "the anger of Hashem was kindled against Yisrael" (Ibid. 3).

27. רֵישֵׁי עַמָּא דְּיָדְעוּ וְלֹא מְחוֹ בִּידַיְיהוּ, אִתְעַנָּשׁוּ בְּקַדְמֵיתָא, דִּכְתִיב, קַח אֶת כָּל רָאשֵׁי הָעָם וְהוֹקַע אוֹתָם לה' נֶגֶד הַשָּׁמֶשׁ. רִבִּי אַבָּא אָמַר, מַאי נֶגֶד הַשָּׁמֶשׁ. נֶגֶד הַבְּרִית דְּאִקְרֵי שֶׁמֶשׁ, וַעֲלֵיהּ אִתְּמַר כִּי שֶׁמֶשׁ וּמָגֵן ה' אֱלֹהִים. שֶׁמֶשׁ וּמָגֵן: דָּא בְּרִית קַדִּישָׁא. מַה שֶּׁמֶשׁ זָרַח וְאַנְהִיר עַל עָלְמָא, אוּף הָכִי בְּרִית קַדִּישָׁא זָרַח וְאַנְהִיר גּוּפָא דב"נ. מָגֵן: מַה מָגֵן אִיהוּ לְאַגָּנָא עֲלֵיהּ דב"נ, אוּף הָכִי בְּרִית קַדִּישָׁא מָגֵן עֲלֵיהּ דב"נ, וּמַאן דְּנָטִיר לֵיהּ, לֵית נִזְקָא בְּעָלְמָא, דְּיָכִיל לְמִקְרַב בַּהֲדֵיהּ וְדָא הוּא נֶגֶד הַשָּׁמֶשׁ.

27. The leaders of the people who know this and do not protest are punished first, as is written: "Take all the chiefs of the people and hang them up before Hashem against the sun" (Ibid. 4). Rabbi Aba said: What is meant by, "against the sun"? It means against the Covenant that is called 'sun', of which it is said, "For Hashem Elohim is a sun and shield" (Tehilim 84:12). "A sun and shield" is the Holy Covenant. In the same way that the sun shines and illuminates the world, the Holy Covenant shines and illuminates the body of man. In the same way that a shield protects the man, so does the Holy Covenant protect the man. And there is no injury that can approach one who protects it. This is: "against the sun."

28. רֵישֵׁי עַמָּא, יִתְפְּסוּן בְּכָל דָּרָא וְדָרָא בְּחוֹבָא דָּא, אִי יָדְעִין וְלֹא מְקַנְּאִין לֵיהּ. בְּגִין דְּחוֹבָא דָּא עֲלַיְיהוּ, לְקַנָּאָה לֵיהּ לְקוּדְשָׁא בְּרִיךְ הוּא בְּהַאי בְּרִית, מַאן דְּאָעִיל קְדוּשָׁה דָּא בִּרְשׁוּתָא אַחֲרָא, עֲלֵיהּ כְּתִיב לֹא יִהְיֶה לְךָ אֱלֹהִים אֲחֵרִים עַל פָּנַי. לֹא תִשְׁתַּחֲוֶה לָהֶם וְלֹא תָעָבְדֵם כִּי אָנֹכִי ה' אֱלֹהֶיךָ אֵל קַנָּא וְכֹלָּא קִנְאָה חֲדָא. וע"ד אִתְדַּחְיָיא שְׁכִינְתָּא מִקַּמֵּיהּ. מַאן דִּמְשַׁקֵּר בִּבְרִית קַדִּישָׁא דְּחָתִים בְּבִשְׂרֵיהּ דב"נ, כְּאִילּוּ מְשַׁקֵּר בִּשְׁמָא דְּקוּדְשָׁא בְּרִיךְ הוּא, מַאן דִּמְשַׁקֵּר חוֹתָמָא דְּמַלְכָּא, מְשַׁקֵּר בֵּיהּ בְּמַלְכָּא, לֵית לֵיהּ חוּלָקָא בֶּאֱלָהָא דְּיִשְׂרָאֵל, אִי לָא בְּחֵילָא דִּתְיוּבְתָּא תָּדִיר.

28. The leaders of the people are punished in every generation if they know of this sin and are not zealous in guarding against it. It is is incumbent upon them to be zealous in upholding this responsibility, for the Holy One,

blessed be He, in this Covenant against all who would bring this holiness in another domain. About this is written: "You shall have no other Elohim before Me, do not bow down to them and do not worship them, for I Hashem your Elohim am a zealous El" (Shemot 20:3-5). And it is all the same zeal, EITHER ONE WHO LIES WITH A GENTILE WOMAN OR ONE WHO WORSHIPS IDOLS. Therefore, the Shechinah is repelled by him. One who is false to the Holy Covenant that is sealed in the flesh of a man is as though he is false to the Holy Name, because one who is false with the seal of the King, WHICH IS THE HOLY COVENANT, is false to the King himself. Therefore, he does not have any part with the Elohim of Yisrael, unless it is through the power of constant repentance.

29. ר' יוֹסֵי פָּתַח וְאָמַר, וַיִּשְׁכְּחוּ אֶת ה' אֱלֹהֵיהֶם וְגוֹ', וַיַּעַזְבוּ אֶת ה'. מַאי וַיִּשְׁכְּחוּ וַיַּעַזְבוּ. דְּדָחוּ מִנַּיְיהוּ בְּרִית קַיָּימָא קַדִּישָׁא, הֲווֹ גָּזְרִין וְלָא פַּרְעִין, עַד דְּאָתַת דְּבוֹרָה וְנָדִיבַת בְּהַאי לְכָל יִשְׂרָאֵל כְּמָה דִּכְתִיב, בִּפְרוֹעַ פְּרָעוֹת בְּיִשְׂרָאֵל בְּהִתְנַדֵּב עָם בָּרְכוּ ה'.

29. Rabbi Yosi opened the discussion saying: "And when they forgot Hashem their Elohim" (I Shmuel 12:9), and "And they forsook Hashem" (Shoftim 2:13). AND HE ASKS: What is: "And when they forgot," and "And they forsook"? AND HE ANSWERS: They repelled from themselves the Holy Covenant, they circumcised but did not uncover until Deborah came and offered this, BY INTRODUCING *Priah* ('UNCOVERING OF THE CORONA') throughout Yisrael, as it says, "In time of tumultuous strife (Heb. *pra'ot*) in Yisrael, when the people willingly offered themselves; praise Hashem" (Shoftim 5:2).

30. מַאן דְּקָטִיל בְּנוֹי, הַהוּא עוֹבָרָא דְּמִתְעַבְּרָא אִתְּתֵיהּ, וְגָרִים לְקַטְלָא לֵיהּ בִּמְעָהָא, דְּסָתִיר בִּנְיָינָא דְּקוּדְשָׁא בְּרִיךְ הוּא וְאוּמָנוּתָא דִּילֵיהּ. אִית מַאן דְּקָטִיל ב"נ. וְהַאי קָטִיל בְּנוֹי.

30. 3) One who slays his children, meaning the embryo that his wife conceived, BY HAVING INTERCOURSE WITH HER ON THE NINETIETH DAY OF CONCEPTION, WHICH HE SLAYS THE EMBRYO and causes it to be killed in her belly, OR HE DOES SOME ACTION THAT CAUSES HER TO ABORT THE EMBRYO. He thus demolishes the building of the Holy One, blessed be He, and His craft. There are people who slay a person, and such a one slays his children.

‎31. תְּלָתָא בִּישִׁין עָבֵיד דְּכָל עָלְמָא לָא יָכִיל לְמִסְבַּל, וְעַל דָּא עָלְמָא מִתְמוֹגְגָא זְעֵיר זְעֵיר, וְלֹא יְדִיעַ, וְקוּדְשָׁא בְּרִיךְ הוּא אִסְתָּלִק מֵעָלְמָא, וְחַרְבָּא וְכַפְנָא וּמוֹתָנָא אַתְיָין עַל עָלְמָא. וְאִלֵּין אִינּוּן: קָטִיל בְּנוֹי, סָתִיר בִּנְיָינָא דְּמַלְכָּא. דָּחֵי שְׁכִינְתָּא, דְּאַזְלָא וּמְשַׁטְּטָא בְּעָלְמָא, וְלָא אַשְׁכָּחַת נַיְיחָא. וְעַל אִלֵּין, רוּחָא דְקוּדְשָׁא בָּכְיָה. וְעָלְמָא אִתְדָּן בְּכָל הָנֵי דִינִין. וַוי לְהַהוּא ב״נ, וַוי לֵיהּ, טָב לֵיהּ דְּלָא יִתְבְּרֵי בְּעָלְמָא.

31. The three evils done, AS EXPLAINED, the whole world can not bear. Therefore, the world deteriorates little by little, although it is not known HOW IT COMES ABOUT. The Holy One, blessed be He, removes Himself from the world, and destruction and famine and death come to the world. These are THE THREE EVILS: he slays his children; he demolishes the structure of the King, NAMELY, HE STONS CONCEPTION WHICH IS THE STRUCTURE OF THE HOLY ONE, BLESSED BE HE; and he repels the Shechinah, who roves in the world but can find no rest. For these evils, the Holy Spirit weeps and the world is judged. Woe to that man, woe to him, better that he was not created in the world.

‎32. זַכָּאִין אִינּוּן יִשְׂרָאֵל, דְּאע״ג דַּהֲווֹ בְּגָלוּתָא דְּמִצְרַיִם, אִסְתָּמְרוּ מִכָּל הָנֵי תְּלָתָא, מִנִּדָּה, וּמִבַּת אֵל נֵכָר, וּמִקְטוֹל זַרְעָא, וְאִשְׁתַּדְּלוּ בְּפַרְהֶסְיָא בִּפְרִיָה וּרְבִיָה. דְּאַף עַל גַּב דִּגְזֵרָה אִתְגְזֵרַת כָּל הַבֵּן הַיִּלּוֹד הַיְאוֹרָה תַּשְׁלִיכוּהוּ, לָא אִשְׁתְּכַח בֵּינֵיהוֹן מַאן דְּקָטִיל עוּבָּרָא בִּמְעָהָא דְּאִתְּתָא, כ״ש לְבָתַר. וּבִזְכוּתָא דָּא נָפְקוּ יִשְׂרָאֵל מִן גָּלוּתָא.

32. Fortunate are Yisrael. Even though they were exiled in Egypt, they were guarded against all these three: from the impurity of menstruation; from daughters of foreign deities; and from killing the children. They attempted ACTIONS in public to awaken the state of being fruitful and multiplying. AS HE SAYS FURTHER: Even though it was decreed that "every son that is born you shall cast into the river" (Shemot 1:22), there was not found among them a person who would kill an embryo in the stomach of a woman, all the more so after BIRTH. Through this merit, Yisrael went out of exile.

‎33. מִנִּדָּה: דְּתָנֵי רַבִּי חִיָּיא מַאי דִכְתִיב וַיַּעַשׂ אֵת הַכִּיּוֹר נְחֹשֶׁת וְאֵת כַּנּוֹ נְחֹשֶׁת בְּמַרְאוֹת הַצּוֹבְאוֹת. מִפְּנֵי מָה זָכוּ נָשִׁין לְהַאי, בְּגִין

דְּאִסְתָּמָרוּ גַרְמַיְיהוּ בְּגָלוּתָא דְמִצְרַיִם, דִּלְבָתַר דְּאִתְדַּכְיָין הֲווֹ אַתְיָין מִתְקַשְּׁטָן וּמִסְתַּכְּלָן בְּמַרְאָה בְּבַעֲלֵיהוֹן, וּמְעוֹרְרָן לוֹן בִּפְרִיָּה וּרְבִיָּה.

33. THEY GUARDED THEMSELVES IN EGYPT from the impurity of menstruation; for Rabbi Chiya taught: What is the verse, "And he made the laver of brass, and its pedestal of brass, of the mirrors of the women assembling" (Shemot 38:8)? Why did the women merit this, TO BRING THE MIRRORS TO THE TABERNACLE? Because they guarded themselves in the exile in Egypt, so that after they became purified from the impurity of their menstruation, they came and adorned themselves and looked in the mirror at their husbands, and aroused them to be fruitful and multiplying. SO THEY WERE GUARDED AGAINST THE IMPURITY OF MENSTRUATION IN THE EXILE OF EGYPT.

34. מִבַּת אֵל נֵכָר, דִּכְתִיב, יָצְאוּ כָּל צִבְאוֹת ה' וְגוֹ'. וּכְתִיב שִׁבְטֵי יָה עֵדוּת לְיִשְׂרָאֵל. עֵדוּת לְיִשְׂרָאֵל וַדַּאי. וְאֵלֶּה שְׁמוֹת בְּנֵי יִשְׂרָאֵל. שִׁבְטֵי בְּנֵי יִשְׂרָאֵל. דַּבֵּר אֶל בְּנֵי יִשְׂרָאֵל.

34. THEY WERE GUARDED IN EGYPT "from the daughter of a foreign El," MEANING FOREIGN WOMEN, as is written: "All the hosts of Hashem left" (Shemot 12:41), and, "The tribes of Yah, as a testimony to Yisrael" (Tehilim 122:4). Assuredly, FOR THERE IS NO MIXTURE OF A FOREIGN NATION, AS WRITTEN: "These are the names of the children of Israel" (Shemot 1:1). "The tribes of the children of Yisrael" (Yehoshea 4:5), "Speak to the children of Yisrael." ALL THIS POINTS OUT THAT THERE IS NO FOREIGN MIXTURE IN THEM.

35. וְאִי תֵּימָא וְהָא כְּתִיב וְהוּא בֶּן אִישׁ מִצְרִי. הָא וַדַּאי חַד הֲוָה, וּפִרְסְמוֹ קְרָא, דִּכְתִיב, וְהוּא בֶּן אִישׁ מִצְרִי וְגוֹ' וְשֵׁם אִמּוֹ שְׁלוֹמִית בַּת דִּבְרִי לְמַטֵּה דָן. פְּרִיָּה וּרְבִיָּה דִּכְתִיב וּבְנֵי יִשְׂרָאֵל פָּרוּ וַיִּשְׁרְצוּ וַיִּרְבּוּ וְגוֹ'. וּמִכָּל הָנֵי אִסְתָּמָרוּ יִשְׂרָאֵל. בְּנֵי יִשְׂרָאֵל עָאלוּ, בְּנֵי יִשְׂרָאֵל נָפְקוּ, הה"ד וְאֵלֶּה שְׁמוֹת בְּנֵי יִשְׂרָאֵל וְגוֹ'.

35. You may ask why it is written: "And he was the son of a Egyptian man..." (Vayikra 24:10-11). AND HE ANSWERS: Certainly there was one, and the verse made him known, as written: "And he was the son of a

Egyptian man…and his mother's name was Shelomit, the daughter of Divri, of the tribe of Dan." THEY WERE OBSERVANT IN EGYPT TO FULFILL being fruitful and multiplying, as it is written: "And the children of Yisrael were fruitful and increased abundantly…" (Shemot 1:7). Assuredly, the children of Yisrael were guarded IN EGYPT from all these: THE IMPURITY OF MENSTRUATION, FOREIGN WOMEN, AND FROM KILLING CHILDREN. Therefore, the children of Yisrael came INTO EGYPT, and the children of Yisrael went out TO FREEDOM. It is written: "And these are the names of the children of Israel who came…" BECAUSE "CAME" SIGNIFIES NOT TO SETTLE, BUT RATHER THAT THEY WOULD GO OUT FROM THERE. AND THIS IS THROUGH THE MERIT OF OBSERVING THE THREE THINGS MENTIONED ABOVE.

6. "Every man came with his household"

A Synopsis
While walking, Rabbi Yosi asks Rabbi Elazar to explain Rabbi Shimon's interpretation of the verse, "And these are the names of the children of Israel…" If this verse refers to God and the heavenly hosts and Chariots who went into captivity with Jacob, he asks, what is the meaning of, "Each man and his household came"? Rabbi Elazar confirms Rabbi Shimon's interpretation and discusses the distinction between "the house of Hashem" and "the house of the king." This leads to a brief explanation of the shifting gender attributed to the King and the various grades of angels: the higher level is always referred to as male-which implies an active quality-in relation to the lower level, which is referred to as female, and implies a passive, receptive quality. Thus, he concludes, symbolically, the title verse refers to the angels, who are called "his house."

Rabbi Yosi then draws from Rabbi's Elazar's explanation to interpret the verse, "A closed garden is my sister…" as a reference to the children of Israel, who must be tended and nurtured, like a garden or vineyard.

The Relevance of the Passage
We learn that a garden must be cultivated, watered, and pruned. Likewise, the Children of Yisrael (which refers to *all* those who walk the spiritual path) must also be refined and cultivated by "watering" them, or nourishing them with Light. A man uses this Light to be pruned like a tree – to uproot and purge all his negative traits and blockages.

The greatest source of Light for human beings is the Temple; specifically, the chamber known as the Holy of Holies. From this sacred place emerges the most powerful spiritual forces known to man.

Here, the Zohar summons forth the energy of the Temple. These forces cultivate, water, and prune the entire earth, transforming our globe into the greatest of all gardens – the Garden of Eden.

The ultimate giving-and-receiving relationship emerges – The Light of the Creator shares with the Vessel (humanity), and the Vessel receives this Light for the sake of sharing pleasure with the Creator. In this scenario, both the Light and the Vessel, both the Creator and the souls of humanity, are in a sharing mode. Perfection of the world and oneness is thus achieved by this remarkable passage.

Our own consciousness is transformed so that we recognize the value of unconditional sharing with others. We become cognizant of the profound pleasure the Creator receives by imparting to mankind. In turn, we deeply cherish all the gifts we have received in our life. Sorrows vanish as fulfillment and thankfulness fill our being.

36. וְאֵלֶּה שְׁמוֹת בְּנֵי יִשְׂרָאֵל. רַבִּי אֶלְעָזָר וְרַבִּי יוֹסֵי הֲווֹ אַזְלֵי בְּאוֹרְחָא, עַד דַּהֲווֹ אַזְלֵי, אָמַר רַבִּי אֶלְעָזָר לְרַבִּי יוֹסֵי, אַפְתַּח פּוּמָךְ, וְיִנְהַרוּן מִילָךְ אָמַר לֵיהּ נִיחָא קַמֵּיהּ דְּמָר, דְּאֶשְׁאַל מִלָּה חֲדָא דְּקַשְׁיָא לִי, הָא שְׁמַעְנָא מִבּוּצִינָא קַדִּישָׁא, דַּהֲוָה אָמַר, וְאֵלֶּה שְׁמוֹת בְּנֵי יִשְׂרָאֵל, יִשְׂרָאֵל סָבָא. כָּל אִינוּן חֵילִין וּמַשְׁרְיָין דְּהֲווֹ נַחְתִּין לְגָלוּתָא בַּהֲדֵי יַעֲקֹב, דִּכְתִיב, אֶת יַעֲקֹב. מַהוּ דִּכְתִיב אִישׁ וּבֵיתוֹ בָּאוּ. אָמַר לֵיהּ, וַדַּאי הָכִי הוּא. אֶלָּא הָא הָא תָּנֵינָן, כָּל דִּמְקַבֵּל מֵאָחֳרָא, אִיהוּ בֵּיתָא מֵהַהוּא דְּיָהִיב, וְעַל דָּא אִישׁ וּבֵיתוֹ בָּאוּ.

36. "And these are the names of the children of Israel" (Shemot 1:1). Rabbi Elazar and Rabbi Yosi were traveling. While they were walking, Rabbi Elazar said to Rabbi Yosi: Open your mouth and let your words illuminate. He said to him: If it pleases my master, may I ask him one thing that I find difficult? I have heard from the Holy Luminary that he used to say that, "And these are the names of the children of Israel," means Yisrael Saba. "WHO CAME INTO EGYPT," MEANS all the hosts and camps OF ANGELS who descended into exile with Jacob, as it is written, "with Jacob"; AND ACCORDING TO THIS IT IS DIFFICULT. Why does it say: "every man came with his household" (Shemot 1:1)? DO ANGELS HAVE HOUSEHOLDS? He said to him: Certainly it is so THAT THE ANGELS CAME, EACH ONE WITH HIS HOUSEHOLD. For so we have learned, anyone who receives from another is considered as household to the giver. Therefore, "every man came with his household," MEANS THE GIVER AND THE RECEIVER, WHICH ALSO APPLIES TO ANGELS.

37. פָּתַח רַבִּי אֶלְעָזָר וְאָמַר, וַיְהִי כְּכַלּוֹת שְׁלֹמֹה לִבְנוֹת אֶת בֵּית ה' וְאֶת בֵּית הַמֶּלֶךְ וְגוֹ'. וְכִי כֵּיוָן דְּאָמַר אֶת בֵּית ה', מַהוּ וְאֶת בֵּית הַמֶּלֶךְ, אִי בְּגִין שְׁלֹמֹה אִתְּמַר, לָאו הָכִי, אֶלָּא אֶת בֵּית ה' דָּא בֵּית הַמִּקְדָּשׁ, וְאֶת בֵּית הַמֶּלֶךְ דָּא קֹדֶשׁ הַקֳּדָשִׁים.

37. Rabbi Elazar opened the discussion saying: "And when Solomon finished building the house of Hashem and the house of the King..." (I

Melachim 9:1). HE ASKS: Since it said "the house of Hashem," what is the meaning of, "the house of the King"? You may reason that of Solomon it is said "THE HOUSE OF THE KING," yet it is not so. Indeed, "the house of Hashem," refers to the Temple and "the house of the King" refers to the Holy of Holies.

38. בֵּית ה׳ דְּאִיהוּ בֵּית הַמִּקְדָּשׁ כְּגוֹן: עֲזָרוֹת וּלְשָׁכוֹת וּבֵית הָאוּלָם וְהַדְּבִיר, דָּא בֵּית הַמִּקְדָּשׁ, וַדַּאי אִקְרֵי בֵּית ה׳. בֵּית הַמֶּלֶךְ: דָּא קֹדֶשׁ הַקֳּדָשִׁים, דְּאִיהוּ פְּנִימָאָה דְּכֹלָּא, הַמֶּלֶךְ סְתָם. מֶלֶךְ דָּא, אע״ג דְּאִיהוּ מֶלֶךְ עִלָּאָה, אִיהוּ נוּקְבָּא לְגַבֵּי נְקוּדָה עִלָּאָה, סְתִימָא דְּכֹלָּא. ואע״ג דְּאִיהוּ נוּקְבָּא, אִיהוּ דְּכוּרָא לְגַבֵּי מֶלֶךְ דִּלְתַתָּא, וּבְגִין כָּךְ כֹּלָּא כְּגַוְונָא דָּא וְעַל דָּא, תַּתָּאֵי, בְּרָזָא דָּא כְּתִיב בְּהוּ, אִישׁ וּבֵיתוֹ בָּאוּ.

38. AND HE EXPLAINS HIS WORDS: "The house of Hashem" is the Temple, that is, the courtyards, chambers, the hall leading to the interior of the Temple and the sanctuary. This is the Temple, WHICH IS MALCHUT. Most certainly, it is called "the house of Hashem." "The house of the King" is the Holy of Holies which is innermost of all, NAMELY BINAH that is called simply 'King'. This King, though he is Supernal King, is considered female in relation to the Highest Point that is concealed from all, WHICH IS CHOCHMAH. But even though it is female, nevertheless it is male compared to the king below, WHICH IS ZEIR ANPIN – MEANING THAT THE HIGHER LEVEL IS ALWAYS CONSIDERED MALE IN RELATION TO THE LOWER, AND THE LOWER IS CONSIDERED FEMALE. YET, IN COMPARISON TO WHAT IS STILL LOWER, IT IS CONSIDERED MALE. AND SO IT IS ALWAYS. Therefore, everything is in this way. Of the lower beings, THE ANGELS THAT DESCENDED WITH JACOB INTO EGYPT, it is written: "every man came with his household," EVEN THOUGH THEY DO NOT HAVE HOUSEHOLDS, FOR "MAN WITH HIS HOUSEHOLD" MEANS MALE AND FEMALE. FOR EVERY HIGHER LEVEL AMONG THEM IS CONSIDERED AS MALE IN RELATION TO THE LOWER LEVEL, AND EVERY LOWER LEVEL IS CONSIDERED AS FEMALE TO THE HIGHER LEVEL AND MALE TO ITS LOWER LEVEL.

39. וְאֵלֶּה שְׁמוֹת, רִבִּי יוֹסֵי פָּתַח וְאָמַר, גַּן נָעוּל אֲחוֹתִי כַלָּה גַּל נָעוּל מַעְיָן חָתוּם. גַּן נָעוּל: דָּא כְּנֶסֶת יִשְׂרָאֵל שֶׁהִיא גַּן נָעוּל. דְּאָמַר רִבִּי אֶלְעָזָר, מַה הַגַּן הַזֶּה צָרִיךְ לִשְׁמוֹר, לַעֲדוֹר, וּלְהַשְׁקוֹת, וְלִזְמוֹר. כָּךְ

כְּנֶסֶת יִשְׂרָאֵל, צְרִיכָה לַעֲדוֹר, וְלִשְׁמוֹר, וּלְהַשְׁקוֹת, וְלִזְמוֹר, וְנִקְרֵאת גַּן, וְנִקְרֵאת כֶּרֶם, מַה הַכֶּרֶם הַזֶּה צָרִיךְ לַעֲדוֹר וּלְהַשְׁקוֹת וְלִזְמוֹר וְלַחְפּוֹר, כָּךְ יִשְׂרָאֵל, הֲדָא הוּא דִּכְתִיב, כִּי כֶרֶם ה׳ צְבָאוֹת בֵּית יִשְׂרָאֵל וּכְתִיב, וַיְעַזְּקֵהוּ וַיְסַקְּלֵהוּ וְגוֹ׳.

39. "And these are the names...". Rabbi Yosi opened the discussion saying: "A garden locked is my sister, my bride, a spring shut up, a fountain sealed" (Shir Hashirm 4:12). "A garden locked," refers to the Congregation of Yisrael, THE NUKVA, as Rabbi Elazar said: Just as one must cultivate a garden, water and prune it, so too does the Congregation of Yisrael needs to be cultivated, watered and pruned, WHICH IS THE SERVICE OF THE RIGHTEOUS – TO RAISE MAYIN NUKVIN ('FEMALE WATERS') AND TO PRUNE THE KLIPOT THAT SURROUND THE NUKVA. Therefore, it is called "garden" and it is also called "vineyard" for Yisrael – MEANING THE HOUSE OF YISRAEL, WHICH IS THE NUKVA – needs to be cultivated, watered and pruned just as the vineyard does. It is written: "For the vineyard of Hashem Tzeva'ot is the House of Yisrael" (Yeshayah 5:7), and, "And he broke ground and cleared away its stones..." (Ibid. 2).

7. The wheels of the holy Chariot travel

A Synopsis
In this long and highly complex section, Rabbi Shimon describes the nature and workings of the Holy Chariot, one of the quintessential emblems of Kabbalah and thus of enormous importance to anyone seriously practising this discipline. It cannot really be summarized but must be read carefully many, many times before it will begin to unfold its profound meaning, which sheds light on numerous related concepts, like the three columns and the secret names of God.

The Relevance of the Passage
The workings of the Ten Sfirot are explored in great detail, but the Zohar speaks in the poetic and concealed language of metaphor and symbolism. Some of the essential treasures revealed in this passage concern the concept of mercy. All of our words, actions and deeds are recorded each moment of our day. The universal law of cause and effect decrees that each negative deed brings the appropriate measure of judgment upon us.

However, we can sweeten this judgment with mercy the moment we accept responsibility for the turmoil that afflicts us.

This section of Zohar annuls all judgments decreed upon mankind through the verse that speaks of the color red transforming into white. Myriad lifetimes of sobbing and wailing cease forevermore as laughter and song are heard throughout the world, for this is the power of Mercy and the ultimate purpose and power of the Zohar.

Later in the passage, we are empowered with the Light of the 42 Letter Name of God – the Ana B'koach meditation – and the 42 supernal angels who descend into this world, in the same way that they accompanied Jacob into Egypt. This connection allows our world to mate with the Upper World, the female to mate with the male. This union causes Light to flow into our life so that all darkness (Egypt) is eternally banished.

תוֹסֶפְתָּא

40. מַתְנִיתִין: אָמַר רִבִּי שִׁמְעוֹן, אֲנַן פַּתְחִין עֵינָנָא חֲמָאן, גַּלְגַּלֵי רְתִיכָתָא קַדִּישָׁתָא נַטְלִין בְּמַטְלָנוֹי, וְקַל שִׁירָתָא בְּסִימָא לְאוּדְנִין, יָאֶה לְלִבָּא, סַלְּקָא וְנַחְתָּא, אַזְלָא וְלָא נַטְלָא, מִזְדַּעְזְעִין אֶלֶף אַלְפִין, וְרִבּוֹא רִבְבָן וּפַתְחִין שִׁירָתָא מִלְּרַע לְעֵילָא.

-32-

Tosefta (addendum)

40. Mishnah. Rabbi Shimon said: We open our eyes and see the wheels of the Holy Chariot traveling in their journeys, and the sound of a song sweet to the ears, WHICH IS BINAH, and good for the heart, SYMBOLIZING MALCHUT, which ascends and descends, and walks but does not travel. Thousands upon thousands tremble, and tens upon tens of thousands start with the singing OF CHOCHMAH from below upwards.

‏41. לְקֶל נְעִימוּתָא הַהוּא, קַיְימִין מַאן דְּקַיְימִין, וּמִתְכַּנְּפִין בְּכְנוּפְיָא לְסְטְרָא דִימִינָא, אַרְבַּע מְאָה וְחַמְשִׁין אַלְפִין מָארֵי דְּעַיְינִין. חַמָּאן וְלָא חַמָּאן, קַיְימִין בְּקִיּוּמֵיהוֹן. תְּרֵין סְטְרִין אָחֲרָנִין אִתְחַוְּורוּ בְּגִינֵיהוֹן. וּלְסְטְרָא דִשְׂמָאלָא מָאתָן וְחַמְשִׁין אַלְפִין.

41. To that pleasant sound FROM THE TRAVELING OF THE WHEELS stand 450,000 eyed ones, who gather into one group on the right side. They see, yet do not see, and are completely present. The two other sides, WHICH ARE LEFT AND CENTER, turn white because of them – MEANING THAT THEIR JUDGMENTS, WHICH ARE RED, ARE CHANGED, BECAUSE THEY RECEIVE CHASSADIM FROM THE RIGHT COLUMN. And on the left side are 250,000.

‏42. אִינּוּן מָארֵיהוֹן דִּיבָבָא, מִיַבְּבִין וּמְיַלְּלִין מֵאֲתַר בֵּית מוֹתְבֵיהוֹן, פַּתְחִין בְּדִינָא וּמְסַיְּימִין בְּדִינָא. מִיַבְּבִין תִּנְיָינוּת, וְדִינָא יָתִיב, וְסְפְרִין פְּתִיחוּ. בֵּיהּ שַׁעֲתָא, סָלִיק מָארֵיהּ דְּדִינָא, דְּקָאֵים עֲלֵיהוֹן, וְיָתִיב בְּכוּרְסַיָּיא דְּדִינָא, וְשִׁירָתָא אִשְׁתְּכַךְ, עַד לָא תִּסְתַּיֵּים דִּינָא.

42. THE 250,000 MENTIONED EARLIER, the weepers sob and wail from their dwellings WHENCE THEY COME, and they commence with Judgment and conclude with Judgment. They sob a second time and the Judgment is revealed, and the books are opened TO LOOK AT THE JUDGMENTS THAT ARE IN THEM. At that moment, the Judge who was standing over them ascends, and sits on the chair of Judgment, and the singing subsides before the Judgment is concluded.

‏43. סָחֲרָן מָארֵי דְּעַיְינִין דִּלְסְטְרָא יְמִינָא, וְעִמְּהוֹן תַּמְנֵיסַר אַלְפִין

אַחֲרָנִין תַּקְעִין, וְלָא מְיַבְּבִין וְלָא מְיַלְּלִין פַּתְחִין שִׁירָתָא, מִזְדַּעְזְעָן מָאתָן וְחַמְשִׁין אַלְפִין מָארֵי דִיבָבָא.

43. Those who have eyes of the right side encircle, together with eighteen thousand others. They blow, THAT IS, DRAW CHASSADIM, WHICH IS CALLED 'BLOWING', A SIMPLE SOUND. AND THEN THOSE do not sob or wail. They commence with singing, DRAWING CHOCHMAH. And the 250,000 ones who sob tremble.

44. תְּקַע תִּנְיָינוּת וְלָא מְיַבְּבִין נָטִיל פַּטְרוֹנָא, מֵהַהוּא כּוּרְסַיָּיא וְיָתִיב בְּכוּרְסַיָּיא דְּוַותְּרָנוּתָא. בֵּיהּ זִמְנָא הוּא מִדְכַּר שְׁמָא קַדִּישָׁא עִלָּאָה רַבָּא, דִּבְהַהוּא שְׁמָא חַיִּים לְכֹלָּא.

44. He blows AND DRAWS CHASSADIM a second time, without sobbing. The Protector, ZEIR ANPIN, travels from that throne OF JUDGMENT and sits in the throne of Mercy TO DRAW MANY CHASSADIM. At that moment he, MEANING ZEIR ANPIN, mentions the Holy Name, YUD HEI VAV HEI, FULLY SPELLED TO AMOUNT NUMERICALLY TO 45: *YUD-VAV-DALET; HEI-ALEPH; VAV-ALEPH-VAV; HEI-ALEPH.* For with this Name, life is drawn for everyone.

45. פָּתַח וְאָמַר זִמְנָא חֲדָא יוֹ"ד הֵ"א וָא"ו הֵ"א כד"א וַיִּקְרָא בְשֵׁם יְהֹוָה. פַּתְחִין כְּקַדְמֵיתָא מָארֵי גַּלְגַּלֵּי קַדִּישִׁין. וְאֶלֶף אַלְפִין, וְרִבּוֹא רִבְבָן, וְאַמְרֵי שִׁירָתָא, מְשַׁבְּחִין וְאָמְרִין, בְּרִיךְ יְקָרָא דה' מֵאֲתָר בֵּית שְׁכִינְתֵּיהּ.

45. He commences, ZEIR ANPIN WHICH IS THE CENTRAL COLUMN, saying one time: *Yud-Vav-Dalet; Hei-Aleph; Vav-Aleph-Vav; Hei-Aleph-YUD-VAV-DALET; HEI-ALEPH; VAV-ALEPH-VAV* ARE THE SECRET OF THE THREE COLUMNS, RIGHT, LEFT, AND CENTRAL, THAT ARE INCLUDED IN ZEIR ANPIN. THE LAST *HEI-ALEPH* IS THE NUKVA THAT RECEIVES FROM THEM, as is written: "And proclaimed the Name of Hashem" (Shemot 34:5). The holy wheels OF THE CHARIOT commence as before and thousands of thousands, WHICH IS THE SECRET OF CHOCHMAH, and tens upon tens of thousands, WHICH IS THE SECRET OF CHASSADIM, ATTIRE THEM AND recite songs. THE ANGELS praise and say: "Blessed is the glory of Hashem from His dwelling place," SO THAT THE SHECHINAH SHALL BE BLESSED FROM ZEIR ANPIN, AND RECEIVE FROM HIM CHOCHMAH ATTIRED IN CHASSADIM.

46. אַתְיָא הַהוּא גִּנְתָּא, דְּאִיהִי טְמִירָא בְּמָאתָן וְחַמְשִׁין עָלְמִין, הוּא שְׁכִינְתָּא יְקָרָא בְּזִיוָהּ, דְּנָפִיק מִזִּיוָא לְזִיוָא, וְזִיוָהּ נָגִיד מִנֵּיהּ, לְד׳ סִטְרִין רֵישִׁין, לְקַיְּימָא, מֵהַהוּא זִיוָא אִתְמְשָׁךְ לְכֻלְּהוּ דְּאִינּוּן לְתַתָּא, וְהַהִיא אִקְרֵי גִּנְתָּא דְּעֵדֶן.

46. Then that garden, NAMELY THE SHECHINAH, comes – which is hidden in 250 worlds. This is the precious Shechinah in Her shine OF CHOCHMAH that goes out from the shine OF CHOCHMAH AND COMBINES AND HIDES in the shine OF CHASSADIM. And the shine is drawn from Her to the four directions – CHESED, GVURAH, TIFERET AND MALCHUT, WHICH ARE THE FOUR branches – in order to provide for them IN MOCHIN. THIS IS THE SECRET OF THE VERSE: "AND FROM THENCE IT WAS PARTED, AND BRANCHED INTO FOUR STREAMS..." (BERESHEET 2:10). And this shine is drawn from Her to all that are below, and she is called 'the Garden of Eden'.

47. פָּתַח תִּנְיָינוּת הַהוּא סָבָא, פַּטְרוֹנָא דְּכֹלָּא וּמִדְכַּר שְׁמֵיהּ יוֹ״ד הֵ״א וָא״ו הֵ״א, וְכֻלְּהוּ פַּתְחֵי בִּתְלֵיסָר מְכִילָן דְּרַחֲמֵי. מָאן חָמֵי כָּל אִלֵּין תַּקִּיפִין, רָאמִין דְּרָאמִין, תַּקִּיפִין דְּתַקִּיפִין, רְתִיכִין קַדִּישִׁין, וּשְׁמַיָּא, וְכָל חֵילֵיהוֹן, מִזְדַּעְזְעִין וּמִתְחַלְחְלָן בְּאֵימָתָא סַגִּיאָה, מְשַׁבְּחָן שְׁמָא קַדִּישָׁא, וְאָמְרִין שִׁירָתָא. זַכָּאִין אִינּוּן נִשְׁמָתְהוֹן דְּצַדִּיקַיָּיא, דְּאִינּוּן בְּהַהוּא עִדּוּנָא, וְיַדְעִין דָּא, עַל הַאי אִתְּמַר מִי לֹא יִרָאֲךָ מֶלֶךְ הַגּוֹיִם כִּי לְךָ יָאָתָה וְגוֹ׳.

(ע״כ תוספתא)

47. That old man commenced speaking again, REFERRING TO ZEIR ANPIN, FOR AFTER HE ASCENDED TO ARICH ANPIN HE IS ALSO CALLED 'OLD'. He protects everything, MEANING BOTH THE DRAWING OF CHOCHMAH AND THE DRAWING OF CHASSADIM, and mentions the name *Yud-Vav-Dalet; Hei-Aleph; Vav-Aleph-Vav; Hei-Aleph*. And they all commence by DRAWING THE LIGHTS FROM the Thirteen Measures of Mercy. Who has

seen these strong lights which are the highest of the high, strongest of the strong! The holy Chariots and the heavens and their hosts tremble and shake with great fear, and praise the Holy Name and recite poetry. Fortunate are the souls of the righteous who are present in this luxuriousness and know this. About this, it is said: "Who would not fear You, King of the nations? For to You it is fitting..." (Yirmeyah 10:7).

End of Tosefta

מח. אָמַר רִבִּי שִׁמְעוֹן, כַּד נַחְתַּת שְׁכִינְתָּא לְמִצְרַיִם, נַחְתַּת חַיָּה חֲדָא, דִּשְׁמָהּ יִשְׂרָאֵל, בְּדִיּוּקְנָא דְּהַהוּא סָבָא, וְאַרְבְּעִין וּתְרֵין שַׁמָּשִׁין קַדִּישִׁין עִמֵּיהּ, וְכָל חַד וְחַד אָת קַדִּישָׁא עִמֵּיהּ, מִשְּׁמָא קַדִּישָׁא, וְכֻלְּהוּ נַחְתָּן עִם יַעֲקֹב לְמִצְרַיִם, הֲדָא הוּא דִכְתִיב, וְאֵלֶּה שְׁמוֹת בְּנֵי יִשְׂרָאֵל הַבָּאִים מִצְרַיְמָה אֵת יַעֲקֹב. א"ר יִצְחָק, מִמַּשְׁמַע דְּקָאָמַר בְּנֵי יִשְׂרָאֵל, וְאַחַר כָּךְ אֵת יַעֲקֹב, וְלֹא נֶאֱמַר אִתּוֹ.

48. Rabbi Shimon said: When the Shechinah descended into Egypt, one living creature OF THE FOUR LIVING CREATURES OF THE HOLY CHARIOT, whose name is Yisrael, descended in the form of that old man MENTIONED IN THE PREVIOUS VERSE, WHO IS ZEIR ANPIN. And 42 holy attendants descended with it, MEANING 42 ANGELS, and each one had a holy letter from the Holy Name OF MEM-BET (42). THESE ANGELS THAT ATTEND THE LIVING CREATURES WHOSE NAME IS YISRAEL ARE CALLED 'THE CHILDREN OF YISRAEL' AND ARE DRAWN FROM THE NAME OF MEM-BET (42), WHICH IS THE SECRET OF THE FIRST THREE SFIROT OF THAT LIVING CREATURES. And they all descended with Jacob into Egypt. This is what is written: "And these are the names of the children of Israel who came into Egypt with Jacob" (Shemot 1:1). Rabbi Yitzchak said: This is the meaning of "the children of Yisrael," "with Jacob," instead of 'with him.'

מט. שָׁאַל רִבִּי יְהוּדָה לְרִבִּי אֶלְעָזָר בר"ש, כֵּיוָן דִּשְׁמַעַת מֵאָבוּךְ, פָּרְשַׁת וְאֵלֶּה שְׁמוֹת בְּרָזָא עִלָּאָה, מַאי קָאָמַר אִישׁ וּבֵיתוֹ בָּאוּ. אָמַר לֵיהּ, הַהוּא מִלָּה דַּהֲוָה אָמַר אַבָּא, אִינוּן הָווּ מַלְאָכִין עִלָּאִין, דְּאִינוּן לְעֵילָא עַל תַּתָּאֵי מִנְהוֹן, הַיְינוּ דִכְתִיב אִישׁ וּבֵיתוֹ בָּאוּ, וְהָכִי אָמַר אַבָּא, כָּל אִינוּן מַלְאָכִין דִּבְדַרְגָּא עִלָּאָה, אִקְרוּן גּוּבְרִין דּוּכְרִין, וְאִינוּן דִּבְדַרְגָּא

תַּתָּאָה מִנְהוֹן, אִתְקְרוּן נוּקְבָתָא בֵּית, דְּאִתְּתָא נוּקְבָּא דִּמְקַבְּלָא מִן דְּכוּרָא.

49. Rabbi Yehuda asked Rabbi Elazar, the son of Rabbi Shimon: You learned from your father the portion of "And these are the names" THAT HE EXPLAINED according to the supernal secret, THAT THE CHILDREN OF YISRAEL ARE 42 HOLY ANGELS, AS EXPLAINED ABOVE. So what is the meaning of, "every man came with his household"? ANGELS DO NOT HAVE A HOUSEHOLD. RABBI ELAZAR said to him: What my father said MEANS the supernal angels, those who are higher than those who are lower among them. This is what is written: "every man came with his household." THE HIGHER ANGEL IS CALLED "MAN" AND THE ONE LOWER THAN HIM IS CALLED "HIS HOUSEHOLD." Likewise, my father said that all the angels in the higher level are called "males" and those in the level below them are called "females," and ARE CALLED "household" because a female receives from the male AND SHE IS LIKE A HOUSE TO HIM.

8. "…with Jacob; every man came with his household"

A Synopsis

In reply to the question posed by Rabbi Yitzchak, Rabbi Elazar affirms that the Shechinah did indeed accompany Jacob into Egypt. A discussion ensues in which Rabbi Elazar, Rabbi Aba, and Rabbi Yehuda each cite verses that indicate that thousands of celestial beings accompanied the Shechinah. Rabbi Elazar explains that in the verse, "And the children of Yisrael journeyed from Raamses to Sukkot about six hundred thousand footmen" (Shemot 12:37), the reference to the children of Israel is an allusion to the celestial hosts, God's servants, who naturally went with God when He went down into Egypt with Jacob, as was promised. Moreover, we're told that the children of Israel hurried to depart from Egypt because they realized these celestial beings were detained for their sake. Rabbi Aba then cites the verse, "Come and behold the works of Hashem Who has made desolations (Heb. *shamot*) in the earth" (Tehilim 46:9), and explains that the word 'desolations' can also be read as 'names'. In corroboration with Rabbi Chiya's statement that earthly counterparts exist for all that is in heaven, Rabbi Aba concludes that just as there are holy names in earth, so are there holy names on heaven. Thus, "And these are the names of the children of Israel," refers to the angels who came to Egypt. Rabbi Yehuda then provides an interpretation of the verse, "Behold the litter, that of Solomon…" (Shir Hashirim 3:7) to reveal that this verse also refers to the angels that went with the Schechinah into Egypt. Finally, while travelling with Rabbi Yosi, Rabbi Chiya deduces that since all of Israel went with Moses to meet his father-in-law, God's heavenly company would certainly have accompanied Him into Egypt.

The Relevance of the Passage

Whenever we find ourselves in spiritual darkness or physical chaos, the Light of the Creator, along with all the supernal angelic forces, is always with us, ready to emancipate us from the slavery and addictions of the material world.

We only have to call upon the holy Names to activate these Divine forces.

These Names are *recited* in the moment we meditate upon this potent passage of Zohar.

All the entities of Light that dwell above are amassed and set into motion. They descend into our world to liberate all humanity from the clutches of the dark side.

50. רִבִּי יִצְחָק הֲוָה קָאֵים קַמֵּיהּ דְּרִבִּי אֶלְעָזָר בַּר רִבִּי שִׁמְעוֹן, אָמַר לֵיהּ שְׁכִינְתָּא נַחְתַּת לְמִצְרַיִם עִם יַעֲקֹב. א"ל וְלָא, וְהָא כְּתִיב אָנֹכִי אֵרֵד עִמְּךָ. אָמַר לֵיהּ תָּא חֲזֵי, שְׁכִינְתָּא נַחְתַּת לְמִצְרַיִם אֶת יַעֲקֹב וְשִׁית מְאָה אַלְפִין רְתִיכִין קַדִּישִׁין עִמָּהּ, וְהַיְינוּ דִּכְתִיב כְּשֵׁשׁ מֵאוֹת אֶלֶף רַגְלִי, תָּנֵינָן שִׁית מְאָה אַלְפִין רְתִיכִין קַדִּישִׁין נַחְתּוּ עִם יַעֲקֹב לְמִצְרַיִם, וְכֻלְּהוּ סְלִיקוּ מִתַּמָּן, כַּד נָפְקוּ יִשְׂרָאֵל מִמִּצְרַיִם. הֲדָא הוּא דִּכְתִיב, וַיִּסְעוּ בְנֵי יִשְׂרָאֵל מֵרַעְמְסֵס סֻכֹּתָה כְּשֵׁשׁ מֵאוֹת אֶלֶף רַגְלִי וְגוֹ'. שֵׁשׁ מֵאוֹת לֹא נֶאֱמַר, אֶלָּא כְּשֵׁשׁ מֵאוֹת, כְּגַוְונָא דְּנָפְקוּ אִלֵּין, כָּךְ נָפְקוּ אִלֵּין.

50. Rabbi Yitzchak was studying before Rabbi Elazar, the son of Rabbi Shimon, and said to him: Did the Shechinah REALLY descend into Egypt with Jacob? He said to him: Did She not? Is it not written: "And I will descend with you" (Beresheet 46:4)? He said to him: Come and behold. The Shechinah descended into Egypt with Jacob and six hundred thousand holy Chariots with Her. This is what is written: "About six hundred thousand footmen" (Shemot 12:37). And we learned that six hundred thousand holy Chariots descended with Jacob into Egypt, and they all ascended from there when the Yisrael left Egypt. This is what is written: "And the children of Yisrael journeyed from Ramses to Sukkot about six hundred thousand footmen" (Ibid.). It does not say 'six hundred thousand', rather it says "about six hundred thousand." THIS IMPLIES THAT as the six hundred thousand BELOW left, so those SIX HUNDRED THOUSAND HOLY CHARIOTS FROM ABOVE WHO WERE WITH THEM left.

51. וְתָא חֲזֵי רָזָא דְּמִלָּה, בְּעִדָּנָא דְּנָפְקוּ אִלֵּין רְתִיכִין קַדִּישִׁין, מַשִּׁירְיָיתָא קַדִּישְׁתָּא, חָמוּ יִשְׂרָאֵל וְיָדְעוּ, דַּהֲווֹ מִתְעַכְּבִין בְּגִינֵיהוֹן, וְכֻלְּהוּ בְּהִילוּ דְּעָבְדוּ יִשְׂרָאֵל, בְּגִינֵיהוֹן הֲוָה, וְהַיְינוּ דִּכְתִיב וְלֹא יָכְלוּ לְהִתְמַהְמֵהַּ, הֲוָה לֵיהּ לְמֵימַר וְלֹא רָצוּ לְהִתְמַהְמֵהַּ אֲבָל לָא כְּתִיב אֶלָּא וְלֹא יָכְלוּ. וְאִתְיְידְעוּ מַמָּשׁ, דְּכֻלְּהוּ בְּנֵי יִשְׂרָאֵל, הֲווֹ בְּנֵי יִשְׂרָאֵל דִּרְקִיעָא, וְהַיְינוּ דִּכְתִיב, בְּנֵי יִשְׂרָאֵל הַבָּאִים מִצְרַיְמָה אֶת יַעֲקֹב, וְעַל דָּא לָא נֶאֱמַר וְאֵלֶּה שְׁמוֹת בְּנֵי יִשְׂרָאֵל הַבָּאִים מִצְרַיְמָה אִתּוֹ, אֶלָּא וְאֵלֶּה שְׁמוֹת בְּנֵי יִשְׂרָאֵל הַבָּאִים מִצְרַיְמָה אֶת יַעֲקֹב, הַבָּאִים מִצְרַיְמָה

-39-

בְּקַדְמֵיתָא וְעִם מִי, אֶת יַעֲקֹב.

51. Come and behold: This is the secret of the matter. When those holy Chariots and holy encampments departed, Yisrael then saw and knew they were being detained FROM LEAVING because of them, SINCE THEY WERE NOT LEAVING. And all the haste of Yisrael was for them. This is the meaning of what is written: "And could not delay" (Shemot 12:39). It should have said, 'And they did not want to delay', but instead it is written: "And could not." AND THIS WAS OUT OF NECESSITY BECAUSE OF THE HOST OF ANGELS THAT WERE TARRYING FOR THEM! And it is actually understood from here that the children of Yisrael IN THE PHRASE were all the children of Yisrael of the firmament – NAMELY THE ANGELS. Thus it is written: "The children of Yisrael who came into Egypt with Jacob" (Shemot 1:1). It does not state, 'And these are the names of the children of Israel who came into Egypt with him', but: "And these are the names of the children of Israel who came into Egypt with Jacob," MEANING who came to Egypt in the beginning, REFERRING TO THE ANGELS, AS STATED PREVIOUSLY. And with whom did they come? With Jacob.

52. א״ר יְהוּדָה, ק״ו, וּמַה כַּד אִשְׁתְּזִיב יַעֲקֹב מִלָּבָן, כְּתִיב, וְיַעֲקֹב הָלַךְ לְדַרְכּוֹ וַיִּפְגְּעוּ בוֹ מַלְאֲכֵי אֱלֹהִים. כַּד נָחַת בְּגָלוּתָא, וְקוּדְשָׁא ב״ה אָמַר, אָנֹכִי אֵרֵד עִמְּךָ מִצְרָיְמָה, לָאו דִּינָא, הוֹאִיל וּפַטְרוֹנָא נַחְתָּא דְּיֵיחָתוּן שַׁמָּשׁוֹי עִמֵּיהּ, הַיְינוּ דִּכְתִּיב הַבָּאִים מִצְרַיְמָה אֶת יַעֲקֹב. רִבִּי יַעֲקֹב דִּכְפַר חָנָן אָמַר מִשְּׁמֵיהּ דר׳ אַבָּא, מַאן אִינּוּן בְּנֵי יִשְׂרָאֵל דְּהָכָא. אִינּוּן דְּאִתְקְרוּן בְּנֵי יִשְׂרָאֵל מַמָּשׁ.

52. Rabbi Yehuda states: We have a situation involving a minor to major inference. At the time when Jacob was saved from Laban, it is written: "And Jacob went on his way, and angels of Elohim met him" (Beresheet 32:2). Then, when he descended into Egypt, the Holy One, blessed be He, said, "I will go down with you into Egypt" (Beresheet 46:4). And if the Master descends, is it not the rule ALL THE MORE SO that His attendants will descend with Him? Thus, it is written: "Who came into Egypt with Jacob" (Shemot 1:1), INSTEAD OF 'WITH HIM'. Rabbi Ya'akov of the village of Chanan asks in the name of Rabbi Aba: Who are the children of Yisrael mentioned here? AND HE ANSWERS: Those who are actually called 'the children of Yisrael', NAMELY THE TRIBES.

53. ר' אַבָּא פָּתַח וְאָמַר, לְכוּ חֲזוּ מִפְעֲלוֹת יְיָ' אֲשֶׁר שָׂם שַׁמּוֹת בָּאָרֶץ. אַל תִּקְרֵי שַׁמּוֹת. אֶלָּא שֵׁמוֹת. וְאַזְלָא הָא כְּהָא דְּאָמַר ר' חִיָּיא, כְּגַוְונָא דִּרְקִיעָא, עָבֵד קוּדְשָׁא בְּרִיךְ הוּא בְּאַרְעָא בִּרְקִיעַ אִית שְׁמָהָן קַדִּישִׁין, בְּאַרְעָא אִית שְׁמָהָן קַדִּישִׁין.

53. Rabbi Aba opened the discussion TO BRING PROOF TO HIS WORDS saying: "Come and behold the works of Hashem who has made desolations (Heb. *shamot*) in the earth" (Tehilim 46:9). Do not pronounce it *shamot*, but rather *shemot* (lit. 'names'). This follows a similar thought expressed by Rabbi Chiya that, as the Holy One, blessed be He, has done in heaven, so has He done on earth. Just as there are holy names in heaven, so are there holy names here on earth. THESE ARE THE NAMES OF THE TRIBES OF WHICH IT IS WRITTEN: "THESE ARE THE NAMES OF THE CHILDREN OF ISRAEL...".

54. אָמַר רְבִּי יְהוּדָה בְּהַהוּא יוֹמָא דְּנָחַת יַעֲקֹב לְמִצְרַיִם, נָחֲתוּ עִמֵּיהּ שִׁתִּין רִבּוֹא דְּמַלְאֲכֵי עִלָּאֵי. ר' יְהוּדָה פָּתַח, הִנֵּה מִטָּתוֹ שֶׁלִּשְׁלֹמֹה שִׁשִּׁים גִּבּוֹרִים סָבִיב וְגוֹ' קוּזְמִיטִין דְּגָלִיפִין בִּקְלַדִיטָא, סָחֲרָן בְּדוּכְתֵּיהּ קוּזְמִיטִין בִּשְׁבִיעָאָה, גְּלִיפִין בִּשְׁתִיתָאָה, הה"ד, שִׁשִּׁים גִּבּוֹרִים סָבִיב לָהּ.

54. Rabbi Yehuda said that six hundred thousand supernal angels descended with Jacob on the day that Jacob descended into Egypt. Rabbi Yehuda commenced TO BRING PROOF OF HIS WORDS: "Behold the litter, that of Solomon. Sixty valiant men are round about it" (Shir Hashirm 3:7). There are locks that are forged to accommodate a key, AND THE KEYS turn inside THE LOCK. The locks are in the seventh SFIRAH OF MALCHUT, and they are carved in the sixth SFIRAH OF YESOD. This is the meaning of what is written: "Sixty valiant men are round about it."

55. הִנֵּה מִטָּתוֹ: דָּא אִיהִי שְׁכִינְתָּא. שֶׁלִּשְׁלֹמֹה: מַלְכָּא דִּשְׁלָמָא דִּילֵיהּ. שִׁשִּׁים גִּבּוֹרִים סָבִיב לָהּ: אִלֵּין אִינּוּן שִׁתִּין רִבּוֹא דְּמַלְאֲכֵי עִלָּאֵי, דְּאִינּוּן מֵחֵילָא דִּשְׁכִינְתָּא, דְּנַחְתַת עִם יַעֲקֹב לְמִצְרַיִם. מִגִּבּוֹרֵי יִשְׂרָאֵל: יִשְׂרָאֵל דִּלְעֵילָּא, הה"ד וְאֵלֶּה שְׁמוֹת בְּנֵי יִשְׂרָאֵל וְגוֹ', אִישׁ וּבֵיתוֹ בָּאוּ: אִינּוּן וְנִימוּסֵיהוֹן.

55. HE CONTINUES TO EXPLAIN THE ENTIRE VERSE AND SAYS: "Behold the litter," refers to the Shechinah, WHICH IS CALLED 'BED'. "Of Solomon" (Shlomo), refers to the King, to Whom the peace (Heb. *shalom*) belongs, ZEIR ANPIN, THE CENTRAL COLUMN THAT BRINGS PEACE BETWEEN RIGHT AND LEFT. "Sixty valiant men are round about it," are the six hundred thousand supernal angels of the host of the Shechinah that descended with Jacob into Egypt. "Of the mighty men of Yisrael," refers to supernal Yisrael, WHICH IS ZEIR ANPIN, FOR GVURAH ('MIGHT') IS DRAWN TO THEM FROM THERE. The verse: "And these are the names of the children of Israel...every man came with his household," REFERS TO them and their customs, BECAUSE "CAME WITH HIS HOUSEHOLD" MEANS HIS WAYS AND CUSTOMS. FOR EVERY ANGEL HAS A PARTICULAR TASK AFTER WHICH HE IS NAMED, AS WE KNOW.

56. ר' חִיָּיא הֲוָה אָזִיל מֵאוּשָׁא לְלוֹד, וַהֲוָה רָכִיב עַל חֲמָרָא, וַהֲוָה ר' יוֹסֵי עִמֵּיהּ, נָחִית ר' חִיָּיא, וְשַׁקְלֵיהּ בִּידוֹי לְר' יוֹסֵי, א"ל, אִי בְּנֵי עָלְמָא יַדְעִין יְקָרָא סַגִּיאָה דְּיַעֲקֹב, בְּשַׁעֲתָא דְּא"ל קוּדְשָׁא בְּרִיךְ הוּא, אָנֹכִי אֵרֵד עִמְּךָ מִצְרַיְמָה, הָווֹ מְלַחֲכֵי עַפְרָא, תְּלַת פַּרְסֵי קָרִיב לְקַבְרֵיהּ, דְּהָכִי מְפָרְשֵׁי מָרָנָא רַבְרְבֵי עָלְמָא, מָארֵיהוֹן דְּמַתְנִיתָא, כְּתִיב וַיֵּצֵא מֹשֶׁה לִקְרַאת חוֹתְנוֹ, אַהֲרֹן חָמָא לְמֹשֶׁה דְּנָפַק, וְנָפַק עִמֵּיהּ, וְאֶלְעָזָר וּנְשִׂיאֵי וְסָבֵי נַפְקוּ עִמֵּיהּ, רָאשֵׁי אֲבָהָן, וּמְעַרְעֵי כְּנִשְׁתָּא, וְכָל יִשְׂרָאֵל נַפְקוּ עִמְּהוֹן, אִשְׁתַּכְּחוּ דְּכָל יִשְׂרָאֵל כֻּלְּהוּ, נָפְקוּ לְקַבְּלֵיהּ דְּיִתְרוֹ, מַאן חָמָא לְמֹשֶׁה דְּנָפִיק וְלָא יִפּוֹק, לְאַהֲרֹן וּלְרַבְרְבֵי דְּנַפְקֵי, וְלָא יִפּוֹק. אִשְׁתְּכַח, דְּבְגִין מֹשֶׁה נָפְקוּ כֻּלְּהוֹן. וּמַה, אִי בְּגִין מֹשֶׁה כָּךְ, בְּגִין קוּדְשָׁא בְּרִיךְ הוּא, כַּד אָמַר אָנֹכִי אֵרֵד עִמְּךָ מִצְרַיְמָה, עאכ"ו.

56. Rabbi Chiya was traveling from Usha to Lod. He was riding on a donkey, and Rabbi Yosi was with him. Rabbi Chiya dismounted, waving his hands toward Rabbi Yosi. He said to him: If the people knew the great respect given to Jacob when the Holy One, blessed be He, said to him: "I will descend with you into Egypt" (Beresheet 46:4), they would lick the dust in the three parasangs around his grave. Thus, our teachers, the greatest men in the world, the sages of the Mishnah expound upon it. It is written: "Moses went out towards his father-in-law" (Shemot 18:7). AND THEY EXPLAIN: When Aaron saw Moses going out, he joined him. Elazar and the princes and the elders accompanied him, and the heads of the house of the

fathers and men of mark in the congregation and all Yisrael accompanied them. So it came about that all of Yisrael went out to meet Jethro, because who would see Moses and Aaron and the princes going out and not accompany them? Thus, because of Moses, they all went out! Now if this occurred because of Moses, when the Holy One, blessed be He, said, "I will descend with you into Egypt," certainly THE WHOLE HEAVENLY COURT DESCENDED WITH HIM. NOW IT IS COMPREHENSIBLE WHY IN THE BEGINNING THE HOLY ONE, BLESSED BE HE, SAID, "I WILL DESCEND WITH YOU INTO EGYPT," WHICH INSINUATES THAT HE ALONE WOULD DESCEND. AND AFTERWARDS IT SAYS, "AND THESE ARE THE NAMES OF THE CHILDREN OF ISRAEL," WHICH MEANS ALL THE HEAVENLY COURT. FOR BY MOSES ALSO, IT IS WRITTEN, "AND MOSES WENT OUT," YET ALL YISRAEL WENT OUT WITH HIM!

9. "The word of Hashem was"

A Synopsis

Upon meeting Rabbi Yosi and Rabbi Chiya immersed in discussion, Rabbi Aba offers an additional verse to reinforce their conclusion that the angels accompanied the children of Israel into Egypt. He alludes to the vision Ezekial revealed to the children of Israel to prove that God had not and would not abandon them in captivity in Babylon. Just as God was with them in Babylon, Rabbi Aba explains, so He and His heavenly company went with them into Egypt.

The Relevance of the Passage

Jacob's soul, like Adam's, embodied all the souls of humanity. Each person who has ever walked this earth was included in Jacob, spiritually speaking. Thus, the reader himself is part of Jacob. This is your story. And the story continues to unfold into this present moment.

The mention of Egypt alludes to our own ego and to the illusionary pleasures of the physical world. We are enslaved to these aspects of our existence.

Yet, the Zohar emphasizes that all the supernal angelic forces and the Shechinah (the Divine Presence) accompanied Jacob into Egypt.
These sacred forces are with us now. They shine their Light upon us and the entire world. We are liberated from *Egypt*. Our soul attains complete dominion over our ego. Now we are free to recognize and enjoy the true and lasting pleasures of life.

This passage also commences the complete revelation of God's truth and wisdom in this world. The Light and the mysteries of the Zohar shine in the hearts of all humanity.

57. עַד דַּהֲווֹ אַזְלֵי, פָּגַע בְּהוּ ר' אַבָּא. א"ר יוֹסֵי, הָא שְׁכִינְתָּא הָכָא, דְּחַד מִמָּארֵיהוֹן דְּמַתְנִיתִין עִמָּנָא. אָמַר ר' אַבָּא, בְּמַאי עַסְקִיתוּ. א"ר יוֹסֵי, בְּהַאי קְרָא, דִּכְתִיב אָנֹכִי אֵרֵד עִמְּךָ מִצְרַיְמָה וְגו'. כַּד נָחַת יַעֲקֹב לְמִצְרַיִם, דִּכְתִיב, וְאֵלֶּה שְׁמוֹת בְּנֵי יִשְׂרָאֵל הַבָּאִים מִצְרַיְמָה, אֶת אוֹלִיף, דְּכֻלְּהוּ נָחֲתוּ עִם יַעֲקֹב לְמִצְרַיִם.

57. While they were still traveling, Rabbi Aba met them. Rabbi Yosi said: Behold the Shechinah is here, because one of the masters of the Mishnah is here with us. Rabbi Aba asked: What are you engaged in? Rabbi Yosi said: "I will descend with you into Egypt" (Beresheet 46:4). When Jacob

descended into Egypt, as written: "Now these are the names of the children of Israel who came into Egypt..." (Shemot 1:1), you learn that they all descended with Jacob into Egypt. THE IMPLICATION IS THAT ALL THE CHARIOTS AND HOSTS DESCENDED WITH JACOB INTO EGYPT AND NOT THE HOLY ONE, BLESSED BE HE, ALONE AS IS IMPLIED IN THE VERSE: "I WILL DESCEND WITH YOU INTO EGYPT."

58. א״ל ר' אַבָּא, וְדָא לְחוּד הֲוַת. פָּתַח וְאָמַר הָיָה הָיָה דְּבַר יְיָ' אֶל יְחֶזְקֵאל בֶּן בּוּזִי הַכֹּהֵן בְּאֶרֶץ כַּשְׂדִּים עַל נְהַר כְּבָר. תְּלַת פְּלוּגְתָּן הָכָא. חֲדָא, דִּתְנֵינָן, אֵין שְׁכִינָה שׁוֹרָה בְּחוּצָה לָאָרֶץ. וַחֲדָא, דְּלָא הֲוָה מְהֵימָן כְּמֹשֶׁה, דִּכְתִיב בֵּיהּ, בְּכָל בֵּיתִי נֶאֱמָן הוּא, וְהוּא, גַּלֵּי וּפַרְסֵם כָּל גִּנְזַיָּיא דְּמַלְכָּא. וַחֲדָא, דְּאִתְחֲזֵי כְּמַאן דְּלָא שְׁלִים בְּדַעְתֵּיהּ.

58. Rabbi Aba said to him: Yet this one was alone. He opened the discussion saying: "The word of Hashem came to Ezekiel the priest, the son of Buzi, in the land of Chaldeans by the river K'var" (Yechezkel 1:3). There are three difficulties here. One difficulty is that we learned that the Shechinah does not dwell outside the land of Yisrael WHILE THE PROPHECY OF EZEKIEL IS IN THE LAND OF CHALDEANS. Another difficulty is that he was not trusted like Moses, as is written: "For he is the trusted one in all My house" (Bemidbar 12:7). But he, EZEKIEL, revealed and publicized all the treasures of the King, MORE THAN MOSES. And another difficulty is that apparently he was not of a wholesome mind, FOR IF HE WAS OF A WHOLESOME MIND HE WOULD NOT HAVE REVEALED SO MUCH.

59. אֶלָּא הָכִי אַסִּיקְנָא בְּמַתְנִיתָא דִּילָן, ח״ו דְּהָא יְחֶזְקֵאל נְבִיאָה שְׁלֵימָא הֲוָה, וּבִרְשׁוּתָא דְקוּדְשָׁא בְּרִיךְ הוּא גַּלֵּי כָּל מַה דְּגַלֵּי. וְכֻלְּהוּ אִצְטְרִיךְ דִּיגַלֵּי וִיפַרְסֵם, עַל חַד תְּרֵין מִמַּה דְּגַלֵּי, דְּהָכִי תְּנַן, מַאן דְּרָגִיל לְמִסְבַּל צַעֲרָא וכו'. וְכֹלָּא אִצְטְרִיךְ, וּמֵעָלְמִין לָא שָׁבִיק קוּדְשָׁא בְּרִיךְ הוּא לְיִשְׂרָאֵל בְּגָלוּתָא, עַד דַּהֲוָה אָתֵי לְמֵידַר דִּיוּרֵיהּ עִמְּהוֹן, כָּל שֶׁכֵּן בְּיַעֲקֹב, דַּהֲוָה נָחִית בְּגָלוּתָא, וְקוּדְשָׁא בְּרִיךְ הוּא וּשְׁכִינְתֵּיהּ, וְקַדִּישִׁין עִלָּאִין, וּרְתִיכִין, דְּנָחֲתוּ כֻּלְּהוּ עִם יַעֲקֹב, הה״ד הַבָּאִים מִצְרַיְמָה אֶת יַעֲקֹב.

59. HE ANSWERS: Rather this is the explanation of our Mishnah. Heaven forbid that he revealed more than necessary, because Ezekiel was perfect in his mind. Whatever he revealed was with the permission of the Holy One, blessed be He, and it was necessary that he reveal whatever he revealed. For so we have learned, "One who is accustomed to bear pain..." (AS MENTIONED EARLIER IN THE ZOHAR, VERSES 7-14) and all was necessary. And never did the Holy One, blessed be He, leave Yisrael in exile before He came and caused His Shechinah to dwell with them. And of course, it was with Jacob, who was descending into exile, that the Holy One, blessed be He, and His Shechinah and the supernal holy beings and the Chariots all descended with Jacob. As it is written: "Who came into Egypt with Jacob" (Shemot 1:1). AND WITH THIS IS THE ANSWER TO THE QUESTION OF RABBI YOSI ABOVE – THAT EVEN THOUGH IT SAYS, "I WILL DESCEND WITH YOU INTO EGYPT," IT DOES NOT IMPLY HE ALONE, BUT RATHER WITH HIS SHECHINAH AND HIS HOSTS AND HIS CHARIOTS. FOR THIS IS THE WAY OF THE HOLY ONE, BLESSED BE HE, IN ALL EXILES, AS EZEKIEL REVEALED BY THE EXILE OF BABYLON.

10. "Come with me from Lebanon, my bride"

A Synopsis

In this section, Rabbi Yitzchak first explains that he who studies Torah and performs good deeds will inherit a complete world, while he whose good deeds are incomplete will inherit according to what he deserves. He who does not study Torah or acquire any good deeds will inherit neither this world nor the World to Come. Following this, a discussion of the title verse begins. Rabbi Yehuda explains that God addressed these words to the Shechinah in the upper Sanctuary and announced that the children of Israel would receive the Torah. This would be their shield in exile, to protect them from the idolatrous and oppressive heathen nations. Rabbi Aba adds that God was first in the company that included the Shechinah and 600,000 ministering angels that descended into Egypt with Him. Rabbi Yitzchak interprets the phrase, "look from the top of Amanah," as referring to the Sanctuary above and below, and "From the top of Senir and Chermon," as signifying Mount Sinai. Finally, Rabbi Yehuda offers a contrasting interpretation of, "from the lions' den," as a reference to the students of the Torah, who are lions and leopards in the Torah.

The Relevance of the Passage

Through the merit of Jacob and all the righteous souls spoken of in the Zohar, we merit a place in the World to Come. Moreover, our actions of reading these very verses become our "good deeds," earning us a portion of the immortal, infinite Light of Creation. And each new day that we embrace these verses and meditate to share its Light with our friends and foes, we add to our good deeds, thereby increasing our share of the World to Come.

The place called *Lebanon* is a code referring to the spiritual domain known as Binah. Binah's Light is super-luminous. Its ultra-radiant rays banish death and discontent. When Binah shines, it is known as the *World to Come*.

Binah shines now.

סֵ. ר׳ אַבָּא פָּתַח וְאָמַר, אִתִּי מִלְּבָנוֹן כַּלָּה אִתִּי מִלְּבָנוֹן תָּבוֹאִי תָּא חֲזֵי וַוי לוֹן בְּנֵי נָשָׁא, דְּלָא יַדְעִין, וְלָא מַשְׁגִּיחִין בְּפוּלְחָנָא דְּמָארֵיהוֹן, דְּתַנְיָא א״ר יִצְחָק, בְּכָל יוֹמָא וְיוֹמָא בַּת קוֹל נַפְקַת מִטּוּרָא דְּחוֹרֵב, וְאָמַר, וַוי לוֹן לִבְנֵי נָשָׁא מִפּוּלְחָנָא דְּמָארֵיהוֹן, וַוי לוֹן לִבְנֵי נָשָׁא מֵעֶלְבּוֹנָה דְּאוֹרַיְיתָא. דְּאָמַר ר׳ יְהוּדָה, כָּל מַאן דְּאִשְׁתַּדַּל בְּאוֹרַיְיתָא

-47-

בְּהַאי עָלְמָא, וּמְסַגֵּל עוֹבָדִין טָבִין יָרִית עָלְמָא שְׁלֵימָא. וְכָל מַאן דְּלָא אִשְׁתַּדַּל בְּאוֹרַיְיתָא בְּהַאי עָלְמָא, וְלָא עָבֵיד עוֹבָדִין טָבִין, לָא יָרִית לָא הַאי וְלָא הַאי. וְהָא תְּנַן, אִית מַאן דְּיָרִית עָלְמֵיהּ כְּפוֹם אַתְרֵיהּ, וּכְפוֹם מַה דְּחָזֵי לֵיהּ. א״ר יִצְחָק, לָא תְּנַן, אֶלָּא מַאן דְּלֵית לֵיהּ עוֹבָדִין טָבִין כְּלָל.

60. Rabbi Aba commenced the discussion and said: "Come with me from Lebanon, my bride, with me from Lebanon" (Shir Hashirm 4:8). Come and behold: Woe to those people who do not know and are not careful of the service to their Creator. For we learned that Rabbi Yitzchak said: Every day a divine voice emanates from Mount Horeb and says, 'Woe is to those WHO DISREGARD the service of their Creator, woe to those who denigrate the honor of the Torah.' For Rabbi Yehuda said: All who study Torah in this world and acquire good deeds will inherit a complete world. And all who do not study Torah in this world and do not do good deeds will not inherit this or that – MEANING NOT THIS WORLD AND NOT THE WORLD TO COME. YOU MAY WONDER WHY IT IS SAID EITHER HE INHERITS A COMPLETE WORLD OR HE LOSES TWO WORLDS, and yet we have learned there is one who inherits according to his station and what is deserving to him, MEANING THERE IS A MIDDLE WAY. Rabbi Yitzchak said: We did not learn THAT ONE DOES NOT HAVE TWO WORLDS, except for one who has no good deed at all. BUT ONE WHO DOES HAVE GOOD DEEDS, EVEN THOUGH THEY ARE INCOMPLETE, INHERITS HIS WORLD ACCORDING TO WHAT HE DESERVES BOTH IN THIS WORLD AND IN THE WORLD TO COME.

61. א״ר יְהוּדָה, אִלְמָלֵי הֲווֹ יַדְעִין בְּנֵי נָשָׁא, רְחִימוּתָא דְּרָחִים קוּדְשָׁא בְּרִיךְ הוּא לְיִשְׂרָאֵל, הֲווֹ שָׁאֲגִין כְּכְפִירַיָּא לְמִרְדַּף אֲבַתְרֵיהּ. דְּתַנְיָא, בְּשַׁעֲתָא דְּנָחַת יַעֲקֹב לְמִצְרַיִם, קָרָא קוּדְשָׁא בְּרִיךְ הוּא לְפָמַלְיָא דִּילֵיהּ אָמַר לְהוֹן, כֻּלְּכוֹן חוּתוּ לְמִצְרַיִם, וַאֲנָא אֵיחוּת עִמְּכוֹן. אָמְרָה שְׁכִינְתָּא רִבּוֹנָא דְּעָלְמָא, אִית צְבָאוֹת בְּלָא מַלְכָּא, אָמַר לָהּ, אֲתִי מִלְּבָנוֹן כַּלָּה, מִלְּבָנוֹן: מֵאַתְרָא דְּעֵדֶן, דְּמִלּוּבָּן בְּכָל עוֹבָדוֹי. כַּלָּה: דָּא שְׁכִינְתָּא, דְּהִיא כַּלָּה בְּחוּפָּה. וְאַזְלָא הָא כְּהָא דְּתַנְיָא א״ר יְהוּדָה, מַאי דִּכְתִיב, וַיְהִי בְּיוֹם כַּלֹּת מֹשֶׁה, כַּלַּת כְּתִיב, בְּיוֹמָא דְּעָאלַת כַּלָּה לַחוּפָּה, וּשְׁכִינְתָּא דָּא הִיא כַּלָּה.

61. Rabbi Yehuda said: If people knew the love that the Holy One, blessed be He, has for Yisrael, they would roar like lions to pursue Him AND ADHERE TO HIM. At the time that Jacob descended into Egypt, the Holy One, blessed be He, summoned His company OF ANGELS and said to them: 'All of you descend into Egypt and I will descend with you'. The Shechinah said, 'Master of the Universe, are there hosts without a king?' FOR THE SHECHINAH IS CONSIDERED THE KING OF THE ANGELS BECAUSE THEY ALL FLOW FROM HER. He said to Her: "Come with me from Lebanon, my bride," you will come with Me from Lebanon from the place of Eden, WHICH IS CHOCHMAH, that is refined in all its actions. "Bride" is the Shechinah, which is the bride under the canopy. It follows what we have learned, that Rabbi Yehuda said: What is the meaning of, "And it came to pass on the day that Moses had finished (Heb. *kalot*)..." (Bemidbar 7:1)? *Kalot* is spelled without a *Vav*, for this is the day that the *kalah* (lit. 'bride') enters the *Chupah* (wedding canopy), and the bride is the Shechinah, WHICH IS IN THE TEMPLE, THE BRIDE UNDER THE CHUPAH.

62. אִתִּי מִלְּבָנוֹן תָּבוֹאִי, מֵאֲתָר בֵּי מַקְדְּשָׁא דִּלְעֵילָא. תְּשׁוּרִי מֵרֹאשׁ אֲמָנָה, מֵרֵישָׁא דְּמַאן. מֵרָאשֵׁיהוֹן דִּבְנֵי מְהֵימָנוּתָא. וּמַאן נִינְהוּ. יַעֲקֹב וּבְנוֹי. מֵרֹאשׁ שְׂנִיר וְחֶרְמוֹן, דְּאִינּוּן עֲתִידִין לְקַבְּלָא אוֹרַיְיתָא דִּילִי, מִטּוּרָא דְּחֶרְמוֹן, וּלְאַגָּנָא עֲלַיְיהוּ בְּגָלוּתְהוֹן. מִמְּעוֹנוֹת אֲרָיוֹת: אִלֵּין אִינּוּן עַמִּין עעכו״ם, דְּדַמְיָין לְאַרְיְוָותָא וּנְמֵרִין, דִּמְעַנִּין לְהוֹן בְּכָל פּוּלְחָנָא דִּקַשְׁיוּ.

62. "...with me from Lebanon..." meaning from the place of the supernal Temple. "Look from the top of Amanah." HE ASKS: From the top of what? AND ANSWERS: From the head (top) of those who have Faith (Heb. *emunah*). And who are they? Jacob and his sons. "From the top of Senir and Chermon," for they are destined to receive My Torah from Mount Chermon – MEANING MOUNT SINAI, WHICH IS CALLED 'CHERMON' – to protect them in exile, WHICH IS CALLED 'CHERMON', DERIVED FROM DESTRUCTION (HEB. *CHEREM*). "From the lions' dens," is in reference to the nations that serve idols, who are compared to lions and leopards that oppress YISRAEL with all types of hard labor.

63. ר' אַבָּא אָמַר, אִתִּי מִלְּבָנוֹן כַּלָּה וְגוֹ'. וְכִי מִלְּבָנוֹן אָתַת, וַהֲלָא לַלְּבָנוֹן עוֹלָה. אֶלָּא א״ר אַבָּא, בְּשַׁעֲתָא דְּנַחֲתַת שְׁכִינְתָּא לְמִצְרַיִם,

נַחְתּוּ בַּהֲדָהּ שִׁתִּין רִבּוֹא שְׁתִּין רִבּוֹא שֶׁל מַלְאֲכֵי הַשָּׁרֵת, וְקוּדְשָׁא בְּרִיךְ הוּא בְּקַדְמֵיתָא הה"ד וַיַּעֲבוֹר מַלְכָּם לִפְנֵיהֶם וה' בְּרֹאשָׁם.

63. Rabbi Aba said: "Come with Me from Lebanon, My bride." AND HE ASKS: Is she coming from Lebanon? Yet she is going up to Lebanon. AND SHE IS ASCENDING TO LEBANON TO RECEIVE CHOCHMAH! THUS, IT SHOULD HAVE SAID, 'ASCEND WITH ME TO LEBANON.' Therefore Rabbi Aba said: When the Shechinah descended into Egypt, six hundred thousand ministering angels descended with Her, and the Holy One, blessed be He, was first, as is written: "And their King passed before them and Hashem at their head" (Michah 2:13).

64. ר' יִצְחָק אָמַר, אִתִּי מִלְּבָנוֹן כַּלָּה, דָּא אִיהִי שְׁכִינְתָּא. אִתִּי מִלְּבָנוֹן תָּבֹאי, מֵאֲתָר בֵּי מַקְדְּשָׁא דִּלְעֵילָא. תָּשׁוּרִי מֵרֹאשׁ אֲמָנָה, מֵאֲתָר בֵּי מַקְדְּשָׁא דִּלְעֵילָא, וּמֵאֲתָר בֵּי מַקְדְּשָׁא דִּלְתַתָּא דְּאָמַר ר' יְהוּדָה, מֵעוֹלָם לֹא זָזָה שְׁכִינְתָּא מִכּוֹתְלֵי דִמְעַרְבָא, דְּבֵי מַקְדְּשָׁא, דִּכְתִיב, הִנֵּה זֶה עוֹמֵד אַחַר כָּתְלֵנוּ. וְהוּא רֹאשׁ אֲמָנָה לְכָל עָלְמָא. מֵרֹאשׁ שְׁנִיר וְחֶרְמוֹן מֵאַתְרָא דְּאוֹרַיְיתָא נָפְקַת לְעָלְמָא, וְלָמָּה. לְאַגָּנָא עַל יִשְׂרָאֵל, מִמְּעוֹנוֹת אֲרָיוֹת: אִלֵּין עַמִּין עעכו"ם. ר' יוּדָן אוֹמֵר, מִמְּעוֹנוֹת אֲרָיוֹת: אִלֵּין אִינוּן ת"ח, דְּעַסְקֵי בְּאוֹרַיְיתָא בִּמְעוֹנוֹת הַמִּדְרָשׁוֹת, וּבְבָתֵּי כְנֵסִיּוֹת, דְּאִינוּן אֲרָיָון וּנְמֵרִים בְּאוֹרַיְיתָא.

64. Rabbi Yitzchak said, "Come with me from Lebanon, my bride," refers to the Shechinah. "…with me from Lebanon…" MEANS from the place of the supernal Temple, WHICH IS BINAH. "Look from the Top of Amanah," MEANS from the place of the Temple above and the Temple below. For Rabbi Yehuda said: The Shechinah has never moved from the western wall of the Temple, as is written: "Behold, he stands behind our wall" (Shir Hashirm 2:9). And He is the top of Amanah for the whole world. "From the top of Senir and Chermon," MEANS from the place whence the Torah went out to the world, MEANING MOUNT SINAI, WHICH IS CALLED 'CHERMON'. And why IS THIS? In order to protect Yisrael. "The lions' dens" (Shim Hashirm 4:8), are the nations who worship idols. Rabbi Yudan says: "The lions' dens," refers to scholars who study the Torah in the Torah academies and synagogues, who are lions and leopards in the Torah.

11. "Seventy souls"

A Synopsis

In reference to the title verse, Rabbi Chiya asks Rabbi Shimon to explain the significance of the number seventy, and why the Torah first enumerates the sons of Jacob as twelve, and then as seventy. Rabbi Shimon's explanation is that seventy corresponds to the seventy nations of the world, and the nation of Israel was equal to all of them. Furthermore, we learn that just as the world cannot exist without the four winds, the other nations of the world cannot exist without Israel, as the twelve tribes illuminate the seventy nations.

The Relevance of the Passage

As the heart furnishes blood to all the organs of the body, Yisrael furnishes spiritual energy to all the nations of the world. This nourishment can only take place through the spiritual secrets of the Torah – the sacred Zohar – which arouses the soul of a man, connecting the soul to the Tree of Life, the source of all joy, wisdom and peace. When there is a deficiency of Light in our world, darkness becomes a naturally occurring phenomenon.

Yisrael creates the Light for the seventy Nations through the Central Column – which is the free will to RESIST all reactive and self-serving impulses in favor of receiving the treasures of this world for the sake of sharing with others.

Each of us is a child of Yisrael. Each time we resist our reactive desires, we nurture the souls of our fellow man with sweetness and Light. Hatred is then banished from the human heart.

Reading these verses nourishes all nations and all mankind with spiritual sustenance. Global conflicts peacefully end and hatred is eternally abolished from the human heart.

65. ר' חִיָּיא הֲוָה יָתִיב קַמֵּיהּ דר"ש, א"ל, מַה חָמַת אוֹרַיְיתָא לְמִמְנֵי בְּנוֹי דְּיַעֲקֹב, דְּאִינּוּן תְּרֵיסָר בְּקַדְמֵיתָא, וּלְבָתַר כֵּן שַׁבְעִים דִּכְתִּיב כָּל הַנֶּפֶשׁ לְבֵית יַעֲקֹב הַבָּאָה מִצְרַיְמָה שִׁבְעִים. ומ"ט שַׁבְעִים וְלָא יַתִּיר. א"ל, לְקַבֵּיל ע' אוּמִין, דְּאִינּוּן בְּעָלְמָא, וְאִינּוּן הֲווֹ אוּמָה יְחִידָאָה לְקַבֵּל כֻּלְּהוֹן.

65. Rabbi Chiya was sitting before Rabbi Shimon. He said to him: In the beginning, why did the Torah count twelve sons of Jacob, yet afterwards

they were seventy, as is written: "All the souls of the house of Jacob who came into Egypt were seventy" (Beresheet 46:27)? And what is the reason that they were seventy and not more? RABBI SHIMON said to him: It corresponds to the seventy nations in the world. They were one nation equal to them all.

‎66. וְתוּ א״ל, תָּא חֲזֵי, קַלְדִּיטִין דְּנָהֲרִין עַנְפִּין יַתְבִין בְּמַטַלְנֵיהוֹן, מְמַנָּן עַל שִׁבְעִין עַמְמִין, נָפְקִין מִתְרֵיסָר גְּלִיפִין קְטוּרִין דְּאִסְתַּחֲרָן בְּמַטַלְנֵיהוֹן, לְמִתְקְלָן לְאַרְבַּע רוּחֵי עָלְמָא, הה״ד, יַצֵּב גְּבוּלוֹת עַמִּים לְמִסְפַּר בְּנֵי יִשְׂרָאֵל. וְהַיְינוּ דִכְתִּיב, כִּי כְּאַרְבַּע רוּחוֹת הַשָּׁמַיִם פֵּרַשְׂתִּי אֶתְכֶם, לְאַחֲזָאָה דְּאִינוּן קַיְימִין בְּגִין יִשְׂרָאֵל. בְּאַרְבַּע לָא נֶאֱמַר, אֶלָּא כְּאַרְבַּע. כְּמָה דְּאִי אֶפְשָׁר לְעָלְמָא בְּלֹא אַרְבַּע רוּחוֹת כַּךְ אִי אֶפְשָׁר לְעָלְמָא בְּלֹא יִשְׂרָאֵל.

66. And he also said to him: Come and behold. Let us consider the keys that illuminate. THEIR BRANCHES ARE SET IN THEIR TRAVELS, MEANING WHEN THEY ARE ILLUMINATING IN THE JOURNEYS OF THE THREE COLUMNS AND ARE APPOINTED OVER THE SEVENTY NATIONS, that emanate from twelve engravings and knots that surround them in their travels IN THE ORDER OF THE THREE COLUMNS, striking against the four directions of the world, THAT IS, CHESED, GVURAH, TIFERET AND MALCHUT. This is what is written: "He set the bounds of the people according to the number of the children of Yisrael" (Devarim 32:8), MEANING THAT THE NUMBER TWELVE THAT IS IN THE CHILDREN OF YISRAEL ILLUMINATES TO THE SEVENTY NATIONS. And this is what is written: "As the four winds of the heavens have I spread you abroad" (Zecharyah 2:10), so THAT THE THREE COLUMNS ILLUMINATE IN ALL THE FOUR DIRECTIONS – CHESED AND GVURAH, TIFERET AND MALCHUT – to show that they exist for the sake of Yisrael, WHO ARE THE TWELVE TRIBES, AS MENTIONED EARLIER. It does not say, 'In the four,' but rather, "As the four," because as it is impossible for the world to exist without the four winds, so it is impossible for the world to exist without Yisrael.

12. "...that let the feet of the ox and the donkey..."

A Synopsis

Rabbi Aba opens a discussion of the meaning of the title verse. He explains that the children of Yisrael are worthy in the sight of God because they "sow beside all waters," that is, according to Righteousness. Reference is then made to the book of Rabbi Yiba Saba. It describes the Chamber of Guilt, which is of the side of Mercy, and the Chamber of Merit, which is of the Other Side. Children, longevity, and sustenance, we learn, do not depend on either Chamber, but rather on *mazal*. The children of Israel cleave to the side of Holiness, thereby banishing the evil symbolized by the union of the ox and the donkey.

The Relevance of the Passage

The Light of *Binah,* the spiritual dimension that resides above the world known as *Zeir Anpin*, illumines your very being. This awesome Light is also known as the *World to Come*, which is defined as a reality where death, turmoil, and pain have no existence. Binah is the essence of perfection, bliss, and never-ending days. It is made ours in this splendid passage, where the lower world is raised into the Upper Heavens.

The Zohar gently pours sweet and clear waters over the world, dissolving and washing away all judgments decreed upon humanity. The wells, springs, and fountains of bitter water that we have created through our negative deeds and actions evaporate as these verses summon forth the warming Light of the Creator and the glowing Light of the righteous souls.

Evil forces and plagues are banished from our reality through the power of Jacob, who embodies all humanity.

67. וַיָּקָם מֶלֶךְ חָדָשׁ. ר' אַבָּא פָּתַח אַשְׁרֵיכֶם זוֹרְעֵי עַל כָּל מָיִם מְשַׁלְּחֵי רֶגֶל הַשּׁוֹר וְהַחֲמוֹר, זַכָּאִין אִינּוּן יִשְׂרָאֵל, דְּקוּדְשָׁא בְּרִיךְ הוּא אִתְרְעֵי בְּהוּ מִכָּל שְׁאָר עַמִּין, וְקָרִיב לוֹן לְגַבֵּיהּ, דִּכְתִיב, וּבְךָ בָּחַר יְיָ' לִהְיוֹת לוֹ לְעַם סְגוּלָה וְגוֹ', וּכְתִיב כִּי חֵלֶק יְיָ' עַמּוֹ יַעֲקֹב חֶבֶל נַחֲלָתוֹ, יִשְׂרָאֵל מִתְדַּבְּקִין בֵּיהּ בְּקוּדְשָׁא בְּרִיךְ הוּא, דִּכְתִיב וְאַתֶּם הַדְּבֵקִים בַּיְיָ' אֱלֹהֵיכֶם חַיִּים כּוּלְּכֶם הַיּוֹם.

67. "Now there arose a new king" (Shemot 1:8). Rabbi Aba commenced: "Blessed are you that sow beside all waters, that let the feet of the ox and

the donkey range freely" (Yeshayah 32:20). Fortunate are Yisrael, whom the Holy One, blessed be He, favored more than all the nations and, and whom He brought close to Him, as it is written: "Hashem has chosen you to be a special possession to Himself…" (Devarim 14:2), and: "For Hashem's portion is His people, Jacob is the lot of His inheritance" (Devarim 32:9). And Yisrael cleave to the Holy One, blessed be He, as it is written: "But you that did cleave to Hashem your Elohim are alive every one of you this day…" (Devarim 4:4).

68. וע"ד זַכָּאִין אִינּוּן קַמֵיה, בְּגִין דְּאִינּוּן זַרְעִין עַל כָּל מָיִם. מַאי עַל כָּל מָיִם. דְּזַרְעִין לִצְדָקָה. וּמַאן דְּזָרַע לִצְדָקָה, כְּתִיב בֵּיה כִּי גָדוֹל מֵעַל שָׁמַיִם חַסְדֶּךָ. מֵעַל שָׁמַיִם: עַל כָּל מַיִם אִיהוּ הֲוֵי, וּמַאן אִיהוּ מֵעַל שָׁמַיִם. דָּא עָלְמָא דְּאָתֵי. וְיִשְׂרָאֵל זַרְעֵי זַרְעָא עַל כָּל מַיִם.

68. And they are therefore righteous before Him, because they sow beside all waters. AND HE ASKS: What is "beside all waters"? AND HE SAYS: They sow for righteousness (Heb. *tzedakah*) – MEANING THEY ELEVATE *MAYIM NUKVIN* ('FEMALE WATERS') TO DRAW MOCHIN INTO MALCHUT, SO SHE WILL BE CALLED '*TZEDAKAH*'. FOR WITHOUT MOCHIN, IT IS CALLED *TZEDEK* (JUSTICE) WITHOUT *HEI*. And of one who sows for righteousness, it is written: "For your kindness is great above (Heb. *me'al*) the heavens (Heb. *shamayim*)…" (Tehilim 108:5). *Me'al shamayim* also means beside all waters (Heb. *al kol mayim*). And what is, "above the heavens"? It is the World to Come, WHICH IS BINAH THAT IS ABOVE ZEIR ANPIN, WHICH IS CALLED "HEAVENS." And Yisrael sow seeds, MEANING THEY ELEVATE *MAYIM NUKVIN* ('FEMALE WATERS') beside (lit. 'above') above all waters, WHICH IS BINAH, IN ORDER TO DRAW MOCHIN TO MALCHUT, SO THAT SHE SHOULD BE CALLED '*TZEDAKAH*'.

69. בְּסִפְרָא דְּרַב יֵיבָא סָבָא הָכִי אָמַר, כְּתִיב בִּגְזֵרַת עִירִין פִּתְגָמָא וּמֵאמַר קַדִּישִׁין שְׁאֶלְתָּא, כָּל דִּינִין דְּהַאי עָלְמָא, וְכָל גְּזֵרִין, וְכָל שְׁאֶלְתִּין, כֻּלְהוּ קַיְימֵי בְּחַד הֵיכָלָא, דְּתַמָּן ע"ב סַנְהֶדְרִין מְעַיְינִין בְּדִינִין דְּעָלְמָא. וְהַהוּא הֵיכָלָא אִקְרֵי הֵיכַל זְכוּתָא, בְּגִין, דְּכַד דַּיְינִין דִּינָא, מְהַפְּכִין בִּזְכוּתָא דְּבַר נָשׁ בְּקַדְמֵיתָא.

69. In the book of Rav Yiba Saba, it says as follows: It is written, "This matter is by the decree of the watchers, and the sentence by the words of the

holy ones" (Daniel 4:14). For all the verdicts in this world and all the decrees and all the questions are all in one chamber, where 72 judges deliberate the sentences of the world. And that chamber is called the 'Chamber of Merit', because when a person is judged, his merit is presented first.

‎70. מַה דְּלָאו הָכִי, בְּדַרְגָּא דְּהַהוּא סִטְרָא אַחֲרָא, דְּתַמָּן אִיהוּ אֲתָר דְּאִקְרֵי חוֹב״ה, בְּגִין דְּכָל עוֹבָדוֹי דְּהַהוּא אֲתָר, דְּנָחָשׁ אֵשֶׁת זְנוּנִים, לָא אִיהוּ אֶלָּא לְמֶהֱפָּכָא בְּחוֹבָה דב״נ, וּלְמִלְשָׁן עַבְדָּא לְמָארֵיה.

70. This is not so in the level of the Other Side, where there is a place called 'Guilt', because all the actions in that place are of the Serpent, the Wife of Harlotry, and their only purpose is to condemn the person and to slander the servant before his Master!

‎71. אִינּוּן דְּהֵיכְלָא דְּזָכוּתָא, אִקְרוֹן מַיִם מְתוּקִים, מַיִם צְלוּלִין. אִינּוּן דְּהֵיכְלָא דְּחוֹבָה, אִקְרוֹן מַיִין מְרִירִין, מֵי הַמָּרִים הַמְאָרְרִים. בְּהַהוּא הֵיכְלָא דְּזָכוּתָא, לָא קַיְימֵי אֲלֵין תְּלַת: בְּנֵי, חַיֵּי, וּמְזוֹנֵי. וְלָאו בְּהַהוּא אֲתָר דְּחוֹבָה, לָא בְּמַיִם מְתִיקָן וּצְלִילָן, וְלָאו בְּמַיִם מְרִירִין מְלַטְטִין.

71. Those that are in the Chamber of Merit are called 'sweet waters', 'clear waters'. Those that are in the Chamber of Guilt are called the 'bitter water' – "The bitter water that causes the curse" (Bemidbar 5:18). In that Chamber of Merit these three are not found: children, longevity, and sustenance; nor are these found in that place of Guilt; nor in the 'sweet and clear waters'; nor in the 'bitter' and 'curse-causing waters'!

‎72. וְעַל דָּא, יִשְׂרָאֵל זַרְעֵי עַל כָּל מַיִם, זַרְעָא קַדִּישָׁא דְּאוֹלִידוּ עַל כָּל מַיִם, אִיהוּ, דְּהָא לָאו נָכוֹן זַרְעָא דִּילְהוֹן אֶלָּא לְעֵילָא. וע״ד אוּקְמוּהָ מ״מ, בְּנֵי חַיֵּי וּמְזוֹנֵי, לָאו בִּזְכוּתָא תַּלְיָא מִלְתָא, אֶלָּא בְּמַזָּלָא קַדִּישָׁא תַּלְיָא מִלְתָא, וַאֲתָר דָּא עַל כָּל מַיָּא אִיהוּ.

72. Therefore, Yisrael sow beside all the waters a holy seed – MEANING THEY ELEVATE *MAYIM NUKVIN* ('FEMALE WATERS') TO SUPERNAL BINAH, WHICH IS CALLED 'ABOVE ALL WATERS' – and they beget above all waters, they whose seed is not appropriate except for above IN BINAH. Therefore, the masters of the Mishnah explain that children, longevity and sustenance are not dependent on THE CHAMBER OF Merit, but rather are dependent upon the Holy Mazal, WHICH IS THE HOLY BEARD OF ARICH ANPIN, WHICH IS ITS ASPECT OF BINAH WHICH HAS EMERGED. This place is "above all waters."

73. מְשַׁלְחֵי רֶגֶל הַשּׁוֹר וְהַחֲמוֹר, דְּלָא אִית לוֹן בְּהַהוּא סִטְרָא בִּישָׁא כְּלוּם, וּמְשַׁדְרָן מִנַּיְיהוּ כָּל חוּלָקִין בִּישִׁין, וּמִתְדַּבְּקִין בְּהַהוּא סִטְרָא טָבָא, דְּכָל קַדּוּשִׁין עִלָּאִין, שׁוֹר וַחֲמוֹר כַּד מִזְדַּוְּוגָן כַּחֲדָא, תְּרֵין פְּגָעִין בִּישִׁין אִינּוּן לְעָלְמָא. שׁוֹר: סִטְרָא דְּדִינָא קַשְׁיָא אִיהוּ, וְאִתְדַּבְּקוּתָא דְּסִטְר קַדִּישָׁא אִיהוּ. חֲמוֹר: כַּד אִזְדְּוַוג בַּהֲדֵיה, דְּאִיהוּ מִסִּטְרָא אַחֲרָא, תְּרֵין פְּגָעִין בִּישִׁין אִינּוּן לְעָלְמָא.

73. "...that let the feet of the ox and the donkey range freely..." They do not contain anything in that side OF THE KLIPOT OF THE OX AND THE DONKEY; for they have banished all the evil parts and cleave to the good side of all supernal holy beings. When the ox and donkey join together, they become two evil plagues of the world. The ox is the side of Severe Judgment and originates in the cleaving of the side of Holiness. When the donkey joins with it from the Other Side OF THE KLIPOT, they become two evil plagues of the world.

74. וְעַל דָּא, שִׁמְעוֹן תּוּקְפָא דְּדִינָא קַשְׁיָא הֲוָה בֵּיה, וְכַד מִזְדַּוְּוגָן כַּחֲדָא, לָא יָכִיל עָלְמָא לְמִסְבַּל, וּבְגִין כָּךְ, לֹא תַחֲרוֹשׁ בְּשׁוֹר וּבַחֲמוֹר יַחְדָּו. וְעַל דָּא, שָׁדַר יַעֲקֹב לְעֵשָׂו מִלָּה דָּא, דִּכְתִיב, וַיְהִי לִי שׁוֹר וַחֲמוֹר. וְאִי לָאו דְּמָאִיךְ יַעֲקֹב גַּרְמֵיה, דְּחִילוּ סַגִּיא נָפַל בֵּיה בְּעֵשָׂו.

74. Hence, Simeon had in him the strength of Severe Judgment, AS HE HAD IN HIMSELF THE ASPECT OF THE OX. And when they combine, the world can not tolerate it. Therefore, "You shall not plow with an ox and an donkey together" (Devarim 22:10). Therefore, Jacob sent this to Esau: "I have oxen and asses" (Beresheet 32:6), MEANING THAT HE SUBJUGATED THEM TO HOLINESS. And had Jacob not humbled himself, a great fear would have fallen on Esau, BECAUSE HE HAD THE POWER TO OVERPOWER THESE TWO FORCES.

13. "Now there arose a new king"

A Synopsis

This section begins with an interpretation of the title verse found in the book of Rabbi Hamnuna Saba. From this, we learn that the rise to power of any nation is a result of the subjugation of the children of Yisrael, as seen in the examples of Egypt, Babylon, and Rome. This is because the nation of Yisrael is equal to all the other nations combined, and therefore when a nation dominates the children of Israel, it's celestial chieftain gains dominion over the chieftains of the other nations.

According to Rabbi Chiya, the impending rise or fall of a nation is announced on earth through small children, simple-minded people and the behavior of birds thirty days before the event. While these proclamations usually go unnoticed, if a nation is deserving, the leaders receive news of the imminent disaster so that they can call their people to repent and return to God while there is still time. When a nation falls from power, Rabbi Yitzchak explains, God first punishes its celestial representative. The chieftain passes through a River of Fire, his power vanishes; then the event is proclaimed above, and later below. This relates to Rabbi Yosi's profound experience, which he describes to Rabbi Elazar, Rabbi Aba, and Rabbi Yehuda while they sit at the gate of Lydda. That morning, Rabbi Yosi tells them, a bird informed him of the raising up of three rulers on earth, and the deposing of an existing ruler. When asked about their identity, the bird threw down three arrows from his right wing, and one from his left wing. On examining these arrows, Rabbi Elazar interprets their significance as an indication of the impending domination of the Egyptians and the children of Israel by three great rulers in Rome. Three children who pass by the Rabbis in succession and announce imminent doom for Egypt reinforce this interpretation. This leads to a discussion of the importance of sages, without whom man would not be able to understand the Torah or God's Commandments.

Finally, Rabbi Yehuda and Rabbi Shimon discuss the title verse, revealing that the "new king" is a reference to the Pharaoh who, like Achashverosh, "arose" through the power of his wealth, and not because he was worthy.

The Relevance of the Passage

When the children of Yisrael are enslaved to their own ego, addicted to their materialistic and primal desires, this spiritual reality is reflected in the physical world. In personal terms, the negative attributes and dark side of our nature become strengthened, empowered, rising to new heights of influence ("Now there arose a new king"). Globally, the Children of Yisrael will then find themselves in exile under the rule of another superpower nation. The great Light that shines in a person's soul is then transferred to the governing nation, allowing it to achieve greatness in the world.

When, however, we truly transform our desires from *selfish receiving* into a genuine *desire to share* and impart to others, we find our own spiritual greatness. We are liberated. The entire nation of Yisrael rises to great heights, no longer in exile or under the rule of a foreign nation.

The other nations of the world subsequently cherish the Children of Yisrael, for they are now receiving their spiritual sustenance.

Here, we elevate the Children of Yisrael (any human being who embraces the spiritual wisdom of the Torah and Zohar) to their ultimate spiritual prominence. The negative forces of darkness dwelling in the Upper Worlds lose their power. Likewise, evil disintegrates here on Earth. Negative nations crumble, corruption ceases, and all humanity recognizes the common spark of divinity that binds all mankind.

Our ego is abolished at the very seed level of its existence. The supernal source of the human ego, the angel called Satan, is crushed and conquered. The nations of the world hold Yisrael dear to their hearts as peace permeates the planet and famine is banished from the planet.

Though we may not be worthy of this miraculous Redemption and transformation, we achieve it on the merit of the sages who love and care for us unconditionally. Their extraordinary Light is ignited with each letter and word of the Zohar that our eyes touch.

75. וַיָּקָם מֶלֶךְ חָדָשׁ עַל מִצְרָיִם. בְּסִפְרָא דְּרַב הַמְנוּנָא סָבָא הָכִי אִתְּמַר, מַאי דִּכְתִיב וַיָּקָם מֶלֶךְ חָדָשׁ עַל מִצְרָיִם, תָּא חֲזֵי, כָּל עַמִּין דְּעָלְמָא, וְכָל מַלְכִין דְּעָלְמָא, לָא אִתְתָּקְפוּ בְּשׁוּלְטָנֵיהוֹן, אֶלָּא בְּגִינַיְיהוּ דְּיִשְׂרָאֵל, מִצְרַיִם לָא הֲווֹ שַׁלְטִין עַל כָּל עָלְמָא, עַד דְּאָתוּ יִשְׂרָאֵל, וְעָאלוּ תַּמָּן בְּגָלוּתָא, כְּדֵין אִתְתָּקְפוּ עַל שְׁאַר עַמִּין דְּעָלְמָא. בָּבֶל לָא אִתְתָּקְפוּ עַל כָּל עַמִּין דְּעָלְמָא, אֶלָּא בְּגִין דְּיִשְׂרָאֵל דְּלֶהֱוֵיָין בְּגָלוּתְהוֹן. אֱדוֹם לָא אִתְתָּקְפוּ עַל כָּל עַמִּין דְּעָלְמָא אֶלָּא בְּגִינֵיהוֹן דְּיִשְׂרָאֵל, דְּלֶהֱוֵיָין בְּגָלוּתְהוֹן. דְּהָא עַמִּין אִלֵּין בְּשִׁפְלוּתָא הֲווֹ בִּשְׁאַר עַמִּין, וּמְאִיכִין הֲווֹ מִכֻּלְּהוּ, וּבְגִין יִשְׂרָאֵל אִתְתָּקְפוּ.

75. "Now there arose a new king over Egypt" (Shemot 1:8). In the book of Rav Hamnuna Saba, it is written thus: what is the meaning of "now there arose a new king over Egypt"? Come and behold: all the nations of the

world and all the kings in the world did not become secure in their dominion save for the sake of Yisrael. Egypt did not rule over the whole world until Yisrael came and entered into exile there. Then they overpowered all the nations of the world. Babylon did not acquire power over all the nations of the world, only so that Yisrael would be in exile by them. Edom acquired power over all the nations of the world only so that Yisrael would be exiled among them. For these nations were once humble among the other nations, and were lower than all of them, and because of Yisrael they became strong.

76. מִצְרַיִם: דִּכְתִּיב מִבֵּית עֲבָדִים. עֲבָדִים אִקְרוּן מַמָּשׁ, דְּהָא מִצְרַיִם בִּשְׁפְלוּתָא דִשְׁאָר עַמִּין הֲווֹ. בָּבֶל: דִּכְתִּיב, הֵן אֶרֶץ כַּשְׂדִּים זֶה הָעָם זֶה לֹא הָיָה. אֱדוֹם: דִּכְתִּיב הִנֵּה קָטֹן נְתַתִּיךָ בַּגּוֹיִם בָּזוּי אַתָּה מְאֹד.

76. Egypt WAS LOWLIER THAN ALL THE NATIONS, for it is written OF THEM: "From the house of bondage" (Shemot 20:2). They are called 'actual slaves', because the Egyptians were [formerly] lowlier than all the nations. Babylon WAS LOWLY, as it is written: "Behold the land of Chaldeans; this people was not" (Yeshayah 23:13). Edom WAS LOWLY, as it is written: "Behold, I make you small among the nations; you are greatly despised" (Ovadyah 1:2).

77. וְכֻלְּהוּ לָא נַטְלוּ תּוּקְפָּא אֶלָּא בְּגִינֵיהוֹן דְּיִשְׂרָאֵל. דְּכַד יִשְׂרָאֵל בְּגָלוּתְהוֹן מִיַּד מִתְתַּקְפֵי עַל כָּל שְׁאָר עַמִּין דְּעָלְמָא. מ״ט, בְּגִין דְּיִשְׂרָאֵל אִינּוּן בִּלְחוֹדַיְיהוּ, לָקֳבֵל כָּל עַמִּין דְּעָלְמָא. כַּד עָאלוּ יִשְׂרָאֵל בְּגָלוּתָא דְּמִצְרַיִם, מִיַּד הֲוָה קַיְימָא לְמִצְרָיִם, וְאִתְתַּקַּף שׁוּלְטָנוּתָא דִּלְהוֹן לְעֵילָּא עַל כָּל שְׁאָר עַמִּין, דִּכְתִּיב וַיָּקָם מֶלֶךְ חָדָשׁ עַל מִצְרָיִם, וַיָּקָם: קַיְימָא הֲוָה לוֹן, דְּאִתְתַּקַּף וְקָם הַהוּא מְמָנָא שׁוּלְטָנָא דְּמִצְרַיִם, וְאִתְיְיהִיב לֵיהּ תּוּקְפָּא וְשָׁלְטָנוּתָא, עַל כָּל מְמָנָן דִּשְׁאָר עַמִּין דְּהָא בְּקַדְמֵיתָא אִית שׁוּלְטָנוּתָא לְהַהוּא מְמָנָא דִּלְעֵילָּא, וּלְבָתַר לְעַמָּא דִּילֵיהּ דִּלְתַתָּא. וּבְגִין כָּךְ, וַיָּקָם מֶלֶךְ חָדָשׁ עַל מִצְרָיִם. דָּא הוּא מְמָנָא דִּלְהוֹן, חָדָשׁ הֲוָה, דְּעַד יוֹמָא הָדֵין לָא הֲוָה לֵיהּ שׁוּלְטָנָא עַל שְׁאָר עַמִּין, וְהַשְׁתָּא אִתְקַם לְשַׁלְטָאָה עַל כָּל שְׁאָר עַמִּין דְּעָלְמָא, וּכְדֵין אִתְקַיַּים תַּחַת שָׁלֹשׁ רָגְזָה אֶרֶץ תַּחַת עֶבֶד כִּי יִמְלוֹךְ.

77. And they all received power only on account of Yisrael; for when Yisrael were in exile among them, they immediately become powerful over all the nations in the world. What is the reason? Because Yisrael alone are comparable to all the nations in the world. When Yisrael began their exile in Egypt, Egypt immediately experienced an elevation and their rule was strengthened above all the nations, as it is written: "Now there arose a new king over Egypt." "Arose," MEANS they rose and became strong! And THE ANGEL, who is the minister appointed to the rule of Egypt, was strengthened and rose. He was given power and dominion over all who were appointed over the other nations, because dominion IS GIVEN first to the one who is appointed above and then to his nation below. Therefore, THE VERSE SAYS, "Now there arose a new king over Egypt." This is the one who was appointed over them. He was new, because until that time, he had no dominion over the other nations; then he was raised to rule over all the nations in the world. Then this was fulfilled: "For three things the earth is disquieted...for a slave when he becomes king..." (Mishlei 30:21) BECAUSE THE EGYPTIANS WERE SLAVES.

78. ר' חִיָּיא אָמַר, תְּלָתִין יוֹמִין עַד לָא יֵיתֵי תּוּקְפָּא לְעַמָּא בְּאַרְעָא, אוֹ עַד לָא תֵּיתֵי תְּבִירוּ לְעַמָּא בְּאַרְעָא, מַכְרְזֵי בְּעָלְמָא הַהוּא מִלָּה, וּלְזִמְנִין דְּאִתְמְסַר הַהוּא מִלָּה בְּפוּמָא דְּרַבְיֵיא, וּלְזִמְנִין לְאִינוּן בְּנֵי נָשָׁא דְּלֵית בְּהוּ דַעְתָּא וּלְזִמְנִין מְסַר הַהוּא מִלָּה אִתְמְסַר בְּפוּמָא דְעוֹפֵי וּמַכְרְזֵי בְּעָלְמָא, וְלֵית מַאן דְּיִשְׁגַּח בְּהוּ. כַּד עַמָּא זַכָּאִין, אִתְמְסַר הַהוּא מִלָּה לְאִינוּן רֵישִׁין זַכָּאִין דְּעָלְמָא, בְּגִין דְּיוֹדִיעוּ לוֹן, וְיתוּבוּן לְמָארֵיהוֹן, וְכַד לָאו אִינוּן זַכָּאִין, הֲוֵי כִּדְקָאמְרַן.

78. Rabbi Chiya said: Thirty days before power comes to a nation on earth or before a crisis comes to a nation on the earth, it is announced in the world. Sometimes it is given over to the mouth of a child, and sometimes to people who have no sense, and sometimes it is given over to the birds and they announce in the world and nobody listens to them. And when people are righteous, it is given over to the leaders, the righteous of the world, so they may notify the people and repent to their Master. And if the people are not righteous, then it is as we said!

79. ר' אֶלְעָזָר, הֲוָה יָתִיב יוֹמָא חַד אַתַּרְעָא דְלוֹד, וַהֲוָה יָתִיב עִמֵּיהּ רַבִּי אַבָּא, וְרַבִּי יְהוּדָה, וְרַבִּי יוֹסֵי. א"ר יוֹסֵי אֵימָא לְכוּ, מַה דְּחָמִית

יוֹמָא דָא בְּצַפְרָא קָמֵית בִּנְהוֹרָא, חָמֵית חַד עוֹפָא, דַּהֲוָה טָאִיס זָקַף לְעֵילָא תְּלַת זִמְנֵי, וּמָאִיךְ חַד, וַהֲוָה אָמַר, עִלָּאֵי עִלָּאֵי, בְּיוֹמָא דָא טָסֵי רְקִיעִין תְּלַת מִמָּנָן זְקִפִין שַׁלְטָנִין עַל אַרְעָא, חַד יָתִיב דְּלָא יָתִיב, אַעְבְּרוּ לֵיהּ בְּנוּרָא דְּדָלִיק, מְעַבְּרִין קַיְימֵיהּ, מְעַבְּרִין שֻׁלְטָנֵיהּ, תְּלַת סַמְכִין שַׁלִיטִין עִלָּאִין, קַיְימִין עַל עָלְמָא.

79. Rabbi Elazar was once sitting in the gate of the city of Lod with Rabbi Aba, Rabbi Yehuda and Rabbi Yosi. Rabbi Yosi said: I will tell you what I saw this morning. I got up with the MORNING light and I saw a bird – THAT IS, AN ANGEL – that was flying. It raised itself three times and lowered itself one time, and was saying: Exalted ones, Exalted ones, on this day the firmaments are soaring. Three upright overseers rule over the world, and one is sitting yet not sitting. HE ALSO WANTS TO STAND AND NOT SIT. He passed through a burning fire, his position is removed and his dominion removed. And three pillars, supernal rulers, stand over the world.

80. רָמֵינָא לְהַהוּא עוֹפָא קָלָא, אֲמֵינָא לֵיהּ עוֹפָא עוֹפָא, אֵימָא לִי תְּלַת דְּקַיְימִין מִמָּנָן, וְחַד דְּמִעַבְּרִין שֻׁלְטָנֵיהּ, מַאן אִינּוּן. רָמָא לִי תְּלַת גִּירִין אִלֵּין מִגַּדְפָּא יְמִינָא, וְדֵין חַד מִשְּׂמָאלָא, וְלָא יָדַעְנָא מַאי רְמִיזָא.

80. I threw a clod of earth towards that bird and I said to it: Bird, Bird, tell me of the three who are appointees and the one who was removed from rulership. Who are they? It cast three arrows at me from the right wing, WHICH IS THE SECRET OF ZEIR ANPIN, and one from the left, WHICH IS THE SECRET OF THE NUKVA. I did not know to what it was alluding – MEANING I DID NOT KNOW THE NEW THOUGHT IT WAS TRYING TO TEACH ME.

81. נָסִיב לְהוּ רִבִּי אֶלְעָזָר, נָחֵית לְהוּ לְנְחִירוֹי, נָפַק דָּמָא מִנְּחִירוֹי. אָמַר, וַדַּאי תְּלַת שַׁלְטָנֵי עַמְמִין קַיְימִין בְּרוֹמֵי בְּאַרְעָא, וּזְמִינִין לְמֶעְבַּד גְּזִרִין בִּישִׁין לְיִשְׂרָאֵל, מִסִּטְרָא דְּרוֹמָאֵי. נָסִיב הַהוּא גִּירָא דְּמִגַּדְפָּא שְׂמָאלָא, אָרַח, וְנָפַק אֶשָׁתָא אוּכְמָא מִנֵּיהּ, אָמַר שֻׁלְטָנָא דְּמִצְרָאֵי אַעְדִּיאוּ וְזַמִּין חַד מַלְכָּא דְּרוֹמָאֵי, לְאַעְבְּרָא בְּכָל אַרְעָא דְמִצְרַיִם,

וּלְמַנָּאָה בְּמִצְרַיִם רַבְרְבֵי תְּרִיסִין, וְסָתִיר בִּנְיָן, וּבָנֵי סְתִירִין. רָמָא לוֹן
ר' אֶלְעָזָר לְאַרְעָא, נָפְלוּ אִלֵּין תְּלַת עַל חַד דְּמִסְטְרָא שְׂמָאלָא.

81. Rabbi Elazar took those arrows, lowered them to his nostrils and blood started to flow from them – AN ALLUSION TO JUDGMENT COLORED RED. He said: Surely there are three rulers among the nations standing in THE CITY OF Rome on earth, BECAUSE THEY ARE DRAWN FROM CHESED, GVURAH AND TIFERET OF ZEIR ANPIN, and they will impose evil laws against Yisrael from the side of the Romans. THIS MEANS THAT THE BLEMISH THAT YISRAEL CAUSED IN CHESED, GVURAH AND TIFERET ENABLED THE ROMANS TO DESTROY THE TEMPLE AND TO IMPOSE EVIL DECREES. He took that arrow THAT THE BIRD THREW from its left wing, smelled it, and a black fire burst forth from it. THIS IS THE LEFT COLOR THAT IS UNIQUE TO THE NUKVA WHICH IS NOT INCLUDED IN THE THREE COLORS OF THE RAINBOW – WHITE, RED AND GREEN, WHICH COME FROM THE THREE COLUMNS CHESED, GVURAH AND TIFERET, AND DO NOT CONTAIN BLACK. He said: They have deposed the rule of the Egyptians WHO DRAW THE LIGHT OF THE LEFT FROM ABOVE DOWN. In the future, a Roman king will pass through the whole land of Egypt and will appoint in Egypt officers and warriors. He will destroy buildings THAT WERE BUILT AND DRAWN FROM THE LEFT SIDE, and will rebuild ruins THAT WERE DESTROYED BECAUSE THEY WERE FROM THE RIGHT, AND EGYPT HAD NO DESIRE FOR THEM. Rabbi Elazar threw those ARROWS to the ground, MEANING THAT HE DREW THEIR ILLUMINATION FROM ABOVE DOWN. The three arrows fell upon the one from the left side AND THE ONE FROM THE LEFT SIDE WAS BURNT, AND THE THREE ARROWS OF THE RIGHT SIDE REMAINED, AS SHALL BE EXPLAINED.

82. עַד דַּהֲווֹ יַתְבֵי, אַעֲבַּר חַד יְנוֹקָא, וַהֲוָה קָארֵי מַשָּׂא מִצְרַיִם הִנֵּה ה'
רוֹכֵב עַל עָב קַל וּבָא מִצְרָיִם. אַעֲבַּר תִּנְיָינָא חַבְרֵיהּ, וְאָמַר, וְאֶרֶץ
מִצְרַיִם תִּהְיֶה שְׁמָמָה. אַעֲבַּר תְּלִיתָאָה חַבְרֵיהּ, וְאָמַר, וְאָבְדָה חָכְמַת
מִצְרָיִם. חָמוּ הַהוּא גִּירָא דְּגַדְפָּא שְׂמָאלָא דְּאִתּוֹקַד, וּתְלַת אַחֲרָנִין
דַּהֲווֹ עֲלֵיהּ לָא אִתּוֹקְדָן.

82. While they were still sitting, a young boy passed by and was reading: "The burden of Egypt. Behold Hashem rides on a light cloud and comes to Egypt" (Yeshayah 19:1). His friend, a second boy, passed and said: "The land of Egypt will be desolate." A third friend passed and said: "The wisdom of Egypt is lost." They saw that the arrow of the left wing was burnt and the arrows that were on it were not burnt.

83. א"ר אֶלְעָזָר, הַאי דְעוֹפָא, וְהַאי דְּדַרְדְקֵי כֹּלָּא הוּא חַד, וְכֹלָּא נְבוּאָה עִלָּאָה הוּא, וּבָעָא קוּדְשָׁא בְּרִיךְ הוּא לְאַחֲזָאָה לָן, סִתְרֵי עִלָּאֵי דְּהוּא עָבֵיד, הה"ד כִּי לֹא יַעֲשֶׂה ה' אֱלֹהִים דָּבָר כִּי אִם גָּלָה סוֹדוֹ אֶל עֲבָדָיו הַנְּבִיאִים.

83. Rabbi Elazar said: That of the bird and that of the boys are all one thing, FOR THE CHILDREN WITH THEIR VERSES ALSO SAID THAT EGYPT – WHICH IS THE LEFT COLUMN THAT ILLUMINATED FROM ABOVE DOWN – WILL BECOME DESOLATE AND WILL BE DESTROYED. This is all a supernal prophecy THAT WAS GIVEN TO BIRDS AND CHILDREN, and the Holy One, blessed be He, wanted to show us the supernal secrets He affected, and this HE HAS SENT TO US. This is what is written: "Surely Hashem Elohim will do nothing, without revealing His secret to His servants the prophets" (Amos 3:7).

84. וְחַכִּימֵי עֲדִיפֵי מִנְּבִיאֵי בְּכָל זְמָן, דְּהָא לִנְבִיאֵי לְזִמְנִין שָׁרַת עֲלַיְיהוּ רוּחַ קוּדְשָׁא, וּלְזִמְנִין לָא, וְחַכִּימִין לָא אַעֲדֵי מִנְּהוֹן רוּחַ קוּדְשָׁא אֲפִילוּ רִגְעָא חֲדָא, דְּיַדְעִין מַה דִּי לְעֵילָא וְתַתָּא, וְלָא בָּעוּ לְגַלָּאָה. א"ר יוֹסֵי כֹּלָּא חָכְמְתָא, וְחָכְמְתָא דר' אֶלְעָזָר יַתִּיר מִכֹּלְּהוּ. רִבִּי אַבָּא אָמַר, אִלְמָלֵא לָא הֲווֹ חַכִּימִין, לָא הֲווֹ יַדְעִין בְּנֵי נָשָׁא, מַהוּ אוֹרַיְיתָא, וּמַה פִּקוּדוֹי דְּמָארֵי עָלְמָא, וְלָא אִתְפְּרְשָׁא רוּחָא דִּבְנֵי נָשָׁא, מֵרוּחָא דִּבְעִירָא.

84. Sages are always superior to prophets, because the Holy Spirit sometimes dwells upon prophets and sometimes does not. As for sages, the Holy Spirit is not removed from them even for a moment, and they know what is above and below though they must not reveal. Rabbi Yosi said: Everything pertains to wisdom and the wisdom of Rabbi Elazar IS SUPERIOR to all. Rabbi Aba said: If not for the sages, people would not know what Torah is and what are the commandments of the Master of the World, and there would be no difference between the spirit of man and the spirit of animals.

85. א"ר יִצְחָק, כַּד אַיְיתֵי קוּדְשָׁא בְּרִיךְ הוּא דִּינָא עַל עַמָּא, בְּקַדְמֵיתָא עָבֵיד דִּינָא, בְּהַהוּא מְמָנָא דִּמְמָנָא עָלַיְיהוּ לְעֵילָא, דִּכְתִיב יִפְקוֹד ה' עַל צְבָא הַמָּרוֹם בַּמָּרוֹם וְעַל מַלְכֵי הָאֲדָמָה עַל הָאֲדָמָה.

85. Rabbi Yitzchak said: When the Holy One, blessed be He, brings Judgment upon a nation, first He judges the minister above who is appointed over them. As it is written: "Hashem will punish the hosts of heaven in the heavens and upon the kings of the earth on the earth" (Yeshayah 24:21) – FIRST ON ALL THE HOSTS OF HEAVEN, MEANING THE APPOINTED ANGEL, AND AFTERWARDS UPON THE KINGS OF THE EARTH.

86. בְּמַאי דִּינָא אִתְּדָן הַהוּא מְמָנָא דִּלְעֵילָא. אַעְבְּרוּ לֵיהּ בְּהַהוּא נְהַר דִּינוּר דְּנָגִיד וְנָפִיק, וּכְדֵין אַעֲדִיו הַהוּא שׁוּלְטָנוּתָא דִּילֵיהּ, וּמִיַּד מַכְרִיזֵי עֲלֵיהּ בִּרְקִיעָא, שׁוּלְטָנוּתָא דִּמְמָנָא פְּלַנְיָא אַעֲדִיו מִנֵּיהּ, עַד דְּמָטֵי הַהוּא קָלָא בְּכָל אִינוּן רְקִיעִין עַד דְּמָטֵי בְּאִינוּן דְּשַׁלְטִין בְּהַאי עָלְמָא, וְנָפִיק קָלָא וְאַכְרִיז בְּכָל עָלְמָא, עַד דְּמָטֵי לְעוֹפֵי וְלִינוֹקֵי, וּלְאִינוּן טִפְּשִׁין דִּבְנֵי נָשָׁא דְּלָא יַדְעִין.

86. HE ASKS: How is Judgment accorded to an appointee above? AND HE ANSWERS: They pass him through the Dinur River that stretches and exits FROM BEFORE HASHEM, and then his dominion is removed. Immediately the announcement that the dominion of a certain appointee has been removed from him reaches the firmament, until it travels throughout the firmaments and reaches those who rule this world, WHO DEPEND UPON THAT APPOINTEE. And the announcement is made throughout the whole world until it reaches the birds and children and those fools among the people who know not WHAT THEY SPEAK.

87. וַיָּקָם מֶלֶךְ חָדָשׁ. רַבִּי חִיָּיא אָמַר, מֶלֶךְ חָדָשׁ, חָדָשׁ מַמָּשׁ הֲוָה. רַבִּי יוֹסֵי אָמַר דַּהֲוָה מְחַדֵּשׁ גְּזֵירִין, דְּלָא חִידֵּשׁ מַלְכָּא אַחֲרָא מִקַּדְמַת דְּנָא. אֲשֶׁר לֹא יָדַע אֶת יוֹסֵף. כָּל הַהוּא טִיבוּ, דְּעָבֵד יוֹסֵף בְּאַרְעָא דְּמִצְרַיִם, דִּכְתִיב, וַיָּבֵא יוֹסֵף אֶת כָּל הַכֶּסֶף בֵּיתָה פַרְעֹה. וְקִיֵּים לוֹן בִּשְׁנֵי כַפְנָא, כָּל הַאי לָא דָּכִיר, וְעָבֵד גַּרְמֵיהּ דְּלָא יָדַע בֵּיהּ.

87. "Now there arose a new king..." (Shemot 1:8). Rabbi Chiya said: "a new king," MEANS actually LITERALLY new. Rabbi Yosi says THAT IT MEANS that he made new decrees that no king had decreed until now. "Who did not know Joseph" (Ibid.), MEANS THAT HE DID NOT KNOW all the good that Joseph did in Egypt, as is written: "And Joseph brought the money to the house of Pharaoh" (Beresheet 47:14), and he kept them alive during the years of famine. He did not remember and pretended not to know ALL THIS.

88. רִבִּי יוֹסֵי וְרִבִּי יְהוּדָה, הֲווֹ יַתְבֵי וְלָעָאן בְּאוֹרַיְיתָא קַמֵיהּ דר"ש, אָמַר רִבִּי יְהוּדָה, הַאי דִּכְתִיב וַיָּקָם מֶלֶךְ חָדָשׁ עַל מִצְרָיִם, וְתָנֵינָן, דְּאִיהוּ קָם מִגַּרְמֵיהּ, מַה דַּהֲוָה שָׁפָל, קָם, וְלָא אִתְחֲזֵי לְמַלְכָּא, וּבְעוּתְרָא קָם. אָמַר רִבִּי שִׁמְעוֹן, כֹּלָּא הָכִי הוּא, כְּגַוְונָא דְּאֲחַשְׁוֵרוֹשׁ דְּלָא אִתְחֲזֵי לְמַלְכָּא, וְקָם מִגַּרְמֵיהּ, וְקָם בְּעוּתְרָא, וּבְעָא לְאוֹבָדָא לְיִשְׂרָאֵל מֵעָלְמָא, אוּף הָכָא, הַאי לָא אִתְחֲזֵי לְמַלְכָּא, וְקָם מִגַּרְמֵיהּ, וּבְעָא לְאוֹבָדָא לְיִשְׂרָאֵל מֵעָלְמָא, דִּכְתִיב וַיֹּאמֶר אֶל עַמּוֹ וְגוֹ', הָבָה נִתְחַכְּמָה לוֹ וְגוֹ', וְכַד הֲוָה קָם מַלְכָּא לְעֵילָא, קָם מַלְכָּא לְתַתָּא.

88. Rabbi Yosi and Rabbi Yehuda were sitting and studying Torah before Rabbi Shimon. Rabbi Yehuda said: It is written, "Now there arose a new king over Egypt." We learn that he arose of himself, one who was humbled arose TO REIGN EVEN THOUGH he was not worthy of ruling, but by THE POWER OF riches he arose. Rabbi Shimon said: So it was similar to Achashverosh, who was not worthy of ruling but he arose to rule by himself, and he arose by THE POWER OF riches and wanted to destroy Yisrael from the world. This is also the case WITH PHARAOH: he was not worthy of ruling, yet he arose and ruled by himself and wanted to destroy Yisrael from the world, as is written: "And he said to his people...come let us deal wisely with them..." (Shemot 1:9-10). When a king arises above, MEANING THE APPOINTED ANGEL, then a king arises below.

14. "The burden of Egypt"

A Synopsis

On their way to Tzipori, Rabbi Elazar, Rabbi Aba, and Rabbi Yosi encounter a Jew who quotes the title verse and then asks them why God Himself came into Egypt, rather than simply exercising His will from above. The reason, we are told, is that God came for the sake of the Shechinah, to raise Her up, as He would do when the Roman captivity of the children of Yisrael ended. God did not go to the Shechinah during Her exile with the children of Yisrael in Babylon because of their sins. In Egypt, however, they remained pure. Whosoever holds the children of Yisrael captive becomes accountable to God, and He punishes their supernal representatives and those who worship them below. God punished Egypt severely, in spite of the relatively good treatment given to the children of Yisrael at first. We may therefore conclude that all the nations who have oppressed the children of Yisrael will receive punishment, including Rome and Assyria – the nation that "oppressed them without cause" and stole their land.

The Relevance of the Passage

In truth, an individual is ill-equipped to triumph successfully over the dark and self-centered tendencies that dominate one's desires. We do not have the power or discipline to confront and conquer our Evil Inclination. Then again, we are not expected to.

Rather, the Kabbalists teach us that the ultimate purpose of life is to evolve an awareness and, consequently, a deep hatred toward our errant and self-indulgent ways. When our realization and revulsion is far greater than our love for selfish-pleasure, then God himself will enter our hearts and our very being to destroy every trace of negativity and selfishness that taints our soul.

Accountability and recognition of one's own faults is perhaps the most difficult attribute a person can evolve. Our natural tendency is to block out any consciousness of our immoral qualities. We find it easier to consider ourselves victims. Sufferers. Blameless. This distorted view is not our conscious intent. Our blindness is real. Nonetheless, disposing of the blinders is the point of our existence. We achieve that here, now, in the moment of this meditation.

The Light of the Creator now enters our very being to destroy *Egypt* (our ego), freeing us forever from the limitations and pain caused by a vain and ungenerous existence.

89. רִבִּי אֶלְעָזָר וְרִבִּי אַבָּא וְרִבִּי יוֹסֵי, הֲווֹ אַזְלֵי מִטְבֶרְיָא לִצְפוֹרִי, עַד

דַּהֲווֹ אָזְלֵי, פָּגַע בְּהוּ חַד יוּדָאי, פָּתַח וְאָמַר, מַשָּׂא מִצְרַיִם הִנֵּה ה'
רוֹכֵב עַל עָב קַל וּבָא מִצְרַיִם וְנָעוּ אֱלִילֵי מִצְרַיִם מִפָּנָיו. תָּא חֲזֵי, כָּל
מַלְכִין דְּעָלְמָא, וְכָל עַמִּין דְּעָלְמָא, לָא חֲשִׁיבֵי כְּלוּם קַמֵּי קוּדְשָׁא בְּרִיךְ
הוּא, דִּכְתִיב, וְכָל דַּיָּירֵי אַרְעָא כְּלָא חֲשִׁיבִין וּכְמִצְבְּיֵהּ עָבֵיד בְּחֵיל
שְׁמַיָּא. וְהָכָא בְּמִצְרַיִם, אַף עַל גַּב דְּכָל אִינּוּן גְּבוּרָאן, וְדַרְעָא מְרַמְּמָא
גַּלֵּי קוּדְשָׁא ב"ה בְּמִצְרַיִם, מַה כְּתִיב הִנֵּה ה' רוֹכֵב עַל עָב קַל וּבָא
מִצְרַיִם. מַאי שְׁנָא, בְּכָל עַמִּין דְּעָלְמָא, דְּלָא הֲוָה הָכִי, דְּהָא קוּדְשָׁא
בְּרִיךְ הוּא גָּזַר גְּזֵרָה וְאִתְעָבֵיד, וְהָכָא אִיהוּ אָתָא, דִּכְתִיב וּבָא מִצְרַיִם.
וּכְתִיב, וְעָבַרְתִּי בְּאֶרֶץ מִצְרַיִם וְגוֹ' אֲנִי ה'.

89. Rabbi Elazar and Rabbi Yosi were journeying from Tiberias to Tzipori. While they were walking, a Jew met them and said: "The burden of Egypt. Behold, Hashem rides on a swift cloud and shall come into Egypt: and the idols of Egypt shall be moved at His presence" (Yeshayah 19:1). Come and behold: All the kings of the world and all the nations of the world are considered as nothing before the Holy One, blessed be He, as is written: "And all the inhabitants of the earth are considered as nothing: and He does according to His will in the host of heaven" (Daniel 4:32). Here in Egypt, despite all these acts of power and the raised hand that the Holy One, blessed be He, revealed, it is written: "Behold, Hashem rides upon a swift cloud and shall come into Egypt." What is the difference? This was not so by all the nations of the world, rather the Holy One, blessed be He, ordered a decree and it was done. Yet here IN EGYPT, He Himself came TO CARRY PUNISHMENT UPON THEM, as is written: "And shall come into Egypt," and: "And I will pass over the land of Egypt... I am Hashem" (Shemot 12:12).

90. אֶלָּא, בְּגִין דְּמַלְכָּא הֲוָה אָתֵי, לְאַפָּקָא לְמַטְרוֹנִיתָא דַּהֲוַות תַּמָּן.
וּבְגִין יְקָרָא דְּמַטְרוֹנִיתָא הֲוָה אָתֵי. וְעַל דָּא הֲוָה קוּדְשָׁא בְּרִיךְ הוּא בָּעֵי
בִּיקָרָה, וְאָתֵי לְגַבָּה לַאֲקָמָא לָה, וּלְמֵיהַב לָה יְדָא, וּלְזַקְפָא לָה, כְּמָה
דְּזַמִּין קוּדְשָׁא בְּרִיךְ הוּא לְמֶעְבַּד בְּסוֹף גָּלוּתָא דֶּאֱדוֹם.

90. AND HE ANSWERS: Because the King came to take out the Queen that was there, and because of the honor of the Queen, WHO IS THE SHECHINAH THAT DESCENDED WITH THEM TO EXILE, He came. Since the Holy One, blessed be He, wanted Her honor, He came to raise Her, and extended His

hand to Her so as to lift Her up, as the Holy One, blessed be He, will do at
the end of the exile of Edom.

91. אָמַר רִבִּי יֵיסָא, אִי הָכִי, דִּבְגִין דְּמַטְרוֹנִיתָא הֲוָה, הָא בְּגָלוּתָא
דְּבָבֶל, מַטְרוֹנִיתָא תַּמָּן הֲוַת, אֲמַאי לָא הֲוָה כָּךְ. אָמַר לֵיהּ, הָא תָּנֵינָן,
דְּחַטָּאָה גָּרַם, דְּנַטְלוּ נָשִׁים נָכְרִיּוֹת, וְאָעִילוּ בְּרִית קַיָּימָא קַדִּישָׁא
בִּרְשׁוּתָא אָחֳרָא. וּבְגִין כָּךְ אִתְאֲבִידוּ מִנְּהוֹן נִסִּין, וְאַתְוָון, דְּאִתְחֲזֵי
לְמֶעְבַּד לְהוּ, מַה דְּלָא הֲוָה הָכִי בְּגָלוּתָא דְּמִצְרַיִם, דְּכֻלְּהוּ הֲווֹ שִׁבְטֵי
יָהּ, בְּנֵי יִשְׂרָאֵל עָאלוּ, בְּנֵי יִשְׂרָאֵל נָפְקוּ.

91. Rabbi Yisa said: If it be so, THAT THE HOLY ONE, BLESSED BE HE,
CAME TO EGYPT because of the Queen, why was it not also thus in the exile
of Babylon when the Queen was also there? He said to him: We have
learned that the sin caused it, because they married foreign women, and they
brought the Holy Covenant into foreign domain. Therefore, the miracles and
signs were lost from them that should have been done for them. Not so in
the exile of Egypt where they were all the Tribes of Yah. The children of
Yisrael came INTO EXILE and the children of Yisrael left EXILE, MEANING
WITHOUT SIN.

92. בְּגָלוּתָא דֶּאֱדוֹם, בָּעֵי קוּדְשָׁא בְּרִיךְ הוּא לְאִתְיַיקְּרָא בְּעָלְמָא,
וּלְמֵיתֵי אִיהוּ לְאַקְמָא לְמַטְרוֹנִיתָא, וּלְנַעֲרָא לָהּ מֵעַפְרָא. וַוי לְמַאן
דְּיֶעְרַע תַּמָּן קַמֵּיהּ, בְּשַׁעֲתָא דְּיֵימָא הִתְנַעֲרִי מֵעָפָר קוּמִי שְׁבִי יְרוּשָׁלַיִם
הִתְפַּתְּחִי מוֹסְרֵי צַוָּארֵךְ. מַאן הוּא מַלְכָּא וְעַמָּא דְּיֵיקוּם קַמֵּיהּ.

92. By the Exile of Edom, the Holy One, blessed be He, wishes to be
honored in the world and to come Himself to uplift the Queen and shake the
dust from Her. Woe to the one who is present before Him at the time when
He will say: "Shake the dust off yourself, arise and sit down, O Jerusalem:
loose yourself from the bands of your neck" (Yeshayah 52:2). Who are the
king and the people who will stand up before Him?

93. וְנָעוּ אֱלִילֵי מִצְרַיִם מִפָּנָיו, אֱלִילֵי מִצְרַיִם, לָאו עַל אַבְנִין וְאַעֵין
אִתְּמַר, אֶלָּא עַל כָּל אִינּוּן דַּרְגִּין מְמָנָן עִלָּאִין, וְעַל אִינּוּן פּוּלְחָנִין

תַּתָּאִין דִּלְהוֹן. וּבְכָל אֲתָר דְּגָלוּ יִשְׂרָאֵל, קוּדְשָׁא בְּרִיךְ הוּא בָּעֵי
עֲלַיְיהוּ, וְאִתְקְבִיל מֵאִינּוּן עַמִּין.

93. "And the idols of Egypt shall be moved from before him" (Yeshayah 19:1). It is written, "the idols of Egypt," not of the stones and trees of which they made the idols; but on all the levels of the supernal appointees and those who worshipped them below, THEY ARE MOVED AND PUNISHED. Wherever Yisrael exiled, the Holy One, blessed be He, seeks them and they are accepted from among those nations.

94. תָּא חֲזֵי, מַה כְּתִיב, כֹּה אָמַר ה' מִצְרַיִם יָרַד עַמִּי בָרִאשׁוֹנָה לָגוּר
שָׁם וְאַשּׁוּר בְּאֶפֶס עֲשָׁקוֹ תּוּרְעֲמָא דְּאִתְרְעַם קוּדְשָׁא בְּרִיךְ הוּא עַל
אַשּׁוּר, וְאָמַר, חָמוּ מַה עָבַד לִי אַשּׁוּר, דְּהָא מִצְרַיִם דַּאֲנָא עֲבָדִית בְּהוּ
כָּל אִינּוּן דִּינִין, וְעַמִּי נַחְתוּ תַּמָּן, לְדַיְּירָא בֵּינַיְיהוּ, וְקַבִּלוֹם מִצְרָאֵי
בֵּינַיְיהוּ, וְיָהֲבוּן לוֹן שְׁפַר אַרְעָא אֶרֶץ גּוֹשֶׁן, וְאע"ג דְּאַעִיקוּ לוֹן
בְּגָלוּתָא, לָא אַעֲדוּ אַרְעָא מִנְּהוֹן, דִּכְתִיב, רַק בְּאֶרֶץ גּוֹשֶׁן אֲשֶׁר שָׁם
בְּנֵי יִשְׂרָאֵל וְגוֹ'. וּמֵיטַב אַרְעָא דְּמִצְרַיִם הֲוָה, דִּכְתִיב בְּמֵיטַב הָאָרֶץ
בְּאֶרֶץ רַעְמְסֵס. וְתוּ, דְּלָא אַעֲדוּ מִדִּלְהוֹן כְּלוּם, דִּכְתִיב וּמִמִּקְנֵה בְּנֵי
יִשְׂרָאֵל וְגוֹ'. וְעכ"ד אִתְדָּנוּ בְּכַמָּה דִּינִין.

94. Come and behold: it is written, "Thus said Hashem, 'My people went down aforetime to Egypt to sojourn there, and Ashur oppressed them without cause'" (Yeshayah 52:4). THIS IS the complaint that the Holy One, blessed be He, made against Assyria. He said: 'See what Assyria has done to Me. To Egypt, upon whom I have rendered all these punishment, My people descended to sojourn among them, and the Egyptians accepted them among them, and gave them the best of the land, which is the land of Goshen. Even though the Egyptians persecuted them in exile, they did not take away the land from them, as is written: "Only in the land of Goshen where the children of Yisrael were..." (Shemot 9:26). It was the best part of the land of Egypt, as is written: "In the best part of the land in the land of Ramses" (Beresheet 47:11), WHICH WAS IN GOSHEN. Moreover, they caused them no loss, as is written: "But of the cattle of the children of Yisrael..." (Shemot 9:6). SO WE SEE THAT THEY DID NOT STEAL THEIR ANIMALS, yet still altogether they were punished with many punishments.

95. אֲבָל אַשּׁוּר בְּאֶפֶס עֲשָׁקוֹ, אַטִּיל לוֹן בְּאַרְעָא דְּסַיְיפֵי עָלְמָא, וְנָטַל לוֹן אַרְעָא דִּלְהוֹן. וּמַה מִצְרָאֵי, דְּעָבְדֵי כָּל הָנֵי טָבָאן לְיִשְׂרָאֵל, אִתְדָּנוּ בְּכָל אִינּוּן דִּינִין. אַשּׁוּר וֶאֱדוֹם וּשְׁאַר עַמִּין, דִּמְעִיקִין לוֹן, וְקַטְלִין לוֹן, וְנַטְלִין לוֹן מָמוֹנֵיהוֹן, עאכ"ו דְקוּדְשָׁא בְּרִיךְ הוּא בָּעֵי לְיַקָּרָא שְׁמֵיהּ עֲלַיְיהוּ, דִּכְתִיב וְהִתְגַּדַּלְתִּי וְהִתְקַדַּשְׁתִּי וְנוֹדַעְתִּי. הָתָם בְּמִצְרַיִם בְּמַלְכָּא חַד, וְהָכָא בְּכָל מַלְכִין דְּעָלְמָא.

95. "And Ashur oppressed them without cause." For they cast them in a land at the end of the world, and took away their land. Now the Egyptians, who had done so many favors for Yisrael, were punished with so many punishments. Then Ashur, Edom and the other nations that oppressed them, and killed them, and took away their money would most certainly be punished. For the Holy One, blessed be He, desired to glorify His Name over them, as is written: "I will magnify Myself and sanctify Myself and I will make Myself known" (Yechezkel 38:23). This happened in Egypt with one king, and IN THE COMPLETE REDEMPTION THAT WILL COME ABOUT, it will be with all the kings of the world.

15. The coming of Messiah

A Synopsis

In this long and complex section, Rabbi Shimon first describes the time when God shall make Himself known throughout the world, which is the prelude to the arrival of the Messiah. We learn that when God reveals His glory to the world, all the nations and their kings will rise up against the children of Yisrael, and the children of Yisrael will suffer greatly. A pillar of fire reaching from heaven to earth will appear for forty days. At this time, the Messiah will rise in Galilee and begin to wage war on the world from there, because this is where the devastation first began. The earth will shake, and everybody will seek refuge in caves and rocky places, as alluded to in the verse, "And they shall go into the holes..." After forty days, a bright star from the east will battle with seven stars surrounding it, extinguishing them night after night for a period of seventy days. Then the one star will be hidden and the Messiah will be concealed in the pillar of fire for twelve months, though it will not be visible to the world. After the twelve months, the Messiah will ascend to receive the power and the crown of the Kingdom. Then the pillar of fire will again be visible on earth and the Messiah will reveal himself and declare war on the world. Many nations will join him to wage war on the nations of the world, which will unite to fight against him. Then a time will come when the world will remain in darkness for fifteen days, and many of the children of Yisrael will perish.

Rabbi Shimon then explains to Rabbi Elazar that the Messiah resides in the lower Garden of Eden, surrounded by saints, angels and the souls of the righteous. There is a concealed place in Eden called "Bird's Nest" which is revealed to the Messiah by the bird that awakens daily in the Garden. In the Bird's Nest is the Cloak of Majesty, and the images of all the nations that banded against Yisrael are woven into this garment. The Messiah enters this place and sees the Patriarchs visiting the ruins of God's Sanctuary and God trying to comfort Rachel, who weeps incessantly. Then he weeps loudly and all of Eden shakes and laments with him. When he cries for a second time, the Holy Throne summons them and they ascend to above. There, God makes them swear to avenge the children of Yisrael through the Messiah and to draw God's goodness towards the children of Yisrael so that they may enjoy His rich rewards. At that time, God will arise to renew the world, and the letters of the Holy Name will shine in perfect union. A mighty star and a flame will then appear in the sky. After forty days, the star will gradually overpower the flame. The star will illuminate twelve pathways for twelve days, and after another twelve days the world will tremble and darkness will fall. A sound shall be heard out of great thunder and lightning, causing the earth to shake and many to die. Then a flame of fire will appear in Rome, and it will burn many towers and places, and many mighty rulers and ministers will perish. For twelve months following, the kings of the nations will unite and persecute the children of Yisrael. Then a tribe will arise in Yisrael, led by the Messiah. The Messiah will be aroused and perfected through the Garden of Eden. He will enter the Bird's Nest, take the Garment of Jealousy, and be hidden there for forty days. After this time, he will ascend to receive God's blessing, and will be crowned with a Holy Crown. He then receives a royal red garment from the mourners of Zion to avenge the destruction of the Temple, and is concealed in the Bird's Nest for thirty days. Then he will descend to earth in a bright light, and no one will know the significance of this light except the sages. He will console Rachel, and she will finally accept consolation, and then the light will settle in the city of Jericho. After twelve months, the Messiah will be revealed to the world in Galilee, and those who study the Torah will surround him and give him additional strength. After waiting for another twelve months, he will raise the Shechinah and gather the exiled from the world. Then God will perform for the children of Yisrael the signs and wonders that He did in Egypt. Rabbi Shimon next discusses the doctrine of Faith contained in the verse, "O Hashem our Elohim; other masters beside you have had dominion…" In exile, we learn, the children of Yisrael are ruled by the Other Side, the Shechinah is separated from Her Spouse, and the two Names of God are also separated. During the first exile, Yisrael had no divine light to guide her. However, upon their return to the Holy Land, not all of the children of Yisrael were Righteous and pure, and therefore the light that returned to guide them was weaker than it had originally been. Consequently, Yisrael was involved in many wars until the destruction of the second Temple, and the Roman captivity was prolonged. After 1266 years, we're told, God shall perform many miracles and wonders, and after another 66 years, the Holy Name will be perfectly engraved, above and below. After a further 132 years, the Holy Land will be purified and God will shake the wicked from the earth and raise the dead. Finally, 144 years later, the remaining dead of Yisrael who are in other lands will also be raised, and the Other Side will be destroyed. Then the Shechinah will be crowned and the holy spirits of the children of Yisrael will be invested with new, holy bodies, and they shall be called 'saints'. After 1266 years, we're now told, God shall perform many miracles and wonders, and after another 66 years, the Holy Name will be perfectly engraved, above and below. After a further 132 years, the Holy Land will be purified and God will shake the wicked from the earth and raise the dead. Finally, 144 years later, the remaining dead of Yisrael who are in other lands will also be raised, and the Other Side will be destroyed. Then, after the seventh millenium, the Shechinah will be crowned and the holy spirits of the children of Yisrael will be invested with new, holy bodies, and they shall be called Holy Ones.

The Relevance of the Passage

In these our final days, the time of Messiah, two realities will coexist – a reality of chaos, suffering, and pain; and a second reality of blessedness, joy, and perfection.

Both existences are available to us. We need only to choose. Those who undertake the labor of self-transformation will find themselves living in Light. Persons who persist on the path of narcissism will dwell in darkness and discontent.

One might ask how both actualities are able to exist side by side. The analogy of sunlight provides profound insight. The sun's rays warm, nourish and sustain life on earth. However, overexposure to these same life-giving emanations of light can also cause damage and destruction.

In our day, the intensity of spiritual Light is at its highest level in history. Those who share, give, love, and care for their fellow human being, thus uprooting all evil impulses from their own nature, become a clear and unobstructed conduit of the Light. Thus, splendid Divine energy flows right through such people, and then to all mankind.

Individuals who are caught up in their own gluttony, mired in materialism, automatically hold on to this intense energy, and it burns severely. They cause the rays to become the fires of Hell. In that case, the flames reduce to ashes all deceitful and inconsiderate characteristics.

Physical wars and destruction on our planet cannot take place if we instigate the only true war worth waging – the war against our own Evil Inclination.

That war is now being won.

And so, this particular passage of Zohar is a great and grand gift to the world. Each verse is a *preemptive strike* against the possibility of global warfare, terror, disease, and suffering, as the Light launched by the gaze of our eyes targets the Satan and the evil within.

The truth of the Creator and the spiritual laws of life take hold within the collective consciousness of humanity. A merciful, kind-hearted, gentle, compassionate, lenient and forgiving redemption unfolds before our eyes. Immortality and the appearance of our departed loved ones is our new and eternal reality.

96. רִבִּי שִׁמְעוֹן זָקַף יְדוֹי וּבָכָה, וְאָמַר, וַוי מַאן דְּיִזְדָּמַן בְּהַהוּא זִמְנָא,
וְזַכָּאָה חוּלָקֵיהּ מַאן דְּיִזְדָּמַן וְיִשְׁתְּכַח בְּהַהוּא זִמְנָא, וַוי מַאן דְּיִזְדָּמַן
בְּהַהוּא זִמְנָא, בְּגִין דְּכַד יֵיתֵי קוּדְשָׁא בְּרִיךְ הוּא לְפַקְדָא לְאַיַּילְתָּא,
יִסְתָּכַּל מַאן אִינוּן דְּקַיְימִין בַּהֲדָה, בְּכָל אִינוּן דְּמִשְׁתַּכְּחֵי עִמָּה, בְּכָל
עוֹבָדוֹי דְּכָל חַד וְחַד, וְלָא יִשְׁתְּכַח זַכָּאי. דִּכְתִיב, וְאַבִּיט וְאֵין עוֹזֵר.
וְכַמָּה עַקְתִּין עַל עַקְתִּין לְיִשְׂרָאֵל.

96. Rabbi Shimon raised his hands, wept and said: Woe to he who is present at that time, and blissful is the portion of he who is present and WILL BE ABLE TO attend at that time. AND HE EXPLAINS: Woe to he who is present at that time, because when the Holy One, blessed be He, comes to visit the Gazelle WHO IS THE SHECHINAH, He will observe who is standing by Her, and all those who are with Her. He will contemplate the actions of each and every one, but no righteous person will be found, as is written: "And I looked and there was none to help" (Yeshayah 63:5). And how many troubles upon troubles will there be for Yisrael.

97. זַכָּאָה מַאן דְּיִזְדָּמַן וְיִשְׁתְּכַח בְּהַהוּא זִמְנָא, בְּגִין דְּהַהוּא דְּיִתְקַיַּים
בְּהַהוּא זִמְנָא בִּמְהֵימָנוּתָא, יִזְכֶּה לְהַהוּא נְהִירוּ דְּחֶדְוָה דְּמַלְכָּא. וְעַל
הַהוּא זִמְנָא כְּתִיב, וּצְרַפְתִּים כִּצְרוֹף אֶת הַכֶּסֶף וּבְחַנְתִּים כִּבְחֹן אֶת
הַזָּהָב וְגוֹ'.

97. Happy is he who is present, because he who is present at that time with Faith, will merit that light of joy of the King. In relation to that time it is written: "And I will refine them as silver is refined, and will try them as gold is tried" (Zecharyah 13:9).

98. לְבָתַר דְּאִינוּן עַקְתִּין מִתְעָרֵי עַל יִשְׂרָאֵל, וְכָל עַמִּין וּמַלְכֵיהוֹן
יִתְיַיעֲטוּן כַּחֲדָא עָלַיְיהוּ, וּמִתְעָרֵי כַּמָּה גְּזֵירִין בִּישִׁין, כֻּלְּהוּ סַלְקֵי
בְּעֵיטָא חֲדָא עָלַיְיהוּ, וְיֵיתוּן עַקְתָּא עַל עַקְתָּא, בַּתְרַיְיתָא מְשַׁכְּחָן
קַמְיַיתָא. כְּדֵין יִתְחֲזֵי חַד עַמּוּדָא דְּאֶשָּׁא, קָאִים מֵעֵלָּא לְתַתָּא, אַרְבְּעִין
יוֹמִין, וְכָל עַמִּין דְּעָלְמָא חָמָאן לֵיהּ.

98. After these troubles have been aroused against Yisrael, all the peoples and their kings will counsel together against them, raise many bad decrees, and come upon them with one mind. There will come troubles upon troubles and the later troubles will cause the earlier ones to be forgotten. Then a pillar of fire shall be seen there, standing from above down for forty days. And all the nations of the world will see it.

99. בְּהַהוּא זִמְנָא, יִתְּעַר מַלְכָּא מְשִׁיחָא, לְנַפְקָא מִגּוֹ גִּנְתָּא דְעֵדֶן, מֵהַהוּא אֲתָר דְּאִתְקְרֵי קַ"ן צִפּוֹ"ר, וְיִתְּעַר בְּאַרְעָא דְגָלִיל, וְהַהוּא יוֹמָא דִּיפּוּק לְתַמָּן, יִתְרְגַּז כָּל עָלְמָא, וְכָל בְּנֵי עָלְמָא מִתְחַבְּאִין גּוֹ מְעַרְתֵּי וְטִנָּרֵי, דְּלָא יַחְשְׁבוּן לְאִשְׁתְּזָבָא. וְעַל הַהוּא זִמְנָא כְּתִיב, וּבָאוּ בִּמְעָרוֹת צוּרִים וּבִמְחִלּוֹת עָפָר מִפְּנֵי פַּחַד ה' וּמֵהֲדַר גְּאוֹנוֹ בְּקוּמוֹ לַעֲרוֹץ הָאָרֶץ.

99. At that time the king, Messiah, will arise to go out of the Garden of Eden from the place called the 'bird's nest' and he will become revealed in the land of Galilee. On the day that MESSIAH goes there, the whole world will tremble and all the people of the world will hide in the caves and CRACKS in the rocks and will not expect to survive. And concerning that time, it is written: "And they shall go into the holes of the rocks, and in the caves of the earth, for fear of Hashem, and for the glory of His majesty, when He arises to shake the earth terribly" (Yeshayah 2:19).

100. מִפְּנֵי פַּחַד ה', דָּא הַהוּא רְגִיזוּ דְּכָל עָלְמָא. וּמֵהֲדַר גְּאוֹנוֹ דָּא מָשִׁיחַ. בְּקוּמוֹ לַעֲרוֹץ הָאָרֶץ, כַּד יְקוּם וְיִתְגְּלֵי בְּאַרְעָא דְגָלִיל, בְּגִין דְּאִיהוּ הוּא אֲתָר קַדְמָאָה דְּאִתְחָרְבָא בְּאַרְעָא קַדִּישָׁא, ובג"כ, יִתְגְּלֵי תַּמָּן קַדְמָאָה לְכָל אֲתָר, וּמִתַּמָּן יִתְּעַר קְרָבִין לְכָל עָלְמָא.

100. AND HE EXPLAINS: "For fear of Hashem," is the trembling of the whole world, "and for the glory OF HIS majesty" is Messiah. "...When He arises to shake the earth terribly..." refers to when MESSIAH will arise and be revealed in the land of Galilee, because this was the first place in the Holy Land that was destroyed BY ASHUR. Therefore, He will be revealed there before any other place, and from there He will stir wars all over the world.

101. לְבָתַר אַרְבְּעִין יוֹמִין, דְּעַמּוּדָא יְקוּם מֵאַרְעָא לִשְׁמַיָּא, לְעֵינֵיהוֹן

דְּכָל עָלְמָא, וּמָשִׁיחַ יִתְגְּלֵי, יְקוּם מִסְטַר מִזְרָח, חַד כּוֹכָבָא מְלַהֲטָא בְּכָל גַּוְונִין, וְשִׁבְעָה כּוֹכָבִין אַחֲרָנִין דְּסַחֲרָן לְהַהוּא כּוֹכָבָא, וְיַגִּיחוּן בֵּיהּ קְרָבָא בְּכָל סִטְרִין, תְּלַת זִמְנִין בְּיוֹמָא, עַד שַׁבְעִין יוֹמִין, וְכָל בְּנֵי עָלְמָא חָמָאן.

101. After 40 days, the pillar will stand from the earth to the heaven before the eyes of the whole world, and Messiah will be revealed. There will arise from the East side a star that will glow with variety of colors, and seven other stars will surround that star and will war with it on all sides, three times a day up to seventy days. And all the people of the world will see.

102. וְהַהוּא כּוֹכָבָא, יַגִּיחַ בְּהוּ קְרָבָא, בְּטִיסִין דְּנוּרָא, מְלַהֲטִין מְנַצְצִין לְכָל עֵבֶר, וּבָטַשׁ בְּהוּ, עַד דְּבָלַע לוֹן, בְּכָל רַמְשָׁא וְרַמְשָׁא, וּבְיוֹמָא אַפִּיק לוֹן. וְיַגִּיחוּן קְרָבָא לְעֵינֵיהוֹן דְּכָל עָלְמָא, וְכֵן בְּכָל יוֹמָא, עַד שַׁבְעִין יוֹמִין. לְבָתַר שַׁבְעִין יוֹמִין, יִתְגְּנִיז הַהוּא כּוֹכָבָא, וְיִתְגְּנִיז מָשִׁיחַ, עַד תְּרֵיסַר יַרְחִין, וְיִתְהַדַר הַהוּא עַמּוּדָא דְּאֶשָׁא כְּמִלְּקַדְּמִין, וּבֵיהּ יִתְגְּנִיז מָשִׁיחַ, וְהַהוּא עַמּוּדָא לָא יִתְחֲזֵי.

102. And that star will do battle with them with flames of fire that will burn and sparkle in every direction, and it will smite them until it will swallow them every night; and by day, AGAIN it shall take them out where they will battle before the eyes of the whole world. And so it shall ensue, every day for seventy days! After seventy days, that star will be hidden and Messiah will be concealed for up to twelve months. Then the pillar of fire will return as originally, and in it Messiah will be concealed, and that pillar is invisible.

103. לְבָתַר תְּרֵיסַר יַרְחִין, יְסַלְּקוּן לֵיהּ לְמָשִׁיחַ, בְּהַהוּא עַמּוּדָא, לְגוֹ רְקִיעָא, וְתַמָּן יְקַבֵּל תּוּקְפָּא וְעִטְרָא דְּמַלְכוּתָא. וְכַד נָחִית, יִתְחֲזֵי הַהוּא עַמּוּדָא דְּאֶשָׁא כְּמִלְּקַדְּמִין, לְעֵינֵיהוֹן דְּכָל עָלְמָא, וְיִתְגְּלֵי לְבָתַר מָשִׁיחַ, וְיִתְכַּנְּשׁוּן לְגַבֵּיהּ עַמִּין סַגִּיאִין, וְיִתְעַר קְרָבִין בְּכָל עָלְמָא. וּבְהַהוּא זִמְנָא יִתְעַר קוּדְשָׁא בְּרִיךְ הוּא גְּבוּרְתֵּיהּ לְכָל עַמִּין דְּעָלְמָא, וּמַלְכָּא מְשִׁיחָא יִתְיְדַע בְּכָל עָלְמָא, וְכָל מַלְכִין דְּעָלְמָא יִתְעָרוּן לְאִתְחַבְּרָא לְאַגָּחָא קְרָבָא בֵּיהּ.

103. After twelve months, Messiah will be elevated within that pillar to the sky, and there he will receive the power and crown of the Kingdom. And when he descends TO THE EARTH, that pillar of fire will again appear as originally, before the eyes of the whole world. Afterwards, Messiah will appear and many nations will gather to him and he will wage wars throughout the entire world. At that time the Holy One, blessed be He, will rise with His might against all the nations of the world. Messiah will be publicly known throughout the world, and all the kings of the world will join together to do battle with Him.

104. וְכַמָּה מְפְרִיצֵי יְהוּדָאִין יִתְהַפְּכוּ לְאָהַדְרָא לְגַבַּיְיהוּ, וְיֵיתוּן עִמְּהוֹן, לְאַגָּחָא קְרָבָא עַל מַלְכָּא מְשִׁיחָא. כְּדֵין יִתְחֲשַׁךְ כָּל עָלְמָא חֲמֵשׁ עֶשְׂרֵה יוֹמִין, וְסַגִּיאִין מֵעַמָּא דְּיִשְׂרָאֵל יְהוֹן מֵתִין בְּהַהוּא חֲשׁוֹכָא. וְעַל דָּא כְּתִיב, כִּי הִנֵּה הַחֹשֶׁךְ יְכַסֶּה אֶרֶץ וַעֲרָפֶל לְאֻמִּים.

104. Many of the oppressors of Yisrael will turn and join THESE NATIONS to war against the king Messiah; then will the world darken for fifteen days. Many of Yisrael will perish during this darkness. Of this it is written: "For, behold, the darkness shall cover the earth, and gross darkness the peoples" (Yeshayah 60:2).

105. פָּתַח וְאָמַר כִּי יִקָּרֵא קַן צִפּוֹר לְפָנֶיךָ בַּדֶּרֶךְ בְּכָל עֵץ אוֹ עַל הָאָרֶץ אֶפְרוֹחִים אוֹ בֵיצִים וְהָאֵם רוֹבֶצֶת וְגוֹ', שַׁלֵּחַ תְּשַׁלַּח אֶת הָאֵם וְגוֹ', הַאי קְרָא אוֹקִימְנָא לֵיהּ, וְאִיהוּ חַד מִפִּקּוּדֵי אוֹרַיְיתָא גְּנִיזִין, וַאֲנָן אִית לָן בֵּיהּ רָזֵי דְּאוֹרַיְיתָא גְּנִיזִין, שְׁבִילִין וְאָרְחִין יְדִיעָן לְחַבְרַיָּיא, בְּאִינּוּן תְּלָתִין וּתְרֵין שְׁבִילִין דְּאוֹרַיְיתָא.

105. He opened the discussion saying: "If a bird's nest chance to be before you in the way in any tree or on the ground, whether they be young ones or eggs, and the mother bird sitting upon the young, or upon the eggs, you shall not take the mother together with the young: but you shall surely let the mother go" (Devarim 22:6). We have explained this verse and it is one of the concealed commandments of the Torah. We have in it concealed secrets of the Torah, paths and ways known to the friends in the 32 paths of the Torah.

106. אָמַר רִבִּי שִׁמְעוֹן לְרִבִּי אֶלְעָזָר בְּרֵיהּ, אֶלְעָזָר, בְּזִמְנָא דְּיִתְּעַר מַלְכָּא מְשִׁיחָא, כַּמָּה אָתִין וְנִסִּין אָחֲרָנִין יִתְּעֲרוּן בְּעָלְמָא. תָּא חֲזֵי, בְּגִנְתָּא דְעֵדֶן דִּלְתַתָּא, אִית אֲתָר חַד גָּנִיז וְטָמִיר דְּלָא אִתְיְדַע, וְאִיהוּ מְרֻקְמָא בְּכַמָּה גַּוְונִין, וּבֵיהּ גְּנִיזִין אֶלֶף הֵיכָלִין דִּכְסוּפִין. וְלֵית מַאן דְּעָיֵיל בְּהוּ, בַּר מָשִׁיחַ, דְּאִיהוּ קָאִים תָּדִיר בְּגִנְתָּא דְעֵדֶן.

106. Rabbi Shimon said to his son Rabbi Elazar: Elazar, when Messiah awakens, so many other signs and miracles will be aroused in the world. Come and behold: in the terrestrial Garden of Eden, there is one place which is concealed and hidden and is not known, and it is woven with many colors. Therein are hidden a thousand pleasant chambers and no one enters them except for Messiah, who is ever present in the Garden of Eden.

107. וְכָל גִּנְתָּא מְסַחֲרָא בְּרָתִיכִין סַגִּיאִין דְּצַדִּיקַיָּיא, וּמְשִׁיחַ קָאִים עֲלַיְיהוּ, וְעַל כַּמָּה חֵילִין וּמַשִׁירְיָין דְּנִשְׁמָתִין דְּצַדִּיקַיָּיא תַּמָּן, וּבְרֵאשֵׁי יַרְחֵי, וּבִזְמַנֵּי, וּבְשַׁבַּתֵּי, מָשִׁיחַ עָאל בְּהַהוּא אֲתָר לְאִשְׁתַּעְשְׁעָא בְּכָל אִינּוּן הֵיכָלִין.

107. The entire Garden is surrounded by many Chariots of the righteous, and Messiah stands over them and over many hosts and camps of souls of the righteous who are there. And Messiah enters that place on the first day of the month and festivals and Shabbatot, WHERE THERE ARE A THOUSAND CHAMBERS OF PLEASURES, to delight in all these chambers.

108. לְגוֹ לְגוֹ מִכָּל אִינּוּן הֵיכָלִין, אִית אֲתָר אָחֲרָא טָמִיר וְגָנִיז דְּלָא אִתְיְדַע כְּלָל, וְאִקְרֵי עֵדֶן. וְלֵית מַאן דְּיָכִיל לְמִנְדַּע בֵּיהּ. וּמָשִׁיחַ אַגְנִיז לְבַר, סַחֲרָנֵיהּ דְּהַהוּא אֲתָר, עַד דְּאִתְגַּלְיֵי לֵיהּ חַד אֲתָר. דְּאִקְרֵי קַן צִפּוֹר, וְאִיהוּ אֲתָר דְּכָרִיז עֲלֵיהּ הַהוּא צִפּוֹר. דְּאִתְּעַר בְּגִנְתָּא דְעֵדֶן בְּכָל יוֹמָא.

108. Innermost from all these THOUSAND chambers OF PLEASURES, there is one place concealed and hidden that is entirely unknown, called 'Eden'. There is no one who can conceive it. Messiah is concealed outside around that place, until a place called 'bird's nest' is revealed to him. This place is announced by the bird, which awakens daily in the Garden of Eden.

109. וּבְהַהוּא אֲתָר, מְרָקְמָן דְּיוּקְנִין דְּכָל שְׁאַר עַמִּין, דְּאִתְכְּנָשׁוּ
עֲלַיְיהוּ דְיִשְׂרָאֵל לְאַבְאָשָׁא לוֹן. עָאל בְּהַהוּא אֲתָר, זָקִיף עֵינוֹי, וְחָזֵי
אֲבָהָן, דְּעָאלִין בְּחָרְבַּן בֵּית אֱלָהָא, עַד דְּחָמֵי לְרָחֵל דְּדִמְעָתָא
בְּאַנְפָּהָא, וְקוּדְשָׁא בְּרִיךְ הוּא מְנַחֵם לָהּ, וְלָא צְבִיאַת לְקַבְּלָא תַּנְחוּמִין,
כְּמָה דְאַתְּ אָמַר, מֵאֲנָה לְהִנָּחֵם עַל בָּנֶיהָ. כְּדֵין. מְשִׁיחַ אָרִים קַלֵּיהּ
וּבְכֵי, וְאִזְדַּעְזַע כָּל גִּנְתָּא דְעֵדֶן, וְכָל אִינּוּן צַדִּיקַיָּא דְּתַמָּן גָּעוּ וּבְכוּ
עִמֵּיהּ.

109. In that place CALLED 'BIRD'S NEST', the images of all the nations that gathered against Yisrael to harm them are woven IN A GARMENT CALLED 'THE CLOAK OF MAJESTY'. MESSIAH enters that place, raises his eyes and sees the patriarchs who entered the house of Elohim that was destroyed, until he sees Rachel with tears on her cheeks. And the Holy One, blessed be He, is consoling her but she refuses to accept condolences, as it is written: "She refuses to be comforted for her children…" (Yirmeyah 31:14). Then, Messiah raises his voice and weeps, and the whole Garden of Eden shakes. All the righteous who are there break down and weep with him.

110. גָּעֵי וּבְכֵי זִמְנָא תִּנְיָינָא, וְאִזְדַּעְזַע הַהוּא רְקִיעַ דְּעַל גַּבֵּי גִּנְתָּא,
אֶלֶף וְחָמֵשׁ מֵאָה רִבּוֹא מַשִּׁרְיָין עִלָּאִין, עַד דְּמָטֵי לְגוֹ כֻּרְסְיָיא עִלָּאָה.
כְּדֵין, קוּדְשָׁא בְּרִיךְ הוּא רָמִיז לְהַהוּא צִפֳּרָא, וְעָאל לְהַהוּא קֵן דִּילָהּ,
וְיָתְבָא לְגַבֵּי מָשִׁיחַ, וְקָרֵי מַה דְּקָרֵי, וְאִתְּעַר מַה דְּאִתְּעַר.

110. He cries bitterly a second time, and the firmament above the Garden trembles. So too do 15,000,000 supernal angels until MESSIAH reaches the supernal throne. Then the Holy One, blessed be He, motions to that bird. It enters its nest, sits next to Messiah, cries whatever it cries and awakens whatever it awakens.

111. עַד דְּמִגּוֹ כֻּרְסְיָיא קַדִּישָׁא, אִתְקְרֵי תְּלַת זִמְנִין הַהוּא קֵן צִפּוֹר,
וּמָשִׁיחַ, וְכֹלָּא סַלְקִין לְעֵילָּא, וְאוֹמֵי לוֹן קוּדְשָׁא בְּרִיךְ הוּא, לְאַעְבְּרָא
מַלְכוּ חַיָּיבָא מִן עָלְמָא, עַל יְדָא דְמָשִׁיחַ, וּלְנָקְמָא נַקְמִין דְּיִשְׂרָאֵל. וְכָל
אִינּוּן טַבְוָון, דְּזַמִּין קוּדְשָׁא בְּרִיךְ הוּא לְמֶעְבַּד לְעַמֵּיהּ. וְתָב הַהוּא קֵן

צִפּוֹר וּמָשִׁיחַ לְדוּכְתֵּיהּ. וְתָב מָשִׁיחַ וְאִתְגְּנִיז גּוֹ הַהוּא אֲתָר כְּמִלְּקַדְמִין.

111. This continues until from the holy throne, WHICH IS BINAH, that same bird's nest is called three times – NAMELY THE THREE COLUMNS, ONE AFTER THE OTHER. Messiah and everyone then ascend above TO BINAH, and the Holy One, blessed be He, makes them swear to remove the Wicked Kingdom from the world through Messiah, to avenge Yisrael and TO DRAW all the goodness that the Holy One, blessed be He, will do for His people. The bird's nest and Messiah then return to their places and Messiah is again concealed in that place, THAT IS, THE BIRD'S NEST, as previously!

112. וּבְזִמְנָא דְּיִתְּעַר קוּדְשָׁא בְּרִיךְ הוּא לְאַתְקָנָא עָלְמִין, וְאִתְנְהִירוּ אַתְוָון דִּשְׁמֵיהּ בִּשְׁלִימוּ, יוּ"ד בְּהֵ"א, וָא"ו בְּהֵ"א, לְמֶהֱוֵי כֹּלָּא בִּשְׁלִימוּ חַד. כְּדֵין יִתְּעַר חַד כֹּכָבָא דְּחֵילָא, בְּאֶמְצַע רְקִיעָא, כְּגַוֶן אַרְגְּוָונָא, לָהִיט וְנָצִיץ בִּימָמָא לְעֵינֵיהוֹן דְּכָל עָלְמָא.

112. At the time that the Holy One, blessed be He, will be aroused to remedy the worlds, and the letters of the Name will illuminate completely. The *Yud* OF THE NAME, WHICH IS CHOCHMAH, WILL ILLUMINATE the *Hei,* WHICH IS BINAH; *Vav* OF THE NAME, WHICH IS TIFERET, WILL ILLUMINATE the SECOND *Hei,* WHICH IS MALCHUT. *YUD-HEI* will be in complete union WITH *VAV-HEI* – THAT IS TO SAY, one awful star will rise, WHICH IS TIFERET, CALLED 'AWFUL', in the middle of the firmament, IT BEING THE CENTRAL COLUMN, of the color purple, THAT AS IT INCLUDES ALL THE COLORS, SO IT INCLUDES ALL THE THREE COLUMNS. It will flame and sparkle by day, MEANING WITH THE LIGHT OF CHASSADIM CALLED 'DAY', before the eyes of the whole world – MEANING ALSO WITH THE LIGHT OF CHOCHMAH, WHICH IS CALLED 'EYES'.

113. וְיָקוּם חַד שַׁלְהוֹבָא דְּאֶשָׁא מִסִּטְרָא דְּצָפוֹן, גּוֹ רְקִיעָא, וְיָקוּם דָּא לָקֳבֵל דָּא אַרְבְּעִין יוֹמִין וְיִתְבַּהֲלוּן כָּל בְּנֵי עָלְמָא. לְסוֹף אַרְבְּעִין יוֹמִין, יַגִּיחוּן קְרָבָא, כֹּכָבָא וְשַׁלְהוֹבָא, לְעֵינֵיהוֹן דְּכֹלָּא, וְיִתְפַּשֵּׁט הַהוּא שַׁלְהוֹבָא בִּיקִידוּ דְּאֶשָׁא, מִסִּטְרָא דְּצָפוֹן, גּוֹ רְקִיעָא, וְיַחֲשׁוֹב לְמִבְלַע הַהוּא כֹּכָבָא, וְכַמָּה שַׁלִּיטִין וּמַלְכִין וְאוּמַיָּא וְעַמְמִיָּא, יִתְבַּהֲלוּן מֵהַאי.

113. A flame of fire will rise from the north side, MEANING FROM THE LEFT COLUMN, FOR AT THE MOMENT THAT CHOCHMAH FROM ABOVE IS DRAWN DOWN, ITS LIGHT IS CONVERTED TO A FLAME OF FIRE in the firmament, and they stand opposite each other for forty days. THE FLAME, WHICH IS FROM THE LEFT COLUMN, SEPARATES ITSELF FROM EACH OF CHOCHMAH AND BINAH, TIFERET AND MALCHUT THAT ARE IN THE CENTRAL COLUMN, EACH MADE UP OF TEN SFIROT, SO THEY ARE FORTY. And all the people of the world will be confused. At the end of forty days, MEANING THE LAST SFIRAH, WHICH IS MALCHUT OF MALCHUT, the star and the flame will wage war before everyone's eyes, and the flame will spread with a fiery conflagration within the firmament on the north side. Many rulers and kings and nations will become confused by this – MEANING, FROM THE STRENGTHENING OF THE FLAME!

114. כְּדֵין יִסְתַּלַק הַהוּא כֹּכָבָא לִסְטַר דָרוֹם, וְיִשְׁלוֹט עַל הַהוּא שַׁלְהוֹבָא, וְהַהוּא שַׁלְהוֹבָא יִתְבְּלַע זְעֵיר זְעֵיר בִּרְקִיעָא, מִקַּמֵּי הַהוּא כֹּכָבָא, עַד דְּלָא יִתְחֲזֵי כְּלָל. כְּדֵין, הַהוּא כֹּכָבָא יַעֲבֵיד אוֹרְחִין בִּרְקִיעַ, בִּתְרֵיסַר תְּחוּמִין, וְקַיְימִין אִינּוּן נְהוֹרִין בִּרְקִיעָא תְּרֵיסַר יוֹמִין.

114. Then the star will ascend to the south side, WHICH IS THE RIGHT COLUMN AND THE LIGHT OF CHESED, AND CHASSADIM WILL AGAIN ILLUMINATE THE WORLD. THUS, it will rule over the flame, and the flame will be swallowed bit by bit in the firmament because of the star, until it is no longer visible. Then the star will make pathways in the sky in twelve borders. AND WHEN ITS THREE COLUMNS WILL BE INCLUDED IN EACH ONE OF CHOCHMAH AND BINAH, TIFERET AND MALCHUT, THREE TIMES FOUR ARE TWELVE PATHWAYS. And these lights will stand in the sky for twelve days. FOR EVEN MALCHUT HERSELF ILLUMINATES ONLY IN THE THREE COLUMNS CHESED, GVURAH AND TIFERET. BUT MALCHUT IN IT DOES NOT ILLUMINATE; THEREFORE, THERE ARE ONLY TWELVE LIGHTS.

115. לְבָתַר תְּרֵיסַר יוֹמִין יִזְדַעְזְעוּן כָּל בְּנֵי עָלְמָא, וְיִתְחֲשַׁךְ שִׁמְשָׁא בְּפַלְגוּת יוֹמָא, כְּמָה דְּאִתְחֲשַׁךְ יוֹמָא דְּאִתְחָרַב בֵּי מַקְדְּשָׁא, עַד דְּלָא יִתְחֲזוּן שְׁמַיָּא וְאַרְעָא. וְיִתְּעַר חַד קָלָא בְּרַעַם וְזִיקִין, וְאִתְחַלְחָלָא אַרְעָא מֵהַהוּא קָלָא, וְכַמָּה חֵילִין וּמַשִׁירְיָין יְמוּתוּן מִנֵּיהּ.

115. WHEN HE DESIRES TO DRAW THEIR ILLUMINATION after twelve days, MEANING TO THE ASPECT OF MALCHUT, all the people of the world will tremble BECAUSE OF THE ATTRIBUTE OF JUDGMENT IN MALCHUT. The sun will be darkened at midday, as it was darkened on the day that the Temple was destroyed, to a point that both heaven and earth will not be visible. And a sound will erupt in thunder and lightning, MEANING A SOUND FROM THE ATTRIBUTE OF JUDGMENT IN MALCHUT. The world will shudder because of that sound, and numerous hosts and companies will perish because of it.

116. וְהַהוּא יוֹמָא, יִתְעַר בְּקַרְתָּא דְרוֹמִי רַבְּתָא, חַד שַׁלְהוֹבָא דְאֶשָּׁא, בְּהַהוּא קָלָא דְיִתְּעַר בְּכָל עָלְמָא. וְיוֹקִיד כַּמָּה מִגְדָּלִין, וְכַמָּה הֵיכָלִין, וְכַמָּה מִגְדָּלִין יִפְּלוּן, וְכַמָּה פַרְדַשְׁכֵּי וְרַבְרְבֵי יִפְּלוּן בְּהַהוּא יוֹמָא וְכֻלְּהוּ, יִתְכַּנְּשׁוּן עֲלָה לְבִישׁ. וְכָל בְּנֵי עָלְמָא לָא יַכְלִין לְאִשְׁתְּזָבָא.

116. And that day, WHICH IS MALCHUT, WILL CAUSE there to be ignited in the great city of Rome – WHICH IS THE SECRET OF BINAH OF KLIPOT – a flame of fire, WHICH IS THE JUDGMENTS OF THE LEFT. That sound will be stirred up in the whole world, WHICH IS FROM THE ATTRIBUTE OF JUDGMENT IN MALCHUT, THAT IS, THESE TWO KINDS OF JUDGMENTS WILL BE COMBINED. It will burn many towers and many palaces, and many towers will collapse and many potentates and ministers will fall on that day. All of them, MEANING ALL OF THE JUDGMENTS, will gather upon it to cause harm. And all the people of the world will be unable to be saved.

117. מֵהַהוּא יוֹמָא, עַד תְּרֵיסַר יַרְחִין, יִתְיַעֲטוּן כָּל מַלְכַיָּא, וְיִגְזְרוּן כַּמָּה גְּזֵרוֹת, וְכַמָּה שְׁמָדוֹת עַל יִשְׂרָאֵל, וְיִצְלְחוּן בְּהוֹן, כְּמָה דְאִתְּמַר זַכָּאָה אִיהוּ מַאן דְּיֶעְרַע תַּמָּן, וְזַכָּאָה אִיהוּ מַאן דְּלָא יֶעְרַע תַּמָּן וְכָל עָלְמָא יְהֵא בְּעִרְבּוּבְיָא סַגְיָא.

117. From that day for twelve months time, THAT IS, UNTIL THE ILLUMINATIONS OF THE TWELVE BOUNDARIES SHALL BE REMEDIED IN MALCHUT AS WELL – BECAUSE IN ZEIR ANPIN THEY ARE CALLED TWELVE DAYS, BUT IN MALCHUT THEY ARE CALLED 'TWELVE MONTHS' – all the kings will counsel and will make numerous decrees and numerous persecutions against Yisrael and they will succeed with them. As we

learned, "Fortunate is he who will chance to be there," MEANING IN THE DAYS OF MESSIAH. Fortunate is he who will not be there, THAT HE WILL BE SAVED FROM THESE JUDGMENTS, and the whole world will be greatly confused.

118. לְסוֹף תְּרֵיסַר יַרְחֵי, יָקוּם שֵׁבֶט מִיִשְׂרָאֵל, דָּא מַלְכָּא מְשִׁיחָא, דְּיִתְּעַר גּוֹ גִּנְתָּא דְּעֵדֶן. וְכָל אִינוּן צַדִּיקַיָּא יַעַטְרוּן לֵיהּ תַּמָּן, וְיַחְגְּרוּן לֵיהּ מָאנֵי זַיִינָא, בְּאַתְוָון רְשִׁימָן דְּמָאנֵי דִּשְׁמָא קַדִּישָׁא.

118. At the end of twelve months, MEANING AFTER THE TWELVE LIGHTS IN MALCHUT ARE RECTIFIED, there will arise a tribe in Yisrael, which is the king Messiah who will awaken in the Garden of Eden. All the righteous will crown him there, and will gird him with weapons with engraved letters of the vessels of the Holy Name.

119. וְקָלָא יִתְפּוֹצֵץ בְּעַנְפֵי אִילָנִין דְּגִנְתָּא, קָרֵי בְּחַיִל, וְאָמַר, אִתְעָרוּ קַדִּישֵׁי עֶלְיוֹנִין, קוּמוּ מִקַּמֵּי מְשִׁיחָא, הָא עִדָנָא לְאִתְחַבְּרָא אִיתְּתָא בְּבַעְלָהּ, וּבַעְלָהּ בָּעֵי לְנַקְמָא לָהּ נוּקְמִין דְּעָלְמָא, וּלְאָקָמָא לָהּ, וּלְאַנְעָרָה לָהּ מֵעַפְרָא.

119. A voice will explode in the branches of the trees in the garden that cries powerfully and says: Awaken, supernal holy ones, arise before Messiah. Behold, it is the time for a wife to join with her husband, MEANING TIFERET WITH MALCHUT. Her husband, TIFERET, wishes to avenge her in the world, raise her and shake the dust off her.

120. כְּדֵין יְקוּמוּן כֻּלְּהוּ, וְיַחְגְּרוּן לֵיהּ כְּמִלְּקַדְמִין מָאנֵי זַיִינֵיהּ, אַבְרָהָם מִימִינֵיהּ, יִצְחָק מִשְׂמָאלֵיהּ, יַעֲקֹב קַמֵּיהּ, מֹשֶׁה רַעְיָא מְהֵימְנָא, עַל כָּל אִלֵּין צַדִּיקַיָּא, אָזִיל וְרָקִיד גּוֹ גִּנְתָּא דְּעֵדֶן.

120. Then they will all arise and will gird him with weapons as before, Abraham at his right, Isaac at his left, Jacob before him, Moses the Faithful Shepherd above all these righteous, walking and dancing in the Garden of Eden.

121. כֵּיוָן דְּאִתְתָּקַן מָשִׁיחַ, עַל יְדָא דְּצַדִּיקַיָּא בְּגִנְתָּא דְּעֵדֶן. יֵעוּל בְּהַהוּא דּוּכְתָּא דְּאִקְרֵי קַ"ן צִפּוֹ"ר כְּמִלְּקַדְמִין, וְחָמֵי תַּמָּן הַהוּא דְּיוּקְנָא דְּחָרְבָּן בֵּית מַקְדְּשָׁא, וְכֻלְּהוּ צַדִּיקַיָּא דְּאִתְקְטָלוּ בֵּיה. כְּדֵין נָטִיל מִתַּמָּן עֶשֶׂר, לְבוּשִׁין, וְאִינוּן אִקְרוּן. עֶשֶׂר לְבוּשֵׁי קִנְאָה. וְיִתְגְּנִיז תַּמָּן אַרְבְּעִין יוֹמִין, דְּלָא אִתְגַּלְיָא כְּלָל.

121. As soon as Messiah is perfected through the righteous in the Garden of Eden, he will enter as before in this place that is called 'bird's nest'. He sees a picture of the destroyed Temple and all the righteous who were killed there. Then, he takes from there ten garments called 'garments of jealousy' to be hidden there for forty days and not to be revealed at all.

122. לְסוֹף אַרְבְּעִין יוֹמִין, קָלָא חַד יִתְּעַר, וְיִתְקְרֵי מִגּוֹ כּוּרְסְיָיא עִלָּאָה, הַהוּא קַ"ן צִפּוֹ"ר בְּמַלְכָּא מְשִׁיחָא דְּאִתְגְּנִיז בֵּיה. וּכְדֵין סַלְקִין לֵיה לְעֵילָּא, וְקוּדְשָׁא בְּרִיךְ הוּא חָמֵי לֵיה לְמַלְכָּא מְשִׁיחָא, מִתְלַבַּשׁ בִּלְבוּשָׁא נוּקְמָא, וְחָגִיר מָאנֵי זַיְינֵי נָטִיל לֵיה, וְנָשִׁיק לֵיה עַל רֵישֵׁיה.

122. At the end of forty days, a voice will stir and will call from the supernal throne, WHICH IS BINAH, to the bird's nest that conceals the King Messiah. Then he is raised up. And the Holy One, blessed be He, sees the King Messiah who is dressed in garments of revenge and is girded with his weapons. He takes him and kisses him on his head.

123. כְּדֵין, מִזְדַּעְזְעָן ג' מְאָה וְתִשְׁעִין רְקִיעִין, וְאַרְמִיז קוּדְשָׁא בְּרִיךְ הוּא לְחַד רְקִיעָא מֵאִינּוּן דַּהֲוָה גָּנִיז מִשֵּׁשֶׁת יְמֵי בְּרֵאשִׁית, וְאַפִּיק מֵחַד הֵיכָלָא דִּבְהַהוּא רְקִיעָא חַד כִּתְרָא גְּלִיפָא, מְחַקְּקָא בִּשְׁמָהָן קַדִּישִׁין. בְּהַהוּא עִטְרָא אִתְעַטַּר קוּדְשָׁא בְּרִיךְ הוּא, כַּד עָבְרוּ יִשְׂרָאֵל יַת יַמָּא, לְמֵיטַל נוּקְמִין מִכָּל רְתִיכֵי פַרְעֹה וּפָרָשׁוֹי, וְאַעְטַר לֵיה לְמַלְכָּא מְשִׁיחָא.

123. Then 390 firmaments tremble and the Holy One, blessed be He, beckoned to one firmament that had been concealed since the Six Days of Creation, and took a crown engraved with holy names from one chamber in that firmament. The Holy One, blessed be He, who crowned Himself with this crown when Yisrael crossed the sea to take revenge on the chariots and riders of Pharaoh, then crowned the King Messiah with THE CROWN.

124. כֵּיוָן דְּאִתְעֲטָּר וְאִתְתַּקָּן בְּכָל הָנֵי תִּקּוּנִין, נָטִיל לֵיהּ קוּדְשָׁא בְּרִיךְ הוּא וְנָשִׁיק לֵיהּ כְּמִלְּקַדְמִין. מַאן חָמֵי, רְתִיכִין קַדִּישִׁין, וּמַשִׁרְיָין עִלָּאִין, דְּסַחֲרִין לֵיהּ, וְיָהֲבִין לֵיהּ מַתְּנָן וּנְבִזְבְּזָן סַגִּיאִין, וְיִתְעֲטָּר מִכֻּלְּהוּ.

124. Once MESSIAH was crowned and perfected with all these perfections, the Holy One, blessed be He, took him and kissed him again. Who saw this? The holy Chariots and companies of supernal angels that surround him and give him presents and many precious things. He is crowned with them all.

125. עָאל תַּמָּן בְּחַד הֵיכְלָא, וְחָמֵי כָּל אִינוּן מַלְאֲכֵי עִלָּאֵי, דְּאִקְרוּן אֲבֵלֵי צִיּוֹן, אִינוּן דְּבָכוּ עַל חָרְבָּן בֵּי מַקְדְּשָׁא, וּבְכָאן תָּדִיר, וְאִינוּן יַהֲבִין לֵיהּ חַד פּוּרְפִּירָא סוּמְקָא, לְמֶעְבַּד נוּקְמִין. כְּדֵין, קוּדְשָׁא בְּרִיךְ הוּא גָּנִיז לֵיהּ בְּהַהוּא קַן צִפּוֹר, וְאִתְכַּסֵּי תַּמָּן תְּלָתִין יוֹמִין.

125. He enters there into one chamber and sees all the supernal angels who are called the 'Mourners of Zion'. They weep over the destruction of the Temple and weep constantly, and they give him a royal purple garment to avenge. Then the Holy One, blessed be He, conceals him in that bird's nest, and he is hidden there for thirty days.

126. לְבָתַר תְּלָתִין יוֹמִין, בְּהַהוּא קַן צִפּוֹר, יֵחוּת מְעַטָּר בְּכָל אִינוּן תִּקּוּנִין מֵעֵילָּא וּמִתַּתָּא, כַּמָּה מַשִׁרְיָין קַדִּישִׁין סַחֲרָנֵיהּ, וְיֵחֲמוּן כָּל עָלְמָא, חַד נְהִירוּ, תָּלֵי מֵרְקִיעָא לְאַרְעָא, וְיֵקוּם שִׁבְעָה יוֹמִין, וְכָל בְּנֵי עָלְמָא יִתְמְהוּן וְיִתְבַּהֲלוּן, וְלָא יִנְדְּעוּן כְּלַל, בַּר אִינוּן חַכִּימִין, דְּיַדְעִין בְּרָזִין אִלֵּין, זַכָּאָה חוּלָקֵיהוֹן.

126. After thirty days, having disappeared in that bird's nest, he will descend ornamented with all those adornments from above, with many holy companies around him, and the whole world will see one light suspended from the sky to the earth. It will remain seven days IN THE SECRET OF CHESED, GVURAH, TIFERET, NETZACH, HOD, YESOD AND MALCHUT IN MALCHUT, AND CAN BE FOUND ILLUMINATING EVEN IN MALCHUT OF MALCHUT. All the inhabitants of the world will wonder and be shocked and will not understand at all, except for those sages who know these secrets – blessed be their portion.

127. וְכָל אִינּוּן שִׁבְעָה יוֹמִין יִתְעַטָּר בְּאַרְעָא, בְּהַהוּא קַ"ן צפּוֹ"ר. בְּאָן אֲתָר. בַּדֶּרֶךְ, דָּא קְבוּרַת רָחֵל, דְּאִיהִי קַיְּימָא בְּפָרָשַׁת אוֹרְחִין. וִיבַשֵּׂר לָהּ, וַיְנַחֵם לָהּ, וּכְדֵין תְּקַבֵּל תַּנְחוּמִין, וְתָקוּם וְתִנַּשִּׁיק לֵיהּ.

127. And all these seven days, he will be adorned on the earth – WHICH IS THE SECRET OF MALCHUT – in that bird's nest, WHICH IS THE SECRET OF THE VERSE: "IF A BIRD'S NEST CHANCE TO BE BEFORE YOU" (DEVARIM 22:6) THAT ALLUDES TO THE KING MESSIAH WHO IS ADORNED WITH A BIRD'S NEST. Where is that place? "In the way," which is the grave of Rachel, for she is placed on the crossroads. MESSIAH IS ALSO ADORNED WITH THE LIGHT OF MALCHUT OF MALCHUT THAT IS CAPABLE OF THE GATHERING OF THE EXILES. Therefore, he will bear these good tidings to her and console her. Then she will accept consolations, UNLIKE AS DESCRIBED PREVIOUSLY: "SHE REFUSES TO BE COMFORTED FOR HER CHILDREN BECAUSE THEY ARE NOT" (YIRMEYAH 31:14). And she will arise and kiss MESSIAH!

128. לְבָתַר יֵקוּם הַהוּא נְהִירוּ מֵהַהוּא אֲתָר, וְשָׁרֵי בִּירִיחוֹ קַרְתָּא דְאִילָנֵי. בְּכָל עֵץ דָּא יְרִיחוֹ. אוֹ עַל הָאָרֶץ, דָּא יְרוּשְׁלֵים. וִיהֵא גָּנִיז בְּהַהוּא נְהִירוּ דְקַ"ן צפּוֹ"ר תְּרֵיסַר יַרְחֵי.

128. Then shall the light arise from that place, THAT IS, RACHEL'S GRAVE, and settle in Jericho, the city of trees, AS IS WRITTEN: "In any tree" (Devarim 22:6) – which is Jericho, THE CITY OF PALM TREES, THAT JOSHUA WAS NOT ABLE TO MEND COMPLETELY. THEREFORE HE SAID, "CURSED BE THE MAN BEFORE HASHEM, THAT RISES UP TO BUILD THIS CITY JERICHO" (YEHOSHUA 6:26), BECAUSE IT IS DRAWN FROM THE ATTRIBUTES OF JUDGMENT WHICH IS IN MALCHUT OF MALCHUT, AND NOW MESSIAH WILL MEND IT WITH THE LIGHT OF THE SEVEN DAYS. "Or

on the ground" (Devarim 22:6), is Jerusalem WHICH IS THE EXTERNAL PART OF MALCHUT, and he will be concealed in that light in the bird's nest for twelve months.

129. בָּתַר תְּרֵיסַר יַרְחֵי, יִזְדְקַף הַהוּא נְהִירוּ בֵּין שְׁמַיָּא וְאַרְעָא, וְיִשְׁרֵי בְּאַרְעָא דְּגָלִיל, דְּתַמָּן הֲוָה שֵׁירוּתָא דְּגָלוּתָא דְּיִשְׂרָאֵל. וְתַמָּן יִתְגְּלֵי מֵהַהוּא נְהִירוּ דְּקַן צִפּוֹר, וְתָב לְאַתְרֵיה. וְהַהוּא יוֹמָא יִזְדַּעְזַע כָּל אַרְעָא כְּמִלְקַדְמִין, מִסַּיְיפֵי שְׁמַיָּא עַד סַיְיפֵי שְׁמַיָּא, וּכְדֵין יֶחֱזוּן כָּל עָלְמָא, דְּהָא אִתְגְּלֵי מַלְכָּא מְשִׁיחָא, בְּאַרְעָא דְּגָלִיל.

129. After twelve months, that light will be stretched between the heaven and the earth and rest on in the land of Galilee, since the exile of Yisrael, NAMELY THE EXILE OF ASHUR, was initiated in Galilee. Then will MESSIAH be revealed from that very same light of the bird's nest, and return to his place. On that day, the whole earth will tremble as earlier, from one end of heaven to the other end, and then the whole world will see that Messiah has been revealed in the land of Galilee!

130. וְיִתְכַּנְּשׁוּן לֵיה כָּל אִינּוּן דְּלָעָאן בְּאוֹרַיְיתָא, וְאִינּוּן זְעִירִין בְּעָלְמָא. וּבִזְכוּת יְנוֹקֵי דְּבֵי רַב, יִתְתַּקַּף חֵילֵיה לְאִתְגַּבְּרָא, וְרָזָא דָּא אֶפְרוֹחִים. וְאִי לָא יִשְׁתַּכְּחוּן אַלֵּין, הָא יְנוֹקֵי דְּיַתְבִין בְּתוּקְפָּא דְּאִמְּהוֹן וְיַנְקֵי, כד״א, גְּמוּלֵי מֵחָלָב עַתִּיקֵי מִשָּׁדָיִם. וְהַיְינוּ אוֹ בֵיצִים, דִּבְגִין אִלֵּין, שַׁרְיָא שְׁכִינְתָּא עִמְּהוֹן דְּיִשְׂרָאֵל בְּגָלוּתָא.

130. And all those who were occupied with Torah, THOSE WHO ARE CALLED IN THE VERSE 'CHILDREN' ('YOUNG'), will gather to him. They are few in the world, and in the merit of school children, the strength OF MESSIAH will grow greatly. And this is the secret of the young IN THE VERSE. And if these are not to be found, then the infants that sit in their mother's lap and suckle, as written, "Those that are weaned from milk, and removed from the breasts" (Yeshayah 28:9); or the "eggs" (Devarim 22:6). It is because of these that the Shechinah dwells with Yisrael in the exile.

131. דְּהָא חַכִּימִין זְעִירִין אִינּוּן דְּיִשְׁתַּכְּחוּן בְּהַהוּא זִמְנָא, וְהַיְינוּ וְהָאֵם רוֹבֶצֶת עַל הָאֶפְרוֹחִים אוֹ עַל הַבֵּיצִים, לֹא תִקַּח הָאֵם עַל הַבָּנִים

-87-

וְיִתְעַכָּב עַד תְּרֵיסַר יַרְחִין אַחֲרָנִין. לְבָתַר, יֵיתֵי בַּעְלָהּ, וְיוֹקִים לָהּ מֵעַפְרָא, כד״א, אָקִים אֶת סֻכַּת דָּוִד הַנֹּפֶלֶת.

131. For the sages WHO ARE CALLED 'CHILDREN' ('YOUNG') will be few in that time, and this is what is meant: "And the mother bird sitting upon the young or upon the eggs, do not take the mother bird together with the young," SINCE THEN THERE WILL BE NO CHILDREN. THEREFORE, DO NOT TAKE THE MOTHER, WHO IS SHECHINAH; and MESSIAH will tarry up to another twelve months. Then her husband, WHO IS ZEIR ANPIN, will come to raise her from the dust as is said, "I will raise up the tabernacle of David that is fallen" (Amos 9:11).

132. בְּהַהוּא יוֹמָא, מַלְכָּא מְשִׁיחָא שָׁארֵי וְיִכְנוֹשׁ גָּלוּתָא, מִסַּיְיפֵי עָלְמָא עַד סַיְיפֵי עָלְמָא, כד״א אִם יִהְיֶה נִדַּחֲךָ בִּקְצֵה הַשָּׁמַיִם וְגוֹ'. מֵהַהוּא יוֹמָא, כָּל אָתִין וְנִסִּין וּגְבוּרָאן דְּעָבַד קוּדְשָׁא בְּרִיךְ הוּא בְּמִצְרַיִם, יַעֲבִיד לוֹן לְיִשְׂרָאֵל, כד״א כִּימֵי צֵאתְךָ מֵאֶרֶץ מִצְרָיִם אַרְאֶנּוּ נִפְלָאוֹת.

132. On that day, Messiah will start to gather the exiled from one end of the world to the other, as it is written: "If your outcast be at the utmost parts of heaven..." (Devarim 30:4). From that day, all the signs and miracles and mighty acts that the Holy One, blessed be He, performed in Egypt, He will perform for Yisrael: "As in the days of your coming out of the land of Egypt I will show him marvelous things" (Michah 7:15).

133. אר״ש, אֶלְעָזָר בְּרִי, כָּל אִלֵּין מִלִּין תִּשְׁכַּח בְּרָזָא דִּתְלָתִין וּתְרֵין שְׁבִילִין דִּבְשְׁמָא קַדִּישָׁא, וְעַד דְּנִסִּין אִלֵּין לָא יִתְעָרוּן בְּעָלְמָא, לָא יִשְׁתְּלִים רָזָא דִשְׁמָא קַדִּישָׁא, וְלָא תִּתְעַר לְאַהֲבָה, כד״א הִשְׁבַּעְתִּי אֶתְכֶם בְּנוֹת יְרוּשָׁלַיִם בִּצְבָאוֹת. בִּצְבָאוֹת: דָּא מַלְכָּא מְשִׁיחָא דְּאִקְרֵי צְבָאוֹת. אוֹ בְּאַיְלוֹת הַשָּׂדֶה שְׁאָר חֵילִין וּמַשִׁרְיָין דִּלְתַתָּא. אִם תָּעִירוּ וְאִם תְּעוֹרְרוּ אֶת הָאַהֲבָה: דָּא יְמִינָא דְּקוּדְשָׁא בְּרִיךְ הוּא, דְּאִקְרֵי אַהֲבָ״ה. עַד שֶׁתֶּחְפָּץ הַהִיא דְּשְׁכִיבַת לְעַפְרָא, וִיהֵא רְעוּתָא דְמַלְכָּא בָּהּ. זַכָּאָה אִיהוּ מַאן דְּיִזְכֵּי לְהַהוּא דָּרָא, זַכָּאָה אִיהוּ בְּעָלְמָא דֵין,

וְזַכָּאָה אִיהוּ בְּעָלְמָא דְּאָתֵי.

133. Rabbi Shimon said: Elazar my son, all these things you shall find in the secret of 32 paths OF CHOCHMAH of the Holy Name. And as long as these miracles do not happen in the world, the secret of the Holy Name will not be completed, nor will love awaken – as it is said: "I charge you, O daughters of Jerusalem by the gazelles for hosts or by the hinds of the fields" (Shir Hashirm 2:7). Hosts refer to the King Messiah, who is so called. "The kinds of the fields," refers to the other hosts and encampments below. "That you stir not up, nor awake my love" (Ibid.), is the right hand of the Holy One, blessed be He, MEANING THE SFIRAH OF CHESED, which is called 'love'. "Till it please," refers to She who lies in the dust, WHICH IS THE SHECHINAH IN EXILE, whom the King should favor her! Righteous is he who will have the merit to be in that generation. He is righteous in this world and righteous in the World to Come.

134. ר' שִׁמְעוֹן אָרִים יְדוֹי בִּצְלוֹ לְקוּדְשָׁא בְּרִיךְ הוּא, וְצַלֵּי צְלוֹתֵיהּ, לְבָתַר דְּצַלֵּי צְלוֹתֵיהּ, אָתוּ ר' אֶלְעָזָר בְּרֵיהּ, וְר' אַבָּא וְיָתְבוּ קַמֵּיהּ. עַד דְּהֲווֹ יַתְבֵי קַמֵּיהּ, חָמוּ חַד נְהִירוּ דִּימָמָא דְּאִתְחֲשָׁךְ, וְאִשְׁתְּקַע חַד צִנּוֹרָא דְּשַׁלְהוֹבָא דְּאֶשָּׁא גּוֹ יַמָּא דִּטְבֶרְיָה, וְאִזְדַּעְזַע כָּל הַהוּא אֲתָר.

134. Rabbi Shimon raised his hands in prayer before the Holy One, blessed be He, and prayed. After he recited his prayer, his son, Rabbi Elazar, and Rabbi Aba sat before him. While they were sitting before him, they saw a ray of daylight become dim, and a conduit of flaming fire, THAT IS, A STREAM OF BURNING FIRE, sink into the sea of Galilee, and the whole place was agitated.

135. אר"ש, וַדַּאי הַשְׁתָּא הוּא עִדָּנָא, דְּקוּדְשָׁא בְּרִיךְ הוּא אִדְכַּר לִבְנוֹי, וְאָחִית תְּרֵין דִּמְעִין לְגוֹ יַמָּא רַבָּא. וְכַד נַחְתִּין, פַּגְעִין בְּהַאי צִנּוֹרָא דְּשַׁלְהוֹבָא דְּאֶשָּׁא, וְיִשְׁתַּקְעוּ דָּא בְּדָא בְּיַמָּא. בָּכָה ר"ש וּבְכוּ חַבְרַיָּיא.

135. Rabbi Shimon said: Certainly now is the time that the Holy One, blessed be He, remembers His children, and He lowers two tears into the Great Sea. As they descend, they touch this conduit of flaming fire and sink

TOGETHER into the sea, one with the other. Rabbi Shimon wept and the friends wept.

136. אר"ש, הָא אִתְּעַרְנָא בְּרָזֵי דְּאַתְוָון דִּשְׁמָא קַדִּישָׁא, בְּסִתְרָא דְּאִתְּעָרוּתָא דִּילֵיהּ, לְגַבֵּי בְּנוֹי, אֲבָל הַשְׁתָּא, אִית לִי לְגַלָּאָה, מַה דְּלָא אִתְיְהִיב רְשׁוּ לב"נ אַחֲרָא לְגַלָּאָה. אֶלָּא זְכוּ דְּדָרָא דָא, יְקַיֵּים עָלְמָא עַד דְּיֵיתֵי מַלְכָּא מְשִׁיחָא. אר"ש לר' אֶלְעָזָר בְּרֵיהּ וּלְרִבִּי אַבָּא, קוּמוּ בְּקִיּוּמַיְיכוּ. קָמוּ ר' אֶלְעָזָר וְר' אַבָּא. בָּכָה ר"ש זִמְנָא אַחֲרָא, אָמַר וַוי מַאן יְקוּם בְּמַה דַּחֲמֵינָא גָּלוּתָא יִתְמְשַׁךְ, מַאן יָכִיל לְמִסְבַּל.

136. Rabbi Shimon said: I have stirred in the secret of the letters of the Holy Name in the secret of the awakening OF THE HOLY ONE, BLESSED BE HE, towards His children. But now I may reveal that which was not permitted to any other person to reveal, but the merit of this generation will preserve the world till the King Messiah will come. Rabbi Shimon said to his son Rabbi Elazar and to Rabbi Aba: Get up on your feet. Rabbi Elazar and Rabbi Aba got up. Rabbi Shimon wept a second time and said: Oh, who will arise then? For what I see is that the exile will be lengthened. Who will be able to endure?

137. אוּף אִיהוּ קָם וְאָמַר ה' אֱלֹהֵינוּ בְּעָלוּנוּ אֲדֹנִים זוּלָתֶךָ לְבַד בְּךָ נַזְכִּיר שְׁמֶךָ הַאי קְרָא אוּקְמוּהָ. אֲבָל בְּהַאי קְרָא אִית רָזָא עִלָּאָה, גּוֹ מְהֵימְנוּתָא. ה' אֱלֹהֵינוּ: דָּא הוּא שֵׁירוּתָא דְּרָזִין עִלָּאִין, אֲתָר דְּמִתַּמָּן נָפְקִין כָּל נְהִירוּ דְּשַׁרְגִּין כֻּלְּהוּ לְאַדְלְקָא. וְתַמָּן תַּלְיָא כָּל רָזָא דִּמְהֵימְנוּתָא, שְׁמָא דָּא שַׁלִּיט עַל כֹּלָא.

137. RABBI SHIMON also got up and said: "O Hashem our Elohim; other masters besides You have had dominion over us. But by You only will we make mention of Your Name" (Yeshayah 26:13). This verse is explained. But this verse contains a supernal secret in the secret of Faith. "Hashem our Elohim," is the beginning of the supernal secrets, NAMELY CHOCHMAH AND BINAH. From these, all the light emanates to kindle all the candles, MEANING THAT ALL THE MOCHIN OF MALE AND FEMALE AND BRIYAH, YETZIRAH AND ASIYAH EMANATE FROM CHOCHMAH AND BINAH THAT ARE CALLED "HASHEM OUR ELOHIM." There is the essence of the entire secret of Faith, WHICH IS FEMALE, MEANING IN THE SECRET OF THE VERSE: "AND OF THE SIDE WHICH HASHEM ELOHIM HAD TAKEN..." (BERESHEET 2:22), WHICH IS THE SECRET OF CHOCHMAH AND BINAH. THE SIDE IS THE SECRET OF THE NUKVA, WHICH IS CALLED 'FAITH'.

138. בְּעָלוּנוּ אֲדֹנִים זוּלָתֶךָ. דְּהָא עַמָּא דְיִשְׂרָאֵל, לֵית מַאן דְּשַׁלִּיט עֲלֵיהּ בַּר שְׁמָא עִלָּאָה דָּא. וְהַשְׁתָּא בְּגָלוּתָא שַׁלִּיט עֲלֵיהּ סִטְרָא אָחֳרָא.

138. "Other masters besides You have had dominion over us." There is no one to dominate over the nation of Yisrael except for the Supernal Name, HASHEM OUR ELOHIM, AS EARLIER MENTIONED. And now in exile, the Other Side holds dominion over it. THIS IS WHAT IS WRITTEN: "OTHER MASTERS BESIDES YOU HAVE HAD DOMINION OVER US."

139. לְבַד בְּךָ נַזְכִּיר שְׁמֶךָ. רָזָא דִשְׁמָא קַדִּישָׁא, כְּלָלָא דְעֶשְׂרִין וּתְרֵין אַתְוָון, וכנ"י לָא מִתְבָּרְכָא אֶלָּא מִגּוֹ שְׁמָא דָא דְּאִקְרֵי בְּךָ, כד"א אֲשֶׁר נִשְׁבַּעְתָּ לָהֶם בָּךְ בְּךָ יְבָרֵךְ יִשְׂרָאֵל. כִּי בְךָ אָרוּץ גְּדוּד. וּבְזִמְנָא דִשְׁלִימוּ אִשְׁתְּכַח, לָא הֲוָה מִתְפָּרֵשׁ דָּא מִן דָּא. וְאָסִיר לְאַפְרָשָׁא דָּא מִן דָּא, אִתְּתָא מִבַּעְלָהּ, לָאו בְּרַעְיוֹנֵי, וְלָאו בְּדַכְירוּ, בְּגִין דְּלָא לְאַחֲזָאָה פְרוּדָא, וְהַשְׁתָּא בְּגָלוּתָא פְרוּדָא אִשְׁתְּכַח, דְּמִגּוֹ עָאקוּ דְּכָל זִמְנָא וְזִמְנָא, אֲנַן עַבְדִּין פְּרוּדָא, לְאַדְכְּרָא הַהוּא שֵׁם, בַּר מִבַּעְלָהּ, בְּגִין דְּאִיהִי שְׁכִיבַת לְעַפְרָא, וְהַיְינוּ לְבַד בְּךָ נַזְכִּיר שְׁמֶךָ.

139. "But by You only will we make mention of Your Name," MEANING the secret of the Holy Name, NAMELY THE NUKVA, is the inclusion of all 22 letters. THEREFORE, SHE IS CALLED 'ET' (ALEPH-TAV), WHICH ALLUDES TO THE 22 LETTERS FROM ALEPH TO TAV. And the Congregation of Yisrael, WHICH IS THE NUKVA, is blessed only through that name called 'Becha' ('by you'), WHICH IS ZEIR ANPIN THAT INCLUDES ALSO 22 LETTERS, LIKE "BECHA" WHICH NUMERICALLY TOTALS 22, as is written: "To whom You did swear by Your own self (Heb. becha)" (Shemot 32:13). "By You (Heb. becha) shall Yisrael bless" (Beresheet 48:20) and "For by You (Heb. becha) I run upon a troop" (Tehilim 18:30) ALL OF WHICH ALLUDE TO ZEIR ANPIN. At the time when perfection was prevalent, ZEIR ANPIN AND THE NUKVA were not separated from each other. And it is

prohibited to separate them one from the other, a wife from her husband, neither in thought, nor by allusion, in order not to show separation. And now in exile, separation is prevalent because of the trouble THAT COMES UPON US at all times, which we cause THROUGH THIS separation by mentioning that name – WHICH IS THE NUKVA away from her husband, ZEIR ANPIN, because she is lying on the dust. This is: "But by You only will we make mention of Your Name..."

140. בַּר מִבַּעְלָה, אֲנָן דַּכְרִין לְהַאי שֵׁם בְּפֵרוּדָא, בְּגִין דַּאֲנַן רְחִיקִין מִינָךְ, וְשַׁלְטִין אַחֲרָנִין עֲלָן, וּשְׁמֶךְ אִיהוּ בְּפֵרוּדָא מִן שְׁמָא דְאִקְרֵי בָּךְ, וְהַאי בְּיוֹמֵי דְגָלוּתָא.

140. HE EXPLAINS: WHEN THE NUKVA is separated from her husband, IT IS CONSIDERED as if we mention this name separately, since we are far from You. AND WE CAUSED that others should rule over us. And Your Name, WHICH IS THE NUKVA, is separated from the name *becha* (lit. 'In You') WHICH IS ZEIR ANPIN, AS MENTIONED EARLIER. And this is so during the days of exile.

141. בְּגִין דְּגָלוּתָא קַדְמָאָה הֲוָה מִבַּיִת רִאשׁוֹן, וּבַיִת רִאשׁוֹן הוּא רָזָא דְה' קַדְמָאָה, וְלָקֳבֵל ע' שְׁנִין דִּילָה, גָּלוּתָא דְּבַיִת רִאשׁוֹן הֲוָה ע' שְׁנִין, וְאִינּוּן ע' שְׁנִין לָא אִשְׁתְּכַחַת אִימָא רְבִיעָא עָלַיְיהוּ, וַהֲוָה פֵּרוּדָא מִן שְׁמָא עִלָּאָה, רָזָא דְה' עִלָּאָה. וּכְדֵין יוּ"ד, רָזָא עִלָּאָה, אִסְתַּלָּק לְעֵילָא לְעֵילָא לְאֵין סוֹף, וּבַיִת רִאשׁוֹן עִלָּאָה קַדִּישָׁא, לָא נָבִיעַ נְבִיעוּ דְמַיִּין חַיִּין, דְּהָא מְקוֹרָא דִּילָה אִסְתַּלָּק.

141. The first exile was since the First Temple and the First Temple is the secret of the first *Hei* OF THE NAME YUD HEI VAV HEI, WHICH IS BINAH. Corresponding to its seventy years, WHICH ARE THE SEVEN LOWER SFIROT CHESED, GVURAH, TIFERET, NETZACH, HOD, YESOD AND MALCHUT, the exile of the First Temple lasted seventy years, SINCE EVERY SFIRAH INCLUDES TEN, TOTALING SEVENTY. During these seventy years, the mother, WHICH IS THE THREE FIRST SFIROT OF BINAH, was not sitting on them and they were separated from the Supernal Name, which is the secret of the first *Hei* OF YUD HEI VAV HEI. Then the *Yud* OF YUD HEI VAV HEI, which is the supernal secret OF BINAH, higher and higher into the

Endless World (Heb. *ein sof*), and the First Temple, WHICH IS BINAH, does not gush forth a flow of living water, because its source, WHICH IS THE *YUD* OF YUD HEI VAV HEI, WHICH IS CHOCHMAH, has departed.

142. וְאִיהִי ע' שְׁנִין בְּגָלוּתָא, בְּגִין דְּאִיהִי ז' שְׁנִין אִקְרֵי, כד"א וַיִּבְנֵהוּ שֶׁבַע שָׁנִים. וְאִי תֵּימָא, דְּשַׁלְטָא מַלְכוּת בָּבֶל לְעֵילָא בְּרָזָא דְּע' שְׁנִין, ח"ו. אֶלָּא בְּזִמְנָא דַּהֲוָה בֵּי מַקְדְּשָׁא קַיָּים, נְהוֹרָא וּנְבִיעוּ דְּאִמָּא עִלָּאָה, הֲוָה נָהִיר וְנָחִית לְתַתָּא. כֵּיוָן דְּחָטוּ יִשְׂרָאֵל, וְאִתְחֲרַב מַקְדְּשָׁא, וְשַׁלְטָא מַלְכוּת בָּבֶל, הֲוָה חָפֵי, וְאַחְשִׁיךְ הַהוּא נְהִירוּ, וְתַתָּאֵי קַדִּישִׁין לָא הֲווֹ נְהִירִין.

142. And it, THE FIRST *HEI* OF YUD HEI VAV HEI, is the seventy years in exile, because it is called 'seven years' as is said: "So was he seven years in building it" (I Melachim 6:38), REFERRING TO THE FIRST TEMPLE, WHICH IS THE FIRST *HEI*. HE ASKS: Would you say that the kingdom of Babylon ruled above in the secret of seventy years, WHICH IS BINAH? Heaven forbid! AND HE ANSWERS: During the time that the Temple existed, the pouring forth of Supernal Ima, WHICH IS BINAH, illuminated and descended below. However, when Yisrael sinned and the Temple was destroyed, the kingdom of Babylon reigned, that light was covered and darkened, and the holy lower beings did not illuminate.

143. כֵּיוָן דְּתַתָּאֵי לָא הֲווֹ נְהִירִין, בְּגִין שָׁלְטָנוּ דְּמַלְכוּתָא דְּבָבֶל. אִסְתַּלָּק הַהוּא נְהוֹרָא, וְהַהוּא מַבּוּעָא עִלָּאָה דַּהֲוָה נָבִיעַ רָזָא דִי', אִסְתַּלָּק לְעֵילָא לְעֵילָא בְּאֵין סוֹף, כְּדֵין אִינּוּן ע' שְׁנִין לָא הֲווֹ נְהִירִין, בְּגִין הַהוּא נְהִירוּ דְּאִתְמְנַע. וְדָא הוּא וַדַּאי גָּלוּתָא דְּע' שְׁנִין.

143. Since the lower beings were not illuminating, because of the dominion of the kingdom of Babylon, that light OF BINAH departed and that supernal emanation that poured forth TO BINAH – which is the secret of *Yud* OF YUD HEI VAV HEI, WHICH IS CHOCHMAH – withdrew higher and higher into the Endless World. Then those seventy years OF BINAH did not illuminate because of that illumination OF THE *YUD* that was prevented FROM ILLUMINATING UPON THE *HEI*. This was certainly the exile of seventy years OF BINAH, WHICH IS THE SECRET OF THE FIRST TEMPLE.

144. כֵּיוָן דְּאַעְדִּיאוּ שֻׁלְטָנוּ דְּבָבֶל, וְשָׁרִיאַת ה"א תַּתָּאָה לְאַנְהֲרָא. יִשְׂרָאֵל כֻּלְּהוּ, לָא אָהַדְרוּ לְאִדְכָּאָה לְמֶהֱוֵי סְגוּלָה שְׁלֵימָתָא כְּמִלְּקַדְמִין, אֶלָּא זְעֵיר זְעֵיר, וְכֵיוָן דִּשְׁלִימוּ לָא אִשְׁתְּכַח, בְּדֵין, י' נְבִיעוּ עִלָּאָה לָא נָחִית כ"כ לְאַנְהֲרָא, כְּמָה דַּהֲוָה כְּמִלְּקַדְמִין, אֶלָּא זְעֵיר בְּעִרְבּוּבְיָא, דְּלָא הֲווֹ דַּכְיָין כְּמִלְּקַדְמִין כְּמָה דְּאִתְחֲזֵי, וְעַל כָּךְ נְבִיעוּ עִלָּאָה, וְלָא נְבִיעַ, וְלָא נָהִיר, אֶלָּא דְּאַהֲדַר לְאַנְהֲרָא זְעֵיר זְעֵיר, מִגּוֹ דַּחֲקָא דִּשְׁמָא.

144. As soon as the reign of Babylon was removed and the second *Hei* OF YUD HEI VAV HEI commenced to illuminate, all of Yisrael did not purify to be a perfect possession as earlier, but rather bit by bit RETURNED FROM THE BABYLONIAN EXILE TO THE LAND OF YISRAEL. And since there was no perfection, the *Yud* OF YUD HEI VAV HEI did not descend to illuminate as it illuminated originally, but rather bit by bit without order, because Yisrael were not purified properly, as before. Therefore, the Supernal Fountain, WHICH IS THE SECRET OF THE YUD OF YUD HEI VAV HEI, did not gush forth and did not illuminate. It returned to illuminate bit by bit because of the need of the Name.

145. וע"ד, אִתְגְּרוּ בְּהוּ בְּיִשְׂרָאֵל קְרָבִין סַגִּיאִין, עַד דְּהַחֹשֶׁךְ יְכַסֶּה אֶרֶץ, וְה', תַּתָּאָה אִתְחֲשָׁךְ, וְנָפְלַת לְאַרְעָא, וּנְבִיעוּ עִלָּאָה אִסְתַּלָּק כְּמִלְּקַדְמִין, בְּגִין דְּמַלְכוּת אֱדוֹם אִתְתַּקַּף, וְיִשְׂרָאֵל אָהַדְרוּ לְסֻרְחָנַיְיהוּ.

145. Therefore, Yisrael were challenged in many wars until the darkness covered the earth and the Lower *Hei*, WHICH IS THE NUKVA, became darkened and fell to the earth. The Supernal Fountain, WHICH IS THE *YUD* OF YUD HEI VAV HEI, withdrew again, because the kingdom of Edom became strong and Yisrael returned to their sins.

146. וע"ד, ה' בַּיִת שֵׁנִי אִתְחֲרַב, וְכָל אִינּוּן תְּרֵיסַר שִׁבְטִין דִּילָהּ, כְּחוּשְׁבַּן מַשִׁרְיָין דִּלְהוֹן, אִינּוּן בְּגָלוּתָא דְּמַלְכוּת אֱדוֹם. וּנְבִיעוּ עִלָּאָה, אִסְתַּלָּק מֵהַהוּא נְבִיעוּ, דְּקַיְימָא עָלָהּ, כד"א, הַצַּדִּיק אָבָד, אָבַד הַהוּא נְבִיעוּ דִּמְקוֹרָא עִלָּאָה, דַּהֲוָה נָגִיד וּמָשִׁיךְ מִלְּעֵילָּא.

146. Therefore, the LOWER *Hei*, WHICH IS the Second Temple that was destroyed, and all its twelve tribes, OF THE LOWER *HEI* – as the number of the legions OF YISRAEL, WHO ARE THE TWELVE TRIBES OF YAH – are in exile of the kingdom of Edom. And the Supernal Fountain, WHICH IS THE *VAV* OF YUD HEI VAV HEI, ZEIR ANPIN, withdrew from that fountain that it supplies, WHICH IS YESOD OF ZEIR ANPIN. As it is said: "the righteous perishes…(lost)" (Yeshayah 57:1) – WHICH IS YESOD, that lost that outpouring of the upper source that flowed from above.

147. וּכְדֵין הֲוָה פֵּרוּדָא בְּהֵ"א, בַּיִת שֵׁנִי, וְאִיהִי בְּגָלוּתָא דֶּאֱדוֹם, בְּכָל אִינּוּן תְּרֵיסַר שְׁבָטִין וּמַשְׁרְיָין דִּילְהוֹן, תְּרֵיסַר שְׁבָטִין סַלְקִין לְחוּשְׁבַּן סַגִּי, וְעַל דְּרָזָא דְּה' הֲוָה בְּהוּ, בְּכָל הַהוּא חוּשְׁבָּנָא, גָּלוּתָא אִתְמְשַׁךְ.

147. Then there was a separation in the *Hei*, WHICH IS the Second Temple, THAT SEPARATED FROM THE *VAV* OF YUD HEI VAV HEI, WHICH IS ZEIR ANPIN, and it GOES INTO the exile in Edom with all these twelve tribes and their legions OF YISRAEL. Twelve tribes add up to a great number, AS WRITTEN BEFORE US, and since the secret of the *Hei* was included in this number, the exile therefore continues A LONG TIME.

148. רָזָא דְּרָזִין לְחַכִּימֵי לִבָּא אִתְמְסָר. י' שְׁבָטִין אֶלֶף שְׁנִין, תְּרֵין שְׁבָטִין מָאתַן שְׁנִין. שָׁרוּ דִּמְעִין לְמִנְפַּל, פָּתַח וְאָמַר, בָּכוֹ תִבְכֶּה בַּלַּיְלָה וְדִמְעָתָהּ עַל לֶחֱיָהּ. לְסוֹף תְּרֵיסַר שְׁבָטִין דְּגָלוּתָא, לֵילְיָא יִתְחֲשַׁךְ לְיִשְׂרָאֵל, עַד דְּיִתְּעַר וָא"ו, לִזְמַן שִׁתִּין וָשִׁית שְׁנִין.

148. The secret of secrets is given over to the wise of heart. The ten tribes are one thousand years. Two tribes are two hundred years. SINCE TWELVE LIGHTS OF THE NUKVA, WHICH ARE CALLED 'TRIBES', ARE DRAWN FROM BINAH, WHOSE SFIROT ARE IN THE SECRET OF HUNDREDS, THEY ARE THEREFORE TWELVE HUNDRED. Tears started to fall – MEANING THAT RABBI SHIMON STARTED WEEPING. He opened the discussion saying, "She weeps sore in the night, and her tears are on her cheeks" (Eichah 1:2). At the end of the twelve tribes of exile, MEANING AT THE END OF ONE THOUSAND AND TWO HUNDRED AS MENTIONED, the night will darken for Yisrael until the *Vav* awakens at the sixty-sixth year.

149. לְבָתַר תְּרֵיסַר שְׁבָטִין, דְּאִינוּן אֶלֶף וּמָאתָן שְׁנִין דְּגָלוּתָא, וּלְבָתַר שִׁתִּין וְשִׁית שְׁנִין בְּחֶשׁוֹכָא דְּלֵילְיָא, כְּדֵין, וְזָכַרְתִּי אֶת בְּרִיתִי יַעֲקֹב. דָּא אִתְעָרוּתָא דְּאָת ו', דְּאִיהוּ נֶפֶשׁ דְּבֵית יַעֲקֹב. וְרָזָא דָּא, כָּל הַנֶּפֶשׁ הַבָּאָה לְיַעֲקֹב מִצְרַיְמָה וְגוֹ' שִׁשִּׁים וָשֵׁשׁ, וְאִיהוּ ו', נֶפֶשׁ דְּבַיִת שֵׁנִי, רָזָא דְּה' תַּתָּאָה, וְדָא ו' רָזָא דְּשִׁשִּׁים וָשֵׁשׁ, שִׁשִּׁים: לְאִתְעָרוּתָא דְּיַעֲקֹב. וְשֵׁשׁ: לְאִתְעָרוּתָא דְּיוֹסֵף. וע"ד אִיהוּ וָ"ו, דְּאִינוּן תְּרֵין בְּחִבּוּרָא חֲדָא, וְרָזָא חֲדָא.

149. At the end of twelve tribes, which are twelve hundred years of exile, and at the end of 66 years of the darkness of night, WHICH IS THE EXILE: "Then will I remember My covenant with Jacob" (Vayikra 26:42), WHICH IS TIFERET. This is the awakening of the letter *Vav* – WHICH IS TIFERET, WHICH IS THE *VAV* OF YUD HEI VAV HEI – which is the soul, MEANING THE INNER PART of the house of Jacob; WHICH IS THE NUKVA THAT IS CALLED THE 'HOUSE OF JACOB'. And this is the secret of: "All the souls that came with Jacob were 66" (Beresheet 46:26), which is *Vav*, the soul of the Second Temple, the secret of the lower *Hei*. And this *Vav* is the secret of 66, sixty for the awakening of Jacob, WHO IS TIFERET, and six for the awakening of Joseph, WHO IS YESOD. Therefore, it is A FULLY SPELLED *Vav* (*Vav-Vav*), WHICH ALLUDES TO TIFERET AND YESOD, which are two in one combination and one secret, BECAUSE YESOD AND TIFERET ARE CONSIDERED AS ONE AND ARE THEREFORE ALLUDED TO IN THE TWO *VAV'S* OF THE FULLY SPELLED *VAV*, WHICH FORM ONE LETTER.

150. מִתַּמָּן וּלְהָלְאָה, יִתְעַר קוּדְשָׁא בְּרִיךְ הוּא לְאִינוּן נִסִּין וְאָתִין דְּקָאמַרָן, וְיִתְעָרוּן עַל יִשְׂרָאֵל אִינוּן עַקְתִין דְּקָאמָרָן, וּכְדֵין, וְאַף אֶת בְּרִיתִי יִצְחָק. וּלְבָתַר כַּד יַגִּיחַ מַלְכָּא מְשִׁיחָא קְרָבִין בְּכָל עָלְמָא בִּימִינָא דְּקוּדְשָׁא בְּרִיךְ הוּא, כד"א יְמִינְךָ ה' נֶאְדָּרִי בַּכֹּחַ. כְּדֵין, וְאַף אֶת בְּרִיתִי אַבְרָהָם אֶזְכֹּר, וּלְבָתַר וְהָאָרֶץ אֶזְכֹּר, דָּא ה' בַּתְרָאָה, בְּהַהוּא זִמְנָא כְּתִיב, וְהָיָה ה' לְמֶלֶךְ עַל כָּל הָאָרֶץ בַּיּוֹם הַהוּא יִהְיֶה ה' אֶחָד וּשְׁמוֹ אֶחָד.

150. From then on, the Holy One, Blessed be He, will stir these miracles and signs that we mentioned earlier, and all the troubles that we said will rise against Yisrael. Then it is said: "And also My covenant with Isaac" (Vayikra 26:42), BECAUSE ISAAC IS THE SECRET OF GVURAH AND JUDGMENT. Afterwards, King Messiah will wage wars throughout the whole world with the right hand of the Holy One, blessed be He, WHICH IS CHESED, as is said: "Your right hand, Hashem, is glorious in power" (Shemot 15:6). Then IT IS SAID: "And also My covenant with Abraham will I remember" (Vayikra 26:42), FOR ABRAHAM IS THE SECRET OF CHESED. Afterwards, "And I will remember the land" (Ibid.), which is the last *Hei* OF YUD HEI VAV HEI; NAMELY, THE NUKVA THAT IS CALLED 'LAND'. About that time it is written: "And Hashem shall be king over all the earth; on that day Hashem shall be One and His Name One" (Zecharyah 14:9).

151. לְסוֹף שִׁתִּין וְשִׁית שְׁנִין אַחֲרָנִין, דְּאִינּוּן מֵאָה וּתְלָתִין וּתְרֵין שְׁנִין, יִתְחֲזוּן אַתְוָון בִּשְׁמָא קַדִּישָׁא, גְּלִיפָן בִּשְׁלִימוּ, עֵילָא וְתַתָּא כַּדְקָא יָאוֹת. וְרָזָא דָּא ה״ה עִלָּאָה וְתַתָּאָה, וְכָל אִינּוּן שְׁבִילִין, דְּאִינּוּן תְּלָתִין וּתְרֵין שְׁנִין דְּכְלִילָן בְּרָזָא דְּאָת ו״ה, ו״ה, רָזָא דִּשְׁלִימוּ דְּמֵאָה וּתְלָתִין וּתְרֵין.

151. After the end of 66 more years, which is 132 years TOGETHER WITH THE AFOREMENTIONED 66, the letters in the Holy Name, OF THE 66, will appear engraved to perfection, above IN TIFERET and below IN THE NUKVA, as is proper. This is the secret of the supernal and lower Hei THAT ARE IN THE LOWER HEI FULLY SPELLED (*HEI-HEI*). SIMILAR TO *VAV*, THAT CONTAINS ANOTHER *VAV* WHEN FULLY SPELLED, AS MENTIONED THAT THE UPPER *VAV* EMANATES THE SECRET OF SIXTY TO THE UPPER *HEI*, AND THE LOWER *VAV* EMANATES THE SECRET OF SIX TO THE LOWER *HEI*. And all these paths, which are 32 years OF THE AFOREMENTIONED 132, are included in the secret of the letters *Vav-Hei*, *Vav-Hei*, THE FIRST *VAV-HEI* BEING TWO TIMES SIXTY, AND THE SECOND *VAV-HEI* BEING TWO TIMES SIX, AS MENTIONED TOGETHER THEY AMOUNT TO 132, OUT OF WHICH, THE NUMBER 32 ALLUDES TO the secret of the completeness of 132, MEANING THAT THE PREPARATION WAS MADE IN THEM TO RECEIVE THE 32 PATHS OF WISDOM FROM THE *YUD* OF YUD HEI VAV HEI, AS WRITTEN BEFORE.

152. לְסוֹף מֵאָה וּתְלָתִין וּתְרֵין שְׁנִין אַחֲרָנִין, יִתְקַיֵּים, לְאֶחֱוֹז בְּכַנְפוֹת הָאָרֶץ וְיִנָּעֲרוּ רְשָׁעִים מִמֶּנָּה. וְיִתְדַּכֵּי אַרְעָא קַדִּישָׁא. וְקוּדְשָׁא בְּרִיךְ הוּא

יִתְּעַר מֵתַיָּיא דְּאַרְעָא קַדִּישָׁא, וְיִקוּמוּן חַיָּילִין חַיָּילִין בְּאַרְעָא דְּגָלִיל.

152. At the end of the other 132 years – AS THOSE 132 THAT WERE COMPLETED IN TIFERET AND THE NUKVA, WHICH ARE VAV-HEI OF YUD HEI VAV HEI, ALSO HAVE TO ILLUMINATE IN CHOCHMAH AND BINAH, WHICH ARE YUD-HEI OF YUD HEI VAV HEI – THE VERSE will be fulfilled: "That it might take hold of the ends of the earth that the wicked might be shaken out of it" (Iyov 38:13). The Holy Land will be purified and the Holy One, blessed be He, will resurrect the dead in the Holy Land, and hosts upon hosts will arise in the Galilee.

153. וּכְדֵין יִתְּעַר סְתִּימוּ דִּנְבִיעוּ עִלָּאָה אָת י׳, וְיִתְקַיְּימוּן תְּלָתִין וּתְרֵין שְׁבִילִין בִּשְׁלִימוּ, לְנַגְדָּא לְתַתָּא, וְיִתְקַיְּימוּן אַתְוָון דִּשְׁמָא קַדִּישָׁא כֻּלְּהוּ בְּקִיּוּמַיְיהוּ ידו״ד, דְּעַד כְּעַן לָא יְהוֹן בִּשְׁלִימוּ.

153. Then will be mended the obstruction, which is in the Supernal Fountain OF YUD HEI VAV HEI – WHICH IS the letter *Yud*, WHICH IS CHOCHMAH – and the 32 paths IN CHOCHMAH will be established in completeness to emanate down. The letters of the Holy Name will be established, all of them completely, MEANING THE NAME Yud Hei Vav Hei, that were not complete heretofore.

154. עַד זְמָן דְּיַנְגִּיד וְיִתְמְשַׁךְ הַהוּא נְבִיעוּ עִלָּאָה, בְּחִבּוּרָה דְּאַתְוָון, גּוֹ ה׳ בַּתְרָאָה, וְדָא אִיהוּ לְסוֹף תַּשְׁלוּם מֵאָה וְאַרְבְּעִין וְאַרְבְּעָה שְׁנִין אַחֲרָנִין דְּיִשְׁתַּלְּמוּן. וְיִתְעָרוּן שְׁאַר מֵתֵי יִשְׂרָאֵל דְּבִשְׁאָר אַרְעָאן.

154. Then shall come the time that the Supernal Fountain will flow and be drawn, WHICH IS *YUD* CONNECTED WITH *HEI-VAV*, WHICH ARE BINAH AND TIFERET, into the last *Hei* OF THE YUD HEI VAV HEI, WHICH IS THE NUKVA. This will be at the culmination of another 144 years. FOR THEY ARE THE SECRET OF THE THIRD 132 TO BE THERE WITH THE TWELVE TRIBES THAT ARE IN THE NUKVA, WHICH TOGETHER ARE 144 YEARS. The other dead in the other countries will be resurrected, NAMELY THE DEAD OUTSIDE OF THE LAND OF YISRAEL.

155. דְּיִשְׁתְּכַח כָּל דָּא בְּחֻשְׁבָּן ח״ת, דְּאִתְיַישִׁיב עָלְמָא וְיִתְבַּסַּם,

וְיִתְעֲבָר סִטְרָא אָחֳרָא מֵעָלְמָא. וְהֵ״א תַּתָּאָה תִּתְמְלֵי מִגּוֹ נְבִיעוּ עִלָּאָה,
וְתִתְעֲטָר וְתִתְנְהִיר בִּשְׁלִימוּ. וּכְדֵין כְּתִיב, וְהָיָה אוֹר הַלְּבָנָה כְּאוֹר
הַחַמָּה וְאוֹר הַחַמָּה יִהְיֶה שִׁבְעָתַיִם.

155. All this adds up to *Chet-Tav*, WHICH ARE TWO TIMES 132, PLUS 144 WHICH TOTALS *TAV-CHET* (= 408). The world will settle and have fragrance, and the Other Side will be removed from the world. And the lower *Hei*, WHICH IS THE NUKVA, will become filled from the Supernal Fountain, WHICH IS *YUD* OF YUD HEI VAV HEI AND THE SECRET OF CHOCHMAH, and be crowned and illuminated perfectly. Then, it is written: "And the light of the moon will be like the light of the sun, and the light of the sun shall be sevenfold" (Yeshayah 30:26).

156. עַד דִּיהֵא שַׁבָּת לַה׳, לְאַלְקָטָא נַפְשִׁין בְּתַעֲנוּגֵי קְדוּשָׁא, כָּל הַהוּא
אֶלֶף שְׁבִיעָאָה, וְדָא אִיהוּ אִתְעָרוּתָא דְרוּחִין קַדִּישִׁין, דְּעַמָּא דְיִשְׂרָאֵל,
לְאִתְלַבְּשָׁא לְבָתַר שַׁבָּת, בְּגוּפִין אַחֳרָנִין קַדִּישִׁין, לְאִתְקְרֵי קַדִּישִׁין,
דִּכְתִיב, וְהָיָה הַנִּשְׁאָר בְּצִיּוֹן וְהַנּוֹתָר בִּירוּשָׁלַם קָדוֹשׁ יֵאָמֶר לוֹ. עַד כָּאן
מִלִּין דְּרָזִין סְתִימִין.

156. There will be a Shabbat for Hashem to gather souls with holy delight, NAMELY TO DRAW ADDITIONAL SOULS IN THE SECRET OF THE SUPERNAL UNION, during the entire seventh millennium, WHICH IS ENTIRELY SHABBAT. This is the stirring of the holy spirits of the nation of Yisrael to clothe themselves after Shabbat – NAMELY AFTER THE SEVENTH MILLENIUM – in other holy bodies, so as to be called 'Holy Ones', as is written: "And it shall come to pass, that he that is left in Zion, and he that remains in Jerusalem shall be called Holy..." (Yeshayah 4:3). Up to this point are words of the concealed secrets.

16. "Now there arose a new king," part two

A Synopsis

Here, Rabbi Yosi explains that God creates new angels every day. The reference to "a new king" in the title verse alludes to the creation of a new supernal representative for Egypt that emanated from the place of Separation. Consequently, "he knew not Joseph," since Joseph represents the sphere where unity rests, called Righteousness.

The Relevance of the Passage

Each action that we perform, be it positive or negative, creates an appropriate spiritual entity that constantly influences our lives. These angelic forces are generated each moment of the day in response to the words we speak and the behavior we exhibit toward others.

When things just happen to go wrong in life, when chaos suddenly materializes for no apparent reason, when life appears unjust, cruel, or blatantly balanced towards the negative, it's the result of negative entities whose accumulative effect tilts our life and the world toward the side of madness and danger. The collective negative deeds of humanity give birth to these influential dark forces. If we continually empower them, their strength grows and they create new nations of terror in the physical world.

The Zohar reveals an important spiritual truth: The Light of the Creator cannot coexist with evil, in the same way that sunlight and darkness cannot manifest concurrently. Likewise, our soul cannot be in the presence of ego. One or the other must prevail. It is our free choice to choose which aspect of our being will lead and direct our lives.

When our Evil Inclination and reactive nature is present, the Light of the Creator is far and distant. When a man subdues his reflexive emotions, the Light of the Creator and the spark of his soul illuminates brilliantly.

Unity and separation correlate to the concept of goodness and turmoil, respectively. Separation, the Zohar tells us, "does not want to know unity," communicating the cosmic principle which states that the unified Light of the Creator cannot rest in places where there is disunity and separation between people. Separation includes disunity among nations, and a rift between two siblings or friends.

This passage seals the cracks, crevices, and chasms that have existed far too long among God's children. Our eyes and hearts are the glue that now conjoin and unite all souls as one, creating a sacred place for the Light of the Creator to occupy with endless luminosity. This Light flows to us through Joseph, from the realm known as *Yesod*, the funnel through which all energy passes en route to our world.

157. וַיָּקָם מֶלֶךְ חָדָשׁ. ר' יוֹסֵי אָמַר, בְּכָל יוֹמָא, קוּדְשָׁא בְּרִיךְ הוּא עָבֵיד מַלְאָכִין שְׁלִיחָן עַל עָלְמָא, דִּכְתִּיב, עוֹשֶׂה מַלְאָכָיו רוּחוֹת. עָשָׂה לָא כְּתִיב, אֶלָּא עוֹשֶׂה, בְּגִין דְּכָל יוֹמָא וְיוֹמָא עוֹשֶׂה. וּבְהַהוּא זִמְנָא אִתְמְנָא מְמָנָא חַד עַל מִצְרַיִם, וְדָא אִיהוּ דִּכְתִּיב וַיָּקָם מֶלֶךְ, חָדָשׁ וַדַּאי.

157. "Now there arose a new king" (Shemot 1:8). Rabbi Yosi says: Every day the Holy One, blessed be He, makes angels into messengers to the world, as is written: "Who makes the winds His messengers" (Tehilim 104:4). It is not written, 'made', but rather, "makes," IN THE PRESENT TENSE, because every day He "makes." And at that time was appointed AN ANGEL as an overseer of Egypt, which is the meaning of: "Now there arose a new king." He is definitely new, FOR HE IS THE OVERSEER THAT THE HOLY ONE, BLESSED BE HE, JUST MADE.

158. אֲשֶׁר לָא יָדַע אֶת יוֹסֵף: דְּהָא מֵאֲתַר דִּפְרוּדָא הֲווֹ, כד"א, וּמִשָּׁם יִפָּרֵד וְקַדְמָאָה מֵהַהוּא פְּרוּדָא, נַהֲרָא דְּמִצְרַיִם אִיהוּ. וּבְגִין כַּךְ אֲשֶׁר לָא יָדַע אֶת יוֹסֵף, אֲתַר דְּכָל יְחוּדָא שַׁרְיָא בֵּיהּ, דְּאִקְרֵי צַדִּיק.

158. "Who knew not Joseph" (Shemot 1:8), because THE OVERSEER was from the place of separation, as is written: "And from thence it was parted, AND BRANCHED INTO FOUR STREAMS" (Beresheet 2:10). The first to separate was the River of Egypt, AS IS WRITTEN: "THE NAME OF THE FIRST WAS PISHON" (IBID. 11), WHICH IS THE RIVER OF EGYPT. Because of this, he knew not Joseph, who is the place where all unity resides, which is called 'righteous'. FOR JOSEPH IS THE SECRET OF YESOD, WHICH IS CALLED 'RIGHTEOUS' BECAUSE ALL THE UNIONS OF ZEIR ANPIN AND THE NUKVA ARE MADE WITH ITS HELP. AND THE SEPARATION DOES NOT WANT TO KNOW THE UNION.

17. The morning star

A Synopsis

Rabbi Elazar and Rabbi Yosi are travelling at dawn when they see two stars shooting across the sky from opposite sides. After explaining that it is the time when the morning stars prepare to glorify God's Name, Rabbi Elazar proceeds to discuss the verse, "To the chief musician upon the morning star..." The "hind of the morning," we're told, indicates the time when the east lightens and the darkness of night disperses. An angel that oversees the east draws a thread of light from the south until the sun rises and illuminates the world. Then a black light comes to unite with the day, as the light of day (which signifies Zeir Anpin) draws the hind of the morning (which signifies the Nukva) to include it. David composed a psalm about this hind when it was separated from day after being included in it. Thus, we learn that the verse, "My El, my El, why have You forsaken me?" mourns the separation of the Nukva from Zeir Anpin.

The Relevance of the Passage

In the opening few verses, our meditation draws threads of Light which crack the *Klipot,* the negative blockages in our soul, thus dispersing the darkness from our being along with the physical chaos in our lives. This super-radiant effect extends to the entire world as the Light shatters the darkness and overwhelms the evil that suffocates human existence. Next, King David, who is the personified will of our entire physical world, is called forth through the mysteries of these verses. He unites our world with paradise above, the source of all Light, commencing our ultimate destiny – eternal existence, song, merriment, joy, and bliss, as we bathe in the Light of the Creator.

159. ר' אֶלְעָזָר וְר' יוֹסֵי הֲוֹו אַזְלֵי בְּאוֹרְחָא, וְקָדִימוּ בִּנְהוֹרָא לְמֵיזָל. חָמוּ חַד כּוֹכָבָא דַּהֲוָה רָהִיט מִסְּטְרָא דָא, וְכוֹכָבָא אַחֲרָא מִסְּטְרָא דָא. א"ר אֶלְעָזָר, הַשְׁתָּא מָטָא זִמְנָא דְכוֹכְבֵי בֹּקֶר לְשַׁבָּחָא לְמָארֵיהוֹן, וְרַהֲטֵי מִדְּחִילוּ וְאֵימָתָא דְּמָארֵיהוֹן, לְשַׁבָּחָא וּלְזַמְּרָא לֵיהּ, הַהַ"ד, בְּרָן יַחַד כּוֹכְבֵי בֹקֶר וַיָּרִיעוּ כָּל בְּנֵי אֱלֹהִים. בְּגִין דְּכֻלְּהוּ בְּיִחוּדָא חֲדָא קָא מְשַׁבְּחָן לֵיהּ.

159. Rabbi Elazar and Rabbi Yosi were walking on the road, and they left before the light of day. They saw a star flying on one side and another THAT WAS FLYING on another side. Rabbi Elazar said: The time has now arrived for the morning stars to praise their Master, and they are running, because of

the fear and terror of their Master to praise and sing BEFORE HIM. This is what is written: "When the morning stars sang together and all the children of Elohim shouted for joy" (Iyov 38:7). Because all the stars together praise before Him.

160. פָּתַח וְאָמַר, לַמְנַצֵּחַ עַל אַיֶּלֶת הַשַּׁחַר מִזְמוֹר לְדָוִד. אַיֶּלֶת הַשַּׁחַר: דְּכַד נְהִירוּ אַנְפּוֹי דְּמִזְרָח, וְאִתְפְּרְשָׁא חֲשׁוֹכָא דְּלֵילְיָא, חַד מְמָנָא אִית לְסְטַר מִזְרָח, וּמָשִׁיךְ חַד חוּטָא דִּנְהִירוּ דִּסְטַר דָּרוֹם, עַד דְּאָתֵי וְנָפִיק שִׁמְשָׁא, וּבָקַע בְּאִינוּן כַּוֵּי רְקִיעָא, וְאַנְהִיר עָלְמָא, וְהַהוּא חוּטָא אַפְרִישׁ חֲשׁוֹכָא דְּלֵילְיָא.

160. He opened the discussion saying: "To the chief musician upon *Ayelet Hashachar* ('the morning star' – lit. 'the hind of dawn'), a psalm of David" (Tehilim 22:1). 'The hind of dawn' MEANS when the east lights up and the darkness of night is dispersed, there is one overseer for the east side – WHICH IS THE SECRET OF THE CENTRAL COLUMN – that draws one thread of light from the south side, WHICH IS THE RIGHT COLUMN, until the sun rises, and cracks the windows of the firmament and illuminates the world. And the thread THAT IT DRAWS FROM THE SOUTH SIDE disperses the darkness of the night.

161. כְּדֵין אַיַּלְתָּא דְּשַׁחֲרָא אָתֵי, וְאָתֵי נְהִירוּ אוֹכָמָא בְּקַדְרוּ, לְאִתְחַבְּרָא בִּימָמָא, וְנָהִיר יְמָמָא. וּנְהִירוּ דִּימָמָא, כָּלִיל וְשָׁאִיב בְּגַוֵּיהּ, לְהַהוּא אַיַּלְתָּא וְעַל הַאי אַיַּלְתָּא, כַּד אִתְפְּרַשׁ מִיּוֹמָא, לְבָתַר דְּכָלִיל לָהּ, אָמַר דָּוִד שִׁירָתָא, דִּכְתִּיב לַמְנַצֵּחַ עַל אַיֶּלֶת הַשַּׁחַר.

161. Then comes the hind of dawn, MEANING THAT a black light comes – WHICH IS THE NUKVA IN THE SECRET OF THE HIND OF DAWN – to unite with the day, WHICH IS ZEIR ANPIN, and the day shines. The light of day includes and draws into it that hind, WHICH IS NUKVA. David composed a psalm about this hind, when she was separated from the day after she was already included in it, as is written: "To the chief musician upon the hind of dawn."

162. וּמַאי קָא אָמַר אֵלִי אֵלִי לָמָה עֲזַבְתָּנִי. דְּהָא אִתְפְּרַשׁ אַיַּלְתָּא דְּשַׁחֲרָא, מִנְּהִירוּ דִּימָמָא. עַד דַּהֲווֹ אַזְלֵי, נָהִיר יְמָמָא, וּמָטָא עִידָן

צְלוֹתָא, א"ר אֶלְעָזָר, נְצַלֵּי צְלוֹתָא וְנֵיזִיל, יָתְבוּ וְצַלּוּ. לְבָתַר קָמוּ
וְאַזְלוּ.

162. And DAVID said: "My El, my El, why have You forsaken me?" (Tehilim 22:2) because the hind of dawn, WHICH IS THE NUKVA, had separated from the light of day, WHICH IS ZEIR ANPIN. THEREFORE, SHE HAD NOTHING TO BESTOW AND HAD LEFT HIM. While they were still walking, daylight appeared and the time for prayer arrived. Rabbi Elazar said: Let us pray and then go. They sat down and prayed, and afterwards they arose and went.

18. Righteous men to whom it happens according to the deeds of the wicked

A Synopsis

In this section, Rabbi Elazar begins by discussing the verse, "There is a vanity..." before the discussion turns to examine the seemingly incongruous system of worldly rewards and punishments. We learn that the world (the Nukva) stands upon the seven vanities (the seven Sfirot of Zeir Anpin). These vanities are the seven pillars that support the world, and they correspond to the seven Firmaments. Just as other Firmaments cleave to and issue from the seven Firmaments, there are other vanities that emanate from the seven vanities, all of which are mentioned by Solomon in his book of Ecclesiastes. The Foundation (Yesod), which emanates from the supernal vanities, is maintained and strengthened by the souls of the Righteous who died before they sinned on earth. Enoch, who was taken before his time to die had arrived, is an example of such a soul. An explanation of the title subject then ensues from a discussion of the two reasons why the Righteous are removed from the world before their time. We learn that when He foresees that the righteous will sin if they live longer, He removes them from the world and they are Judged as though they had sinned. Conversely, He allows wicked men to live if He foresees that they will repent or that they will have Righteous children. Another interpretation of the verse relating to the title quotation reveals that God is glorified by both the deeds of the Righteous and the good deeds that the wicked perform. Finally, Rabbi Elazar provides further insight into the verse, "All things have I seen in the days of my vanity..." (Kohelet 7:15). When Solomon was granted wisdom, we're told, he saw everything at the time when the moon reigned. "A just man who perishes in his righteousness" is an allusion to the Foundation of the world and the Nukva, which have no power during the time of the exile. Therefore, supernal blessings do not reach a just man in exile and he "perishes in his righteousness." "And there is a wicked man who prolongs his life in his wickedness," alludes to Samael and his wife, the Serpent, who gives strength and peace to the other kings that rule Yisrael in exile.

The Relevance of the Passage

Here we acquire the proactive awareness and courage to resist reactive impulses, borne of vanity, *before* they lead us into sin. The Light we draw is now used to cleanse and purify the wicked who dwell in our midst, infusing our spiritual and physical environment with luminous forces of positivity and goodness.

18. Righteous men to whom it happens according to the deeds of the wicked

The sins of our generation are atoned for by the righteous sages of antiquity, whose Light and merit are summoned forth as our eyes dance across the letters of these sacred pages.

Each of us possesses a portion of goodness and wickedness. Immense Light erupts in our world each time we triumph over our wicked traits. By meditating upon our own negative qualities now, this Light shines from one end of the universe to the other.

The powers of evil nations and Kings vanish. The evil angels known as Samael and Lilit (do not pronounce these names) are banished forevermore from reality. The energy of King David rises in this passage, elevating the dimension known as Malchut, our physical world, into the sphere of the Upper World.

163. פָּתַח ר' אֶלְעָזָר וְאָמַר יֵשׁ הֶבֶל אֲשֶׁר נַעֲשָׂה עַל הָאָרֶץ אֲשֶׁר יֵשׁ צַדִּיקִים אֲשֶׁר מַגִּיעַ אֲלֵיהֶם כְּמַעֲשֵׂה הָרְשָׁעִים וְגוֹ' אָמַרְתִּי שֶׁגַּם זֶה הָבֶל. הַאי קְרָא אוּקְמוּהָ וְאִתְּמַר, אֲבָל יֵשׁ הֶבֶל, שְׁלֹמֹה מַלְכָּא עֲבַד סִפְרָא דָא, וְאוֹקִים לֵיהּ עַל שִׁבְעָה הֲבָלִים, דְּעָלְמָא קַיְּימָא עֲלַיְיהוּ.

163. Rabbi Elazar opened the discussion, saying: "There is a vanity (Heb. *hevel*) which is done upon the earth; that there are just men to whom it happens according to the deeds of the wicked... I said that this also is vanity" (Kohelet 8:14). This verse was explained, but THE WORDS, "There is vanity," MEAN THAT King Solomon wrote this book and based it on seven vanities, WHICH ARE THE SEVEN SFIROT OF ZEIR ANPIN, WHICH IS THE LIGHT OF THE RUACH. AND THE SEVEN LOWER SFIROT OF RUACH ARE CALLED 'VANITIES'. The world, WHICH IS THE NUKVA, is based on them, AS ITS SEVEN SFIROT ARE UPHELD BY THE SEVEN SFIROT – CHESED, GVURAH, TIFERET, NETZACH, HOD, YESOD AND MALCHUT OF ZEIR ANPIN. FOR THE NUKVA IS THE SECRET OF SPEECH, AND THERE IS NO SPEECH WITHOUT AIR (HEB. *HEVEL*) THAT BEATS UPON THE FIVE ARTICULATION PLACES IN THE MOUTH, AS IS KNOWN.

164. וְאִינוּן שִׁבְעָה עַמּוּדִין סַמְכִין דְּעָלְמָא, לָקֳבֵל שִׁבְעָה רְקִיעִים, וְאִלֵּין אִינוּן: וִילוֹ"ן. רְקִי"עַ, שְׁחָקִי"ם זְבוּ"ל. מָעוֹ"ן. מָכוֹ"ן. עֲרָבוֹ"ת. וּלְקָבְלַיְיהוּ הֶבֶל הֲבָלִים אָמַר קֹהֶלֶת הֶבֶל הֲבָלִים הַכֹּל הָבֶל.

164. These seven vanities are called 'the seven pillars that support the world', WHICH IS THE NUKVA, and they correspond to the seven firmaments. And these are: Curtain, Firmament, Skies, Temple, Dwelling, Institute, Heaven. "'Vanities of Vanities,' said Kohelet, 'vanities of vanities; all is vanity'" (Kohelet 1:2), corresponds to them. WE HAVE HERE SEVEN VANITIES. BECAUSE "VANITY OF VANITIES," ARE THREE, TOGETHER WITH "VANITY OF VANITIES," THERE ARE SIX, AND WITH "VANITY," MENTIONED AT THE END OF THE VERSE, IT EQUALS SEVEN.

165. כְּמָה דְּאִינוּן שִׁבְעָה רְקִיעִין, וְאִית אַחֲרָנִין דְּדַבְקִין בְּהוּ, וּמִתְפַּשְּׁטֵי וְנַפְקֵי מִנַּיְיהוּ, הָכִי נָמֵי אִית הֲבָלִים אַחֲרָנִין, דְּמִתְפַּשְּׁטֵי וְנַפְקֵי מֵאִלֵּין, וְכֻלְּהוּ אָמַר שְׁלֹמֹה.

165. As there are seven firmaments, and there are other firmaments that are attached to them and spread out and emanate from them – WHICH ARE THE SEVEN FIRMAMENTS THAT ARE IN THE NUKVA – so there are other vanities, MEANING OF THE NUKVA, that spread out and emanate from these SEVEN VANITIES OF ZEIR ANPIN. Solomon mentioned them all IN HIS BOOK OF KOHELET.

166. וְהָכָא רָזָא דְּחָכְמְתָא אִית בֵּיהּ. יֵשׁ הֶבֶל, דְּנַפְקָא מֵאִינוּן הֲבָלִים עִלָּאִין, דְּעָלְמָא קַיְּימָא עֲלַיְיהוּ, וְדָא נַעֲשָׂה עַל הָאָרֶץ, וְאִתְקַיַּים בְּקִיּוּמֵיהּ, וְאִתְתַּקַּף בְּתוּקְפֵּיהּ בְּעוֹבְדֵי אַרְעָא, וּבְסַלִּיקוּ דְּסַלְקָא מֵאַרְעָא, וְדָא אִתְמָנָא עַל אַרְעָא, וְכָל תּוּקְפָּא וְקִיּוּמָא דִּילֵיהּ, בְּאִינוּן נִשְׁמָתִין דְּצַדִּיקַיָּא, דְּאִתְלְקִיטוּ מֵאַרְעָא, כַּד אִינוּן זַכָּאִין, עַד לָא סָרְחוּ, בְּעוֹד דְּיָהֲבֵי רֵיחָא טָב, כְּגוֹן חֲנוֹךְ, דִּכְתִיב בֵּיהּ, וְאֵינֶנּוּ כִּי לָקַח אוֹתוֹ אֱלֹהִים. וְנָטַל לֵיהּ עַד לָא מָטָא זִמְנֵיהּ, וְאִשְׁתְּעֲשַׁע בֵּיהּ, וְכֵן שְׁאַר זַכָּאִין דְּעָלְמָא.

166. And here is the secret of Chochmah, meaning in the verse: "There is a vanity," THE ASPECT OF YESOD OF THE VANITIES, that emanates from the supernal vanities AFOREMENTIONED, upon which the world, WHICH IS THE NUKVA, is based. And this is THE MEANING OF: "Which is done upon the earth" (Kohelet 8:14), MEANING ON THE NUKVA THAT IS CALLED 'EARTH'. "WHICH IS DONE," MEANS THAT YESOD is maintained and its power is strengthened by the tillers of earth, WHO ARE THE RIGHTEOUS, and in the elevation OF THEIR *MAYIN NUKVIN* ('FEMALE WATERS') that rise from the earth. And this, YESOD, is appointed TO POUR upon the earth. All its might and existence is from the souls of the righteous that were gathered from the earth, MEANING THEY DIED while being righteous, before they sinned, when they were still emanating a fragrant scent. For example, it is written about Enoch: "And he was not, for Elohim took him" (Beresheet 5:24). For He took him before his time had arrived TO DIE, and He delighted in him. And it is so with the other righteous of the world.

167. דְּתָנֵינָן, עַל תְּרֵין מִלִּין, צַדִּיקַיָּא מִסְתַּלְּקֵי מֵעָלְמָא, עַד לָא יִמְטֵי זִמְנַיְיהוּ, חַד, עַל חוֹבֵי דָרָא, דְּכַד אַסְגִּיאוּ חַיָּיבַיָּא בְּעָלְמָא, אִינּוּן זַכָּאִין דְּמִשְׁתַּכְּחֵי בֵּינַיְיהוּ, אִתְּפְּסוּן בְּחוֹבֵיהוֹן, וְחַד כַּד אִתְגְּלֵי קָמֵי קוּדְשָׁא בְּרִיךְ הוּא דְּיִסְרְחוּן לְבָתַר, סָלִיק לוֹן מֵעָלְמָא, עַד לָא מָטָא זִמְנַיְיהוּ, הה"ד, אֲשֶׁר יֵשׁ צַדִּיקִים אֲשֶׁר מַגִּיעַ אֲלֵיהֶם כְּמַעֲשֵׂה הָרְשָׁעִים, מָטֵי עָלַיְיהוּ דִּינָא דִּלְעֵילָא, כְּאִילוּ עָבְדוּ חוֹבִין וְעוֹבָדִין דִּרְשִׁיעַיָּיא.

167. We learned that two things cause the righteous to leave the world before their time: One, because of the sins of the generation; when the wicked multiply in the world then the righteous who are among them are punished for their sins. Another is when it is revealed before the Holy One, blessed be He, that they will sin later on. He then removes them from the world before their time. This is what is written: "There are just men to whom it happens according to the deeds of the wicked." They are treated as though they had sinned and acted wicked by celestial justice.

168. דְּהָא זִמְנָא חֲדָא, שָׁאִיל רַבִּי יוֹסֵי ב"ר יַעֲקֹב, אִישׁ כְּפַר אוֹנוֹ בְּזִמְנָא דְּרַבִּי עֲקִיבָא וְחַבְרוֹי אִסְתַּלָּקוּ מֵעָלְמָא, וּמִיתוּ בְּהַהוּא גַּוְונָא, לְרַבִּי מֵאִיר, אָמַר לֵיהּ, וְכִי כְּתִיב דָּא בְּכָל אוֹרַיְיתָא כֻּלָּהּ, אָמַר לֵיהּ וְלָא, וְהָא אָמַר שְׁלֹמֹה, אֲשֶׁר יֵשׁ צַדִּיקִים אֲשֶׁר מַגִּיעַ אֲלֵיהֶם כְּמַעֲשֵׂה הָרְשָׁעִים. מָטֵי עָלַיְיהוּ דִּינָא מִלְּעֵילָא, כְּאִילוּ עָבְדוּ חוֹבִין וְעוֹבָדִין דִּרְשִׁיעַיָּיא. וְיֵשׁ רְשָׁעִים שֶׁמַּגִּיעַ אֲלֵיהֶם כְּמַעֲשֵׂה הַצַּדִּיקִים, יַתְבֵי בְּשֶׁקֶט

וּשְׁלָם בְּהַאי עָלְמָא, דִּינָא לָא מָטָא עָלַיְיהוּ, כְּאִילוּ עָבְדוּ עוֹבָדִין דְּצַדִּיקַיָּיא.

168. One time, Rabbi Yosi ben Rabbi Ya'akov, the leader of Kfar Ono asked Rabbi Meir about the time that Rabbi Akiva and his friends passed from the world and died in that manner, MEANING THAT THEY WERE KILLED BY THE AUTHORITIES. He said to him: Is it written anywhere in the Torah thus, THAT RIGHTEOUS PEOPLE SHOULD SUFFER SO? RABBI MEIR said to him: It is not WRITTEN SO, and did not Solomon say, "There are just men to whom it happens according to the deeds of the wicked"? They are judged from above as though they sinned and acted like the wicked. "There are wicked men, to whom it happens according to the deeds of the righteous" (Kohelet 8:14). They sit quietly and peacefully in this world and Judgment does not reach them as though they had acted like righteous people.

169. אֲמַאי, אִי בְּגִין דְּאִתְגְּלֵי קָמֵי קוּדְשָׁא בְּרִיךְ הוּא, דִּיתוּבוּן בִּתְיוּבְתָּא, אוֹ דְּיִפּוֹק מִנַּיְיהוּ זַרְעָא, דִּיהֵא קְשׁוֹט בְּעָלְמָא, כְּגוֹן תֶּרַח דְּנָפַק מִנֵּיהּ זַרְעָא דִּקְשׁוֹט, אַבְרָהָם. אָחָז, דְּנָפַק מִנֵּיהּ חִזְקִיָּהוּ. וּשְׁאַר חַיָּיבִין דְּעָלְמָא. וּבְגִין כָּךְ, בְּסִטְרָא דָא, וּבְסִטְרָא דָא, הֶבֶל דְּקָאֲמָרָן, נַעֲשָׂה וְאִתְתַּקַּף עַל הָאָרֶץ, כִּדְקָאֲמָרַן.

169. HE ASKS: Why DOES IT HAPPEN TO THEM ACCORDING TO THE RIGHTEOUS? AND HE ANSWERS: Either because it is revealed before the Holy One, blessed be He, that they will repent, or that a righteous person will descend from them, as Terah, from whom emanated the true seed of Abraham; or Achaz from whom came Hezekiah. AND SO the other wicked of the world. Therefore on both sides, MEANING BY THE RIGHTEOUS AND THE WICKED, vanity IS DONE that we said, and is strengthened upon the earth, as we have said.

170. ד"א יֵשׁ הֶבֶל אֲשֶׁר נַעֲשָׂה עַל הָאָרֶץ, כִּדְקָאֲמָרַן דְּאִתְתַּקַּף עַל עָלְמָא. בְּמַאי, בְּגִין דְּיֵשׁ צַדִּיקִים אֲשֶׁר מַגִּיעַ אֲלֵיהֶם כְּמַעֲשֵׂה הָרְשָׁעִים, מָטָאן לִידַיְיהוּ כְּאִינוּן עוֹבָדִין דְּחַיָּיבַיָּא, כְּגוֹן בַּת עע"ז, אוֹ חַד מֵאִינוּן עוֹבָדִין, דְּאִינוּן מִמַּעֲשֵׂה הָרְשָׁעִים, וְאִינוּן קַיְימֵי בְּקִיּוּמַיְיהוּ, מִדְּחִילוּ

-109-

18. Righteous men to whom it happens
according to the deeds of the wicked

דְּמָארֵיהוֹן, וְלָא בָּעָאן לְאִסְתַּאֲבָא, כְּגוֹן כַּמָּה זַכָּאֵי קְשׁוֹט דְּמָטוּ לִידַיְיהוּ כְּעוֹבָדִין אִלֵּין, וְאִינוּן גְּבוֹרֵי כֹּחַ, דְּעַבְדֵּי רְעוּתָא דְּמָארֵיהוֹן, וְלָא חָטָאוּ. וְעַל דָּא, הֶבֶל נַעֲשָׂה עַל הָאָרֶץ וְאִתְתַּקַּף בְּתוּקְפֵּיהּ.

170. Another explanation OF THE VERSE: "There is a vanity which is done upon the earth." As we said, ITS MEANING IS that it prevails in the world. How? Because "there are just men, to whom it happens according to the deeds of the wicked," meaning that the actions of sinners confront them – SUCH AS a daughter of idol worshippers, or other actions that are actions of the wicked – but they make their stand AND DO NOT SIN, because of fear of their Master, and they do not wish to become impure. Like many truly righteous, they are confronted by similar actions. And they are valiant for they have done the desire of their Master and did not sin. On this is written: "Vanity has been done of the earth," and its might grows strong.

171. וְיֵשׁ רְשָׁעִים שֶׁמַּגִּיעַ אֲלֵיהֶם כְּמַעֲשֵׂה הַצַּדִּיקִים, מָטֵי לִידַיְיהוּ חַד מִצְוָה, דְּאִיהוּ עוֹבָדָא דְּצַדִּיקַיָּא, וְזַכָּאן בָּהּ, וְעַבְדִין יָתָהּ. כְּגוֹן לִסְטִים מְקַפְּחָא הֲוָה מִשְׁתַּכַּח בְּטוּרַיָּא, בַּהֲדֵי אִינוּן לִסְטִים עע"ז, וְכַד הֲוָה יוּדָאי אַעֲבַר תַּמָּן, הֲוָה מְשֵׁזִיב לֵיהּ, וְנָטִיר לֵיהּ מִנַּיְיהוּ, וַהֲוָה קָרֵי עֲלֵיהּ רִבִּי עֲקִיבָא, יֵשׁ רְשָׁעִים אֲשֶׁר מַגִּיעַ אֲלֵיהֶם כְּמַעֲשֵׂה הַצַּדִּיקִים.

171. "Again, there are wicked men to whom it happens according to the deeds of the righteous." IT IS when they are presented with a good deed, which is an action of the righteous, that they merit it and fulfill it. For example, there was a JEWISH murderer in the hills with heathen murderers, and when a Jew would pass by there he would save him and guard him from the others. Rabbi Akiva would declare of him: "There are wicked men to whom it happens according to the deeds of the righteous."

172. וּכְגוֹן הַהוּא חַיָּיבָא, דַּהֲוָה בִּשְׁבָבוּתֵיהּ דְּרִבִּי חִיָּיא, דְּלֵילְיָא חַד פָּגַע בָּהּ בְּהַהִיא אִתְּתָא דַּהֲוַת אַזְלַת לְבֵי בְרַתָּהּ. בָּעָא לְמִתְקַף בָּהּ, אָמְרָה לֵיהּ, בְּמָטוּ מִינָךְ, אוֹקִיר לְמָרָךְ, וְלָא תֶּחֱטָא גַּבַּאי. שַׁבְקָהּ וְלָא חָב בָּהּ. הֲוֵי אוֹמֵר, וְיֵשׁ רְשָׁעִים אֲשֶׁר מַגִּיעַ אֲלֵיהֶם כְּמַעֲשֵׂה הַצַּדִּיקִים

אָמַרְתִּי שֶׁגַּם זֶה הָבֶל, כְּמָה דְּאִתְתְּקַף הַהוּא הֶבֶל, בַּהֲדֵי אִינּוּן צַדִּיקַיָּא,
דְּמָטוּ לִידַיְיהוּ עוֹבְדֵי דְּחַיָּיבַיָּא, וְלָא חָטָאן. אוּף הָכִי, אִתְתְּקַף בַּהֲדֵי
אִינּוּן חַיָּיבַיָּא, דְּמָטֵי לִידַיְיהוּ עוֹבְדֵי דְּאִינּוּן צַדִּיקַיָּא, וְעַבְדֵי לְהוּ.

172. Another instance is that wicked person who was the neighbor of Rabbi
Chiya, who met a woman one night who was going to her daughter's home.
He wanted to rape her. She said to him: I beg of you, honor your Master and
do not sin by me. He left her and did not sin by her. He said: "There are
wicked men to whom it happens according to the deeds of the righteous: I
said that this also is vanity," meaning that vanity becomes powerful by the
righteous to whom it happens according to the deeds of the wicked, yet they
do not sin. Similarly, it becomes powerful by the wicked to whom it
happens according to the deeds of the righteous, and they do fulfill them.

173. דְּתָנֵינָן עָבֵד קוּדְשָׁא בְּרִיךְ הוּא צַדִּיקִים וּרְשָׁעִים בְּעָלְמָא. וְכַמָּה
דְּאִתְיָיקַר אִיהוּ בְּעָלְמָא, בְּעוֹבְדֵי דְּצַדִּיקַיָּא, הָכִי נָמֵי אִתְיָיקַר אִיהוּ
בְּרַשִּׁיעַיָּיא, כַּד עַבְדֵי עוֹבָדֵי טָבָא בְּעָלְמָא. כְּמָה דְּאַתְּ אָמַר, אֶת הַכֹּל
עָשָׂה יָפֶה בְעִתּוֹ. וַוי לַחַיָּיבָא, כַּד עָבֵיד גַּרְמֵיה רַע, וְאִתְתְּקַף בְּחוֹבֵיה,
כְּמָה דְּאַתְּ אָמַר, אוֹי לְרָשָׁע רָע וְגוֹ'.

173. For we have learned, the Holy One, blessed be He, has made righteous
and wicked people in the world. Just as He is honored in the world by the
actions of the righteous, so He is honored by the wicked when they do good
actions in the world. As is written: "He has made every thing beautiful in its
time" (Kohelet 3:11). Woe to the wicked when he does evil to himself and
strengthens in his sins, as it is written: "Alas! it shall be ill with the
wicked..." (Yeshayah 3:11).

174. תּוּ פָּתַח וְאָמַר, אֶת הַכֹּל רָאִיתִי בִּימֵי הֶבְלִי וְגוֹ'. הַאי קְרָא אוּף
הָכִי אוּקְמוּהָ חַבְרַיָּיא, אֲבָל כַּד אִתְיְהִיב חָכְמָה לִשְׁלֹמֹה, חָמָא כּוּלָּא,
בְּזִמְנָא דְּשַׁלְטָא סִיהֲרָא, יֵשׁ צַדִּיק דָּא עַמּוּדָא דְּעָלְמָא. אוֹבֵד: כד"א,
הַצַּדִּיק אָבָד, בְּזִמְנָא דְּגָלוּתָא בְּצִדְקוֹ: בְּגִין דְּהִיא שְׁכִיבַת לְעַפְרָא, צֶדֶק
דָּא, כָּל זִמְנָא דְּיִשְׂרָאֵל בְּגָלוּתָא, אִיהִי עִמְּהוֹן בְּגָלוּתָא, וּבְגִין כָּךְ,
צַדִּיק אוֹבֵד בְּצִדְקוֹ. דְּהָא לָא מָטָאן לְגַבֵּיה אִינּוּן בִּרְכָּאן עִלָּאִין.

18. Righteous men to whom it happens according to the deeds of the wicked

174. Again, he opened the discussion saying: "All things have I seen in the days of my vanity..." (Kohelet 7:15). This passage was also explained by the friends. When wisdom was granted to Solomon, he saw everything when the moon reigned, WHICH IS NUKVA WHEN SHE IS FULL, BECAUSE SOLOMON RECEIVED FROM HER. "There is a just man." This is the pillar of the world, MEANING THE FOUNDATION THAT THE WORLD STANDS UPON is lost, as is written: "The righteous perishes" (Yeshayah 57:1) at the time of exile, WHEN HE CAN NOT BESTOW ABUNDANCE ON ANYONE AND IS CONSIDERED AS LOST. "In his righteousness," REFERS TO THE NUKVA THAT IS CALLED 'RIGHTEOUSNESS', because when she lies on the dust, THE RIGHTEOUS MAN HAS NO ONE UPON WHOM TO BESTOW ABUNDANCE, AND THEREFORE HE IS LOST IN HIS RIGHTEOUSNESS. As long as Yisrael are in exile, righteousness is with them in exile, and therefore, "there is a just man who perishes in his righteousness" (Kohelet 7:15), because the supernal blessings do not reach him.

175. וְיֵשׁ רָשָׁע מַאֲרִיךְ בְּרָעָתוֹ, דָּא סמאל, דְּאוֹרִיךְ שֶׁקֶט וְשַׁלְוָה לֶאֱדוֹם, בְּמַאי בְּרָעָתוֹ. בְּהַהִיא רָעָה אִתְּתֵיהּ, נָחָשׁ תַּקִּיפָא, דְּהָא לָא מָטָא עֲלַיְיהוּ שֶׁקֶט וְשַׁלְוָה, אֶלָּא בְּגִין דְּאִתְדַּבַּק בְּהַהִיא נוּקְבָּא. כְּגַוְונָא דָּא לִשְׁאַר מַלְכְּוָון, עַד דְּקוּדְשָׁא בְּרִיךְ הוּא יָקִים מֵעַפְרָא, לְהַהִיא סוּכַּת דָּוִד הַנּוֹפֶלֶת, דִּכְתִיב אָקִים אֶת סֻכַּת דָּוִד הַנֹּפָלֶת.

175. "And there is a wicked man who prolongs his life in his wickedness" (Ibid.). This is Samael who prolongs the quiet and tranquillity to Edom. How does he do this? By "his wickedness," BECAUSE HE IS WICKED, AND HIS WIFE IS CALLED 'WICKEDNESS', for she is a strong serpent. For they receive quiet and tranquility only because SAMAEL cleaves to that female, AND HIS FEMALE GIVES THEM THIS. Similarly, he supplies the other kings, THAT YISRAEL ARE IN EXILE AMONG THEM. This is until the Holy One, blessed be He, raises the fallen tabernacle of David, WHICH IS THE NUKVA WHO IS FALLEN DURING EXILE, as is written: "I will raise the tabernacle of David that is fallen" (Amos 9:11).

19. "And there went a man of the house of Levi"

A Synopsis

Rabbi Yosi begins the discussion with an interpretation of the verse, "My beloved has gone down to His garden…" We learn that this is a reference to the children of Yisrael, who are filled with the fragrance of the World to Come. The righteous souls that inhabit the lower Garden of Eden, which emit a fragrance when God descends into this place, belong to those who lived in this world or who will someday descend to dwell there. These souls have the outward form that was or will be their likeness on earth, and the impression of the spirit is engraved within. When the spirit leaves the body, it returns to the Garden in the form of the body it wore in this world because the spirit is like a seal, an inward engraving that produces an outward protrusion. The discussion then turns to the meaning of the title verse. This, we're told, is a reference to Gabriel, who is also called 'Night', and his relationship to the souls of the Righteous. Gabriel takes the soul from the Garden and delivers it to the body of the righteous at the time of birth, and he guards it. Another explanation of the title verse interprets it as a reference to Amran, who was told by a celestial voice to marry Jochebed because their son would bring the time of the redemption of Yisrael closer. When they united, the Shechinah was with them and She never ceased to cleave to their son, Moses. Jochebed saw that "he was a goodly son," because when he was born he was marked with the sign of the Covenant (he was born circumcised), and the house was filled with light.

The Relevance of the Passage

The Light of Binah, known as the World to Come, now illuminates our souls. Binah's Light represents immortality and infinite joy. Thus, the power of this passage triggers the demise of the Angel of Death, generating a reality of deathlessness in a world of peace and contentment. The fragrances of the Garden of Eden emanate from our soul and all the righteous souls in history join with us in eternal unification.

The power of Moses ignites to commence and seal our final Redemption, unifying this world with the Divine Presence called Shechinah. This wondrous effect is achieved through the purifying Light that is aroused through the ritual known as circumcision. All negative forces are hereby cut off eternally from our world.

176. וַיֵּלֶךְ אִישׁ מִבֵּית לֵוִי. רִבִּי יוֹסֵי פָּתַח דּוֹדִי יָרַד לְגַנּוֹ לַעֲרוּגוֹת הַבּוֹשֶׂם וְגוֹ'. לְגַנּוֹ: דָּא כְּנֶסֶת יִשְׂרָאֵל, בְּגִין דְּהִיא עֲרוּגַת הַבּוֹשֶׂם,

דְּאִיהִי כְּלִילָא מִכָּל זִינֵי בּוּסְמִין וְרֵיחִין דְּעָלְמָא דְּאָתֵי. בְּשַׁעֲתָא
דְּקוּדְשָׁא בְּרִיךְ הוּא נָחִית לְגִנְתָּא דָא כָּל אִינּוּן נִשְׁמָתְהוֹן דְּצַדִּיקַיָּא,
מִתְעַטְּרָן תַּמָּן, כֻּלְּהוּ יַהֲבֵי רֵיחָא, כמד״א וְרֵיחַ שְׁמָנַיִךְ מִכָּל בְּשָׂמִים,
אִלֵּין אִינּוּן נִשְׁמָתְהוֹן דְּצַדִּיקַיָּא, דְּאָמַר רִבִּי יִצְחָק, כָּל אִינּוּן נִשְׁמָתִין
דְּצַדִּיקַיָּא, דַּהֲווֹ בְּהַאי עָלְמָא, וְכָל אִינּוּן נִשְׁמָתִין, דִּזְמִינִין לְנַחֲתָּא
לְהַאי עָלְמָא, כֻּלְּהוּ בְּגִנְתָּא דָא קַיְּימִין.

176. "And there went a man of the house of Levi" (Shemot 2:1). Rabbi Yosi opened the discussion saying: "My beloved is gone down to his garden to the bed of spices" (Shir Hashirm 6:2). His garden is the Congregation of Yisrael, WHICH IS THE NUKVA, because she is a "bed of spices," included with all kinds of spices and fragrances of the World to Come, WHICH IS BINAH. At the time that the Holy One, blessed be He, descends to this garden, WHICH IS THE NUKVA, all the souls of the righteous adorn themselves there, MEANING THAT THEY RECEIVE MOCHIN AND ILLUMINATIONS. They all exude fragrance, as is written: "The smell of your ointments than (or 'from') all spices" (Shir Hashirm 4:10). These are the souls of the righteous, WHO ARE CALLED 'SPICES', AND AFTER THEM, THE NUKVA IS CALLED 'A BED OF SPICES'. For Rabbi Yitzchak said: All these souls of the righteous who were in this world, and all the souls that will descend in the future to this world, are in this garden, WHICH IS THE NUKVA.

177. בְּגִנְתָּא דִי בְּאַרְעָא, כֻּלְּהוּ קַיְּימִין בְּדִיּוּקְנָא וְצִיּוּרָא דַּהֲווֹ קַיְּימִין
בְּהַאי עָלְמָא, וְסִתְרָא וְרָזָא דָא אִתְמְסַר לְחַכִּימֵי. רוּחָא דְּנָחִית לִבְנֵי
נָשָׁא, דְּאִיהוּ מִסִּטְרָא דְּנוּקְבָּא, מִתְגַּלְּפָא תָּדִיר בְּגִלּוּפָא כְּהַאי חוֹתָם.
צִיּוּרָא דְּגוּפָא דְּבַר נָשׁ בְּהַאי עָלְמָא, בָּלִיט לְבַר, וְרוּחָא אִתְגְּלִיף לְגוֹ.
כַּד אִתְפַּשַּׁט רוּחָא מִן גּוּפָא, הַהוּא רוּחַ בָּלִיט בְּגִנְתָּא דְּאַרְעָא, בְּצִיּוּרָא
וְדִיּוּקְנָא דְּגוּפֵיהּ מַמָּשׁ דִּבְהַאי עָלְמָא, בְּגִין דַּהֲוָה תָּדִיר כַּחוֹתָם.

177. In the terrestrial Garden of Eden, they all retain the form and image that they had in this world, and their secrets and mystery were given over to the sages. The spirit that descends to people, which is of the female side, is always engraved on like a seal, WHOSE LETTERS ARE ETCHED. This is because the form of the body in this world protrudes outward, and the spirit

is engraved internally. When the spirit removes itself from the body AND ASCENDS TO THE TERRESTRIAL GARDEN OF EDEN, that spirit protrudes in the terrestrial Garden of Eden in the form and shape of the body exactly as in this world, because it is always like a seal.

178. וְעַל דָּא אָמְרָה אִיהִי, שִׂימֵנִי כַחוֹתָם, מַה חוֹתָם גָּלִיף בְּגְלוּפָא לְגוֹ, וְאִתְצְיַיר בְּצִיּוּרָא בְּלִיטָא לְבַר. אוּף הָכִי אִיהִי רוּחָא, דַּהֲוָה מִסְטְרָא דִּילָה, כְּהַאי גַּוְונָא מַמָּשׁ בְּהַאי עָלְמָא, גָּלִיף בְּגְלוּפָא לְגוֹ, וְכַד אִתְפָּשַׁט מִן גּוּפָא, וְעָאל בְּגִנְתָא דְּאַרְעָא, אֲוִירָא דְּתַמָּן בָּלִיט הַהוּא גְּלוּפָא לְאִתְצַיְירָא לְבַר, וְאִתְצַיַּיר בְּצִיּוּרָא בְּלִיטָא לְבַר, כְּגַוְונָא דְּצִיּוּרָא דְּגוּפָא בְּהַאי עָלְמָא.

178. And therefore she said: "Set me as a seal" (Shir Hashirm 8:6). As a seal is engraved inwards, and THAT WHICH IS SEALED takes shape with an outward protruding form, so is the spirit that is from her side in that way exactly in this world; it is engraved inwards, AS WRITTEN EARLIER IN THE PREVIOUS VERSE. When it removes itself from the body and enters the terrestrial Garden of Eden, in the air there – MEANING THAT IT CLEAVES THERE TO ITS LEVEL, WHICH IS THE SPIRIT IN THE GARDEN OF EDEN PROTRUDING FROM THAT ENGRAVING WHICH IS INWARDS to assume a shape – it takes shape with a form that protrudes outwardly as the configuration of the body was in this world.

179. נִשְׁמָתָא, דְּאִיהִי מֵאִילָנָא דְּחַיָּיא, אִתְצַיַּיר תַּמָּן לְעֵילָא, בְּהַהוּא צְרוֹרָא דְּחַיֵּי, לְאִתְעַנְגָּא בְּנוֹעַם יְיָ', כְּמָה דְאַתְּ אָמֵר לַחֲזוֹת בְּנוֹעַם יְיָ' וּלְבַקֵּר בְּהֵיכָלוֹ.

179. The soul OF THE PERSON which is born of the Tree of Life, FROM ZEIR ANPIN, is formed there above in that bundle of life, WHICH IS MALCHUT, to delight in the beauty of Hashem, as is written: "To behold the beauty of Hashem, and to inquire in His temple" (Tehilim 27:4).

180. וַיֵּלֶךְ אִישׁ מִבֵּית לֵוִי, דָּא גַּבְרִיאֵל, כמד"א וְהָאִישׁ גַּבְרִיאֵל אֲשֶׁר רָאִיתִי בֶחָזוֹן וְגוֹ'. מִבֵּית לֵוִי: דָּא כנ"י, דְּאַתְיָא מִסְטְרָא דִּשְׂמָאלָא. וַיִּקַּח אֶת בַּת לֵוִי דָּא נִשְׁמָתָא.

180. "And there went a man of the house of Levi." This is Gabriel, as written: "And the man Gabriel whom I saw in a vision" (Daniel 9:21). The house of Levi is the Congregation of Yisrael, WHICH IS MALCHUT, that comes from the left side, BECAUSE GABRIEL IS FROM THE LEFT SIDE. "And took to wife a daughter of Levi" (Shemot 2:1); that is, the soul.

181. דְּתָנֵינָן, בְּשַׁעֲתָא דְּאִתְיְילִיד גּוּפָא דְּצַדִּיק, בְּהַאי עָלְמָא, קוּדְשָׁא בְּרִיךְ הוּא קָרֵי לֵיהּ לְגַבְרִיאֵל, וְנָטִיל הַהִיא נִשְׁמָתָא דִּי בְּגִנְתָּא, וְנַחְתָּא לָהּ לְהַאי גוּפָא דְּצַדִּיקַיָּא, דְּאִתְיְילִיד בְּהַאי עָלְמָא, וְאִיהִי אִתְפְּקַד עָלָהּ וְנָטִיר לָהּ.

181. For we have learned that at the time that the body of a righteous is born in this world, the Holy One, blessed be He, calls Gabriel. Gabriel takes that soul that is in the Garden, WHICH IS MALCHUT, and lowers it to the body of the righteous man who is born in this world, and he, GABRIEL, is appointed over it and guards it.

182. וְאִי תֵּימָא, הַהוּא מַלְאָכָא דְּאִתְמָנָא עַל רוּחֵיהוֹן דְּצַדִּיקַיָּא, לַיְלָה שְׁמֵיהּ, וְאַתְּ אַמְרַתְּ דְּאִיהוּ גַבְרִיאֵל. הָכִי הוּא וַדַּאי, בְּגִין דְּאָתֵי מִסִּטְרָא דִּשְׂמָאלָא, וְכָל מַאן דְּאָתֵי מִסִּטְרָא דִּשְׂמָאלָא הָכִי אִקְרֵי.

182. You may ask why the angel who is appointed over the spirits of the righteous is named 'Night', and yet you say that he is Gabriel? Most certainly HIS NAME IS NIGHT, because he comes from the left side and everything that comes from the left side is called 'NIGHT', BUT HIS NAME IS ACTUALLY GABRIEL.

183. וַיֵּלֶךְ אִישׁ: דָּא עַמְרָם. וַיִּקַּח אֶת בַּת לֵוִי: דָּא יוֹכֶבֶד. וּבַת קוֹל נַחְתַּת וְאָמְרַת לֵיהּ לְאִזְדַּוְּוגָא בָּהּ, דְּהָא קָרִיב זִמְנָא דְּפוּרְקָנָא דְּיִשְׂרָאֵל, עַל יְדָא דִּבְרָא דְּאִתְיְילִיד מִנַּיְיהוּ.

183. "And there went a man." This is Amran. "And took to wife a daughter of Levi." This is Jochebed. A heavenly voice came down and said to Amran that he should marry her because the time for the redemption of Yisrael is near, and it will come through the son that shall be born from them.

184. וְקוּדְשָׁא בְּרִיךְ הוּא סִיַּיע בֵּיה, דְּתָנֵינָן, שְׁכִינְתָּא שַׁרְיָא עַל
עַרְסַיְיהוּ וּרְעוּתָא דִּלְהוֹן בִּדְבֵקוּתָא חֲדָא, הֲוָה בָּה בִּשְׁכִינְתָּא, וע״ד, לָא
אִתְעֲדֵי שְׁכִינְתָּא, מֵהַהוּא בְּרָא דְּאוֹלִידוּ לְקַיְּימָא, דִּכְתִּיב וְהִתְקַדִּשְׁתֶּם
וִהְיִיתֶם קְדוֹשִׁים. ב״נ דִּמְקַדֵּשׁ גַּרְמֵיה מִלְּרַע, קוּדְשָׁא בְּרִיךְ הוּא מְקַדֵּשׁ
לֵיה לְעֵילָא, כְּמָה דִּרְעוּתָא דִּלְהוֹן הֲוָה בִּדְבֵקוּתָא דִּשְׁכִינְתָּא. הָכִי
אִתְדַּבְּקָא שְׁכִינְתָּא, בְּהַהוּא עוֹבָדָא מַמָּשׁ דְּעָבְדוּ.

184. And the Holy One, blessed be He, assisted him, for we learned the Shechinah dwelt on their bed and that their intention when they cleaved together was on the Shechinah. Therefore, the Shechinah was not removed from the son whom they bore, so as to fulfill what is written: "And you shall sanctify yourselves and you shall be holy" (Vayikra 11:44). A person sanctifies himself from below, so the Holy One, blessed be He, sanctifies him from above. As their intention was the cleaving of the Shechinah, so did the Shechinah cleave to their very actions.

185. א״ר יִצְחָק, זַכָּאִין אִינּוּן צַדִּיקַיָּא דִּרְעוּתָא דִּלְהוֹן בִּדְבֵקוּתָא
דְּקוּדְשָׁא בְּרִיךְ הוּא תָּדִיר, וְכְמָה דְּאִינּוּן מִתְדַּבְּקִין בֵּיה תָּדִיר, הָכִי נָמֵי
אִיהוּ אִתְדַּבָּק בְּהוּ, וְלָא שָׁבִיק לוֹן לְעָלְמִין. וַוי לְרַשִׁיעַיָּיא, דִּרְעוּתָא
דִּלְהוֹן, וּדְבֵקוּתָא דִּלְהוֹן, מִתְרַחֲקָא מִנֵּיה. וְלָא דִּי לְהוּ דְּמִתְרַחֲקָן
מִנֵּיה, אֶלָּא דְּמִתְדַּבְּקָן בְּסִטְרָא אַחֲרָא. תָּא חֲזֵי, עַמְרָם דְּאִתְדַּבָּק בֵּיה
בְּקוּדְשָׁא בְּרִיךְ הוּא. נָפַק מִנֵּיה מֹשֶׁה, דְּקוּדְשָׁא בְּרִיךְ הוּא לָא אַעֲדֵי
מִנֵּיה לְעָלְמִין, וּשְׁכִינְתָּא אִתְדַּבְּקַת בַּהֲדֵיה תָּדִיר, זַכָּאָה חוּלָקֵיה.

185. Rabbi Yitzchak said: Fortunate are the righteous, whose desire is to cleave to the Holy One, blessed be He, always. As they cleave to Him constantly, thus does He cleave to them and never leaves them. Woe to the wicked, that their desire and cleaving are far removed from Him, FROM THE HOLY ONE, BLESSED BE HE. For not only are they distanced from Him, but they also cleave to the Other Side, MEANING THE SIDE OF IMPURITY. Come and behold: from Amran who cleaved to the Holy One, blessed be He, Moses came. The Holy One, blessed be He, never turned from him, and the Shechinah cleaved to him always; thus, blessed is his lot.

186. וַתַּהַר הָאִשָּׁה וַתֵּלֶד בֵּן וַתֵּרֶא אוֹתוֹ כִּי טוֹב הוּא. מַאי כִּי טוֹב הוּא. אָמַר רִבִּי חִיָּיא, דְּאִתְיְלִיד מָהוּל. בְּגִין, דְּרָזָא דִּבְרִית, טוֹב אִקְרֵי, דִּכְתִּיב אִמְרוּ צַדִּיק כִּי טוֹב.

186. "And the woman conceived and she bore a son: and when she saw that he was a goodly son" (Shemot 2:2). HE ASKS: What is the meaning of, "that he was a goodly son"? Rabbi Chiya said: The meaning is that he was born circumcised, because the secret of the covenant is called 'good', as is written: "Say of the righteous, that it shall be well ('good') with him" (Yeshayah 3:10), AND THE RIGHTEOUS IS THE SECRET OF THE COVENANT.

187. רִבִּי יוֹסֵי אָמַר, נְהִירוּ דִּשְׁכִינְתָּא דְּנָהִיר בֵּיהּ חָמָאת, דִּבְשַׁעֲתָא דְּאִתְיְלִיד אִתְמַלְיָא כָּל בֵּיתָא נְהוֹרָא, דִּכְתִּיב וַתֵּרֶא אוֹתוֹ כִּי טוֹב הוּא, וּכְתִיב וַיַּרְא אֱלֹהִים אֶת הָאוֹר כִּי טוֹב. וְעַל דָּא כִּי טוֹב הוּא כְּתִיב, וְכֹלָּא הֲוָה.

187. Rabbi Yosi said: She saw the light of the Shechinah that shone in him. For at the time that he was born, the entire house was filled with light, as is written: "And when she saw that he was a goodly son," and, "Elohim saw the light that it was good" (Beresheet 1:4). AND AS GOOD ALLUDES TO LIGHT, SO HERE GOOD ALLUDES TO LIGHT. And hence it is written, "that he was a goodly son." Everything was included in him; HE CONTAINED THE LIGHT OF THE SHECHINAH, AND ALSO, AS WAS WRITTEN EARLIER, HE WAS BORN CIRCUMCISED.

20. "And she hid him three months"

A Synopsis
In his discussion of the title verse, Rabbi Yehuda explains the significance of "three months" and reveals that the "ark of papyrus" is an allusion to the Ark of the Covenant, while the "child" signifies Yisrael. Another explanation of the verse, "A man of the House of Levi" interprets this as a reference to God, Who went from the place where Aba and Ima (the supernal Mother and Father) unite as the Foundation.

The Relevance of the Passage
This passage draws the original primordial Light that illuminated Mount Sinai. This Light was so effulgent, it banished all darkness from the universe, including disease, discontent, and death itself. Our meditation serves to complete our keeping of the 613 precepts – the transformation of our Desire to Receive into the Desire to Receive for the Sake of Sharing.

We connect to the realm known as Yesod, which is alluded to by the creature known as Leviathan or whale, which represents immeasurable joy in our life, in our world. This joy is the Shechinah, the Divine Presence, which means we are now, in this moment, united with the Shechinah forevermore.

The three Hebrew months known as Tamuz, Av, and Tevet are windows through which severe judgment flow into our word. These windows are now permanently shut. Judgment can no longer affect us personally, or any part of humanity.

The colors of Light that shimmer in our reading banish demons and all evil forces from this world.

The Zohar teaches us that our physical dimension corresponds to the Hebrew letter Hei ה and the supernal world above is denoted by the letter Vav ו.

The letter Hei ה spelled out alphabetically is Hei-Aleph הא. Vav ו spelled out alphabetically is Vav-Aleph-Vav ואו.

The letters Vav-Aleph-Vav ואו and Hei-Aleph הא appear in this passage to ignite and seal our unification with the Upper World.

Moreover, these letters ensure that we are redeemed in a process that embodies compassion and sweetness.

188. וַתִּצְפְּנֵהוּ שְׁלֹשָׁה יְרָחִים, ג' יְרָחִים מַאי קָא מַיְירֵי. אָמַר ר'

יְהוּדָה, רֶמֶז הוּא דְּקָא רָמַז, דְּלָא אִשְׁתְּמוֹדַע מֹשֶׁה בְּזֹהֲרָא עִלָּאָה, עַד
ג' יְרָחִים. דִּכְתִּיב בַּחֹדֶשׁ הַשְּׁלִישִׁי, דְּהָא כְּדֵין אִתְיְהִיבַת תּוֹרָה עַל יְדוֹי,
וּשְׁכִינְתָּא אִתְגַּלְיָא, וְשַׁרְיָא עֲלוֹי לְעֵינֵיהוֹן דְּכֹלָּא, דִּכְתִּיב וּמֹשֶׁה עָלָה
אֶל הָאֱלֹהִים וַיִּקְרָא אֵלָיו יְיָ', וְלֹא יָכְלָה עוֹד הַצְּפִינוֹ, דְּעַד הַהוּא
שַׁעְתָּא, לָא אִשְׁתְּמוֹדַע מִלּוּלֵיהּ בְּקוּדְשָׁא ב"ה, וּכְתִיב מֹשֶׁה יְדַבֵּר
וְהָאֱלֹהִים יַעֲנֶנּוּ בְקוֹל.

188. "And she hid him three months" (Shemot 2:2). HE ASKS: What is the
significance of three months? Rabbi Yehuda said: It is an allusion to THE
VIRTUE OF Moses not being recognized by the supernal radiance for three
months, as is written: "In the third month" (Shemot 19:1). For then the
Torah was given through him, and the Shechinah was revealed and dwelt
upon him before everyone's eyes, as is written: "And Moses went up to the
Elohim, and the Hashem called to him" (Ibid. 3). THIS IS WHAT IS WRITTEN:
"And when she could no longer hide him" (Shemot 2:3). For until that time,
his communication with the Holy One, blessed be He, was not known. And
then it is written: "Moses speaks, and the Elohim answers him by a voice"
(Shemot 19:19).

189. וַתִּקַּח לוֹ תֵּבַת גּוֹמֶא, רֶמֶז עַל הָאָרוֹן, דְּלוּחוֹת קַיְימָא עָאלִין
בְּגַוֵּיהּ, תֵּיבַת גּוֹמֶא, אֲרוֹן הַבְּרִית אִיהוּ. וַתַּחְמְרָה בַחֵמָר וּבַזָּפֶת דְּהָא
הָאָרוֹן הֲוָה מְחוּפֶּה מִלְּגָו וּמִלְּבַר. רִבִּי יְהוּדָה אָמַר, דָּא הִיא אוֹרַיְיתָא,
דְּהֶחֱמִירָה קוּדְשָׁא בְּרִיךְ הוּא בְּמִצְוֹת עֲשֵׂה וּבְמִצְוֹת לֹא תַּעֲשֶׂה.

189. "She took for him a box (lit. 'ark') made of papyrus" (Shemot 2:3).
This is an allusion to the ark in which the tablets of the covenant came. "An
ark made of papyrus" is the Ark of the Covenant. "And daubed it with slime
clay and with pitch," because the ark was overlaid inside and out. Rabbi
Yehuda said: This is the Torah that the Holy One, blessed be He, inscribed
with positive commandments and negative commandments.

190. וַתָּשֶׂם בָּהּ אֶת הַיֶּלֶד, אֵלּוּ יִשְׂרָאֵל, כד"א כִּי נַעַר יִשְׂרָאֵל וָאֹהֲבֵהוּ.
וַתָּשֶׂם בַּסּוֹף דְּלָא הֲווֹ פְּקוּדֵי אוֹרַיְיתָא חוּמְרָא לְמֶעְבַּד, עַד סוֹף, דְּעָאלוּ
יִשְׂרָאֵל לְאַרְעָא, לְסוֹף אַרְבְּעִין שְׁנִין. עַל שְׂפַת הַיְאֹר: עַל מֵימְרָא
דְּאִינּוּן דְּמוֹרִים אוֹרַיְיתָא וְחוּקָה לְיִשְׂרָאֵל.

190. "…and put the child in it…" (Ibid. 3). These are Yisrael, as is said: "When Yisrael was still a youth, I loved him" (Hoshea 11:1). "And she laid it in the rushes (Heb. *suf*)" (Ibid.), so there was no obligation to perform the commandments of the Torah until the end (Heb. *sof*), when Yisrael came to the land at the end of forty years. "…by the river's brink (Heb. *safah*)…" meaning according to the speech of those who teach Torah and laws to Yisrael. BECAUSE THE WORD "*SAFAH*" IS LIKE THE WORD 'LANGUAGE' (HEB. *SAFAH*) AND SPEECH, AND THE WORD "*YEOR*" ('RIVER') HAS THE MEANING OF *MOREH* ('TEACHER').

191. ד"א וַיֵּלֶךְ אִישׁ, דָּא קוּדְשָׁא בְּרִיךְ הוּא, דִּכְתִּיב יְיָ' אִישׁ מִלְחָמָה. מִבֵּית לֵוִי, דָּא קוּדְשָׁא בְּרִיךְ הוּא, אֲתָר דְּחָכְמָה עִלָּאָה, וְהַהוּא נָהָר, מִתְחַבְּרָן כַּחֲדָא, וְלָא מִתְפָּרְשִׁין לְעָלְמִין. מִבֵּית לֵוִי דְּאַשְׁרֵי לְוְיָתָן לְחִידוּ בְּעָלְמָא, הה"ד, לִוְיָתָן זֶה יָצַרְתָּ לְשַׂחֶק בּוֹ. וַיִּקַּח אֶת בַּת לֵוִי, דָּא קוּדְשָׁא בְּרִיךְ הוּא, אֲתָר דְּנָהִירוּ דְּסִיהֲרָא נָהִיר.

191. Another explanation: "A man," refers to the Holy One, blessed be He, as is written: "Hashem is a Man of war" (Shemot 15:3). "Of the house of Levi," refers to the Holy One, blessed be He, WHO WENT FROM the place where the supernal Chochmah, THIS BEING SUPERNAL ABA, and that river, WHICH IS SUPERNAL IMA, join together and never separate. HE WENT FROM THE PLACE OF THE YESOD OF SUPERNAL ABA AND IMA. "Of the house of Levi" IS DERIVED FROM THE WORD *LEVIATHAN*, MEANING YESOD; He caused the *Leviathan* (lit. 'whale') to dwell in this world to bring joy into the world, WHICH IS THE SHECHINAH. It is written: "There is the Leviathan, whom You have made to play therein" (Tehilim 104:26). "And took to wife a daughter of Levi." This is the Holy One, blessed be He, MEANING the place where the light of the moon illuminates, WHICH IS THE SHECHINAH.

192. וַתַּהַר הָאִשָּׁה וַתֵּלֶד בֵּן. הָאִשָּׁה וַדַּאי, כד"א לְזֹאת יִקָּרֵא אִשָּׁה. בְּקַדְמֵיתָא בַּת לֵוִי, וְהָכִי הוּא וַדַּאי, וְכִי בַּת לֵוִי בְּקַדְמֵיתָא, וְהַשְׁתָּא אִשָּׁה. אֶלָּא הָכִי הוּא וַדַּאי, וְהָכִי אוֹלִיפְנָא, אִתְּתָא עַד לָא אִזְדַּוְּוגַת, אִתְקְרִיאַת בַּת פְּלוֹנִי, בָּתַר דְּאִזְדַּוְּוגַת אִתְקְרִיאַת אִשָּׁה. וְהָכָא, בַּת, וְאִשָּׁה, וְכַלָּה, חַד דַּרְגָּא אִיהוּ.

192. "And the woman conceived, and bore a son." The woman, MEANING THE SHECHINAH IS most certainly CALLED A 'WOMAN', as is written: "She shall be called woman" (Beresheet 2:23), AND "THIS" IS THE NAME OF THE SHECHINAH. Originally she was a daughter of Levi, WHICH IS YESOD OF ABA AND IMA THAT IS CALLED 'LEVIATHAN', AS MENTIONED EARLIER, and it is certainly so, AS ABA AND IMA BUILT THE NUKVA. THEREFORE, HE ASKS: Originally she was a daughter of Levi and now she is a woman? AND HE ANSWERS: It is certainly so, as we have learned, that a woman is called the daughter of so and so before she marries, MEANING BY THE NAME OF HER FATHER AND MOTHER. After she marries, she is called a woman BY HER OWN NAME and here, daughter, woman and bride, are all one level, MEANING THE SHECHINAH.

193. וַתִּצְפְּנֵהוּ שְׁלֹשָׁה יְרָחִים. אִלֵּין תְּלַת יַרְחִין, דְּדִינָא קַשְׁיָא שַׁרְיָא בְּעָלְמָא וּמַאי נִינְהוּ. תַּמּוּז, אָב, טֵבֵת, מַאי מַשְׁמַע. דְּעַד לָא נָחַת מֹשֶׁה לְעָלְמָא, שְׁכִיחַ הֲוָה אִיהוּ לְעֵילָּא, וְעַל דָּא אִזְדַּוְּוגַת בֵּיהּ שְׁכִינְתָּא, מִיּוֹמָא דְּאִתְיְלִיד. מִכָּאן אָמַר רַבִּי שִׁמְעוֹן, רוּחֵיהוֹן דְּצַדִּיקַיָּא, שְׁכִיחִין אִינּוּן לְעֵילָּא, עַד לָא יֶחֱתוּן לְעָלְמָא.

193. "She hid him three months" (Shemot 2:2). These are the three months in which Severe Judgment is prevalent in the world. And which are they? THEY ARE *Tamuz*, *Av*, and *Tevet* IN WHICH THERE IS NO REVELATION OF THE SHECHINAH BECAUSE OF THE JUDGMENTS IN THE WORLD. HE ASKS: What is he trying to tell us? AND HE ANSWERS THAT HE IS TELLING US THAT before Moses descended to this world, he was above WITH THE SHECHINAH. Therefore, the Shechinah joined with him from the day he was born. From this Rabbi Shimon derived that the spirits of the righteous were above IN THE GARDEN OF EDEN before they descended into this world.

194. וְלֹא יָכְלָה עוֹד הַצְּפִינוֹ וְגו'. מַאי וַתִּקַּח לוֹ תֵּבַת גֹּמֶא. דְּחָפַת לֵיהּ בְּסִימָנָהָא, לְמֶחֱוֵי נָטִיר מֵאִינּוּן נוּנֵי יַמָּא, דְּשָׁאטִין בְּיַמָּא רַבָּא, דִּכְתִּיב שָׁם רֶמֶשׂ וְאֵין מִסְפָּר. וְהִיא חָפַת לֵיהּ, לְמֶחֱוֵי נָטִיר מִנַּיְיהוּ, בְּחָפוּ יַקִּירָא, דִּתְרֵין גַּוְונִין חִוָּור וְאוּכָם, וְאָנַח לֵיהּ לְמֹשֶׁה בֵּינַיְיהוּ, דְּיִשְׁתְּמוֹדַע עִמְּהוֹן, בְּגִין דִּזְמִין לְסַלְּקָא בֵּינַיְיהוּ זִמְנָא אַחֲרָא, לְקַבְּלָא אוֹרַיְיתָא.

194. "And when she could no longer hide him..." (Ibid. 3). HE ASKS: What is the meaning of, "She took for him a box made of papyrus"? HE ANSWERS: She covered him with signs, so that he should be protected from the fish that swam in the Great Sea, MEANING KLIPOT AND DEMONS, as is written: "Where there are creeping things innumerable" (Tehilim 104:25). She covered him, to be guarded against them, with a precious cover of two colors, white and black. THE SLIME IS WHITE, WHICH IS THE SECRET OF THE RIGHT COLUMN, AND THE PITCH IS BLACK, WHICH IS THE SECRET OF THE LEFT COLUMN THAT IS MIXED WITH MALCHUT OF THE ATTRIBUTE OF JUDGMENT. THEN THE RED IN IT CONVERTS TO BLACK, WHICH IS THE SECRET OF OUR SAGES – THAT BLACK IS REALLY RED THAT HAS BEEN AFFECTED. And she placed Moses, WHO IS THE SECRET OF THE CENTRAL COLUMN, among them so that he should be recognized with them AS THE SECRET OF DA'AT WHICH IS THE CENTRAL COLUMN, because he was going to ascend among them at a different time, to receive the Torah.

195. וַתֵּרֶד בַּת פַּרְעֹה לִרְחוֹץ עַל הַיְאוֹר. דָּא אִיהִי דְּאַתְיָא מִסִּטְרָא דִּשְׂמָאלָא דְּדִינָא קַשְׁיָא, כְּמָה דְּאַתְּ אָמַר, לִרְחוֹץ עַל הַיְאוֹר, עַל הַיְאוֹר דַּיְיקָא, וְלֹא עַל הַיָּם.

195. "And the daughter of Pharaoh came down to wash herself at the river" (Shemot 2:5). This DAUGHTER OF PHARAOH came from the left side of the Strict Judgment as is written: "To wash herself at the river" – in the river and not in the sea. THE SEA ALLUDES TO MALCHUT OF HOLINESS, BUT THE RIVER IS THE ATTRIBUTE OF STRICT JUDGMENT OF THE LEFT SIDE. AND THE EGYPTIANS MADE IT THEIR IDOL, AND SINCE THE DAUGHTER OF PHARAOH BATHED THERE, SHE WAS ALSO OF STRICT JUDGMENT.

196. וְאִי תֵּימָא, וְהָא כְּתִיב, וּמַטְּךָ אֲשֶׁר הִכִּיתָ בּוֹ אֶת הַיְאוֹר, וּמֹשֶׁה לָא מָחָא אֶלָּא יַמָּא, וְקַרְיֵיהּ יְאוֹר. אֶלָּא יְאוֹר הֲוָה דְּמָחָא אַהֲרֹן ע"י דְּמֹשֶׁה, וְשַׁוְיֵיהּ קְרָא דְּאִיהוּ עָבִיד.

196. And you may ask why, then, it is written: "And your rod, with which you smote the river" (Shemot 17:5). Moses smote only the sea, which THE VERSE also calls a 'river'. SO THE TERM 'RIVER' IS NOT PRECISE. AND HE ANSWERS: Aaron smote the river through Moses, and the verse considers it as though he himself did it.

.197 כה"ג, וַיִּמָּלֵא שִׁבְעַת יָמִים אַחֲרֵי הַכּוֹת ה' אֶת הַיְאוֹר. וְאַהֲרֹן הִכָּהוּ. אֶלָּא עַל דְּאָתָא מִסִּטְרָא דְּקוּדְשָׁא בְּרִיךְ הוּא, קָרֵיהּ קְרָא אַחֲרֵי הַכּוֹת ה', לְבָתַר קָרֵייהּ בִּשְׁמָא דְּמֹשֶׁה. וְנַעֲרוֹתֶיהָ הוֹלְכוֹת עַל יַד הַיְאוֹר, אִלֵּין שְׁאַר מַשִּׁרְיָין דְּאַתְיָין מִסִּטְרָא דָּא.

197. Similarly, it is written: "And seven days were completed, after Hashem had smitten the river" (Shemot 7:25), even though Aaron smote it. But since it came from the Holy One, blessed be He, the Torah refers to it as, "after Hashem smote." Thus, afterwards it is called in the name of Moses, BECAUSE AARON DID IT AT HIS INSTRUCTION. "And her maidens walked along by the river's side" (Shemot 2:5), are the other companies who came from that side OF THE RIVER.

.198 וַתִּפְתַּח וַתִּרְאֵהוּ אֶת הַיֶּלֶד. וַתִּרְאֵהוּ וַתֵּרֶא מִבָּעֵי לֵיהּ. מַאי וַתִּרְאֵהוּ. אָמַר רִבִּי שִׁמְעוֹן, לֵית לָךְ מִלָּה בְּאוֹרַיְיתָא, דְּלֵית בָּהּ רָזִין עִלָּאִין וְיַקִּירִין. אֶלָּא הָכִי אוֹלִיפְנָא, רְשִׁימָא דְּמַלְכָּא וּמַטְרוֹנִיתָא אִשְׁתְּכַח בֵּיהּ, וְאִיהוּ רְשִׁימָא דְּוָא"ו הֵ"א. וּמִיַּד וַתַּחְמֹל עָלָיו וְגוֹ'. עַד כָּאן לְעֵילָּא, מִכָּאן וּלְהָלְאָה לְתַתָּא, בַּר מֵהַאי קְרָא.

198. "And when she had opened it, she saw (him,) the child" (Ibid. 6). HE ASKS: It is written: "She saw him," but it should say 'she saw'. Why, then, does it state: "She saw him?" Rabbi Shimon said: There is nothing in the Torah that does not have supernal and precious secrets. For this is what we learned, that the mark of the King and Queen, MEANING TIFERET AND MALCHUT, are found in him. It is the mark of Vav- Hei; FOR VAV IS TIFERET AND HEI IS MALCHUT. THEREFORE IT SAYS, "SHE SAW HIM (HEB. TIR'EHU)"; WHICH IS SPELLED WITH EXTRA VAV AND HEI. Immediately, WHEN SHE SAW THIS, "she had compassion on him" (Ibid.). Until this point, the Torah talks about THE SUPERNAL WORLDS above. From here and further, it talks about THE WORLDS below, except for this verse: "AND HIS SISTER STOOD ..." (Ibid. 4).

21. "And his sister stood afar off"

A Synopsis
Initially, a discussion of the title verse identifies "his sister" as the children of Yisrael, from whom Zeir Anpin is concealed at a distance. The discussion then turns to reinforce the idea that the Righteous, and especially Moses, are known above before they descend to this world, and their souls are drawn from a high place. We learn that just as the body has both a mother and father, the soul also has a mother and father. Indeed, everything above and below is produced by a male and a female. Finally, a further interpretation of the title verse reveals that, "And his sister stood," is lower Wisdom, which would stand "afar off" when Judgment accused Yisrael for their sins. Then the Shechinah distanced Herself from them too.

The Relevance of the Passage
Each of us contains a spark of divinity, a portion of our soul that is truly Righteous. Here we connect to the ultimate root of our soul, to the innermost depth and highest grade. All the souls of the Righteous above, and those among us, impregnate us in this moment, to elevate us to the highest possible level. We become one.

We learn that the Shechinah, the Divine Presence, distances itself from this world each time we behave with any form of reactivity, including intolerance, anger, envy, impatience, greed, selfishness, and the like.

These verses reconnect us to this Divine Light so that it is no longer far off, but rather near to us, one with us, at all times and without end.

199. וַתֵּתַצַּב אֲחוֹתוֹ מֵרָחוֹק וְגוֹ'. וַתֵּתַצַּב אֲחוֹתוֹ, אֲחוֹתוֹ דְּמַאן. אֲחוֹתֵיהּ, דְּהַהוּא דְּקָרָא לִכְנֶסֶת יִשְׂרָאֵל אֲחוֹתִי. כְּמָה דְאַתְּ אָמֵר, פִּתְחִי לִי אֲחוֹתִי רַעְיָתִי. מֵרָחוֹק: כְּמָה דְאַתְּ אָמַר מֵרָחוֹק ה' נִרְאָה לִי.

199. "And his sister stood afar off..." (Shemot 2:4). HE ASKS: Whose sister? AND HE ANSWERS: The sister of he who called the Congregation of Yisrael "my sister," MEANING ZEIR ANPIN, as is said: "Open to me my sister, my love" (Shir Hashirm 5:2) – MEANING THE SHECHINAH STOOD BY MOSES TO GUARD HIM. "Afar off" is as is written: "Hashem appeared of old (also: 'from afar') to me" (Yirmeyah 31:2), MEANING THAT KEEPING IS NOT IN THE OPEN, BUT RATHER HIDDEN, FROM A DISTANCE.

200. מַשְׁמַע, דְּאִינּוּן זַכָּאִין, עַד לָא נַחְתּוּ לְעָלְמָא, אִשְׁתְּמוֹדְעָאן אִינּוּן

לְעֵילָּא, לְגַבֵּי כֹּלָּא, וְכָל שֶׁכֵּן מֹשֶׁה. וּמַשְׁמַע נָמֵי, דְּנִשְׁמָתֵהוֹן
דְּצַדִּיקַיָּא, אִתְמְשָׁכוּ מֵאֲתַר עִלָּאָה, כְּמָה דְּאוֹקִימְנָא. וְרָזָא דְּמִלָּה
אוֹלִיפְנָא, דְּמַשְׁמַע, דְּאָב וָאֵם אִית לְנִשְׁמָתָא, כְּמָה דְּאִית אָב וָאֵם
לְגוּפָא בְּאַרְעָא, וּמַשְׁמַע, דְּבְכָל סִטְרִין, בֵּין לְעֵילָּא, בֵּין לְתַתָּא, מִדְּכַר
וְנוּקְבָּא אִתְיָין כֹּלָּא וּמִשְׁתַּכְחֵי. וְהָא אוּקְמוּהָ רָזָא, דִּכְתִיב, תּוֹצֵא
הָאָרֶץ נֶפֶשׁ חַיָּה. הָאָרֶץ: דָּא כְּנֶסֶת יִשְׂרָאֵל. נֶפֶשׁ חַיָּה: נַפְשָׁא דְּאָדָם
קַדְמָאָה עִלָּאָה, כְּמָה דְּאִתְּמַר. אָתָא רַבִּי אַבָּא וּנְשָׁקֵיה. אָמַר וַדַּאי
שַׁפִּיר קָאֲמַרְתְּ, וְהָכִי הוּא וַדַּאי זַכָּאָה חוּלָקֵיה דְּמֹשֶׁה נְבִיאָה מְהֵימְנָא,
עַל כָּל שְׁאַר נְבִיאֵי עָלְמָא.

200. It seems that the righteous are known above before their descent to the world; this refers to all THE RIGHTEOUS, and all the more so to Moses. THEREFORE IT IS SAID OF HIM, "SHE SAW HIM" (SHEMOT 2:6) SPELLED WITH *HEI-VAV*, WHICH IS THE SECRET OF THE IMPRESSION MADE BY THE KING AND THE QUEEN, AS ALREADY MENTIONED. And it is also understood that the souls of the righteous are drawn from a high place, as we explained IN THE PASSAGE: "AND THERE WENT A MAN OF THE HOUSE OF LEVI" (IBID. 1) – WHICH IS THE SECRET OF YESOD OF CHOCHMAH AND BINAH, WHICH IS A HIGH PLACE. The secret of this is what we learned from here: that the soul has a father and a mother, WHICH ARE ZEIR ANPIN AND THE NUKVA, BECAUSE MAN IS ZEIR ANPIN AND THE DAUGHTER OF LEVI IS THE NUKVA. Similarly, there is a father and mother to the body on earth. And it appears that in all aspects, whether above or below, everything comes forth from a male and a female, and we have explained the secret of the passage: "Let the earth bring forth living creatures" (Beresheet 1:24). "The earth," refers to the Congregation of Yisrael, WHO IS NUKVA. "Living creatures" (lit. 'soul'), is the soul of Adam, as we explained – BECAUSE ZEIR ANPIN AND NUKVA ARE FATHER AND MOTHER OF THE FIRST MAN, AS WE EXPLAINED. Rabbi Aba came and kissed him. He said: Assuredly, you are speaking beautifully and it is definitely so. Fortunate is the portion of Moses, the faithful prophet, above all the other prophets of the world.

201. ד"א וַתֵּתַצַּב אֲחוֹתוֹ דָּא הִיא חָכְמָה, כְּמָה דְּאַתְּ אָמַר, אֱמוֹר
לַחָכְמָה אֲחוֹתִי אָתְּ. אָמַר רַבִּי יִצְחָק, מֵעוֹלָם לָא אִתְעֲדִיאַת גְּזֵרַת דִּינָא

מֵעָלְמָא, דְּהָא בְּכָל שַׁעֲתָא דְּהֲווּ יִשְׂרָאֵל חָטָאן, הֲוָה דִּינָא מְקַטְרְגָא
עִמְּהוֹן, וּכְדֵין, וַתֵּתַצַּב אֲחוֹתוֹ מֵרָחוֹק. כְּמָה דְאַתְּ אָמַר מֵרָחוֹק ה'
נִרְאָה לִי.

201. "And his sister stood." This is Chochmah, THE NUKVA THAT IS
CALLED THE 'LOWER CHOCHMAH'. As is said: "Say to wisdom, 'You are
my sister" (Mishlei 7:4). Rabbi Yitzchak said: The decree of Judgment was
never removed from the world. For every time that Yisrael sinned,
Judgment accused them, and then "his sister stood afar off." FOR THE
SHECHINAH DISTANCED HERSELF FROM THEM, as is said: "Hashem
appeared from afar to me."

22. "And the daughter of Pharaoh came down"

A Synopsis

The opening discussion of the title verse reveals that it contains an allusion to the attribute of Judgment that comes down to bathe in the blood of Yisrael when they separate from and neglect the Torah. Rabbi Yehuda then speaks about the importance of repentance and prayer, especially prayer accompanied by weeping. The Shechinah stands over Yisrael and argues their merits. When She saw the children of Yisrael repent before God with tearful supplications, She had great compassion for them and considered them as gentle and good in contrast to the other stubborn and hard-hearted nations.

Rabbi Yitzchak then reiterates the concept that the redemption of Yisrael depends on weeping. We learn that the tears Esau wept before his father over his lost birthright brought Yisrael into captivity. When the force of Esau's tears is exhausted, the redemption of Yisrael will arrive.

The Relevance of the Passage

When a man succumbs to his Evil Inclination – his impulsive, reactive desires that gratify himself alone – he severs his connection to the Light of the Creator. The result is darkness and judgment.

We learn that genuine tears of remorse can atone for our failures and our misdeeds incited by our own selfishness, because the Zohar states that "there is no gate that these tears can not enter."

As we awaken remorse now, tears of Light flow to the highest supernal dimensions to wash away harsh judgments, severe verdicts, and deadly decrees set forth against us and against the world.

These tears now soften even the hardest of hearts. They soften our own hearts and the hearts of our enemies.

The love and tears that a mother sheds for her children is, perhaps, the strongest force of energy and love in the universe.

Rachel, the mother of all the world's children, weeps for us now, for our pain, for our suffering, for our self-imposed exile from the Creator. Upon her merit, we are Redeemed, everlastingly.

The love of a mother stirs and inspires. As we draw this unconditional flow of love to our souls now, we are enlightened and thus motivated to emulate constantly the ways of our Creator, which is to express unending care and concern for others.

Our exile is ended. Tears of joy are the only tears we shall ever know.

202. וַתֵּרֶד בַּת פַּרְעֹה לִרְחֹץ עַל הַיְאוֹר. בְּשַׁעֲתָא דַּהֲוּו פָּסְקֵי יִשְׂרָאֵל מֵאוֹרַיְיתָא, מִיָּד וַתֵּרֶד בַּת פַּרְעֹה לִרְחֹץ עַל הַיְאוֹר. הֲוַת נַחְתַּת מִדַּת הַדִּין, לְאִסְתַּחֲאָה מִדְּמָא דְּיִשְׂרָאֵל, עַל עֶלְבּוֹנָה דְּאוֹרַיְיתָא. וְנַעֲרוֹתֶיהָ הֹלְכוֹת עַל יַד הַיְאוֹר, אִלֵּין אוּמַיָּא, דְּאִינּוּן אַזְלִין וְרַדְפִין אֲבַתְרַיְיהוּ, עַל יַד הַיְאוֹר, עַל סִבַּת עֶלְבּוֹנָה דְּאוֹרַיְיתָא, וְאִינּוּן דְּמוֹרִים בָּה, דְּרָפוּ יְדַיְיהוּ מִינָה.

202. "And the daughter of Pharaoh came down to wash herself at the river" (Shemot 2:5). When Yisrael severed themselves from the Torah, "the daughter of Pharaoh came down to wash herself at the river," immediately. The attribute of Judgment, WHICH IS CALLED 'THE DAUGHTER OF PHARAOH', would come down to wash herself with the blood of Yisrael, MEANING WITH THEIR BLEMISH, because of the disregard of the Torah – BECAUSE 'RIVER' MEANS TORAH. "And her maidens walked along by the river's side," because of the disregard to the Torah, for those who studied it loosened their hands from it.

203. א"ר יְהוּדָה, כָּל מִלִּין דְּעָלְמָא, תַּלְיָין בִּתְשׁוּבָה, וּבִצְלוֹתָא דְּצַלֵּי ב"נ לְקוּדְשָׁא בְּרִיךְ הוּא, וְכָל שֶׁכֵּן, מַאן דְּאוֹשִׁיד דִּמְעִין בִּצְלוֹתֵיהּ, דְּלֵית לָךְ תַּרְעָא, דְּלָא עָאלִין אִינּוּן דִּמְעִין. מַה כְּתִיב וַתִּפְתַּח וַתִּרְאֵהוּ אֶת הַיֶּלֶד. וַתִּפְתַּח, דָּא שְׁכִינְתָּא, דְּקַיְימָא עֲלַיְיהוּ דְּיִשְׂרָאֵל, כְּאִימָּא עַל בְּנִין, וְהִיא פָּתְחָה תָּדִיר בִּזְכוּתֵיהוֹן דְּיִשְׂרָאֵל.

203. Rabbi Yehuda said: Everything in the world depends upon repentance and prayer that the person prays to the Holy One, blessed be He – one who sheds tears during his prayer especially, for there is no gate that these tears can not enter. It is written: "And when she had opened it, she saw the child" (Ibid.). "And she opened," refers to the Shechinah, who stands over Yisrael as a mother over her children, and She always opens with the merit of Yisrael.

204. כֵּיוָן שֶׁפָּתְחָה, וַתִּרְאֵהוּ אֶת הַיֶּלֶד, יֶלֶד שַׁעֲשׁוּעִים. דְּאִינּוּן יִשְׂרָאֵל, דְּמִתְחַשָּׁאן קָמֵי מַלְכֵיהוֹן בְּכֹלָּא, וּמִיָּד דְּמִתְחַנְּנָן קָמֵי קוּדְשָׁא בְּרִיךְ הוּא, הַדְרֵי בִּתְשׁוּבָה, וּבָכָאן קָמֵיהּ, כִּבְרָא דְּבָכֵי קָמֵי אֲבוֹי, מַה כְּתִיב,

וְהִנֵּה נַעַר בּוֹכֶה. כֵּיוָן דְּבָכֵי, אִתְעֲדוּ כָּל גְּזֵרִין בִּישִׁין דְּעָלְמָא, מַה כְּתִיב וַתַּחְמוֹל עָלָיו, אִתְּעַר עֲלוֹי בְּרַחֲמִים, וּמְרַחֵם לֵיהּ.

204. As soon as she opened it, "she saw the child," MEANING "a darling child" (Yirmeyah 31:19), referring to Yisrael who are constantly sinning before their King. But they immediately beseeched the Holy One, blessed be He, returned in repentance, and wept before Him as a son weeps before his father. As is written: "Behold, a weeping boy" (Shemot 2:6). Since he wept, all the difficult decrees were removed from him. It is written: "And she had compassion on him" (Ibid.), because she was stirred with compassion and she pitied him.

205. וַתֹּאמֶר מִיַּלְדֵי הָעִבְרִים זֶה, דְּאִינּוּן רַכֵּי לִבָּא, וְלָא מִיַּלְדֵי העכו״ם, דְּאִינּוּן קְשֵׁי קְדַל, וּקְשֵׁי לִבָּא. מִיַּלְדֵי הָעִבְרִים רַכֵּי לִבָּא מֵאֲבָהָן וּמֵאִמְּהָן לְאָתָבָא קַמֵּי מָארֵיהוֹן. וַתִּקְרָא אֶת אֵם הַיֶּלֶד. שֶׁהָיְתָה בּוֹכָה, הה״ד, קוֹל בְּרָמָה נִשְׁמָע נְהִי בְּכִי תַמְרוּרִים רָחֵל מְבַכָּה עַל בָּנֶיהָ וְגוֹ', הוּא בּוֹכֶה וְאֵם הַיֶּלֶד הִיא בּוֹכָה.

205. "And said: 'This is one of the Hebrews' children'" (Ibid.). For they are soft-hearted, not children of the idol worshippers, who are stiff-necked and hard-hearted. "...the Hebrews' children..." are soft-hearted in THE MERIT OF the fathers and mothers, to repent before their Master. "And the maid went and called the child's mother" (Ibid. 8). THIS IS IN REFERENCE TO RACHEL THE MATRIARCH who was weeping. This is the verse: "A voice was heard in Rama, lamentation, and bitter weeping: Rachel weeping for her children..." (Yirmeyah 31:14). And he is crying, MEANING YISRAEL, and the mother of the child is weeping, REFERRING TO RACHEL, THE MOTHER OF YISRAEL.

206. א״ר יְהוּדָה, לְזִמְנָא דְּאָתֵי מַה כְּתִיב, בִּבְכִי יָבוֹאוּ וּבְתַחֲנוּנִים וְגוֹ'. מַהוּ בִּבְכִי יָבוֹאוּ. בִּזְכוּת בְּכִי דְּאֵם הַיֶּלֶד, שֶׁהִיא רָחֵל, יָבוֹאוּ וְיִתְכַּנְּשׁוּן מִן גָּלוּתָא. וְאָמַר רִבִּי יִצְחָק, פּוּרְקָנָא דְּיִשְׂרָאֵל לָא תַּלְיָא אֶלָּא בִּבְכִי, כַּד יִשְׁתַּלְּמוּן וְיִכְלוּן, בְּכִי דְּמָעוֹת דְּבָכָה עֵשָׂו קַמֵּי אָבִיו, דִּכְתִיב וַיִּשָּׂא עֵשָׂו קוֹלוֹ וַיֵּבְךְּ. וְאִינּוּן דְּמָעִין, אֲחִיתוּ לְיִשְׂרָאֵל בְּגָלוּתֵיהּ. כֵּיוָן דְּיִכְלוּן אִינּוּן דְּמָעִין בְּבִכְיָה דְּיִשְׂרָאֵל, יִפְקוּן מִגָּלוּתֵיהּ, הה״ד בִּבְכִי יָבוֹאוּ

וּבְתַחֲנוּנִים אוֹבִילֵם.

206. Rabbi Yehuda said: Into the future, this is what is written, "They shall come with weeping, and with supplications will I lead them" (Ibid. 8). HE ASKS: What is the meaning of, "They shall come with weeping"? AND HE ANSWERS: In the merit of the weeping of the mother of the child, THE MOTHER OF YISRAEL, who is Rachel, they will come, and will be gathered from the exile. Rabbi Yitzchak said: The redemption of Yisrael is dependent only upon weeping, MEANING when the tears that Esau wept before his father will be finished and come to an end. THEN THEY WILL BE REDEEMED, as is written: "And Esau raised his voice and wept" (Beresheet 27:38). These tears lowered Yisrael into exile. THEREFORE, as soon as these tears cease through the weeping of Yisrael, they will go out of exile. This is the meaning of: "They shall come with weeping, and with supplications will I lead them."

23. "And he looked this way and that"

A Synopsis

This section discusses the episode wherein Moses kills an Egyptian who is beating an Yisrael. "He looked this way and that," we're told, to see if the Egyptian proclaimed the Divine Unity, performed any good works, or would produce a righteous son. Though wicked men often beget good sons, and these are especially precious to God since they represent light from darkness, Moses saw through the Holy Spirit that the Egyptian would not have such a son.

The Relevance of the Passage

Darkness becomes a powerful positive force the moment it is transformed into Light, for it creates unparalleled brilliance. Light from darkness is far more luminous than Light from Light.

Our most negative and wicked traits can be harnessed to change this world absolutely, bringing us endless joy the moment we own up to their existence and transform them into positive traits.

Instead of feeling shame, guilt, dishonor, and disgrace over our own evil impulses; instead of denying their existence, we should immediately acknowledge them (as painful as that may be) and ask the Light to transform our evil qualities into their opposite state.

This passage uproots our negative traits, allowing them to give birth to their opposite. From evil emerges divine goodness. From selfishness is born selflessness. Greed gives way to generosity. Spitefulness engenders kindness and compassion. Our greatest weaknesses now become our greatest strengths, and the Light that shimmers uplifts all humanity.

The most corrupt and sinful aspects of our society now transform, giving birth to divinity, purity, and blessings.

The negative traits within us, and the negative beings in our world that cannot be altered into positivity and goodness, are now banished forever, freeing us from their destructive influences.

207. וַיִּפֶן כֹּה וָכֹה. חָמָא בְּאִלֵּין נ' אַתְוָון, דְּמִיַחֲדִין לֵיה יִשְׂרָאֵל בְּכָל יוֹמָא, שְׁמַע יִשְׂרָאֵל פַּעֲמַיִם, דְּאִית בְּהוֹן כ"ה כ"ה תְּרֵי זִמְנֵי, וְלָא חָמָא בֵּיה. וַיִּפֶן כֹּה וָכֹה וְגוֹ'. כֹּה וָכֹה, אָמַר רִבִּי אַבָּא, כֹּה חָמָא, אִי הֲווֹ בֵּיה עוֹבָדִין דְּכַשְׁרָן. וָכֹה אִי זַמִּין לְנָפְקָא מִנֵּיה בְּרָא מְעַלְיָא, מִיַּד וַיַּרְא כִּי אֵין אִישׁ. חָמָא בְּרוּחַ קוּדְשָׁא, דְּלָא זַמִּין לְנָפְקָא מִנֵּיה בְּרָא מְעַלְיָא.

207. "And he looked this way [Heb. *koh* (*Caf-Hei*)] and that (*koh*)" (Shemot 2:12). SINCE he saw in these fifty letters that Yisrael proclaim twice every day the prayer: "Shma Yisrael" (Hear O Yisrael), that contains *Caf-Hei* (= 25) and *Caf-Hei* LETTERS twice; but he did not see THAT THE EGYPTIAN WOULD BE SAYING THEM. "And he looked *Koh* and *Koh*." Rabbi Aba said: THE FIRST *Koh* IS BECAUSE he looked to see whoever possessed good deeds, and THE SECOND *Koh* IS BECAUSE he desired to perceive whether a righteous son would emerge from him. Immediately, "he saw that there was no man" (Ibid.) he saw by the Holy Spirit that no righteous son would not emerge from him.

208. דְּאָמַר רְבִּי אַבָּא, כַּמָּה חַיָּיבִין אִינּוּן בְּעָלְמָא, דְּמָפְקֵי בְּנֵי מְעַלְיָא, יַתִּיר מֵאִינּוּן זַכָּאִין. וְהַהוּא בְּרָא מְעַלְיָא דְּנָפַק מִן חַיָּיבָא, אִיהוּ מְעַלְיָא יַתִּיר, לְמֶהֱוֵי טָהוֹר מִטָּמֵא. נְהוֹרָא מִגּוֹ חֲשׁוֹכָא. חָכְמְתָא מִגּוֹ טִפְּשׁוּתָא. וְדָא אִיהוּ מְעַלְיָא מִכֹּלָּא.

208. Rabbi Aba said: How many wicked people are there in the world who beget good children, more than the righteous. And that good son who comes from the wicked person is even better because he is pure from impure, light from darkness, wisdom from foolishness and this is the best of all.

24. "And he sat by the well"

A Synopsis

In this section we learn that God allowed Moses to see all through the Holy Spirit, so that he would kill the Egyptian and go to the same well to which Jacob came. While Jacob "looked" at the well, Moses "sat" by the well, which reveals that although both were of the same level of Holiness, Moses ascended higher than Jacob. This well, Rabbi Yitzchak tells Rabbi Yosi, is not the same well that Isaac and Abraham dug. Rather, it was created at the same time that the world was created, and its mouth was created by Shabbat eve at twilight. There follows a description of the system of unification of the three Columns and the roles of the Sfirot within this system. After, Rabbi Yehuda quotes the verse, "And the priest of Midian has seven daughters..." and questions how the daughters could have drawn water from Jacob's well when there was a large stone covering its mouth. Rabbi Chiya resolves this difficulty, explaining that there was no longer a stone covering the mouth of the well because Jacob removed it, as it was no longer needed.

The Relevance of the Passage

Much is concealed from the eyes of men. However, when our consciousness is raised, and when we evolve and elevate spiritually into genuine and proactive people, we see more. We perceive more. We sense more. Consequently, we reject evil. We recognize negative forces in all their nefarious and clever disguises.

We're told that Moses looked at an Egyptian and killed him merely by his gaze. This alludes to the power of the eyes. *Egypt* is a metaphor pertaining to our personal impious impulses. As our own eyes peruse these verses, we do away with the "Egyptian" within us. We connect to the Holy Spirit and we view life, forevermore, through the eyes of our soul.

The Zohar's discussion concerning the well, the Central Column, the Sfirah known as Tiferet, and its connection to Moses and Jacob, connects the reader to the power of his own free will, which is the embodiment of the Central Column.

Kabbalistically, the physical world and humanity is founded upon Three Columns, three distinct forces which are:

Right Column: A positive (+), proton force of imparting and sharing, or the human soul.

Left Column: A negative (-), electron force of receiving and desire, or the human ego and all of its indulgent longings.

Central Column: The neutron force of balance and Resistance or the free will to stop the power of our ego and connect instead to the Right Column force of sharing.

Kabbalist Rav Ashlag explains the dynamics of the Three Columns as it relates to human behavior: Rav Ashlag says a man's mission in life is to transform his Left Column's *Desire to Receive*, into the *Desire to Receive for the Sake of Sharing.* The moment of transformation occurs when we apply resistance against the Left Column which seeks to receive endlessly for the self alone. The spiritual path of Kabbalah involves utilizing the Left Column for the purpose of receiving for the sake of sharing with others. This is how the Children of Yisrael become the Light for all the nations. Lacking a Central Column, a person falls under the sway of the Left Column, and darkness is the inevitable result. Moses and Jacob are the personification of the Central Column.

Here we draw upon their spiritual might so that we possess the courage and strength to resist all Left Column urges and instead, dedicate ourselves to giving love, kindness, and Light to everyone in our lives.

Each time we resist our egocentric urges, we immediately unite Malchut, our world, with Tiferet, the Upper World. This is referred to by the Zohar as "perfecting Malchut" and "the pursuit of Righteousness." Each act of resistance allows us to drink from the divine well of Light that fills the Upper Worlds.

This passage allows us to make the complete perfection of Malchut, empowering all mankind with the Central Column and the wisdom and power to forever resist selfishness and evil. The well is open and the Divine Waters pour over all Creation.

209. וַיַּרְא וַיַּרְא דְּהָכָא, כֹּלָּא בְּרוּחַ קוּדְשָׁא אִסְתָּכַּל וְחָמָא, וּבְגִין כַּךְ אִסְתָּכַּל בֵּיהּ וְקַטַל לֵיהּ, וְקוּדְשָׁא בְּרִיךְ הוּא סַבֵּב כֹּלָּא, לְמִהַךְ לְהַהוּא בֵּירָא, כְּמָה דְּאָזַל יַעֲקֹב לְגַבֵּי הַהוּא בֵּירָא, דִּכְתִיב, וַיֵּשֶׁב עַל הַבְּאֵר. בְּיַעֲקֹב כְּתִיב, וַיַּרְא וְהִנֵּה בְאֵר. בְּמֹשֶׁה כְּתִיב, וַיֵּשֶׁב בְּאֶרֶץ מִדְיָן וַיֵּשֶׁב עַל הַבְּאֵר. בְּגִין דְּמֹשֶׁה וְיַעֲקֹב, אע"ג דִּבְדַרְגָּא חֲדָא הֲווֹ, אִסְתָּלַק מֹשֶׁה בְּהַאי יַתִּיר מִנֵּיהּ.

209. HE ASKS: WHAT IS THE ALLUSION IN THE MENTIONING OF "HE SAW" TWICE? "And he saw AN EGYPTIAN MAN...and when he saw THAT THERE IS NO MAN.." (Shemot 2:11-12). AND HE ANSWERS: He observed

and saw everything with the Holy Spirit. Therefore he looked at him and killed him, MEANING THAT HE KILLED HIM BY LOOKING AT HIM. THEREFORE, IT SAYS A SECOND TIME "HE SAW." And the Holy One, blessed be He, caused all this so that MOSES should go to that well as Jacob went to that well, as it is written "and he sat down by a well" (Ibid. 15). HE ASKS: By Jacob, it is written, "And he looked, and behold a well in the field" (Beresheet 29:2), while by Moses it says, "And dwelt in the land of Midian: and he sat down by a well". BY JACOB, IT DID NOT SAY 'SAT', BUT ONLY "HE LOOKED." AND HE ANSWERS: IT IS BECAUSE even though Moses and Jacob were on one level, MEANING THE CENTRAL COLUMN, IN ALL Moses became elevated more than him – BECAUSE JACOB IS THE ASPECT OF TIFERET AND MOSES IS THE ASPECT OF DA'AT, WHICH IS THE INNER PART OF TIFERET. AND THE INNER MEANING OF THE WELL IS MALCHUT, THE SPOUSE OF TIFERET, AND SINCE MOSES WAS THE INNER PART OF TIFERET, THEREFORE BY HIM IT SAYS, "SAT" AND BY JACOB ONLY, "HE SAW."

210. רִבִּי יוֹסֵי וְרִבִּי יִצְחָק הֲווֹ אַזְלֵי בְּאוֹרְחָא. אָמַר רִבִּי יוֹסֵי, הַהוּא בְּאֵר דְּחָמָא יַעֲקֹב, וְחָמָא מֹשֶׁה, אִי דָּא הֲוָה הַהוּא בֵּירָא, דְּחָפַר אַבְרָהָם וְיִצְחָק. א״ל לָאו. אֶלָּא, בְּשַׁעֲתָא דְּאִתְבְּרֵי עָלְמָא, אִתְבְּרֵי הַאי בֵּירָא. וּבְעֶרֶב שַׁבָּת בֵּין הַשְּׁמָשׁוֹת, אִתְבְּרֵי פּוּמָא דִּילֵיהּ, וְהַאי אִיהוּ בְּאֵר דְּחָמוּ יַעֲקֹב וּמֹשֶׁה.

210. Rabbi Yosi and Rabbi Yitzchak were traveling on the road. Rabbi Yosi said: The well that Jacob and Moses saw was the same well that Abraham and Isaac dug, WHICH ARE THE TWO COLUMNS, RIGHT AND LEFT OF ZEIR ANPIN. He said to him: No, THE WELL OF JACOB AND MOSES WAS NOT OF THE SAME STATUS AS THE WELL THAT ABRAHAM AND ISAAC DUG. This well was created at the same time that the world was created, and by Shabbat eve at twilight, the mouth of the well was created. And this is the well that Jacob and Moses saw. THEREFORE IT SAYS, "AND HE SAT DOWN BY A WELL."

(תוֹסֶפְתָּא)

211. מַתְנִיתִין. אִינּוּן דְּרַדְפֵּי קְשׁוֹט, אִינּוּן דְּתַבְעֵי רָזָא דִּמְהֵימְנוּתָא. אִינּוּן דְּאִתְדַּבָּקוּ בְּקִשּׁוּרָא מְהֵימְנָא. אִינּוּן דְּיַדְעִין אוֹרְחוֹי דְּמַלְכָּא

עִלָּאָה. קְרִיבוּ שְׁמָעוּ.

Tosefta (Addendum)

211. Mishnah. Those who pursue righteousness, THAT IS, WHO PURSUE TO PERFECT MALCHUT THAT IS CALLED 'RIGHTEOUSNESS', THROUGH THREE COLUMNS, RIGHT, LEFT AND CENTRAL OF ZEIR ANPIN. Those who FORCIBLY demand the secret of Faith, WHICH IS THE SECRET OF EXTENDING THE LEFT COLUMN TO MALCHUT WHICH IS CALLED 'FAITH'. Those who have adhered with the bond of Faith, WHICH IS THE BOND WHICH IS IN THE RIGHT COLUMN, those who know the ways of the Supernal King – WHICH IS ZEIR ANPIN, THE SECRET OF THE CENTRAL COLUMN. THE MASTER OF THE TOSEFTA CALLS THEM AND SAYS TO THEM: Draw near and hearken. THOSE WHO ARE PURSUING TO PERFECT MALCHUT TO ILLUMINATE HER WITH THE THREE COLUMNS, HEARKEN THE SYSTEM OF THIS UNIFICATION, HOW IT IS DONE.

212. כַּד סְלִיקוּ תְּרֵין, וְנַפְקוּ לְקַדְמוּת חַד, מְקַבְּלִין לֵיהּ בֵּין תְּרֵין דְּרוֹעִין. תְּרֵין נַחְתֵּי לְתַתָּא תְּרֵין אִינּוּן, חַד בֵּינַיְיהוּ. תְּרֵין אִלֵּין מוֹתְבָא דִּנְבִיאֵי יַנְקִין בְּהוּ. חַד בֵּינַיְיהוּ, חַבּוּרָא אִיהוּ דְּכֹלָּא, אִיהוּ נָטִיל מִכֹּלָּא.

212. When the two COLUMNS, CHOCHMAH AND BINAH, ascend and emerge towards the one CENTRAL COLUMN, they receive it between the two arms, WHICH ARE CHESED AND GVURAH. DUE TO THEIR RECEPTION OF THE CENTRAL COLUMN, CHOCHMAH AND BINAH DESCENDED TO BECOME CHESED AND GVURAH. FOR THE FIRST THREE OF THE FIRST THREE SFIROT WERE GONE FROM THEM. MALCHUT CANNOT AS YET RECEIVE CHOCHMAH FROM THEM, AS THE LIGHT OF CHASSADIM PREVAILS, WHILR CHOCHMAH THERE IS HIDDEN. Until the two, WHICH ARE CHESED AND GVURAH, descend below, MEANING THAT THEY BECOME NETZACH AND HOD, they are two, AS THE MAIN MOCHIN ARE TWO, RIGHT AND LEFT, THAT BECOME NETZACH AND HOD, and one between them – MEANING THAT THEY NEED THE CENTRAL COLUMN TO RECONCILE BETWEEN THEM, AND THAT IS YESOD. THE ARBITRATOR BETWEEN CHESED AND GVURAH IS CALLED 'TIFERET', AND THE ARBITRATOR BETWEEN NETZACH AND HOD IS CALLED 'YESOD'. AND HE EXPLAINED HIS WORDS: These two, THAT DESCENDED BELOW, are the place from which the prophets gain nourishment; NAMELY NETZACH AND

HOD. There is one between them, WHICH IS YESOD. It joins everything, BOTH THE RIGHT COLUMN AND THE LEFT COLUMN; it receives from everything, BOTH CHOCHMAH AND CHASSADIM, SINCE IT IS THE CENTRAL COLUMN THAT SUSTAINS THEIR ILLUMINATION, AND THEREFORE IT ALSO RECEIVES THEIR ILLUMINATION TO ITSELF. FOR THIS IS THE RULE: ALL THE ILLUMINATIONS THAT THE LOWER CAUSES TO BE SUSTAINED AMONG THE SUPERNAL IT TOO ATTAINS IN THEIR ENTIRETY.

213. הַהוּא בֵּירָא קַדִּישָׁא, קָאֵים תְּחוֹתַיְיהוּ, חַקְלָא דְתַפּוּחִין קַדִּישִׁין אִיהוּ מֵהַאי בֵּירָא אַתְשַׁקְיָין עֶדְרַיָּיא, כָּל אִינוּן רְתִיכִין, כָּל אִינוּן מָארֵי דְגַדְפִּין. תְּלָת קַיְימִין רְבִיעִין עַל הַאי בֵּירָא. הַאי בֵּירָא מִנַּיְיהוּ אִתְמְלֵי. אֲדֹנָ"י אִתְקְרֵי, עַל דָּא כְּתִיב, אֲדֹנָי יְיָ' אַתָּה הַחִלּוֹת וְגוֹ'. וּכְתִיב וְהָאֵר פָּנֶיךָ עַל מִקְדָּשְׁךָ הַשָּׁמֵם לְמַעַן אֲדֹנָי, אֲדוֹן כָּל הָאָרֶץ, הה"ד הִנֵּה אֲרוֹן הַבְּרִית אֲדוֹן כָּל הָאָרֶץ. בֵּיהּ גָּנִיז חַד מְקוֹרָא קַדִּישָׁא, דְּנָבִיעַ בֵּיהּ תָּדִיר, וְאַמְלֵי לֵיהּ, יְיָ' צְבָאוֹת אִקְרֵי. בְּרִיךְ הוּא לְעָלַם וּלְעָלְמֵי עָלְמִין.

(ע"כ תוספתא)

213. That holy well, WHICH IS MALCHUT, WITH THE MOCHIN OF THE FIRST THREE SFIROT, is situated under them, MEANING UNDER NETZACH, HOD, AND YESOD – that is, the field of holy apple trees. From that well they would water the flocks – WHO ARE all these Chariots OF ANGELS, and all these ANGELS have wings. Three were found lying by this well. THEY ARE THE THREE SFIROT NETZACH, HOD AND YESOD, AS MENTIONED, and this well is filled by them IN THE LIGHT OF THE THREE FIRST SFIROT, and it is called 'Adonai'. About this is written: "Adonai Elohim, you have begun..." (Devarim 3:24), and: "And cause Your face to shine upon Your sanctuary that is desolate for the sake of Adonai, the Master of the whole earth" (Daniel 9:17). WHEN IT HAS THE THREE FIRST SFIROT, IT IS REFERRED TO IN THE MASCULINE, MASTER. This is what is written: "Behold the Ark of the Covenant (of) the Master of the whole earth..." (Yehoshua 3:11). In it is concealed one holy source, THAT IS YESOD, that flows into it constantly and fills it. And it is called Hashem Tzeva'ot, blessed is He, for ever and ever.

(End of Tosefta)

214. וּלְכֹהֵן מִדְיָן שֶׁבַע בָּנוֹת וַתָּבֹאנָה וַתִּדְלֶנָה וְגוֹ'. א"ר יְהוּדָה, אִי בֵּירָא דָא, אִיהוּ בֵּירָא דְיַעֲקֹב, הָא כְּתִיב בֵּיהּ, וְנֶאֶסְפוּ שָׁמָּה כָל הָעֲדָרִים וְגָלְלוּ וְגוֹ'. וְהָכָא בְּנוֹת יִתְרוֹ לָא אִצְטְרִיכוּ לְהַאי. אֶלָּא וַתָּבֹאנָה וַתִּדְלֶנָה בְּלָא טוֹרַח אַחֲרָא.

214. "Now the priest of Midian has seven daughters and they came and drew water" (Shemot 2:16). Rabbi Yehuda said: If this well was the well of Jacob, is it not written BY JACOB: "And there were: all the flocks gathered and they rolled the stone from the well's mouth" (Beresheet 29:3)? Yet here the daughters of Jethro did not need this. They just came and drew water without any other effort – MEANING OF ROLLING THE STONE FROM THE MOUTH OF THE WELL.

215. א"ר חִיָּיא, יַעֲקֹב אַעֲדֵי לָה מִן בֵּירָא, דְּהָא כְּתִיב, כַּד מִתְכַּנְּשֵׁי תַּמָּן כָּל עֲדָרַיָּיא, וְהֵשִׁיבוּ אֶת הָאֶבֶן. וּבְיַעֲקֹב, לָא כְּתִיב וַיָּשֶׁב אֶת הָאֶבֶן, דְּהָא לָא אִצְטְרִיךְ לְבָתַר כֵּן, דְּהָא בְּקַדְמֵיתָא מַיָּא לָא הֲווֹ סַלְקִין, כֵּיוָן דְּאָתָא יַעֲקֹב, סְלִיקוּ מַיָּא לְגַבֵּיהּ, וְהַהוּא אַבְנָא, לָא הֲוָה עַל פּוּם בֵּירָא, וּבְגִין כָּךְ וַתָּבֹאנָה וַתִּדְלֶנָה.

215. Rabbi Chiya answered: Jacob removed THE STONE from the well. It is written that when the flocks gathered there, they "put the stone back upon the well's mouth" (Ibid.). But by Jacob it is not written that 'he put the stone back', because afterwards there was no more need for the stone, since originally the water would not rise. But when Jacob came, the water rose toward him BECAUSE THE WATER INCREASED. Therefore, that stone was no longer on the mouth of the well, SINCE THEY DID NOT NEED PROTECTION ANYMORE. Therefore, IT SAYS BY THE DAUGHTERS OF JETHRO, that they "came and drew," WITHOUT ANY EFFORT OF ROLLING THE STONE.

25. "Come from the four winds, O breath"

A Synopsis

Rabbi Elazar begins by quoting the title verse and asks how Ezekiel could have prophesied on the wind when it is clearly written that man cannot control the wind. The answer to this question, we're told, is that he prophesied by God's will. Furthermore the spirit (wind) was embodied in material form in this world, and Ezekiel called to it to come from the region where it resides. This place is not the Garden of Eden, Rabbi Elazar explains, but rather the Throne that stands on four pillars. The soul ascends from the Garden to the Throne and then descends to the world, and just as the body is taken from the four regions of the world, the spirit is taken from the four pillars of the Throne.

This discussion prompts the Jew who sits with the companions to describe his remarkable experience in the desert. He tells them that after entering a fragrant cavern, he found himself in a remarkable place where he encountered a man with a scepter who gave him a bundle of writings to give to the Fellowship. This man then struck him with his scepter, causing him to fall asleep. In his dream, he heard many voices and saw crowds of people arriving at that place. When the man with the scepter touched them with it and spoke to them, they proceeded on and then flew up into the air and disappeared. When he awoke, the Jew continues, the man with the scepter explained that the crowds in his dream were Righteous spirits on their way to the Garden of Eden. He then proceeded to discuss the relationship between the four elements of the body and the four spiritual elements of the body. After concluding his story, the Jew gives the bundle of writings to Rabbi Elazar. When he opens them, a flame explodes and envelops Rabbi Elazar. This allows him to gain new spiritual insight before the bundle flies from his hand, and though he is left grateful and happy, Rabbi Elazar tells nothing of this to his colleagues.

The Relevance of the Passage

This complex section of Zohar discourses on the origins and make-up of spirit, the four elements that create the body and the structure of the Upper and Lower worlds. These words purify and thus correct our body and soul so that we attain the Garden of Eden in this world.

Our consciousness is raised to the greatest of heights so that we now perceive the secrets of life.

The water on earth and the water that comprises the very cells of our body is reverted back to its original and primordial state, prior to the Flood at the time of Noah.

This ignites immortality as water, the life-blood of the planet, and the human body transforms it into healing waters. The deepest secrets and mysteries concerning water are revealed to the world. Through water, we achieve the blissful and eternal state known as the Garden of Eden.

216. ר' אֶלְעָזָר ור' אַבָּא הֲווֹ אַזְלֵי מִטְּבֶרְיָא לְצִפֹּרִי. עַד דַּהֲווֹ אַזְלֵי, פָּגַע בְּהוּ חַד יוּדָאי, אִתְחַבָּר בַּהֲדַיְיהוּ, א"ר אֶלְעָזָר, כָּל חַד לֵימָא מִלָה דְּאוֹרַיְיתָא.

216. Rabbi Elazar and Rabbi Aba were traveling from Tiberias to Tzipori. While they were walking, a Jew met them. He joined them. Rabbi Elazar said: Let everyone say a word of Torah.

217. פָּתַח אִיהוּ וְאָמַר, וַיֹּאמֶר אֵלַי הִנָּבֵא בֶּן אָדָם הִנָּבֵא אֶל הָרוּחַ וְאָמַרְתָּ אֶל הָרוּחַ וְגוֹ'. מֵהַאי קְרָא יְדַעְנָא, אֲתָר דְּהָרוּחַ נַפְקָא מִנֵּיהּ, וְכִי יָכִיל הֲוָה יְחֶזְקֵאל לְנַבְּאָה עַל הָרוּחַ, וְהָא כְּתִיב אֵין אָדָם שַׁלִּיט בָּרוּחַ לִכְלוֹא אֶת הָרוּחַ. אֶלָּא, בַּר נָשׁ לָא יָכִיל לְשַׁלְטָאָה בָּרוּחַ, אֲבָל קוּדְשָׁא בְּרִיךְ הוּא אִיהוּ שַׁלִּיט בְּכֹלָּא, וְעַל מֵימְרֵיהּ הֲוָה מִתְנַבֵּי יְחֶזְקֵאל. וְתוּ דְּהָא רוּחַ הֲוָה בְּגוּפָא בְּהַאי עָלְמָא, וּבְגִין כָּךְ אִתְנַבֵּי עֲלֵיהּ, מֵאַרְבַּע רוּחוֹת בֹּאִי הָרוּחַ, מֵהַהוּא אֲתָר דְּאִתְּחָם בְּסַמְכוֹי בְּאַרְבַּע סִטְרִין דְּעָלְמָא.

217. RABBI ELAZAR opened the discussion saying: "Then He said to me, 'Prophesy to the breath, prophesy, son of man, and say to the breath ('wind')'..." (Yechezkel 37:9). From this passage, I know from which place the wind emerges, for how was Ezekiel able to prophesy the wind, seeing as it is written: "Man does not have power over the wind to control the wind" (Kohelet 8:8). Man can not control the wind, but the Holy One, blessed be He, rules over everything and Ezekiel was prophesying by His command. Furthermore, the spirit (or: 'wind') was already in a body in this world, BECAUSE THERE WERE DEAD IN THE CAVE, WHOM HE RESURRECTED. Therefore, he prophesied to it, "Come from the four winds, O wind" (Yechezkel 37:9), MEANING from that place which pillars serve as borders at the four winds of the world – WHICH ARE THE SECRET OF THE LOWER THRONE, WHICH IS MALCHUT, THE THRONE FOR ZEIR ANPIN. IT HAS

FOUR PILLARS IN THE SECRET OF THE FOUR DIRECTIONS OF THE
WORLD, WHICH ARE CHESED AND GVURAH, TIFERET AND MALCHUT,
WHERE THE SPIRIT STAYS BEFORE IT RETURNS INTO A BODY IN THIS
WORLD.

218. דְּלִיג הַהוּא יוּדָאי קַמֵּיהּ, אָמַר לֵיהּ רִבִּי אֶלְעָזָר, מַאי חָמֵית. אָמַר
מִלָּה חֲמֵינָא. אָמַר לֵיהּ מַאי הִיא. אָמַר לֵיהּ רוּחַ בְּנֵי אָדָם, אִי אִתְלְבַּשׁ
בג"ע בִּלְבוּשָׁא דְּדִיּוּקְנָא בְּגוּפָא דְּהַאי עָלְמָא, הֲוָה לֵיהּ לְמִכְתַּב, כֹּה
אָמַר ה' מג"ע בּוֹאִי הָרוּחַ, מַהוּ מֵאַרְבַּע רוּחוֹת.

218. That Jew WHO JOINED THEM sprang up before him. Rabbi Elazar said
to him: What did you see? He answered: I saw something. He said to him:
What is it? He replied: If the spirit of people is attired in the Garden of Eden
in the form and image of the body of this world, AND IT RESIDES THERE, it
should have been written IN THE PASSAGE: 'Come from the Garden of
Eden, O breath (or: 'spirit').' Why does it say, "From the four winds"?

219. א"ל, רוּחָא לָא נַחְתָּא לְהַאי עָלְמָא, עַד דְּסַלְקָא מִגִּנְתָּא דְּאַרְעָא,
לְגוֹ כּוּרְסְיָיא, דְּקַיְימָא עַל אַרְבַּע סַמְכִין. כֵּיוָן דְּסַלְקָא תַּמָּן, אִשְׁתַּאֲבָא
מִגּוֹ הַהוּא כּוּרְסְיָיא דְּמַלְכָּא, וְנַחְתָּא לְהַאי עָלְמָא, גּוּפָא אִתְנְטִיל
מֵאַרְבַּע סִטְרֵי עָלְמָא, רוּחַ אוּף הָכִי אִתְנְטִיל מֵאַרְבַּע סִטְרֵי דְּכוּרְסְיָיא,
דְּמִתְתַּקְּנָא עֲלַיְיהוּ.

219. He said to him: The spirit does not descend to this world, until it
ascends from the earthly Garden of Eden to the throne – WHICH IS
MALCHUT that stands on four pillars, WHICH ARE CHESED, GVURAH,
TIFERET AND MALCHUT. When the spirit ascends there, it draws into itself
from that throne of the King and descends to this world. The body receives
from the four directions of the world, WHICH ARE THE FOUR ELEMENTS:
FIRE, AIR, WATER AND EARTH. The spirit also receives from the four
directions of the throne. THEY ARE CHESED, GVURAH, TIFERET AND
MALCHUT. Thus, it becomes perfected through them.

220. אָמַר לֵיהּ הַהוּא בַּר נָשׁ, דְּלִיגָא דְּקָא דְּלִיגְנָא קַמַּיְיכוּ, מִלָּה
חֲמֵינָא מֵהַאי סִטְרָא. בְּגִין דְּיוֹמָא חֲדָא הֲוֵינָא אָזִיל בְּמַדְבְּרָא, וַחֲמֵינָא

אִילָנָא חַד דְּמַרְגַּג לְמֶחֱזֵי, וְחַד מְעַרְתָּא תְּחוֹתֵיהּ, קָרִיבְנָא גַּבֵּיהּ
וַחֲמֵינָא הַהִיא מְעַרְתָּא, דְּסַלְקָא רֵיחִין מִכָּל זִינֵי רֵיחִין דְּעָלְמָא.
אִתְתַּקַּפְנָא בְּגַרְמָאי וְאַעֵילְנָא בְּהַהִיא מְעַרְתָּא, וְנָחִיתְנָא בְּדַרְגִּין יְדִיעָן
בְּגוֹ דּוּכְתָּא חֲדָא, דַּהֲווֹ בֵּיהּ אִילָנִין סַגִּיאִין וְרֵיחִין וּבוּסְמִין, דְּלָא
יָכִילְנָא לְמִסְבַּל.

220. That man said to him: When I jumped before you it WAS BECAUSE I saw something on this subject. One day I was walking in the desert and I saw a tree, which was pleasant to behold, and there was a cave under it. I approached it, and saw that from that cave emanated different scents. I braced myself and entered that cave, and descended certain steps in a place that had many trees, fragrances, and spices that I could not endure.

221. וְתַמָּן חֲמֵינָא חַד בַּר נָשׁ, וְשַׁרְבִיטָא חַד בִּידֵיהּ. וַהֲוָה קָאִים בְּחַד
פִּתְחָא, כֵּיוָן דְּחָמָא לִי, תָּוַהּ וְקָם לְגַבָּאי. אָמַר לִי, מָה אַתְּ הָכָא, וּמָאן
אַתְּ, אֲנָא דָּחִילְנָא סַגִּיא, אֲמֵינָא לֵיהּ, מָארֵי מִן חַבְרַיָּיא אֲנָא, כַּךְ וְכַךְ
חֲמֵינָא בְּמַדְבְּרָא, וְעָאלְנָא בְּהַאי מְעַרְתָּא, וְנָחִיתְנָא הָכָא.

221. And there I saw a man with a scepter in his hand, standing in an entrance. When he saw me he was surprised, and stood by me. He said to me: What are you doing here and who are you? I became very frightened. I said to him: Sir, I am one of the friends and as I saw such and such in the desert, I entered this cave and came down here.

222. אָמַר לִי, הוֹאִיל וּמִן חַבְרַיָּיא אַנְתְּ, טוֹל הַאי קִיטְרָא דִּכְתָבָא, וְהַב
לֵיהּ לְחַבְרַיָּיא, אִינּוּן דְּיַדְעִין רָזִין דְּרוּחֵיהוֹן דְּצַדִּיקַיָּא, בָּטַשׁ בִּי בְּהַהוּא
שַׁרְבִיטָא, וְדָמִיכְנָא. אַדְהָכִי, חֲמֵינָא כַּמָּה חֵילִין וּמַשִׁירְיָין גּוֹ שֵׁינָתָא,
דַּהֲווֹ אַתְיָין בְּאוֹרְחָא, לְהַהוּא דּוּכְתָּא. וְהַהוּא גַּבְרָא בָּטַשׁ בְּהַהוּא
שַׁרְבִיטָא, וְאָמַר בְּאוֹרְחָא דְּאִילָנֵי זִילוּ. אַדְהָכִי דַּהֲווֹ אַזְלֵי, פַּרְחֵי
בַּאֲוִירָא וְסַלְקֵי, וְלָא יְדַעְנָא לְאָן אֲתָר. וּשְׁמַעְנָא קָלִין דְּמַשִׁירְיָין
סַגִּיאִין, וְלָא יְדַעְנָא מֵאָן אִיהוּ. אִתְעַרְנָא, וְלָא חֲמֵינָא מִידִי, וְדָחִילְנָא
בְּהַהוּא אֲתָר.

222. He said to me: Since you are one of the friends, accept this bundle of writings and give it to the friends, to those who know the secrets of the spirits of the righteous ones. He struck me with the wand THAT WAS IN HIS HAND and I fell asleep. During my sleep, I saw many hosts and companies that were coming along the way to that place, and then that man struck with his wand and told them: Go by way of the trees. While they were still going, they flew in the air and ascended but I do not know where. And I heard the sounds of many hosts, and I did not know who they were. I awoke and saw nothing. And I was frightened in that place.

223. אַדְהָכִי, חֲמֵינָא לְהַהוּא בַּר נָשׁ, אָמַר לִי, חָמֵית מִידִי, אֲמֵינָא לֵיהּ, חֲמֵינָא גּוֹ שֵׁינָתָא כַּךְ וְכַךְ. אָמַר, בְּהַהוּא אָרְחָא אַזְלֵי רוּחֵיהוֹן דְּצַדִּיקַיָּא, גּוֹ גִנְתָּא דְּעֵדֶן לְאָעֲלָא תַמָּן. וּמַה דְּשַׁמְעַת מִנַּיְיהוּ, הוּא, דְּקַיְימֵי בְּגִנְתָּא בְּדִיּוּקְנָא דְּהַאי עָלְמָא וְחַדָּאן בְּרוּחֵיהוֹן דְּצַדִּיקַיָּא דְּעָאלִין תַּמָּן.

223. Meanwhile, I saw that man. He asked me: Have you seen something? I said to him: I saw something. I saw in my sleep such and such. He said: On that road, the spirits of the righteous go to the Garden of Eden to enter there. And what you heard from them, MEANING THE SOUNDS OF MANY HOSTS, IS BECAUSE they are standing in the Garden in their forms of this world, and they are rejoicing with the righteous who are coming there.

224. וּכְמָה דְּגוּפָא אִתְבְּנֵי בְּהַאי עָלְמָא, מִקְּטוּרָא דְּאַרְבַּע יְסוֹדֵי, וְאִתְצַיַּיר בְּהַאי עָלְמָא. אוּף הָכִי רוּחָא, אִתְצַיַּיר בְּגִינְתָּא, מִקְּטוּרָא דְּאַרְבַּע רוּחִין דְּקַיְימָא בְּגִנְתָּא, וְהַהוּא רוּחָא, אִתְלַבְּשָׁא תַּמָּן, וּמִתְצַיְּירַת מִנַּיְיהוּ, בְּצִיּוּרָא דְּדִיּוּקְנָא דְּגוּפָא, דְּאִתְצַיַּיר בְּהַאי עָלְמָא. וְאִלְמָלֵא אִינוּן אַרְבַּע רוּחִין, דְּאִינוּן אֲוִירִין דְּגִנְתָּא, רוּחָא לָא מִתְצַיְּירָא בְּצִיּוּרָא כְּלָל, וְלָא אִתְלַבְּשָׁא בְּהוּ.

224. As the body is built in this world by the binding of the four elements, FIRE, AIR, WATER AND EARTH, and is formed from them in this world, so the spirit is formed of the four spirits that stand in the Garden of Eden, WHICH ARE CHESED, GVURAH, TIFERET AND MALCHUT. The spirit is enveloped there and is formed in the image of the body that is formed in this world. And if not for these four spirits which are the air in the Garden –

MEANING CHESED, GVURAH, TIFERET AND MALCHUT FROM THE LIGHT OF CHASSADIM, THAT IS CALLED 'AIR' – they would not form any image at all and no spirit would be enveloped there.

225. אִינּוּן ד' רוּחִין, קְטִירִין אִלֵּין בְּאִלֵּין כַּחֲדָא, וְהַהוּא רוּחַ אִתְצַיָּיר וְאִתְלַבַּשׁ בְּהוּ, כְּגַוְונָא דְגוּפָא אִתְצַיָּיר בְּקִטּוּרֵי, דְּד' יְסוֹדֵי עָלְמָא. וּבְגִין כָּךְ, מֵאַרְבַּע רוּחוֹת בּוֹאִי הָרוּחַ, מֵאִינּוּן אַרְבַּע רוּחִין דג״ע, דְּאִתְלַבְּשָׁא וְאִתְצַיָּירֵת בְּהוּ, וְהַשְׁתָּא טוֹל הַאי קִטְרָא דִכְתָבָא וְזִיל לְאָרְחָךְ, וְהַב לֵיהּ לְחַבְרַיָּיא.

225. These four spirits are intertwined one with another, and the spirit is formed and wrapped with them, as the body is formed in the joining of the four elements of the world: FIRE, AIR, WATER AND EARTH. Therefore, EZEKIEL SAID: "Come from the four winds, O wind" (Yechezkel 37:9), MEANING these four spirits of the Garden of Eden with which it is clothed and formed. And now accept this bundle of writings and go on your way and give it to the friends.

226. אָתָא רִבִּי אֶלְעָזָר, וְאִינּוּן חַבְרַיָּיא, וְנַשְׁקוּהוּ בְּרֵישֵׁיהּ, א״ר אֶלְעָזָר, בְּרִיךְ רַחֲמָנָא, דְּשַׁדְרָךְ הָכָא, דְּוַדַּאי דָּא הוּא בְּרִירָא דְמִלָּה, וְקוּדְשָׁא בְּרִיךְ הוּא אַזְמִין לְפוּמִי הַאי קְרָא. יְהַב לוֹן הַהוּא קִיטְרָא דִכְתָבָא, כֵּיוָן דְּנָטַל לֵיהּ רִבִּי אֶלְעָזָר, וּפָתַח לֵיהּ, נָפַק אֲפוּתָא דְאֶשָּׁא, וְאַסְחַר לֵיהּ, חָמָא בֵּיהּ מַה דְּחָמָא, וּפָרַח מִן יְדוֹי.

226. Rabbi Elazar and the friends approached the Jew, kissing him on the forehead. Rabbi Elazar said: Blessed is the Merciful who sent you here, because this is certainly clarification of the matter. The Holy One, blessed be He, brought to my mouth this passage: "COME FROM THE FOUR WINDS," SO THAT YOU WOULD REVEAL TO ME ITS SECRET. The man gave him the bundle of writings. As soon as Rabbi Elazar took it and opened it, a conflagration emerged and surrounded him. He saw in the bundle of writings what he saw, and the bundle flew out of his hands.

227. בָּכָה ר' אֶלְעָזָר, וְאָמַר מַאן יָכִיל לְקַיְּימָא בְּגִנְזַיָּיא דְמַלְכָּא, ה׳ מִי יָגוּר בְּאָהֳלֶךָ מִי יִשְׁכּוֹן בְּהַר קָדְשֶׁךָ. זַכָּאָה הַאי אוֹרְחָא, וְהַהִיא שַׁעֲתָא

דְּאִעְרַעְנָא בָּךְ. וּמֵהַהוּא יוֹמָא הֲוָה חַדֵּי רְבִּי אֶלְעָזָר, וְלֹא אָמַר כְּלוּם לְחַבְרַיָּיא, עַד דַּהֲווֹ אַזְלֵי, פָּגְעוּ בְּחַד בֵּירָא דְּמַיָּא, קַיְימוּ עָלֵיהּ, וְשָׁתוּ מִן מַיָּא.

227. Rabbi Elazar wept and said: Who can fathom the secrets of the King, as it is written: "Hashem, who shall abide in Your tent? Who shall dwell in Your holy hill?" (Tehilim 15:1). Blessed is the way and the moment that we met you. And from that day, Rabbi Elazar rejoiced and said nothing to his friends OF WHAT HE SAW IN THE WRITINGS. While they were still traveling, they came upon a well of water, stood there and drank of the water.

26. The well of Moses and Jacob

A Synopsis

In this section, Rabbi Elazar discourses on the well of Jacob and Moses. The waters of this well arose towards Jacob and he found his spouse, Rachel, there. Similarly, when Moses came across the well, the waters rose towards Moses and he joined there with his spouse, Tziporah. The discussion then turns to Jethro, a heathen priest who renounced paganism and ceased to worship idols. Because of this renunciation, Jethro's people excommunicated him and they drove his daughters away so they could not water his flock. Through the Holy Spirit, Moses knew that their mistreatment was caused by their rejection of idolatry, and so Moses helped Jethro's daughters. With the help of a metaphorical example, Rabbi Chiya then explains that their rescue was actually due to the Egyptian whom Moses killed.

The Relevance of the Passage

Kabbalistically, water represents purification and Light. Both Moses and Jacob met their soul mates by a well, alluding to the spiritual principle that states that a man merits and unites with his soul mate only when he has purified himself through spiritual transformation.

Meditating upon this passage literally transports our soul to the well of Moses and Jacob so that we may meet our true soul mate, or deeply enrich existing marital relationships.

We draw water from the well to cleanse our soul, wash away our iniquities, and thus cause the ultimate soul mate unification – the marriage of our physical world with the supernal world of Light.

Towards the end of this passage, we're told that after Moses had killed the Egyptian man, he fled and came upon the well, where he met his wife, Tziporah. In turn, Moses was also able to help the daughters of Jethro water their flock. For this reason, the daughters say "an Egyptian man delivered us." The Egyptian is given credit because it was he who caused Moses to come to Midyan, the place of the well.

One basic idea emerges from this story. We find out that our dark side, the Egyptian man, allows us to come closer to the Light of the Creator. Namely, our negative qualities let us fulfill our most deepest need and most profound desire – to become the cause and creators of our own fulfillment, because in the moment that we identify and banish our egocentric features, we arouse Light. Thus, we have become responsible and the cause for our own joy.

Jethro represents the transformation from Idol-worshipper to one who truly knows the one Light of the Creator. This is us. To one degree or another, each person has idol-worship in his nature, be it the worship of money, the veneration of prestige and power, the adulation of cultural icons, or the adoration of acceptance by other people. But again, these negative traits allow us to attain affinity with the Creator as soon as we eradicate them and transform ourselves.

Here the Zohar purges idol-worshipping from our nature. Another discharge of Light is released to extricate extreme meanness (Egyptian) from our hearts.

228. א״ר אֶלְעָזָר, זַכָּאָה חוּלְקֵיהוֹן דְּצַדִּיקַיָּא, יַעֲקֹב עֲרַק מִקַּמֵּי אֲחוּי, וְאִזְדְּמַן לֵיה בֵּירָא, כֵּיוָן דְּבֵירָא חָמָא לֵיה, מַיָּא אִשְׁתְּמוֹדְעוּ לְמָארֵיהוֹן, וְסַלְקִין לְגַבֵּיה, וְחַדוּ בַּהֲדֵיה, וְתַמָּן אִזְדְּוְוּגַת לֵיה בַּת זוּגֵיה. מֹשֶׁה עֲרַק מִקַּמֵּי פַּרְעֹה, וְאִזְדְּמַן לֵיה הַהוּא בֵּירָא, וּמַיְיָן חָמוּ לֵיה, וְאִשְׁתְּמוֹדְעוּ לְמָארֵיהוֹן, וְסַלְקוּ לְגַבֵּיה, וְתַמָּן אִזְדְּוְוּגַת לֵיה בַּת זוּגֵיה.

228. Rabbi Elazar said: Blessed is the portion of the righteous. Jacob fled from his brother and he chanced upon a well, WHICH IS THE SECRET OF NUKVA. As soon as the well saw him, the waters recognized their master, and they rose toward him, IN THE SECRET OF *MAYIN NUKVIN* ('FEMALE WATERS'). And they rejoiced with him and then his soulmate, RACHEL, joined him. Moses fled from Pharaoh and chanced upon that well, and the waters saw him and recognized their master and rose towards him, IN THE SECRET OF *MAYIN NUKVIN,* and there he was joined by his soulmate, TZIPORAH.

229. מַה בֵּין מֹשֶׁה לְיַעֲקֹב, יַעֲקֹב כְּתִיב בֵּיה, וַיְהִי כַּאֲשֶׁר רָאָה יַעֲקֹב אֶת רָחֵל וְגוֹ'. וַיִּגַּשׁ יַעֲקֹב וַיָּגֶל אֶת הָאֶבֶן וְגוֹ'. מֹשֶׁה מַה כְּתִיב בֵּיה, וַיָּבוֹאוּ הָרוֹעִים וַיְגָרְשׁוּם וַיָּקָם מֹשֶׁה וַיּוֹשִׁעָן וְגוֹ'. בְּוַדַּאי יָדַע הֲוָה מֹשֶׁה, כֵּיוָן דְּחָמָא מַיָּא דְסַלְקִין לְגַבֵּיה, דְּתַמָּן תִּזְדְּמַן לֵיה בַּת זוּגֵיה. וְתוּ, דְּהָא רוּחַ קוּדְשָׁא, לָא אִתְעָדֵי מִנֵּיה לְעָלְמִין וּבֵיה הֲוָה יָדַע, דְּצִפּוֹרָה תֶּהֱוֵי בַּת זוּגֵיה. אָמַר מֹשֶׁה, וַדַּאי יַעֲקֹב אָתָא לְהָכָא, וּמַיָּא סְלִיקוּ לְגַבֵּיה, אִזְדְּמַן לֵיה בַּר נָשׁ דְּאַכְנִישׁ לֵיה לְבֵיתֵיה, וְיָהַב לֵיה כָּל מַה דְּאִצְטְרִיךְ. אֲנָא אוּף הָכִי.

229. What was the difference between Moses and Jacob? MEANING THERE IS REALLY NO DIFFERENCE BETWEEN MOSES AND JACOB. It is written of

Jacob: "And it came to pass that when Jacob saw Rachel...and rolled the stone..." (Beresheet 29:10). Of Moses it is written: "And the shepherds came and drove them away: but Moses stood up and helped them" (Shemot 2:17). After he saw the waters rising towards him, certainly Moses knew that he would find his soulmate there. Also, the Holy Spirit never departed from him, and through it he knew that Tziporah would be his wife. Moses said: 'Certainly when Jacob came here and the waters rose towards him, someone came to him who took him to his home and gave him all his needs. So will it be with me!'

230. אָמַר הַהוּא בַּר נָשׁ, הָכִי אוֹלִיפְנָא, דְּיִתְרוֹ כּוֹמֶר לכו"ם הֲוָה. כֵּיוָן דְּחָמָא דכו"ם לֵית בָּה מַמָּשׁוּ. אִתְפְּרַשׁ מִפּוּלְחָנָא דִּילֵהּ. קָמוּ עַמָּא וְנִדּוּהוּ. כֵּיוָן דְּחָמָא בִּנְתֵיהּ, הֲווֹ מִתַרְכָן לוֹן, דְּהָא בְּקַדְמֵיתָא אִינּוּן הֲווֹ רַעֲאָן עָאנֵיהּ. כֵּיוָן דְּחָמוּ מֹשֶׁה בְּרוּחַ קוּדְשָׁא, דְּעַל מִלָּה דכו"ם הֲווֹ עַבְדֵּי, מִיַּד וַיָּקָם מֹשֶׁה וַיּוֹשִׁעָן וַיַּשְׁקְ אֶת צֹאנָם. וְאִתְעֲבֵיד קִנְאָה לְקוּדְשָׁא בְּרִיךְ הוּא בְּכֹלָּא.

230. That man said: So have I learned that Jethro was a priest to idols; as soon as he saw that there is nothing in idolatry, he separated from its service. The people arose and excommunicated him. When the people saw his daughters COMING TO WATER HIS SHEEP, they drove them away. For originally, they THEMSELVES herded his sheep, SINCE HE WAS THEIR PRIEST. As soon as Moses saw, by the Holy Spirit, that they were doing this because of the matter of idolatry, "Moses stood up and helped them, and watered their flock." And all this was done through zealousness for the Holy One, blessed be He.

231. אָמַר לֵיהּ רִבִּי אֶלְעָזָר, אַנְתְּ לְגַבָּן, וְלָא יְדַעְנָא שְׁמָךְ. אָמַר, אֲנָא יוֹעֶזֶר בֶּן יַעֲקֹב. אָתוּ חַבְרַיָּיא וּנְשָׁקוּהוּ, אָמְרוּ, וּמָה אַנְתְּ לְגַבָּן, וְלָא הֲוֵינָן יַדְעִין בָּךְ. אָזְלוּ כַּחֲדָא כָּל הַהוּא יוֹמָא לְיוֹמָא אַחֲרָא אִזְפוּהוּ תְּלָת מִילִין, וְאָזִיל לְאוֹרְחֵיהּ.

231. Rabbi Elazar said to him: You are with us but we do not know your name. He said: I am Yoezer, the son of Jacob. The friends came and kissed him and said: You have been with us and we did not know you. They

walked together all that day and the morrow they escorted him three miles and he went on his way.

232. וַתּאמַרְן אִישׁ מִצְרִי הִצִּילָנוּ. רַבִּי חִיָּיא אָמַר, הָא אוּקְמוּהָ חַבְרַיָּיא, דְּנִצְנְצָא בְּהוּ רוּחַ קוּדְשָׁא, וְאָמְרוּ, וְלֹא יָדְעוּ מָה אָמְרוּ. לְבַר נָשׁ, דַּהֲוָה יָתִיב בְּמַדְבְּרָא, וַהֲווֹ יוֹמִין דְּלָא אָכַל בִּשְׂרָא. יוֹמָא חַד אָתָא דּוּבָא לְנַטְלָא חַד אִימְרָא, עָרַק אִימְרָא, וְדוּבָא אֲבַתְרֵיה, עַד דְּמָטוּ לְגַבֵּי הַהוּא בַּר נָשׁ לְמַדְבְּרָא, חָמָא אִימְרָא, וְאַתְקִיף בֵּיה וּשְׁחָטֵיה וְאָכַל בִּשְׂרָא.

232. "And they said: 'An Egyptian man delivered us'" (Shemot 2:19). Rabbi Chiya said: The friends explained this to mean that the Holy Spirit flickered in them WHEN THEY SAID "AN EGYPTIAN MAN DELIVERED US." They spoke but did not know what they spoke. FOR EXAMPLE, a man was dwelling in a wilderness and many days passed that he ate no food. One day, a bear came to catch a lamb. The lamb fled and the bear PURSUED him until they reached that man in the wilderness. He saw the lamb, grabbed it, slaughtered it and ate the meat. WE FIND THAT THE BEAR CAUSED THAT MAN TO EAT FOOD. ALSO, HERE THE EGYPTIAN THAT WAS KILLED BY MOSES CAUSED MOSES TO FLEE AND COME TO MIDIAN, TO THE WELL. THEREFORE, THEY SAID: "AN EGYPTIAN MAN DELIVERED US," WITH THE HOLY SPIRIT, MEANING THE EGYPTIAN MAN THAT MOSES KILLED.

27. "I am black, but comely"

A Synopsis
In answer to questions regarding the verse, "And these are the names of the children of Israel," Rabbi Yehuda explains the title verse, "I am black but comely..." This, we learn, is a reference to the Shechinah who is described as "black" because Yisrael are in captivity, but "comely" because they cleave to the Torah and good deeds. For this, the children of Yisrael will inherit the heavenly Jerusalem.

The Relevance of the Passage
The Zohar emanates spiritual forces that end our personal and global Exile upon the merit of the Torah's awesome powers. The Heavenly Jerusalem becomes our world, a place of boundless blessings and endless fulfillment.

Any area or aspect of our personal life that is in exile or darkness is redeemed and eternally illuminated.

233. ד״א וְאֵלֶּה שְׁמוֹת בְּנֵי יִשְׂרָאֵל. רִבִּי יְהוּדָה פָּתַח וְאָמַר, שְׁחוֹרָה אֲנִי וְנָאוָה וְגוֹ', שְׁחוֹרָה אֲנִי וְנָאוָה, דָּא כְּנֶסֶת יִשְׂרָאֵל, דְּהִיא שְׁחוֹרָה מִן גָּלוּתָא, וְנָאוָה, דְּהִיא נָאוָה בְּאוֹרַיְיתָא, וּבְפִקּוּדִין, וּבְעוֹבָדִין דְּכַשְׁרָן. בְּנוֹת יְרוּשָׁלַם, דְּעַל דָּא, זַכָּאִין לְיָרְתָאָה יְרוּשְׁלֵם דִּלְעֵילָא. כְּאָהֳלֵי קֵדָר, אַף עַל גַּב דְּהִיא קוֹדֶרֶת בְּגָלוּתָא, בְּעוֹבָדִין הִיא כִּירִיעוֹת שְׁלֹמֹה, כִּירִיעוֹת, דְּמַלְכָּא דִשְׁלָמָא כֹּלָּא דִּילֵיהּ.

233. Another explanation of: "And these are the names of the children of Israel" (Shemot 1:1). HE WAS PRESENTED WITH THIS DIFFICULTY: YISRAEL IS THE NAME OF GREATNESS, AND SO WHY IS THIS NAME MENTIONED WHEN THEY CAME TO THE EXILE IN EGYPT? AND WHY DOES HE REPEAT AFTERWARDS "WITH JACOB," WHICH IS THE NAME OF SMALLNESS? AND TO ANSWER THIS, Rabbi Yehuda opened the discussion saying: "I am black, but comely..." (Shir Hashirm 1:5). "I am black, but comely," refers to the Congregation of Yisrael, THAT IS, THE SHECHINAH that is black from the exile, "but comely" with Torah, commandments and good deeds THAT YISRAEL DO. "O, daughters of Jerusalem"; THESE ARE THE SOULS, WHO ARE OCCUPIED WITH TORAH AND THE PRECEPTS. Therefore, they merit inheriting the celestial Jerusalem, WHICH IS THE SHECHINAH. "Like the tents of Kedar" (Ibid.) – although she is blackened

(Heb. *koderet*) in exile, STILL IN ALL in actions she is "like the curtains of Solomon" (Heb. *Shlomo*), MEANING like the curtains, WHICH IS THE SECRET OF THE LIGHTS of the King, to Whom peace (Heb. *shalom*) belongs, WHICH IS ZEIR ANPIN.

28. "Make haste, my beloved"

A Synopsis

When Rabbi Chiya the Great goes to visit Rabbi Shimon bar Yochai to learn from the masters of the Mishnah, he see a curtain of fire behind which Rabbi Shimon and his students converse. Deciding to listen to the conversation from outside of the house, he hears an explanation of the title verse. According to the masters, we learn that this verse signifies the longing of Yisrael for God, as they implore Him not distance Himself from them without looking back.

Rabbi Shimon then hears Rabbi Chiya weeping outside of the house and tells his students that the Shechinah is with him. Knowing that the Shechinah will protect him from being burned by the fiery curtain, Rabbi Elazar is about to go and bring him in when he hears a voice that stops him. Rabbi Chiya then quotes the title verse and the curtain parts, a sign granting Rabbi Chiya permission to enter. Rabbi Shimon then stands up and the fire moves from the place where he stands to Rabbi Chiya, causing him to become mute. Rabbi Chiya enters with his eyes lowered and is unable to speak until Rabbi Elazar passes his hand over Rabbi Chiya's mouth. Rabbi Chiya then expounds upon his newfound insight: "It is good to die in the good golden fire that is burning." This is the place of Rabbi Shimon bar Yochai. From here, sparks fly on all sides and ascend to the 370 Chariots, each of which then separates into thousands until it reaches the Ancient of Days, who sits on a throne. The throne trembles, and this trembling penetrates to 260 worlds until it reaches the righteous in Eden and is heard throughout all the Firmaments. When Rabbi Shimon expounds on the Torah, all the celestial beings listen to his voice in silence. After he concludes, all rejoice and the souls and angels come to kneel before God, raising up the secrets of the spices that are in Eden to the Ancient of Days. Rabbi Shimon then explains that six levels of Holiness (Sfirot) descended with Jacob into Egypt, and corresponding to these are the six levels of Yisrael and the six steps to the supernal throne. Each of the aforementioned six are equal to ten, and so there are sixty in all, corresponding to the sixty mighty men that surround the Shechinah. When Rabbi Chiya points out that there are seven Sfirot, Rabbi Shimon explains that the level of Malchut is not counted because it does not illuminate of itself.

The Relevance of the Passage

The Zohar speaks of a "fiery curtain" that separates Rabbi Chiya from Rabbi Shimon and his companions. This curtain refers to the concealment of the supernal Light from our own eyes. The curtain's existence is the cause of darkness in our world.

Rav Ashlag's profound commentary explains that our world generates no Light of its own. Rather, the Light that animates our existence radiates from six candles. These six candles are the six dimensions that are enfolded into one, known collectively as Zeir Anpin. The curtain separates these six dimensions from our dimension.

The notion of multiple dimensions was unimaginable among the scientific and lay community during the time of Rabbi Shimon. Yet, today, physics concurs with Kabbalah that indeed, the universe consists of ten dimensions and that six of them curled up into one at the moment of physical creation.

This realm of the six is the source of all our joy. It is where wisdom, love, happiness, and all information dwell. When we make contact with this realm, at will or inadvertently, Light flows to our soul, resulting in happiness, joy, awareness, discovery, and enlightenment.

The ultimate purpose of existence is to remove this curtain gradually through spiritual elevation, so that infinite Light and joy may shine upon the world. But during the course of a lifetime, a man often falls to great depths of darkness; there are times when his suffering seems unbearable, and the hurt feels unendurable. However, the Light of the Creator incandesces with super-radiance, without end. The souls of humanity requested that this awesome Light be hidden by the curtain until we, by our own hand, reveal its full splendor by means of climbing the spiritual ladder. The rungs on this ladder are known as the Fifty Gates of Binah.

Prior the worldwide dissemination of the Zohar, which began in the 20th century, it could take numerous lifetimes for a soul to reach the highest rung on the ladder. Fortunately, our meditation upon this sacred Book of Splendor now elevates us to the fiftieth gate. The Light of Binah floods our darkness with iridescent streams of Celestial Light that soothes our pain and heals humanity to the point of perfection. This is attainable upon the greatness and prominence of the soul of Rabbi Shimon, the author of the Zohar.

The actual words that speak of this saintly sage's eminence imbues our own souls with greatness.

234. רִבִּי חִיָּיא רַבָּא, הֲוָה אָזִיל לְגַבֵּי מָארֵיהוֹן דְּמַתְנִיתָא, לְמֵילַף מִנַּיְיהוּ. אָזַל לְגַבֵּי רִבִּי שִׁמְעוֹן בֶּן יוֹחָאי, וְחָמָא פַּרְגּוֹד חַד, דַּהֲוָה פָּסִיק בְּבֵיתָא. תָּוָה רִבִּי חִיָּיא, אָמַר, אֶשְׁמַע מִלָּה מִפּוּמֵיה מֵהָכָא.

234. Rabbi Chiya Raba went to the masters of the Mishnah to learn from them. He went to Rabbi Shimon bar Yochai, and saw a curtain OF FIRE that

divided the house. AND RABBI SHIMON AND HIS STUDENTS WERE IN THE INSIDE OF THE CURTAIN. Rabbi Chiya was mystified and said: I will hear a word from his mouth from here, FROM OUTSIDE THE FIERY CURTAIN.

235. שָׁמַע דַּהֲוָה אָמַר, בְּרַח דּוֹדִי וּדְמֵה לְךָ לִצְבִי אוֹ לְעוֹפֶר הָאַיָּלִים. כָּל כְּסוּפָא דְּכָסִיפוּ יִשְׂרָאֵל מִקּוּדְשָׁא בְּרִיךְ הוּא הוּא, דְּאר"ש, תַּאֲוָתָם שֶׁל יִשְׂרָאֵל, שֶׁיִּהְיֶה הַקּוּדְשָׁא בְּרִיךְ הוּא לֹא הוֹלֵךְ וְלֹא מִתְרַחֵק, אֶלָּא בּוֹרֵחַ כַּצְּבִי אוֹ כְּעוֹפֶר הָאַיָּלִים.

235. He heard THE VOICE OF ONE OF THE STUDENTS OF RABBI SHIMON, who said: "Make haste, my beloved, and be you like a gazelle or a young hart" (Shir Hashirm 8:14). All the longings that Yisrael had for the Holy One, blessed be He, were AS Rabbi Shimon said: the desire of Yisrael is that the Holy One, blessed be He, should not distance Himself, but rather run like a gazelle or a young deer.

236. מ"ט, אר"ש, אֵין חַיָּה בָּעוֹלָם עוֹשָׂה כְּמוֹ הַצְּבִי אוֹ כְּעוֹפֶר הָאַיָּלִים, בִּזְמָן שֶׁהוּא בּוֹרֵחַ הוֹלֵךְ מְעַט מְעַט, וּמַחֲזִיר אֶת רֹאשׁוֹ לַמָּקוֹם שֶׁיָּצָא מִמֶּנּוּ, וּלְעוֹלָם תָּמִיד הוּא מַחֲזִיר אֶת רֹאשׁוֹ לַאֲחוֹרָיו. כָּךְ אָמְרוּ יִשְׂרָאֵל, רבש"ע, אִם אָנוּ גּוֹרְמִים שֶׁתִּסְתַּלֵּק מִבֵּינֵינוּ, יְהִי רָצוֹן, שֶׁתִּבְרַח כְּמוֹ הַצְּבִי אוֹ כְּמוֹ עוֹפֶר הָאַיָּלִים, שֶׁהוּא בּוֹרֵחַ וּמַחֲזִיר אֶת רֹאשׁוֹ לְמָקוֹם שֶׁהִנִּיחַ, הה"ד, וְאַף גַּם זֹאת בִּהְיוֹתָם בְּאֶרֶץ אוֹיְבֵיהֶם לֹא מְאַסְתִּים וְלֹא גְעַלְתִּים לְכַלֹּתָם. ד"א, הַצְּבִי כְּשֶׁהוּא יָשֵׁן, הוּא יָשֵׁן בְּעַיִן אַחַת, וְהָאַחֶרֶת הוּא נֵעוֹר, כָּךְ אָמְרוּ יִשְׂרָאֵל לְקוּדְשָׁא בְּרִיךְ הוּא, עֲשֵׂה כְּמוֹ הַצְּבִי, שֶׁהִנֵּה לֹא יָנוּם וְלֹא יִישָׁן שׁוֹמֵר יִשְׂרָאֵל.

236. Rabbi Shimon said: What is the reason that there is no animal in the world who does as the gazelle or young deer, which when he flees, goes a measure and turns his head to the place whence he left. He always turns his head backwards. So did Yisrael say: 'Master of the Universe, if we cause that You ascend from us, may it please You to flee like a gazelle or young deer who flees, and turns his head to the place that he left' – MEANING THE PLACE HE WAS BEFORE, FROM WHERE HE FLED. This is what is written: "And yet for all that, when they are in the land of their enemies, I will not cast them away, nor will I abhor them, to destroy them utterly" (Vayikra. 26:44). Another explanation is that the deer sleeps with one eye, while the other eye is awake. So did Yisrael say to the Holy One, blessed be He: 'Do as the deer; "Behold, the Guardian of Yisrael neither slumbers nor sleeps" (Tehilim 121:4)'.

237. שָׁמַע רִבִּי חִיָּיא וְאָמַר, אִי עִלָּאִין עַסְקִין בְּבֵיתָא, וַאֲנָא יָתִיב אַבְרַאי, בָּכָה. שָׁמַע ר"ש וְאָמַר, וַדַּאי שְׁכִינְתָּא לְבָרָא, מַאן יִפּוֹק. אָמַר רִבִּי אֶלְעָזָר בְּרֵיהּ. אִי אֲנָא קָלֵינָא, לָא קָלֵינָא דְּהָא שְׁכִינְתָּא בָּרָא מִנָּנָא, לֵיעוֹל שְׁכִינְתָּא, וְתִיהֱוֵי אֶשָּׁתָא שְׁלֵימָתָא. שָׁמַע קָלָא דְּאָמַר, עַד לָא סַמְכִין אִסְתַּמְּכוּ, וְתַרְעִין לָא אִתְתַּקְּנוּ, וּמְזוּטְרֵי דְּבוּסְמַיָּא דְּעֵדֶן דִּכְעָן הוּא, לָא נָפַק ר' אֶלְעָזָר.

237. Rabbi Chiya heard and said: Those higher ones are occupied WITH TORAH inside the house and I sit outside. He wept. Rabbi Shimon heard and said: Assuredly, the Shechinah is outside, MEANING WITH RABBI CHIYA, who will go out AND BRING HIM IN. His son Rabbi Elazar said: If I am burned BY GOING OUT THROUGH THE FIERY CURTAIN, I will yet not be burned because the Shechinah is outside BY RABBI CHIYA. Let the Shechinah enter and the fire OF THE CURTAIN will be complete. Rabbi Elazar heard a voice that said: The pillars have not yet been supported, WHICH IS THE SECRET OF THE THREE COLUMNS, and the gates have still not been completed, MEANING THE FIFTY GATES OF BINAH, and he is now of the smaller spice trees of Eden, MEANING OF THE SMALLEST SOULS WHO ARE CALLED "SPICES". THEREFORE, Rabbi Elazar did not go out TO BRING HIM IN.

238. יָתִיב רִבִּי חִיָּיא, בָּכָה וְאִתְגַּנַּח, פָּתַח וְאָמַר, סוֹב דְּמֵה לְךָ דוֹדִי לִצְבִי אוֹ לְעֹפֶר הָאַיָּלִים. אִתְפְּתַח תַּרְעָא דְּפַרְגּוֹדָא, לָא עָיֵיל רִבִּי חִיָּיא, זָקִיף רִבִּי שִׁמְעוֹן עֵינוֹי וְאָמַר, ש"מ אִתְיְהִיב רְשׁוּתָא לְמַאן דְּאִיהוּ אַבְרַאי וַאֲנָן לְגוֹ. קָם רִבִּי שִׁמְעוֹן, אָזַל אֶשָּׁא מְדוּכְתֵּיהּ, עַד דּוּכְתָּא דְּרִבִּי חִיָּיא, אָמַר רִבִּי שִׁמְעוֹן, קוּזְטִיפָא דִּנְהוֹרָא דְּקַלִּיטְרָא לְבַר, וַאֲנָא הָכָא לְגוֹ, אִתְאַלַּם פּוּמֵיהּ דְּרִבִּי חִיָּיא.

238. Rabbi Chiya sat, wept and sighed. He opened the discussion, saying: "Turn, my beloved, and be you like a gazelle or young hart" (Shir Hashirm

2:17), MEANING ACCORDING TO THE EXPLANATION THAT HE HEARD
FROM RABBI SHIMON – THAT EVEN THOUGH THAT HE WAS FLEEING, HE
TURNED HIS HEAD BACK AND DID NOT DISTANCE HIMSELF, AND THEN
the gate of the curtain opened. BUT Rabbi Chiya did not enter. Rabbi
Shimon raised his eyes AND SAW THAT THE ENTRANCE OF THE CURTAIN
OPENED. He said: Apparently, permission has been granted to whoever is
outside, yet we are inside, AND WE MUST NOT BRING HIM IN. Rabbi
Shimon stood up and the fire moved from its place to the place of Rabbi
Chiya. Rabbi Shimon said: The spark of the ingathering light HAS ALREADY
SPREAD outside, TO RABBI CHIYA, yet I am here inside AND I MUST NOT
BRING HIM IN. Rabbi Chiya's mouth became mute BECAUSE OF THE FIRE
THAT SPREAD TOWARDS HIM.

239. כֵּיוָן דְּעָאל לְגוֹ, מַאִיךְ עֵינוֹי, וְלָא זָקִיף רֵישֵׁיה. אָמַר רִבִּי שִׁמְעוֹן
לְרִבִּי אֶלְעָזָר בְּרֵיה, קוּם אַעְבָּר יָדָךְ אֲפוּמֵיה, דְּלָא יָדַע בְּהַאי, דְּלָא
רָגִיל בֵּיה. קָם רִבִּי אֶלְעָזָר, אַעְבָּר יְדֵיה אֲפוּמֵיה דְּרִבִּי חִיָּיא, פָּתַח
פּוּמֵיה רִבִּי חִיָּיא, וְאָמַר, חָמָא עֵינָא מַה דְּלָא חֲמֵינָא, אִזְדְּקַף דְּלָא
חֲשִׁיבְנָא, טָב לְמֵימַת בְּאֶשָּׁא דְּדַהֲבָא טָבָא דָּלִיק.

239. As soon as RABBI CHIYA entered inside, he lowered his eyes and did
not raise his head. Rabbi Shimon said to his son Rabbi Elazar: Pass your
hand over the mouth OF RABBI CHIYA because he does not know about this,
as he is not accustomed to it, AND DOES NOT KNOW WHAT TO DO. Rabbi
Elazar arose and passed his hand over Rabbi Chiya's mouth. Rabbi Chiya
opened his mouth and said: My eye has seen what I have not EVER seen and
my stature has straightened, for I have never thought SO. It is good to die in
the good golden fire that is burning.

240. בְּאֲתָר דְּשְׁבִיבִין זַרְקִין לְכָל עִיבָר, וְכָל שְׁבִיבָא וּשְׁבִיבָא, סָלִיק
לִתְלַת מְאָה וְשַׁבְעִין רְתִיכִין. וְכָל רְתִיכָא, אִתְפְּרַשׁ לְאֶלֶף אַלְפִין,
וְרִבּוֹא רִבְוָון, עַד דְּמָטוּ לְעַתִּיק יוֹמִין, דְּיָתִיב עַל כֻּרְסְיָיא, וְכֻרְסְיָיא
מִזְדַּעְזְעָא מִנֵּיה, לְמָאתָן וְשִׁתִּין עָלְמִין.

240. In the place OF RABBI SHIMON BAR YOCHAI, which casts sparks to all
sides, every single spark ascends to 370 Chariots. THEN, every single
Chariot separates to thousands, and tens of thousands, until it reaches Atik
Yomin that sits on a throne. And the throne trembles from it to 260 worlds.

241. עַד דְּמָטָא לַאֲתָר עֵדוּנָא דְּצַדִּיקַיָּיא, עַד דְּאִשְׁתְּמַע בְּכָל רְקִיעִין, וְכָל עֶלָּאִין וְתַתָּאִין, וְכֻלְּהוּ בְּזִמְנָא חֲדָא, תַּוְוהִין וְאַמְרִין, הָדֵין הוּא רַבִּי שִׁמְעוֹן בֶּן יוֹחַאי, דַּהֲוָה מַרְעִישׁ כֹּלָּא, מַאן יָכִיל לְמֵיקַם קַמֵּיהּ. דֵּין הוּא רשב"י, דִּבְשַׁעֲתָא דְּפָתַח פּוּמֵיהּ לְמִשְׁרֵי לְמִלְעֵי בְּאוֹרַיְיתָא, צַיְיתִין לְקָלֵיהּ, כָּל כֻּרְסְוָון וְכָל רְקִיעִין וְכָל רְתִיכִין, וְכָל אִינּוּן דִּמְשַׁבְּחֵי לְמָרֵיהוֹן.

241. Until RABBI SHIMON BAR YOCHAI reaches the place of Eden of the righteous, until THE SUPERIORITY OF RABBI SHIMON BAR YOCHAI is heard throughout the firmaments, those above and below at the same time are amazed and say: Is this Rabbi Shimon bar Yochai who shook everything up? Who can stand before him? This is Rabbi Shimon whos voice, at the moment he opens his mouth to start occupying himself with Torah, all the thrones, and all the firmaments, and all the Chariots hearken to, and also all those that praise their Master.

242. לֵית דְּפַתְחִין וְלֵית דִּמְסַיְּימִין, כֻּלְּהוּ מִשְׁתַּכְּחִין, עַד לָא אִשְׁתְּמַע בְּכָל רְקִיעַיָּא דִּלְעֵילָּא וְתַתָּא, פְּטָרָא. כַּד מְסַיֵּים רַבִּי שִׁמְעוֹן לְמִלְעֵי בְּאוֹרַיְיתָא, מַאן חָמֵי שִׁירִין, מַאן חָמֵי חֶדְוָתָא, דִּמְשַׁבְּחִין לְמָרֵיהוֹן, מַאן חָמֵי קָלִין דְּאַזְלִין בְּכֻלְּהוּ רְקִיעִין. אַתְיָין כֻּלְּהוּ בְּגִינֵיהּ דר"ש, וְכַרְעִין וְסָגְדִּין קַמֵּי דְּמָרֵיהוֹן, סַלְקִין רֵיחִין דְּבוּסְמִין דְּעֵדֶן, עַד עַתִּיק יוֹמִין, וְכָל הַאי בְּגִינֵיהּ דר"ש.

242. There is no one to open TO SING PRAISES, and there is no one to end HIS SONG OF PRAISE. THAT IS TO SAY, THOSE WHO ARE IN THE MIDDLE OF THEIR PRAISES DO NOT FINISH THEIR PRAISES, FOR they are all there TO HEARKEN TO THE VOICE OF RABBI SHIMON BAR YOCHAI. It comes to a point that no utterance is heard in all the heavens above and below. When Rabbi Shimon concludes his occupation with Torah, who has seen songs, who has seen joy of those that praise their Master, who has seen the voices that permeate all the heavens. And because of Rabbi Shimon they all come, MEANING ALL THE SOULS AND ANGELS, and kneel and bow before their Master, raising up the secrets of the spices that are in Eden, WHICH IS THE SECRET OF THE ILLUMINATION OF CHOCHMAH, until Atik Yomin. And all this is because of Rabbi Shimon.

243. פָּתַח רִבִּי שִׁמְעוֹן פּוּמֵיהּ וְאָמַר, שִׁית דַּרְגִּין נַחְתּוּ עִמֵּיהּ דְּיַעֲקֹב לְמִצְרַיִם וְכָל חַד וְחַד עֲשָׂרָה אֶלֶף רִבּוֹא. וּלְקָבְלֵיהוֹן שִׁית דַּרְגִּין לְיִשְׂרָאֵל. וּלְקָבְלֵיהוֹן שִׁית דַּרְגִּין לְכֻרְסְיָיא דִּלְעֵילָא. וּלְקָבְלֵיהוֹן שִׁית דַּרְגִּין לְכֻרְסְיָיא דִּלְתַתָּא. דִּכְתִיב שֵׁשׁ מַעֲלוֹת לַכִּסֵּא. הה"ד רִבְבָה כְּצֶמַח הַשָּׂדֶה נְתַתִּיךְ וְגו', הֲרֵי שִׁית. וּלְקָבְלֵיהוֹן כְּתִיב, וּבְנֵי יִשְׂרָאֵל פָּרוּ וַיִּשְׁרְצוּ וַיִּרְבּוּ וַיַּעַצְמוּ וְגו'.

243. Rabbi Shimon opened his mouth and said: Six levels descended with Jacob to Egypt. THEY ARE CHESED, GVURAH, TIFERET, NETZACH, HOD AND YESOD. And each one EXPANDS TO ten, WHEN THEY ARE IN THE ILLUMINATION OF ZEIR ANPIN ALONE. THEN THEY ARE SIXTY, AND ARE one thousand WHEN THEY RECEIVE THE ILLUMINATION OF CHOCHMAH, WHICH IS THE SECRET OF THOUSANDS. THEN, THEY ARE SIXTY THOUSAND, UP TO ten thousand, WHEN RECEIVING THE ILLUMINATION OF CHASSADIM FROM ATIK, AND THEY ARE SIX HUNDRED THOUSAND. And corresponding to them are six levels to Yisrael – BECAUSE FROM YISRAEL THEY DESCEND TO JACOB. Corresponding to them are six steps to the supernal throne, WHICH ARE CHESED, GVURAH AND TIFERET OF ZEIR ANPIN THAT INCLUDES NETZACH, HOD AND YESOD. And corresponding to them are the six steps to the lower throne, WHICH IS MALCHUT, WHICH ARE CHESED, GVURAH, TIFERET, NETZACH, HOD AND YESOD as is written: "The throne had six steps" (I Melachim 10:19). This is the meaning of: "I will cause you to increase like the plant of the field" (Yechezkel 16:7), WHICH IS THE FIRST GRADE; "AND YOU DID INCREASE," WHICH IS THE SECOND; "AND GROW BIG," THE THIRD; "AND YOU DID COME TO POSSESS GREAT ATTRACTIONS," THE FOURTH; "YOUR BREASTS WERE FIRM," THE FIFTH; "AND YOUR HAIR WAS GROWN," THE SIXTH. Correspondingly, it is written: "And the children of Yisrael were fruitful" (Shemot 1:7), WHICH IS THE FIRST; "and increased abundantly," THE SECOND; "and multiplied," THE THIRD; "and grew," THE FOURTH; "EXCEEDINGLY," THE FIFTH; AND "MIGHTY," THE SIXTH.

244. תָּא חֲזֵי, כָּל חַד וְחַד סָלִיק לַעֲשָׂרָה, וַהֲווֹ שִׁתִּין, וְאִינוּן שִׁתִּין גַּבְרִין דִּבְסַחֲרָנֵי שְׁכִינְתָּא, וְאִינוּן שִׁתִּין רִבְבָן, דְּנַפְקוּ עִם יִשְׂרָאֵל מִגָּלוּתָא, וּדְעָאלוּ עִם יַעֲקֹב בְּגָלוּתָא.

244. Come and behold: each one OF THE AFOREMENTIONED SIX EXTREMITIES equals ten – MEANING FROM THE ILLUMINATION OF ZEIR ANPIN ITSELF, WHOSE SFIROT ARE COUNTED BY TENS, AS AFOREMENTIONED – and THE SIX EXTREMITIES become sixty. THEN they are the sixty valiant men who surround the Shechinah, AS IS WRITTEN: "BEHOLD THE LITTER, THAT OF SOLOMON" (SHIR HASHIRM 3:7), WHICH IS THE SHECHINAH THAT IS CALLED 'BED'. "SIXTY VALIANT MEN ARE ROUND ABOUT IT, OF THE MIGHTY MEN OF YISRAEL." And they are six hundred thousand," WHEN SHE RECEIVES THE ILLUMINATION OF CHASSADIM FROM ATIK YOMIN AS MENTIONED ABOVE, that emerged with Yisrael from the exile, and came with Jacob to the exile.

245. אָמַר לֵיהּ ר' חִיָּיא, וְהָא הֲווֹ שִׁבְעָה, וְסַלְקִין לְשַׁבְעִין, אָמַר לֵיהּ ר' שִׁמְעוֹן, שַׁבְעִין לָאו מֵהָכָא, וְאִי ס"ד שִׁבְעָה, הָא כְּתִיב וְשִׁשָּׁה קָנִים יוֹצְאִים מִצִּדֶּיהָ שְׁלֹשָׁה קְנֵי מְנוֹרָה וְגו'. וְקָנֶה הָאֶחָד הָאֶמְצָעִי לָאו בְּחֻשְׁבָּנָא, דִּכְתִיב אֶל מוּל פְּנֵי הַמְּנוֹרָה יָאִירוּ וְגו'.

245. Rabbi Chiya said to him: But they are seven: CHESED, GVURAH, TIFERET, NETZACH, HOD, YESOD AND MALCHUT. AND WHEN EACH ONE BECOME TEN they add up to seventy, AND NOT SIXTY. Rabbi Shimon said to him that seventy does not apply here, BECAUSE HERE ARE CONSIDERED THE LEVELS THAT ILLUMINATE, AND THE LEVEL OF MALCHUT DOES NOT ILLUMINATE OF ITSELF. And if you wish to consider seven, MEANING TO COUNT ALSO MALCHUT WITH THE SIX EXTREMITIES, it is written: "And six branches shall come out of its sides; three branches of the candlestick out of the one side..." (Shemot 25:32). FOR THEY CORRESPOND TO CHESED, GVURAH, TIFERET, NETZACH, HOD AND YESOD, and one branch that is central, WHICH IS MALCHUT, is not counted, as it is written: "...the seven lamps shall give light towards the body of the candlestick..." (Bemidbar 8:2). BECAUSE MALCHUT DOES NOT ILLUMINATE ONHER OWN, SHE ONLY RECEIVES FROM THE SIX CANDLES.

29. Wherefore exile, and wherefore to Egypt

A Synopsis

Rabbi Elazar begins the discussion by asking his father why God allowed Yisrael to go into exile, and why into Egypt. After receiving encouragement from his father, he interprets the verse, "There are sixty queens, eighty concubines and young women without number." We then learn that God scattered all the nations across the earth and appointed supernal ministers over them, taking Yisrael as His portion. Indeed, God created the world for the sake of Yisrael and endowed it with permanence through Abraham (Wisdom), Isaac (Understanding) and Jacob (Knowledge). Once the twelve Tribes were born to Jacob, the supernal pattern was complete, as ordained from the beginning. If Yisrael assimilated with other nations, all the worlds would become tainted. Therefore, God caused Yisrael to wander the earth until they fell among the Egyptians, who made them slaves and despised them and their customs. Because the Egyptians hated them and would not mingle with them, they became perfected completely within the Holy Seed (without any mixture of foreign people) and the guilt of the other nations became complete.

The Relevance of the Passage

The term Yisrael is a code for the human soul, the person who successfully nullifies the base impulses of his body in favor of the longings of his soul.

The other nations of the world correspond to all our negative desires, borne of ego. Negative angelic forces govern and incite these negative urges, whereas the Light of the Creator inflames the Light of our soul.

Using the power of the Three Column System, the free will to resist selfishness, we can purify ourselves and gain freedom from our egocentric and self-indulgent inclinations, which are known in Kabbalistic terminology as Egypt.

Purification and true spiritual greatness is found when we go into the chaos of this world (Egypt), when we willingly confront our self-centeredness, and use the power of Kabbalah to eradicate every ounce of egotism from our being. We attain purification from the Light cast through these ancient verses. The perfection that has been our destiny since the birth of the cosmos is achieved through our interaction with the letters composing this passage.

246. עַד דַּהֲווֹ יַתְבֵי, אר"א לְרבִּי שִׁמְעוֹן אֲבוֹי, מֶה חָמָא קוּדְשָׁא בְּרִיךְ הוּא, לְנַחְתָּא יִשְׂרָאֵל, לְמִצְרַיִם בְּגָלוּתָא. א"ל חֲדָא שְׁאֶלְתָּא אַתְּ

שָׁאִיל, אוֹ תְּרֵין. א״ל תְּרֵין. גָּלוּתָא לָמָה. וּלְמִצְרַיִם לְמָה. א״ל תְּרֵין אִינּוּן וְאִתְחֲזָרוּ לְחַד. א״ל קוּם בְּקִיּוּמָךְ בְּגִינָךְ יִתְקְיָּים לְעֵילָּא, מִשְּׁמָךְ הַאי מִלָּה, אֵימָא בְּרִי אֵימָא.

246. While they were still sitting, Rabbi Elazar said to his father, Rabbi Shimon: Why did the Holy One, blessed be He, cause Yisrael to go down to Egypt in exile? He said to him: Are you asking one question or two questions? RABBI ELAZAR said to him: Two. I AM ASKING: why the exile? And why, PARTICULARLY, in Egypt? Rabbi Shimon said to him: They are two questions that result in one question! RABBI SHIMON said to him: Establish yourself, THAT IS, IN YOUR LEVEL. Because of this you will be established above, IN THE HEAVENLY YESHIVAH, speak in your name. Speak up, my son, speak up.

247. פָּתַח וְאָמַר שִׁשִּׁים הֵמָּה מְלָכוֹת וּשְׁמוֹנִים פִּילַגְשִׁים. שִׁשִּׁים הֵמָּה מְלָכוֹת, אִינּוּן גִּבְרַיָּא דִלְעֵילָּא מֵחֵילָא דִּגְבוּרָא דְּאִתְאַחֲדָן בְּגָלִיפִין, דְּחֵיוָתָא קַדִּישָׁא דְּיִשְׂרָאֵל. וּשְׁמוֹנִים פִּילַגְשִׁים, מְמָנָן בְּגָלִיפוֹי דִּתְחוֹתוֹי. וְעָלְמוֹת אֵין מִסְפָּר, כד״א הֲיֵשׁ מִסְפָּר לִגְדוּדָיו. וְעִם כָּל דָּא כְּתִיב, אַחַת הִיא יוֹנָתִי תַמָּתִי אַחַת הִיא לְאִמָּה, דָּא הִיא שְׁכִינְתָּא קַדִּישָׁא דְּנָפְקָא מִתְּרֵיסַר זִיהֲרָא, דְּזֹהֲרָא דְּנָהִיר לְכֹלָּא, וְאִיהִי אִתְקְרֵי אִמָּא.

247. He opened the discussion saying: "There are sixty queens, eighty concubines and young women without number" (Shir Hashirm 6:8). "There are sixty queens," are the mighty men of above, from the side of Gvurah, who hold onto the inscriptions, MEANING THE EXTERIORS, of the holy living creature of Yisrael, WHICH IS MALCHUT, AND ARE THEREFORE BAMED AFTER IT: "SIXTY QUEENS." THEY ARE THE ANGELS WHO ARE APPOINTED OVER THE NATIONS, AS WRITTEN FURTHER. "And eighty concubines" are THE ANGELS who are appointed in the inscriptions of the queens which are under THE SIXTY QUEENS. THEREFORE, THEY ARE CALLED 'CONCUBINES' AND NOT 'QUEENS'. "And young women without number," is as is written: "Is there any number to His armies?" (Iyov 25:3). And yet it is written: "My Dove, my undefiled is but one, she is the only one of her mother..." (Shir Hashirm 6:9). This is the Holy Shechinah that emerges from twelve lights, AND IS the shine that illuminates everything. Therefore she is called 'mother', AS IT IS WRITTEN: "SHE IS THE ONLY ONE OF HER MOTHER."

248. כְּגַוְונָא דָּא עָבִיד קוּדְשָׁא בְּרִיךְ הוּא בְּאַרְעָא, זָרִיק לְכָל עַמִּין לְכָל
עִיבָר, וּמְנֵי עֲלֵיהֶן רַבְרְבֵי, הה״ד אֲשֶׁר חָלַק ה׳ אֱלֹהֶיךָ אוֹתָם לְכָל
הָעַמִּים, וְהוּא נָסִיב לְחוּלָקֵיה כְּנִשְׁיתָּא דְּיִשְׂרָאֵל, הה״ד כִּי חֵלֶק ה׳
עַמּוֹ יַעֲקֹב חֶבֶל נַחֲלָתוֹ. וְקָרָא לָה אַחַת הִיא יוֹנָתִי תַמָּתִי אַחַת הִיא
לְאִמָּה, דָּא הִיא שְׁכִינַת יְקָרֵיה, דְּאַשְׁרֵי בֵּינַיְהוֹן, אַחַת הִיא וּמְיוּחֶדֶת
לֵיה. רָאוּהָ בָנוֹת וַיְאַשְּׁרוּהָ, כד״א רַבּוֹת בָּנוֹת עָשׂוּ חָיִל וְאַתְּ עָלִית עַל
כֻּלָּנָה. מְלָכוֹת וּפִילַגְשִׁים וַיְהַלְלוּהָ, אִלֵּין רַבְרְבֵי עַמִּין דְּאִתְפַּקְדָן
עֲלַיְיהוּ.

248. Similarly, the Holy One, blessed be He, did in this world. He cast all the nations to every side and appointed overseers over them, as is written: "Which Hashem your Elohim has allotted to all the nations" (Devarim 4:19). And He, MEANING THE HOLY ONE, BLESSED BE HE, took as His portion the Congregation of Yisrael. This is written: "For Hashem's portion is His people, Jacob is the lot of His inheritance" (Devarim 32:9). And He called it: "My Dove, my undefiled is but one, she is the only one of her Mother." This is the Shechinah of His glory, which He caused to dwell among them. She is the only one and is selected for Him. "The daughters saw her and called her happy," as is written: "Many daughters have done virtuously, but you excel them all" (Mishlei 31:29). "And the queens and the concubines praised her" (Shir Hasirim 6:9). These were the Princes of the nations that were appointed over them.

249. וְעוֹד רָזָא דְּמִלָּה הִיא דִּתְנַן בַּעֲשָׂרָה מַאֲמָרוֹת נִבְרָא הָעוֹלָם, וְכַד
תִּסְתַּכַּל תְּלָתָא אִינּוּן, וְעָלְמָא בְּהוּ אִתְבְּרֵי, בְּחָכְמָה וּבִתְבוּנָה וּבְדַעַת,
וְעָלְמָא לָא אִתְבְּרֵי אֶלָּא בְּגִינֵיהוֹן דְּיִשְׂרָאֵל, כַּד בָּעָא לְקַיְּימָא עָלְמָא,
עָבֵד לְאַבְרָהָם בְּרָזָא דְּחָכְמָה. לְיִצְחָק, בְּרָזָא דִּתְבוּנָה. לְיַעֲקֹב בְּרָזָא
דְּדַעַת. וּבְהַאי אִתְקְרֵי, וּבְדַעַת חֲדָרִים יִמָּלְאוּ. וּבְהַהִיא שַׁעֲתָא
אִשְׁתַּכְלַל כָּל עָלְמָא. וּמִדְּאִתְיְלִידוּ לְיַעֲקֹב תְּרֵיסַר שִׁבְטִין, אִשְׁתַּכְלַל
כֹּלָּא, כְּגַוְונָא דִּלְעֵילָא.

249. And another secret we have learned is that the world was created by ten sayings, but when you observe it closely, they are really three through

which the world was created – NAMELY Chochmah, Tevunah and Da'at. And the world was created only for Yisrael. When the Holy One, blessed be He, wanted to preserve the world, He did for Abraham with the secret of Chochmah, for Isaac with the secret of Tvunah, and for Jacob with the secret of Da'at. It is written: "And by knowledge are the chambers filled" (Mishlei 24:4). THIS IS THE SECRET OF CHESED, GVURAH AND TIFERET, WHICH ARE ABRAHAM, ISAAC AND JACOB. THEY ROSE TO BECOME CHOCHMAH, BINAH AND DA'AT. At that moment, the entire world was perfected. And when the twelve tribes were born to Jacob, WHICH ARE THE SECRET OF THE TWELVE DIAGONAL BORDERS, everything was perfected IN THIS WORLD as above IN ATZILUT.

250. כַּד חָמָא קוּדְשָׁא בְּרִיךְ הוּא חֶדְוָותָא סַגִּיאָה דְּהַאי עָלְמָא תַּתָּאָה, דְּאִשְׁתַּכְלַל כְּגַוְונָא דִּלְעֵילָא, אָמַר, דִּילְמָא ח"ו יִתְעָרְבוּן בִּשְׁאַר עַמָּמִין, וְיִשְׁתְּאַר פְּגִימוּתָא בְּכֻלְּהוּ עָלְמִין. מַה עָבֵד קוּדְשָׁא בְּרִיךְ הוּא, טִלְטֵל לְכֻלְּהוּ מֵהָכָא לְהָכָא, עַד דְּנַחְתּוּ לְמִצְרַיִם, לְמֵידָר דִּיּוּרֵיהוֹן בְּעַם קְשֵׁי קָדָל, דִּמְבַזִּין נִמּוּסֵיהוֹן, וּמְבַזִּין לְהוֹן לְאִתְחַתְּנָא בְּהוּ, וּלְאִתְעָרְבָא בַּהֲדַיְיהוּ, וַחֲשִׁיבוּ לְהוֹן עַבְדִּין. גּוּבְרִין גָּעֲלִין בְּהוֹן, נוּקְבָתָא גָּעֲלָן בְּהוֹן עַד דְּאִשְׁתַּכְלַל כֹּלָּא בְּזַרְעָא קַדִּישָׁא, וּבֵין כָּךְ וּבֵין כָּךְ שְׁלִים חוֹבָא דִּשְׁאַר עַמִּין, דִּכְתִיב כִּי לֹא שָׁלֵם עֲוֹן הָאֱמוֹרִי עַד הֵנָּה. וְכַד נָפְקוּ, נָפְקוּ זַכָּאִין קַדִּישִׁין, דִּכְתִיב שִׁבְטֵי יָהּ עֵדוּת לְיִשְׂרָאֵל. אָתָא ר' שִׁמְעוֹן וּנְשָׁקֵיהּ בְּרֵישֵׁיהּ, א"ל קָאִים בְּרִי בְּקִיּוּמָךְ, דְּשַׁעְתָּא קַיְימָא לָךְ.

250. When the Holy One, blessed be He, saw the great joy of this world when it was perfected as above, He said: 'Heaven forbid that THE TWELVE TRIBES become mixed among the other nations and there will remain a blemish in all the worlds.' What did the Holy One, blessed be He, do? He caused them to move from here to there until they descended to Egypt to settle in their homes among a stiff-necked people who ridiculed their customs, were too scornful to intermarry with them and to mingle with them, and considered them slaves. The men scorned them and the women scorned them, until they became perfected completely into a holy seed, WITHOUT ANY MIXTURE OF A FOREIGN PEOPLE. In the meantime, the sin of the nations was completed as is written: "For the iniquity of the Amorites is not yet full" (Beresheet 15:16). When they left, they left holy and righteous as is written: "The tribes of Yah, as a testimony for Yisrael"

(Tehilim 122:4). Rabbi Shimon came and kissed him on his head, and said to him: stand in your position, my son – MEANING AT YOUR LEVEL – for the moment is at your command.

30. "He did neither eat bread nor drink water"

A Synopsis

After two days of continual discussion without food or water, Rabbi Shimon quotes the title verse to Rabbi Elazar. He observes that since they were caught up in Divine contemplation for just two days, forgetting to eat or drink, it is understandable that when Moses "was there with Hashem forty days and forty nights, he did neither eat bread nor drink water."

Upon hearing this, Rabbi Shimon ben Gamliel compares Rabbi Shimon to a fearful lion, different to other lions. He explains that Rabbi Shimon is so close to God that he does not order a fast for what he prays for; he simply decrees and God fulfills. Moreover, he may even annul God's decrees, for as God rules over man, the righteous man rules over God.

The Relevance of the Passage

God neither punishes nor rewards. The Light of God is an endless force of sharing and goodness, in existence for all eternity. If we liken this force to electrical current, we understand that one can interact with the force in a positive and productive manner or one can short-circuit and cause oneself extreme pain.

When we channel the Light of the Creator in a sharing manner, we are pure conduits of Divine energy. As Light flows through us to others, we experience endless joy and fulfillment.

We when we connect to this Force through ego, we short-circuit and we hurt.

One who masters one's own ego receives infinite Light, power, and oneness with the God. Thus, the ability of achieving mind over matter and absolute control over the physical reality is placed in the palm of one's hands. This is our destiny.

For millennia, mankind did not internalize this truth; and therefore, humanity failed to achieve this level of control.

Thus, the Light of the Creator gave us the gift of the Zohar. On the merit of Rabbi Shimon, the revered Kabbalist who attained the highest level of spirituality and control, we can now annul all decrees set forth against this world and against ourselves. We can shift the destiny of humanity from a Final Redemption of pain, suffering, and destruction to one of mercy, compassion, and wonders.

251. יָתִיב ר' שִׁמְעוֹן, ור' אֶלְעָזָר בְּרֵיה קָאִים וּמְפָרֵשׁ מִלֵּי דְרָזֵי

דְּחָכְמְתָא, וַהֲווֹ אַנְפּוֹי נְהִירִין כְּשִׁמְשָׁא. וּמִלִּין מִתְבַּדְּרִין וְטָאסִין בִּרְקִיעָא. יָתְבוּ תְּרֵין יוֹמִין דְּלָא אָכְלוּ וְלֹא שָׁתוּ, וְלָא הֲווֹ יַדְעִין אִי הֲוָה יְמָמָא אוֹ לֵילְיָא. כַּד נָפְקוּ, יָדְעוּ דַּהֲווֹ תְּרֵין יוֹמִין דְּלָא טָעֲמוּ מִידִי. קָרָא עַל דָּא רִבִּי שִׁמְעוֹן, וַיְהִי שָׁם עִם ה' אַרְבָּעִים יוֹם וְאַרְבָּעִים לַיְלָה לֶחֶם לֹא אָכַל וְגוֹ'. וּמָה אִי אֲנַן בְּשַׁעֲתָא חֲדָא כָּךְ, דִּקְרָא אַסְהִיד בֵּיהּ, וַיְהִי שָׁם עִם ה' אַרְבָּעִים יוֹם וְגוֹ', עַל אַחַת כַּמָּה וְכַמָּה.

251. Rabbi Shimon sat while his son, Rabbi Elazar, stood and explained the secrets of the words of wisdom, and his face shone like the sun. And the word spread and flew in the sky. They sat two days and neither ate nor drank, and they did not know if it was day or night. When they went out, they realized that already two days had passed and they had eaten nothing. Rabbi Shimon exclaimed: "And he was there with Hashem forty days and forty nights, he did neither eat bread nor drink water" (Shemot 34:28). If for us, WHO MERITED TO CLEAVE TO HASHEM for a while it was so, THAT AND WE SPENT TWO DAYS IN THE LIGHT OF HASHEM AND DID NOT KNOW WHERE WE WERE, with Moses, about whom the Torah bears witness: "And he was there with Hashem forty days" – it is much more so.

252. כַּד אָתָא רִבִּי חִיָּיא קַמֵּיהּ דְּרִבִּי, וְסָח לֵיהּ עוֹבָדָא, תָּוָה רִבִּי, וְאָמַר לֵיהּ ר' שִׁמְעוֹן בֶּן גַּמְלִיאֵל אָבוֹי, בְּרִי, ר' שִׁמְעוֹן בֶּן יוֹחַאי אַרְיָא, וְרִבִּי אֶלְעָזָר בְּרֵיהּ אַרְיָא, וְלָאו ר' שִׁמְעוֹן כִּשְׁאַר אַרְיָוָותָא, עֲלֵיהּ כְּתִיב אַרְיֵה שָׁאַג מִי לֹא יִירָא וְגוֹ'. וּמָה עָלְמִין דִּלְעֵילָּא מִזְדַּעְזְעִין מִינֵּיהּ, אֲנַן עאכ"ו. גּוּבְרָא דְּלָא גָּזַר תַּעֲנִיתָא לְעָלְמִין עַל מַה דְּשָׁאִיל וּבָעֵי, אֶלָּא הוּא גּוֹזֵר, קוּדְשָׁא בְּרִיךְ הוּא מְקַיֵּים. קוּדְשָׁא בְּרִיךְ הוּא גּוֹזֵר, וְאִיהוּ מְבַטֵּל. וְהַיְינוּ דִּתְנָן, מַאי דִּכְתִיב מוֹשֵׁל בָּאָדָם צַדִּיק מוֹשֵׁל יִרְאַת אֱלֹהִים, הַקּוּדְשָׁא בְּרִיךְ הוּא מוֹשֵׁל בָּאָדָם, וּמִי מוֹשֵׁל בְּהַקּוּדְשָׁא בְּרִיךְ הוּא, צַדִּיק. דְּאִיהוּ גּוֹזֵר גְּזֵרָה, וְהַצַּדִּיק מְבַטְּלָהּ.

252. When Rabbi Chiya came before Rabbi and told him the story, Rabbi was amazed. His father, Rabbi Shimon ben Gamliel said to him: My son, Rabbi Shimon ben Yochai is a lion, and his son Rabbi Elazar is a lion, and Rabbi Shimon is not like the other lions. About him is written: "A lion has roared, who will not fear?" (Amos 3:8). Now that the higher worlds tremble before him, we certainly do. He is man who never decreed a fast for what he asked or prayed for. He would just decree and the Holy One, blessed be He, would fulfill. The Holy One, blessed be He, decrees and he annuls. This is what we learned of the meaning of the passage: "He that rules over men must be just, ruling in the fear of Elohim" (II Shmuel 23:3). The Holy One, blessed be He, rules over man, and who rules over the Holy One, blessed be He, but the righteous man. For He decrees and the righteous man annuls it.

31. Twelve mountains of balsam trees

A Synopsis

This section begins with reference to Rabbi Yehuda's comment that although God delights in the prayers of the Righteous, He does not always grant their requests. There follows an account illustrating this idea. Once, during a drought, Rabbi Eliezer prayed and decreed forty fasts to no avail, yet after Rabbi Akiva prayed, the wind and rain came immediately. Seeing Rabbi Eliezer's chagrin, Rabbi Akiva stood before the congregation and told them a parable. In it, he compared Rabbi Eliezer to a friend of a king who loved him so dearly that he delayed granting his friend's request in order to prolong his visit. In contrast, the king instantly granted the requests of his servant in order to dispense with him quickly. Rabbi Eliezer then tells Rabbi Akiva his dream, in which he saw the verse, "Therefore pray you not for this people..." and reveals that he was crestfallen because although he knew another could pray for them, the congregation thought he was of a lower degree than Rabbi Akiva. Rabbi Eliezer then describes the dream in which he saw twelve mountains of balsam trees; the one who wears a breastplate and Efod entered and prayed to God to have mercy on the world. He explains that there are eighteen mountains of balsam. The Righteous souls enter there, and from there 49 aromas ascend daily to Eden. These correspond to the 49 pure aspects and the 49 impure aspects of the Torah, the 49 letters of the names of the twelve Tribes, and the 49 day interval between the exodus and the handing of the Torah to Yisrael. The one who wears the breastplate sits on a holy throne supported by the four pillars, the Patriarchs, who receive from the twelve stones that illuminate in the breastplate. They raise their eyes and see the sparks that glitter on 620 sides of the Crown, on which the Holy Name is engraved. Then the pillars tremble, "And the heavens become revealed like a book" (Yeshayah 34:4).

The Relevance of the Passage

Here we are connected to the Light of the Creator in a warm and loving embrace. This connection is of a permanent nature, so that we are constantly in the presence of the Creator. This ensures absolute fulfillment of our prayers.

Moreover, humility is aroused within us. Humbleness is the key that unlocks the gates of heaven. This further ensures the answering of our prayers and the arrival of lasting peace and countless blessings.

Though our generation may not really merit a merciful Redemption, we can achieve it upon the merit of Rabbi Shimon, Rabbi Elizar, Rabbi Akiva, and the worldwide presence of this sacred Book of Splendor.

Our collective meditation upon these verses unites our world to the fiftieth Gate – Binah, a realm of boundless bliss! All 49 spiritual levels leading up to Binah are now perfected by the words that speak of the "49 fragrances," the "illuminating stones," and the "engravings of the breastplate."

The story of humanity now arrives to a glorious conclusion after so many chapters of persecution and pain. Happily Ever After is our new reality.

253. תְּנָן, אָמַר ר' יְהוּדָה, אֵין לְךָ דָּבָר בַּחֲבִיבוּתָא קָמֵי קוּדְשָׁא בְּרִיךְ הוּא, כְּמוֹ תִּפְלָתָן שֶׁל צַדִּיקִים, וְאַף עַל גַּב דְּנִיחָא לֵיה, זִמְנִין דְּעָבֵיד בָּעוּתְהוֹן, זִמְנִין דְּלָא עָבֵיד.

253. We learned that Rabbi Yehuda said: There is nothing that is so cherished by the Holy One, blessed be He, as the prayers of the righteous. Even though it pleases Him, sometimes He grants their request and sometimes He does not.

254. ת"ר, זִמְנָא חֲדָא הֲוָה עָלְמָא צְרִיכָא לְמִטְרָא, אָתָא רִבִּי אֱלִיעֶזֶר, וּגְזַר אַרְבְּעִין תַּעֲנִיתָא, וְלָא אָתָא מִטְרָא, צַלֵּי צְלוֹתָא, וְלָא אָתָא מִטְרָא. אָתָא רִבִּי עֲקִיבָא, וְקָם וְצַלֵּי, אָמַר מַשִּׁיב הָרוּחַ, וְנָשַׁב זִיקָא, אָמַר וּמוֹרִיד הַגֶּשֶׁם, וְאָתָא מִטְרָא. חָלַשׁ דַּעְתֵּיה דְּרִבִּי אֱלִיעֶזֶר, אִסְתָּכַּל רִבִּי עֲקִיבָא בְּאַנְפּוֹי.

254. The sages have taught that one time the world needed rain. Rabbi Eliezer came and decreed forty fasts, but rain did not come. He prayed, but rain did not come. Rabbi Akiva came, stood and prayed. He said: "He makes the wind to blow," and the wind blew strong and powerful. He said: "And He makes the rain fall" and rain came. Rabbi Elazar was crestfallen. Rabbi Akiva looked into his face AND SENSED HE WAS DISCOURAGED.

255. קָם רִבִּי עֲקִיבָא קָמֵי עַמָּא וְאָמַר, אֶמְשׁוֹל לָכֶם מָשָׁל, לְמָה הַדָּבָר דּוֹמֶה, רִבִּי אֱלִיעֶזֶר דָּמֵי לְרְחִימָא דְּמַלְכָּא, דִּרְחִים לֵיה יַתִּיר, וְכַד עָאל קָמֵי מַלְכָּא, נִיחָא לֵיה, וְלָא בָּעֵי לְמֵימְתָן לֵיה בָּעוּתֵיה בִּבְהִילוּ, כִּי הֵיכִי דְּלָא לִיתְפְּרַשׁ מִנֵּיה, דְּנִיחָא לֵיה דְּלִישְׁתַּתָּעֵי בַּהֲדֵיה. וַאֲנָא דָּמֵי לְעַבְדָּא

דְּמַלְכָּא, דִּבְעָא בָּעוּתֵיה קַמֵּיה, וְלָא בָּעֵי מַלְכָּא דְּלֵיעוּל לְתַרְעֵי
פַּלְטְרִין, וכ״ש דְּלִישְׁתָּעֵי בַּהֲדֵיה, אָמַר מַלְכָּא, הָבוּ לֵיה בָּעוּתֵיה
בִּבְהִילוּ, וְלָא לֵיעוּל הָכָא. כָּךְ רִבִּי אֱלִיעֶזֶר אִיהוּ רְחִימָא דְּמַלְכָּא, וַאֲנָא
עַבְדָּא, וּבָעֵי מַלְכָּא לְאִשְׁתָּעֵי בַּהֲדֵיה כָּל יוֹמָא, וְלָא יִתְפְּרִישׁ מִנֵּיה.
וַאֲנָא, לָא בָּעֵי מַלְכָּא דְּאִיעוּל תַּרְעֵי דְּפַלְטְרִין. נָח דַּעְתֵּיה דְּרִבִּי
אֱלִיעֶזֶר.

255. Rabbi Akiva stood up before the people and said: I will give an
example similar to the situation. Rabbi Eliezer is compared to the friend of
the king, who is cherished exceedingly. And when he appears before the
king, he is very pleasantly accepted, and the king does not want to grant him
his wish quickly so that he will not leave him, because it is so pleasant to
speak with him. But I am likened to the servant of the king who makes a
request of him, and the king does not want him to enter the gates of the
palace, and naturally does not want to speak to him. The king says: Grant
his request immediately and do not let him enter here. Similarly, Rabbi
Eliezer is the friend of the King and I am a servant. The king desires to
speak with him constantly and not to be away from him. But as for me, the
King does not want me to enter the gates of the palace, THEREFORE HE
GRANTS MY WISH IMMEDIATELY. Rabbi Eliezer regained his composure.

256. א״ל, עֲקִיבָא, תָּא וְאֵימָא לָךְ מִלְּתָא, דְּאִתְחֲזֵיָא לִי בְּחֶלְמָא הַאי
פְּסוּקָא, דִּכְתִיב, וְאַתָּה אַל תִּתְפַּלֵּל בְּעַד הָעָם הַזֶּה וְאַל תִּשָּׂא בַעֲדָם
רִנָּה וּתְפִלָּה וְאַל תִּפְגַּע בִּי. תָּא חֲזֵי, תְּרֵיסָר טוּרֵי אֲפַרְסְמוֹנָא, עָאל.
הַהוּא דְּלָבִישׁ חוּשְׁנָא וְאֵפוֹדָא, וּבָעֵא מִן קוּדְשָׁא בְּרִיךְ הוּא, לְמֵיחָס עַל
עָלְמָא וְעַד הָאִידָנָא תָּלֵי אִיהוּ. אִי הָכִי אֲמַאי חָלַשׁ דַּעְתֵּיה דְּרִבִּי
אֱלִיעֶזֶר. מִשּׁוּם בְּנֵי נָשָׁא, דְּלָא יַדְעִין בְּהַאי.

256. RABBI ELIEZER said to him: Akiva, come and I will tell you
something. In a dream, there appeared to me the passage: "Therefore pray
you not for this people; lift up neither cry nor prayer for them, nor make
intercession to Me" (Yirmeyah 7:16). Behold, DUE TO THE SINS OF THE
GENERATION, THE PRAYER ON THEIR BEHALF IS NOT ACCEPTED, AND
STILL IT SAYS, "THEREFORE PRAY YOU NOT FOR THIS PEOPLE." THIS
IMPLIES THAT OTHERS MAY PRAY ON THEIR BEHALF. THEREFORE I WAS

NOT ANSWERED, BUT YOU WERE ANSWERED. AND MORE THAN THIS, THERE ARE CERTAIN THINGS ON WHOSE BEHALF NO RIGHTEOUS MAN IN THE WORLD CAN PRAY. Come and behold: twelve mountains of balsam trees. THE ONE WHO RAISES FEMALE WATERS, the one who wears the breastplate and Efod, enters and prays to the Holy One, blessed be He, BY RAISING FEMALE WATERS TO BINAH, to have mercy on the world. Until now, his prayer is still suspended, THAT IS, IT HAS NOT BEEN ACCEPTED. FOR THESE ARE THINGS FOR WHICH PRAYERS ARE NOT ACCEPTED. AND HE ASKS: If so, why was Rabbi Eliezer crestfallen, SINCE HE SAW IN HIS DREAM, "THEREFORE PRAY YOU NOT..." FROM WHICH IT IS UNDERSTOOD THAT ANOTHER MAY PRAY. AND HE ANSWERS: That was because of the people who did not know this. THEY THOUGHT THAT HE WAS ON A LOWER DEGREE THAN RABBI AKIVA.

257. אָמַר רִבִּי אֱלִיעֶזֶר תַּמְנֵי סְרֵי טוּרֵי אֲפַרְסְמוֹנָא עִלָּאִין, עָאלִין נִשְׁמָתְהוֹן דְּצַדִּיקַיָּא, וְאַרְבְּעִין וְתִשְׁעָה רֵיחִין, סַלְקִין בְּכָל יוֹמָא, עַד הַהוּא אֲתָר דְּאִתְקְרֵי עֵדֶן, דִּי לְקָבֵל דָּא, אִתְיְהִיבַת אוֹרַיְיתָא, בְּמ"ט פָּנִים טָמֵא, וּבְמ"ט פָּנִים טָהוֹר. מ"ט אַתְוָון בִּשְׁמָהֹן דְּשִׁבְטֵי. מ"ט יוֹמִין לְקַבְּלָא אוֹרַיְיתָא. מ"ט יוֹמִין קַדִּישִׁין עִלָּאִין קַיְימִין, לְמֵיטַל רְשׁוּתָא בְּכָל יוֹמָא מֵאֲבָנִין זְהִירִין, דִּגְלֵיפָאן בְּהַהוּא חוּשְׁנָא.

257. Rabbi Eliezer said: There are eighteen mountains of supernal balsam trees. The souls of the righteous enter BY RAISING FEMALE WATERS. And 49 fragrances, WHICH IS THE SECRET OF THE FIFTY GATES OF BINAH LESS ONE, ascend daily FROM BINAH to that place called 'Eden', WHICH IS CHOCHMAH. Corresponding to this, the Torah was given in 49 impure aspects and in 49 pure aspects, FOR BECAUSE OF THE LACK OF THE FIFTIETH GATE, THERE EVOLVED 49 IMPURE ASPECTS IN ACCORDANCE WITH THE SECRET OF THE VERSE: "THE ELOHIM HAS MADE THE ONE AS WELL AS THE OTHER" (KOHELET 7:14). The 49 letters in the names of the tribes AND LIKEWISE the 49 days OF THE SFIRAH OF THE OMER, in order to receive the Torah, FOR THEY CONTAIN 49 supernal days OF THE MALE AND FEMALE, are going to receive permission, MEANING TO BECOME PERFECTED daily from THESE 49 DAYS, the illuminating stones THAT ARE FILLED in the engraving of that breastplate.

258. וְהַהוּא דְּלָבִישׁ חוּשְׁנָא, יָתִיב בְּכָרְסְיָיא קַדִּישָׁא יַקִּירָא, דְּאַרְבַּע

סַמְכִין קַיְימִין מִסְתַּכְּלִין בְּחוֹשְׁנָא, עַל מֵימְרֵיהּ עָאלִין, וְעַל מֵימְרֵיהּ
נָפְקִין, זַקְפָן עַיְינִין וּמִסְתַּכְּלִין לְעֵילָא, חָמָאן צִיצָא, דְּלָהִיט בְּשִׁית מְאָה
וְעֶשְׂרִין עִיבָר, וּשְׁמָא קַדִּישָׁא עִלָּאָה, גְּלִיף עֲלֹוי, מִזְדַּעְזְעָן וּמִתְחַלְחֲלָן.
קְטִירֵי בְּסִטְרוֹי דִּימִינָא קַדִּישָׁא, דִּשְׂמָאלָא נָטִיל בִּידוֹי סַמְכֵי שְׁמַיָּא,
עָלִיל לוֹן, וְגַלֵּי לוֹן. הֲדָא הוּא דִּכְתִיב, וְנָגֹולּוּ כַסֵּפֶר הַשָּׁמָיִם.

258. And he who wears the breastplate, BEING ZEIR ANPIN IN THE MOCHIN OF GREATNESS, sits on the precious holy throne, MEANING THAT HE ILLUMINATES WITHIN MALCHUT THAT IS CALLED 'THRONE'. The four pillars OF THIS THRONE, WHO ARE MICHAEL, GABRIEL, URIEL AND RAPHAEL, stand and observe the breastplate – MEANING THAT THEY RECEIVE FROM THE TWELVE STONES THAT ARE ILLUMINATING IN IT. By the word OF THE WEARER OF THE BREASTPLATE do they come, and according to his word do they leave. They raise their eyes and look up, and see the sparks that glitter in 620 sides, WHICH ALLUDES TO KETER, WHOSE NUMERICAL VALUE IS 620, BECAUSE IT IS BOUND UPON THE FOREHEAD AND SKULL, WHICH IS THE SECRET OF KETER. And the Holy Name is engraved on it. And THE AFOREMENTIONED PILLARS tremble and shake, bound on the right side, WHICH IS ZEIR ANPIN, while the left, WHICH IS MALCHUT, takes into its hands the pillars of heaven – WHICH IS THE SECRET OF THE THREE COLUMNS IN ZEIR ANPIN, WHICH IS CALLED 'HEAVEN'. It clears them and reveals them. This is what is written: "And the heavens become revealed like a book" (Yeshayah 34:4).

32. "I went down into the garden of nuts"

A Synopsis

Rabbi Eliezer begins by explaining and expounding upon the meaning of the title verse to Rabbi Akiva. The "garden," we learn, is the garden that comes out of Eden, and it signifies the Shechinah. The "nut," which has four sections, signifies the holy Chariot, and the phrase "I went down" signifies a penetration to the inner meaning. In answer to Rabbi Chiya's question regarding the symbolic significance of the (dirt of the) nut's shell, Rabbi Eliezer reveals its meaning through its connection with the almonds. Although the two types of almond, bitter and sweet, imply an illusion to severe Judgment and Holiness, every open illusion to almonds in the Torah describes only their aspect of Judgement. He then draws a comparison between the Hebrew words for 'almonds', 'watched' and 'hasten', which reinforces their aspect of Judgment.

The Relevance of the Passage

Much good is accomplished through our visual embrace of this passage. We draw the Shechinah into our lives. We crack open the shells known as Klipah that conceal sparks of Light. This action reveals the Divine Energy that has been concealed since the time of Creation. This revelation removes all manner of judgment, from the smallest to the most severe. In addition, our efforts illumine all the supernal secrets concealed inside the Torah so that the ultimate truth of the Creator is revealed to all humanity.

259. א״ל ר׳ עֲקִיבָא, מַהוּ דִּכְתִיב, אֶל גִּנַּת אֱגוֹז יָרַדְתִּי. א״ל תָּא חֲזֵי, הַהוּא גִּנְתָּא נָפְקָא מֵעֵדֶן, וְדָא הִיא שְׁכִינְתָּא. אֱגוֹז: דָּא הִיא רְתִיכָא עִלָּאָה קַדִּישָׁא, דְּאִינּוּן אַרְבַּע רֵישִׁין דְּנַהֲרִין, דְּמִתְפָּרְשָׁן מִן גִּנְתָּא, כְּהַאי אֱגוֹזָא, דְּאִינּוּן אַרְבַּע רֵישִׁין קַדִּישִׁין לְגוֹ. וּמַאי דְּאָמַר יָרַדְתִּי, כְּמָה דִּתְנָן, יָרַד פְּלוֹנִי לַמֶּרְכָּבָה.

259. Rabbi Akiva said to him: What is the meaning of the passage, "I went down into the garden of nuts" (Shir Hashirm 6:11)? He said to him: Come and behold. This garden comes out of Eden, and this is the Shechinah. Nut is the holy supernal Chariot, which is the four headwaters of the rivers that separates from the garden, WHICH IS THE SECRET OF THE FOUR FACES — NAMELY THE FACE OF A LION, THE FACE OF AN OX, THE FACE OF AN EAGLE, THE FACE OF A MAN. This nut has four holy heads inside,

MEANING IN ITS FRUIT, AND IT ALSO HAS FOUR KLIPOT ('PEELS') THAT COVER THE FRUIT, WHICH ALLUDES TO THE FOUR KLIPOT: A STORM WIND; A GREAT CLOUD; A FIRE FLARING UP; AND A BRIGHTNESS, LIKE THE SUPERNAL CHARIOT. And when he said: "I went down," IN "I WENT DOWN INTO THE GARDEN OF NUTS," it is as we learned that so and so descended to the Chariot.

260. א״ל ר׳ עֲקִיבָא, אִי הָכִי, הֲוָה לֵיהּ לְמֵימַר, לֶאֱגוֹז יָרַדְתִּי, מַהוּ אֶל גִּנַּת אֱגוֹז יָרַדְתִּי. א״ל, מִשּׁוּם דְּהִיא שְׁבָחָא דֶּאֱגוֹזָא. מָה אֱגוֹזָא, טְמִירָא וּסְתִימָא מִכָּל סִטְרוֹי, כַּךְ רְתִיכָא דְּנָפְקָא מִגִּנְתָּא, סְתִימָא מִכָּל סִטְרוֹי. מַה אִינּוּן אַרְבַּע קְרִישִׁין דִּי בֶּאֱגוֹזָא, מִתְחַבְּרָן בְּהַאי גִּיסָא, וּמִתְפָּרְשָׁן מֵהַאי גִּיסָא. כַּךְ רְתִיכָא, מִתְחַבְּרָן בְּאַחֲדוּתָא בְּחֶדְוָותָא בִּשְׁלִימוּתָא, וּמִתְפָּרַשׁ כָּל חַד בְּעַבְרוֹי, עַל מַה דְּאִתְמָנֵי הַה״ד, הוּא הַסּוֹבֵב אֵת כָּל אֶרֶץ הַחֲוִילָה הוּא הַהוֹלֵךְ קִדְמַת אַשּׁוּר, וְכֵן כּוּלָּם.

260. Rabbi Akiva said to him: If so, he should have said: 'I went down into the nut', WHICH IS THE CHARIOT. Why does it say, "I went down into the garden of nuts"? He said to him: Because THE GARDEN, WHICH IS MALCHUT, has all that is goodly in the nuts, FOR THEY GROW IN AND EMERGE FROM THIS GARDEN, WHICH IS MALCHUT. THEREFORE, HE MENTIONS THE GARDEN SPECIFICALLY. AND HE CONTINUES TO EXPLAIN HIS WORDS, AS TO WHY THE CHARIOT WAS ALLUDED TO IN THE NUT. Just as the nut is hidden and concealed from all sides IN ITS PEEL, so the Chariot that emerges from the garden, WHICH IS MALCHUT, is concealed from all sides. All these four heads in the nut are attached to each other on this side, MEANING IN THEIR CENTER, and separate on this side, OUTWARDLY. Thus, THE FOUR ASPECTS OF the Chariot attain each other in unity, in joy, in completeness, and they separate, each one to its individual aspect for which it was appointed. This is what is written: "That it is which compasses the whole land of Chavilah" (Beresheet 2:11). Likewise, "that is it which goes toward the east of Ashur" (Ibid. 14). It is the same with the rest of them.

261. אָמַר רִבִּי עֲקִיבָא, הַאי לְכלּוּכָא דְּהִיא בִּקְלִיפוֹי דֶּאֱגוֹזָא, לְמָאי רְמִיזָא. אָמַר לֵיהּ, אע״ג דְּאוֹרַיְיתָא לָא גַּלֵּי לֵיהּ, בְּהַאי גַּלֵּי.

261. Rabbi Akiva said: This dirt in the peel of the nut, MEANING IN THE FOUR KLIPOT THAT SURROUND IT, to what do they allude? He said to him: Even though the Torah did not reveal it, BECAUSE THE TORAH SPEAKS ONLY ON THE ASPECT OF GOOD IN THE NUT, it did reveal in this – MEANING IN THE ALMONDS – AS WILL BE EXPLAINED WILL THAT THE TORAH SPEAKS ABOUT THE FOUR KLIPOT OF THE ALMOND IN PARTICULAR, ALLUDING TO JUDGMENT, AND NOT THEIR GOOD ASPECT.

262. תָּא חֲזֵי, שְׁקֵדִים, מִנְּהוֹן מְרִירָן, וּמִנְּהוֹן מְתִיקָן, וּרְמִיזָא אִית לוֹן, אִית מָארֵי דְּדִינָא קַשְׁיָא, וְאִית מָארֵי דְּשֵׁירוּתָא, אֲבָל כָּל רְמִיזָא דְּגַלֵּי בְּאוֹרַיְיתָא חָזִינָן דְּדִינָא הֲוֵי, וְהָכִי הוּא לִירְמְיָהוּ, אַחֲזוֹ לֵיהּ בְּדִינָא, דִּכְתִיב, מַקֵּל שָׁקֵד אֲנִי רוֹאֶה. מַאי שָׁקֵד. שְׁקֵדִים מַמָּשׁ. וְכֵן בְּמַטֵּה אַהֲרֹן, וַיִּגְמוֹל שְׁקֵדִים. וּמִן תֵּיבוּתָא מַמָּשׁ, אִשְׁתְּמַע, דְּהוּא דִּינָא קַשְׁיָא. דִּכְתִיב, וַיִּשְׁקוֹד ה' עַל הָרָעָה. וְכֵן שׁוֹקֵד אֲנִי עַל דְּבָרִי, וְכֵן כּוּלָּם. אָמַר לֵיהּ ר' עֲקִיבָא, מַשְׁמַע כָּל מַה דְּעָבֵד קוּדְשָׁא בְּרִיךְ הוּא, לְמֵילַף מִנֵּיהּ חָכְמְתָא סַגִּיאָה, דִּכְתִיב כָּל פָּעַל ה' לַמַּעֲנֵהוּ. ר' אֶלְעָזָר אָמַר מֵהָכָא, דִּכְתִיב, וַיַּרְא אֱלֹהִים אֶת כָּל אֲשֶׁר עָשָׂה וְהִנֵּה טוֹב מְאֹד. מַהוּ מְאֹד. לְמֵילַף מִנֵּיהּ חָכְמְתָא עִלָּאָה.

262. Come and behold: Some almonds are bitter BECAUSE OF THEIR PEELS, and some are sweet, implying that some are of Severe Judgment, TO WHICH THE BITTER ALMONDS ALLUDE, and some serve HOLINESS, TO WHICH THE SWEET ALMONDS ALLUDE. But we see that every open allusion TO THEM in the Torah is about Judgment, AND DOES NOT DISCUSS THE GOOD IN THEM – THE SWEET ONES. And so it is in Jeremiah, who was shown the Judgment THAT IS IN THEM as is written: "I see a rod of an almond tree (Heb. *shaked*)" (Yirmeyah 1:11). What is the meaning of *shaked*? Actual almonds – "AND IT WAS SAID TO HIM, 'FOR I WILL HASTEN (HEB. *SHOKED*) MY WORD TO PERFORM IT'" (IBID. 12), MEANING TO UPROOT, CRUSH, DESTROY AND DEMOLISH... It is written by the rod of Aaron: "And yielded almonds" (Bemidbar 17:23), AND IT BECAME A SIGN TO THE REBELLIOUS PEOPLE. SO WE SEE THAT THE TORAH SPEAKS ONLY OF THEIR ASPECT OF JUDGMENT. And from the word itself, THAT THEY ARE CALLED 'ALMONDS' (HEB. *SHKEDIM*) it is understood that it refers to Severe Judgment, as is written: "And Hashem watched (Heb.

yishkod) over the evil" (Daniel 9:14). And, "I will hasten My word," and so all of them. SO IT IS CLEAR THAT THE WORD "*SHAKED*" REFERS TO SEVERE JUDGMENT. Rabbi Akiva said to him: It seems that one could gain much wisdom from everything the Holy One, blessed be He, does, as is written: "Whatever Hashem has done is for His own purpose" (Mishlei 16:4). Rabbi Elazar says: We learn it from these words, "And Elohim saw everything that He had made and, behold, it was very good" (Beresheet 1:31). That is the meaning of "very" – IT IS GOOD to learn supernal Wisdom from it.

33. "The one as well as the other"

A Synopsis

The discussion here begins with an interpretation of the title verse, revealing that the earthly realm corresponds symbolically in all its aspects to the heavenly realm. Rabbi Aba's comment regarding human ignorance of lost wisdom pertaining to the natural world leads to a discourse on the classification of trees and herbs and their relationships to divine elements. We learn that it is forbidden to "sow your field with mingled seed" because each seed has an individual name, a separate secret, and an appointed supervisor above. Planting mixed seeds mingles their authority and their names. This concept also applies to the twelve Tribes, and explains the Scriptural emphasis on the names of these tribes, as seen in the verse, "These are the names of the children of Israel."

The Relevance of the Passage

Our entire physical world, down to the smallest detail, including the laws of nature, like the process of a seed giving birth to a tree bearing fruit, mirrors and corresponds to spiritual forces that occupy the supernal realms.

The knowledge and awareness of this awesome truth has been lost to mankind, and we have thus disconnected ourselves from the Upper World. When one possesses the wisdom that identifies the relationship between our world and the Upper world, one immediately acquires the power to ignite and summon the spiritual forces of Light.

The Zohar possesses all this divine wisdom. Hence, in the act of meditating upon its verses, the reader reaches into the supernal dimensions to taste of the heavenly fruits and spiritual herbs that will heal our bodies and souls.

Just as each living creature possesses its own unique DNA, composed of the genetic alphabet, each living entity on Earth has its own unique "name--spiritual DNA – including the trees and herbs that grow from the Earth.

Here we connect to the spiritual DNA level of our world to capture the divine essence of reality. Strangely enough, our diversity is the quintessence of our underlying unity. For instance, when sunlight shines through a prism, the white ray of light refracts into the seven colors of the rainbow. Each color has its own unique name and frequency. However, when they unite as one, they create a perfect and complete ray of white sunlight.

Each of us has a unique "name" and "color" in the spectrum of Creation. Yet each of us is also a part of the one Light of the Creator.

When we love our neighbor as ourselves, and we show respect and awe for the trees, flowers, and herbs that populate our planet, we unite as one Divine Light to heal and bless all the world.

This spectacular unification and arousal of blessings occurs now.

263. א"ר יְהוּדָה, מַאי דִּכְתִּיב, גַּם אֶת זֶה לְעֻמַּת זֶה עָשָׂה הָאֱלֹהִים. כְּגַוְּונָא דִרְקִיעָא, עָבֵד קוּדְשָׁא בְּרִיךְ הוּא בְּאַרְעָא, וְכֻלְּהוּ רְמִיזָא לְמַה דִּלְעֵילָא. דְּכַד הֲוָה חָמֵי ר' אַבָּא, חַד אִילָנָא, דְּאִבֵיהּ אִתְעֲבֵיד עוֹפָא דְּפָרַח מִנֵּיהּ, הֲוָה בָּכֵי וְאָמַר, אִי הֲווֹ בְּנֵי נָשָׁא יַדְעֵי לְמַאי רְמִיזָאן, הֲווֹ מְבַזְעֶן מַלְבּוּשֵׁיהוֹן עַד טַבּוּרֵיהוֹן, לְמַאי דְּאִתְנְשֵׁי חָכְמָה מִנְּהוֹן. כ"ש בִּשְׁאַר מַה דְּעָבֵד קוּדְשָׁא בְּרִיךְ הוּא בְּאַרְעָא.

263. Rabbi Yehuda said: What is the meaning of that which is written, "The Elohim has made the one as well as the other" (Kohelet 7:14)? IT INSTRUCTS US THAT similar to those things that are in heaven, the Holy One, blessed be He, made on earth, AND ALL THAT THERE IS ON THE EARTH alludes to what is above IN THE SKY. For when Rabbi Aba saw a tree whose fruits were ripe and from which the birds flew, he wept and said: If people knew what they were suggesting, they would rend their clothes down to their navel, for the fact that this wisdom was forgotten by them. Even more so for the other things that the Holy One, blessed be He, has made on earth.

264. כְּדְאָמַר ר' יוֹסֵי, אִלָנִין, אִינּוּן דְּאִתְחֲזֵי מִנְּהוֹן חָכְמְתָא, כְּגוֹן חָרוּבָא, דְּקַל, פְּסְתּוּקָא, וְכַדּוּמֶה לוֹן, כֻּלְּהוּ בְּחַד רְכִיבָא אִתְרְכָבוּ. כָּל אִינּוּן דְּעַבְדִּין פֵּירִין, בַּר מִתַּפּוּחִין, רָזָא חֲדָא אִינּוּן, בַּר שְׁבִילִין דְּאִתְפָּרְשָׁן.

264. As Rabbi Yosi said: The trees from which wisdom is visible – meaning the Carob tree, Palm tree, and Ground Nut tree, WHICH IS A KIND OF NUT TREE, and those similar to them – were all grafted into one, because all these trees that produce fruit, except for apples, WHICH ARE NETZACH, HOD AND YESOD, have the same principle, WHICH ALLUDES TO TIFERET. That is, except for the paths in which they are separate, BECAUSE EVERY TREE HAS A UNIQUE PATH IN WHICH IT ILLUMINATES.

265. כָּל אִינּוּן דְּלָא עַבְדִּין פֵּירִין, וְאִינּוּן רַבְרְבִין, בַּר מֵעַרְבִין דְּנַחֲלָא, דְּאִית לְהוּ רָזָא בִּלְחוֹדוֹי כְּגַוְונָא דִּלְעֵילָא, מֵחַד יְנִיקָא יָנִיקוּ, וְכָל חַד מֵאִינּוּן דְּאִינְהוּ זוּטְרֵי, בַּר מֵאֵזוֹבָא, מֵאִימָּא חֲדָא אִתְיְלִידוּ.

265. All these trees that do not produce fruits, all the large ones – except for the willow, which has its own secret similar to above, WHICH ARE NETZACH AND HOD – gain nourishment from one source. THEY GAIN NOURISHMENT FROM THE EXTERIOR PART, WHICH IS THE MEANING OF ANOTHER EL THAT DOES NOT PRODUCE FRUIT. And every one of the small trees except for the Hyssop, WHICH ALLUDES TO YESOD, were born of one mother, MEANING THE NUKVA.

266. כָּל עֶשְׂבִּין דְּאַרְעָא, דְּאִתְמְנֵי עֲלֵיהוֹן רַבְרְבִין תַּקִּיפִין בִּשְׁמַיָּא. כָּל חַד וְחַד רָזָא בִּלְחוֹדוֹי, כְּגַוְונָא דִּלְעֵילָא, וּבְגִין כָּךְ כְּתִיב, שָׂדְךָ לֹא תִזְרַע כִּלְאָיִם. דְּכָל חַד וְחַד עָאל בִּלְחוֹדוֹי, וְנָפִיק בִּלְחוֹדוֹי, הה"ד, הֲיָדַעְתָּ חֻקּוֹת שָׁמָיִם אִם תָּשִׂים מִשְׁטָרוֹ בָאָרֶץ. וּכְתִיב לְכֻלָּם בְּשֵׁם יִקְרָא. וּמָה בְּכָל מַה, דְּבְעָלְמָא רָזָא בִּלְחוֹדוֹי וְלָא בָּעָא קוּדְשָׁא בְּרִיךְ הוּא לְגַלָּאָה לוֹן, וּלְעַרְבְּבָא לוֹן, וּקְרָאן בִּשְׁמָהָן. בְּנֵי יַעֲקֹב דְּאִינּוּן שִׁבְטִין קַדִּישִׁין, דְּאִינּוּן קִיּוּמָא דְּעָלְמָא, עַל אַחַת כַּמָּה וְכַמָּה, הה"ד וְאֵלֶּה שְׁמוֹת בְּנֵי יִשְׂרָאֵל.

266. All the herbs of the earth have powerful ministers appointed over them in heaven. FOR THERE IS NO PLANT ON EARTH THAT DOES NOT HAVE A STAR AND CONSTELLATION IN THE SKY THAT PRODS IT AND SAYS: GROW. Each and every one of them has a separate secret, similar to above, JUST AS THEY HAVE INDIVIDUAL APPOINTED SUPERVISORS ABOVE THEM. Therefore it is written: "You shall not sow your field with mingled seed" (Vayikra 19:19), because each one enters alone and emerges alone. FOR NO APPOINTEE MINGLES WITH ANOTHER, AND ONE WHO PLANTS MINGLED SEEDS, MINGLES THEIR AUTHORITY, ONE WITH ANOTHER. This is the meaning: "Do you know the ordinances of the heavens, can you establish His dominion in the earth" (Iyov 38:33), and: "He calls them all by names" (Yeshayah 40:26). Everything in the world has its own secret and the Holy One, blessed be He, did not want to reveal it FROM ITS PLACE and mix it WITH ANOTHER, and thus called, EACH AND EVERY ONE by name. The sons of Jacob, who are holy tribes, who maintain the world, all the more so, as it is written: "These are the names of the children of Israel" (Shemot 1:1).

34. The children of Yisrael, the children of Jacob

A Synopsis

This discussion provides greater insight into the verse, "These are the names of the children of Israel." Rabbi Yosi first reinforces this verse as an indication of the importance of the twelve Tribes who sustain the world. His comment on the title names reveals a lack of distinction between the terms; this relates closely to the death and descent of Joseph and his brothers and is the subject of the discourse that ensues. We learn that the Shechinah and the supernal angels went with Jacob and his sons into Egypt while he was alive. Then, after the death of Joseph and the tribes, Yisrael descended into exile, and the Shechinah (with the twelve Tribes inscribed in Her) and the supernal angels descended with them. Consequently, Yisrael became known as the children of Jacob, since they descended to the level of the children of Jacob.

The Relevance of the Passage

The power to end our exile and control the twelve constellations and the entire physical world, and to ascend to the ultimate spiritual heights known as "Yisrael," is imbued in the reader.

267. ר׳ יוֹסֵי בַּר׳ יְהוּדָה אָמַר, אִילוּ נֶאֱמַר אֵלֶּה שְׁמוֹת, מַשְׁמַע דְּהָכִי הוּא. הַשְׁתָּא דִּכְתִיב וְאֵלֶּה שְׁמוֹת, מַשְׁמַע דְּעַל הָרִאשׁוֹנִים מוֹסִיף, מַה הָרִאשׁוֹנִים בְּנֵי יַעֲקֹב, אַף כָּאן בְּנֵי יַעֲקֹב.

267. Rabbi Yosi ben Rabbi Yehuda said: If it had said: 'These are the names', it would infer that this is so! AS RABBI YEHUDA SAID THAT: "AND THESE ARE THE NAMES OF THE CHILDREN OF ISRAEL," REFERS TO THE IMPORTANCE OF THE TRIBES WHO SUSTAIN THE WORLD. But now that it is written: "And these are the names," WITH AN ADDED *VAV* ('AND'), it infers that it is adding on to the first ones. Just as the first ones were the children of Jacob, so these are also the children of Jacob.

268. א״ר יְהוּדָה, ח״ו, בְּשַׁעְתָּא דְּאָמַר קוּדְשָׁא בְּרִיךְ הוּא, אָנֹכִי אֵרֵד עִמְּךָ מִצְרַיְמָה, ס״ד דִּשְׁכִינְתָּא תֵּיחוֹת עִמֵּיהּ בְּהַהִיא שַׁעְתָּא מַמָּשׁ, אֶלָּא, בְּשַׁעְתָּא דַּהֲוַת יְרִידָה לִבְנוֹהִי, נַחְתַּת שְׁכִינְתָּא, הה״ד, אָנֹכִי אֵרֵד עִמְּךָ מִצְרַיְמָה, וְאָנֹכִי אַעַלְךָ גַם עָלֹה, כָּל זִמְנָא דְּיֶהֱוֵי לָךְ עֲלִיָּיה,

כִּבְיָכוֹ״ל עֲלָיָיה אִית לִי, וּבְשַׁעֲתָא דִיהֲוֵי לָךְ יְרִידָה, כִּבְיָכוֹ״ל אָנֹכִי
אֵרֵד עִמְּךָ. וְעַד דְּמִית יוֹסֵף וְכָל אָחוּי, וַהֲוַת לוֹן יְרִידָה, קָמַת שְׁכִינְתָּא
וְנַחְתַּת עִמְּהוֹן, כְּמָה דְּנַחְתוּ אִלֵּין, כַּךְ נַחְתוּ אִלֵּין.

268. Rabbi Yehuda said TO RABBI YOSI BEN RABBI YEHUDA: Heaven
forbid that when the Holy One, blessed be He, said: "I will descend with
you to Egypt," that it should occur to you that the Shechinah descended with
Him, precisely in that moment. THIS WAS BECAUSE RABBI YEHUDA
THOUGHT THE IMPLICATION OF RABBI YOSI BEN RABBI YEHUDA WAS
THAT THEY WERE IN THE LEVEL OF THE CHILDREN OF JACOB, MEANING
'DESCENDING', IMMEDIATELY UPON THEIR ARRIVAL IN EGYPT. But rather,
the Shechinah descended at the time his children experienced descent. This
is what is written: "I will go down with you into Egypt; and I will also
surely bring you up again" (Beresheet 46:4), MEANING THAT as long as you
will ascend, then I will also ascend; and when you descend, I will descend
with you. After Joseph and all his brothers died and they descended, the
Shechinah also descended with them. And as they descended, MEANING
THE CHILDREN OF YISRAEL, so did these descend, MEANING THE
SHECHINAH AND HER HOSTS.

269. אָמַר ר' יוֹסֵי בַּר' יְהוּדָה, מַה כְּתִיב לְעֵיל מִנֵּיהּ, וַיָּמָת יוֹסֵף בֶּן
מֵאָה וָעֶשֶׂר שָׁנִים וְגוֹ', בְּהַהִיא שַׁעֲתָא דְּמִית יוֹסֵף, וְכֻלְּהוּ שִׁבְטִין, וַהֲוָה
לוֹן יְרִידָה, נַחְתוּ בְּנֵי יִשְׂרָאֵל בְּגָלוּתָא, וּשְׁכִינְתָּא וּמַלְאֲכֵי עִלָּאֵי נַחְתוּ
עִמְּהוֹן, הה״ד, וְאֵלֶּה שְׁמוֹת בְּנֵי יִשְׂרָאֵל, דְּאִינּוּן אִתּוֹסְפוּ עַל קַדְמָאֵי
לְמֵיחַת בְּגָלוּתָא.

269. Rabbi Yosi ben Rabbi Yehuda, said TO HIM: It is written above, "And
Joseph died, being 110 years old" (Beresheet 50:26). At the time that Joseph
and all the tribes died and descended, the children of Yisrael descended into
exile, and the Shechinah and the supernal angels descended with them,
MEANING AS RABBI YEHUDA SAID. This is what is written: "And these are
the names of the children of Israel"; THE VAV OF "VE'ELEH" ('AND
THESE') is added to the first ones that descended into exile AFTER THE
DEATH OF JOSEPH AND HIS BROTHERS. THEREFORE, THEY MUST BE
THE CHILDREN OF JACOB, NAMELY IN DESCENT.

270. א״ל, אִי הָכִי, יַעֲקֹב הֲוָה מִית אוֹ לָא. א״ל מִית. א״ל, וּמַהוּ דִּכְתִּיב הַבָּאִים מִצְרַיְמָה אֶת יַעֲקֹב, אִי בְּחַיֵּי, אֵימָא אֶת יַעֲקֹב, וְאִי בָּתַר דְּמִית, אַפִּיק מִתַּמָּן אֶת יַעֲקֹב. אֶלָּא תָּא חֲזֵי, לָא אָמַר קְרָא הַיּוֹרְדִים מִצְרַיְמָה אֶת יַעֲקֹב, דְּעַד כְּעַן לָא הֲוַת יְרִידָה לְיַעֲקֹב, אֶלָּא הַבָּאִים, אוֹלִיפְנָא דְּאָתוּ עִמֵּיהּ דְּיַעֲקֹב, וְאַזְלוּ לְהוֹן, עַד דְּנַחֲתוּ אִלֵּין בְּגָלוּתָא, נַחֲתוּ אִלֵּין עִמְּהוֹן, הה״ד וְאֵלֶּה שְׁמוֹת וְגוֹ'.

270. RABBI YEHUDA said to him: If so, was Jacob dead or not? He said to him: He was dead! So he said to him: It is written, "Who came to Egypt with Jacob" (Shemot 1:1). If he was alive, IT IS POSSIBLE to say "with Jacob," BUT IF THE TORAH IS SPEAKING of after his death, remove "with Jacob," SINCE HE HAD ALREADY DIED — SINCE THE *VAV* ('AND') ADDS TO THE FIRST ONES. But come and behold: the verse does not say 'who came (lit. 'come') into Egypt with Jacob' but IT IS WRITTEN: "who came." For until then, there was no descent for Jacob. And we learn that THE SHECHINAH AND THE TWELVE TRIBES THAT ARE IN HER came with Jacob TO EGYPT, and went from there until the descent into exile, MEANING AFTER THE DEATH OF JACOB AND THE TRIBES. And then those descended with them, MEANING THE SHECHINAH AND THE TWELVE TRIBES IN HER. Therefore the passage: "And these are the names OF THE CHILDREN OF ISRAEL," REFERS TO THEIR GREAT LEVEL AND IMPORTANCE, SINCE IT REFERS TO THE DAYS OF ASCENT AND NOT THE DAYS OF DESCENT.

271. ר' דּוֹסְתָּאִי אָמַר, בְּכָל יוֹמָא וְיוֹמָא הֲווֹ אַתְיָין, וְאַזְלִין לוֹן, הה״ד הַבָּאִים מִצְרַיְמָה, וְלָא כְּתִיב אֲשֶׁר בָּאוּ, וְהַיְינוּ דִּכְתִּיב הַבָּאִים מִצְרַיְמָה בְּקַדְמֵיתָא אֶת יַעֲקֹב. וּלְבָתַר כַּד הֲוַת לוֹן יְרִידָה אִישׁ וּבֵיתוֹ בָּאוּ. וְתָּא חֲזֵי, בְּנֵי יַעֲקֹב כֻּלְּהוּ הֲווֹ מֵתִין בְּהַהוּא זִמְנָא וְנַחֲתוּ אִלֵּין וְאִלֵּין.

271. Rabbi Dustai said: Every day they would come, THE SHECHINAH AND THE TWELVE TRIBES THAT WERE IN HER, and leave. This is what is written: "Who come into Egypt," IN THE PRESENT TENSE, and not 'Who came', IN THE PAST TENSE. This means that in the beginning it is written, "Who come into Egypt with Jacob," BEFORE THE DESCENT, and when they descended, it is written: "Every man came with his household" (Shemt 1:1), IN PAST TENSE. Come and behold: the children of Jacob had already died by that time, and the others descended INTO EXILE.

272. רִבִּי יוֹסֵי וְרִבִּי אֶלְעָזָר אָמְרוּ, הַאי פַּרְשְׁתָּא מִלְּין עִלָּאִין אִית בָּהּ, דִּתְנָן, בְּשַׁעֲתָא דְּנַחְתּוּ אִלֵּין רְתִיכִין וּמַשִּׁרְיָין קַדִּישִׁין, דְּיוֹקְנֵיהוֹן דְּשִׁבְטִין, דִּגְלִיפִין לְעֵילָּא, כֻּלְּהוּ עָאלָן לְמֵידַר עִמְּהוֹן. הה"ד, אִישׁ וּבֵיתוֹ בָּאוּ, וּכְתִיב רְאוּבֵן שִׁמְעוֹן לֵוִי.

272. Rabbi Yosi and Rabbi Elazar said: This portion contains lofty subjects. For we learned that at the time these holy companies and Chariots descended, WHICH ARE the form of the TWELVE tribes which are engraved above IN THE SHECHINAH, they all came to sojourn with them. This is the meaning of: "Every man came with his household," WHICH ALLUDES TO THE ANGELS WHO CAME TO SOJOURN IN EGYPT WITH THE CHILDREN OF YISRAEL, and: "Reuben, Simeon, Levi..." (Ibid. 2). THEY ALLUDE TO THE FORMS OF THE TWELVE TRIBES IN THE SHECHINAH.

273. ד"א וְאֵלֶּה שְׁמוֹת בְּנֵי יִשְׂרָאֵל הַבָּאִים מִצְרַיְמָה אֵת יַעֲקֹב וְגוֹ'. אִתְחֲזַר פַּרְשְׁתָּא דָא, לָמָּה דא"ר יוֹסֵי בְּרִבִּי יְהוּדָה, וְכֹלָּא הֲוָה.

273. Another explanation of: "And these are the names of the children of Israel who came into Egypt with Jacob...": HE HAD DIFFICULTY UNDERSTANDING WHY IT OPENED WITH "THE CHILDREN OF YISRAEL," AND CONCLUDED WITH "JACOB," AND SAYS: This portion reverted FROM THE CHILDREN OF YISRAEL TO JACOB. IT IS according to what Rabbi Yosi ben Rabbi Yehuda, said earlier – THAT THE CHILDREN OF YISRAEL DESCENDED TO THE LEVEL OF THE CHILDREN OF JACOB. And it all occurred, MEANING THAT ALL THE LITERAL EXPLANATIONS ARE TRUE.

35. "Every man came with his household"

A Synopsis

A discussion of the title verse elaborates on a concept mentioned in the previous section – that the Tribes descended into Egypt twice, once when alive and once when dead. According to Rabbi Elazar, when the children of Yisrael went into exile, all the souls of the tribes gathered at the cave of Machpelah. They cried to Jacob, lamenting that a heathen nation had enslaved Yisrael. This awakened the spirit of Jacob, and after gaining permission from God, Jacob, the Tribes, the Shechinah and the supernal angels descended into Egypt. Thus, even in death Jacob did not separate from Yisrael.

The Relevance of the Passage

This potent passage transports our soul to the Cave of Machpelah, where we connect to the souls of the Twelve Tribes and to the Patriarch Jacob. We summon as well the strength of Joseph and all the supernal angelic forces to initiate and complete our ascension out of our own personal Egypt – our ego or reactive nature, including all the chaotic darkness brought about by our self-centered impulses.

274. וְתָּא חֲזֵי, רַבִּי אֶלְעָזָר בֶּן עֲרָךְ, כַּד הֲוָה מָטֵי לְהַאי פָּסוּק, הֲוָה בָּכֵי, דְּתַנְיָא, א"ר אֶלְעָזָר בֶּן עֲרָךְ, בְּשַׁעֲתָא דְּאַזְלוּ יִשְׂרָאֵל בְּגָלוּתָא, אִתְכְּנָשׁוּ כֻּלְּהוּ נִשְׁמָתְהוֹן דְּשִׁבְטִין, לְמְעַרְתָּא דְּכַפֶלְתָּא, צָוְוחוּ וְאָמְרוּ: סָבָא סָבָא, כְּאֵבָא דִּבְנִין לָאו בַּלְאוּתָא דְּעָלְמָא דֵּין, בָּנֶיךָ כֻּלְּהוּ מִשְׁתַּעְבְּדִין בְּקַשְׁיוּ, עִם אַחֲרָן עַבְדִין בְּהוּ נוּקְמִין דְּעָלְמָא.

274. Come and behold: when Rabbi Elazar ben Arach reached this passage: "AND THESE ARE THE NAMES..." he would weep. Rabbi Elazar ben Arach said: We learned that when the children of Yisrael went into exile, all the souls of the tribes gathered at the cave of Machpelah. They cried and said: 'Grandfather, grandfather, there is no greater labor in pain of the children, there is no greater labor in this world THAT IT. Your children are all enslaved WITH HARD LABOR by others, who execute upon them ALL MANNERS OF vengeance in the world.'

275. בְּהַהִיא שַׁעֲתָא, אִתְעַר רוּחֵיהּ דְּהַהוּא סָבָא, רְשׁוּתָא שָׁאִיל, וְנָחִית, קָרָא קוּדְשָׁא בְּרִיךְ הוּא לְכָל רְתִיכוֹי וּמַשְׁרְיָיתֵיהּ, וּמַלְכֵיהוֹן בְּרָאשֵׁיהוֹן. וְנָחֲתוּ כֻּלְּהוּ עִם יַעֲקֹב וְעִם שִׁבְטוֹהִי. שִׁבְטִין נָחֲתוּ חַיִּין עִם

אֲבוּהוֹן, וּשְׁבָטִין נַחְתּוּ מֵתִים עִם אֲבוּהוֹן, הה"ד וְאֵלֶּה שְׁמוֹת בְּנֵי
יִשְׂרָאֵל הַבָּאִים מִצְרָיְמָה וְגוֹ' וּכְתִיב רְאוּבֵן שִׁמְעוֹן לֵוִי וְגוֹ'. וּתָא חֲזֵי,
מֵתִים הֲווֹ, וְנַחְתּוּ, וּכְתִיב וְיוֹסֵף הָיָה בְמִצְרָיִם. אָמַר רִבִּי אַבָּא, בְּהַאי
אִתְקְרֵי כְּרַחֵם אָב עַל בָּנִים.

275. At that moment, the spirit of that grandfather was stirred, MEANING JACOB, requested permission. and descended INTO EGYPT. The Holy One, blessed be He, summoned His companies and Chariots, and their King, WHICH IS THE SHECHINAH at their head. And they all descended with Jacob and his tribes. The tribes descended alive with their father TO EGYPT. They also descended dead with their father TO EGYPT. This is what is written: "And these are the names of the children of Israel who came into Egypt...Reuben, Simeon, Levi..." (Shemot 1:1-2). Come and behold: now they are dead, AS MENTIONED EARLIER, yet they descended TO EGYPT. And it was written: "And Joseph was in Egypt" (Ibid. 5). FOR HIS SPIRIT DID NOT LEAVE EGYPT AFTER HIS DEATH, THAT HE SHOULD HAVE TO RETURN AND DESCEND AS THE OTHER TRIBES DID. Rabbi Aba said: After this he, JOSEPH, is called: "As a father pities his children" (Tehilim 103:13), BECAUSE HE DID NOT LEAVE THEM, EVEN AFTER HIS DEATH.

36. The dead know of the pain of the living

A Synopsis

This section consists chiefly of a parable in which Rabbi Yehuda and Rabbi Aba participate. While travelling, the two come across a place where they decide to spend the night. They lay down to sleep, resting their heads on some raised ground under which is a grave. A voice from this grave speaks to them, and they learn that it belongs to a Jew who is unable to enter the Garden of Eden because his young son was stolen by an abusive heathen. He tells the Rabbis that not only do the dead know of the sufferings of the living, but without the prayers of the dead, they would not survive for half a day. The voice then tells them his son is being beaten at that moment and orders them to leave. Rabbi Yehuda and Rabbi Aba run for half a mile and wait until morning, at which time they see a man with blood running from his shoulders. When they question him, they discover that he is Lachma bar Livai, the son of the dead man. Yet, they do not converse with him or return to the grave sight out of fear.

Rabbi Yehuda then explains the two promises God made to Jacob: that He would go down into exile with Jacob, and that He would raise Jacob from his grave to witness the joy of the celestial company that dwelled with Yisrael in captivity. Finally, Rabbi Shimon interprets the verse, "A new king arose..." revealing that Egypt was not granted dominion over all the nations until after Joseph's death.

The Relevance of the Passage

We are never alone. If we should fall to the greatest depth of sin and darkness, we are never by ourselves. The Light, the supernal angelic forces, and the souls of the Righteous sages are constantly with us to aid us in the moment we choose to transform and embrace the spiritual path of correction.

The prayers of the righteous souls now blanket our world with protection, healing, and Light as we read this passage. The energy arising here launches the process known as the Resurrection of the Dead. It completes our Final Redemption with tender mercy and kindness, for this is the ultimate attribute of spiritual Light and is the desire of the great sages. In the process, the supernal forces responsible for provoking our Evil Inclination are eternally relieved of their duties, as goodness and freedom reigns supreme.

276. רִבִּי יְהוּדָה בַּר שָׁלוֹם, הֲוָה אָזִיל בְּאוֹרְחָא, וְרִבִּי אַבָּא הֲוָה עִמֵּיהּ, עָאלוּ לְחַד אַתְרָא, וּבָתוּ תַּמָּן, אָכְלוּ, כַּד בָּעוּ לְמִשְׁכַּב, שָׁווּ רֵישַׁיְיהוּן

בְּהַהוּא תְּלָא דְּאַרְעָא, דַּהֲוָה חַד קַבְרָא תַּמָּן, עַד דְּלָא דְּמִיכוּ, קָרָא חַד
קָלָא מִן קַבְרָא, אָמַר זַרְעָא לְאַרְעָא אַזְלָא, תְּרֵיסַר שְׁנִין הֲוָה דְּלָא
אִתְעָרִית, בַּר הָאִידָנָא, דְּפַרְצוּפָא דִּבְרִי חֲמֵינָא הָכָא.

276. Rabbi Yehuda bar Shalom was traveling with Rabbi Aba. They entered a place and lodged there. They ate and when they wanted to lie down, they lay their heads on a mound of earth where there was a grave. Before they fell asleep, someone called from the grave and said: MY seed is going into the ground – MEANING GOING TO WASTE. It has been twelve years that I have not awakened, except now, for I see the face of my son here!

277. א״ר יְהוּדָה, מַאן אַתְּ. א״ל יוּדָאי אֲנָא, וַאֲנָא יָתִיב נְזִיפָא, דַּאֲנָא
לָא יָכִילְנָא לְמֵיעַל, בְּגִין הַהוּא צַעֲרָא דִּבְרִי, דְּגַנְבֵיהּ הַהוּא עכו״ם, כַּד
אִיהוּ הֲוָה זְעֵירָא, וְאַלְקֵי לֵיהּ כָּל יוֹמָא, וְצַעֲרָא דִּילֵיהּ דָּחֵי לִי לְמֵיעָאל
בְּדוּכְתָּאי, וּבְהַאי אַתְרָא לָא אִתְעָרִית, בַּר הָאִידָנָא.

277. Rabbi Yehuda said: Who are you? He said to him: I am a Jew, and I sit alone, AS IN EXCOMMUNICATION. For I can not enter THE GARDEN OF EDEN because of the pain of my son who was stolen, when he was still small, by a heathen who beats him every day. His pain prevents me from entering my place, and I awoke just now in this place.

278. אָמַר לֵיהּ וְאַתּוּן יַדְעִין בְּצַעֲרָא דְּחַיֵּי. א״ל, שָׁרֵי קַבְרִי, אִי לָאו
בָּעוּתָא דִּילָן עַל חַיֵּי, לָא יִתְקַיְּימוּן פַּלְגּוּת יוֹמָא בְּעָלְמָא, וְהָאִידָנָא
אִתְעָרִית הָכָא, דַּהֲווֹ אַמְרִין לִי כָּל יוֹמָא, דְּלַעֲגָלָא יֵיתֵי בְּרִי הָכָא, וְלָא
יָדַעְנָא אִי בְּחַיֵּי אִי בְּמוֹתָא.

278. He said to him: Do you know the pain of the living? He said to him: I SWEAR by the minister of my grave that were it not for our prayers for the living, they would not survive in the world for even a half day. I awoke here, for they were telling me every day that my son would come here soon, but I do not know if alive or after his death.

279. א״ל רִבִּי יְהוּדָה, מַאי עֲבִידְתַּיְיכוּ בְּהַהוּא עָלְמָא. אִתְרְגִישׁ קַבְרָא,

וְאָמַר, אַזִילוּ קוּמוּ, דְּהָאִידָנָא יַלְקוּן לִבְרִי, תַּווֹהוּ, וְעָרְקוּ מִתַּמָּן
כְּפַלְגּוּת מִיל, יָתְבוּ עַד דְּנָהִיר צַפְרָא. קָמוּ לְמֵיזַל, חָמוּ חַד בַּר נָשׁ,
דַּהֲוָה רָהִיט וְעָרַק, וַהֲוָה שָׁתִית דָּמָא אֲכַתְפוֹי, אַחֲדוּ בֵּיהּ, וְסָח לְהוּ
עוֹבָדָא, אָמְרוּ לֵיהּ מַה שְׁמָךְ. אָמַר לְהוּ, לַחְמָא בַּר לֵיוָאֵי. אָמְרוּ, וּמַה
לֵיוָאֵי בַּר לַחְמָא הֲוָה הַהוּא מֵיתָא, וּמִסְתָּפֵינָא לְאִשְׁתְּעוּיֵי יַתִּיר
בַּהֲדֵיהּ. לָא אֲהַדְרוּ. אָמַר רִבִּי אַבָּא, הַאי דְּאָמְרוּ, דִּצְלוֹתְהוֹן דְּמֵתַיָּיא,
מְגִינָן עַל חַיֵּי. מְנָלָן. דִּכְתִיב וַיַּעֲלוּ בַנֶּגֶב וַיָּבֹא עַד חֶבְרוֹן.

279. Rabbi Yehuda said to him: What do you do in that world? The grave rumbled and he said: Go, arise, for now they are beating my son. They were amazed and fled from there about a half a mile. They sat until morning light. They rose to go and saw a man who was running and fleeing FROM HIS MASTER – AS HE WAS SAVED FROM HIM BY THE PRAYERS OF HIS DEAD FATHER. And he was bleeding from his shoulders. They held him and he told them THE STORY OF THE HEATHEN WHO KIDNAPPED HIM WHEN HE WAS A CHILD, AND WHO BEAT HIM UNTIL HE STARTED TO BLEED. They said to him: What is your name? He said to them: Lachma bar Livai. They said: Was not Livai bar Lachma THE NAME OF that deceased? We are afraid to talk with him anymore! They did not return to him. Rabbi Aba said: This is what they said – that the prayers of the dead protect the living. How do we know? IT IS because it is written: "And they went up to the Negev and he came to Cherubs" (Bemidbar 13:22), MEANING TO PRAY AT THE GRAVE OF THE PATRIARCHS, THAT THEY WOULD PRAY FOR THEM.

280. א"ר יְהוּדָה, תָּא חֲזֵי, תְּרֵין נִדְרִין נָדַר קוּדְשָׁא בְּרִיךְ הוּא לְיַעֲקֹב.
חַד, דְּיֵיחוּת עִמֵּיהּ לְמֵידַר עִמֵּיהּ בְּגָלוּתָא, וְחַד דְּיֵסְקִינֵיהּ מִקִּבְרֵיהּ,
לְמֶחֱמֵי חֶדְוָותָא דְּסִיַּיעְתָּא קַדִּישָׁא דְּדַיְירֵי עִם בְּנוֹהִי, הה"ד, אָנֹכִי אֵרֵד
עִמְּךָ מִצְרַיְמָה אָנֹכִי אֵרֵד עִמְּךָ בְּגָלוּתָא. וְאָנֹכִי אַעַלְךָ גַם עָלֹה, כד"א
וְהַעֲלֵיתִי אֶתְכֶם מִקִּבְרוֹתֵיכֶם עַמִּי. וּכְתִיב שֵׁשָׁם עָלוּ שְׁבָטִים וְגוֹ'.

280. Rabbi Yehuda said: Come and behold. The Holy One, blessed be He, made two vows to Jacob. He would descend with him and sojourn with him in exile, and He would raise him from his grave to see the joy of the holy camp OF THE CHARIOTS AND THE ANGELS, who sojourned with his children IN EXILE DURING THE REDEMPTION. This is the meaning of: "I will go down with you into Egypt" (Beresheet 46:4), MEANING I will descend with you into exile. "And I will surely bring you up again," MEANING DURING THE REDEMPTION, BECAUSE "BRING YOU UP" IS AN EXPRESSION OF REDEMPTION, as is written: "And I will bring you up from your graves, My people" (Yechezkel 37:12), and: "There the tribes used to go up..." (Tehilim 122:4).

281. ד"א וַיָּקָם מֶלֶךְ חָדָשׁ עַל מִצְרָיִם וְגוֹ', אר"ש, בְּהַהוּא יוֹמָא, אִתְיְהִיב לֵיהּ רְשׁוּתָא לְשָׂרוֹ שֶׁל מִצְרַיִם, עַל כָּל שְׁאַר עַמִּין, דְּתָנָא, עַד דְּלָא מִית יוֹסֵף, לָא אִתְיְהִיב שׁוּלְטָנוּ לְשַׁלְטָנָא דְּמִצְרַיִם עַל יִשְׂרָאֵל, כֵּיוָן דְּמִית יוֹסֵף, כְּדֵין וַיָּקָם מֶלֶךְ חָדָשׁ עַל מִצְרָיִם, וַיָּקָם: כְּמַאן דַּהֲוָה מָאִיךְ וְקָם.

281. Another explanation of: "Now there arose a new king..." (Shemot 1:8) Rabbi Shimon said: On that day, permission was granted to the Minister of Egypt to be SUPERIOR over all the other nations. For we learned that before Joseph died, Egypt was not granted dominion over Yisrael, but when Joseph died, "Now there arose a new king." "Arose" MEANS as one who was lowly and arose, FOR ON THAT DAY THE MINISTER OF EGYPT AROSE TO BE GREAT, AS MENTIONED EARLIER.

37. "While the king was reclining at his board"

A Synopsis
Rabbi Yitzchak opens with the first of three interpretations of the title verse. Rabbi Tanchum concludes this section by explaining that every nation has a minister above and the rise of one minister coincides with the fall of another. Thus, when God gave dominion to the minister of Egypt, he gained dominion only because of Yisrael.

The Relevance of the Passage
The ultimate intent behind the giving of the Torah on Mount Sinai to Moses is accomplished for each reader, and the world, through the power of these heavenly verses.

The Torah, viewed through the lens of Kabbalah, is an awesome instrument of power designed to uproot and banish each and every one of our negative desires and reactive traits that are embedded in our nature. In truth, a man does not possess the power to accomplish this profound task on his own. Rather, our accountability and acknowledgment of the various wicked aspects of our character is the effort we must exert. Once we identify and accept responsibility for these reprehensible characteristics, the Light of the Torah is free to cleanse them from our being.

As we connect to this particular passage, the reader should self-reflect on all of his nefarious qualities. Recall moments of intolerance, envy, anger, insensitivity, narrow-mindedness, jealousy, rage, impatience, selfishness, and self-indulgence. The more difficult and painful it is to admit these misdeeds, the more powerful will be the result you will achieve.

This action will allow the Zohar to purge now the underlying traits that caused these reactive moments in the first place. The foul fragrances and darkness that arise from such behavior dissipate forever. The heavenly fragrances of the Torah now permeate our entire existence.

282. רִבִּי יִצְחָק פָּתַח, עַד שֶׁהַמֶּלֶךְ בִּמְסִבּוֹ נִרְדִּי נָתַן רֵיחוֹ. עַד שֶׁהַמֶּלֶךְ: דָּא קוּדְשָׁא בְּרִיךְ הוּא. הה"ד, כֹּה אָמַר יְיָ' מֶלֶךְ יִשְׂרָאֵל. וּכְתִיב וַיְהִי בִישׁוּרוּן מֶלֶךְ. בִּמְסִבּוֹ: בֵּין כַּנְפֵי הַכְּרוּבִים. נִרְדִּי נָתַן רֵיחוֹ, דְּגָרְמוּ לְאִסְתַּלְּקָא מִבֵּינֵיהוֹן.

282. Rabbi Yitzchak opened the discussion saying: "While the king was reclining at his board, my nard sent forth its fragrance" (Shir Hashirm 1:12).

"While the king," refers to the Holy One, blessed be He, as is written: "Thus says Hashem, the King of Yisrael" (Yeshayah 44:6), and: "And he was King in Yeshurun" (Devarim 33:5). "While the King was reclining at his board," MEANS between the wings of Cherubs THAT WERE ON THE ARK OF THE TESTIMONY. "My nard gave forth its fragrance," MEANS THEY CAUSED THE HOLY ONE, BLESSED BE HE, to depart from among them, AND "GIVES FORTH ITS FRAGRANCE" MEANS THEIR BAD ODOR!

283. ד"א, עַד שֶׁהַמֶּלֶךְ בִּמְסִבּוֹ, בְּעוֹד דְּקוּדְשָׁא בְּרִיךְ הוּא הֲוָה יָהִיב אוֹרַיְיתָא לְיִשְׂרָאֵל, דִּכְתִּיב וַיְהִי שָׁם עִם ה' אַרְבָּעִים יוֹם וְאַרְבָּעִים לַיְלָה לֶחֶם לֹא אָכַל וְגוֹ'. בְּעוֹד דַּהֲוָה כְּתִיב אוֹרַיְיתָא לְיִשְׂרָאֵל, שָׁבְקוּ רֵיחֵיהוֹן טָב, וְאָמְרוּ אֵלֶּה אֱלֹהֶיךָ יִשְׂרָאֵל.

283. Another explanation of : "While the King was reclining at his board," meaning while the Holy One, blessed be He, was still giving the Torah to Yisrael, as it is written: "And he was there with Hashem forty days and forty nights" (Shemot 34:28). While he was still writing the Torah for Yisrael, they abandoned their good fragrance and said: "These are your Elohim, Yisrael" (Shemot 32:4). THE MEANING OF "SENT FORTH" IS 'ABANDONED.'

284. ד"א עַד שֶׁהַמֶּלֶךְ בִּמְסִבּוֹ, בְּעוֹד דַּהֲוָה קוּדְשָׁא בְּרִיךְ הוּא נָחִית עַל טוּרָא דְּסִינַי, לְמִיהַב אוֹרַיְיתָא לְיִשְׂרָאֵל, נִרְדִּי נָתַן רֵיחוֹ, דִּכְתִּיב נַעֲשֶׂה וְנִשְׁמָע.

284. Another explanation of: "While the King was reclining at His board." While the Holy One, blessed be He, was still descended on Mount Sinai to give the Torah to Yisrael, "my nard sent forth its fragrance," MEANING, LITERALLY, THAT IT GAVE ITS GOOD FRAGRANCE. It is written THAT THEY SAID: "Will we do, and obey" (Shemot 24:7).

38. Yisrael corresponds to all the other nations of the world

A Synopsis

Continuing the discussion of the previous section, Rabbi Yitzchak explains that the single nation of Yisrael is equivalent to all of the seventy other nations, and therefore whoever rules over Yisrael dominates the whole world. Because of this powerful status, the children of Yisrael are subjected to the rule of other nations in order that the world may be elevated through them. Rabbi Yitzchak also explains the great symbolic significance of the numbers one and seventy in this context. Seventy is the number of nations, the number of Yisrael who came into Egypt, and the number of Names for God, while God is One and Yisrael is one, on a par with the rest of the world.

The Relevance of the Passage

When we are born into this world, our Evil Inclination (the body) is given dominion over our soul. Our purpose in life is to gradually conquer all of the various aspects of our Evil Inclination.

This effort allows us to perfect our soul and, in turn, correct our physical body. Heaven on Earth will materialize for all mankind when a significant amount of people achieve this ultimate transformation.

Reading these passages of Zohar is equivalent to attaining that transformation – such is the power of these divine verses.

Yisrael can be likened to the heart of the human body, whereas the other nations of the world correspond to all the organs.

If the heart cannot deliver sufficient blood to each area of the body, illness and disease inevitably set in.

Personally, each time we resist a reactive urge, a powerful *heart beat* propels Light through the spiritual arteries that interconnect all nations. The Light that is generated becomes the "blood" that nourishes the body, the soul, and all the nations of the world.

If we do not undertake this spiritual path, the other nations experience malnutrition. This is the underlying cause behind hatred towards Yisrael and, on a personal level, the reason for the chaos and darkness in our own lives.

Hence, each of our actions simultaneously contributes to or subtracts from our personal welfare and the global state of the world. *All* is interconnected.

Here, the readers of the Zohar play the role of the heart, nourishing all the world with spiritual Light, healing the wounds between the nations, and healing personal ailments. The entire body of mankind is

unified by this effort. Love becomes the blood that courses through
our spiritual veins – which are the relationships that connect one man
to another, one nation to a second.

285. רִבִּי תַּנְחוּם אָמַר, כָּל אוּמָה וְאוּמָה אִית לָה שַׂר לְעֵילָא, וְכַד
קוּדְשָׁא בְּרִיךְ הוּא יָהִיב שֻׁלְטָנוּתָא לְדֵין, אַנְחִית לְדֵין, וְכַד יָהִיב
שֻׁלְטָנוּתָא לְהַהוּא שַׂר, לֵית לֵיהּ שֻׁלְטָנוּתָא, אֶלָּא בְּגִין יִשְׂרָאֵל, הה"ד
הָיוּ צָרֶיהָ לְרֹאשׁ.

285. Rabbi Tanchum said: Every nation has a minister above and when the
Holy One, blessed be He, gives dominion to one, He humbles another.
When He gave dominion to that Minister OF EGYPT, he had that dominion
only because of Yisrael. This is the meaning of: "Her adversaries have
become the chief" (Eichah 1:5).

286. רִבִּי יִצְחָק אָמַר, יִשְׂרָאֵל אִינּוּן לָקֳבֵיל כָּל שְׁאַר אוּמִין דְּעָלְמָא,
מַה שְׁאַר עַמִּין אִינּוּן שִׁבְעִים, אוּף יִשְׂרָאֵל אִינּוּן שִׁבְעִים, הה"ד, כָּל
הַנֶּפֶשׁ לְבֵית יַעֲקֹב הַבָּאָה מִצְרַיְמָה שִׁבְעִים. וּמַאן דְּשָׁלִיט עַל יִשְׂרָאֵל,
כְּאִילּוּ שָׁלִיט עַל כָּל עָלְמָא.

286. Rabbi Yitzchak said: Yisrael corresponds to all the other nations of the
world. As all the other nations are seventy, Yisrael is also seventy. It is
written: "All the souls of the House of Jacob who came into Egypt were
seventy" (Beresheet 46:27). And it is as if he who rules over Yisrael, rules
over the whole world.

287. רִבִּי אַבָּא אָמַר מֵהָכָא, וּבְנֵי יִשְׂרָאֵל פָּרוּ וַיִּשְׁרְצוּ וְגוֹ', הָא שִׁבְעָה.
וְכָל דַּרְגָּא לַעֲשָׂרָה, הָא שִׁבְעִים. מַה כְּתִיב בַּתְרֵיהּ, וַיָּקָם מֶלֶךְ חָדָשׁ עַל
מִצְרָיִם.

287. Rabbi Aba said: From here IT IS UNDERSTOOD THAT YISRAEL IS
SEVENTY, AS IS WRITTEN: "And the children of Yisrael were fruitful, and
increased abundantly and multiplied and became exceedingly mighty"
(Shemot 1:7). We have here seven LEVELS, and every level INCLUDES ten;
thus, there are seventy. What is written after this? "Now there arose a new

king over Egypt" (Ibid. 8). BY REASON OF HIS DOMINION OVER YISRAEL, THAT CORRESPONDS TO THE SEVENTY NATIONS, HE WAS CONSIDERED AS A NEW KING.

288. אָמַר רַב הוּנָא, אֲמַאי אִשְׁתַּעְבִּידוּ יִשְׂרָאֵל בְּכָל הָאוּמִין, בְּגִין דְּיִשְׁתְּאַר בְּהוֹן עָלְמָא, דְּאִינּוּן לָקֳבֵיל כָּל עָלְמָא, וּכְתִיב, בַּיּוֹם הַהוּא יִהְיֶה ה' אֶחָד וּשְׁמוֹ אֶחָד. וּמַה הוּא חַד, אוּף יִשְׂרָאֵל חַד, דִּכְתִּיב גּוֹי אֶחָד בָּאָרֶץ. מַה שְׁמֵיהּ חַד, וְנִתְפְּרַשׁ בְּע', אוּף יִשְׂרָאֵל חַד, וְנִתְפְּרַשׁ בְּשַׁבְעִין.

288. Rabbi Huna said: Why were Yisrael enslaved among all the nations? It was in order that the world should be elevated through them. For they correspond to the whole world. And it is written: "On that day Hashem shall be One and His Name One" (Zecharyah 14:9). As THE HOLY ONE, BLESSED BE HE, is One, so is Yisrael one, as is written: "one nation in the earth" (II Shmuel 7:23). As the name OF THE HOLY ONE, BLESSED BE HE, is One and is explained in seventy NAMES, Yisrael is also one and interpreted by seventy.

39. "For a slave when he becomes king"

A Synopsis

Rabbi Yehuda begins the discussion by interpreting the title verse, explaining that it refers to Egypt, whom God despises more than any other nation, and Ishmael, who torments and persecutes Yisrael for their Faith. Following this we learn of an incident involving Rabbi Yehoshua, who saw a meeting between a Jew and an Arab with his son. The Arab told his son to insult the Jew and spit in his face, however when the boy grabbed the Jew's beard, Rabbi Yehoshua prayed to the Patriarchs and the earth opened up and swallowed the Arabs.

The Relevance of the Passage

Everyone has two aspects within their nature – selfish desire, also known as the Evil Inclination; and a will to share, or the Good Inclination.

The soul's desire to impart is known by the code word "Yisrael." Our selfish impulses are termed "Egypt" or "Ishmael."

When we, as individuals, allow our egocentric urges to dominate our life, we end up treating others with unkindness, intolerance, and cruelty. The negative energy this creates arouses the dark side in our Arab brothers which, in turn, leads to hatred toward the Children of Yisrael. Moreover, these negative traits disconnect us from the Light that permeates the Upper World.

When we resist our selfish impulses, we connect to Light and illuminate all existence. This Light nourishes our Arab brothers and arouses love for Yisrael. This, and only this, ends the conflict and uproots the hatred that has long existed between Muslims and Jews.

Our gentle reading of these verses swallows up all our evil tendencies and impulses. We arouse Light and Love within all Arabs as the Light banishes these negative qualities from our core being.

Each word we glance over generates harmony, tolerance, and true love among all the souls of humanity and between our own body and our soul.

289. רַבִּי יְהוּדָה פָּתַח, תַּחַת שָׁלשׁ רָגְזָה אֶרֶץ וְגו', תַּחַת עֶבֶד כִּי יִמְלוֹךְ, דְּתַנְיָא לֵית לָךְ אוּמָא מְכִיכָא וּקְלִילָא וְנִבְזֵית קַמֵּי קוּדְשָׁא בְּרִיךְ הוּא, כְּוָותַיְיהוּ דְּמִצְרָאֵי, וְיָהִיב לוֹן קוּדְשָׁא בְּרִיךְ הוּא שָׁלְטָנוּתָא בְּגִינַיְיהוּ דְּיִשְׂרָאֵל. וְשִׁפְחָה כִּי תִירַשׁ גְּבִירְתָּהּ, דָּא הָגָר, דְּאוֹלִידַת

לְיִשְׁמָעֵאל, שֶׁעָשָׂה כַּמָּה רָעוֹת לְיִשְׂרָאֵל, וְשָׁלַט בָּהֶם, וְעִנָּה אוֹתָם בְּכָל
מִינֵי עִנּוּיִין, וְגָזַר עֲלֵיהֶם כַּמָּה שְׁמָדוֹת, וְעַד הַיּוֹם הֵם שׁוֹלְטִים עֲלֵיהֶם,
וְאֵינָם מַנִּיחִים לָהֶם לַעֲמוֹד בְּדָתָם. וְאֵין לְךָ גָּלוּת קָשָׁה לְיִשְׂרָאֵל כְּמוֹ
גָּלוּת יִשְׁמָעֵאל.

289. Rabbi Yehuda opened the discussion saying: "For three things the earth is disquieted...for a slave when he becomes king" (Mishlei 30:21). We learned that there is no nation as lowly, despised and degraded before the Holy One, blessed be He, as the Egyptians. And the Holy One, blessed be He, gave them dominion because of Yisrael. "And a handmaid that is heir to her mistress" (Ibid.), is Hagar, who bore Ishmael who has done so much evil to Yisrael, dominated them and oppressed them with all kinds of oppressions, and decreed against them many devastations. They dominate Yisrael to this day, and do not permit them to observe their religion. There has been no exile as hard on Yisrael as the exile of Ishmael.

290. ר' יְהוֹשֻׁעַ הֲוָה סָלִיק לִירוּשָׁלֵם, וַהֲוָה אָזִיל בְּאוֹרְחָא, חָמָא חַד
עַרְבָאָה, דַּהֲוָה אָזִיל בְּאוֹרְחָא, וּבְרֵיהּ עִמֵּיהּ. פָּגְעוּ בְּיוּדָאי חַד. אָמַר
לִבְרֵיהּ, הַאי יוּדָאי גָּעֲלָא, דְּמָאִיס בֵּיהּ מָרֵיהּ. נְוֹל לֵיהּ, וְרָקִיק לֵיהּ
בְּדִיקְנֵיהּ ז' זִמְנִין, דְּאִיהוּ מִזַּרְעָא דְּרָאמִין, דַּאֲנָא יָדַעְנָא דְּמִשְׁעַעְבְּדָן
בְּהוּ שַׁבְעִין עַמְמִין, אָזִיל בְּרֵיהּ וְאָחִיד בְּדִיקְנֵיהּ. אָמַר רַבִּי יְהוֹשֻׁעַ
רָאמִין רָאמִין, גּוֹזַרְנָא עַל עִלָּאִין, דְּיֵחֲתוּן לְתַתָּא. עַד לָא סַיֵּים
אִתְבְּלָעוּ בְּאַתְרַיְיהוֹן.

290. Rabbi Yehoshua was going up to Jerusalem and, as he was traveling, he saw an Arab walking with his son. They met a Jew. THE ARAB said to his son: This is a loathsome Jew who is despised by his Master. Soil him and spit into his beard seven times, for he is of the seed of high ones – MEANING FROM ABRAHAM, ISAAC AND JACOB, yet I know that seventy nations are subjugating them! His son went and grasped the beard OF THE JEW. Rabbi Yehoshua said: Lofty one, lofty ones, MEANING THAT HE PRAYED IN THE MERIT OF THE PATRIARCHS, I decree on the high ones, MEANING ON THE ARAB AND HIS SON WHO CONSIDERED THEMSELVES HIGHER THAN THE YESRAEL, that they should descend down under. Before Rabbi Yehoshua finished his words, they were swallowed up IN THE GROUND where they stood.

40. "Before the day cools"

A Synopsis

Rabbi Yitzchak opens with an explanation of the title verse. We learn that the subjugation of Yisrael will end after one thousand years, whereupon God will appear in the terrestrial Jerusalem to purify it. At this time, He will drive the heathen nations from the Holy City and shake the wicked out of the earth. If the exile lasts longer than one thousand years, we're told, it is because Yisrael will not return in repentance to God.

The Relevance of the Passage

Often, we know that a particular behavioral action is positive and beneficial to our life. Nevertheless, another voice inside us persuades us to avoid it and procrastinate. Likewise, we are all-too-often aware that certain behavior is extremely detrimental. We routinely vow not to engage in such actions. Yet these same voices compel us into the misdeed, even though we do not really want to.

When we allow our negative and wicked impulses to rule over our own positive traits and good intentions, the nations of the world are empowered, measure for measure, to rule over Yisrael. Meditating with deep conviction on the words presented here shakes and dislodges all the disobedient impulses that govern our daily behavior. We stir repentance in our hearts for all our iniquities caused by these negative traits. Genuine repentance and deep remorse are unimaginably powerful forces; and through them, we now achieve our final purification and correction.

Our soul achieves dominion over our lives. In turn, Yisrael is purified with great mercy and is empowered so that her relationship with the other nations of the world is strengthened, founded upon unconditional mutual love and respect.

Permanent world peace is achieved through our spiritual actions performed here, for they have infinitely more power and might than the military or political actions that take place in the physical realm.

291. רִבִּי יִצְחָק פָּתַח, עַד שֶׁיָּפוּחַ הַיּוֹם וְנָסוּ הַצְּלָלִים וְגו', עַד שֶׁיָּפוּחַ הַיּוֹם, הַאי קְרָא עַל גָּלוּתָא דְּיִשְׂרָאֵל אִתְּמַר, דְּאִינּוּן יִשְׁתַּעְבְּדוּן בְּגָלוּתָא, עַד דְּיִסְתַּיֵּים הַהוּא יוֹמָא דְּשָׁלְטָנוּתָא דְּאוּמִין. דִּתְנָן, א"ר יִצְחָק, אֶלֶף שְׁנִין הוּא שָׁלְטָנוּתָא דְּכָל אוּמִין כַּחֲדָא, עֲלַיְיהוּ דְּיִשְׂרָאֵל. וְלֵית לָךְ אוּמָה דְּלָא יִשְׁתַּעְבֵּד בְּהוֹן. וְיוֹמָא חֲדָא, הוּא לְקַבְלֵיהּ דִּכְתִיב,

וְהָיָה יוֹם אֶחָד הוּא יִוָּדַע לַיְיָ' וְגוֹ'.

291. Rabbi Yitzchak opened the discussion saying: "Before the day cools, and the shadows flee away" (Shir Hashirm 4:6). "Before the day cools" refers to the exile of Yisrael, and that they would be subjugated in exile until that day when the rule of the nations will end. For we have learned that Rabbi Yitzchak said that the dominion of all nations together over Yisrael would last one thousand years. There is no nation that would not subjugate them. The one day corresponds to the words "but it shall be one particular day which shall be known as Hashem's..." (Zecharyah 14:7).

292. ד"א, עַד שֶׁיָּפוּחַ הַיּוֹם קֹדֶם דְּיִפּוּחַ הַהוּא יוֹמָא דְּאוּמִין. וְנָסוּ הַצְּלָלִים, אִינּוּן שׁוּלְטָנִין דְּשַׁלְטוּ עֲלַיְיהוּ. אֵלֶךְ לִי אֶל הַר הַמּוֹר, אָמַר קוּדְשָׁא בְּרִיךְ הוּא, אֵלֶךְ לִי, לְנַעֲרָא הָאוּמוֹת מִירוּשְׁלֵם דְּהוּא הַר הַמּוֹר, כְּמָה דִּכְתִיב, בְּהַר הַמּוֹרִיָּה אֲשֶׁר בִּירוּשָׁלַם. וְאֶל גִּבְעַת הַלְּבוֹנָה, דָּא בֵּי מַקְדְּשָׁא דִּי בְּצִיּוֹן, דִּכְתִיב בֵּיהּ יְפֵה נוֹף מְשׂושׂ כָּל הָאָרֶץ הַר צִיּוֹן וְגוֹ', כד"א, לֶאֱחֹז בְּכַנְפוֹת הָאָרֶץ וְיִנָּעֲרוּ רְשָׁעִים מִמֶּנָּה. כְּהַאי דְּאָחִיד בְּטַלִּית, לְנַעֲרָא טְנוּפָא מִנָּהּ.

292. Another explanation. "Before the day cools," meaning before that day the nations will cool. "And the shadows flee away," are the governments that dominate them. "I will get me to the mountain of myrrh" (Shir Hashirm 4:6), said the Holy One, blessed be He: 'I will betake myself to shake the nations from Jerusalem, which is the mountain of myrrh, as is written: 'on the mountain of Moria that is in Jerusalem' (II Divrei Hayamim 3:1). "And to the hill of frankincense," is the Temple that is in Zion, about which is written: "Fair in situation, the joy of the whole earth; Mount Zion" (Tehilim 48:3). AND THIS IS ALSO TO SHAKE OUT FROM THERE ALL THE WICKED PEOPLE, as is written: "To grasp the corners of the earth and to shake all the wicked people from it" (Iyov 38:13), as one holds a garment to shake all the filth from it.

293. א"ר יוֹסֵי, עָתִיד קוּדְשָׁא בְּרִיךְ הוּא לְאִתְגַּלְּיָיא בִּירוּשְׁלֵם דִּלְתַתָּא, וּלְדַכְּאָה יָתָהּ מִטְּנוּפֵי עֲמַמְיָא, עַד דְּלָא אִשְׁתְּלִים הַהוּא יוֹמָא דְּאוּמִין. דא"ר חִיָּיא, לֵית שׁוּלְטָנוּ לְאוּמִין עֲלַיְיהוּ דְּיִשְׂרָאֵל, אֶלָּא יוֹמָא חֲדָא

לְחוּד, דְּהוּא יוֹמוֹ שֶׁל הַקּוּדְשָׁא בְּרִיךְ הוּא, וְהוּא אֶלֶף שָׁנִים. הה"ד,
נְתָנַנִי שׁוֹמֵמָה כָּל הַיּוֹם דָּוָה. יוֹמָא חַד לְחוּד, וְלָא יַתִּיר.

293. Rabbi Yosi said: The Holy One, blessed be He, will eventually be
revealed in terrestrial Jerusalem, and purify it from the filth of the nations,
before that day of the nations is complete. For Rabbi Chiya said: The
dominion of the nations over Yisrael last only one day, and that is the day of
the Holy One, blessed be He, which is one thousand years long. This is what
is written: "He has made me desolate and faint all the day" (Eichah 1:13),
meaning one day only, and no more.

294. א"ר יוֹסֵי, אִי יַתִּיר יִשְׁתַּעְבְּדוּן, לָא עַל פּוּם גְּזֵרַת מַלְכָּא הוּא,
אֶלָּא עַל דְּלָא בַּעְיָין לְמֵיהֲדַר לְקַבְּלֵיהּ, וּכְתִיב וְהָיָה כִּי יָבוֹאוּ עָלֶיךָ כָּל
הַדְּבָרִים הָאֵלֶּה וְגוֹ', וּכְתִיב, אִם יִהְיֶה נִדַּחֲךָ בִּקְצֵה הַשָּׁמַיִם מִשָּׁם
יְקַבֶּצְךָ וְגוֹ'.

294. Rabbi Yosi said: If they are subjugated more than one thousand years,
it is not because of the decree of the King, but rather because they do not
wish to return IN REPENTANCE before Him. And it is written: "And it shall
be when all these things come upon you... THEN YOU WILL RETURN TO
HASHEM YOUR ELOHIM" (Devarim 30:1-2), and: "If your outcasts be at the
utmost part of heaven, from there will Hashem gather you..." (Ibid. :4).

41. "And he said to his people"

A Synopsis

Rabbi Shimon begins the discussion by explaining that the title verse refers to the supernal minister over Egypt who revealed to the Egyptians that the minister over Yisrael was stronger than theirs. Rabbi Shimon then clarifies the distinction between "King of Egypt," which refers to the supernal minister over Egypt, and "Pharaoh, the King of Egypt," which refers to the actual Pharaoh. Similarly, we learn from Rabbi Yitzchak that in the title verse, "the people of the children of Yisrael," refers to the children of the supernal Yisrael above. While the other nations are called the people of their appointed rulers, Yisrael are called the people of Hashem because they are the only nation directly under God. Rabbi Yochanan then asks about Balak's reference to Yisrael in the verse, "Behold, there is a people come out from Egypt." Rabbi Yitzchak explains that sorcerers prefer to avoid all ambiguity, and therefore when referring to someone, they mention only the mother's name because only maternal descent is certain. Moreover, the demons also adhere to this strict code. Rabbi Aba, however, interprets Balak's reference as one of contempt that implies that the origin of Yisrael is unknown. The discussion then turns to expound upon the concept that God punishes His own children first so that they will guard against sin more than the other nations. Rabbi Yosi provides a personal incident to illustrate this idea, and concludes that God punishes students of the Torah so that they will not separate themselves from the Tree of Life (the Torah) for even a moment.

Finally, we learn from an episode involving Rabbi Yitzchak that an earthquake is a physical sign of the appointment of a minister in heaven who will cause suffering to Yisrael. This is in accordance with the verse, "For three things the earth is disquieted..."

The Relevance of the Passage

A man's wicked tendencies are not part of his soul, nor do they emanate from the Light of the Creator. Each selfish and unkind impulse is rooted in a higher, negative force that attempts to seduce us into immoral behavior, minute by minute, hour by hour, day by day. Genuine positive change can only occur when we uproot the source of our dark side. Instead of treating the symptoms and branches, we must probe to the unseen cause and seed, the spiritual DNA level of our darkest impulses. This passage of sacred texts delves deeply into our spiritual being to extract the root of our Evil Inclination. This Light also reaches into the Upper Worlds to banish forever the negative forces (the snake) that nurture our dark side.

Not only do we rise above all negative cosmic influences that have ruled human existence for millennia, but we transform these dark and demonic forces into positive forces of Light that do our soul's bidding. Light becomes the only reality, and peace and tranquility become our eternal treasures, as the truth of the Torah shines throughout the world.

Finally, this passage heals the earth, preventing earthquakes from taking place, for there are no longer any negative forces dwelling on high to trigger their occurrence.

295. וַיֹּאמֶר אֶל עַמּוֹ הִנֵּה עַם בְּנֵי יִשְׂרָאֵל. א״ר שִׁמְעוֹן תָּא חֲזֵי, דְּהָא עַל כָּל פָּנִים מַלְאָכָא שַׁלְטוֹנָא דְּמְמָנָא עַל מִצְרָאֵי הֲוָה, וְהָכִי הוּא, דְּרוּבָא דְּפַרְשְׁתָּא לָא אִתְּמַר, אֶלָּא מֶלֶךְ מִצְרַיִם סְתָם, וְהַיְינוּ מְמָנָא רַבְרְבָא עַל מִצְרָאֵי. פַּרְעֹה מֶלֶךְ מִצְרַיִם, פַּרְעֹה מַמָּשׁ.

295. "And he said to his people, 'Behold the people of the children of Yisrael'" (Shemot 1:9). Rabbi Shimon said: Come and behold. In all instances, a ruling angel was appointed over Egypt AND SAID TO HIS PEOPLE, "BEHOLD, THE CHILDREN OF YISRAEL..." And so it is in the majority of the portion that says plainly, "king of Egypt," meaning the minister who is appointed over Egypt. However, when it is written: "Pharaoh, the King of Egypt," IT IS actually Pharaoh, AND NOT THE ANGEL, WHO IS APPOINTED OVER THEM!

296. א״ר שִׁמְעוֹן, לְפִיכָךְ כְּתִיב, וַיֹּאמֶר כְּלוֹמַר אַכְנִיס בְּלִבְּהוֹן מִלְּתָא דָא, כד״א, כִּי יְיָ' אָמַר לוֹ קַלֵּל אֶת דָּוִד. מַחֲשֶׁבֶת הַלֵּב בִּלְבַד. וְכֵן וַיֹּאמֶר הָמָן בְּלִבּוֹ, וְכֵן וַיֹּאמֶר בְּלִבּוֹ הַלָּבֶן מֵאָה שָׁנָה. אוּף הָכָא נָמֵי, אַכְנִיס מַחֲשַׁבְתָּא בְּלִבְּהוֹן, דְּאָמְרוּ רַב וְעָצוּם מִמֶּנּוּ. מַאי מִמֶּנּוּ. ר״ל מְמָנָא דִּילְהוֹן, אִינוּן אָמְרוּ בְּלַבַּיְיהוּ, דְּחֵילָא וְתוּקְפָּא דִּילְהוֹן, רַבְרְבָא וְתַקִּיפָא מִמֶּנּוּ, מְשׁוּלְטָנָא דִּילְהוֹן.

296. Rabbi Shimon said: Therefore it is written, "And he said TO HIS PEOPLE," MEANING I will introduce this into their hearts THAT THEY SHOULD THINK SO. As the Torah says, "Because Hashem said to him, 'Curse David'" (II Shmuel 16:10), MEANING the thought of his heart alone, THAT HASHEM INTRODUCED INTO HIS HEART. Also, "And Haman said in

his heart" (Ester 6:6), and so, "And he said in his heart, 'Shall a child be born to him that is a hundred years old?'" (Beresheet 17:17). THE MEANING OF "HE SAID" IS also to introduce a thought into their hearts, that they should say IN THEIR HEARTS. "More and mightier than we" (Shemot 1:9). Why does it say "than we"? It means, than the angel who is appointed over them, because they thought in their hearts that Elohim and their power, THAT IS, OF YISRAEL, is greater and stronger than us – than THE APPOINTED ANGEL who rules over Egypt.

297. ר' יִצְחָק אָמַר, כָּל אוּמִין דְּעָלְמָא, מַשְׁכִין תּוּקְפָּא מִשָּׂרֵיהוֹן, וְיִשְׂרָאֵל נַגְדִּין חֵילֵיהוֹן מִקּוּדְשָׁא בְּרִיךְ הוּא, וְאִינּוּן אִתְקְרוּן עַמָּא דַּיְיָ', וְלָא עַמָּא דְּשׁוּלְטָנַיָּא. ר' יְהוּדָה אָמַר, הָכָא אִתְקְרוּן עַמּוֹ, דִּכְתִּיב וַיֹּאמֶר אֶל עַמּוֹ, וְהָתָם כְּתִיב, רָאֹה רָאִיתִי אֶת עֳנִי עַמִּי, עַמִּי מַמָּשׁ, יִשְׂרָאֵל אִקְרוּן עַם יְיָ', וּשְׁאַר אוּמִין אִקְרוּן, עַמּוֹ דְּשׁוּלְטָנָא דִּילְהוֹן דִּכְתִּיב, כִּי כָּל הָעַמִּים יֵלְכוּ אִישׁ בְּשֵׁם אֱלֹהָיו וַאֲנַחְנוּ נֵלֵךְ בְּשֵׁם יְיָ' אֱלֹהֵינוּ לְעוֹלָם וָעֶד.

297. Rabbi Yitzchak said: All the nations of the world draw strength from the Ministers WHO ARE APPOINTED IN HEAVEN over them. And the children of Yisrael draw their powers from the Holy One, blessed be He. And they are called 'the people of Hashem', and not 'the people of a ruler WHO WAS APPOINTED'. Rabbi Yehuda said: Here, the Egyptians are called the people OF THE APPOINTED, as is written: "And he said to his people," and there it is written, "I have surely seen the affliction of My people" (Shemot 3:7), MEANING actually, "My people." Yisrael are called 'the people of Hashem', and the other nations are called 'the people of their appointed rulers', as it is written: "For let all people walk, everyone in the name of his Elohim, and we will walk in the name of Hashem our Elohim, forever and ever" (Michah 4:5).

298. אָמַר רִבִּי אַבָּא, הַאי פְּסוּקָא, הֲוָה לֵיהּ לְמֵימַר בְּנֵי יִשְׂרָאֵל רַב וְעָצוּם מִמֶּנּוּ, מַהוּ עַם בְּנֵי. אֶלָּא עַם בְּנֵי יִשְׂרָאֵל מַמָּשׁ, מֵהַהוּא יִשְׂרָאֵל דִּלְעֵילָּא, דַּחֲשִׁיבוּ דְּעַם בְּנֵי יִשְׂרָאֵל הֲווֹ, וְלָא עַם יְיָ', וּכְתִיב וַיָּקוּצוּ מִפְּנֵי בְּנֵי יִשְׂרָאֵל, וְלָא כְּתִיב מִפְּנֵי עַם בְּנֵי יִשְׂרָאֵל, אֶלָּא מִפְּנֵי בְּנֵי יִשְׂרָאֵל מַמָּשׁ.

298. Rabbi Aba said: This passage should have read, 'The children of Yisrael are more and mightier than we'. Why does it say: "the people of the children..."? AND HE ANSWERS: It means the actual people of the children of Yisrael, THAT IS, THE PEOPLE OF THE CHILDREN OF YISRAEL OF BELOW, WHICH IS THE CORPOREAL YISRAEL WHO IS DRAWN from that Yisrael of above, WHICH IS ZEIR ANPIN. SINCE THE PEOPLE ARE NOT CONNECTED TO THE SUPERNAL YISRAEL, THEY ADDED THE WORD "PEOPLE" because they thought that they were the people of the children of Yisrael OF BELOW, and not the people of Hashem, WHICH IS ZEIR ANPIN. It is written: "And they were mortified on account of the children of Yisrael" (Shemot 1:12), instead of, 'On account of the people of the children of Yisrael', WHICH IS YISRAEL OF BELOW. FOR EVENTUALLY, THEY RECOGNIZED THAT THEY WERE THE SUPERNAL CHILDREN OF YISRAEL OF ABOVE, MEANING THE PEOPLE OF HASHEM.

299. רִבִּי יוֹחָנָן הֲוָה קָאִים קַמֵּיהּ דְּר' יִצְחָק, אָמַר, מֶה חָמָא בָּלָק לְמֵימַר, הִנֵּה עַם יָצָא מִמִּצְרַיִם, וְלֹא אָמַר הִנֵּה עַם בְּנֵי יִשְׂרָאֵל. א"ל ר' יִצְחָק, בָּלָק מְכַשֵּׁף גָּדוֹל הֲוָה, וְכֵן דֶּרֶךְ הַמְכַשְּׁפִים לָקַחַת הַדָּבָר שֶׁאֵין בּוֹ חֲשָׁדָא, וְכֵן אֵין מַזְכִּירִין לְעוֹלָם שֵׁם אָבִיו שֶׁל אָדָם, אֶלָּא שֵׁם אִמּוֹ, דָּבָר שֶׁאֵין בּוֹ חֲשָׁדָא.

299. Rabbi Yochanan was before Rabbi Yitzchak. He said: Why did Balak choose to say, "Behold, there is a people come out from Egypt" (Bemidbar 22:5), and did not say, "Behold the people of the children of Yisrael." Rabbi Yitzchak said to him: Balak was a great sorcerer, and it is the way of sorcerers to select a matter that is completely certain. Similarly, they never mention the father's name of a person, but rather his mother's name, which is certain. THEREFORE, BILA'AM DID NOT MENTION THE CHILDREN OF YISRAEL, WHICH IS THE NAME OF THE FATHER.

300. דְּכֵן דֶּרֶךְ הַשֵּׁדִים, דִּמְעַיְּינִים בְּהַהוּא מִלָּה דְּקָאמְרֵי לְהוּ, אִי אִיהוּ כְּדִיבָא, מוֹדִיעִין לֵיהּ מִלִּין כְּדִיבִין, וְאִי הוּא קְשׁוֹט, כָּל מַה דְּאַמְרִין לְזִמְנָא זְעֵירָא קוּשְׁטָא הוּא, כָּל שֶׁכֵּן לְמֶעְבַּד עֲבִידְתָּא. רִבִּי אֲחָא אָמַר, בָּלָק אוֹרְחָא דְּקַלָּנָא נָקַט, הִנֵּה עַם יָצָא מִמִּצְרַיִם, כְּלוֹמַר, דְּלֵית אֲנָן יַדְעִין מִמָּאן אִינּוּן.

300. This is the way of the demons. They examine the matter that is said to them BY THE SORCERERS. If it is false, they notify them with false words. And if it is true, whatever they tell them is true at least for a short time. Especially if the sorcerers desire an action of them, THEY ARE PARTICULARLY CAUTIOUS TO SAY THE TRUTH, THAT IS BEYOND SUSPICION. THEREFORE, THEY DO NOT MENTION THE NAME OF A PERSON'S FATHER. Rabbi Acha said: Balak used a degrading tone, "Behold, there is a people come out from Egypt," meaning we do not know where they are from.

301. אָמַר רַבִּי יוֹחָנָן, מִפְּנֵי מַה עַמָּא דִּרְבָרְבִין נְטִירִין, וְעַמָּא דְּקוּדְשָׁא בְּרִיךְ הוּא לָא נְטִירִין. אָמַר רַבִּי יִצְחָק, לָא דָּמֵי מִסְכְּנָא לַעֲתִירָא. מִסְכְּנָא בָּעֵי לְנַטְרָא דִּילֵיה, עֲתִירָא לָא נָטִיר דִּילֵיה, וְכָל שֶׁכֵּן דְּיִשְׂרָאֵל, אִינוּן מִמַּלְכָּא דְּרָחִים קְשׁוֹט וְדִינָא. וְדִינָא קַדְמָאָה עָבֵיד בְּגוֹבְרִין דְּבֵיתֵיה, דְּבָעֵי דְּאִינוּן לֶהֱוֵון נְטִירִין מֵחַטָּאָה יַתִּיר מִכֻּלְּהוּ הֲדָא הוּא דִכְתִיב, רַק אֶתְכֶם יָדַעְתִּי מִכֹּל מִשְׁפְּחוֹת הָאֲדָמָה וְגוֹ'.

301. Rabbi Yochanan said: Why is it that a people THAT IS UNDER THE GUIDANCE of ministers guard themselves, and the people of the Holy One, blessed be He, do not guard themselves? Rabbi Yitzchak said: The poor man is not comparable to the rich man. The poor man needs to guard what is his, BECAUSE PEOPLE ARE NOT AFRAID TO CHALLENGE HIM. The rich man does not guard his possessions, BECAUSE EVERYONE IS AFRAID TO CHALLENGE HIM. All the more so, Yisrael are UNDER THE GUIDANCE OF a King who loves Truth and Justice. And He does justice with His household first, because He wants them to be protected against sin more than all THE NATIONS. This is what is written: "You only have I known of all the families of the earth" (Amos 3:2).

302. רַבִּי יוֹסֵי נָפַק לְאוֹרְחָא, וַהֲוָה רַבִּי אַחָא בַּר יַעֲקֹב אָזִיל עִמֵּיהּ, עַד דַּהֲווֹ אַזְלֵי שָׁתִיק רַבִּי יוֹסֵי, וְהִרְהֵר בְּמִלֵּי דְעָלְמָא. וְרַבִּי אַחָא הִרְהֵר בְּמִלֵּי דְאוֹרַיְיתָא. חָמָא רַבִּי יוֹסֵי חַד חִוְיָא, דַּהֲוָה רָהִיט אֲבַתְרֵיהּ. אָמַר רַבִּי יוֹסֵי לְרַבִּי אַחָא, חֲזֵית הַאי חִוְיָא דְּרָהִיט אֲבַתְרָאי. אָמַר לֵיהּ רַבִּי אַחָא, אֲנָא לָא חֲמֵינָא לֵיהּ. רָהַט רַבִּי יוֹסֵי וְחִוְיָא אֲבַתְרוֹי. נָפַל רַבִּי יוֹסֵי, וְדָמָא שָׁתַת וְנָחַת מֵחוֹטָמוֹי, שָׁמַע דַּהֲווֹ אַמְרִין, רַק אֶתְכֶם יָדַעְתִּי מִכֹּל מִשְׁפְּחוֹת הָאֲדָמָה וְגוֹ', אָמַר רַבִּי יוֹסֵי, וּמַה עַל שַׁעֲתָא חֲדָא כָּךְ,

מַאן דְּמִתְיָיאֵשׁ מִנָּהּ עַל אַחַת כַּמָּה וְכַמָּה.

302. Rabbi Yosi went on the road and Rabbi Acha bar Ya'akov went with him. While they were traveling, Rabbi Yosi kept quiet FROM WORDS OF THE TORAH, and reflected on worldly things. But Rabbi Acha CONTINUED to meditate on the words of the Torah. Rabbi Yosi saw a snake that was running after him. Rabbi Yosi said to Rabbi Acha: Do you see the snake that is chasing me? Rabbi Acha said to him: I do not see it. Rabbi Yosi ran with the snake after him. Rabbi Yosi fell and blood flowed from his nose. He heard them saying, "You only have I known of all the families of the earth." DUE TO THIS, HE WAS SAVED FROM THE SNAKE. Rabbi Yosi said: If for just one moment I CEASED FROM THE WORDS OF TORAH and TURNED TO WORLDLY THINGS, AND THIS HAPPENED TO ME, it is much worse for one who has suspended his mind entirely FROM WORDS OF TORAH.

303. פָּתַח וְאָמַר, כִּי ה' אֱלֹהֶיךָ בֵּרַכְךָ בְּכֹל מַעֲשֵׂה יָדֶךָ יָדַע לֶכְתְּךָ וְגוֹ' הַמּוֹלִיכֲךָ וְגוֹ', נָחָשׁ שָׂרָף וְעַקְרָב וְגוֹ', נָחָשׁ שָׂרָף לָמָּה הָכָא. אֶלָּא, לְקָחַת עוֹנְשָׁן מִיִּשְׂרָאֵל, כָּל זְמָן שֶׁמִּתְפָּרְשִׁין מִן עֵץ הַחַיִּים. דִּכְתִיב כִּי הוּא חַיֶּיךָ וְאֹרֶךְ יָמֶיךָ.

303. He opened the discussion saying: "For Hashem your Elohim has blessed you in all the work of your hand: He knows your walking through..." (Devarim 2:7). "Who led you...venomous serpents and scorpions" (Devarim 8:15). HE ASKS: Why were there venomous serpents here IN THE WILDERNESS? AND HE ANSWERS: To punish Yisrael any time they separate from the Tree of Life, of which it is written: "For he is your life, and the length of your days" (Devarim 30:20).

304. תָּא חֲזֵי, אָמַר רִבִּי חִיָּיא, כְּתִיב חוֹשֵׂךְ שִׁבְטוֹ שׂוֹנֵא בְנוֹ וְגוֹ'. וּכְתִיב אָהַבְתִּי אֶתְכֶם אָמַר ה'. וּכְתִיב, וְאֶת עֵשָׂו שָׂנֵאתִי. מַהוּ שָׂנֵאתִי, דִּכְתִיב חוֹשֵׂךְ שִׁבְטוֹ שׂוֹנֵא בְנוֹ. כְּלוֹמַר שָׂנֵאתִי אוֹתוֹ, וְעַל כֵּן חָשַׂכְתִּי שֵׁבֶט מֵהֶם, כָּל שֶׁכֵּן וְכָל שֶׁכֵּן תַּלְמִידֵי חֲכָמִים, דְּלָא בָּעֵי קוּדְשָׁא בְּרִיךְ הוּא דְיִתְפָּרְשׁוּן מֵעֵץ הַחַיִּים אֲפִילוּ רִגְעָא חֲדָא.

304. Come and behold. Rabbi Chiya said: It is written, "He that spares his rod hates his son..." (Mishlei 13:24) and, "'I have loved you,' says Hashem"

(Malachi 1:2), and also: "And I hated Esau" (Ibid. 3). What does "hate" REFER TO? It is written: "He that spares his rod hates his son," meaning: I hate him, therefore, I spare his rod from him. This is even more so with Torah scholars; HE DOES NOT SPARE HIS ROD FROM THEM, for the Holy One, blessed be He, does not want them to become separated from the Tree of Life, even for one moment.

305. וַיֹּאמֶר אֶל עַמּוֹ. יָהַב לְהוֹן עֵיטָא, לְמֶעְבַּד עִמְּהוֹן בִּישָׁא. אָמַר רִבִּי תַּנְחוּם, יַדְעִין הֲווֹ מִצְרָאֵי בְּאִצְטַגְנִינוּת דִּלְהוֹן, שֶׁסוֹפָן לְמִלְקֵי בְּגִין יִשְׂרָאֵל, וּלְכָךְ אַקְדִּים שׁוּלְטָנָא דִּלְהוֹן, לְמֶעְבַּד עִמְּהוֹן בִּיש.

305. "And he said to his people" (Shemot 1:9). He gave them advice in order to do evil with them. Rabbi Tanchum said: The Egyptians knew by their knowledge of astrology that they would eventually be smitten because of Yisrael. Therefore, their Minister did evil to them first.

306. רִבִּי יִצְחָק פָּגַע בְּהַהוּא טוּרָא, וְחָמָא חַד בַּר נָשׁ דַּהֲוָה נָאִים תְּחוֹת חַד אִילָן. יָתִיב תַּמָּן, אַדְהֲוָה יָתִיב, חָמָא אַרְעָא דְּמִתְחַלְחֲלָא, וְאִתְּבַּר הַהוּא אִילָנָא, וְנָפַל, וְחָמָא בְּקִיעִין גּוּמִין בְּאַרְעָא, וְאַרְעָא סַלְקָא וְנַחְתָּא.

306. Rabbi Yitzchak came upon a mountain and saw a man sleeping under a tree. RABBI YITZCHAK sat down there. While he was sitting, he noticed the earth moving, and saw that tree break and fall. He saw fissure holes in the earth, and the earth was rising and falling

307. אִתְּעַר הַהוּא גַּבְרָא, צָוַוח לְקָבְלֵיהּ דְּרִבִּי יִצְחָק, וְאָמַר לֵיהּ יוּדָאי יוּדָאי, בְּכֵי וְנָהִים, דְּהָאִידָנָא מְקִיּמִין בִּרְקִיעָא חַד רַבְרְבָא מְמָנָא שֶׁלְטָנָא עִלָּאָה, וְהוּא זַמִּין לְמֶעְבַּד עִמְּכוֹן בִּישׁ סַגִּי, וְהַאי רְגָשָׁא דְּאַרְעָא בְּגִינֵיכוֹן הֲוָה. דְּכָל זִמְנָא דְּרַגְשָׁא אַרְעָא, כַּד קָם מְמָנָא, דְּיַעֲבֵיד עִמְּכוֹן בִּישָׁא.

307. The man awoke and screamed towards Rabbi Yitzchak: Jew, Jew, cry and wail, because now they are setting up in heaven a minister, a supernal ruler, who is destined to do great evil with your people. These tremors in the

earth are because of you, for whenever the earth rumbles it is when a minister arises in the heaven, who will do evil with you!

308. תָּוָוה רִבִּי יִצְחָק וְאָמַר, וַדַּאי כְּתִיב, תַּחַת שָׁלֹשׁ רָגְזָה אֶרֶץ, וּכְתִיב תַּחַת עֶבֶד כִּי יִמְלוֹךְ. מִמָּנָא דַּהֲוָה תְּחוֹת שֻׁלְטָנָא אַחֲרָא, וּמָלִיךְ, וְיָהֲבִין לֵיהּ שֻׁלְטָנָא, וכ״ש כַּד שָׁלִיט בְּיִשְׂרָאֵל.

308. Rabbi Yitzchak was astonished and said: It is certainly written, "For three things the earth is disquieted...for a slave when he becomes king" ((Mishlei 30:21-22). ITS MEANING refers to a minister who was ORIGINALLY SUBJUGATED under a different ruler, AND NOW that he rules, and they give him dominion, THE SCRIPTURE SAYS THAT THE EARTH QUAKES and, moreover, when THAT APPOINTED ONE rules over Yisrael, CERTAINLY THE EARTH QUAKES AND IS DISQUIETED.

309. א״ר חָמָא בַּר גּוּרְיָא, כַּד אֲנַח לְיִשְׂרָאֵל תְּחוֹת שֻׁלְטָנוּתָא דְּאוּמִין, יָתִיב וְגָעֵי וּבָכֵי, הֲדָא הוּא דִכְתִיב, בְּמִסְתָּרִים תִּבְכֶּה נַפְשִׁי. אָמַר רִבִּי יוֹסֵי, בְּמִסְתָּרִים דַּוְוקָא.

309. Rabbi Chama bar Guria said: When the Holy One, blessed be He, placed Yisrael under the dominion of other nations, He sat and wailed and wept. This is what is written: "My soul shall weep in secret" (Yirmeyah 13:17). Rabbi Yosi said: "In secret" is precise, THAT IS, IN THE WORLD OF ATZILUT.

42. "Behold, the mighty ones shall cry outside"

A Synopsis

Rabbi Elazar tells Rabbi Yehuda that the title verse refers to God's ministers who weep in the outer chambers when God, Who is in the inner chambers, is sad and weeping. We learn that these are called angels of peace, and are distinct from the various other types of angels. Rabbi Yehuda then asks why the ministers of the other nations oppress Yisrael knowing that this causes God to suffer. Rabbi Elazar's reply indicates that they carry out their duties in accordance with God's will.

The Relevance of the Passage

Reality resembles a mirror. Every deed we perform, each emotion we display, and every word we speak is reflected back to our lives in equal measure, and in identical tone, by the universe. When we curse, we create a negative angel, a negative force that inevitably influences our life in a negative fashion. Likewise, deeds of kindness and the moments where we resist our reactive, egocentric impulses arouse angels of peace. Their influence blankets us with protection and blessings. The events and circumstances that transpire before us are the cumulative results of our positive and negative interactions with the people we encounter on a daily basis. Moreover, the state of the world is merely the sum total of mankind's interactions.

The angels of peace, we're told, derive from the spiritual dimension known as Binah. Binah's Light signifies immortality and infinite bliss.

These verses of Zohar were given to us so that we may now establish a connection to Binah and arouse endless angels of peace who will bring a bounty of blessings to this world. These blessings and spiritual influences will now banish conflict, hatred, judgment, and intolerance from our lives, and will give birth to an existence of paradise for all mankind.

310. רִבִּי יְהוּדָה עָאל לְגַבֵּיהּ דְּרִבִּי אֶלְעָזָר, אַשְׁכְּחֵיהּ דַּהֲוָה יָתִיב, וִידֵיהּ בְּפוּמֵיהּ, וַהֲוָה עָצִיב. אָמַר לֵיהּ, בְּמַאי קָא עָסִיק מַר. אָמַר לֵיהּ דִּכְתִּיב, בְּאוֹר פְּנֵי מֶלֶךְ חַיִּים. אִי טַרְנָא עָצִיב, וכ״ש דְּגָעֵי וּבְכֵי, שַׁמְּשׁוֹי מַאי עַבְדֵּי, הֲדָא הוּא דִכְתִּיב, הֵן אֶרְאֶלָּם צָעֲקוּ חוּצָה. מַאי חוּצָה. מָרֵיהוֹן בְּגוֹ, וְאִינוּן לְבַר. מָרֵיהוֹן בְּבָתֵּי גַוָּאי, וְאִינוּן בְּבָתֵּי בָרָאֵי. בָּתֵּי גַוָּאי מַאי אִינוּן. אָמַר רִבִּי יִצְחָק, אִינוּן מֵעֲשָׂרָה כִּתְרֵי מַלְכָּא.

310. Rabbi Yehuda came to Rabbi Elazar and found him sitting with his hand in his mouth. He was sad. He asked him: With what is Sir occupied? He said to him that it is written: "In the light of the King's countenance is life" (Mishlei 16:15). If the Master is sad and especially IF HE weeps and wails, what do His ministers do? It is written: "Behold, the mighty ones shall cry outside" (Yeshayah 33:7). "...outside..." meaning that their Master is within, AS IS WRITTEN: "MY SOUL WEEPS IN SECRET," and they are outside. Their Master is in the inner rooms, WHICH ARE IN ATZILUT, while they are in the outer rooms, WHICH ARE IN BRIYAH, YETZIRAH AND ASIYAH. HE ASKS: What are the inner rooms? Rabbi Yitzchak said: They are from the ten crowns of the King, MEANING OF THE TEN SFIROT OF ZEIR ANPIN IN ATZILUT.

311. מַלְאֲכֵי שָׁלוֹם מַר יִבְכָּיוּן, וְכִי יֵשׁ מַלְאָכִים שֶׁאֵינָם שֶׁל שָׁלוֹם. אָמַר לֵיהּ אִין. תָּא חֲזֵי, אִית מָארֵי דְּדִינָא קַשְׁיָא, וְאִית מָארֵי דְּדִינָא דְּלָא קַשְׁיָא, וְאִית מָארֵי דִּינָא וְרַחֲמָנוּתָא. וְאִית מָארֵי דְּרַחֲמָנוּתָא דְּלֵית בְּהוּ דִּינָא כְּלָל. וְאִלֵּין אִתְקְרוּן מַלְאֲכֵי שָׁלוֹם. וְעַל אִינּוּן דִּלְתַתָּא, כְּתִיב, אַלְבִּישׁ שָׁמַיִם קַדְרוּת וְשַׂק אָשִׂים כְּסוּתָם. וּכְתִיב וְנָמַקּוּ כָּל צְבָא הַשָּׁמַיִם.

311. "The ambassadors of peace shall weep bitterly" (Ibid.). HE ASKS: Are there any angels who are not for peace? He said to him: Yes. Come and behold: there are angels who are of Severe Judgment, WHO ARE DRAWN FROM THE ASPECT OF GVURAH. There are those of Judgment not severe, WHO ARE DRAWN FROM MALCHUT. And there are those who have Judgment and Mercy WHO ARE DRAWN FROM TIFERET. And there are those of Mercy that contain no Judgment at all, WHO ARE DRAWN FROM BINAH, and they are called the 'angels of peace'. Pertaining to these ANGELS of below, WHICH ARE EXTERNAL, it is written: "I clothe the heavens with blackness, and I make sackcloth their covering" (Yeshayah 50:3), and: "And all the host of heaven shall rot away" (Yeshayah 34:4).

312. אִי הָכִי, כָּל אִינּוּן שׁוּלְטָנִין דִּמְמָנָן עַל שְׁאַר עַמִּין, כַּד חָמָאן לְמָארֵיהוֹן עָצִיב, לְמָאי עַבְדִין פָּרוֹכָא לִבְנוֹהִי. א"ר אֶלְעָזָר, לָא עַבְדִי אֶלָּא מַאי דְּאִתְפַּקְּדוּ, וּרְעוּתָא דְּמָארֵיהוֹן עַבְדִין.

312. HE ASKS: If this is so, then why do all the ministers who are appointed over the other nations enslave His children with heavy labor when they see that their Master is sad, BECAUSE OF THE SUBJUGATION OF YISRAEL? Rabbi Elazar said: They only do that which is incumbent upon them, and they are doing the desire of their Master!

43. Two tears sink into the great abyss

A Synopsis

Rabbi Dustai explains that when the children of Yisrael are delivered to the supernal ministers of the other nations, twelve courts convene and the Master weeps. Then two tears sink into the great abyss, and both the higher and the lower celestial beings descend multiple levels. We also learn that when God delivered Yisrael into the power of the supernal minister of Egypt, He made seven decrees that Egypt should subjugate them, and seven decrees bestowing benefits on Yisrael.

The Relevance of the Passage

Our slavery to our own Evil Inclination and to the negative influences of the Twelve Signs is ended. All judgments forever cease. Our soul now achieves eternal dominion over the negative influences of the body. Likewise, Yisrael begins to shine brightly to nourish all the world with Divine Light, creating peace and unconditional love between Arabs, Jews and all the peoples of the world. The spiritual truths and Light of the Zohar expand throughout the world bringing joy and peace to all humanity.

313. ר' דּוֹסְתָּאי אָמַר בְּעִדָנָא דְּאִתְמַסְּרָן בְּנוֹי דְּקוּדְשָׁא ב״ה, לְשׁוּלְטָנֵי עַמְמִין, מִתְכַּנְפִין תְּרֵיסַר בָּתֵּי דִינִין, וּמִשְׁתַּקְעָן גּוֹ תְּהוֹמָא רַבָּה, גָּעֵי טַרְנָא, גָּעִין, וּרְהִיטָן וְנַחְתִּין תְּרֵין דִּמְעִין לִשְׁקִיעָא דְּיַמָּא רַבָּה, הה״ד מִשְׁפָּטֶיךָ תְּהוֹם רַבָּה. וּמִתְגַּלְגְּלָן עִלָּאִין לְתַתָּא, אִתְבַּקְעָן תַּתָּאִין, וְנַחְתִּין מָאתַן וְאַרְבְּעִין דַּרְגִּין הה״ד אַרְיֵה שָׁאָג מִי לֹא יִירָא.

Z

313. Rabbi Dustai said: As soon as the children of the Holy One, blessed be He, are given over to the rulers of the nations, twelve courts will convene, MEANING MALCHUT HAS TWELVE PERMUTATIONS OF ADONAI, WHICH CONTAINS THE LETTERS OF *DINA* ('JUDGMENT'). SINCE THE UNION OF YUD HEI VAV HEI ADONAI WAS ABOLISHED, IN WHICH THE TWELVE PERMUTATIONS OF ADONAI RECEIVED FROM THE TWELVE PERMUTATIONS OF YUD HEI VAV HEI, THE TWELVE PERMUTATIONS OF ADONAI GATHERED and sank in the great Abyss, WHICH IS BINAH. The Master, WHICH IS BINAH, weeps by raising the voice CALLED 'WAILINGS'. Two teardrops fell FROM THE EYE SOCKETS, WHICH IS BINAH, to the depths of the Great Sea, WHICH IS MALCHUT. This is the meaning of: "Your Judgments are a great deep" (Tehilim 36:7). Those above rolled downward,

and the lower beings broke asunder and descended 240 levels. This is what is written, "The lion has roared, who will not fear" (Amos 3:8).

314. תָּנָא, בְּשַׁעֲתָא דְּמָסַר קוּדְשָׁא בְּרִיךְ הוּא לְיִשְׂרָאֵל לְשָׂרָא דְּמִצְרָאֵי, גָּזַר עֲלַיְיהוּ ז' גְּזֵרוֹת, שֶׁיִּשְׁעַבְּדוּ בְּהוֹן מִצְרָאֵי. הה"ד וַיְמָרְרוּ אֶת חַיֵּיהֶם בַּעֲבוֹדָה קָשָׁה בְּחוֹמֶר וּבִלְבֵנִים וְגו'. וְלָקֳבְלֵיהוֹן שִׁבְעָה לְטָב, וּבְנֵי יִשְׂרָאֵל פָּרוּ, וַיִּשְׁרְצוּ, וַיִּרְבּוּ, וַיַּעַצְמוּ, בִּמְאֹד, מְאֹד, וַתִּמָּלֵא הָאָרֶץ אוֹתָם.

314. We learned that at the time that the Holy One, blessed be He, gave Yisrael to the Minister of Egypt, He made seven decrees that Egypt should subjugate them. This is what is written: "And they made their lives bitter, with hard bondage in the mortar and in brick, and all manner of bondage in the field, all their bondage, wherein they made them serve was with rigor" (Shemot 1:14). He correspondingly made seven to the good: "And the children of Yisrael were fruitful and increased abundantly, and multiplied and grew exceedingly mighty; and the land was filled with them" (Ibid. 7).

44. "Come, let us deal wisely with them"

A Synopsis

The title verse, we learn, refers to the ministering angels that agreed in their judgment against the supernal children of Yisrael. Rabbi Yitzchak compares them to thorns and thistles continually stinging Yisrael so that they would not multiply and grow stronger.

The Relevance of the Passage

All judgments are banished from this earthly plane. Pain and suffering are vanquished from our reality. As a rose is lifted out from the thorns, all the world elevates out of the judgment and hurt that has tormented mankind throughout the ages. All that remains is the sweet fragrance of a supernal rose, and the reality of Heaven on Earth.

315. הָבָה נִתְחַכְּמָה לוֹ. רִבִּי יוֹסֵי אָמַר, אֵין הָבָה אֶלָּא לְשׁוֹן הַזְמָנָה, לְמֶעְבַּד דִּינָא. כְּמָה דְאַתְּ אָמַר, הָבָה נֵרְדָה. הָבָה תָמִים. אָמַר רִבִּי יוֹחָנָן, הָבָה כּוּלָם, לְשׁוֹן הַסְכָּמָה וְהַזְמָנָה. כְּמוֹ הָבָה נִבְנֶה לָנוּ עִיר. הָבוּ לָכֶם עֵצָה. הָבוּ לַה' בְּנֵי אֵלִים.

315. "Come, let us deal wisely with them" (Shemot 1:10). Rabbi Yosi said: "Come (Heb. *hava*)" is an expression of preparation to execute judgment, as is said, "Come, let us go down" (Beresheet 11:7). "Give (Heb. *hava*) a perfect lot" (I Shmuel 14:41). Rabbi Yochanan said: *Hava* is always an expression of agreement and invitation, as in, "Come, let us build us a city" (Beresheet 11:4). "Give counsel" (II Shmuel 16:20); "ascribe (Heb. *havu*) to Hashem, O you mighty" (Tehilim 29:1).

316. רִבִּי יִצְחָק אָמַר, הָבָה נִתְחַכְּמָה לוֹ נֶהֱוֵי בְהַסְכָּמַת דִּינָא לְגַבֵּיהּ. פֶּן יִרְבֶּה, וְרוּחַ הַקֹּדֶשׁ אוֹמֶרֶת כֵּן יִרְבֶּה, וְכֵן יִפְרוֹץ. וּמַלְאֲכֵי הַשָּׁרֵת הָווּ לְהוּ לְשֹׁכִּים וְלִצְנִינִים הה"ד, וַיָּקוּצוּ מִפְּנֵי בְּנֵי יִשְׂרָאֵל. דַּהֲווֹ מִתְעַקְצֵי מִמַּלְאֲכֵי הַשָּׁרֵת, כְּהָנֵי קוֹצֵי דְמִתְעַקְצֵי בְּהוּ אִינָשֵׁי.

316. Rabbi Yitzchak said: "Come, let us deal wisely with him," MEANING: we will agree in Judgment concerning them. "Lest they multiply" (Shemot 1:10); and the Holy Spirit says, "So would it multiply and so would it spread." And the ministering angels were to them as thistles and thorns.

This is what is written: "And they were mortified (Heb. *yakutzu*) on account of the children of Yisrael" (Ibid. 12). ITS MEANING IS THAT THE SUPERNAL CHILDREN OF YISRAEL, WHO ARE THE ANGELS, AS SAID EARLIER, were being stung by the ministering angels, like the thorns (Heb. *kotz*) that prick people.

45. "And against all the Elohim of Egypt I will execute Judgments!"

A Synopsis

The discussion in this section encompasses the Judgments that God executed against the Egyptians. According to Rabbi Yochanan, when Moses spoke the words of the title verse, Dumah, the supernal minister of Egypt, ran in fear. His authority was taken from him and he was appointed as minister over Gehenom, to judge the souls of the wicked. After punishing the gods of Egypt, causing the Egyptian idols to melt or rot, God commanded the public desecration of the lamb, the chief Egyptian deity. He then punished the nation itself. Rabbi Shimon, son of Rabbi Yosi, then comments that the premonition of all these events is apparent in the Pharaoh's words, "Come, let us deal wisely with them; lest they multiply, and it shall come to pass, when any war should chance..."

The Relevance of the Passage

The negative influences of the stars, particularly of the lamb Aries, which represents the God of Egypt, are rescinded. The false icons and trappings of material existence are exposed for what they really are – temporary moments of pleasure at the cost of eternal fulfillment and joy. As our eyes dance across the Zohar's verses, billions of minds are awakened to the enduring and true fulfillment that is the Light of the Creator.

False gods that inhabit our world crumble as our eyes fall upon these verses. Deceptive temptations of our shallow material existence are banished from this world, freeing us to pursue and acquire unending spiritual joy and fulfillment. All our traits and impulses borne of our Evil Inclination are purged from our core being. All forms of corruption and crookedness that exist in our world are shattered forever, paving the way for eternal goodness and justice.

317. א״ר יוּדָאי א״ר יִצְחָק, מַה הֲוָה מַחֲשַׁבְתְּהוֹן דְּמִצְרָאֵי, דְּמִמְנַע מִיִשְׂרָאֵל פְּרִיָה וּרְבִיָּה, וְשָׁלְטָנָא דִּמְמָנָא עֲלֵיהוֹן דְּאָעִיל בְּלִבְּהוֹן כָּךְ. אֶלָּא, אָמַר לְהוֹן, הֲווֹ יַדְעִין, דְּזַמִּין בְּרָא חֲדָא לְמֵיפַק מִיִשְׂרָאֵל, דְּיִתְעֲבֵיד דִּינָא בֵּאֱלֹהֵיהוֹן עַל יְדֵיה.

317. Rabbi Yudai said, said Rabbi Yitzchak: What was the thought of the Egyptians to prevent Yisrael from being fruitful and multiplying, AND THE THOUGHT OF the minister who was appointed over them to bring this into their hearts? BECAUSE "AND HE SAID TO HIS PEOPLE," REFERS TO THEIR

MINISTER? AND HE ANSWERS: But he said to them, 'know that one son will emerge from Yisrael and punishment will be done by his hand against your Elohim.'

318. דְּאָמַר רִבִּי יוֹחָנָן, בְּשָׁעָה שֶׁאָמַר מֹשֶׁה, וּבְכָל אֱלֹהֵי מִצְרַיִם אֶעֱשֶׂה שְׁפָטִים הָלַךְ דּוּמָה שָׂרוֹ שֶׁל מִצְרַיִם, ד' מֵאוֹת פַּרְסָה. אָמַר לֵיהּ קוּדְשָׁא בְּרִיךְ הוּא, גְּזֵרָה נִגְזְרָה לְפָנַי, דִּכְתִיב יִפְקֹד יְיָ' עַל צְבָא הַמָּרוֹם בַּמָּרוֹם וְגוֹ'. בְּאוֹתָהּ שָׁעָה נִטְלָה הַשְּׂרָרָה מִמֶּנּוּ, וְנִתְמַנָּה דּוּמָה שַׂר שֶׁל גֵּיהִנָּם, לִידוֹן שָׁם נַפְשׁוֹת הָרְשָׁעִים. וְרִבִּי יְהוּדָה אוֹמֵר עַל הַמֵּתִים נִתְמַנָּה.

318. For Rabbi Yochanan said: When Moses said, "And against all the Elohim of Egypt I will execute judgments" (Shemot 12:12). Dumah, the Minister of Egypt went four hundred parasangs FROM GREAT FEAR. The Holy One, blessed be He, said to him: 'A decree was decreed before Me, AND IT CAN NOT BE RESCINDED for it is written: "Hashem shall punish the host of the high ones on high..." (Yeshayah 24:21). At that moment, his authority was removed and Dumah was appointed TO BE the minister of Gehenom, to judge the souls of the wicked there. And Rabbi Yehuda said: He was appointed over the dead.

319. אָמַר רִבִּי חֲנִינָא, כְּתִיב וּבֵאלֹהֵיהֶם עָשָׂה יְיָ' שְׁפָטִים. וְכִי בֵּאלָהּ שֶׁל כֶּסֶף, וְשֶׁל זָהָב, וְשֶׁל עֵץ, וְשֶׁל אֶבֶן, יֵשׁ שְׁפָטִים. אֶלָּא אָמַר רִבִּי יוֹסֵי, שֶׁל כֶּסֶף וְשֶׁל זָהָב הָיוּ נִתָּכִים מֵאֲלֵיהֶם, וְשֶׁל עֵץ מִתְרַקְבִין.

319. Rabbi Chanina said: It is written, "Upon their Elohim Hashem inflicted punishments" (Bemidbar 33:4). AND HE ASKS: Are there punishments upon Elohim of silver or of gold or of wood or of stone? Rabbi Yosi said: Those of silver or gold melted of themselves, and those of wood rotted.

320. אָמַר רִבִּי אֶלְעָזָר, אֱלוֹהַּ שֶׁל מִצְרַיִם שֶׂה הָיָה, וְצִוָּה הַקּוּדְשָׁא בְּרִיךְ הוּא לַעֲשׂוֹת בּוֹ שְׁפָטִים, לִשְׂרוֹף אוֹתוֹ בָּאֵשׁ, כְּמָה דְאַתְּ אָמַר, פְּסִילֵי אֱלֹהֵיהֶם תִּשְׂרְפוּן בָּאֵשׁ. כְּדֵי שֶׁיְּהֵא רֵיחוֹ נוֹדֵף. וְעוֹד, רֹאשׁוֹ עַל כְּרָעָיו וְעַל קִרְבּוֹ. וְעוֹד, שֶׁעַצְמוֹתָיו מוּשְׁלָכִים בַּשּׁוּק. וְזֹאת הָיְתָה

לְמִצְרַיִם קָשֶׁה מִכּוּלָן, הֲדָא הוּא דִכְתִיב, שְׁפָטִים.

320. Rabbi Elazar said: The deity of Egypt was a lamb and the Holy One, blessed be He, commanded the execution of punishments upon it, to burn it in fire, as is written: "The carvings of their Elohim shall you burn with fire" (Devarim 7:25), in order that its odor should spread, and, "its head, with its legs, and its entrails," IN A DISRESPECTFUL WAY. Furthermore, its bones shall be thrown in the marketplace. And this was the hardest of all to Egypt. This is the meaning of punishments.

321. אָמַר רִבִּי יְהוּדָה בֵּאלֹהֵיהֶם מַמָּשׁ וְזֶהוּ שַׂר שֶׁלָהֶם, לְקַיֵּים, יִפְקוֹד ה' עַל צְבָא הַמָּרוֹם בַּמָּרוֹם וְעַל מַלְכֵי הָאֲדָמָה עַל הָאֲדָמָה. וְכָל זֶה הָיוּ יוֹדְעִים הַחֲכָמִים שֶׁבָּהֶם, וְכ"ש שַׂר שֶׁלָהֶם. עַל כֵּן כְּתִיב, הָבָה נִתְחַכְּמָה לוֹ.

321. Rabbi Yehuda said: Upon their very Elohim DID HE EXECUTE JUDGMENTS, and this is their minister, to fulfill: "Hashem shall punish the hosts of the high ones on high, and the kings of the earth upon the earth" (Yeshayah 24:21). Their sages, and of course their minister, knew all this. Therefore it is written, "Come, let us deal wisely."

322. רִבִּי יוֹחָנָן אָמַר, הַרְבֵּה ע"ז הָיוּ בְמִצְרַיִם, וְנִילוּס אֱלוֹהַּ שֶׁלָהֶם הָיָה, וּבִכְלַל אֱלֹהֵיהֶם הָיָה הוּא, וּבְכוּלָם עָשָׂה ה' שְׁפָטִים. אָמַר רִבִּי אַבָּא, הָא דְר' יוֹחָנָן דַיְיקָא, וּפְשִׁיטָא, מִשׁוּם דֶאֱלֹהֵיהֶם נִלְקִים בַּתְּחִלָה, ואח"כ הָאוּמָה, וְכֵן נִילוּס נִלְקָה בַּתְּחִלָה, וְהָעֵצִים וְהָאֲבָנִים, הה"ד וַיְהִי הַדָם בְּכָל אֶרֶץ מִצְרַיִם וּבָעֵצִים וּבָאֲבָנִים, שֶׁהָיוּ לָהֶם אֱלֹהוּת מַמָּשׁ. וְאָמַר רִבִּי יִצְחָק, עַל צְבָא הַמָּרוֹם בַּמָּרוֹם כְּתִיב, וְנִילוּס לֹא הָיָה בַּמָּרוֹם. א"ר יוֹחָנָן, רוֹב מֵימָיו כְּדוּגְמָתָן בַּמָּרוֹם. אָמַר רִבִּי יִצְחָק, שַׂר שֶׁלָהֶם נִלְקָה בַּתְּחִלָה, ואח"כ שְׁאַר אֱלֹהֵיהֶם.

322. Rabbi Yochanan said: There were many idols in Egypt and the Nile RIVER was their deity, and the Holy One, blessed be He, executed judgments on all of them. Rabbi Aba said: This OPINION of Rabbi Yochanan is exact and clear, since their deities were smitten first, then the nation. The Nile also was smitten first, and the wood and stones THAT THEY WORSHIPPED. This is what is written: "That there may be blood throughout all the land of Egypt, both in vessels of wood, and in vessels of stones" (Shemot 7:19), that were for them their actual Elohim. And Rabbi Yitzchak said TO RABBI YOCHANAN: It is written, "the hosts of the high ones on high," yet the Nile was not on high, BUT RATHER ON THE EARTH. Rabbi Yochanan said: Because of the vast amount of water of the Nile, it appeared as though THE RIVER was on high. Rabbi Yitzchak said: Their minister was smitten first and afterwards the rest of their Elohim!

323. רִבִּי שִׁמְעוֹן בְּרִבִּי יוֹסֵי אוֹמֵר, לָקוּת אוּמָה שֶׁל מִצְרַיִם מַמָּשׁ, לָא הָיָה אֶלָּא בַּיָּם, דִּכְתִּיב, לֹא נִשְׁאַר בָּהֶם עַד אֶחָד. וְקוֹדֶם זֶה, נַעֲשָׂה שְׁפָטִים בֵּאלֹהֵיהֶם. וע״ד כְּתִיב, הָבָה נִתְחַכְּמָה לוֹ פֶּן יִרְבֶּה וְהָיָה כִּי תִקְרֶאנָה. וְנִתְנַבְּאוּ עַל הֶעָתִיד, כְּפִי מַה שֶׁאֵירַע לָהֶם. וְנוֹסַף גַּם הוּא עַל שׂוֹנְאֵינוּ, נִבְּאוּ עַל מַחֲנוֹת עֶלְיוֹנִים, שֶׁיִּהְיוּ שְׁרוּיִים בְּתוֹכָם. וְנִלְחַם בָּנוּ, נִבְּאוּ עַל מַה דִּכְתִּיב ה׳ יִלָּחֵם לָכֶם וְגוֹ׳. וְעָלָה מִן הָאָרֶץ, כְּמָה דְאַתְּ אָמַר וּבְנֵי יִשְׂרָאֵל יוֹצְאִים בְּיַד רָמָה.

323. Rabbi Shimon, the son of Rabbi Yosi, said: The actual smiting of the nation of Egypt was done only by the sea, as is written: "There remained of them not even one" (Shemot 14:28). Before, judgments were executed upon their Elohim, and therefore it is written: "Come, let us deal wisely with them; lest they multiply, and it shall come to pass, when any war should chance" (Shemot 1:10). They prophesied about the future according to what occurred to them. "They also join our enemies" (Ibid.); they prophesied about the supernal camps OF ANGELS that would dwell among them, "and fight against us." They prophesied about the words: "Hashem shall fight for you" (Shemot 14:14). "And so go up out of the land," as is said: "And the children of Yisrael went out with a high hand" (Ibid. 8).

46. "The song of songs, which is Solomon's"

A Synopsis

Rabbi Elazar expounds upon the title verse, explaining that God after created heaven and earth and the divisions of day and night, He created angels to sing praises by day, and angels to sing praises at night. The angels that sing by day are on the right side, while the angels that sing by night are on the left side. The angels of the night include all three Columns, and they are above all the other singers. When they listen to the songs of the children of Yisrael by day, they gain knowledge and understanding of matters that they were unable to grasp previously. Heaven and earth, signifying the Male and the Female, also gain strength through this singing. Rabbi Nechemyah then explains that he who achieves knowledge of the celestial singing will also merit profound knowledge of the Torah and Wisdom, through which he will learn what was and what will be. It was in this way that both David and Solomon gained knowledge. Indeed, through that song, Solomon was able to penetrate the essence of Wisdom and he then composed many proverbs and wrote a book that he called "The Song of Songs."

Rabbi Elazar then explains that the supernal singers began to sing at Levi's birth, however their singing was not perfected until after Moses was born, Aaron was anointed, and the Levites became sanctified. Because the actions of the lower beings complete the supernal ones, when the singing of below issued from the tribes of Levi, all were sanctified above and below and the worlds became one, with one King dwelling over them.

We learn that the singers of below are called Levites because they are joined to and united with the singers above. Also, the seed of Levi is joined to the Shechinah through Moses, Aaron, and Miriam. Before the birth of these three figures, the supernal singers could not perform their function.

We're also told that Levi's descendant Amram was called this because the mightiest nation descended from him. However, his name is not mentioned because he secretly left his wife and later returned to her. When this happened, God rebuked the heavenly singers and they ceased their song until God extended His right hand to Amram.

The Relevance of the Passage

Melodies that sing out in heartbreakingly beautiful chords from the distant heavens are heard all over the world as we read these stirring verses of Zohar. Each passage of this Book of Splendor is supernal sheet music; each letter, a divine musical note expressing bliss and happiness in a song that will never end: This is the song of the soul.

The aching sounds of children crying, men wailing, and women sobbing forever cease as the music of the spheres fills our being with a joy that defies all forms of language.

Supernal wisdom permeates all existence, settling upon our souls like petals made of Light.

Judgments are removed from this earthly plane. Day and Night meld into one, creating an eternal *moment* of Light.

324. וַיֵּלֶךְ אִישׁ מִבֵּית לֵוִי וַיִּקַּח אֶת בַּת לֵוִי. רִבִּי אֶלְעָזָר פָּתַח, שִׁיר הַשִּׁירִים אֲשֶׁר לִשְׁלֹמֹה. תָּנָא, כְּשֶׁבָּרָא הַקָּדוֹשׁ בָּרוּךְ הוּא אֶת עוֹלְמוֹ, עָלָה בְּחֶפֶץ לְפָנָיו, וּבָרָא אֶת הַשָּׁמַיִם בִּימִינוֹ וְהָאָרֶץ בִּשְׂמֹאלוֹ, וְעָלָה בְּחֶפֶץ לְפָנָיו, לְנַהוֹג הַיּוֹם וְהַלַּיְלָה. וּבָרָא הַמַּלְאָכִים הַמְמוּנִּים בְּחַסְדּוֹ, בַּיּוֹם. וּבָרָא הַמַּלְאָכִים הַמְמוּנִּים לוֹמַר שִׁירָה בַּלַּיְלָה. הֲדָא הוּא דִּכְתִיב, יוֹמָם יְצַוֶּה יְיָ' חַסְדּוֹ וּבַלַּיְלָה שִׁירֹה עִמִּי. אֵלוּ מִיָּמִין, וְאֵלוּ מִשְׂמֹאל, אֵלוּ מַקְשִׁיבִים שִׁירַת הַיּוֹם, שִׁירָתָם שֶׁל יִשְׂרָאֵל קָדוֹשׁ. רִבִּי יִצְחָק אָמַר, אוֹתָם שֶׁאוֹמְרִים שִׁירָה בַּלַּיְלָה, מַקְשִׁיבִים שִׁירָתָם שֶׁל יִשְׂרָאֵל בַּיּוֹם, הֲדָא הוּא דִּכְתִיב, חֲבֵרִים מַקְשִׁיבִים לְקוֹלֵךְ.

324. "And there went a man of the house of Levi, and took to wife a daughter of Levi" (Shemot 2:1). Rabbi Elazar opened the discussion saying: "The song of songs, which is Solomon's" (Shir Hashirm 1:1). We learned that when the Holy One, blessed be He, WHICH IS BINAH, created His world, He so wished and created the heavens, WHICH IS ZEIR ANPIN, with His right hand, WHICH IS THE SECRET OF CHASSADIM, and the earth, WHICH IS THE NUKVA, with His left hand, WHICH IS THE SECRET OF GVUROT. And He so desired to guide the day and the night, THAT THEY SHOULD BE PAIRED IN THE SECRET OF THE PASSAGE: "AND THERE WAS EVENING AND THERE WAS MORNING, ONE DAY" (BERESHEET 1:5). He created the angels, WHO ARE DRAWN FROM ZEIR ANPIN, who are appointed by His kindness by day, and He created the angels who are appointed to sing praises by night. FOR THE SONG IS THE SECRET OF THE ILLUMINATION OF CHOCHMAH THAT IS DRAWN THROUGH THE NUKVA, THAT IS CALLED 'NIGHT'. This is what is written, "Hashem will command His steadfast love (Heb. *chesed*) in the daytime" (Tehilim 42:9), THROUGH THE ANGELS WHO ARE APPOINTED OVER CHESED, "and in the night His song shall be with me" (Ibid.), THROUGH THE ANGELS WHO ARE

APPOINTED OVER THE SINGING, those on the right, MEANING THOSE APPOINTED OVER CHESED, and those on the left, MEANING THOSE APPOINTED OVER THE SINGING. Those OF THE RIGHT listen to the singing of the day, the singing of holy Yisrael, BECAUSE YISRAEL SINGS PRAISES BY DAY. Rabbi Yitzchak said: Those who say songs of praise by night listen to the singing of Yisrael by day, as is written: "The companions hearken for your voice" (Shir Hashirm 8:13).

325. אָמַר רִבִּי שִׁמְעוֹן, כַּת אַחַת, כְּלוּלָה מִשָּׁלֹשׁ כִּתּוֹת, אוֹמֶרֶת שִׁירָה בַּלַּיְלָה. הֲדָא הוּא דִכְתִיב, וַתָּקָם בְּעוֹד לַיְלָה וַתִּתֵּן טֶרֶף לְבֵיתָהּ.

325. Rabbi Shimon said: One group, WHICH IS THE LEFT COLUMN, is comprised of three groups, MEANING THAT IT IS COMPRISED OF ALL THREE COLUMNS, and recites songs during the night. This is the meaning of: "She rises also while it is yet night and gives food to her household" (Mishlei 31:15).

326. אָמַר רִבִּי אֶלְעָזָר, עֲשָׂרָה דְּבָרִים נִבְרְאוּ בְּיוֹם רִאשׁוֹן, מֵהֶם מִדַּת לַיְלָה, וּמֵהֶם מִדַּת יוֹם, וְעַל מִדַּת לַיְלָה כְּתִיב, וַתָּקָם בְּעוֹד לַיְלָה וַתִּתֵּן טֶרֶף לְבֵיתָהּ. כד"א, אַפּוֹ טָרָף. וּכְתִיב, וְטָרַף וְאֵין מַצִּיל. וְחֹק לְנַעֲרוֹתֶיהָ, כְּמָה דְאַתְּ אָמַר חֹק וּמִשְׁפָּט. חֻקָּיו וּמִשְׁפָּטָיו. כִּי חֹק לְיִשְׂרָאֵל הוּא מִשְׁפָּט וְגוֹ'. מִכָּאן שמה"ד שׁוֹלֶטֶת בַּלַּיְלָה.

326. Rabbi Elazar said: Ten things were created on the first day, among them being the attribute of night, WHICH IS MALCHUT, and the attribute of day, WHICH IS TIFERET. It is written about the attribute of night: "She rises also while it is yet night, and gives food (Heb. teref) to her household." FOR FOOD IS JUDGMENTS, as is written: "He tears (Heb. taraf) me in His wrath" (Iyov 16:9), MEANING THE WRATH OF HASHEM TORE ME. It is also written: "...and tears in pieces, and none can deliver" (Michah 5:7). As for, "and a portion (Heb. chok) to her maidens" (Mishlei 31:15), rations are also Judgments, AS IS WRITTEN: "a statute (Heb. chok) and an ordinance" (Shemot 15:25), and "His statutes and His ordinances" (Tehilim 147:19). "For this is a statute for Yisrael, an ordinance of the Elohim of Jacob" (Tehilim 81:5). From here, IT IS UNDERSTOOD that the attribute of Judgment rules at night.

327. וְתָנָא, אֵלּוּ הָאוֹמְרִים שִׁירָה בַּלַּיְלָה, אֵלּוּ הֵם שָׁרִים עַל כָּל בַּעֲלֵי שִׁיר. וּכְשֶׁפוֹתְחִין הַחַיִּים שִׁירָה, מוֹסִיפִים הָעֶלְיוֹנִים כֹּחַ, לָדַעַת וּלְהַכִּיר וּלְהַשִּׂיג מַה שֶּׁלֹא הִשִּׂיגוּ. שָׁמַיִם וָאָרֶץ, מוֹסִיפִין כֹּחַ בְּהַאי שִׁירָה.

327. We learned that those who sing praises at night are singers WHO RISE above all those who sing. When the living, MEANING THE LOWER BEINGS, start singing, the supernal ones gain added strength to know and to recognize and to grasp what they could not grasp before. Heaven and earth, WHICH ARE MALE AND FEMALE, ALSO gain added strength through this singing.

328. אָמַר רבִּי נְחֶמְיָה, אַשְׁרֵי הַזּוֹכֶה לָדַעַת בְּאוֹתוֹ שִׁיר, דְּתַנְיָא הַזּוֹכֶה בְּאוֹתוֹ שִׁיר, יָדַע בְּעִנְיָנֵי הַתּוֹרָה וְהַחָכְמָה, וְיַאֲזִין וְיַחְקוֹר וְיוֹסִיף כֹּחַ וּגְבוּרָה בַּמֶּה שֶׁהָיָה, וּבַמֶּה שֶׁעָתִיד לִהְיוֹת, וּבָזֶה זָכָה שְׁלֹמֹה לָדַעַת.

328. Rabbi Nechemyah said: Fortunate is one who achieves knowledge of that singing, MEANING THAT MOCHIN OF THE ILLUMINATION OF CHOCHMAH. For we learned, the one who merits the singing will know the subjects of Torah and wisdom, and will hear and ascertain and add strength and power in what was, and into what is going to be. And by this, Solomon gained knowledge.

329. דְּתָנֵי רבִּי שִׁמְעוֹן, דָּוִד ע״ה, יָדַע בָּזֶה, וְתִקֵּן שִׁירִים וְתוּשְׁבָּחוֹת הַרְבֵּה, וְרָמַז בָּהֶם הָעֲתִידוֹת לָבוֹא, וְהוֹסִיף כֹּחַ וּגְבוּרָה בְּרוּחַ הַקּוֹדֶשׁ. יָדַע בְּעִנְיָינֵי הַתּוֹרָה וְהַחָכְמָה, וְאִזֵּן וְחִקֵּר וְהוֹסִיף כֹּחַ וּגְבוּרָה בִּלְשׁוֹן הַקּוֹדֶשׁ.

329. For Rabbi Shimon taught that David, may he rest in peace, knew of this, MEANING HE ACHIEVED THE MOCHIN OF CHOCHMAH INSIDE DA'AT. THEREFORE, he composed many songs and praises, and in them alluding to what would come in the future. He added strength and power through the Holy Spirit, WHICH IS THE SECRET OF THE NUKVA AT THE TIME THAT IT IS RECEIVING DA'AT FROM HOLINESS, WHICH IS THE SECRET OF CHOCHMAH. He knew the subjects of Torah and Wisdom, and heard and ascertained and added strength and power in the Holy Language, WHICH IS THE SECRET OF THE NUKVA WHEN IT IS RECEIVING DA'AT FROM HOLINESS, WHICH IS THE SECRET OF CHOCHMAH.

330. וּשְׁלֹמֹה זָכָה יוֹתֵר בְּאוֹתוֹ הַשִּׁיר, וְיָדַע הַחָכְמָה, וְאִזֵּן וְחִקֵּר וְתִקֵּן מְשָׁלִים הַרְבֵּה, וְעָשָׂה סֵפֶר מֵאוֹתוֹ הַשִּׁיר מַמָּשׁ, וְהַיְינוּ דִּכְתִיב, עָשִׂיתִי לִי שָׁרִים וְשָׁרוֹת. כְּלוֹמַר, קָנִיתִי לִי לָדַעַת שִׁיר, מֵאוֹתָן הַשִּׁירִים הָעֶלְיוֹנִים, וַאֲשֶׁר תַּחְתָּם. וְהַיְינוּ דִּכְתִיב, שִׁיר הַשִּׁירִים, כְּלוֹמַר, שִׁיר, שֶׁל אוֹתָם שָׁרִים שֶׁל מַעְלָה. שִׁיר, שֶׁכּוֹלֵל כָּל עִנְיְינֵי הַתּוֹרָה וְהַחָכְמָה, וְכֹחַ וּגְבוּרָה, בְּמַה שֶׁהָיָה, וְעָתִיד לִהְיוֹת, שִׁיר שֶׁהַשָּׁרִים שֶׁל מַעְלָה מְשׁוֹרְרִים.

330. And Solomon gained more merit through the song and achieved wisdom, and weighed and searched and composed many proverbs, and wrote a book from that very poem, as written: "I acquired men singers and women singers" (Kohelet 2:8). This means: I learned the science of poetry from those lofty poems, and those lower than them. This is the meaning of the words, "The song of songs:" a song of all those singers of above, a song which includes all that pertains to the Torah and to wisdom, to strength and might, what was and what will be; a song that the singers above sing.

331. א״ר אֶלְעָזָר, אֵלּוּ הַשָּׁרִים, עָמְדוּ, עַד שֶׁנּוֹלַד לֵוִי, אֲבָל מִשֶּׁנּוֹלַד לֵוִי וְאֵילָךְ אָמְרוּ שִׁיר. כֵּיוָן שֶׁנּוֹלַד מֹשֶׁה וְנִמְשַׁח אַהֲרֹן, וְנִתְקַדְּשׁוּ הַלְוִיִּם, נִשְׁלָם הַשִּׁיר, וְעָמְדוּ עַל מִשְׁמְרוֹתָם.

331. Rabbi Elazar said: All those who sing, MEANING THE SUPERNAL SINGERS, stopped SINGING PRAISES until Levi was born. Since the birth of Levi and afterwards, they said praises, BUT IT WAS STILL NOT COMPLETE. When Moses was born and Aaron was anointed and the Levites became sanctified, the singing became complete. And they stood, THE SUPERNAL SINGERS, on their watches.

332. וְאָמַר רִבִּי אֶלְעָזָר, בְּאוֹתָהּ שָׁעָה שֶׁנּוֹלַד לֵוִי, פָּתְחוּ לְמַעְלָה וְאָמְרוּ, מִי יִתֶּנְךָ כְּאָח לִי יוֹנֵק שְׁדֵי אִמִּי אֶמְצָאֲךָ בַחוּץ אֶשָּׁקְךָ גַּם לֹא יָבוּזוּ לִי. כֵּיוָן שֶׁיָּצְאוּ מִשֵּׁבֶט לֵוִי הַמְשׁוֹרְרִים שֶׁל מַטָּה, וְנִתְקַדְּשׁוּ כּוּלָם, וְעָמְדוּ עַל מִשְׁמְרוֹתָם, וְנִתְקַדְּשׁוּ אֵלֶּה לְנוֹכַח אֵלֶּה, חֲבֵרִים כְּאֶחָד, וְהָעוֹלָמוֹת אֶחָד, וּמֶלֶךְ אֶחָד שׁוֹכֵן עֲלֵיהֶם, בָּא שְׁלֹמֹה, וְעָשָׂה סֵפֶר מֵאוֹתוֹ שִׁיר שֶׁל אוֹתָם שָׁרִים, וְנִסְתַּם הַחָכְמָה בּוֹ.

332. Rabbi Elazar also said: At the moment of Levi's birth, they opened above and said THAT THE SHECHINAH SAID TO ZEIR ANPIN, "O that you were as my brother, that sucked the breasts of my mother! When I should find You outside, and would kiss you; and none would scorn me" (Shir Hashirm 8:1). "O THAT YOU WERE MY BROTHER," MEANING THAT YOU SHOULD GIVE ME CHOCHMAH, BECAUSE FROM THE POINT OF VIEW OF CHOCHMAH, ZEIR ANPIN AND THE NUKVA ARE CALLED 'BROTHER' AND 'SISTER'. "THAT SUCKED THE BREASTS OF MY MOTHER," FOR THEN THEY BOTH SUCK FROM BINAH, AND ARE OF AN EQUAL LEVEL. "WHEN I SHOULD FIND YOU OUTSIDE, AND WOULD KISS YOU," FOR THE ILLUMINATION OF CHOCHMAH WITHOUT CHASSADIM IS ON THE OUTSIDE. SHE ASKED HIM TO KISS HIM AND SHINE FROM HIM ALSO WHEN SHE IS OUTSIDE. "AND NONE WOULD SCORN ME" REFERS TO THE KLIPOT THAT ARE ROUSED ON THE OUTSIDE TO SCORN THE SHECHINAH, AS IT IS WRITTEN: "SIN CROUCHES AT THE DOOR" (BERESHEET 4:7). As soon as the singing of below emerged from the tribe of Levi, DIVIDING INTO RIGHT AND LEFT, PRIESTS AND LEVITES, they were all sanctified, standing on their watches – MEANING THE SUPERNAL MINISTERS and THESE ANGELS became sanctified, corresponding to these LEVITES – companions as one. BECAUSE THE ACTIONS OF THE LOWER BEINGS COMPLETE THE SUPERNAL ONES, THEN the worlds BECOME as one and one King dwells over them. AFTER ALL THESE PREPARATIONS, Solomon came and composed a book from the song of those singers, AS MENTIONED, and the wisdom was concealed in it!

333. א"ר יְהוּדָה, לָמָּה נִקְרְאוּ הַשָּׁרִים שֶׁל מַטָּה לְוִיִּם, עַל שֶׁנִּלְוִים וְנֶחְבָּרִים לְמַעְלָה כְּאֶחָד. וְהַשּׁוֹמֵעַ, נִלְוָה וְנִדְבָּק נַפְשׁוֹ לְמַעְלָה. וע"כ אָמְרָה לֵאָה, יִלָּוֶה אִישִׁי אֵלַי. רִבִּי תַּנְחוּם אָמַר, שֶׁבְּכֹל נִלְוָה זֶרַע לֵוִי עִם הַשְּׁכִינָה, בְּמֹשֶׁה וְאַהֲרֹן וּמִרְיָם, וּבְכָל זַרְעוֹ אַחֲרָיו, וְהֵם הַנִּלְוִים אֶל ה' לְשָׁרְתוֹ.

333. Rabbi Yehuda said: Why are the singers of below called Levites? IT IS because they are attached (Heb. *nilvim*) and joined as one above. THE REASON BEING that the soul of the one who hears the singing became attracted and attached above TO HASHEM. Therefore Leah said: "Will my husband be joined to me" (Beresheet 29:34). Rabbi Tanchum said: THE REASON HE WAS CALLED LEVI IS BECAUSE the seed of Levi is entirely attached to the Shechinah by Moses, Aaron and Miriam, and to all his children after him. They are attached to Hashem to serve Him.

334. תָּא חֲזֵי, בְּשָׁעָה שֶׁעָמְדוּ הַמְשׁוֹרְרִים לְמַעְלָה, לֹא עָמְדוּ עַל מִשְׁמַרְתָּם, עַד שֶׁנּוֹלְדוּ שְׁלֹשָׁה הָאַחִים: מֹשֶׁה, אַהֲרֹן, וּמִרְיָם. תֵּינַח מֹשֶׁה וְאַהֲרֹן, מִרְיָם לָמָּה. אָמַר רַבִּי יוֹסֵי, הַהֲ"ד, כד"א, וַתַּעַן לָהֶם מִרְיָם.

334. Come and behold: at the time that the poets stood above, they did not keep their post until the three siblings, Moses, Aaron and Miriam, were born. This may apply to Moses and Aaron, but why Miriam? Rabbi Yosi said: It is written: "And women singers" (Kohelet 2:8), and, "And Miriam answered them" (Shemot 15:21).

335. תָּאנָא, בְּאוֹתָהּ שָׁעָה שֶׁנּוֹלַד לֵוִי, נָטְלוֹ הַקּוּדְשָׁא בְּרִיךְ הוּא, וּבְחֲרוּ מִכָּל אֶחָיו וְהוֹשִׁיבוֹ בָאָרֶץ, וְהוֹלִיד לִקְהָת, וּקְהָת הוֹלִיד לְעַמְרָם, וְהוּא הוֹלִיד לְאַהֲרֹן וּמִרְיָם. פֵּירַשׁ מֵאִשְׁתּוֹ, וְהֶחֱזִירָהּ, בְּאוֹתָהּ שָׁעָה הָיוּ הַמְשׁוֹרְרִים שֶׁל מַעְלָה עוֹמְדִים וּמְשׁוֹרְרִים, גָּעַר בָּהֶם הַקּוּדְשָׁא בְּרִיךְ הוּא, וְנִשְׁתַּכַּךְ הַשִּׁיר, עַד שֶׁנָּטָה קַו יְמִינוֹ, וְהוֹשִׁיט לְעַמְרָם.

335. We have learned that when Levi was born, the Holy One, blessed be He, took him and chose him from all his brothers, and set him in the land. And he begot Kohath, and Kohath begot Amram, who begot Aaron and Miriam. He separated from his wife, and when he brought her back, the singers above were singing. The Holy One, blessed be He, reproved them, and the song ceased until He stretched out His right hand and extended it to Amram.

336. מ"ט נִקְרָא עַמְרָם. שֶׁיָּצָא מִמֶּנּוּ עַם רָם עַל כָּל רָמִים, וְלֹא נִזְכַּר שְׁמוֹ. מ"ט לֹא נִזְכַּר שְׁמוֹ. רַבִּי יְהוּדָה אָמַר בְּשֵׁם רַבִּי אַבָּהוּ, מִפְּנֵי שֶׁבְּצִנְעָא הָלַךְ, וּבְצִנְעָא חָזַר לְאִשְׁתּוֹ, כְּדֵי שֶׁלֹּא יַכִּירוּ בּוֹ, הַהֲ"ד וַיֵּלֶךְ אִישׁ, וְלֹא נֶאֱמַר וַיֵּלֶךְ עַמְרָם בְּפַרְהֶסְיָא. וַיִּקַח אֶת בַּת לֵוִי, אַף הִיא בְּצִנְעָא חָזְרָה, וְלֹא נִזְכְּרָה שְׁמָהּ.

336. Why was he called Amram? Because a mighty nation (Heb. *am ram*) over all mighty nations descended from him. Why was his name not mentioned? In the name of Rabbi Abahu, Rabbi Yehuda said it was because he discreetly left and secretly returned to his wife, so that he would not be recognized, as written: "And there went a man," instead of, 'And Amram went', openly. "And took to wife a daughter of Levi" (Shemot 2:1). She also returned in secret, and was not mentioned by name.

47. "And there went a man"

A Synopsis
While Rabbi Abahu interprets the title verse as a reference to Gabriel, who brought Amram's wife back to him, Rabbi Yehuda states that it refers to Amram, who decided to marry his wife because he was urged to do so from above. Rabbi Yitzchak then explains that Amram was not worthy to give birth to Moses until he obtained a portion in the Shechinah by marrying "a daughter of Levi". He was then worthy of bearing a son with a great voice, to whom God attached His Name, "Good". Amram himself then merited a divine voice, and in this way he advanced to a higher level.

The Relevance of the Passage
Through Moses, the children of Yisrael merited redemption and freedom from bondage in Egypt. Moses was able to achieve this miracle because the Creator "united his Name over him." That means that Moses was attached to the Upper World and thus was able to elevate this entire lower world.

In this passage, we draw upon the power of the Shechinah, Moses and the Holy Name of God יהוה to merit and effect our final and eternal unification with the realm called Zeir Anpin. This merging of two worlds unleashes endless Light, freeing humanity from the clutches of the negative forces and demons who have imprisoned us since the dawn of physical existence.

337. וַיֵּלֶךְ אִישׁ. רִבִּי אֲבָהוּ אָמַר, וַיֵּלֶךְ אִישׁ, זֶה גַּבְרִיאֵל. דִּכְתִּיב, וְהָאִישׁ גַּבְרִיאֵל. שֶׁהָלַךְ הוּא וְהֶחֱזִירָהּ לְעַמְרָם. רִבִּי יְהוּדָה אָמַר, עַמְרָם מַמָּשׁ הָיָה, וְלֹא נִזְכַּר שְׁמוֹ, מִפְּנֵי שֶׁהֲלִיכָה זוֹ לֹא הָיְתָה מִמֶּנּוּ לְהִזְדַּוֵּוג לְאִשְׁתּוֹ, אֶלָּא מִלְמַעְלָה.

337. Rabbi Abahu said: "And there went a man" (Shemot 2:1), refers to Gabriel, as it is written, "And the man Gabriel" (Daniel 9:21), for he went and returned her to Amram. Rabbi Yehuda said it was actually Amram, but his name is not mentioned because he was not going to mate with his wife out of his own volition, but rather from above. BECAUSE THE URGING OF THE HOLY ONE, BLESSED BE HE, PREVAILED ON HIM, HE WENT.

338. רִבִּי יִצְחָק אָמַר, בְּאַהֲרֹן וּמִרְיָם לֹא נֶאֱמַר זִיוּוּג אֲבוֹתָם בַּתּוֹרָה,

וּבְמֹשֶׁה כְּתִיב וַיִּקַּח אֶת בַּת לֵוִי, לְהוֹרוֹת, שֶׁהַשְּׁכִינָה נִקְרֵאת עַל שֵׁם
לֵוִי. וְלֹא הָיָה עַמְרָם רָאוּי לְהוֹלִיד לְמֹשֶׁה, עַד שֶׁנָּטַל חֵלֶק בַּשְּׁכִינָה,
וְהוֹלִיד לְמֹשֶׁה. הֲדָא הוּא דִכְתִיב, וַיִּקַּח אֶת בַּת לֵוִי. וּלְפִיכָךְ כְּתִיב,
וַתֵּרֶא אוֹתוֹ כִּי טוֹב הוּא.

338. Rabbi Yitzchak said: WHY IS IT THAT by Aaron and Miriam the union of their parents is not mentioned in the Torah, but by Moses is written: "And took to wife a daughter of Levi" (Shemot 2:1)? AND HE ANSWERS: IT IS to show that the Shechinah is named after 'Levi', and Amram was not worthy to beget Moses until he took part with the Shechinah. Then did he beget Moses This is what is written: "And took to wife a daughter of Levi," WHICH IS SHECHINAH. Therefore, it is written: "And when she saw that he was a goodly (lit. 'good')..." MEANING THAT THE SHECHINAH DWELT ON HIM.

339. רַבִּי אֶלְעָזָר אָמַר, זָכָה עַמְרָם שֶׁיָּצָא מִמֶּנּוּ בֵּן, שֶׁזָּכָה לְקוֹל גָּדוֹל,
דִּכְתִיב וְהָאֱלֹהִים יַעֲנֶנּוּ בְקוֹל. וְעַמְרָם זָכָה לְבַת קוֹל, דִּכְתִיב וַיִּקַּח אֶת
בַּת לֵוִי. כְּלוֹמַר, בַּת קוֹל. וּלְפִיכָךְ כְּתִיב וַיֵּלֶךְ. כְּלוֹמַר, שֶׁהָלַךְ לְמַדְרֵגָה
זוֹ. תָּאנָא, כְּשֶׁנּוֹלַד מֹשֶׁה, יִיחֵד הַקּוּדְשָׁא בְּרִיךְ הוּא שְׁמוֹ עָלָיו, דִּכְתִיב
וַתֵּרֶא אוֹתוֹ כִּי טוֹב הוּא. וּכְתִיב, טוֹב ה' לַכֹּל. וּכְתִיב, טַעֲמוּ וּרְאוּ כִּי
טוֹב ה'.

339. Rabbi Elazar said: Amram merited that there should emerge from him a son who would merit a great voice, WHICH IS ZEIR ANPIN, as is written: "And the Elohim answered him by a voice" (Shemot 19:19). And Amram merited a divine voice, WHICH IS MALCHUT, as is written: "And took to wife a daughter of Levi," meaning a divine voice (lit. 'a daughter of a voice'). Therefore it says, "And there went," meaning he went to this level! We learned that when Moses was born, the Holy One, blessed be He, united His name over him, as is written: "And when she saw that he was good..." AND GOOD IS THE NAME OF THE HOLY ONE, BLESSED BE HE, as is written: "Hashem is good to all" (Tehilim 145:9), and "O taste and see that Hashem is good" (Tehilim 34:9). HENCE, THE HOLY ONE, BLESSED BE HE, IS CALLED 'GOOD'.

48. "And the king of Egypt died"

A Synopsis

Rabbi Yehoshua of Sachnin explains that God did not remember or hear the prayers of Yisrael until the time when the supernal minister of Egypt fell from power, as signified by the title verse.

The Relevance of the Passage

Egypt represents our negative and wicked character traits, and Egypt's minister or King is the root seed of our evil. When we offer up our negative traits by admitting them to ourselves during prayer and meditation and to others during moments of conflict, our prayers then ascend to the Upper World. The act of acknowledgment is the key that unlocks the gates of heaven so that all our prayers will be answered.

As we recall our most vile traits in this moment, and peruse the text of the Zohar, we eradicate the root level of all evil in ourselves, and in this world. All our prayers for peace, endless joy, and eternal life are henceforth answered.

340. וַיְהִי בַיָּמִים הָרַבִּים הָהֵם. רַבִּי יְהוֹשֻׁעַ דְּסַכְנִין אָמַר, וַיְהִי בַיָּמִים הָרַבִּים הָהֵם, סוֹף גָּלוּתָם הָיָה, שֶׁהָיוּ יִשְׂרָאֵל מְשׁוּעֲבָּדִים בְּכָל עֲבוֹדָה. בַּיָּמִים הָרַבִּים הָהֵם, שֶׁהָיוּ רַבִּים לְיִשְׂרָאֵל בְּמִצְרַיִם, וְכֵיוָן שֶׁנִּשְׁתַּלַּם קֵץ גָּלוּתָם, מַה כְּתִיב, וַיָּמָת מֶלֶךְ מִצְרַיִם. מ״ט. שֶׁהוּרַד שַׂר מִצְרַיִם מִמַּעֲלָתוֹ, וְנָפַל מִגַּאֲוָתוֹ. וְכֵיוָן שֶׁנָּפַל מֶלֶךְ מִצְרַיִם, שֶׁהוּא שַׂר שֶׁלָּהֶן, זָכַר הַקּוּדְשָׁא בְּרִיךְ הוּא לְיִשְׂרָאֵל, וְשָׁמַע תְּפִלָּתָם.

340. "And it came to pass in the course of those many days" (Shemot 2:23). Rabbi Yehoshua of Sachnin said it was at the end of their exile that Yisrael were subjugated with all kinds of labor. "In the course of those many days." They were many to THE SOJOURN OF Yisrael in Egypt, MEANING THAT THE END HAD ARRIVED. Since the end of their exile was complete, it is written: "And the king of Egypt died" (Ibid.). What is the meaning? IT IS that the Minister of Egypt was lowered from his high position and fell from his glory. THEREFORE, THE TORAH SAYS ABOUT HIM, "AND THE KING OF EGYPT DIED," SINCE HIS DESCENT WAS CONSIDERED BY HIM AS DEATH. Since the king of Egypt who was their minister fell, the Holy One, blessed be He, remembered Yisrael and heard their prayers.

341. אָמַר רַבִּי יְהוּדָה, בֹּא וּרְאֵה שֶׁכָּךְ הוּא, שֶׁכָּל זְמַן שֶׁהַשַּׂר שֶׁלָּהֶם

נִתְּנָה לוֹ שְׂרָרָה עַל יִשְׂרָאֵל, לֹא נִשְׁמַע צַעֲקָתָם שֶׁל יִשְׂרָאֵל, כֵּיוָן שֶׁנָּפַל הַשַּׂר שֶׁלָּהֶם, כְּתִיב וַיָּמָת מֶלֶךְ מִצְרַיִם, וּמִיָּד וַיֵּאָנְחוּ בְנֵי יִשְׂרָאֵל מִן הָעֲבוֹדָה וַיִּזְעָקוּ וַתַּעַל שַׁוְעָתָם אֶל הָאֱלֹהִים. שֶׁעַד אוֹתָהּ שָׁעָה לֹא נַעֲנוּ בְּצַעֲקָתָם.

341. Rabbi Yehuda said: Come and behold. As RABBI YEHOSHUA OF SACHNIN SAID, as long as the minister held sway over Yisrael, the cries of Yisrael were not heard. But as soon as their minister fell, it is written: "And the king of Egypt died." Immediately, "the children of Yisrael sighed by reason of their bondage, and they cried, and their beseeching rose to the Elohim" (Ibid.). BUT until that time, their beseeching was not answered.

49. Two tears into the Great Sea

A Synopsis

Rabbi Elazar explains that when God has mercy on Yisrael, He suppresses the attribute of Judgment by dropping two tears (signifying two attributes of Judgment) into the Great Sea (signifying the Sea of Wisdom) in order to sweeten them. In this way, He turns the attribute of Justice into the attribute of Compassion.

Rabbi Yitzchak then clarifies the apparent contradiction in the verse, "Behold, Egypt marched after them," explaining that it refers to the deposed and powerless supernal minister of Egypt.

Finally, Rabbi Aba answers Rabbi Yosi's question regarding the verse, "Behold, the day of Hashem comes…" This, we're told, refers to the day on which God will Judge the heathen nations and their ministers will fall from power.

The Relevance of the Passage

All our negative impulses originate in a supernal negative force or evil angel that attempts to influence and manipulate us throughout our day. Each time we yield to an evil urge, we strengthen that supernal angel. His influence grows stronger in the world. Moreover, he is now free to inflict judgment upon us.

Every time we resist a wicked impulse, we diminish the negative angel's power. In addition, each time we shed tears of repentance for our misdeeds and make the effort to abolish the traits that originally caused them, we awaken the compassionate force of mercy, which tempers and sweetens judgments decreed against us.

Thus, we learn that our every deed is vital to the world and stands like a lock-keeper with his hands upon the wheel: a turn to the left, and the river of Light is shut out; a turn to the right, and it pours through again in a torrent of blinding Glory that overflows its banks, washing away darkness and judgment.

Our own tearful meditation upon these holy verses now turns the wheel to the right, unleashing mercy, compassion, and clemency into our world. These awesome forces of kindness ensure that our Redemption unfolds in a gentle and pleasant manner, as opposed to one filled with pain and suffering.

342. אָמַר רִבִּי אֶלְעָזָר, בֹּא וּרְאֵה רַחֲמָנוּתוֹ שֶׁל הַקָּדוֹשׁ בָּרוּךְ הוּא, כְּשֶׁהוּא מְרַחֵם עַל יִשְׂרָאֵל, כּוֹפֶה למדה״ד, וּמוֹרִידָהּ, וּמְרַחֵם עֲלֵיהֶם. וְהַיְינוּ דִּתְנָן, שֶׁהַקָּדוֹשׁ בָּרוּךְ הוּא מוֹרִיד שְׁתֵּי דְמָעוֹת לַיָּם הַגָּדוֹל. מַאן

אִינּוּן שְׁתֵּי דְמָעוֹת. אָמַר רִבִּי יוֹסֵי, לָאו מִלָּא בְּרִירָא הִיא, דְּהָא א״ל לְאוֹבָא טַמְיָא, דְּהוּא כָּדִיב, וּמִלֵּיהּ כְּדִיבָן.

342. Rabbi Elazar said: Come and behold the compassion of the Holy One, blessed be He. When He has mercy for Yisrael, He subjugates the attribute of Judgment, lowers it, and has compassion for them. We learned that the Holy One, blessed be He, drops two tears into the Great Sea. HE ASKS: What are the two tears? Rabbi Yosi said: It is not clear. We see that one should say to a medium who obtains information through the bones of the dead that he and his words are false.

343. א״ר אֶלְעָזָר, לָאו בָּתַר אוֹבָא טַמְיָא אַזְלִינָן, דִּבְרִירָא דְמִלָּה הוּא, דִּתְנַן, בַּעֲשָׂרָה כִּתְרֵי מַלְכָּא, אִית תְּרֵין דִּמְעִין לְקוּדְשָׁא בְּרִיךְ הוּא, וְהֵן שְׁתֵּי מִדּוֹת דִּין, שֶׁהַדִּין בָּא מִשְּׁתֵּיהֶן, כד״א, שְׁתַּיִם הֵנָּה קוֹרְאוֹתַיִךְ. וּכְשֶׁהַקּוּדְשָׁא בְּרִיךְ הוּא זוֹכֵר אֶת בָּנָיו, הוּא מוֹרִיד אוֹתָם לַיָּם הַגָּדוֹל, שֶׁהוּא יָם הַחָכְמָה לְהַמְתִּיקָן, וְהוֹפֵךְ מִדַּת הַדִּין לְמִדַּת רַחֲמִים, וּמְרַחֵם עֲלַיְיהוּ. א״ר יְהוּדָה, שְׁתֵּי דְמָעוֹת, שֶׁמֵּהֶם בָּאִים הַדְּמָעוֹת, מֵהֶם בָּא הַדִּין.

343. Rabbi Elazar said: We do not follow the Klipah of necromancy. IT IS NOT SO, RATHER the clarification of the matter is, because we learned that in the ten Sfirot of the King there are two tears to the Holy One, blessed be He, and they are two attributes of Judgment. Judgment comes from both of them, as is written: "These two things have befallen you" (Yeshayah 51:19). And when the Holy One, blessed be He, remembers His children, He lowers them to the Great Sea, the Sea of Wisdom, WHICH IS MALCHUT, to sweeten them. THEN the attribute of Judgment IN MALCHUT is changed into the attribute of Mercy and has compassion for them. Rabbi Yehuda said: There are two tears, from where the tears come, and Judgment comes.

344. א״ר יְהוּדָה כְּתִיב, וְהִנֵּה מִצְרַיִם נוֹסֵעַ אַחֲרֵיהֶם. וא״ר יוֹסֵי זֶה שַׂר שֶׁל מִצְרַיִם, הוּא, וְאַתְּ אָמַרְתְּ וַיָּמָת מֶלֶךְ מִצְרַיִם, זֶה שַׂר שֶׁל מִצְרַיִם. א״ר יִצְחָק, הַאי מִלָּה קָא מְסַיֵּיעַ לְהַהוּא דִּלְעֵילָא, כְּתִיב הָכָא וְהִנֵּה מִצְרַיִם, וּכְתִיב הָתָם וַיָּמָת מֶלֶךְ מִצְרַיִם. מְלַמֵּד דְּעַכְשָׁיו לֹא הָיָה מֶלֶךְ,

דְּהוֹרִידוּהוּ מִגְּדוּלָתוּ. וּלְפִיכָךְ כְּתִיב, וְהִנֵּה מִצְרַיִם, וְלָא כְּתִיב מֶלֶךְ מִצְרַיִם. וּמַה דְּאָמַר וַיָּמָת. כד"א כִּי מֵתוּ כָּל הָאֲנָשִׁים הַמְבַקְשִׁים אֶת נַפְשֶׁךָ.

344. Rabbi Yehuda said: It is written, "And behold, Egypt marched after them" (Shemot 14:10). And Rabbi Yosi said: This is the minister of Egypt. IT APPEARS THAT HE WAS STILL IN AUTHORITY AT THE TIME THE CHILDREN OF YISRAEL LEFT EGYPT, yet you say that, "And the king of Egypt died" (Shemot 2:23), refers to the minister of Egypt, AND THIS WAS BEFORE YISRAEL LEFT EGYPT. Rabbi Yitzchak said these words OF RABBI YOSI ARE NOT CONTRADICTORY, BUT EVEN maintain the above explanation of the passage, WHICH IS THAT THE KING OF EGYPT DIED. For it is written here: "And, behold, Egypt," and there, "And the king of Egypt died." This teaches that AFTER THE EXODUS FROM EGYPT, there was no king, because BEFOREHAND they had removed him from his high position. Therefore, it is written: "And, behold, Egypt" instead of, 'And, behold, the king of Egypt.' "And...died," DOES NOT MEAN THAT HE WAS NULLIFIED ALTOGETHER, ONLY THAT THEY REMOVED HIM FROM HIS HIGH POSITION AND HE COULD NO LONGER HARM, as is written: "For all the men are dead who sought your life" (Shemot 4:19). THIS MEANS THAT THEY CAN NO LONGER DO HARM; ALSO "DIED" HERE MEANS THAT HE COULD NO LONGER DO HARM BECAUSE HE HAD BEEN REMOVED FROM HIS HIGH POSITION!

345. א"ר יִצְחָק א"ר יְהוֹשֻׁעַ, בֹּא וּרְאֵה, כָּל מַלְכֵי מִצְרַיִם פַּרְעֹה שְׁמָם. וּבְכָאן לֹא נֶאֱמַר אֶלָּא מֶלֶךְ מִצְרַיִם סְתָם. וּבִמְקוֹמוֹ פַּרְעֹה, וְהוּא פַּרְעֹה מַמָּשׁ. תָּא חֲזֵי, בְּעוֹד דְּאִית שׁוּלְטָנוּתָא דִּלְעֵילָא, אִית שׁוּלְטָנוּתָא בְּעַמָּא דִּלְתַתָּא, אִתְעֲדֵי שׁוּלְטָנוּתָא דִּלְעֵילָא, אִתְעֲדֵי שׁוּלְטָנוּתָא דִּלְתַתָּא.

345. Said Rabbi Yitzchak, said Rabbi Yehoshua: Come and behold. All the kings of Egypt were named Pharaoh, yet here it says merely that the king of Egypt DIED, AND DOES NOT SAY 'PHARAOH, THE KING OF EGYPT'. THAT IS BECAUSE WHAT IS BEING DISCUSSED IS THE MINISTER OF EGYPT, AS MENTIONED EARLIER, AND IF IT WERE WRITTEN 'Pharaoh' instead, then it would actually mean Pharaoh AND NOT THE MINISTER OF EGYPT. Come and behold: as long as there is rule over the nation above BY THE

MINISTER, there is rule over the nation below. When dominion above is removed FROM THE MINISTER OF THE NATION, then dominion below is also removed.

346. א"ר יוֹסֵי, כְּתִיב הִנֵּה יוֹם בָּא לַיְיָ' וְגו' וְהָיָה יוֹם אֶחָד הוּא יִוָּדַע לַיְיָ' וְגו'. וְכִי שְׁאַר יוֹמִין לָאו אִינּוּן דִּילֵיהּ. אֶלָּא אָמַר רְבִּי אַבָּא, מְלַמֵּד, שֶׁשְּׁאַר הַיָּמִים, נִתָּנִים לְשָׂרִים, וְאוֹתוֹ יוֹם, אֵינוֹ שֶׁל הַשָּׂרִים, אֶלָּא שֶׁל הַקּוּדְשָׁא בְּרִיךְ הוּא, כְּדֵי לַעֲשׂוֹת דִּין בעכו"ם. מִפְּנֵי שֶׁבְּבֹאוֹתוֹ יוֹם, יִפְּלוּ כָּל הַשָּׂרִים מִמַּעֲלָתָם. וע"ד כְּתִיב, וְנִשְׂגַּב ה' לְבַדּוֹ בַּיּוֹם הַהוּא. שֶׁאוֹתוֹ יוֹם לֹא יִהְיֶה מַעֲלָה לְשָׂרִים.

346. Rabbi Yosi said: It is written, "Behold, the day of Hashem comes..." (Zecharyah 14:1), "but it shall one day be known as Hashem's..." (Ibid. 7). HE ASKS: And are not the rest of the days also Hashem's? Rabbi Aba said: It teaches that the other days are given over to the ministers, and that day will be of the Holy One, blessed be He, and not the ministers' in order to execute judgment upon the heathen. On that day, all the ministers will fall from their high positions and it is therefore written: "And Hashem alone will be exalted on that day" (Yeshayah 2:17). Because on that day, the ministers will have no exaltation.

50. Does Hashem have a sword?

A Synopsis
Rabbi Aba and Rabbi Yitzchak discourse on the sword of God, by which He executes Justice. The verse that describes the angel of God, who stands "with a drawn sword in his hand," signifies that he was granted permission to execute Judgment. The words of the Angel of Death, "and I will reveal their place of slaughter," refer to the disclosure of the sin that is the cause of death. Finally, the verse, "And he put up his sword again into its sheath," signifies the return of the permission to execute Judgment to the Judge to whom it belongs, God.

The Relevance of the Passage
The souls of humanity deeply desired in the beginning the opportunity to express their inherited Godly trait that allows them to become the *cause* and *creators* of their own fulfillment. Accordingly, free will was the necessary feature to allow man the possibility of truly *earning* his happiness. For this reason, *time* was brought into existence to separate and distance *cause* from *effect*. Namely, if man was instantly rewarded each time he opposed his evil urge, he would transform his behavior at once. Likewise, if man experienced judgment the moment he committed a misdeed, he would, straight away, refrain from such behavior.

However, animals will curb their behavior when there is an immediate reprimand or reward. A human being's soul is of a much higher grade than an animal. Thus, rewards and punishments are delayed, through time, to create the illusion of injustice and disorder. Under this scenario, one must now strive with great effort to resist temptation and conquer one's evil impulses. One must work hard to acquire deep wisdom and evolve acute insight so that one may perceive the underlying order beneath the chaos. One must exert tremendous effort to learn the spiritual laws of life in order to recognize the cause and effect relationship that exists in our world.

This is how human beings become the *cause* of our own fulfillment.

The Creator, respecting this desire for free will and our need to become the cause of our Light, implanted time and the law of cause and effect into this world when it was created. Each time we sin (the cause), an equal measure of judgment will be decreed against us (the effect) by the natural laws of the universe. When a our misdeeds become so great over the course of our life, the judgments reach a critical mass, and death becomes the ultimate effect.

This is the underlying meaning behind the phrase "the sword of the Creator is full of blood."

God permits the natural universal laws of cause and effect to exact their toll upon humanity so that each one of us may earn and merit the infinite Light that is our destiny.

However, thousands of years of judgment and suffering have already occurred. Moreover, for the first time in human history, this holy Book of Zohar and its profound spiritual truths and Light has reached the people. Our time of *earning* is effectively over.

With the assistance of the Zohar and our own consciousness, we now ignite the Light of the Creator in this world. *Time* is hereby removed from the cause-and-effect process. We experience immediate Light and joy with each act of kindness, with each good deed. The wicked experience immediate judgment with every negative action. The world undergoes immediate transformation, where Light and immortality are the only reality.

347. א"ר אַבָּא, כְּשֶׁהַקּוּדְשָׁא בְּרִיךְ הוּא עוֹשֶׂה דִין בַּשָּׂרִים שֶׁל מַעֲלָה, מַה כְּתִיב, כִּי רִוְּתָה בַּשָּׁמַיִם חַרְבִּי. וְכִי חֶרֶב אִית לַיְיָ׳. אֶלָּא אָמַר רַבִּי יִצְחָק, חֶרֶב אִית לֵיהּ, דִּכְתִיב, חֶרֶב לַיְיָ׳ מָלְאָה דָּם. וּכְתִיב וּבְחַרְבּוֹ אֶת כָּל בָּשָׂר.

347. Rabbi Aba said: When the Holy One, blessed be He, executes judgment upon the ministers above, it is written: "For my sword is sated in heavens" (Yeshayah 34:5). AND HE ASKS: Does Hashem have a sword? Rabbi Yitzchak said: He does have a sword, as it is written: "The sword of Hashem is full of blood" (Ibid. 6) and, "And with His sword, upon all flesh..." (Ibid. 66:16).

348. א"ר אַבָּא, הַחֶרֶב הַזֶּה הוּא הַדִּין שֶׁעוֹשֶׂה, דִּכְתִיב, וַיַּרְא אֶת מַלְאַךְ ה׳ עוֹמֵד בֵּין הָאָרֶץ וּבֵין הַשָּׁמַיִם וְחַרְבּוֹ שְׁלוּפָה בְּיָדוֹ. וְכִי חֶרֶב שְׁלוּפָה הָיְתָה בְּיַד הַמַּלְאָךְ, אֶלָּא, שֶׁהָיְתָה הָרְשׁוּת נְתוּנָה בְּיָדוֹ לַעֲשׂוֹת דִּין.

348. Rabbi Aba said: With this sword Hashem accomplishes the Judgment that He performs, as is written: "And saw the angel of Hashem standing between the earth and the heaven, with a drawn sword in his hand" (I Divrei Hayamim 21:16). AND HE ASKS: Was there a drawn sword in the hand of the angel? AND HE ANSWERS: Rather, it means he was granted permission to execute punishment, AND THIS PERMISSION IS TERMED "SWORD."

349. וְהָא אָמַר ריב"ל, אָמַר לִי מַלְאָךְ הַמָּוֶת, אִי לָאו דְּחַיְיסְנָא לִיקָרָא
דִּבְרִיָּיתָא, פָּרַעְנָא לְהוּ בֵּית הַשְּׁחִיטָה, כִּבְהֵמָה. א"ר אַבָּא, כֹּלָא מִשׁוּם
דְּאִתְיְיהִיב רְשׁוּתָא בִּידֵיה, לְמֶעְבַּד גְּמַר דִּינָא, הה"ד, וְחַרְבּוֹ שְׁלוּפָה
בְּיָדוֹ, הָרְשׁוּת נְתוּנָה בְּיָדוֹ לַעֲשׂוֹת דִּין. אִי הָכִי מַאי וַיָּשֶׁב חַרְבּוֹ אֶל
נְדָנָהּ. אָמַר רַבִּי אַבָּא, שֶׁנֶּחֱזַר הַדִּין לְבַעַל הַדִּין, וְהָרְשׁוּת לְמִי
שֶׁהָרְשׁוּת שֶׁלּוֹ.

349. HE RAISE A DIFFICULTY. For Rabbi Yehoshua bar Levi, said: The
Angel of Death told me, 'Were it not for my consideration for the honor of
creatures, I would reveal the place of slaughter (the slit in the neck) just like
in an animal.' SO IT APPEARS THAT THERE IS AN ACTUAL SWORD IN THE
HANDS OF THE ANGEL OF DEATH. Rabbi Aba said: Everything, MEANING
WHEREVER IT IS WRITTEN "SWORD" BY THE SUPERNAL ONES, INFERS
permission was granted to him to execute judgment, AND NOT THE ACTUAL
USING OF A SWORD. "AND I WILL REVEAL THEIR PLACE OF SLAUGHTER,"
MEANS THAT HE WILL REVEAL THE CAUSE OF DEATH, MEANING THE SIN,
WHICH IS LIKE A PLACE OF SLAUGHTER, WHICH IS THE CAUSE OF DEATH
OF THE ANIMAL. It is written: "With his sword drawn in his hand"
(Yehoshua 5:13), as permission was given to him to execute judgment. HE
ASKS: If so, what is the meaning of the passage: "And he put up his sword
again into its sheath" (I Divrei Hayamim 21:27)? Rabbi Aba said: IT MEANS
that the Judgment was returned to the Judge, and the permission TO
EXECUTE JUDGMENT WAS RETURNED to the one who possesses the
permission, MEANING TO HASHEM.

51. "And the children of Yisrael sighed"

A Synopsis

From the discourse on the title verse, we learn that this refers to the supernal children of Yisrael above. Rabbi Elazar then describes the nature of the punishment that the ministers of the other nations receive when God Judges them. We learn that they are made to pass through the River of Fire, the fire that defeats fire, where they lose their power and positions to ministers of other nations, who rule in their place.

The Relevance of the Passage

Our cries and laments ascend into Heaven, returning an equal measure of Light that forever soothes our sorrows and heals our troubles. The energy flowing from this mystical text painlessly burns away all our negative characteristics. This energy reaches into the Upper Worlds to banish the root of all evil at its very source. This generates love, respect, and unity between Yisrael and all the nations of the world.

350. וַיֵּאָנְחוּ בְּנֵי יִשְׂרָאֵל, וַיִּתְאַנְּחוּ לָא כְּתִיב, אֶלָּא וַיֵּאָנְחוּ, כְּלוֹמַר, נִתְאַנְּחוּ לוֹ לְמַעְלָה שֶׁהָאֲנָחָה הָיְתָה בִּשְׁבִילָם לְמַעְלָה.

350. "And the children of Yisrael sighed" (Shemot 2:23). HE ASKS: It is not written 'they sighed' with a reflexive form, WHICH WOULD SIGNIFY THAT THEY SIGHED BECAUSE OF THEIR OWN TROUBLES, but rather with a transitive form, WHICH CAN BE CONSTRUED TO MEAN THAT THEY POSSIBLY SIGHED BECAUSE OF THE TROUBLES OF OTHERS. HE ANSWERS: That is to say they sighed from above, that the sighing was for them from above, MEANING THAT THE ANGELS SIGHED FOR THE CHILDREN OF YISRAEL.

351. ר' בְּרֶכְיָה אָמַר, בְּנֵי יִשְׂרָאֵל דִּלְעֵילָא הֲווֹ, וּמַאן אִינּוּן בְּנֵי יִשְׂרָאֵל. אִינּוּן דְּאִתְקְרוּן בְּנֵי פוּלְחָנָא. כְּלוֹמַר, אוֹתָם שֶׁהֵם מִן הָעֲבוֹדָה שֶׁל מַעְלָה. וַתַּעַל שַׁוְעָתָם אֶל הָאֱלֹהִים, שֶׁעַד אוֹתָהּ שָׁעָה לָא עָלְתָה שַׁוְעָתָם לְפָנָיו.

351. Rabbi Brachyah said: THE PASSAGE, "THE CHILDREN OF YISRAEL SIGHED," refers to the children of Yisrael above, MEANING THE ANGELS. THE CONCLUSION OF THE PASSAGE: "FROM THE LABOR" IS TO TEACH who are the children of Yisrael IN THIS PASSAGE. Those who are called

"those who serve," mean those who are of the supernal service; NAMELY THE MINISTERING ANGELS. THEREFORE, IT IS NOT NECESSARY TO DEDUCE THIS FROM THE FACT THAT IT IS NOT WRITTEN WITH A REFLEXIVE VERB AS THE WORDS OF THE PREVIOUS PARAGRAPH. "And their cry rose up to the Elohim" TEACHES US that until that hour their cry did not rise up before Him.

352. א״ר יִצְחָק כַּד עָבֵיד קוּדְשָׁא בְּרִיךְ הוּא דִּינָא בְּפָמַלְיָיא שֶׁל מַעְלָה, הַהוּא דִּינָא מַאי הֲוֵי. אָמַר רבִּי אֶלְעָזָר, מַעְבַּר לְהוּ בְּהַהוּא נְהַר דִּינוּר, וְאַעְבַּר לוֹן מִשׁוּלְטָנֵיהוֹן, וּמָנֵי שׁוּלְטָנִין אַחֲרָנִין דִּשְׁאָר עַמִּין. א״ל וְהָא כְּתִיב מְשָׁרְתָיו אֵשׁ לוֹהֵט. א״ל, אִית אֶשָׁא קַשְׁיָא מֵאֶשָׁא, וְאִית אֶשָׁא דְּדַחְיָא אֶשָׁא.

352. Rabbi Yitzchak said: When the Holy One, blessed be He, punishes the company of supernal ministers, NAMELY THE MINISTERING ANGELS, AND THE MINISTERS OF THE SEVENTY NATIONS, what is the nature of that punishment? Rabbi Elazar said: He has them pass through the Dinur River, and depose them from their positions, and appoints different ministers of the other nations. He said to him: But it is written: "The flames of fire His ministers" (Tehilim 104:4). THUS, HOW DOES THIS AFFECT THEM IF THEY PASS THROUGH THE RIVER OF FIRE? He said to him: There is fire that is stronger than fire, and there is fire that rejects fire. THEREFORE, EVEN THOUGH THEY ARE OF FIRE, THE FIRE OF THE RIVER OF FIRE IS STRONGER. AND THERE, PUNISHMENT IS DONE TO THE FIERY ANGELS.

52. A sigh, a cry, a wail

A Synopsis

Rabbi Yitzchak discusses the distinction between a sigh, a cry and a wail. We learn that crying involves words, while wailing is crying without words. Because it comes from the heart, prayer with wailing is the most powerful form of prayer. Rabbi Brachyah gives the example of Samuel, who "wailed to Hashem all night" because this form of prayer allows the closest access to God. The intensity of this silent expression of prayer and sorrow is such that it can effect a change in the decreed Judgment for the individual, since wailing dominates the aspect of Justice in this world and the World to Come.

The Relevance of the Passage

Tears emerge from the eyes, so it is fitting that our eyes now commence the greatest of all wails simply by allowing them to caress the words that adorn this passage. Our heartfelt meditation here gathers the wailings and unutterable emotions of the Righteous throughout history and sends them heavenward. A torrent of healing Light is summoned forth, and all judgments decreed upon this world are repealed.

353. אָמַר רִבִּי יִצְחָק, תְּלַת עִנְיָינֵי הָכָא: אֲנָחָה, שַׁוְעָה, צְעָקָה. וְכָל חַד מִתְפָּרְשָׁא מֵאַחֲרָא. אֲנָחָה: כְּתִיב, וַיֵּאָנְחוּ בְּנֵי יִשְׂרָאֵל. צְעָקָה: דִּכְתִּיב, וַיִּזְעָקוּ. שַׁוְעָה: דִּכְתִּיב, וַתַּעַל שַׁוְעָתָם. וְכָל חַד בִּלְחוֹדוֹי מִתְפָּרְשָׁא, וְכֻלְּהוּ עָבְדוּ יִשְׂרָאֵל. אָמַר רִבִּי יְהוּדָה, צְעָקָה וְשַׁוְעָה עָבְדוּ, אֲנָחָה לָא עָבְדוּ, מַשְׁמַע מִדִּכְתִּיב וַיֵּאָנְחוּ וּלְמַעְלָה הָיְתָה הָאֲנָחָה בִּשְׁבִילָם.

353. Rabbi Yitzchak said: There are three subjects here: a sigh, a cry, a wail, and each one is different from the other. THEY ARE NOT SIMILAR TO EACH OTHER. "Sigh" as is written, "And the children of Yisrael sighed" (Shemot 2:23); "wail" as written, "And they wailed" (Ibid.); and "cry" as is written, "And their cry went up to Hashem." Each one is explained individually, and Yisrael did all of them. Rabbi Yehuda said: Yisrael did cry and wail, but they did not sigh! This is implied from what is written: "And they sighed," INSTEAD OF USING THE REFLEXIVE VERB, as there was sighing for them from above.

354. צְעָקָה וְשַׁוְעָה בְּמַאי אִתְפָּרְשָׁן, אָמַר רִבִּי יִצְחָק, אֵין לָךְ שַׁוְעָה,

אֶלָּא בַּתְּפִלָּה. שֶׁנֶּאֱמַר, שִׁמְעָה תְפִלָּתִי יְיָ' וְשַׁוְעָתִי הַאֲזִינָה. אֵלֶיךָ יְיָ'
שִׁוַּעְתִּי. שִׁוַּעְתִּי אֵלֶיךָ וַתִּרְפָּאֵנִי. צְעָקָה שֶׁצּוֹעֵק וְאֵינוֹ אוֹמֵר כְּלוּם. אָמַר
רִבִּי יְהוּדָה, הִלְכָּךְ גְּדוֹלָה צְעָקָה מִכּוּלָּן, שֶׁצְּעָקָה הִיא בַּלֵּב. הה"ד,
צָעַק לִבָּם אֶל יְיָ'. צְעָקָה וּזְעָקָה דָּבָר אֶחָד הוּא, וְזֶה קָרוֹבָה לְהַקּוּדְשָׁא
בְּרִיךְ הוּא, יוֹתֵר מִתְּפִלָּה וַאֲנָחָה, דִּכְתִיב כִּי אִם צָעֹק יִצְעַק אֵלַי שָׁמֹעַ
אֶשְׁמַע צַעֲקָתוֹ.

354. HE ASKS: How are wailing and crying different? Rabbi Yitzchak said:
There is no crying, except in prayer! As written: "Hear my prayer, Hashem,
and give ear to my cry" (Tehilim 39:13), AND SO, "But to You have I cried,
Hashem" (Tehilim 88:14) and, "I cried to You and You have healed me"
(Tehilim 30:3). SO WE SEE THAT "CRY" MEANS WORDS OF PRAYER, and
"wailing" means wailing without saying anything, MEANING WITHOUT
WORDS. Rabbi Yehuda said: Wailing is therefore greater than all of them,
because wailing is in the heart. This is written: "Their heart wailed to
Adonai" (Eichah 2:18). Wailing and crying out in prayer are closer to the
Holy One, blessed be He, than prayer and sighing, for it is written: "And
they wail to Me, I will surely hear their wail!" (Shemot 22:22).

355. אָמַר רִבִּי בְּרֶכְיָה, בְּשָׁעָה שֶׁאָמַר הַקּוּדְשָׁא בְּרִיךְ הוּא לִשְׁמוּאֵל,
נִחַמְתִּי כִּי הִמְלַכְתִּי אֶת שָׁאוּל לְמֶלֶךְ. מַה כְּתִיב, וַיִּחַר לִשְׁמוּאֵל, וַיִּזְעַק
אֶל יְיָ' כָּל הַלַּיְלָה. הִנִּיחַ הַכֹּל, וְלָקַח צְעָקָה, מִשּׁוּם דְּהִיא קָרוֹבָה
לְקוּדְשָׁא בְּרִיךְ הוּא יַתִּיר מִכֻּלְּהוּ, הה"ד, וְעַתָּה הִנֵּה צַעֲקַת בְּנֵי יִשְׂרָאֵל
בָּאָה אֵלָי.

355. Rabbi Brachyah said: The Holy One, blessed be He, said to Samuel, "I
regret that I have set up Saul to be king" (II Shmuel 15:11). It is written: "It
grieved Samuel, and he wailed to Hashem all night" (Ibid.). He forsook
everything, MEANING SIGHING AND CRYING, and took to bewailing because
it is closer to the Holy One, blessed be He, than all of them. This is what is
written: "And now, behold the wail of the children of Yisrael have come
before Me" (Shemot 3:9).

356. ת"ר, הַאי מַאן דְּצַלֵּי וּבָכֵי וְצָעִיק, עַד לָא יָכִיל לְמִרְחַשׁ

בִּשְׁפְוָותֵיה, הַאי צְלוֹתָא שְׁלֵימָתָא דְּהִיא בְּלִבָּא, וּלְעוֹלָם לָא הַדְרָא רֵיקַנְיָא. אָמַר רִבִּי יְהוּדָה, גְּדוֹלָה צְעָקָה, שְׁקוֹרֵעַ גְּזַר דִּינוֹ שֶׁל אָדָם מִכָּל יָמָיו.

356. The sages taught that it is considered a complete prayer in the heart when one prays and weeps and wails until he can no longer move his lips. It never returns empty, but rather is accepted. Rabbi Yehuda said: Wailing has great value, for it tears the decreed judgment of a person from all his days.

357. רִבִּי יִצְחָק אָמַר, גְּדוֹלָה צְעָקָה, שְׁמוֹשֶׁלֶת עַל מִדַּת הַדִּין שֶׁל מַעְלָה. רִבִּי יוֹסֵי אָמַר, גְּדוֹלָה צְעָקָה, שְׁמוֹשֶׁלֶת בְּעוֹה"ז וּבְעוֹה"ב. בִּשְׁבִיל צְעָקָה נוֹחֵל הָאָדָם הָעוֹה"ז וְהָעוֹה"ב, דִּכְתִיב, וַיִּצְעֲקוּ אֶל ה' בַּצַּר לָהֶם מִמְּצוּקוֹתֵיהֶם יַצִּילֵם.

357. Rabbi Yitzchak said: Wailing is of great value for it has power over the attribute of Judgment above. Rabbi Yosi said: Wailing is of great value for it has power in this world and in the World to Come. Because of wailing, a person acquires this world and the World to Come, as is written: "They wailed to Hashem in their distress. He delivered them from their afflictions" (Tehilim 107:6).

53. "My beloved is mine, and I am his: he feeds among the lilies"

A Synopsis

Rabbi Shimon first discourses on the creation of the upper and lower worlds. He explains that God created both worlds at the same moment by one thought. He chose the angels to be His servants in the upper realm and He chose Yisrael to be His children in the lower realm. In the title verse, "My beloved is mine, and I am His," signifies the reciprocation of this filial relationship between God and Yisrael.

Rabbi Shimon then interprets the symbolic meaning of, "He feeds among the roses." This, we're told, signifies that God leads this world from the attribute of Judgment, alluded to by the red color of the rose, to the attribute of Mercy, alluded to by the white color of the nectar. Rabbi Aba then expounds upon the spiritual significance of the scent of the rose, and explaining that this is why we smell the myrtle at the end of Shabbat.

Another explanation of the title verse interprets it as an allusion to the sinner, who is called 'red', who puts a sacrificial offering into the fire, which is also red, and then sprinkles the blood around the altar. The white smoke that rises from the burnt offering alludes to the conversion of the attribute of Justice into the attribute of Compassion. The burning of incense involves the same principle, since both the offering and the scent of the offering is red and white. Rabbi Yosi then explains that this also applies to the individual, who must offer red and white in order to obtain atonement. Since the destruction of the Temple, man must sacrifice his own fat (white) and blood (red) by fasting. The fasting causes the body to weaken and burn, symbolizing the sacrificial fire, and the scent that rises from his mouth is then an altar of atonement.

The section concludes with alternative explanations of the title verse, one of which points out that just as roses could not exist without thorns, the Righteous would not be recognizable without the wicked.

The Relevance of the Passage

The essential purpose behind our creation was for the Creator to bestow endless joy upon His created beings. Thus, God created an infinite *Desire to Receive* all that He could share. This *Desire to Receive* is man's essential feature and core being. In fact, this entire universe, known as Malchut, is comprised of this great Desire.

The Light corresponds to the Creator's Will to Share. This infinite sharing aspect is embodied by the Upper World, known as Zeir Anpin. When Malchut (our world) is joined with Zeir Anpin (the

Upper World), the Divine act of sharing can now manifest. Our world and our souls receive infinite Light.

This section, notably paragraph 359, unites Zeir Anpin with Malchut, the Light of the Creator with our souls. Untold pleasure and serenity fills our lives.

Later in this passage, the Zohar's poetic references to the red rose and its white nectar ignite the forces of mercy and compassion, so that judgment and evil may be purged from our world. The traits that compel us to sin cease to exist, as the scent of Light emanating from this passage eradicates them.

We summon forth the power of the ancient sacrifices to cleanse away our iniquities. As we meditate upon this action, we must acknowledge and sacrifice our own self-indulgent qualities, which correspond to the fat burned upon the altar. Our remorseful reading becomes our personal atonement for all of our iniquities. We also share this energy with the world, causing humanity to atone for its collective sins throughout history.

358. וּמֹשֶׁה הָיָה רוֹעֶה אֶת צֹאן יִתְרוֹ חוֹתְנוֹ כֹּהֵן מִדְיָן. רִבִּי שִׁמְעוֹן פָּתַח, דּוֹדִי לִי וַאֲנִי לוֹ הָרוֹעֶה בַּשּׁוֹשַׁנִּים. אר"ש, אוֹי לָהֶם לַבְּרִיּוֹת, שֶׁאֵינָם מַשְׁגִּיחִים וְאֵינָם יוֹדְעִים, בְּשָׁעָה שֶׁעָלָה בְּמַחֲשָׁבָה לִפְנֵי הַקָּדוֹשׁ ב"ה, לִבְרוֹא עוֹלָמוֹ, כָּל הָעוֹלָמוֹת עָלוּ בְּמַחֲשָׁבָה אַחַת, וּבְמַחֲשָׁבָה זוֹ נִבְרְאוּ כּוּלָם, הה"ד, כֻּלָּם בְּחָכְמָה עָשִׂיתָ. וּבְמַחֲשָׁבָה זוֹ, שֶׁהִיא הַחָכְמָה, נִבְרָא הָעוֹלָם הַזֶּה, וְהָעוֹלָם שֶׁל מַעְלָה.

358. "Now Moses kept the flock of Jethro his father-in-law, the priest of Midian" (Shemot 3:1). Rabbi Shimon opened the discussion, saying: "My Beloved is mine, and I am his: he feeds among the lilies" (Shir Hashirim 2:16). Rabbi Shimon said: Woe to people who do not pay attention and do not know that all the worlds arose in one thought at the moment it arose in thought before the Holy One, blessed be He, to create His world. And with this thought were they all created, as it is written: "In wisdom have You made them all" (Tehilim 104:24). And with this thought, which is wisdom, this world and the world above were created.

359. נָטָה יְמִינוֹ, וּבָרָא הָעוֹלָם שֶׁל מַעְלָה. נָטָה שְׂמֹאלוֹ, וּבָרָא הָעוֹלָם הַזֶּה, הה"ד, אַף יָדִי יָסְדָה אֶרֶץ וִימִינִי טִפְּחָה שָׁמָיִם. קוֹרֵא אֲנִי אֲלֵיהֶם

יַעַמְדוּ יַחְדָּו. וְכֻלָּם בְּרֶגַע אַחַת נִבְרְאוּ, וְעָשָׂה הָעוֹלָם הַזֶּה, כְּנֶגֶד הָעוֹלָם שֶׁל מַעְלָה. וְכָל מַה שֶּׁיֵּשׁ לְמַעְלָה, כְּדוּגְמָתוֹ לְמַטָּה. וְכָל מַה שֶּׁיֵּשׁ לְמַטָּה, כְּדוּגְמָתוֹ בַּיָּם. וְהַכֹּל אֶחָד. בָּרָא בָּעֶלְיוֹנִים הַמַּלְאָכִים, בָּרָא בעוה"ז בְּנֵי אָדָם, בָּרָא בַּיָּם לִוְיָתָן, כד"א לְחַבֵּר אֶת הָאֹהֶל לִהְיוֹת אֶחָד.

359. He stretched out His right hand and created the world above, WHICH IS ZEIR ANPIN. He stretched out His left hand and created this world, WHICH IS MALCHUT. This is what is written: "My hand has also laid the foundation of the earth," WHICH IS MALCHUT, "and My right hand has spanned the heavens," WHICH IS ZEIR ANPIN. "When I call to them, they stand up together" (Yeshayah 48:13). All of them were created in a moment, and He made this world corresponding to the world above. The model of all that is above EMERGED below, FOR THERE IS NOTHING BELOW THAT HAS NO ROOT IN THE HIGHER WORLDS. The sea is the model of all that there is below ON THE EARTH, and it is all one. He created angels in the higher worlds. He created people in this world. He created a Leviathan in the sea, as is written: "To couple the tent together, that it might be one" (Shemot 36:18).

360. כְּתִיב בָּאָדָם, כִּי בְּצֶלֶם אֱלֹהִים עָשָׂה אֶת הָאָדָם. וּכְתִיב, וַתְּחַסְרֵהוּ מְעַט מֵאֱלֹהִים. אִי בְּנֵי נָשָׁא יַקִּירִין בְּעוֹבָדוֹי כָּל הַאי, וְאִינוּן מִתְאַבְּדִין מֵעֲפָר דְּבֵירָא, בַּמֶּה אַתְיָין לְשַׁאֲבָא מִנֵּיהּ. וּבָחַר בָּעֶלְיוֹנִים, וּבָחַר בְּיִשְׂרָאֵל, לָעֶלְיוֹנִים לֹא קָרָא בָּנִים, לַתַּחְתּוֹנִים קָרָא בָּנִים. הה"ד בָּנִים אַתֶּם לַה' אֱלֹהֵיכֶם. הוּא קָרָא לָהֶם בָּנִים, וְהֵם קָרְאוּ לוֹ אָב, דִּכְתִיב כִּי אַתָּה אָבִינוּ. וּכְתִיב דּוֹדִי לִי וַאֲנִי לוֹ. הוּא בָּחַר בִּי, וַאֲנִי בָּחַרְתִּי בּוֹ.

360. It is written about Adam: "For in the image of Elohim made He man" (Beresheet 9:6), and: "Yet You have made him a little lower than the angels" (Tehilim 8:5). If people are so precious with their actions yet they perish from the dust of the well, MEANING THEY PERISH THROUGH THE KLIPOT THAT CLING TO THE DUST OF MALCHUT, WHICH IS CALLED 'WELL', how can they come to draw SUSTENANCE from the well? And He chose those above, THE ANGELS, and He chose Yisrael. He did not call those above children, but those below He did call 'children'. This is what is written: "You are the children of Hashem your Elohim" (Devarim 14:1). He called them children and they called Him Father, as is written: "For You are our Father" (Yeshayah 63:16), and also: "My Beloved is mine, and I am his" (Shir Hashirm 2:16). He chose me and I chose Him.

361. הָרוֹעֶה בַּשׁוֹשַׁנִּים, הוּא רוֹעֶה בַּשׁוֹשַׁנִּים, אע"פ שֶׁהַקּוֹצִים סָבִיב לָהֶם, וְאֵין אַחֵר יָכוֹל לִרְעוֹת בַּשּׁוֹשַׁנִּים כְּמוֹתוֹ. ד"א הָרוֹעֶה בַּשׁוֹשַׁנִּים, מַה שׁוֹשָׁן זֶה הוּא אָדוֹם, וּמֵימָיו לְבָנִים, כַּךְ הַקּוּדְשָׁא בְּרִיךְ הוּא, מַנְהִיג עוֹלָמוֹ, ממה"ד למה"ר. וּכְתִיב אִם יִהְיוּ חֲטָאֵיכֶם כַּשָּׁנִים כַּשֶּׁלֶג יַלְבִּינוּ.

361. "He feeds among the lilies." He grazes among the lilies even though the thorns surround them, MEANING THE KLIPOT, and no other can feed among the roses as He. Another explanation of, "He feeds among the lillies," is that as the lily is red and the nectar THAT IS SUCKED FROM IT is white, so the Holy One, blessed be He, leads His world from the attribute of Judgment, ALLUDED TO BY THE RED, to the attribute of Mercy, WHICH IS ALLUDED TO IN THE COLOR WHITE. As it is written: "Though your sins be like scarlet, they shall be white as snow" (Yeshayah 1:18).

362. רְבִּי אַבָּא הֲוָה אָזִיל בְּאוֹרְחָא, וַהֲוָה עִמֵּיהּ רְבִּי יִצְחָק. אַדְהֲווֹ אַזְלֵי, פָּגַע בְּאִינוּן וְרָדִים, נָטַל חַד רְבִּי אַבָּא בִּידוֹי וַהֲוָה אָזִיל. פָּגַע בְּהוּ רְבִּי יוֹסֵי, אָמַר וַדַּאי שְׁכִינְתָּא הָכָא, וַאֲנָא חֲמֵינָא בִּידוֹי דְּרְבִּי אַבָּא, לְמֵילַף חָכְמְתָא סַגִּיאָה, דְּהָא יָדַעְנָא, דְּרְבִּי אַבָּא לָא נָטַל הַאי, אֶלָּא לְאַחֲזָאָה חָכְמְתָא.

362. Rabbi Aba was traveling on the road with Rabbi Yitzchak. They came upon some roses. Rabbi Aba took one ROSE in his hands and continued walking. Rabbi Yosi met them and said: It is certain that the Shechinah is here. I see a rose in the hands of Rabbi Aba AND THAT HE IS to learn FROM IT much wisdom, because I know he took it only to teach that wisdom.

363. אָמַר רְבִּי אַבָּא, תִּיב בְּרִי תִּיב. יָתְבוּ. אָרַח רְבִּי אַבָּא בְּהַהוּא וַרְדָא, אָמַר, וַדַּאי אֵין הָעוֹלָם מִתְקַיֵּים אֶלָּא עַל הָרֵיחַ. דְּהָא חֲזֵינָא דְּלֵית נַפְשָׁא מִתְקַיְּימָא אֶלָּא עַל רֵיחָא. וְעַל דָּא, הֲדַס בְּמוֹצָאֵי שַׁבָּת.

363. Rabbi Aba said: Sit, my son, sit. They sat down. Rabbi Aba smelled that rose. He said the world is definitely maintained only by scent. FOR IT IS THE SECRET OF THE MOCHIN OF THE ILLUMINATION OF CHOCHMAH THAT RADIATE FROM BELOW UPWARDS, AS DOES SCENT. Because I see that the soul is maintained only through scent, therefore we smell the myrtle at the end of Shabbat IN ORDER TO DRAW THE MOCHIN OF THE ILLUMINATION OF CHOCHMAH, WHICH IS THE SECRET OF ITS SCENT, AS ALREADY MENTIONED.

364. פָּתַח וְאָמַר דּוֹדִי לִי וַאֲנִי לוֹ הָרוֹעֶה בַּשּׁוֹשַׁנִּים. מִי גָּרַם לִי, שֶׁאֲנִי לְדוֹדִי וְדוֹדִי לִי, מִפְּנֵי שֶׁהוּא מַנְהִיג עוֹלָמוֹ בַּשּׁוֹשַׁנִּים. מַה שׁוֹשָׁן יֵשׁ בּוֹ רֵיחַ, וְהוּא אָדֹם, מוֹצְקִין אוֹתוֹ, וְהוּא מִתְהַפֵּךְ לַלָּבָן, וּלְעוֹלָם רֵיחוֹ לֹא זָז. כָּךְ הַקּוּדְשָׁא בְּרִיךְ הוּא, מַנְהִיג עוֹלָמוֹ בְּדֶרֶךְ זֶה, שֶׁאִלְמָלֵא כֵּן לֹא יִתְקַיֵּים הָעוֹלָם בִּשְׁבִיל הָאָדָם הַחוֹטֵא. וְהַחוֹטֵא נִקְרָא אָדֹם, כְּמָה דְאַתְּ אָמַר, אִם יִהְיוּ חֲטָאֵיכֶם כַּשָּׁנִים כַּשֶּׁלֶג יַלְבִּינוּ, מַקְרִיב קָרְבָּנוֹ לָאֵשׁ שֶׁהוּא אָדֹם. זוֹרֵק הַדָּם, סָבִיב לַמִּזְבֵּחַ שֶׁהוּא אָדֹם. מִדַּת הַדִּין אָדֹם, מוֹצְקִין אוֹתוֹ, וְעוֹלֶה הֶעָשָׁן כֻּלּוֹ לָבָן, וְאָז הָאָדֹם נֶהְפָּךְ לְלָבָן, נֶהְפָּךְ מִדַּת הַדִּין לְמִדַּת הָרַחֲמִים.

364. He opened the discussion, saying: "My beloved is mine, and I am his: he feeds among the lilies" (Shir Hashirm 2:16), MEANING that my Beloved is mine and I am His, because He leads His world with lilies. The lily has a scent and it is red, yet squeeze it and it turns white. But its scent never leaves, and the Holy One, blessed be He, does lead His world in this way, for otherwise the world would not exist, because of the sinner. And the sinner is called 'red', as written: "Through your sins be like scarlet, they shall be white as snow." SIMILARLY, THE SINNER makes his offering to fire, which is red, then sprinkles the blood, which is red, around the altar. So is the attribute of Judgment ALLUDED TO IN red. Squeeze it, MEANING WHEN THE OFFERING IS BURNED ON THE ALTAR, and the smoke rises all white. Then the red turns into white, WHICH INDICATES THAT the attribute of Judgment turns into the attribute of Mercy.

365. וְתָא חֲזֵי, כָּל מדה"ד, אֵין צָרִיךְ הָרֵיחַ שֶׁלּוֹ, אֶלָּא מִצַּד אוֹדֶם. וְהַיְינוּ דְּאָמַר רבּי יְהוּדָה, מַה דִּכְתִּיב, וַיִּתְגּוֹדְדוּ כְּמִשְׁפָּטָם וְגו' עַד שְׁפָךְ

דָּם עֲלֵיהֶם. אֶלָּא הָיוּ יוֹדְעִים, שֶׁלֹּא יַשִּׂיגוּ מִמִּדַּת הַדִּין כִּרְצוֹנָם, זוּלָתִי בָּאוֹדֶם.

365. Come and behold: the attribute of Judgment needs its scent only from the red part, BECAUSE THE SCENT, WHICH IS THE SECRET OF THE ILLUMINATION OF CHOCHMAH, IS NOT DRAWN FROM THE WHITE PART – WHICH IS THE RIGHT COLUMN WHICH IS ENTIRELY CHASSADIM – BUT RATHER FROM THE RED PART, WHICH IS THE LEFT COLUMN, FROM WHICH SOURCE IS CHOCHMAH. And Rabbi Yehuda said that it is written: "And they cut themselves according to their fashion with swords and lances till the blood gushed out upon them" (I Melachim 18:28), but they knew that they would not get from the attribute of judgment, WHICH IS MALCHUT, what they wanted – NAMELY, TO DRAW THE CHOCHMAH FROM ABOVE TO BELOW, WHICH ALL IDOL WORSHIPERS WANT – except with red – MEANING THROUGH THE LEFT COLUMN, WHICH IS RED. AND THEY THEREFORE CUT THEMSELVES WITH SWORDS UNTIL BLOOD GUSHED OVER THEM, IN ORDER TO ATTRACT THE RED.

366. אָמַר רַבִּי יִצְחָק, וְעוֹד, אוֹדֶם וְלָבָן נִקְרָב לְעוֹלָם, וְהָרֵיחַ עוֹלֶה מִשְׁתֵּיהֶן. מַה הַשּׁוֹשָׁן אָדוֹם וְלָבָן, כָּךְ רֵיחַ הַקָּרְבָּן. וְהַקָּרְבָּן, מֵאָדוֹם וְלָבָן. בֹּא וּרְאֵה מֵרֵיחַ הַקְּטוֹרֶת, שֶׁהַשַּׁמָּנִים, מֵהֶם אֲדוּמִים, וּמֵהֶם לְבָנִים, כְּגוֹן הַלְּבוֹנָה, שֶׁהוּא לָבָן, מֹר דְּרוֹר אָדוֹם, וְהָרֵיחַ עוֹלֶה מֵאָדוֹם וְלָבָן. וְעַ"כ מַנְהִיג עוֹלָמוֹ בַּשּׁוֹשַׁנִּים, שֶׁהוּא אָדוֹם וְלָבָן. וּכְתִיב לְהַקְרִיב לִי חֵלֶב וָדָם.

366. Rabbi Yitzchak said: moreover, red and white, WHICH ARE LEFT AND RIGHT, are always close and the scent arises from them both. This is BECAUSE THE CHOCHMAH, WHICH IS IN THE LEFT, IS NOT ABLE TO ILLUMINATE WITHOUT BEING CLOTHED WITH THE LIGHT OF CHASSADIM, THAT IS IN THE RIGHT. AND THEREFORE, as the lily is red and white, so is the scent of the offering and the offering ITSELF is of red and white. Come and behold: from the scent of the incense, some of the spices are red and some are white; namely, the frankincense is white, pure myrrh is red, and the scent rises from red and white. Therefore, He leads His world in lilies, which are red and white. And it is written: "To offer Me the fat and the blood" (Yechezkel 44:15). THE FAT IS WHITE AND THE BLOOD IS RED.

367. כְּנֶגֶד זֶה, אָדָם מַקְרִיב חֶלְבּוֹ וְדָמוֹ, וּמִתְכַּפֵּר לוֹ, זֶה אָדוֹם, וְזֶה לָבָן. מַה הַשּׁוֹשָׁן שֶׁהוּא אָדוֹם וְהוּא לָבָן, אֵין מוֹצְקִין אוֹתוֹ לַחֲזוֹר כֻּלּוֹ לָבָן, אֶלָּא בָּאֵשׁ. כָּךְ הַקָּרְבָּן אֵין מוֹצְקִין אוֹתוֹ לַחֲזוֹר כֻּלּוֹ לָבָן, אֶלָּא בָּאֵשׁ. עַכְשָׁיו, מִי שֶׁיּוֹשֵׁב בְּתַעֲנִיתוֹ, וּמַקְרִיב חֶלְבּוֹ וְדָמוֹ, אֵינוֹ נִצְמָק לַחֲזוֹר כֻּלּוֹ לָבָן, אֶלָּא בָּאֵשׁ. דְּאר״י, מִתּוֹךְ תַּעֲנִיתוֹ שֶׁל אָדָם, מַחֲלִישִׁין אֵבָרָיו, וְגוֹבֵר עָלָיו הָאֵשׁ, וּבְאוֹתָהּ שָׁעָה, צָרִיךְ לְהַקְרִיב חֶלְבּוֹ וְדָמוֹ בְּאוֹתוֹ הָאֵשׁ, וְהוּא הַנִּקְרָא מִזְבֵּחַ כַּפָּרָה.

367. Correspondingly, a person who offers his fat and blood is granted atonement, for the one is red and the other is white. Just as the lily, which is red and white, is not cast to turn completely white, save in fire, similarly the offering is not cast so as to turn it completely white, except in fire. Now one who fasts and offers his fat and blood does not get thin so as to turn completely white, save in fire. For Rabbi Yitzchak said, through the fasting of man, his limbs become weakened and the fire gains control over him, and at that time he must offer his fat and blood in that fire, and that is called 'the Altar of Atonement'.

368. וְהַיְינוּ דְּרַבִּי אֶלְעָזָר, כַּד הֲוָה יָתִיב בְּתַעֲנִיתָא, הֲוָה מְצַלֵּי וְאָמַר, גָּלוּי וְיָדוּעַ לְפָנֶיךָ ה׳ אֱלֹהַי וֵאלֹהֵי אֲבוֹתַי, שֶׁהִקְרַבְתִּי לְפָנֶיךָ חֶלְבִּי וְדָמִי, וְהִרְתַּחְתִּי אוֹתָם בַּחֲמִימוּת חוּלְשַׁת גּוּפִי, יְהִי רָצוֹן מִלְּפָנֶיךָ, שֶׁיְּהֵא הָרֵיחַ הָעוֹלֶה מִפִּי בְּשָׁעָה זוֹ, כְּרֵיחַ הָעוֹלֶה מֵהַקָּרְבָּן בָּאֵשׁ הַמִּזְבֵּחַ, וְתִרְצֵנִי.

368. This is what Rabbi Elazar would pray and say when he fasted: It is revealed and known before You, Hashem, my Elohim and the Elohim of my fathers, that I have offered up before You my fat and blood, and I have seethed them with the heat of the weakness of my body. May it be Your will that the scent that rises from my mouth at this moment shall be as the scent that rises from an offering in the fire of the altar, and You shall favor me.

369. נִמְצָא, שֶׁאָדָם הוּא מַקְרִיב בְּתַעֲנִיתוֹ הַחֵלֶב וְהַדָּם, וְהָרֵיחַ שֶׁעוֹלֶה מִפִּיו, הוּא מִזְבֵּחַ כַּפָּרָה, וּלְפִיכָךְ תִּקְּנוּ הַתְּפִלָּה בִּמְקוֹם הַקָּרְבָּן, וּבִלְבַד שֶׁיִּתְכַּוֵּין לְמָה דְּאַמְרָן. אָמַר רַבִּי יִצְחָק, מִכָּאן וּלְהָלְאָה כְּתִיב, כָּל דָּבָר

אֲשֶׁר יָבוֹא בָאֵשׁ תַּעֲבִירוּ בָאֵשׁ וְטָהֵר. אָמַר רִבִּי יוֹסֵי, כְּשֶׁהָיָה בֵּית הַמִּקְדָּשׁ קַיָּים, אָדָם מַקְרִיב קָרְבְּנוֹ בְּעִנְיָן זֶה, וּמִתְכַּפֵּר לוֹ. עַכְשָׁיו, תְּפִלָּתוֹ שֶׁל אָדָם מְכַפֵּר לוֹ בִּמְקוֹם הַקָּרְבָּן, כִּי הַאי גַּוְונָא.

369. So we find that a person offers in his fasting the fat and blood, and the scent that rises from his mouth is an altar of atonement. Therefore, they instituted prayer in place of the offering, with the stipulation that one should intend that which we said. Rabbi Yitzchak said: From here and further it is written, "Everything that passes through the fire, you shall make it go through fire, and it shall be clean" (Bemidbar 31:23), MEANING THAT THROUGH THE FIRE IT HAS BEEN RETURNED TO BE ENTIRELY WHITE. Rabbi Yosi said: When the Temple was in existence, a person would offer his sacrifices in this manner, IN THE SECRET OF THE RED AND WHITE AND THE SCENT THAT RISES FROM THEM, AND ITS RETURN TO WHITENESS THROUGH THE FIRE, AS EXPLAINED. And he is granted atonement. Now, the prayer of a person atones for him in place of the offering in that way, OF THE INTENTION CONCERNING THE OFFERING.

370. דָּבָר אַחֵר, דּוֹדִי לִי וַאֲנִי לוֹ הָרוֹעֶה בַּשּׁוֹשַׁנִּים. מַה הַשּׁוֹשַׁנִּים קוֹצִין מְצוּיִין בְּתוֹכָם, אַף הַקָּדוֹשׁ בָּרוּךְ הוּא, מַנְהִיג עוֹלָמוֹ בְּצַדִּיקִים וּרְשָׁעִים. מַה הַשּׁוֹשַׁנִּים, אִלְמָלֵא הַקּוֹצִים, אֵין הַשּׁוֹשַׁנִּים מִתְקַיְּימִין. כָּךְ אִלְמָלֵא הָרְשָׁעִים, אֵין הַצַּדִּיקִים נִיכָּרִים. דְּאָמַר רִבִּי יְהוּדָה, בְּמָה הַצַּדִּיקִים נִיכָּרִים, מִתּוֹךְ שֶׁיֵּשׁ רְשָׁעִים, דְּאִלְמָלֵא רְשָׁעִים אֵין הַצַּדִּיקִים נִיכָּרִים. ד"א הָרוֹעֶה בַּשּׁוֹשַׁנִּים, הַמַּנְהִיג עוֹלָמוֹ בְּשֵׁשׁ שָׁנִים, וְהַשְּׁבִיעִית שַׁבָּת לַה'. ד"א בַּשּׁוֹשַׁנִּים, בְּאוֹתָם שֶׁשּׁוֹנִים בַּתּוֹרָה.

370. Another explanation OF THE PASSAGE: "My Beloved is mine, and I am his: he feeds among the lilies" (Shir Hashirim 2:16). Just as lilies have thorns prevalent among them, the Holy One, blessed be He, conducts His world with righteous and wicked people. Just as lilies could not exist without the thorns, the righteous would not be recognizable were it not for the wicked. For Rabbi Yehuda said: How are the righteous recognized? Because there are wicked people. Another explanation: "He feeds among the lilies," He leads His world in six years. BECAUSE THE WORD "SHOSHANIM" ('LILIES') IS COMPOSED OF THE LETTERS SHESH-SHANIM (SIX YEARS), and the seventh is Shabbat to Hashem. Another explanation:

"Among the lilies," MEANS by those who study the Torah, BECAUSE "*SHOSHANIM*" HAS THE SAME DERIVATION AS *SHONEH* ('TO STUDY').

54. "Now Moses kept the flock"

A Synopsis

Rabbi Chiya begins the discourse on the title verse by explaining that as a worthy shepherd guides his flock to good pastures and treats them tenderly, God guides His children on the straight and righteous path. We learn that God saw that Moses was a wise and considerate shepherd over Jethro's flock and He knew that Moses would lead Yisrael with these same qualities. Therefore, God made him king over all of Yisrael. Rabbi Yehuda then expounds upon the qualities and benefits of a good leader of Yisrael.

Rabbi Yosi follows this discussion with a discourse on Moses' journey to Mount Sinai. We learn that both Moses and the mountain were prepared for each other from the time of Creation. As soon as Moses saw it, he knew it was the mountain of God and he was drawn to it. He saw birds flying from the mountain and falling at his feet, and interpreting this sign, he led Yisrael "far away into the desert," and ascended the Mountain alone. From this, there follows a discussion of the fiery flame in which God appeared to Moses. We learn that this flame represents Judgment, since the flame appeared at the time of Minchah. In their discussion, the Rabbis also explain that because the evening is a time of Judgment and the morning is a time of Mercy, it is proper to eat bread in the morning and meat at night.

The Relevance of the Passage

Pain, hurt, suffering, and turmoil occur in our lives when we veer off the path of spiritual growth. The afflictions of life are signs and guideposts that attempt to set us back on course. However, our ego attempts to explain away these misfortunes as random chaos. If we pay heed to our ego, then the pain becomes even greater.

This passage proactively awakens all humanity to the truth of our existence – to the value and priceless benefits of positive behavior, of deeds of kindness, and of unconditional love for friends and foes. In turn, the pain of life vanishes.

Finally, the spiritual energy of the cosmic morning, which is mercy, blankets the world with a glorious radiance. Judgments are overturned. Darkness is banished from the world. Goodness and Light reign supreme as we achieve our ultimate destiny – infinite fulfillment through our unification with the Light of the Creator.

‎371. וּמֹשֶׁה הָיָה רוֹעֶה אֶת צֹאן יִתְרוֹ חוֹתְנוֹ כֹּהֵן מִדְיָן. רִבִּי חִיָּיא פָּתַח

‎וְאָמַר, מִזְמוֹר לְדָוִד יְיָ׳ רוֹעִי לֹא אֶחְסָר. כְּלוֹמַר, יְיָ׳ רוֹעִי: יְיָ׳ הָרוֹעֶה

שֶׁלִּי. מַה הָרוֹעֶה מַנְהִיג אֶת הַצֹּאן, וּמוֹלִיכָם לְמִרְעֶה טוֹב, לְמִרְעֶה שָׁמֵן, בִּמְקוֹם נַחֲלֵי מָיִם, מְיַשֵּׁר הֲלִיכָתָן בְּצֶדֶק וּבְמִשְׁפָּט. אַף הַקָּדוֹשׁ בָּרוּךְ הוּא, כְּתִיב בִּנְאוֹת דֶּשֶׁא יַרְבִּיצֵנִי עַל מֵי מְנוּחוֹת יְנַהֲלֵנִי נַפְשִׁי יְשׁוֹבֵב.

371. "Now Moses kept the flock of Jethro his father-in-law, the priest of Midian" (Shemot 3:1). Rabbi Chiya opened the discussion, saying: "A Psalm of David, Hashem is my shepherd; I shall not want" (Tehilim 23:1). "Hashem is my shepherd," means "the shepherd of mine." In the same way that a shepherd leads his sheep and brings them to a good pasture, to a fat pasture, to a place of a stream of water, he straightens their path with righteousness and Justice. Also of the Holy One, blessed be He, it is written, "He makes me to lie down in green pastures, He leads me beside the still waters. He restores my soul" (Ibid. 2-3).

372. אָמַר רִבִּי יוֹסֵי, דֶּרֶךְ הָרוֹעֶה, לִנְהוֹג בְּצֶדֶק אֶת צֹאנוֹ, לְהַרְחִיקָם מִן הַגָּזֵל, לְהַנְהִיגָם בְּמִישׁוֹר, וְהַשֵּׁבֶט בְּיָדוֹ שֶׁלֹּא יַטּוּ יָמִין וּשְׂמֹאל. כָּךְ הַקָּדוֹשׁ בָּרוּךְ הוּא, הוּא רוֹעֶה אֶת יִשְׂרָאֵל לְהַנְהִיגָם בְּמִישׁוֹר, וּבְכָל עֵת הַשֵּׁבֶט בְּיָדוֹ שֶׁלֹּא יַטּוּ יָמִין וּשְׂמֹאל.

372. Rabbi Yosi said: The way of the shepherd is to lead his flock with righteousness, to distance them from stealing, to lead them on a plain, and at all times the rod is in his hand so that they do not turn off right or left. So does the Holy One, blessed be He, do. He herds Yisrael, leading them on a plain, with the rod constantly in His hand, so they will not turn right or left.

373. דָּבָר אַחֵר וּמֹשֶׁה הָיָה רוֹעֶה, אָמַר רִבִּי יוֹסֵי, תֵּדַע לָךְ, שֶׁכָּל זְמַן שֶׁהָרוֹעֶה חָכָם לְנַהֵל אֶת צֹאנוֹ, הוּא מוּכָן לְקַבֵּל עוֹל מַלְכוּת שָׁמַיִם. אִם הָרוֹעֶה שׁוֹטֶה, עָלָיו נִקְרָא תִּקְוָה לִכְסִיל מִמֶּנּוּ.

373. Another explanation of: "Now Moses kept the flock." Rabbi Yosi said: Know that as long as the shepherd is skillful in managing his sheep, he is ready to accept the yoke of the Kingdom of Heaven. If the shepherd is a simpleton, it is said of him: "There is more hope of a fool than of him" (Mishlei 26:12).

374. אָמַר רִבִּי יְהוּדָה, מֹשֶׁה חָכָם הָיָה, וּבָקִי לִנְהוֹג אֶת צֹאנוֹ. בֹּא וּרְאֵה, מִדָּוִד, שֶׁנֶּאֱמַר וְהִנֵּה רוֹעֶה בַּצֹּאן. לְלַמֶּדְךָ שֶׁדָּוִד חָכָם גָּדוֹל הָיָה, וְהָיָה רוֹעֶה צֹאנוֹ כַּדִּין וְכַשּׁוּרָה. לְפִיכָךְ, עֲשָׂהוּ הַקֻּדְשָׁא בְּרִיךְ הוּא מֶלֶךְ עַל כָּל יִשְׂרָאֵל. וְלָמָּה צֹאן וְלֹא בָּקָר. אָמַר רִבִּי יְהוּדָה, יִשְׂרָאֵל נִקְרָאִים צֹאן. שֶׁנֶּאֱמַר, וְאַתֵּן צֹאנִי צֹאן מַרְעִיתִי אָדָם אַתֶּם. וּכְתִיב, כְּצֹאן קֳדָשִׁים כְּצֹאן יְרוּשָׁלָיִם.

374. Rabbi Yehuda said: Moses was wise and knowledgeable in leading his flock. Come and behold: we learn this from David, "And he is tending the sheep" (I Shmuel 16:11), which teaches us that he was very wise and tended his sheep properly and appropriately. The Holy One, blessed be He, therefore made him king over all of Yisrael. And why sheep and not cows? Because Yisrael are named sheep, as written: "But you My flock, the flock of My pasture, are men" (Yechezkel 34:31), and, "Like the flock of sacrifices, like the flock of Jerusalem" (Yechezkel 36:38).

375. מַה הַצֹּאן, כְּשֶׁיִּקְרְבוּ עַל הַמִּזְבֵּחַ, בִּשְׁבִילָם זוֹכֶה לְחַיֵּי הָעוֹלָם הַבָּא. כָּךְ הַמַּנְהִיג לְיִשְׂרָאֵל כַּדִּין וְכַשּׁוּרָה, בִּשְׁבִילָם זוֹכֶה לְחַיֵּי הָעוֹלָם הַבָּא. וְעוֹד, הָרוֹעֶה אֶת הַצֹּאן, כְּשֶׁהַצֹּאן יוֹלֶדֶת, הָרוֹעֶה נוֹטֵל אוֹתָם טְלָאִים בְּחֵיקוֹ, כְּדֵי שֶׁלֹּא יִלְאוּ וְיִגְעוּ, וּמוֹלִיכָם אַחֲרֵי אִמּוֹתָם, וּמְרַחֵם עֲלֵיהֶם. כָּךְ הַמַּנְהִיג לְיִשְׂרָאֵל, צָרִיךְ לְהַנְהִילָם בְּרַחֲמִים, וְלֹא בְּאַכְזָרִיּוּת. וְכֵן אָמַר מֹשֶׁה, כִּי תֹאמַר אֵלַי, שָׂאֵהוּ בְחֵיקֶךָ וְגוֹ'.

375. As one attains life in the World to Come due to the sheep, when they are offered upon the altar, he who leads Yisrael properly attains due to them life in the World to Come. Furthermore, he who herds the sheep takes the lambs to his bosom when the ewes give birth, so that they will not tire and be fatigued, and the shepherd carries the lambs after their mothers, and pities them. So should the leader of Yisrael lead them mercifully and without cruelty. And thus did Moses say, "That You should say to me, 'Carry them in your bosom'" (Bemidbar 11:12).

376. מַה הָרוֹעֶה אֶת הַצֹּאן, כְּשֶׁהוּא רוֹעֶה טוֹב, מַצִּיל אֶת הַצֹּאן מִן הַזְּאֵבִים, וּמִן הָאֲרָיוֹת. כָּךְ הַמַּנְהִיג לְיִשְׂרָאֵל, אִם הוּא טוֹב, מַצִּילָן מִן

הָעַכּוּ"ם, וּמִדִּין שֶׁל מַטָּה, וּמִדִּין שֶׁל מַעְלָה, וּמַדְרִיכָן לְחַיֵּי הָעוֹלָם הַבָּא. כָּךְ מֹשֶׁה, רוֹעֶה נֶאֱמָן הָיָה, וְרָאָה הַקּוּדְשָׁא בְּרִיךְ הוּא, שֶׁכְּדַאי הוּא לִרְעוֹת אֶת יִשְׂרָאֵל, בְּאוֹתוֹ הַדִּין מַמָּשׁ, שֶׁהָיָה רוֹעֶה אֶת הַצֹּאן, לַכְּשָׂבִים, כְּפִי הָרָאוּי לָהֶן. וְהַנְּקֵבוֹת כְּפִי הָרָאוּי לָהֶן.

376. As a good shepherd saves the sheep from the wolves and lions, the leader of Yisrael, if he is good, saves them from the heathen and the Judgment of below and of above, and guides them into the life of the World to Come. Moses was such a Faithful shepherd, and the Holy One, blessed be He, saw that he was worthy of shepherding Yisrael, using the same principles that he used to tend to the sheep, the lambs according to their needs and to the females according to their needs.

377. וּלְפִיכָךְ כְּתִיב, וּמֹשֶׁה הָיָה רוֹעֶה אֶת צֹאן יִתְרוֹ חוֹתְנוֹ, וְלֹא שֶׁלּוֹ, דְּאָמַר רַבִּי יוֹסֵי, וְכִי מַה שֶּׁנָּתַן אֶת צִפּוֹרָה בִּתּוֹ לְמֹשֶׁה, לֹא נָתַן לוֹ צֹאן וּבָקָר, וַהֲלֹא יִתְרוֹ עָשִׁיר הָיָה. אֶלָּא מֹשֶׁה לֹא הָיָה רוֹעֶה אֶת צֹאנוֹ, כְּדֵי שֶׁלֹּא יֹאמְרוּ בִּשְׁבִיל שֶׁהָיָה צֹאנוֹ עִמּוֹ, הָיָה רוֹעֶה אוֹתָן בְּטוֹב. וְלָכֵן כְּתִיב אֶת צֹאן יִתְרוֹ חוֹתְנוֹ, וְלֹא אֶת שֶׁלּוֹ. כֹּהֵן מִדְיָן, רַבִּי תַּנְחוּם אָמַר, אַף עַל גַּב שֶׁהָיָה עוֹבֵד כּוּ"ם, בִּשְׁבִיל שֶׁעָשָׂה עִמּוֹ חֶסֶד, הָיָה רוֹעֶה צֹאנוֹ כַּדִּין וְכַשּׁוּרָה, בְּמִרְעֶה טוֹב שָׁמֵן וְדָשֵׁן.

377. It is therefore written: "Now Moses kept the flock of Jethro his father-in-law" (Shemot 3:1) and not his own. Rabbi Yosi said: As he gave Moses his daughter Tziporah to wife, did he not give him cows and sheep, for Jethro was rich? But Moses did not tend to his own sheep, lest one would say that since his flock was with him, he tended to them well. Therefore, it says, "The flock of Jethro his father-in-law" and not his own. "The priest of Midian": Rabbi Tanchum said: Though he was an idolater, since he was kind by him, he tended to his flock properly, in a good, fatty and rich pasture.

378. וַיִּנְהַג אֶת הַצֹּאן אַחַר הַמִּדְבָּר. רַבִּי יוֹסֵי אָמַר, מֹשֶׁה, מִיּוֹם שֶׁנּוֹלַד, לֹא זָזָה מִמֶּנּוּ רוּחַ הַקֹּדֶשׁ. רָאָה בְּרוּחַ הַקֹּדֶשׁ, שֶׁאוֹתוֹ מִדְבָּר הָיָה קָדוֹשׁ, וּמוּכָן לְקַבֵּל עוֹל מַלְכוּת שָׁמַיִם עָלָיו. מַה עָשָׂה, הִנְהִיג אֶת

הַצֹּאן אַחַר הַמִּדְבָּר. רַבִּי יִצְחָק אָמַר, אַחַר הַמִּדְבָּר עכ״פ, וְלֹא בַּמִּדְבָּר, שֶׁלֹּא רָצָה שֶׁיִּכָּנְסוּ בְּתוֹכוֹ, אֶלָּא הִרְחִיקָם אַחַר הַמִּדְבָּר.

378. "And he led the flock far away into the desert" (Ibid.). Rabbi Yosi said: Since the day that Moses was born, the Holy Spirit did not move away from him. He saw through the Holy Spirit that that desert was holy, and prepared to receive upon it the yoke of heavenly kingdom. What did he do? He led the flock to the desert. Rabbi Yitzchak said: "Far away (lit. 'after') the desert" and not in the desert, for he did not want them to come into it but led them away from the desert.

379. וַיָּבֹא אֶל הַר הָאֱלֹהִים חֹרֵבָה, הוּא לְבַדּוֹ בְּלֹא צֹאן. אר״י, הַאי אַבְנָא, דִּמְקַבְּלָא פַרְזְלָא, כַּד חָמֵי לֵיהּ, מְדַלְגָא עִילוֹי. כַּךְ מֹשֶׁה וְהַר סִינַי, כְּשֶׁנִּרְאוּ זֶה עִם זֶה, דְּלֵג עָלָיו. הה״ד, וַיָּבֹא אֶל הַר הָאֱלֹהִים חֹרֵבָה.

379. "And came to the mountain of the Elohim to Horeb" (Shemot 3:1). He alone CAME without the sheep. Rabbi Yitzchak said: There is a stone that draws and receives metal, and THE METAL jumps on it when it sees it. So with Moses and mount Sinai: when they appeared to each other he jumped on it. This is what is written: "And he came to the mountain of Elohim to Horeb."

380. א״ר אַבָּא, מוּכָנִים הָיוּ מִשֵּׁשֶׁת יְמֵי בְּרֵאשִׁית, זֶה עִם זֶה. וְאוֹתוֹ הַיּוֹם, נִתְרַגֵּשׁ הָהָר לְמוּל מֹשֶׁה. וְכֵיוָן שֶׁרָאָהוּ שֶׁנִּכְנַס לְתוֹכוֹ, וְדִלֵּג בּוֹ, עָמַד הָהָר. מְלַמֵּד, שֶׁשְּׂמֵחִים הָיוּ זֶה עִם זֶה.

380. Rabbi Aba said: They were designated from the six days of Creation, the one together with the other. On that day, the mountain quaked before Moses. When he saw him entering it and jumping upon it, the mountain quieted. This teaches us that they were happy with each other.

381. א״ר יַנַּאי, יוֹדֵעַ הָיָה מֹשֶׁה, שֶׁאוֹתוֹ הַר, הַר הָאֱלֹהִים הוּא. דִּכְתִיב וַיָּבֹא אֶל הַר הָאֱלֹהִים. דְּתָנָן, מָה רָאָה מֹשֶׁה בְּאוֹתוֹ הַר, רָאָה עוֹפוֹת שֶׁהָיוּ פוֹרְחִים, וּפוֹרְשִׂים כַּנְפֵיהֶם וְלֹא הָיוּ נִכְנָסִים בּוֹ.

381. Rabbi Yanai said: Moses knew that the mountain was the mount of Elohim, as written: "And came to the mountain of the Elohim." We learned what Moses saw on that mountain. He saw birds fly, spreading their wings yet not approaching it.

382. רבִּי יִצְחָק אוֹמֵר, רָאָה הָעוֹפוֹת פּוֹרְחִים וְטָסִים מִשָּׁם, וְנוֹפְלִים לְרַגְלָיו שֶׁל מֹשֶׁה, מִיַּד הִרְגִּישׁ בָּעִנְיָן, וְהֶעֱמִיד אֶת הַצֹּאן אַחַר הַמִּדְבָּר, וְהוּא נִכְנַס לְבַדּוֹ.

382. Rabbi Yitzchak says: He saw birds flying and soaring from there, falling at Moses' feet. He immediately noticed it, and stood the flock away from the desert and entered alone.

383. וַיֵּרָא מַלְאַךְ ה' אֵלָיו בְּלַבַּת אֵשׁ מִתּוֹךְ הַסְּנֶה. רבִּי תַּנְחוּם אוֹמֵר, שְׁעַת הַמִּנְחָה הָיְתָה, שֶׁמִּדַּת הַדִּין שׁוֹלֶטֶת בּוֹ. רבִּי יוֹחָנָן אָמַר, וְהָא כְּתִיב, יוֹמָם יְצַוֶּה יְיָ' חַסְדּוֹ. מִדַּת חֶסֶד קָאָמַר, וְלֹא מה"ד. אָמַר רבִּי יִצְחָק, מִשֶּׁיּוֹצֵא הָאוֹר, עַד שֶׁנּוֹטֶה לָרֶדֶת, נִקְרָא יוֹם, וְהוּא מִדַּת חֶסֶד. מִשֶּׁנּוֹטֶה לָרֶדֶת, נִקְרָא עֶרֶב, וְהוּא מה"ד. וְהַיְינוּ דִּכְתִיב, וַיִּקְרָא אֱלֹהִים לָאוֹר יוֹם.

383. "And the angel of Hashem appeared to him in a flame of fire out of the midst of a bush" (Shemot 3:2). Rabbi Tanchum said: It was the time for the afternoon prayer, upon which the attribute of Judgment has sway. Rabbi Yochanan said that it is written: "Hashem will command his Chesed in the daytime" (Tehilim 42:9). It mentions the attribute of Chesed, not the attribute of Judgment. Rabbi Yitzchak said: When the light sets until it descends, it is called 'day', which is the attribute of Chesed. Once it descends, it is called evening, which is the attribute of Judgment, as written: "And Elohim called the light day" (Beresheet 1:5).

384. א"ר יוֹחָנָן, שְׁעַת הַמִּנְחָה הוּא, מוּ' שָׁעוֹת וּלְמַטָּה. דְּתַנְיָא ר' יִצְחָק אוֹמֵר, מ"ד בֵּין הָעַרְבַּיִם תֹּאכְלוּ בָשָׂר וּבַבֹּקֶר תִּשְׂבְּעוּ לָחֶם. בֵּין הָעַרְבַּיִם, דְּהוּא שַׁעֲתָא דְּדִינָא תֹּאכְלוּ בָשָׂר. וּכְתִיב, הַבָּשָׂר עוֹדֶנּוּ בֵּין שִׁנֵּיהֶם וְאַף יְיָ' חָרָה בָעָם. מִשּׁוּם, דְּבֵין הָעַרְבַּיִם, דִּינָא דְּמַלְכוּתָא

-259-

שָׁלִיט. וּבַבֹּקֶר תִּשְׂבְּעוּ לָחֶם, מִשּׁוּם דְּאִקְרֵי חֶסֶד הַהוּא שַׁעֲתָא, וּכְתִיב, חֶסֶד אֵל כָּל הַיּוֹם. וּכְתִיב, וַיִּקְרָא אֱלֹהִים לָאוֹר יוֹם. דְּאִיהוּ מִצַּפְרָא.

384. Rabbi Yochanan said: The time of Minchah is from the sixth hour or less. As we learned, Rabbi Yitzchak said that it is written: "At evening you shall eat meat, and in the morning you shall be filled with bread" (Shemot 16:12). At twilight, the time of Judgment, "you shall eat meat." And it is written: "And while the meat was yet between their teeth... the wrath of Hashem was inflamed against the people" (Bemidbar 11:33). This is because at twiligjt, the Judgment of Malchut has sway. "And in the morning you shall be filled with bread," since that time is considered Chesed. It is also written: "The Mercy of El endures continually (lit. 'all the day')" (Tehilim 52:3), and, "And Elohim called the light day," which is in the morning.

385. רִבִּי תַּנְחוּם אוֹמֵר, דָּא סוּמָק, וְדָא חִוָּור. סוּמָק: בֵּין הָעַרְבַּיִם. דִּכְתִיב, בֵּין הָעַרְבַּיִם תֹּאכְלוּ בָשָׂר. וְחִוָּורָא: בְּצַפְרָא. דִּכְתִיב, וּבַבֹּקֶר תִּשְׂבְּעוּ לָחֶם. רִבִּי יִצְחָק אָמַר, כְּתִיב, וְשָׁחֲטוּ אוֹתוֹ כָּל קְהַל עֲדַת יִשְׂרָאֵל בֵּין הָעַרְבַּיִם וְגוֹ'. דְּהַהוּא שַׁעֲתָא לְמֶעְבַּד דִּינָא. רִבִּי יְהוּדָה אָמַר, יַלְפִינָן מִשְׁנֵי כְבָשִׂים שֶׁבְּכָל יוֹם, הָאֶחָד מִתְקָרֵב כְּנֶגֶד מִדַּת הַחֶסֶד, וְהב' כְּנֶגֶד מה"ד.

385. Rabbi Tanchum said: The one is red and the other is white; red at twilight, as written: "At evening you shall eat meat," and white in the morning, as written: "And in the morning you shall be filled with bread." Rabbi Yitzchak said: It is written, "And the whole assembly of the congregation of Yisrael shall kill it towards evening" (Shemot 12:6), which is the time to execute judgment. Rabbi Yehuda said: We have deduced from the two daily sheep, one is offered to correspond to the attribute of Chesed, and the second corresponds to Judgment.

386. וא"ר יְהוּדָה, מ"ד, אֶת הַכֶּבֶשׂ הָאֶחָד תַּעֲשֶׂה בַבֹּקֶר, וְלָא כְּתִיב אֶת הַכֶּבֶשׂ הָרִאשׁוֹן, אֶלָּא אֶת הַכֶּבֶשׂ הָאֶחָד, מְיוּחָד, כְּנֶגֶד מִדַּת הַחֶסֶד. דִּבְכָל מָקוֹם, שֵׁנִי, לֹא נֶאֱמַר בּוֹ כִּי טוֹב.

386. Rabbi Yehuda also said: Why is it written, "The one lamb shall you offer in the morning" (Bemidbar 28:4). Instead of 'The first lamb'? But "The one lamb," sole one to corresponds to the attribute of Chesed. For it never says of the second that it was good.

387. רִבִּי תַּנְחוּם אָמַר, לְפִיכָךְ, יִצְחָק תִּקֵּן תְּפִלַּת הַמִּנְחָה, שֶׁהוּא כְּנֶגֶד מה"ד. א"ר יִצְחָק, מִכָּאן, אוֹי לָנוּ כִּי פָּנָה הַיּוֹם כִּי יִנָּטוּ צִלְלֵי עָרֶב. כִּי פָּנָה הַיּוֹם: זֶה מִדַּת הַחֶסֶד. כִּי יִנָּטוּ צִלְלֵי עָרֶב: שֶׁכְּבָר גָּבַר מה"ד. אַבְרָהָם תִּקֵּן תְּפִלַּת שַׁחֲרִית, כְּנֶגֶד מִדַּת הַחֶסֶד.

387. Rabbi Tanchum said: Isaac therefore composed the prayer of Minchah, which corresponds to the attribute of Judgment. Rabbi Yitzchak said: From this, "Woe to us! For the day declines, for the shadows of the evening are lengthened" (Yirmeyah 6:4). "For the day declines" is the attribute of Chesed. "For the shadows of the evening are lengthened," for the attribute of Judgment has already gained the ascendancy. Abraham composed the morning prayer corresponds to the attribute of Chesed.

388. ת"ר, בְּהַהִיא שַׁעֲתָא דְּעָאל מֹשֶׁה לְטוּרָא דְּסִינַי, מ"ט אִתְגְּלֵי לֵיהּ בְּשַׁלְהוֹבֵי אֶשָּׁתָא, דְּהוּא דִּינָא. א"ר יַעֲקֹב כְּעֵין שַׁעֲתָא הֲוָה גָּרִים. ר' יוֹסֵי אָמַר, כֹּלָּא לְחַד גִּזְעָא אִשְׁתָּרְשָׁא. כְּתִיב, וַיָּבֹא אֶל הַר הָאֱלֹהִים חֹרֵבָה. וּכְתִיב, וּבְחֹרֵב הִקְצַפְתֶּם אֶת יְיָ'. וּכְתִיב, וַיֵּרָא מַלְאַךְ יְיָ' אֵלָיו בְּלַבַּת אֵשׁ מִתּוֹךְ הַסְּנֶה. מִתּוֹךְ שֶׁהֵם עֲתִידִים לִהְיוֹת כַּסְּנֶה, כְּהַאי דִּכְתִיב, קוֹצִים כְּסוּחִים בָּאֵשׁ יִצַּתּוּ.

388. The sages taught why He appeared to Moses in a fiery flame, which is Judgment, at the time that Moses ascended on Mount Sinai. Rabbi Ya'akov said: Then the time caused it, MEANING IT WAS THE TIME OF JUDGMENT, NAMELY THE TIME OF MINCHAH. Rabbi Yosi said: Everything, MEANING THE FLAME OF FIRE, THE NAME HOREB AND THE BUSH, is all rooted to one stem. It is written: "He came to the mountain of the Elohim to Horeb" (Shemot 3:1), "And at Horeb you angered Hashem" (Devarim 9:8), and: "And the angel of Hashem appeared to him in a flame of fire out of the midst of a bush" (Shemot 3:2), MEANING they would eventually be like a bush, as it is written: "As thorns cut down, burned in fire" (Yeshayah 33:12). THE PLACE CAUSED IT, FOR YISRAEL WOULD EVENTUALLY SIN

THERE, AND BECOME LIKE A BUSH. THEREFORE, HE APPEARED IN A FIERY FLAME, WHICH IS JUDGMENT, THAT BURNS UP THE WICKED, AS WRITTEN: "THORNS CUT DOWN, BURNED IN FIRE."

55. "out of the midst of a bush"

A Synopsis

Rabbi Yehuda first explains that the burning bush is an allusion to the fire of Gehenom that punishes but does not utterly destroy the wicked. Thus, it signifies God's compassion towards the wicked.

We then learn that God appeared to Moses in the flame of fire because Moses was unlike all the other prophets, and only he was able to approach the flame without being burned by it. This was because Moses' soul was drawn from a place from where no other was drawn; his unique connection to Mercy allowed him to confront Judgment without fear. Rabbi Shimon then establishes that although Bila'am was Moses' counterpart, Bila'am drew strength from the lower crowns and he acted according to impurity below, while Moses drew from the holy Crown above and his actions were performed according to Holiness. This follows the duality inherent in all aspects of the universe.

Finally, Rabbi Yochanan refers to Rabbi Yitzchak's interpretation of the title verse to explain that the burning bush was a sign to reassure Moses that Yisrael would not succumb under the burden of their oppression.

The Relevance of the Passage

The Light cast by this narrative painlessly burns away our sins and egocentric qualities from our nature, so that we now merit the World to Come, which really means the arrival of Heaven on Earth. Our fears of judgment are expunged from our being. When we are born into this world, our dark side and our soul have equal power. Our free will is to choose which voice we will follow.

This good-and-evil duality exists in the world at large. We now stamp out the darkness and tip the scales completely over to the side of good. Evil is banished from all existence. All wicked people of the world are rendered powerless. Their reign of terror is ended as the Zohar's Light successfully overthrows the powers of darkness.

Through the Holy Names that appear in this book of Zohar, and upon the merit of Moses, this becomes our ultimate exodus out of evil, our final and complete redemption and lasting freedom from the bondage of darkness.

The Light now shines from one end of the world to the other. And we bathe and bask forevermore in its pleasing and pleasurable radiance.

389. אָמַר ר' יְהוּדָה, מִכָּאן לָמַדְנוּ, רַחֲמָנוּתוֹ שֶׁל מָקוֹם עַל הָרְשָׁעִים,

דִּכְתִיב, וְהִנֵּה הַסְּנֶה בּוֹעֵר בָּאֵשׁ, לַעֲשׂוֹת בָּהֶם דִּין בָּרְשָׁעִים, וְהַסְּנֶה אֵינֶנּוּ אֻכָּל, אֵין לָהֶם כְּלָיָה. בּוֹעֵר בָּאֵשׁ, עכ״פ רֶמֶז, לָאֵשׁ שֶׁל גֵּיהִנָּם. אֲבָל הַסְּנֶה אֵינֶנּוּ אֻכָּל, לִהְיוֹת בָּהֶם כְּלָיָה.

389. Rabbi Yehuda said: From here we learn the compassion of the Place, MEANING OF THE HOLY ONE, BLESSED BE HE, towards the wicked, for it is written, "and behold, the bush burned with fire" (Shemot 3:2), to punish the wicked with it, AS MENTIONED ABOVE. "But the bush was not consumed" (Ibid.), meaning that they were not utterly destroyed. "Burned with fire" is all the same an allusion to the fire of Gehenom, MEANING EVEN THOUGH THE FIRE APPEARED TO MOSES, WHO WAS RIGHTEOUS, IT IS NONETHELESS AN ALLUSION TO THE FIRE OF GEHENOM WHICH IS FOR THE WICKED. "But the bush was not consumed," so it does not destroy them utterly.

390. ד״א וַיֵּרָא מַלְאַךְ יְיָ׳ אֵלָיו בְּלַבַּת אֵשׁ. מ״ט לְמֹשֶׁה בְּלַבַּת אֵשׁ, וְלִשְׁאָר נְבִיאִים לָא. א״ר יְהוּדָה, לָאו מֹשֶׁה כִּשְׁאָר נְבִיאִים. דִּתְנַן, מַאן דְּקָרִיב לְאֶשָּׁא בֵּיהּ אִתּוֹקַד, וּמֹשֶׁה קָרִיב לְאֶשָּׁא וְלָא אִתּוֹקַד. דִּכְתִיב, וּמֹשֶׁה נִגַּשׁ אֶל הָעֲרָפֶל אֲשֶׁר שָׁם הָאֱלֹהִים. וּכְתִיב, וַיֵּרָא מַלְאַךְ יְיָ׳ אֵלָיו בְּלַבַּת אֵשׁ מִתּוֹךְ הַסְּנֶה.

390. Another explanation of: "And the angel of Hashem appeared to him in a flame of fire" (Ibid.). HE ASKS: Why did He appear to Moses in a flame of fire, and not to the other prophets. Rabbi Yehuda said: Moses is not like the other prophets, for we learned that everyone who approaches the fire is burnt by it. Yet Moses approached it and was not burnt, as it is written: "And Moses drew near to the thick darkness where the Elohim was" (Shemot 20:18), and, "And the angel of Hashem appeared to him in a flame of fire out of the midst of a bush."

391. רִבִּי אַבָּא אָמַר, הַאי דְּמֹשֶׁה, אִית לְאִסְתַּכְּלָא בֵּיהּ בְּחָכְמְתָא עִלָּאָה, עַל מַה כְּתִיב, כִּי מִן הַמַּיִם מְשִׁיתִיהוּ. מַאן דְּאִתְמְשָׁךְ מִן מַיָּא, לָא דָחִיל מִנּוּרָא. דְּתַנְיָא אָמַר רִבִּי יְהוּדָה, מֵאֲתָר דְּאִתְגְּזַר מֹשֶׁה, לָא אִתְגְּזַר בַּר נָשׁ אָחֳרָא. א״ר יוֹחָנָן, בַּעֲשָׂרָה דַּרְגִּין אִשְׁתַּכְלַל. דִּכְתִיב,

בְּכָל בֵּיתִי נֶאֱמָן הוּא. וְלֹא נֶאֱמָן בֵּיתִי. זַכָּאָה חוּלָקֵיהּ דב"נ, דְּמָרֵיהּ
אַסְהִיד כְּדֵין עֲלוֹי.

391. Rabbi Aba said: IN THIS SUBJECT of Moses, we should observe it with supernal Wisdom. Why is it written: "Because I drew him out of the water" (Shemot 2:10)? THIS COMES TO TEACH US that one who is drawn from water, WHICH IS CHESED, does not fear fire, WHICH IS JUDGMENT. Rabbi Yehuda said: Because we have learned the place from where THE SOUL OF Moses was derived, no other person was derived. Rabbi Yochanan said he was composed of the ten levels OF ZEIR ANPIN as is written: "He is the trusted one in all My house" (Bemidbar 12:7), WHICH IS THE NUKVA. It is not written: 'the trusted of My house', WHICH WOULD IMPLY THE TRUSTED OF THE NUKVA, BUT RATHER IT IS WRITTEN, "HE IS THE TRUSTED," WHICH MEANS THE TRUSTED OF ZEIR ANPIN, WHICH IS HIGHER THAN THE NUKVA. Blessed is the portion of the person whose Master testifies of him thus.

392. אָמַר רַב דִּימִי, וְהָא כְּתִיב וְלֹא קָם נָבִיא עוֹד בְּיִשְׂרָאֵל כְּמֹשֶׁה.
וְאָמַר ריב"ל, בְּיִשְׂרָאֵל לֹא קָם, אֲבָל באוה"ע קָם, וּמַנוֹ בִּלְעָם. א"ל,
וְדַאי שַׁפִּיר קָאמַרְתְּ, אִשְׁתִּיק. כַּד אָתָא רשב"י, אָתוּ, שָׁאִילוּ קָמֵיהּ
הַאי מִלָּה.

392. Rav Dimi said: Is it not written, "And there arose not a prophet since in Yisrael like Moses" (Devarim 34:10)? And Rabbi Yehoshua bar Levi said: In Yisrael none arose but among the nations of the world there did arise, and who is he? He is Bila'am. SO HOW CAN YOU SAY THAT NO OTHER PERSON WAS HEWN FROM THE PLACE THAT MOSES WAS HEWN? Rabbi Elazar said to him: Certainly, you speak well. He remained silent. When Rabbi Shimon bar Yochai came, they asked him this matter.

393. פָּתַח וְאָמַר, קוּטִיפָא דְּקַרְנְטֵי, אִתְעָרְבָא בַּאֲפַרְסְמוֹנָא טָבָא ח"ו.
אֶלָּא, וְדַאי כָּךְ הוּא, באוה"ע קָם, וּמַנוֹ בִּלְעָם. מֹשֶׁה עוֹבָדוֹי לְעֵילָא,
וּבִלְעָם לְתַתָּא. מֹשֶׁה, אִשְׁתַּמַּשׁ בְּכִתְרָא קַדִּישָׁא דְּמַלְכָּא עִלָּאָה לְעֵילָא.
וּבִלְעָם, אִשְׁתַּמַּשׁ בְּכִתְרִין תַּתָּאִין דְּלָא קַדִּישִׁין לְתַתָּא. וּבְהַהוּא גּוָונָא
מַמָּשׁ כְּתִיב, וְאֶת בִּלְעָם בֶּן בְּעוֹר הַקּוֹסֵם הָרְגוּ בְּנֵי יִשְׂרָאֵל בֶּחָרֶב. וְאִי

סַלְקָא דַעְתָּךְ יַתִּיר, זִיל שָׁאִיל לְאַתְנֵיהּ. אָתָא רְבִי יוֹסֵי, וְנָשַׁק יְדוֹי, אָמַר, הָא חַמְרָא דְלִבָאי נָפַק לְבַר.

393. RABBI SHIMON opened the discussion, saying: Heaven forbid that the fluid flowing from the bloom FLOWER, THAT HAS A FOUL ODOR, would mix, with the good balsam – MEANING, ARE YOU, HEAVEN FORBID, COMPARING THE WICKED BILA'AM, TO OUR MASTER MOSES? But certainly this is THE MEANING OF: "Among the nations of the world there did arise, who is Bila'am's": Moses' actions were above IN HOLINESS and Bila'am below IN IMPURITY. Moses utilized the holy crown of the Supernal King, WHICH IS ZEIR ANPIN above. Bila'am utilized the lower crowns, which are unholy below. And in that manner precisely it is written: "And Bila'am, the son of Beor the sorcerer, the children of Yisrael slew by the sword" (Yehoshua 13:22). WE SEE THAT HE IS CALLED "THE SORCERER" BECAUSE HIS ACTIONS WERE IN IMPURITY, and if you can not conceive that he did more THAN THIS, look to his mule. FOR HE BECAME IMPURE WITH HER AND COPULATED WITH HER, AS OUR SAGES OF BLESSED MEMORY SAID. Rabbi Yosi came and kissed his hands and said: Behold, the stone that was in my heart has gone, MEANING THAT THIS QUESTION WEIGHED UPON HIS HEART LIKE A STONE IN HIS HEART AND NOW IT HAS LEFT AND HE IS RELEASED FROM IT.

394. דְּהָכָא מַשְׁמַע, דְּאִית עֶלָּאִין וְתַתָּאִין, יְמִינָא וּשְׂמָאלָא, רַחֲמֵי וְדִינָא, יִשְׂרָאֵל וְעכו"ם. יִשְׂרָאֵל, מִשְׁתַּמְּשִׁין בְּכִתְרִין עֶלָּאִין קַדִּישִׁין. עכו"ם, בְּכִתְרִין תַּתָּאִין דְּלָא קַדִּישִׁין. אִלֵּין דִּימִינָא, וְאִלֵּין דִּשְׂמָאלָא, וְעכ"פ, מִתְפָּרְשִׁין נְבִיאֵי עֶלָּאֵי מִנְּבִיאֵי תַּתָּאֵי. נְבִיאֵי דְקוּדְשָׁא, מִנְּבִיאֵי דְּלָאו דְּקוּדְשָׁא.

394. From this, THE WORDS OF RABBI SHIMON, it appears that there are those above and those below, right and left, Mercy and Judgment, the children of Yisrael and the heathen. Yisrael utilize the crowns of above, which are holy. The heathen utilize the crowns of below, which are not holy. Those OF YISRAEL are of the right, and those OF THE HEATHEN are of the left. Nevertheless, the upper prophets OF YISRAEL differ from the lower prophets OF THE HEATHEN; the prophets of holiness are separate from the prophets that are not from holiness.

395. אָמַר רִבִּי יְהוּדָה, כְּגַוְונָא דַּהֲוָה מֹשֶׁה, פָּרִישׁ מִכָּל נְבִיאֵי, בִּנְבוּאָה
קַדִּישָׁא עִלָּאָה. כַּךְ הֲוָה בִּלְעָם, פָּרִישׁ מִשְׁאָר נְבִיאֵי וְחָרָשֵׁי, בִּנְבוּאָה
דְּלָאו קַדִּישָׁא לְתַתָּא. וע״כ מֹשֶׁה הֲוָה לְעֵילָּא, וּבִלְעָם לְתַתָּא, וְכַמָּה
דַּרְגִּין וְדַרְגִּין מִתְפָּרְשִׁין בֵּינַיְיהוּ.

395. Rabbi Yehuda said: Just as Moses differed from all the prophets in the holy supernal prophecy, Bila'am was similarly separate from the other prophets below, the magicians of non holy prophecy. Moses nevertheless was above and Bila'am below, and many levels divided them.

396. אָמַר רִבִּי יוֹחָנָן אָמַר רִבִּי יִצְחָק, מֹשֶׁה הֲוָה מְהַרְהֵר וְאוֹמֵר, שֶׁמָּא
ח״ו יִשְׂרָאֵל יִכְלוּ בְּהַאי עֲבוֹדָה קָשָׁה, הֲדָא הוּא דִּכְתִיב, וַיַּרְא
בְּסִבְלוֹתָם. לְפִיכָךְ, וַיֵּרָא מַלְאַךְ יְיָ' אֵלָיו בְּלַבַּת אֵשׁ וְגוֹ', וַיַּרְא וְהִנֵּה
הַסְּנֶה בּוֹעֵר בָּאֵשׁ וְגוֹ'. כְּלוֹמַר, מְשׁוּעְבָּדִים הֵם בַּעֲבוֹדָה קָשָׁה, אֲבָל
וְהַסְּנֶה אֵינֶנּוּ אֻכָּל. זַכָּאִין אִינּוּן יִשְׂרָאֵל, דְּקוּדְשָׁא בְּרִיךְ הוּא פָּרִישׁ לוֹן
מִכָּל עַמִּין, וְקָרָא לוֹן בְּנִין, דִּכְתִיב בָּנִים אַתֶּם לַה' אֱלֹהֵיכֶם.

396. Rabbi Yochanan said in the name of Rabbi Yitzchak, that Moses thought and said: 'Perhaps, heaven forbid, Yisrael will expire from this hard labor', as it is written: "And looked on their burdens" (Shemot 2:11). Therefore, "the angel of Hashem appeared to him in a flame of fire...and he looked, and, behold, the bush burned with fire" (Shemot 3: 2). That is, they are enslaved to hard labor, but "the bush was not consumed"; NAMELY, THEY DO NOT PERISH IN EXILE, AS MENTIONED ABOVE. Happy are Yisrael that the Holy One, blessed be He, separated them from all nations and called them 'children', as it is written: "You are the children of Hashem your Elohim" (Devarim 14:1).

VAERA

Names of the articles

1. "And I appeared...by the name of El Shadai, but by My name, Hashem, I was not known to them"

A Synopsis

This passage begins with: "And Elohim spoke to Moses and said to him, 'I am Hashem, and I appeared to Abraham, Isaac and Jacob as El Shadai.'" Rabbi Aba talks about "Trust in Hashem forever...for Yad Hashem is an everlasting rock," and we hear many interpretations of this scripture. One is that people have permission to observe and understand up to the level of Hashem but no higher. Rabbi Yehuda offers the interpretation that the world was created with justice and is sustained by the name Hashem. Next the discussion moves to Moses, who said, "Adonai why did you do wrong to this nation. Why did you send me etc. And from the time that I have come to Pharaoh to speak in your name it has become worse for these people and you did not deliver your people." Rabbi Yehuda wonders how anyone can talk to God like this without being punished, and Rabbi Yitzchak replies that it was because Moses had authority over Malchut like someone over his household – thus he was able to speak without fear. We hear next of judgment and mercy being joined together, and then of the reason for the name 'El Shadai.' We are told a parable about a king and his daughter to clarify that Yud Hei Vav Hei spoke to Abraham, Isaac and Jacob only through his somewhat lower intermediary, El Shadai – and El Shadai is Malchut. Next Rabbi Yosi changes the topic to the verse: "The earth is Hashem's and the fullness thereof, the world, and they that dwell in it." He tells us that 'the earth' means The Holy Land, and that it receives the first of the blessings and the water from Hashem. Afterwards the rest of the world receives what is left over. Rabbi Yosi also talks about the verse: "For he founded it upon seas." He says that the seas are the seven pillars or Sfirot upon which the world is supported. The Sea of Galilee – Malchut – rules over them. Rabbi Yehuda does not like the phrase 'rules over them,' and he contends that Malchut receives from the Sfirot; thus the Sea of Kineret is filled from them. Rabbi Shimon explains why Jacob does not rule over the land of Yisrael like Moses does, saying that Jacob forsook the higher realms for the lower world. Therefore Yud hei vav hei spoke to him only in the name El Shadai. Lastly we learn from Rabbi Chiya that everyone who is circumcised and observes the sign of the covenant is righteous and inherits the land, as in the verse: "And I have also established My covenant with them to give them the land of Canaan."

1. "And I appeared...by the name of El Shadai, but by My name, Hashem, I was not known to them"

The Relevance of the paragraph

In this section there are four names for God: El Shadai, Adonai, Hashem and Yud Hei Vav Hei. Because of their different levels of development, Moses and Jacob received messages from different aspects or manifestations of God. As each of us seeks and resonates to our own spiritual level, we can think about this concept while trying to raise ourselves higher and higher – thus becoming ever more worthy to hear the voice of the One God.

١. וַיְדַבֵּר אֱלֹהִים אֶל מֹשֶׁה וַיֹּאמֶר אֵלָיו אֲנִי יְיָ' וָאֵרָא אֶל אַבְרָהָם אֶל יִצְחָק וְאֶל יַעֲקֹב בְּאֵל שַׁדַּי וְגוֹ'. רִבִּי אַבָּא פָּתַח, בִּטְחוּ בַיְיָ' עֲדֵי עַד כִּי בְּיָהּ יְיָ' צוּר עוֹלָמִים. בִּטְחוּ בַיְיָ', כָּל בְּנֵי עָלְמָא בַּעְיָין לְאִתְתַּקְפָא בֵּיהּ בְּקוּדְשָׁא בְּרִיךְ הוּא, וּלְמֶהֱוֵי רָחֲצָנוּ דִּלְהוֹן בֵּיהּ.

1. "And Elohim spoke to Moses and said to him, 'I am Hashem and I appeared to Abraham, to Isaac, and to Jacob, by the name of El Shadai...'" (Shemot 6:2-3). Rabbi Aba opened the discussion saying, "Trust in Hashem forever (Heb. *adei ad*), for Yah Hashem is an everlasting rock" (Yeshayah 26:4). "Trust in Hashem" MEANS THAT all the people of the world have to strengthen themselves in the Holy One, blessed be He, and trust in Him.

٢. אִי הָכִי מַהוּ עֲדֵי עַד. אֶלָּא, בְּגִין דִּיהֵא תָּקְפָּא דְּבַר נָשׁ, בַּאֲתַר דְּאִיהוּ קִיּוּמָא וְקִשּׁוּרָא דְּכֹלָּא, וְאִקְרֵי עַד, וְהָא אוּקְמוּהָ, כְּמָה דְאַתְּ אָמֵר, בַּבֹּקֶר יֹאכַל עַד. וְהַאי עַד, אֲתַר דְּאָחִיד לְכָל סְטְרִין, לִסְטְרָא דָא, וּלְסִטְרָא דָא, לְאִתְקַיְּימָא, וּלְאִתְקַשְּׁרָא קִשּׁוּרָא, דִּי לָא לָא תַּעְדֵי.

2. HE ASKS, If so, what is the meaning of "adei ad"? AND ANSWERS, It means that the strength of a person should be in the place which sustains and connects everything, and which is called "ad," WHICH IS ZEIR ANPIN, as is written: "In the morning he shall devour the prey (Heb. *ad*)" (Beresheet 49:27). "Ad" is the place that unites this side and that side, MEANING THAT IT IS THE CENTRAL COLUMN THAT CONNECTS THE RIGHT SIDE AND THE LEFT SIDE TO EACH OTHER, for sustenance and connecting, NAMELY, SO THAT THE TWO COLUMNS ARE SUSTAINED, AND THEIR ILLUMINATIONS ARE LINKED TO EACH OTHER, a connection that will not be destroyed.

3. וְהַאי עַד, תִּיאוּבְתָּא דְכֹלָּא בֵּיהּ, כְּמָה דְאַתְּ אָמֵר, עַד תַּאֲוַת גִּבְעוֹת
עוֹלָם. מַאן אִינּוּן גִּבְעוֹת עוֹלָם. אִלֵּין אִינּוּן תְּרֵין אִמָּהָן נוּקְבֵּי, יוֹבֵל,
וּשְׁמִטָּה, דְּאִקְרוּן גִּבְעוֹת עוֹלָם. עוֹלָם: כְּמָה דְאַתְּ אָמֵר, מִן הָעוֹלָם וְעַד
הָעוֹלָם.

3. And everything directs its desire towards "Ad," as written: "to (Heb. *ad*) the utmost bound (or desire) of the everlasting hills" (Beresheet 49:26). Who are the everlasting hills? These are the two matriarchs, MEANING BINAH AND MALCHUT, WHICH ARE females AND ARE CALLED Jubilee and Sabbatical year. BINAH IS CALLED YOVEL (ENG. JUBILEE) AND MALCHUT SHMITAH (ENG. SABBATICAL YEAR), and both are called "everlasting hills (lit. 'hills of the world')." EACH ONE OF THEM IS CALLED A HILL OF THE WORLD. THEY ARE CALLED 'world' as you say "from everlasting to everlasting (lit. 'from the world to the world')" (Tehilim 106:48), MEANING BINAH AND MALCHUT, FOR BOTH ARE CALLED 'WORLD'.

4. וְתִיאוּבְתָּא דִּילְהוֹן בְּהַאי עַד, דְּאִיהוּ קִיּוּמָא דְּכָל סִטְרִין. תִּיאוּבְתָּא
דְּיוֹבְלָא לְגַבֵּי דְעַד, לְאַעְטְרָא לֵיהּ, וּלְנַגְדָּא עָלֵיהּ בִּרְכָּאן, וּלְאַרְקָא
עָלֵיהּ מַבּוּעִין מְתִיקִין, הֲדָא הוּא דִכְתִיב, צְאֶינָה וּרְאֶינָה בְּנוֹת צִיּוֹן
בַּמֶּלֶךְ שְׁלֹמֹה בַּעֲטָרָה שֶׁעִטְּרָה לּוֹ אִמּוֹ. תִּיאוּבְתָּא דִּשְׁמִטָּה, לְאִתְבָּרְכָא
מִנֵּיהּ, וּלְאִתְנַהֲרָא מִנֵּיהּ. וַדַּאי הַאי עַד תַּאֲוַת גִּבְעוֹת עוֹלָם אִיהוּ.

4. And they desire Ad, WHICH IS ZEIR ANPIN, SINCE BEING THE CENTRAL COLUMN, it sustains all sides, MEANING THE RIGHT SIDE AND THE LEFT SIDE. AND THEREFORE, Jubilee, WHICH IS BINAH, desires Ad, to adorn it WITH THE TOP THREE SFIROT, and to pour on it blessings, WHICH IS THE SECRET OF THE ABUNDANT FLOW OF CHASSADIM, and to pour sweet springs onto it, WHICH ARE THE SECRET OF CHOCHMAH SWEETENED WITH CHASSADIM. This is the meaning of: "Go forth, O daughters of Zion, and behold King Solomon with the crown with which his mother crowned him" (Shir Hashirim 3:11). KING SOLOMON (HEB. *SHLOMO*) IS THE SECRET OF THE KING THAT THE PEACE (HEB. *SHALOM*) IS HIS, WHICH IS ZEIR ANPIN; HIS MOTHER IS THE SECRET OF BINAH. Sabbatical year, WHICH IS MALCHUT, desires Ad, THAT IS ZEIR ANPIN, to be blessed by it and to illuminate from it. THUS the everlasting hills, WHICH ARE BINAH

1. "And I appeared...by the name of El Shadai, but by My name, Hashem, I was not known to them"

AND MALCHUT, assuredly desire Ad, THE ONE TO POUR ON IT ITS ABUNDANCE AND THE OTHER TO RECEIVE.

5. בְּגִין כַּךְ, בִּטְחוּ בַיְיָ' עֲדֵי עַד, דְּהָא מִתַּמָּן וּלְעֵילָא, אֲתָר טָמִיר וְגָנִיז אִיהוּ, דְּלָא יָכִיל לְאִתְדַּבְּקָא. אֲתָר הוּא, דְּמִנֵּיהּ נָפְקוּ וְאִצְטַיְּירוּ עָלְמִין, הֲדָא הוּא דִּכְתִּיב, כִּי בְּיָהּ יְיָ' צוּר עוֹלָמִים וְהוּא אֲתָר גָּנִיז וְסָתִים, וע"ד בִּטְחוּ בַיְיָ' עֲדֵי עַד, עַד הָכָא אִית רְשׁוּ לְכָל ב"נ לְאִסְתַּכְּלָא בֵּיהּ, מִכָּאן וּלְהָלְאָה, לֵית לֵיהּ רְשׁוּ לב"נ לְאִסְתַּכְּלָא בֵּיהּ, דְּהָא אִיהוּ גָּנִיז מִכֹּלָּא, וּמַאן אִיהוּ יָהּ יְדֹוָד. דְּמִתַּמָּן אִצְטַיְּירוּ עָלְמִין כֻּלְּהוּ, וְלֵית מַאן דְּקָאִים עַל הַהוּא אֲתָר.

5. Therefore THE VERSE SAYS, "Trust in Hashem forever" (Yeshayah 26:4), WHICH IS ZEIR ANPIN. For from there up, NAMELY CHOCHMAH AND BINAH, WHICH ARE ABOVE ZEIR ANPIN, the place is covered and hidden, as none can conceive it. It is a place from which the worlds, WHICH ARE MALE AND FEMALE, emerge and are formed. This is the meaning of: "For Yah Hashem is an everlasting rock." YAH IS CHOCHMAH, *YUD HEI VAV* Hei IS BINAH, AND THEY DESIGN AND PRODUCE THE WORLDS THAT ARE MALE AND FEMALE. This place is hidden and concealed. Therefore, THE SCRIPTURE SAYS, "Trust in Hashem forever (Heb. *adei ad*)," TO TEACH that up to here, TO ZEIR ANPIN WHICH IS CALLED AD, everyone is permitted to observe. From here and further, MEANING IN CHOCHMAH AND BINAH AS MENTIONED, no one is permitted to observe because it is concealed from everyone. And what is THE PLACE THAT IS PROHIBITED TO BE OBSERVED-IT IS Yah, Yud Hei Vav Hei, WHICH ARE CHOCHMAH AND BINAH whence all the worlds were formed, and no one is able to understand that place, IN ORDER TO CONCEIVE ANYTHING.

6. א"ר יְהוּדָה, קְרָא אוֹכַח עֲלֵיהּ, דִּכְתִּיב כִּי שְׁאַל נָא לְיָמִים רִאשׁוֹנִים וְגוֹ'. עַד הָכָא אִית רְשׁוּ לב"נ לְאִסְתַּכְּלָא, מִכָּאן וּלְהָלְאָה לֵית מַאן דְּיָכִיל לְמֵיקָם עֲלֵיהּ.

6. Rabbi Yehuda said, The scripture proves this, THE PRECLUSION OF UNDERSTANDING ABOVE ZEIR ANPIN. For is written: "For ask now the

days that are past...FROM ONE SIDE OF HEAVEN (WHICH IS ZEIR ANPIN) TO THE OTHER" (Devarim 4:32). SO IT IS EXPRESSED IN THE SCRIPTURE THAT QUESTIONING AND UNDERSTANDING PERTAIN ONLY TO THE LEVEL OF HEAVEN, WHICH IS ZEIR ANPIN, FROM ONE SIDE TO THE OTHER. Up to here, one is permitted to observe, but from here and further, MEANING ABOVE ZEIR ANPIN, no one can comprehend it.

7. ד"א בְּטְחוּ בַיְיָ' עֲדֵי עַד, כָּל יוֹמוֹי דְּבַר נָשׁ, בָּעֵי לְאִתַּתְקְפָא בֵּיהּ בְּקוּדְשָׁא בְּרִיךְ הוּא, וּמַאן דְּשַׁוֵּי בֵּיהּ, בִּטְחוֹנֵיהּ וְתוּקְפֵּיהּ כַּדְקָא יָאוֹת, לָא יַכְלִין לְאַבְאָשָׁא לֵיהּ, כָּל בְּנֵי עָלְמָא. דְּכָל מַאן דְּשַׁוֵּי תּוּקְפֵּיהּ בִּשְׁמָא קַדִּישָׁא, אִתְקַיָּים בְּעָלְמָא.

7. Another explanation OF THE PASSAGE: "Trust in Hashem forever" IS THAT a person has to strengthen himself in the Holy One, blessed be He, throughout his life. No one can harm one who properly places his trust and strength in Him, since one who places his strength in the Holy Name endures forever.

8. מַאי טַעֲמָא, בְּגִין דְּעָלְמָא, בִּשְׁמֵיהּ קַדִּישָׁא אִתְקַיָּים. הה"ד כִּי בְּיָהּ יְיָ' צוּר עוֹלָמִים: צַיָּיר עָלְמִין. דְּהָא בִּתְרֵין אַתְוָון, אִתְבְּרוּן עָלְמִין, עָלְמָא דֵּין, וְעָלְמָא דְּאָתֵי. עָלְמָא דָּא, בְּדִינָא אִתְבְּרֵי, וְעַל דִּינָא קַיְימָא, הה"ד, בְּרֵאשִׁית בָּרָא אֱלֹהִים. מ"ט, בְּגִין דְּיִתְנַהֲגוּן בְּנֵי נָשָׁא בְּדִינָא, וְלָא יִפְּקוּן מֵאוֹרְחָא לְבַר.

8. HE ASKS, What is the reason, AND ANSWERS, since the world endures by His Holy Name. This is the meaning of: "For Yah Hashem is an everlasting (lit. 'worlds') rock (Heb. tzur)" (Yeshayah 26:4), WHICH MEANS the former (Heb. tzayar) of worlds. For by two letters were the worlds created, this world and the World to Come. This world was created with Judgment and is maintained, NAMELY EXISTS, on Judgment. This is the meaning of: "In the beginning Elohim created" (Beresheet 1:1), AS THIS NAME ALLUDES TO JUDGMENT. The reason is so that people would conduct themselves according to judgment (law) and would not digress from the path.

9. תָּא חֲזֵי כְּתִיב וַיְדַבֵּר אֱלֹהִים אֶל מֹשֶׁה, גְּזֵירַת דִּינָא דְּקַיְימָא עֲלֵיהּ,

1. "And I appeared...by the name of El Shadai, but by My name, Hashem, I was not known to them"

מַה כְּתִיב לְעֵילָּא, וַיָּשָׁב מֹשֶׁה אֶל ה', וַיֹּאמֶר אֲדֹנָ"י, בְּאָלֶ"ף דָּלֶ"ת נוּ"ן
יוֹ"ד. חָמֵי תּוּקְפָּא דְּמֹשֶׁה, בְּשֵׁירוּתָא דִּנְבִיאוּתֵיהּ, לָא נָח רוּחֵיהּ בְּהַאי
אֲתָר, אָמַר, אֲדֹנָי לָמָה הֲרֵעֹתָה לָעָם הַזֶּה וְגוֹ', וּמֵאָז בָּאתִי אֶל פַּרְעֹה
לְדַבֵּר בִּשְׁמֶךָ הֵרַע לָעָם הַזֶּה וְהַצֵּל לֹא הִצַּלְתָּ אֶת עַמֶּךָ. מַאן הוּא
דְּיֵימָא כְּדֵין, אֶלָּא מֹשֶׁה, דְּיָדַע, דְּהָא דַּרְגָּא אָחֳרָא עִלָּאָה זַמִּין לֵיהּ.

9. Come and see: It is written, "And Elohim spoke to Moses" (Shemot 6:1). THE NAME ELOHIM ALLUDES TO the decree of Judgment that is looming over him. It is written before: "And Moses returned to Hashem, and said, Adonai" (Shemot 5:22) spelled Aleph Dalet Nun Yud, WHICH IS THE NAME OF MALCHUT. See the strength of Moses, THAT AS SOON AS he started prophesying, his spirit did not rest at this place, WHICH IS MALCHUT. He said, "Adonai, why have You dealt ill with this people? why is it that You have sent me? for since I came to Pharaoh to speak in Your name he has done evil to this people; neither have You delivered your people at all" (Ibid. 22-23). Who CAN talk like this? Only Moses who knew that a another, higher level THAN MALCHUT was intended for him, BECAUSE HE WAS A CHARIOT TO ZEIR ANPIN, WHICH IS THE HUSBAND OF QUEEN.

10. אָמַר רִבִּי יִצְחָק, בְּשֵׁירוּתָא דְּאִתְיְהִיב לֵיהּ בֵּיתָא, פָּקִיד לָהּ, כְּבָר
נָשׁ דְּפָקִיד לְבֵיתֵיהּ, וְאָמַר כָּל מַאן דְּבָעֵי בְּלָא דְּחִילוּ. אוּף הָכִי מֹשֶׁה,
לְבֵיתֵיהּ קָאֲמַר, וְלָא דָחִיל.

10. Rabbi Yitzchak said, at first, the house, WHICH IS MALCHUT, was given to him, FOR BEING A CHARIOT TO ZEIR ANPIN, WHICH IS THE HUSBAND OF MALCHUT, HE MERITED THE LEVEL OF MALCHUT AS HIS HOUSE, AS IT IS A HOUSE FOR ZEIR ANPIN. THEREFORE, he commanded it like a man would command his household, and spoke whatever he wished to without fear. Moses too spoke to his household, WHICH IS MALCHUT, without fear.

11. דָּבָר אַחֵר וַיְדַבֵּר אֱלֹהִים, גְּזֵרַת דִּינָא, וַיֹּאמֶר אֵלָיו אֲנִי יְיָ', דַּרְגָּא
אָחֳרָא דְּרַחֲמֵי. וְהָכָא אִתְקַשַּׁר כּוֹלָּא כַּחֲדָא, דִּינָא וְרַחֲמֵי. הֲדָא הוּא
דִּכְתִיב, וַיֹּאמֶר אֵלָיו אֲנִי יְיָ'. אָמַר רִבִּי שִׁמְעוֹן אִי כְּתִיב וַיְדַבֵּר אֱלֹהִים

אֶל מֹשֶׁה אֲנִי ה', הַוֵינָא אָמַר הָכִי. אֶלָּא לָא כְּתִיב, אֶלָּא וַיְדַבֵּר אֱלֹהִים אֶל מֹשֶׁה בְּקַדְמֵיתָא, וּלְבָתַר וַיֹּאמֶר אֵלָיו אֲנִי ה', דְּמַשְׁמַע דַּרְגָּא בָּתַר דַּרְגָּא.

11. Another explanation of: "And Elohim spoke": THIS IS the decree of Judgment, AS THE NAME ELOHIM IS JUDGMENT, NAMELY MALCHUT. "And said to him, 'I am Hashem'": This is a different grade, NAMELY, ZEIR ANPIN which is Mercy, and here everything is connected together, Judgment and Mercy TOGETHER, WHICH IS GREAT WHOLENESS. This is the meaning of: "And said to him, 'I am Hashem'", WHICH IS THE ATTRIBUTE OF MERCY. Rabbi Shimon said, If it were written: "And Elohim spoke to Moses, 'I am Hashem'", I would say THAT FOR HIM JUDGMENT AND MERCY WERE LINKED TOGETHER. But it is not written so. Rather, it is first written: "And Elohim spoke to Moses" and then: "And said to him, 'I am Hashem,'" which means they are a grade after another grade INSTEAD OF JUDGMENT AND MERCY LINKED TOGETHER.

12. וְאָמַר רִבִּי יוֹסֵי, מֹשֶׁה, אִלְמָלֵא דַהֲוָה מָארֵיהּ דְּבֵיתָא, אִישׁ הָאֱלֹהִים, אִתְעַנַּשׁ עַל מַה דְּאָמַר, אֲבָל בְּגִינֵי הַאי, לָא אִתְעַנַּשׁ. לְבַר נָשׁ דְּנָפַל לֵיהּ קְטָטָה בִּדְבֵיתְהוּ, וְאָמַר לָהּ מִלִּין, שָׁרִאַת הִיא לְאִתְרַעֲמָא, כֵּיוָן דְּשָׁאֲרִית מִלָּה, הֲוָה תַּמָּן מַלְכָּא, נָטַל מַלְכָּא מִלָּה, וְהִיא שָׁתְקַת וּפַסְקַת לְמַלְלָא. אָמַר לֵיהּ מַלְכָּא, וְכִי לָא יָדַעְתְּ דַּאֲנָא הוּא מַלְכָּא, וּמִקָּמַאי מַלִּילַת מִלִּין אִלֵּין, כִּבְיָכוֹל אוּף הָכִי מֹשֶׁה, וַיָּשָׁב מֹשֶׁה אֶל יְיָ' וַיֹּאמַר אֲדֹנָי לָמָה הֲרֵעוֹתָה וְגו'. מִיָּד, וַיְדַבֵּר אֱלֹהִים אֶל מֹשֶׁה, שָׁארֵי לְאִתְרַעֲמָא, מִיָּד נָטַל מַלְכָּא מִלָּה וַיֹּאמֶר אֵלָיו אֲנִי יְיָ' וְלָא יָדַעְתְּ דַּאֲנָא הוּא מַלְכָּא, וּמִקָּמַאי מַלִּילַת מִלִּין אִלֵּין.

12. Rabbi Yosi said, Had not Moses been the master of the house, AS IS WRITTEN ABOUT HIM: "A PRAYER BY MOSES, the man of Elohim" (Tehilim 90:1), he would have been punished for saying TO ADONAI, "WHY HAVE YOU dealt ill WITH THIS PEOPLE..." (SHEMOT 5:22). But since HE WAS THE MASTER OF THE HOUSE, he was not punished. THIS IS LIKENED TO a man who had a quarrel with his wife, WHO WAS THE KING'S DAUGHTER, and spoke to her IMPROPER words. She started to complain, but as soon as she started speaking, the king, who was present, took over the matter, and she became silent and stopped speaking. The king said TO HER HUSBAND, Don't you know that I am the king, and that it is in my presence that you spoke these words? Similarly, so to speak, with Moses, AS IS WRITTEN, "And Moses returned to Hashem and said 'Adonai, why have You dealt ill...'" Immediately "Elohim spoke to Moses," WHICH IS THE ATTRIBUTE OF JUDGMENT BECAUSE THE KING'S DAUGHTER started to complain. Immediately, the King took up the complaint, "And said to him 'I am Hashem.'" Did you not know that I am King, and it is in My presence that you spoke these words?

13. וָאֵרָא אֶל אַבְרָהָם אֶל יִצְחָק וְאֶל יַעֲקֹב בְּאֵל שַׁדָּי. אֲמַאי שָׁנֵי שְׁמָא הָכָא מֵאִלֵּין דִּלְעֵילָּא. אֶלָּא לְמַלְכָּא, דַּהֲוָה לֵיהּ בְּרַתָּא, דְּלָא אִתְנְסִיבַת, וַהֲוָה לֵיהּ רְחִימָא. כַּד בָּעֵי מַלְכָּא לְמַלְּלָא בְּהַהוּא רְחִימָא, מְשַׁדַּר לִבְרַתֵּיהּ לְמַלְּלָא עִמֵּיהּ, וַהֲוָה מַלְכָּא עַל יְדָא דִּבְרַתֵּיהּ, מְמַלֵּיל עִמֵּיהּ. אָתָא זִמְנָא דִּבְרַתֵּיהּ לְאִתְנַסְּבָא, הַהוּא יוֹמָא דְּאִתְנְסִיבַת, אָמַר מַלְכָּא, קָרוֹן לָהּ לִבְרַתָּא, קְרוֹסְפּוּנְיָא מַטְרוֹנִיתָא. וְאָמַר לָהּ, עַד הָכָא, מַלִּילְנָא עַל יְדָךְ, לְמַאן דְּמַלִּילְנָא מִכָּאן וּלְהָלְאָה אֲנָא אֵימָא לְבַעֲלִיךְ, וְהוּא יֵימָא לְמַאן דְּאִצְטְרִיךְ. לְיוֹמִין, אָמַר לָהּ בַּעֲלָהּ מִלִּין קַמֵּי מַלְכָּא, עַד דְּהִיא שָׁרְאַת לְמַלְּלָא, נָטַל מַלְכָּא מִלָּה, אָמַר לֵיהּ, וְלָאו אֲנָא מַלְכָּא, דְּעַד יוֹמָא דָּא לָא מַלִּיל אֵינָשׁ עִמִּי, אֶלָּא עַל יְדָא דִּבְרַתִּי, וַאֲנָא יָהֵיבְנָא לָךְ בְּרַתִּי, וּמַלִּילְנָא עִמָּךְ בְּאִתְגַּלְיָא, מַה דְּלָא עֲבִידְנָא לְאָחֳרָא.

13. "And I appeared to Abraham, to Isaac, and to Jacob by, the name of El Shadai." Why did He use a different name than the names before, WHICH WERE ADONAI, YUD HEI VAV HEI ELOHIM, AND HERE HE SAID EL SHADAI. HE ANSWERS, THIS IS LIKENED to a king who had an unmarried daughter, and also a beloved friend. When the king wanted to speak with his beloved friend, he used to send his daughter to speak to him and thus the king spoke to him through his daughter. The time has come for his daughter to marry. On the day she married, the king said to her, precious queen, until now I spoke through you to whomever I wished to. From now on, I will tell your husband and he will speak with whomever it is necessary. After some

time, the husband said HARSH words to her in the king's presence. Before she started to talk, the king took the cause and said to him, am I not the king? Until this day no person spoke to me except through my daughter. And I gave you my daughter, and I spoke to you openly, a thing I have not done for any other person.

14. כָּךְ, וָאֵרָא אֶל אַבְרָהָם אֶל יִצְחָק וְאֶל יַעֲקֹב בְּאֵל שַׁדָּי, כַּד אִיהִי בְּבֵיתִי וְלָא אִתְנְסִיבַת, וְלָא מַלִּילוּ עִמִּי אַנְפִּין בְּאַנְפִּין, כְּמָה דְּעֲבִידְנָא לָךְ. וְאַתְּ, בְּשֵׁירוּתָא דְּמִלּוּלָךְ, מַלִּילַת לִבְרַתִּי קַמָּאי מִלִּין אִלֵּין, אֶלָּא בְּגִינֵי כָּךְ, וָאֵרָא אֶל אַבְרָהָם אֶל יִצְחָק וְאֶל יַעֲקֹב בְּאֵל שַׁדָּי וּשְׁמִי יְיָ' לֹא נוֹדַעְתִּי לָהֶם, לְמַלְּלָא עִמְּהוֹן בְּדַרְגָּא דָּא דְּעִמָּךְ מַלִּילְנָא.

14. Similarly, "And I appeared to Abraham, to Isaac, and to Jacob, by the name of El Shadai," WHICH IS THE NAME OF MALCHUT BEFORE SHE UNITED WITH ZEIR ANPIN FACE TO FACE. THIS MEANS, I APPEARED TO THE PATRIARCHS BY THE NAME OF EL SHADAI, WHICH IS MALCHUT when she was unmarried in My house. I was not spoken to face to face as I did with you, and you, at the beginning of your speech, said to My daughter in My presence such words. Therefore, IT IS WRITTEN: "And I appeared to Abraham, to Isaac, and to Jacob, by the name of El Shadai, but by My name, Hashem, I was not known to them," THAT IS, to speak to them in the grade in which I spoke to you.

15. רִבִּי יוֹסֵי פָּתַח, לְדָוִד מִזְמוֹר לַיְיָ' הָאָרֶץ וּמְלוֹאָהּ תֵּבֵל וְיוֹשְׁבֵי בָהּ. הָאָרֶץ: דָּא אַרְעָא קַדִּישָׁא דְּיִשְׂרָאֵל, דְּאִיהִי קַיְימָא לְאִתְשַׁקְיָיא מִנֵּיהּ, וּלְאִתְבָּרְכָא מִנֵּיהּ בְּקַדְמֵיתָא, וּלְבָתַר מִנָּהּ אִתְשַׁקְיָיא עָלְמָא כֹּלָּא. תֵּבֵל וְיוֹשְׁבֵי בָהּ: דָּא שְׁאָר אַרְעָאן, דְּשַׁתְאָן מִינָהּ, מְנָא לָן. דִּכְתִיב, וְהוּא יִשְׁפֹּט תֵּבֵל בְּצֶדֶק.

15. Rabbi Yosi opened the discussion saying, "A psalm of David. The earth is Hashem's and the fullness thereof; the world, and they that dwell in it" (Tehilim 24:1). The earth refers to the Holy land of Yisrael that is the first to be blessed by Him and watered by Him, BY HASHEM. Afterwards, the whole world is watered from it. "The world, and they that dwell in it" refers to the rest of the lands that drink from it. How do we know this? From the

words: "And He will judge the world in righteousness" (Tehilim 9:9).

16. כִּי הוּא עַל יַמִּים יְסָדָהּ, אִלֵּין שִׁבְעָה עַמּוּדִים, דְּאַרְעָא סְמִיכָא עֲלַיְיהוּ. וְאִינּוּן שִׁבְעָה יַמִּים. וְיַם כִּנֶּרֶת שַׁלְטָא עֲלַיְיהוּ. א״ר יְהוּדָה, לָא תֵּימָא דְּשַׁלְטָא עֲלַיְיהוּ, אֶלָּא דְּאִתְמַלְיָיא מִנַּיְיהוּ. וְעַל נְהָרוֹת יְכוֹנְנֶהָ, מַאן אִינּוּן נְהָרוֹת. אֶלָּא, כד״א, נָשְׂאוּ נְהָרוֹת קוֹלָם יִשְׂאוּ נְהָרוֹת דָּכְיָם, אִינּוּן נְהָרוֹת, כד״א, וְנָהָר יוֹצֵא מֵעֵדֶן לְהַשְׁקוֹת אֶת הַגָּן, וּבְגִין כַּךְ, וְעַל נְהָרוֹת יְכוֹנְנֶהָ.

16. "For He has founded it upon seas" (Tehilim 24:2). There are seven pillars, WHICH ARE SEVEN SFIROT - CHESED, GVURAH, TIFERET, NETZACH, HOD, YESOD AND MALCHUT OF ZEIR ANPIN, on which the earth supports itself, and which are seven seas. The Sea of Kineret (Galilee), WHICH IS MALCHUT, rules over them. Rabbi Yehuda said, Do not say it rules over them BECAUSE MALCHUT DOES NOT RULE OVER THE SEVEN SFIROT OF ZEIR ANPIN, but THE SEA OF KINERET is filled from them, BECAUSE MALCHUT RECEIVES FROM THEM: "And established it on the rivers" (Ibid.) HE ASKS, Which rivers are being referred to? AND HE ANSWERS, It is written: "The floods have lifted up, Hashem, the floods (lit. 'rivers') have lifted up their voice" (Tehilim 93:3), WHICH ARE THE SFIROT OF YESOD OF ZEIR ANPIN WHICH IS CALLED RIVER, as written: "And a river went out from Eden to water the garden" (Beresheet 2:10). Therefore, IT IS WRITTEN: "He established it on the rivers."

17. תָּא חֲזֵי, הַאי אֶרֶץ, אִקְרֵי אֶרֶץ יִשְׂרָאֵל. יַעֲקֹב דְּאִיהוּ יִשְׂרָאֵל, אֲמַאי לָא שַׁלִּיט עַל דָּא כְּמֹשֶׁה, דְּהָא כְּתִיב וָאֵרָא אֶל אַבְרָהָם אֶל יִצְחָק וְאֶל יַעֲקֹב בְּאֵל שַׁדָּי וְלָא יַתִּיר.

17. Come and see, this land, WHICH IS MALCHUT, is called BY THE NAME the land of Yisrael WHEN FACE TO FACE WITH ZEIR ANPIN THAT IS CALLED YISRAEL. HE ASKS, Why does not Jacob, who is Israel, rule over it like Moses? FOR HE IS ALSO A CHARIOT TO ZEIR ANPIN, WHICH IS CALLED YISRAEL. For it is written: "And I appeared to Abraham, to Isaac, and to Jacob, by the name of El Shadai", WHICH IS THE NAME OF THE NUKVA, BEFORE SHE UNITES WITH ZEIR ANPIN, and no more.

18. אֶלָּא, יַעֲקֹב הָא אוֹקִימְנָא, נָטַל בֵּיתָא דִּלְתַתָּא, וְאִשְׁתְּבִיק מִנֵּיהּ
בֵּיתָא דִּלְעֵילָּא. וְעִם בֵּיתָא דִּלְתַתָּא, אַתְקִין בֵּיתָא דִּלְעֵילָּא, בִּתְרֵיסַר
שְׁבָטִין, בְּשַׁבְעִין עַנְפִּין, וְהָא אוּקְמוּהָ. מֹשֶׁה, נָטַל בֵּיתָא דִּלְעֵילָּא,
וְשָׁבִיק בֵּיתָא דִּלְתַתָּא. וע״ד, כְּתִיב בְּיַעֲקֹב בְּאֵל שַׁדָּי. בְּאֵל שַׁדָּי מַלִּיל
עִמֵּיהּ קוּדְשָׁא בְּרִיךְ הוּא, וְלָא יַתִּיר. וּשְׁמִי יְיָ׳ לֹא נוֹדַעְתִּי לָהֶם,
לְמַלְּלָא עִמְּהוֹן בְּדַרְגָּא דָא דְּאִיהוּ עִלָּאָה.

18. HE ANSWERS, We have already established that Jacob took the terrestrial house, THAT IS, IN THIS WORLD. Therefore, he lost the celestial house, WHICH IS MALCHUT, but with the terrestrial house, THAT IS, THE FOUR WIVES, he reestablished the celestial house, WHICH IS MALCHUT, with twelve tribes, with seventy branches REFERRING TO ITS SEVENTY NAMES, WHICH IS THE MEANING OF THE SEVENTY SOULS WHO CAME TO EGYPT. And we have already established that Moses took the celestial house, WHICH IS MALCHUT, and forsook the terrestrial house BECAUSE HE SEPARATED FROM HIS WIFE. Therefore, it is written of Jacob: "By the name of El Shadai," AS MENTIONED. BECAUSE ONLY by the name El Shadai did the Holy One, blessed be He, speak to him and no more THAN THIS. "But by My name, Hashem, I was not known to them," MEANING to speak to them in this level OF YUD HEI VAV HEI, which is superior.

19. וָאֵרָא אֶל אַבְרָהָם אֶל יִצְחָק וְאֶל יַעֲקֹב. א״ר חִיָּיא, תּוּשְׁבְּחָן
דַּאֲבָהָן יַעֲקֹב הֲוָה, דְּהוּא שְׁלִימוּ דְּכֹלָּא. בְּכֻלְּהוּ כְּתִיב, אֶל אַבְרָהָם, אֶל
יִצְחָק, וּבֵיהּ אִתּוֹסַף אָת חַד, דִּכְתִיב, וְאֶל יַעֲקֹב. אִתּוֹסַף בֵּיהּ ו׳,
לְאַחֲזָאָה דְּאִיהוּ שְׁלֵימָא יַתִּיר מִכֻּלְּהוּ. וְעִם כָּל דָּא, לָא זָכָה
לְאִשְׁתַּמְּשָׁא בֵּיהּ כְּמֹשֶׁה.

19. "And I appeared to Abraham, to Isaac, and to Jacob." Rabbi Chiya said, The glory of the patriarchs was Jacob, who was all-perfect. By all, it is written "to Abraham, to Isaac," but by him a letter was added, as is written: "and (= Vav) to Jacob." The letter Vav was added to him to show that he was more whole than them all. But notwithstanding, he did not merit uniting with it, WITH MALCHUT, like Moses did, AS EARLIER MENTIONED.

20. וְגַם הֲקִמֹתִי אֶת בְּרִיתִי אִתָּם לָתֵת לָהֶם אֶת אֶרֶץ כְּנַעַן, בְּגִין

1. "And I appeared...by the name of El Shadai, but by My name, Hashem, I was not known to them"

דְּאִתְגְּזָרוּ. דְּכָל מַאן דְּאִתְגְּזַר, יָרִית אַרְעָא, דְּהָא לָא יָרִית אַרְעָא, אֶלָּא
צַדִּיק, וְכָל מַאן דְּאִתְגְּזַר, אִקְרֵי צַדִּיק. דִּכְתִּיב וְעַמֵּךְ כֻּלָּם צַדִּיקִים
לְעוֹלָם יִירְשׁוּ אָרֶץ, כָּל מַאן דְּאִתְגְּזַר, וְנָטִיר הַאי אָת קַיָּימָא, אִקְרֵי
צַדִּיק, תָּא חֲזֵי מִן יוֹסֵף, דְּכָל יוֹמוֹי לָא אִקְרֵי צַדִּיק, עַד דְּנָטִיר הַהוּא
בְּרִית, אָת קַיָּימָא קַדִּישָׁא. כֵּיוָן דְּנָטַר לֵיהּ, אִקְרֵי צַדִּיק, יוֹסֵף הַצַּדִּיק.

20. "And I have also established my covenant with them to give them the land of Canaan" (Shemot 6:4). IT IS because they were circumcised. For all who are circumcised inherit the land. THEREFORE THE TORAH SAYS, "TO GIVE THEM THE LAND OF CANAAN." For the land is inherited only by a righteous person and everyone who is circumcised is called righteous, as is written: "Your people also shall be all righteous, they shall inherit the land forever" (Yeshayah 60:21). Everyone who is circumcised and observes the sign of the covenant is called righteous. Come and learn this from Joseph, who was not called righteous in his life until he observed that covenant, the sign of the holy covenant. Once he observed it BY THE INCIDENT OF THE WIFE OF POTIFAR, he was called righteous, namely, Joseph the righteous.

2. Visible and invisible colors

A Synopsis

Rabbi Elazar wonders why in the passage: "And I appeared to Abraham, to Isaac and to Jacob etc.," it says, "And I appeared" rather than "And I spoke." Rabbi Shimon explains the secret of visible and invisible colors. The patriarchs saw the visible colors of El Shadai that are the reflection of the supernal colors. Moses was the only person to be able to see the higher colors of Chesed-Gvurah-Tiferet. Next Rabbi Shimon turns to: "And they who are wise shall shine like the brightness of the firmament; and they who turn many to righteousness like the stars for ever and ever," saying that the 'wise' are the kind of person who understands higher matters intuitively because they are too deep for words. He explains that there are four lights: the light that illuminates, the light that shines, purple light and the light that does not illuminate. These correspond to Chesed, Gvurah, Tiferet and Malchut. The three higher lights are reflected in Malchut. We are told that there are three colors in the eye – white, red and green – which are like the three colors of Zeir Anpin. The pupil of the eye is black, the mirror that does not illuminate. Rabbi Shimon says that the secret of seeing the three concealed lights is to close your eyes and turn them inwardly toward Cholam, Shuruk and Chirik – the three places that receive love, power and beauty. When the eye is closed it sees the higher colors as did Moses, but when it is open it sees only the lower colors. This explains why Moses was spoken to by Yud Hei Vav Hei but the patriarchs were spoken to by El Shadai. Finally, Rabbi Shimon tells us that one is not allowed to greet a wicked person, but if one greets a righteous person it is the same as though he were greeting Hashem.

21. רִבִּי שִׁמְעוֹן הֲוָה יָתִיב יוֹמָא, חַד, וְרִבִּי אֶלְעָזָר בְּרֵיהּ, וְרִבִּי אַבָּא עִמֵּיהּ. א״ר אֶלְעָזָר, הַאי קְרָא דִּכְתִּיב, וָאֵרָא אֶל אַבְרָהָם אֶל יִצְחָק וְאֶל יַעֲקֹב וְגוֹ׳. מַהוּ וָאֵרָא, וַאֲדַבֵּר מִבָּעֵי לֵיהּ. אָמַר לֵיהּ, אֶלְעָזָר בְּרִי, רָזָא עִלָּאָה אִיהוּ.

21. One day Rabbi Shimon was sitting one day with his son Rabbi Elazar, and Rabbi Aba. Rabbi Elazar said, in the passage: "And I appeared to Abraham, to Isaac, and to Jacob..." (Shemot 6:3), why is "And I appeared" stated? It should state 'And I spoke.' RABBI SHIMON said to him, Elazar my son, this is a very high secret.

22. תָּא חֲזֵי, אִית גַּוְונִין דְּמִתְחַזְיָין, וְאִית גַּוְונִין דְּלָא מִתְחַזְיָין. וְאִלֵּין וְאִלֵּין, אִינוּן רָזָא עִלָּאָה דִּמְהֵימְנוּתָא, וּבְנֵי נָשָׁא לָא יַדְעִין לֵיהּ, וְלָא מִסְתַּכְּלִין בֵּיהּ. וְאִלֵּין דְּמִתְחַזְיָין, לָא זָכָה בְּהוּ בַּר נָשׁ, עַד דְּאָתוּ אֲבָהָן, וְקַיְּימוּ עֲלַיְיהוּ. וְעַל דָּא כְּתִיב וָאֵרָא, דְּחָמוּ, אִינוּן גַּוְונִין דְּאִתְגַּלְיָין.

22. Come and see: There are visible colors and invisible colors. And both are a high secret of the Faith, but people neither know it nor observe it. No one was worthy of the visible COLORS until the patriarchs came and understood them, THAT IS, CONCEIVED THEM. Of this it is written: "And I appeared," since they saw the visible colors.

23. וּמַאן גַּוְונִין דְּאִתְגַּלְיָין. אִינוּן דְּאֵל שַׁדָּי, דְּאִינוּן חֵיזוּ דִּגְוָונִין עִלָּאִין, וְאִלֵּין אִתְחַזְיָין. וּגְוָונִין דִּלְעֵילָּא, סְתִימִין דְּלָא אִתְחַזְיָין, לָא קָאֵים אִינִישׁ עֲלַיְיהוּ, בַּר מֹשֶׁה. וְעַל דָּא כְּתִיב, וּשְׁמִי יְיָ' לֹא נוֹדַעְתִּי לָהֶם, לָא אִתְגְּלֵיתִי לוֹן בְּגַוְונִין עִלָּאִין. וְאִי תֵּימָא, דַּאֲבָהָן לָא הֲווֹ יַדְעֵי בְּהוּ. אֶלָּא הֲווֹ יַדְעֵי, מִגּוֹ אִינוּן דְּאִתְגַּלְיָין.

23. And which colors appeared? They are of El Shadai, WHICH IS MALCHUT, which are the reflection of the supernal colors, WHICH ARE IN CHESED, GVURAH AND TIFERET OF ZEIR ANPIN. These are THE visible COLORS, WHICH MEANS THAT THEY CONTAIN CHOCHMAH. And the colors above, IN CHESED, GVURAH AND TIFERET OF ZEIR ANPIN, which are concealed since they are invisible, WHICH MEANS THEY DO NOT CONTAIN CHOCHMAH BUT ONLY THE LIGHT OF CHASSADIM, no person understood them TO PERCEIVE THEM THERE, IN ZEIR ANPIN, except for Moses. Of this it is written: "But by My name, Hashem, I was not known to them" (Ibid.), WHICH MEANS I did not appear to them in the superior colors IN CHESED, GVURAH AND TIFERET OF ZEIR ANPIN, WHICH IS CALLED *YUD HEI VAV HEI*. And if you claim that the patriarchs did not know THE NAME YUD HEI VAV HEI, WHICH IS CHESED, GVURAH AND TIFERET OF ZEIR ANPIN; THIS IS UTTERLY IMPOSSIBLE, FOR THE PATRIARCHS ARE A CHARIOT TO CHESED, GVURAH AND TIFERET OF ZEIR ANPIN. But rather, they knew it from those colors that were visible IN MALCHUT.

24. כְּתִיב וְהַמַּשְׂכִּילִים יַזְהִירוּ כְּזֹהַר הָרָקִיעַ וּמַצְדִּיקֵי הָרַבִּים כַּכּוֹכָבִים

לְעוֹלָם וָעֶד. וְהַמַּשְׂכִּילִים יַזְהִירוּ, מַאן אִינּוּן מַשְׂכִּילִים. אֶלָּא דָּא הוּא,
הַהוּא חָכָם דְּיִסְתַּכַּל מִגַּרְמֵיהּ מִלִּין, דְּלָא יָכִילִין בְּנֵי נָשָׁא לְמַלְלָא
בְּפוּמָא, וְאִלֵּין אִקְרוּן מַשְׂכִּילִים. יַזְהִירוּ כְּזֹהַר הָרָקִיעַ, מַאן הוּא
הָרָקִיעַ. דָּא הוּא רְקִיעַ דְּמֹשֶׁה, דְּקַיְּימָא בְּאֶמְצָעִיתָא, וְהַאי זֹהַר דִּילֵיהּ,
אִיהוּ סָתִים, וְלָא אִתְגַּלְיָיא מִגּוֹ דִּילֵיהּ קַיְּימָא עַל הַהִיא רְקִיעָא דְּלָא
נָהִיר, דְּאִתְחַזְיָין בֵּיהּ גַּוְונִין, וְאִינּוּן גַּוְונִין אע"ג דְּאִתְחַזְיָין בֵּיהּ, לָא
זַהֲרֵי כְּזֹהֲרָא בְּגִין דְּאִינּוּן גַּוְונִין סְתִימִין.

24. It is written: "And they who are wise shall shine like the brightness of the firmament; and they who turn many to righteousness like the stars for ever and ever" (Daniel 12:3). HE ASKS, In "And they who are wise shall shine," who are the wise ones. HE ANSWERS, This refers to the wise one who will perceive on his own LOFTY things that people cannot utter by mouth BECAUSE OF THEIR GREAT HEIGHT. And these are called "wise ones." "Shall shine like the brightness of the firmament": HE ASKS, What is the firmament? HE ANSWERS, This is the firmament of Moses, which is situated in the center, NAMELY, ZEIR ANPIN, WHICH IS THE SECRET OF THE CENTRAL COLUMN THAT INCLUDES THE TWO COLUMNS AS WELL, THE RIGHT AND THE LEFT. And its brightness is concealed and not revealed IN CHOCHMAH THAT IS CALLED BRIGHTNESS, THOUGH ITS LIGHT IS GREAT. By means of its color THAT INCLUDES ALL THREE COLORS, it is situated over and shines on the firmament that does not illuminate, WHICH IS MALCHUT, in which the colors are visible, WHICH MEANS IT ILLUMINATES WITH CHOCHMAH WHICH IS CALLED SIGHT. And even though these colors are visible in it, they do not illuminate like the brightness of those of unrevealed colors, WHICH ARE THE COLORS OF ZEIR ANPIN THAT IS CALLED THE ILLUMINATING FIRMAMENT.

25. תָּא חֲזֵי, אַרְבַּע נְהוֹרִין אִינּוּן. תְּלַת מִנַּיְיהוּ סְתִימִין, וְחַד
דְּאִתְגַּלְיָיא: נְהוֹרָא דְּנָהִיר. נְהוֹרָא דְּזָהֲרָא. וְאִיהוּ נָהִיר כְּזִהֲרוּ דִּשְׁמַיָּא
בְּדַכְיוּ. נְהוֹרָא דְּאַרְגְּוָונָא, דְּנָטִיל כָּל נְהוֹרִין. נְהוֹרָא דְּלָא נָהִיר אִסְתַּכַּל
לְגַבֵּי אִלֵּין, וְנָטִיל לוֹן, וְאִתְחַזְיָין אִינּוּן נְהוֹרִין בֵּיהּ, כַּעֲשָׁשִׁיתָא, לָקֳבֵל
שִׁמְשָׁא.

25. Come and see: There are four lights. Three of them are concealed,

NAMELY, CHESED, GVURAH AND TIFERET, and one, NAMELY, MALCHUT, is revealed. THEY ARE: (A) The shining light, WHICH IS CHESED AND THE RIGHT COLUMN; (B) the bright light, WHICH IS GVURAH AND THE LEFT COLUMN. And it shines like the brightness of the heaven for its clarity. THEREFORE IT IS REFERRED TO AS SHINING. (C) purple light, WHICH IS TIFERET AND THE CENTRAL COLUMN that receives all the lights, FOR THE CENTRAL COLUMN INCLUDES THE RIGHT AND THE LEFT; and (D) the light that does not illuminate, WHICH IS MALCHUT, that looks to these THREE ABOVE MENTIONED LIGHTS and receives them. These lights are visible in it like a reflector, which is A PLATE OF POLISHED METAL placed against the sun, AND THE SUN IS SEEN IN IT. SO THE THREE LIGHTS OF ZEIR ANPIN THAT IS CALLED SUN ARE VISIBLE IN MALCHUT, AND IN THIS RESPECT MALCHUT IS CALLED A REFLECTOR THAT RECEIVES FROM THE SUN AND THE SUN IS SEEN IN IT.

26. וְאִלֵּין תְּלַת דְּקָאמְרָן, סְתִימִין וְקַיְּימִין עַל הַאי דְּאִתְגַּלְיָיא. וְרָזָא דָא עֵינָא תָּא חֲזֵי, בְּעֵינָא אִית תְּלַת גַּוְונִין, דְּאִתְגַּלְיָין רְשִׁימִין בֵּיהּ, וְכֻלְּהוּ לָא מִזְדַּהֲרֵי, בְּגִין דְּקַיְּימֵי בִּנְהוֹרָא דְּלָא נָהִיר. וְאִלֵּין אִינּוּן כְּגַוְונָא דְּאִינּוּן סְתִימִין דְּקַיְּימֵי עֲלַיְיהוּ וְאִלֵּין אִינּוּן דְּאִתְחַזְיָין לַאֲבָהָן, לְמִנְדַּע אִינּוּן סְתִימִין דְּמִזְדַּהֲרִין, מִגּוֹ אִלֵּין דְּלָא מִזְדַּהֲרֵי. וְאִינּוּן דְּמִזְדַּהֲרֵי וְאִינּוּן סְתִימִין, אִתְגַּלְיָין לְמֹשֶׁה, בְּהַהוּא רְקִיעָא דִּילֵיהּ. וְאִלֵּין קַיְּימֵי, עַל אִינּוּן גַּוְונִין דְּאִתְחַזְיָין בֵּיהּ בְּעֵינָא.

26. And those three LIGHTS we mentioned ABOVE are concealed IN THEIR PLACE IN ZEIR ANPIN, and are situated over this FOURTH, visible LIGHT, WHICH IS MALCHUT. THAT IS TO SAY, THE THREE LIGHTS FLOW TO THE FOURTH LIGHT, WHERE THE THREE LIGHTS BECOME REVEALED AND SHINE WITH CHOCHMAH. This secret is the eye. Come and see: there are three colors in the eye, WHITE, RED AND GREEN, that are visible THROUGH THE ILLUMINATION OF CHOCHMAH, AND were imprinted on it, NAMELY, ON THE FOURTH LIGHT THAT IS IN IT, WHICH IS THE BLACK OF THE EYE. None of them shines because they are placed in the light that does not shine, FOR THEIR MAIN SOURCE IS THE BLACK IN THE EYE, WHICH IS MALCHUT, WHICH IS THE MIRROR THAT DOES NOT ILLUMINATE. And these THREE COLORS THAT ARE IN THE EYE are like those THREE COLORS OF ZEIR ANPIN, which are hidden and are situated over them, THAT IS, THEY ARE THE ASPECTS OF THE THREE COLUMNS OF ZEIR ANPIN BUT

ILLUMINATE AND APPEAR IN THE PLACE OF MALCHUT. And they are the ones that appeared to the patriarchs in order to know and perceive these hidden THREE IN ZEIR ANPIN that appeared from within those that did not illuminate, MEANING THE THREE IN MALCHUT. And those that are bright yet hidden, WHICH ARE THE THREE IN THE PLACE OF ZEIR ANPIN, were revealed to Moses in his firmament. And these are situated over AND POUR ABUNDANCE TO these THREE colors that are visible in the eye, MEANING THOSE THAT APPEARED TO THE PATRIARCHS.

27. וְרָזָא דָּא סָתִים עֵינָךָ, וְאַסְחַר גַּלְגַּלָּךָ, וְיִתְגַּלְיָין אִינּוּן גְּווֹנִין דְּנַהֲרִין, דְּמִזְדַּהֲרֵי, וְלָא אִתְיְיהִיב רְשׁוּ לְמֶיחֱמֵי, אֶלָּא בְּעַיְינִין סְתִימִין, בְּגִין דְּאִינּוּן סְתִימִין עִלָּאִין, קַיְימֵי עַל אִינּוּן גְּווֹנִין דְּאִתְחַזְיָין, דְּלָא מִזְדַּהֲרֵי.

27. And it is a secret, THAT HE WHO WISHES TO SEE THE THREE CONCEALED IN ZEIR ANPIN, IS TOLD: Close your eyes, MEANING THAT HE SHOULD NOT DRAW CHOCHMAH WHICH IS CALLED EYES, and turn the EYE balls TOWARDS THREE PLACES-CHOLAM, SHURUK AND CHIRIK-THAT DRAW THE THREE COLUMNS OF CHESED, GVURAH AND TIFERET AS MENTIONED. In this way, the THREE colors IN ZEIR ANPIN will appear that illuminate WITH CHASSADIM and shine FROM THE BRIGHTNESS OF THE LEFT COLUMN. YET THEY ARE HIDDEN AND COVERED, since permission is given to see only with closed eyes these THREE hidden superior COLORS IN ZEIR ANPIN that are situated over AND POUR ABUNDANCE TO these three colors that are visible IN MALCHUT that do not shine.

28. וְעַל דָּא קָרֵינָן, מֹשֶׁה זָכָה בְּאַסְפָּקְלַרְיָא דְּנָהֲרָא דְּקַיְימָא עַל הַהוּא דְּלָא נָהֲרָא. שְׁאָר בְּנֵי עָלְמָא, בְּהַהוּא אַסְפָּקְלַרְיָא דְּלָא נָהֲרָא. וַאֲבָהָן הֲווֹ חָמָאן מִגּוֹ אִלֵּין גְּווֹנִין דְּאִתְגַּלְיָין, אִינּוּן סְתִימִין, דְּקַיְימֵי עֲלַיְיהוּ דְּאִינּוּן דְּלָא נָהֲרִין, וע"ד כְּתִיב, וָאֵרָא אֶל אַבְרָהָם אֶל יִצְחָק וְאֶל יַעֲקֹב בְּאֵל שַׁדָּי, בְּאִינּוּן גְּווֹנִין דְּאִתְחַזְיָין.

28. And of this we learned that Moses merited the illuminating mirror, THE THREE COLUMNS OF ZEIR ANPIN AS MENTIONED that is placed over AND

ILLUMINATES TO that MIRROR, which does not illuminate. Other people WERE WORTHY of the mirror, which does not illuminate ONLY, WHICH IS MALCHUT. But the patriarchs saw from within these three colors that appear IN MALCHUT those hidden THREE COLORS that are situated over them AND SHINE ON THEM, WHICH ARE THE THREE COLUMNS OF ZEIR ANPIN, which THREE VISIBLE IN MALCHUT do not shine. SO WE CONCLUDE THAT ALSO THE PATRIARCHS CONCEIVED CHESED, GVURAH AND TIFERET OF ZEIR ANPIN, THOUGH NOT FROM THEIR PLACE IN ZEIR ANPIN, BUT ONLY FROM CHESED, GVURAH AND TIFERET THAT ARE RECEIVED IN MALCHUT AND APPEAR THERE. Therefore it is written: "And I appeared to Abraham, to Isaac, and to Jacob, by the name of El Shadai", that is, by the THREE colors that are visible IN MALCHUT THAT IS CALLED EL SHADAI.

29. וּשְׁמִי יְיָ' לֹא נוֹדַעְתִּי לָהֶם, אִלֵּין גַּוְונִין עִלָּאִין סְתִימִין דְּזָהֲרִין, דְּזָכָה בְּהוּ מֹשֶׁה לְאִסְתַּכְּלָא בְּהוֹן. וְרָזָא דָּא, דְּעֵינָא סָתִים וְגַלְיָא. סָתִים, חָמֵי אַסְפַּקְלַרְיָא דְּנָהֲרָא, אִתְגַּלְיָיא, חָמֵי אַסְפַּקְלַרְיָא דְּלָא נָהֲרָא. וְעַל דָּא, וָאֵרָא, בְּאַסְפַּקְלַרְיָא דְּלָא נָהֲרָא, דְּאִיהוּ בְּאִתְגַּלְיָיא, בֵּיהּ כְּתִיב רְאִיָּה. בְּאַסְפַּקְלַרְיָא דְּנָהֲרָא דְּאִיהוּ בִּסְתִימוּ, כְּתִיב בֵּיהּ יְדִיעָה, דִּכְתִיב לֹא נוֹדַעְתִּי. אָתוּ רַבִּי אֶלְעָזָר וְרַבִּי אַבָּא וְנָשְׁקוּ יְדוֹי. בָּכָה רַבִּי אַבָּא, וְאָמַר, וַוי כַּד תִּסְתַּלַּק מֵעָלְמָא, וְיִשְׁתְּאַר עָלְמָא יָתוֹם מִינָּךְ, מַאן יָכִיל לְאַנְהָרָא מִלִּין דְּאוֹרַיְיתָא.

29. "But by My name, Hashem, I was not known to them": These are the supernal colors that are hidden yet illuminate, THE SECRET OF CHESED, GVURAH AND TIFERET OF ZEIR ANPIN THAT IS CALLED YUD HEI VAV HEI that Moses merited to observe. And this is the secret reason why the eye is SOMETIMES closed and SOMETIMES, IF IT IS OPEN, IS visible. IF IT IS closed, it sees the illuminating mirror, WHICH IS CHESED, GVURAH AND TIFERET OF ZEIR ANPIN, AND IF IT IS open, it sees the mirror that does not illuminate, WHICH IS MALCHUT, AS MENTIONED. Therefore, THE VERSE SAYS, "And I appeared" in the mirror that does not illuminate, which is revealed, AS THE THREE COLORS ARE VISIBLE IN IT. Sight is mentioned in relation to it. BUT in relation to the illuminating mirror, WHICH IS ZEIR ANPIN, which is concealed, THAT IS, SIGHT DOES NOT PERTAIN TO IT, knowledge is mentioned, as is written: "BUT BY MY NAME, HASHEM, I was not known." AND IT DOES NOT SAY 'I DID NOT APPEAR,' SINCE SIGHT

APPLIES ONLY TO MALCHUT. Rabbi Elazar and Rabbi Aba approached and kissed the hands OF RABBI SHIMON. Rabbi Aba wept and said, Woe, when you are gone from the world and the world will remain orphaned from you. Who will be able to illuminate THEN the words of Torah?

30. פָּתַח רִבִּי אַבָּא וְאָמַר, וַאֲמַרְתֶּם כֹּה לֶחָי וְאַתָּה שָׁלוֹם וּבֵיתְךָ שָׁלוֹם וְכֹל אֲשֶׁר לְךָ שָׁלוֹם. וַאֲמַרְתֶּם כֹּה לֶחָי, וְכִי דָוִד לָא הֲוָה יָדַע בֵּיה בְּנָבָל, דְּאִיהוּ אָמַר בְּגִינֵיה, וַאֲמַרְתֶּם כֹּה לֶחָי, אֶלָּא, הַהוּא יוֹמָא טָבָא דר"ה הֲוָה, וְקוּדְשָׁא בְּרִיךְ הוּא יָתִיב בְּדִינָא עַל עָלְמָא, וּבְגִין קוּדְשָׁא בְּרִיךְ הוּא קָאָמַר, וַאֲמַרְתֶּם כֹּה, לֶחָי, לְקַשְׁרָא כֹּה, לֶחָי, דְּכָל חַיִּין בֵּיה תַּלְיָין. וְאַתָּה שָׁלוֹם, מַאי וְאַתָּה אַתָּה מִבְּעֵי לֵיה. אֶלָּא, וְאַתָּה כֹּלָּא לְקוּדְשָׁא בְּרִיךְ הוּא קָאָמַר, בְּגִין לְקַשְׁרָא קִשְׁרָא דִּמְהֵימָנוּתָא וְכַדְקָא יֵאוּת.

30. Rabbi Aba opened the discussion saying, "And thus (Heb. koh) shall you say so to him, a hearty greeting (lit. 'to the living')! Peace be both to you, and peace to your house, and peace to all that you have" (I Shmuel 25:6). HE ASKS, IT IS WRITTEN, "And you shall say koh to the living," WHICH MEANS THAT RICHES AND HONOR BEFIT A LIVING MAN, THAT IS, A RIGHTEOUS MAN. Did not David know Naval TO BE EVIL, to have said of him, SAYING TO HIM: "koh to the living?" HE ANSWERS, That day was the holy day of Rosh Hashanah (the Jewish New Year) and the Holy One, blessed be He, was sitting in judgment over the world. For the Holy One, blessed be He, he said, "And you shall say koh to the living" in order to attach 'koh' WHICH IS MALCHUT, to the 'living', WHICH IS YESOD OF ZEIR ANPIN, from which all life comes. "Peace be both to you." HE ASKS, What is "both to you?" IT SHOULD SAY 'YOU', SO WHEREFORE IS 'VAV (BOTH)?' HE ANSWERS, "both to you" refers to the Holy One, blessed be He, in order to connect the link of Faith, WHICH IS MALCHUT, WHICH IS CALLED "YOU" TO ZEIR ANPIN THAT IS CALLED VAV as is proper. THEREFORE, "BOTH TO YOU" IS SPELLED WITH A VAV.

31. מִכָּאן אוֹלִיפְנָא, דְּהָא לְבַר נָשׁ חַיָּיבָא, אָסוּר לְאַקְדְּמָא לֵיה שְׁלָם, וְאִי אִצְטְרִיךְ, יַקְדִּים לֵיה כְּדָוִד, דְּבָרִיךְ לֵיה לְקוּדְשָׁא בְּרִיךְ הוּא, וְאִתְחֲזֵי דִּבְגִינֵיה קָאָמַר. וְאִי תֵּימָא דְּרַמָּאוּת הֲוָה. לָאו. דְּהָא כָּל מַאן

דְּסָלִיק לֵיהּ לְקוּדְשָׁא בְּרִיךְ הוּא, וְאִתְחֲזֵי דִּבְגִינֵיהּ קָאָמַר, לָאו רְמָאוּת הוּא. וּמַאן דְּאַקְדִּים שְׁלָם לְזַכָּאָה, כְּאִילּוּ אַקְדִּים לֵיהּ לְקוּדְשָׁא בְּרִיךְ הוּא, כ"ש מַר, דְּאִיהוּ שְׁלָמָא לְעֵילָא וְתַתָּא.

31. From this I deduce that it is forbidden to be the first to greet a wicked person and, if he is forced TO DO SO, he should be the first TO GREET like David who blessed the Holy One, blessed be He, though it seemed he spoke to him, NAVAL. And if you say it was deception, it is not so because it is not considered deception for anyone to offer up HIS WORDS to the Holy One, blessed be He, though it seems he spoke TO A PERSON. BECAUSE THIS IS THE WAY OF THE RIGHTEOUS, WHO SEEMINGLY SPEAK TO A PERSON, BUT OFFER THEIR WORDS TO THE HOLY ONE, BLESSED BE HE, IN ORDER TO FULFILL THE PASSAGE: "I HAVE SET HASHEM ALWAYS BEFORE ME" (TEHILIM 16:8). Whoever is the first to greet a righteous person, it is as though he is the first to greet the Holy One, blessed be He, and all the more so my master, MEANING RABBI SHIMON, who is the peace of above and below.

3. The four elements – fire, air, water, earth

A Synopsis

Rabbi Chizkiyah tells us that when man was created he was made from the dust of the Temple of below, and that the four winds of the world – Chesed, Gvurah, Tiferet and Malchut – became joined there. These four winds joined in the four elements of the world: fire, air, water and dust. Furthermore, the four directions of the world joined in the four elements. In this way the body of man is composed of and joins together the lower world and the world above. Next Rabbi Chizkiyah says that gold, silver, copper and iron are emitted from fire, air, water and dust. He explains further that fire stands in the direction of north, air in the east, water in the south and dust in the west. Opposites are combined, in that fire has power of heat and dryness, and it combines with the cold moist north. Water combines with the hot dry south. The east draws from them both so it is hot and moist. Fire and water circulate back and forth between these directions. They are in conflict, though, because fire wants to burn up water and water wants to extinguish fire. It is the air that reconciles them, as is seen in: "And the wind of Elohim hovers upon the surface of the water." Dust, then, receives from fire, water and air. The air is hot and moist because it draws from fire and water. Because dust is cold and dry it can receive from all of them. Next we are told how the metals are created from earth, air, fire and water. When the dust fused with fire, water and air to produce gold, silver and copper, the dirt became stronger and brought forth other metals. It also produced four rivers where the twelve precious stones are found that correspond to the twelve tribes and the twelve oxen under the sea. However, the main sustenance of the world is still the air, or spirit. Without it nothing could exist. The soul, Nefesh, could not exist without the air, Ruach. This is the secret of: "Also, that the soul be without knowledge is not good." Rabbi Shimon says that man's body was created from the dust of Malchut yet his soul was given to him from the dust of Binah. When he was created from the dust of above and below the fire, air and water of above and below were combined in him. This is how man was completed with a body and a soul.

The Relevance of the paragraph

At last we are told how the elements that make up the world are combined in the human being, and how the spirit sustains everything. We can use the images of fire, water and air circulating and exchanging properties to remind ourselves what amazing creatures we are, well suited to the amazing creation of the world we inhabit. Another thing to contemplate while reading this section is the question of whether the elements could ever have combined at all if they hadn't done so in the human being, and if this isn't the essential reason for the creation of mankind.

32. וָאֵרָא אֶל אַבְרָהָם אֶל יִצְחָק וְאֶל יַעֲקֹב בְּאֵל שַׁדָּי וּשְׁמִי יְיָ׳ לֹא נוֹדַעְתִּי לָהֶם. רִבִּי חִזְקִיָּה פָּתַח, אַשְׁרֵי אָדָם לֹא יַחְשֹׁב ה׳ לוֹ עָוֹן וְגוֹ׳. כַּמָּה אִינוּן בְּנֵי נָשָׁא אֲטִימִין, דְּלָא יָדְעִין, וְלָא מִסְתַּכְּלָן, עַל מַה קַיְימִין בְּעָלְמָא. דְּהָא קוּדְשָׁא בְּ״ה כַּד בָּרָא עָלְמָא, עָבֵד לֵיהּ לְבַר נָשׁ בְּדִיּוּקְנָא דִּילֵיהּ, וְאַתְקִין לֵיהּ בְּתִקּוּנוֹי, בְּגִין דְּיִשְׁתַּדַּל בְּאוֹרַיְיתָא, וְיֵהַךְ בְּאוֹרְחוֹי.

32. "And I appeared to Abraham, to Isaac, and to Jacob, by the name of El Shadai, but by My name, Hashem, I was not known to them" (Shemot 6:3). Rabbi Chizkiyah opened the discussion saying, "Blessed is the man to whom Hashem imputes no iniquity..." (Tehilim 32:2). How obtuse are people who do not know and do not observe why they are in the world. For when the Holy One, blessed be He, created the world, He made man in His image and made him the way He did, in order that he should be occupied with the Torah and walk in His ways.

33. דְּהָא כַּד אִתְבְּרֵי אָדָם, מֵעַפְרָא דְּמַקְדְּשָׁא דִּלְתַתָּא אִתַּתְקַן וְאַרְבַּע סִטְרֵי דְּעָלְמָא, אִתְחַבְּרוּ בְּהַהוּא אֲתָר דְּאִקְרֵי בֵּי מַקְדְּשָׁא. וְאִינוּן אַרְבַּע סִטְרִין דְּעָלְמָא, אִתְחַבְּרוּ בְּאַרְבַּע סִטְרִין, דְּאִינוּן יְסוֹדִין דְּעָלְמָא, אֵ״שׁ רוּ״חַ וּמַיִ״ם וְעָפָ״ר, וְאִתְחַבְּרוּ אַרְבַּע סִטְרִין אִלֵּין, בַּד׳ יְסוֹדִין דְּעָלְמָא, וְאַתְקִין מִנַּיְיהוּ קוּדְשָׁא בְּרִיךְ הוּא חַד גּוּפָא בְּתִקּוּנָא עִלָּאָה. וְהַאי גּוּפָא, אִתְחַבַּר מִתְּרֵין עָלְמִין, מֵעָלְמָא דָּא תַּתָּאָה, וּמֵעָלְמָא דִּלְעֵילָּא.

33. For when Adam was created, he was composed of the earth of the terrestrial Temple, WHICH IS MALCHUT THAT IS CALLED EARTH, THOUGH IT IS MALCHUT SWEETENED BY BINAH, WHICH IS CALLED THE EARTH OF THE TERRESTRIAL TEMPLE. And the four directions of the world, WHICH ARE CHESED, GVURAH, TIFERET AND MALCHUT, were joined to that place called the Temple, MEANING IN MALCHUT THAT IS MITIGATED BY BINAH. These four directions joined in four aspects, which are the elements,

WHICH ARE fire, air, water and earth, WHICH ARE THE INNER PART OF
CHESED, GVURAH, TIFERET AND MALCHUT, and the four directions
joined the four elements. The Holy One, blessed be He, formed from them
one body of supernal arrangement, WHICH IS BINAH, MEANING THAT
MALCHUT IN IT WAS REFINED IN BINAH. THUS, this body is composed of
two worlds, this lower world, WHICH IS MALCHUT, and the world above,
WHICH IS BINAH.

34. אר"ש, תָּא חֲזֵי, ד' קַדְמָאֵי אִינּוּן רָזָא דִּמְהֵימָנוּתָא. וְאִינּוּן אֲבָהָן
דְּכָלְהוּ עָלְמִין. וְרָזָא דִּרְתִיכָא עִלָּאָה קַדִּישָׁא. וְאִינּוּן ד' יְסוֹדִין: א"ש
רו"ח וּמַיִ"ם וְעָפָ"ר. אִלֵּין אִינּוּן רָזָא עִלָּאָה. וּמֵאִינּוּן נָפְקִין, זָהָ"ב
וָכֶסֶ"ף וּנְחֹשֶׁ"ת וּבַרְזֶ"ל. וּתְחוֹת אִלֵּין מַתָּכָאן אַחֲרָנִין, דְּדַמְיָין לוֹן.

34. Rabbi Shimon said, Come and see: The four first ones, WHICH ARE THE
FOUR DIRECTIONS, are the secret of the Faith, WHICH IS THE NUKVA THAT
IS CORRECTED BY THEM. They are the patriarchs of all the worlds,
BECAUSE ALL THE WORLDS, BINAH, ZEIR ANPIN AND MALCHUT IN
ATZILUT AND THE THREE WORLDS BRIYAH, YETZIRAH AND ASIYAH
WERE FORMED FROM CHESED, GVURAH, TIFERET AND MALCHUT,
WHICH ARE THREE COLUMNS, AND MALCHUT THAT RECEIVES FROM
THEM. And they are the secret of the supernal holy Chariot, MEANING
BINAH, WHICH IS A CHARIOT TO CHOCHMAH. And these four elements —
fire, air, water and earth — are a supernal secret CONTAINED IN THE FOUR
DIRECTIONS, MEANING THAT THEY ARE THE INNER PART OF CHESED,
GVURAH, TIFERET AND MALCHUT. Gold, silver, brass, and iron originate
in these four ELEMENTS, MEANING THAT GOLD ORIGINATES FROM THE
UNION OF ZEIR ANPIN AND MALCHUT UNDER THE DOMINATION OF FIRE
OF THE LEFT COLUMN; SILVER ORIGIAES IN THE UNION OF ZEIR ANPIN
AND MALCHUT UNDER THE DOMINATION OF WATER OF THE RIGHT
COLUMN; BRASS ORIGINATES IN THE DOMINATION OF THE CENTRAL
COLUMN AND IRON IN MALCHUT WHEN IT IS NOT UNITED WITH ZEIR
ANPIN. Under these FOUR, there are other similar metals. FROM THE GOLD
METAL A GREEN METAL ALLOY IS PRODUCED AND FROM THE SILVER
METAL, LEAD, ETC.

35. תָּא חֲזֵי. א"ש רו"ח וּמַיִ"ם וְעָפָ"ר, אִלֵּין אִינּוּן קַדְמָאֵי וְשָׁרְשִׁין
דִּלְעֵילָּא וְתַתָּא, וְתַתָּאִין וְעֶלְאִין עֲלַיְיהוּ קַיְימִין. וְאִלֵּין אִינּוּן אַרְבַּע,

לְאַרְבַּע סִטְרֵי עָלְמָא, וְקַיְּימִין בְּאַרְבַּע אִלֵּין: צָפוֹ"ן, וְדָרוֹ"ם, וּמִזְרָ"ח, וּמַעֲרָ"ב. אִלֵּין אִינּוּן אַרְבַּע סִטְרִין דְּעָלְמָא, וְקַיְּימִין בְּאַרְבַּע אִלֵּין. אֵ"שׁ לְסְטַר צָפוֹ"ן. רוּ"חַ לְסְטַר מִזְרָ"ח. מַיִ"ם לְסְטַר דָּרוֹ"ם. עָפָ"ר לְסְטַר מַעֲרָ"ב. וְאַרְבַּע אִלֵּין, בְּאַרְבַּע אִלֵּין קְטִירִין, וְכֻלְּהוּ חַד, וְאִלֵּין עַבְדֵי אַרְבַּע מַתָּכָאן, דְּאִינּוּן זָהָ"ב וְכֶסֶ"ף וּנְחֹשֶׁ"ת וּבַרְזֶ"ל הָא אִינּוּן תְּרֵיסַר, וְכֻלְּהוּ חַד.

35. Come and see, fire, air, water and earth are the first ones and the roots above and below; upper and lower beings are based on them. These four ELEMENTS – FIRE, AIR, WATER AND EARTH – correspond to the four directions, BECAUSE THE RELATION BETWEEN THEM IS THAT OF AN OUTER TO THE INNER. THEREFORE, THEY are situated in these four – north, south, east and west – which are the four directions, and the four ELEMENTS abide in them. Fire IS to the north side, WHICH IS THE VOWEL SHURUK, THE LEFT COLUMN AND THE SFIRAH OF GVURAH. Air is to the east side, WHICH IS THE VOWEL CHIRIK, THE CENTRAL COLUMN AND THE SFIRAH OF TIFERET. Water is to the south side, WHICH IS THE VOWEL CHOLAM, THE RIGHT COLUMN AND THE SFIRAH OF CHESED. Earth is to the west, WHICH IS THE SFIRAH OF MALCHUT THAT RECEIVES THE THREE, FIRE, AIR AND WATER. And these four ELEMENTS – FIRE, AIR, WATER EARTH – are connected to the four DIRECTIONS – NORTH, SOUTH, EAST AND WEST. And they are all one, EXCEPT THEY ARE WRAPPED ONE WITHIN THE ANOTHER AS OUTER AND INNER. And these FIRE, AIR, WATER AND EARTH produce four metals, NAMELY BY MEANS OF UNION WITH MALCHUT, which are gold, silver, brass and iron. And together there are twelve ASPECTS, and are all one, NAMELY THREE COLUMNS AND MALCHUT THAT RECEIVES THEM. AND THEY ARE THUS THREE TIMES FOUR, BECAUSE THE FIRST EIGHT ARE INNER AND OUTER, AND THE FOUR METALS ARE PRODUCED BY THEM, AS SHALL BE SAID.

36. תָּא חֲזֵי, אֵשׁ הוּא בִּשְׂמָאלָא, לִסְטַר צָפוֹן, דְּהָא אֵשׁ, תּוּקְפָּא דַּחֲמִימוּתָא בֵּיהּ, וְיָבִישׁוּ דִּילֵיהּ תַּקִּיף. וְצָפוֹן בְּהִפּוּכָא דִּילֵיהּ הוּא, וְאִתְמְזִיג חַד בְּחַד וְאִיהוּ חַד. מַיִם לִימִינָא, וְהוּא לִסְטַר דָּרוֹם. וְקוּדְשָׁא בְּרִיךְ הוּא, לְחַבְּרָא לוֹן כַּחֲדָא, עָבֵיד מִזְגָּא דָּא כְּמִזְגָּא דָּא.

36. Come and see: Fire is in the Left COLUMN to the north side, WHICH IS

GVURAH. Because in the fire are the power of the heat and the power of the dryness. Its opposite is the north, WHICH IS COLD AND MOIST. The one blends with the other and they are one. Water is in the Right COLUMN and is to the south side, WHICH IS CHESED AND IS HOT AND DRY, AS SHALL BE SAID. And the Holy One, blessed be He, in order to join them together, made the disposition of the one as the disposition of the other.

37. צָפוֹן אִיהוּ קַר וְלַח, אֶשָּׁא חַם וְיָבֵשׁ. אַחֲלַף לוֹן לִסְטַר דָּרוֹם. דָּרוֹם, אִיהוּ חַם וְיָבֵשׁ. מַיִם קָרִים וְלַחִים. וְקוּדְשָׁא בְּרִיךְ הוּא מָזִיג לוֹן כְּחַד דְּנַפְקֵי מַיָּא מִדָּרוֹם, וְעָאלִין בְּגוֹ צָפוֹן. וּמִצָּפוֹן נַגְדֵי מַיָּא. נָפִיק אֶשָּׁא מִצָּפוֹן, וְעָאל בְּתוּקְפָּא דְּדָרוֹם, וּמִדָּרוֹם נָפִיק תּוּקְפָּא דַּחֲמִימוּתָא לְעָלְמָא. בְּגִין דְּקוּדְשָׁא בְּרִיךְ הוּא אוֹזִיף דָּא בְּדָא, וְכָל חַד וְחַד אוֹזִיף לְחַבְרֵיהּ מִדִּילֵיהּ כַּדְקָא חֲזֵי לֵיהּ. כְּגַוְונָא דָּא רוּחַ וּמִזְרָח, בְּגִין דִּיוֹזִיף כָּל חַד לְחַבְרֵיהּ, וְאִתְכְּלִיל דָּא בְּדָא, לְאִתְחַבְּרָא כְּחַד.

37. HE EXPLAINS FURTHER, IN the north, WHICH is cold and moist, WAS fire PLACED, WHICH IS hot and dry. SIMILARLY, He switched them in the south side. IN the south, WHICH is hot and dry, water WAS PLACED, WHICH IS cold and moist. NOW HE EXPLAINS THE BLENDING TOGETHER THAT HE AFFECTED. AND HE SAYS, And the Holy One, blessed be He, blended them as one, because water emerges from the south and enters into the north, and water flows from the north. SIMILARLY fire emerges from the north and comes into the power of the south, and the power of heat emerges into the world from the south. WE SEE THAT THE NORTH BRINGS FORTH WATER THAT APPERTAINS TO THE SOUTH, AND THE SOUTH PRODUCES HEAT THAT APPERTAINS TO THE NORTH because the Holy One, blessed be He, CAUSED them to borrow from each other. And each one lent the other of its own, as appropriate. Similarly, the wind and the east side, WHICH ARE HOT AND MOIST, CONTAINS TWO OPPOSITES BECAUSE HEAT COMES FROM THE FIRE, WHICH IS IN THE NORTH, AND MOISTURE COMES FROM WATER, WHICH IS IN THE SOUTH, in order that they should lend one to the other, to be included and join with each other.

38. תָּא חֲזֵי, אֶשָּׁא מִסִּטְרָא דָּא, מַיִם מִסִּטְרָא דָּא. וְאִינוּן מַחֲלוֹקֶת. עָאל רוּחַ בֵּינַיְיהוּ, וְאָחִיד לִתְרֵין סִטְרִין. הֲדָא הוּא דִכְתִיב וְרוּחַ אֱלֹהִים מְרַחֶפֶת עַל פְּנֵי הַמָּיִם. דְּהָא אֶשָּׁא קָאִים לְעֵילָא בְּסִטְרָא דָּא. וּמַיִם

קָיְימֵי. רוּחָא אָעִיל בֵּינַיְיהוּ, וְאָחִיד לִתְרֵין סִטְרִין, וְאַפְרִישׁ מַחֲלוֹקֶת.
עָפָר מַיָּא קַיְימֵי עָלֵיהּ וְרוּחָא וְאֶשָּׁא וּמְקַבְּלָא מִכֻּלְּהוּ, בְּחֵילָא דִּתְלָתָא
אִלֵּין דְּקַיְימֵי עָלָהּ.

38. HE EXPLAINS THE OPPOSITES CONTAINED IN THE AIR AND IN THE EAST, AND SAYS, Come and see, fire is on the one side, SOUTH, and water is on the other, NORTH. They are in conflict, AS FIRE WANTS TO BURN THE WATER AND WATER WANTS TO EXTINGUISH FIRE. Air comes between them and holds both sides together, UPHOLDING THEM BOTH, as is written: "And a wind from Elohim moved over the surface of the water" (Beresheet 1:2). For fire is situated above to the SOUTH side and water to the NORTH side. Air comes between them, holds both sides and settles the quarrel. The water, air and fire stand over the earth, and by means of the three over it, it receives from all of them.

39. תָּא חֲזֵי, רוּחַ וּמִזְרָח. מִזְרָח, חַם וְלַח, רוּחַ, חַם וְלַח אִיהוּ, וּבְגִינֵי
כַּךְ, אָחִיד לִתְרֵין סִטְרִין, דְּהָא אֵשׁ חַם וְיָבֵשׁ, וּמַיִם קָרִים וְלַחִים, רוּחַ
אִיהוּ חַם וְלַח, סִטְרָא דְּאִיהוּ חַם, אָחִיד בְּאֶשָּׁא. סִטְרָא דְּאִיהוּ לַח,
אָחִיד בְּמַיָּא. וְעַל דָּא אַסְכִּים בֵּינַיְיהוּ, וְאַפְרִישׁ מַחֲלוֹקֶת דְּאֶשָּׁא וּמַיָּא.

39. HE EXPLAINS FURTHER, SAYING, Come and see, air IS TO the east. BEHOLD, the east is hot and moist AND SO air is hot and moist. Therefore, it is attached to both sides, since fire is hot and dry and water is cold and moist. SO the hot aspect in air, which is hot and moist, is attached to fire and the cold aspect in it is attached to water. It therefore brought peace and nullified the conflict between fire and water.

40. עָפָר אִיהוּ קַר וְיָבֵשׁ, וע״ד מְקַבֵּל עָלֵיהּ כֻּלְּהוּ, וְכֻלְּהוּ עַבְדֵי בֵּיהּ
עֲבִידְתַּיְיהוּ, וּמְקַבְּלָא מִכֻּלְּהוּ, לְאַפָּקָא בְּחֵילַיְיהוּ מְזוֹנָא לְעָלְמָא. בְּגִין
דִּבְמַעֲרָב אִתְאֲחִיד עַפְרָא, דְּאִיהוּ קַר וְיָבֵשׁ. וְסִטְרָא דְּאִיהוּ קַר, אָחִיד
בְּצָפוֹן דְּאִיהוּ קַר וְלַח, דְּהָא קְרִירָא אִתְאֲחִיד בִּקְרִירָא. בג״כ צָפוֹן
אִתְאֲחִיד בַּמַּעֲרָב בְּסִטְרָא דָּא. דָּרוֹם דְּאִיהוּ חַם וְיָבֵשׁ, בְּהַהוּא יְבֵישׁוּתָא
דִּילֵיהּ, אָחִיד לִיבֵשׁוּתָא דְּמַעֲרָב בְּסִטְרָא אָחֳרָא, וְאִתְאֲחִיד מַעֲרָב
בִּתְרֵין סִטְרִין.

40. Earth is cold and dry; therefore, it can receive upon itself all of them, NAMELY THE FIRE, WATER AND AIR. They all perform their tasks by it, and it receives from all of them in order to produce by their powers sustenance to the world. Because the earth is attached to the west, being cold and dry LIKE THE WEST, and the cold aspect IN THE EARTH is attached to the north, which is cold and moist, because cold is attached to cold, therefore, the north is attached to the west from the one side. That which is dry in the south, which is hot and dry, is attached to the dryness of the west on the other side OF THE WEST. And so the west is attached to the two sides.

41. וְכֵן אִתְאֲחִיד דָּרוֹם בְּמִזְרָח, דְּהָא חֲמִימוּתָא דְּדָרוֹם, אִתְאֲחִיד בֵּיהּ בַּחֲמִימוּתָא דְּמִזְרָח. וּמִזְרָח אִתְאֲחִיד בַּצָּפוֹן דְּהָא לַחוּתָא דִּילֵיהּ אִתְאֲחִיד בְּלַחוּתָא דְּצָפוֹן. הַשְׁתָּא אִשְׁתְּכַח דְּרוֹמִי״ת מִזְרָחִי״ת. מִזְרָחִי״ת צְפוֹנִי״ת. צְפוֹנִי״ת מַעֲרָבִי״ת. מַעֲרָבִי״ת דְּרוֹמִי״ת וְכֻלְּהוּ כְּלִילָן דָּא בְּדָא, לְאִשְׁתַּלְשְׁלָא חַד בְּחַד.

41. The south similarly is attached to the east, for the heat of the south fuses with the heat of the east. Similarly the east is attached to the north, because its moistness fuses with the moistness of the north. Now there is south-east, MEANING THAT THEY ADHERE TO EACH OTHER THROUGH THEIR MUTUAL HEAT, north-east, THROUGH THEIR MUTUAL MOISTNESS, north-west THROUGH THEIR MUTUAL COLDNESS, and south-west THROUGH THEIR MUTUAL DRYNESS. They all are combined with each other, for they evolve from one to another.

42. כְּגַוְונָא דָא, צָפוֹן עָבֵיד דַּהֲבָא. דְּמִסְטְרָא דְּתוּקְפָּא דְּאָשָּׁא, אִתְעֲבֵיד דַּהֲבָא. וְהַיְינוּ דִּכְתִיב, מִצָּפוֹן זָהָב יֶאֱתֶה. דְּאֵשׁ אִתְאֲחִיד בֶּעָפָר, וְאִתְעֲבֵיד דַּהֲבָא. וְהַיְינוּ דִּכְתִיב, וְעַפְרוֹת זָהָב לוֹ. וְרָזָא דָא, שְׁנַיִם כְּרוּבִים זָהָב.

42. In a similar way, north produces gold, because gold is formed by the potency of the fire. This is the meaning of: "From the north comes forth gold" (Iyov 37:22), since fire fuses with the earth and gold is formed. This is the meaning of: "He has gold dust" (Iyov 28:6), and the secret meaning of "two gold Cherubs" (Shemot 25:18).

43. מַיִם אִתְאֲחִיד בְּעָפָר, וּקְרִירוּתָא בְּלָחוּתָא עָבֵיד כֶּסֶף, הַשְׁתָּא הָא עָפָר אִתְאֲחִיד בִּתְרֵין סִטְרִין, בַּזָּהָב וּבַכֶּסֶף, וְאִתְיְיהִיב בֵּינַיְיהוּ. רוּחָא אָחִיד לְמַיִם, וְאָחִיד לְאֵשׁ, וְאַפִּיק תְּרֵין כְּחַד, דְּאִיהוּ עֵין נְחֹשֶׁת קָלָל. וְעָפָר דְּקָאמְרָן, כַּד אִיהוּ בִּלְחוֹדוֹי, בְּבִישׁוּ וּקְרִירוּ דִּילֵיה, נָפִיק בַּרְזֶל, וְסִימָנֵיךְ, אִם קֵהָה הַבַּרְזֶל וְגוֹ'.

43. Water fuses with earth, and the coldness OF THE EARTH with the moistness OF THE WATER produces silver, WHICH IS THE SECRET OF THE LIGHT OF CHASSADIM IN THE SOUTH, WHICH FLOWS FROM ABOVE DOWNWARDS. WHEN IT FUSES WITH THE COLDNESS AND DRYNESS IN THE EARTH, THE DRYNESS OF THE EARTH IS VOIDED AND BECOMES MOIST, MEANING THAT IT FLOWS FROM ABOVE DOWNWARDS. THIS GRADE OF EARTH IS CALLED SILVER. Now earth is attached to two sides, to gold and silver, and is placed between them. Air holds to water and fire, BEING THE CENTRAL COLUMN AS MENTIONED, and brings them both out as one which is CONSIDERED: "like burnished brass" (Daniel 10:6). When earth is on its own, with its coldness and dryness, it produces iron, as mentioned. This is deduced from: "If the iron is blunt (Heb. *kehah*)..." (Kohelet 10:10). EARTH, WHICH IS MALCHUT, IS CALLED THE DARK (HEB. *KEHAH*) HAND BECAUSE MALCHUT IS THE SECRET OF THE HAND TEFILIN, AS IS KNOWN.

44. וְהַאי עָפָר, אִתְאֲחִיד בְּכֻלְּהוּ, וְכֻלְּהוּ עַבְדִין בֵּיה כְּגַוְונָא דִּלְהוֹן. תָּא חֲזֵי, בְּלָא עָפָר, לֵית זָהָב וְכֶסֶף וּנְחֹשֶׁת, דְּהָא כָּל חַד וְחַד אוֹזִיף לְחַבְרֵיה מִדִּילֵיה, לְאִתְקַשְּׁרָא דָּא בְּדָא. וְאִתְאֲחִיד עָפָר בְּכֻלְּהוּ, בְּגִין דִּתְרֵין סִטְרִין אֲחִידָן לֵיה, אֵשָׁא וּמַיָּא. וְרוּחָא אִתְקְרִיב בֵּיה, בְּגִין אִלֵּין תְּרֵין וְעָבֵיד בֵּיה עֲבִידְתָּא.

44. This earth fuses with them all, NAMELY WITH FIRE, AIR AND WATER, and they all produce with it according to their likeness. FIRE PRODUCES GOLD, WHICH IS LIKE IT AND SO DOES WATER PRODUCE SILVER, WHICH IS LIKE IT. Come and see: Without earth, there is neither gold, silver nor brass, because each one lends to the other of its characteristics IN ORDER to combine one with the other. And the earth fuses with all of them because the two sides, fire and water, fuse with it. FOR THE COLDNESS IN IT FUSES

WITH THE WATER AND THE DRYNESS IN IT FUSES WITH THE FIRE. And air, WHICH IS ZEIR ANPIN, is attracted to it because IT COMBINES these two – FIRE AND WATER – and performs its deed by it. AIR ALSO COMBINES FIRE AND WATER, FOR THE HEAT IN IT IS FROM FIRE AND THE MOISTNESS IN IT IS FROM WATER.

45. אִשְׁתְּכַח, דְּכַד אִתְחַבַּר עַפְרָא בַּהֲדַיְיהוּ, עָבֵיד וְאוֹלִיד עַפְרָא אַחֲרָנִין, כְּגַוְּונָא דִּלְהוֹן. כְּגַוְּונָא דְּזָהָב, אוֹלִיד עַפְרָא סוֹסְפִיתָא יְרוֹקָא, דְּאִיהוּ כְּגַוְּונָא דְּדַהֲבָא מַמָּשׁ. כְּגַוְּונָא דִּכְסֶף, אוֹלִיד עוֹפֶרֶת. כְּגַוְּונָא דִּנְחֹשֶׁת עִילָאָה, אוֹלִיד קָסִיטְרָא דְּאִיהוּ נְחֹשֶׁת זוּטָא. כְּגַוְּונָא דְּבַרְזֶל, אוֹלִיד בַּרְזֶל, וְסִימָנָךְ בַּרְזֶל בְּבַרְזֶל יָחַד.

45. We find that when the earth fused WITH FIRE, WATER AND AIR THAT PRODUCED WITH IT GOLD, SILVER AND BRASS, EARTH ACQUIRED STRENGTH. EARTH made and produced other METALS similar TO GOLD, SILVER AND BRASS. In the likeness of gold, the earth produces dross OF GOLD, which is green just like real gold. In the likeness of silver, it produces lead, WHICH IS LIKE SILVER, and in the likeness of the superior brass, it produces tin, which is called brass minor. In the likeness of iron, it produces a DIFFERENT kind of iron. This is derived from: "Iron sharpens iron" (Mishlei 27:17). IT SHOWS THAT THERE ARE TWO KINDS OF IRON.

46. תָּא חֲזֵי, אֵשׁ רוּחַ מַיִם וְעָפָר, כֻּלְּהוּ אֲחִידָן דָּא בְּדָא, וְאִתְקַשְׁרָן דָּא בְּדָא. וְלָא הֲוֵי בְּהוּ פְּרוּדָא. וְעָפָר דָּא, כַּד אִיהוּ אוֹלִיד לְבָתַר, לָא מִתְקַשְׁרָן דָּא בְּדָא בְּאִינוּן עֶלָּאֵי, כְּמָה דְּאַתְּ אָמֵר, וּמִשָּׁם יִפָּרֵד וְהָיָה לְאַרְבָּעָה רָאשִׁים, בְּאִלֵּין הֲוֵי פְּרוּדָא.

46. Come and see: Fire, air, water and earth are all attached to each other and connected to one another. There is no division between them. THEREFORE THERE IS NO DISCONNECTION BETWEEN GOLD, SILVER AND BRASS THAT EMERGED FROM THEM. But those that earth produces afterwards, NAMELY THE DROSS OF GOLD, LEAD, TIN AND IRON, do not connect with each other as those superior do, NAMELY GOLD, SILVER AND BRASS THAT EMERGE FROM FIRE, WATER AND AIR, WHEN COMBINED WITH EARTH. This is stated in the verse: "And from thence it was parted,

and branched into four streams" (Beresheet 2:10). Among those there is division.

47. בְּגִין דְּהָא עָפָר, כַּד אִיהוּ אוֹלִיד בְּחֵילָא דִּתְלַת עִלָּאֵי, אַפִּיק אַרְבְּעָה נַהֲרִין, דְּתַמָּן מִשְׁתַּכְּחֵי אַבְנֵי יְקָר, וּבַאֲתַר חַד אִינּוּן, דִּכְתִּיב שָׁם הַבְּדֹלַח וְאֶבֶן הַשֹּׁהַם. וְאִלֵּין אַבְנֵי יְקָר אִינּוּן תְּרֵיסַר, וְאִינּוּן לְאַרְבַּע סִטְרֵי עָלְמָא, לָקֳבֵיל תְּרֵיסַר שְׁבָטִין, דִּכְתִּיב וְהָאֲבָנִים תִּהְיֶין עַל שְׁמוֹת בְּנֵי יִשְׂרָאֵל שְׁתֵּים עֶשְׂרֵה עַל שְׁמוֹתָם. וְאִלֵּין תְּרֵיסַר בָּקָר, דְּאִינּוּן תְּחוֹת יַמָּא.

47. Since when the earth produced by the power of the three upper ones, it brought forth ON ITS OWN four rivers, where there are precious stones. They concentrate in one place, NAMELY IN THE RIVER PISHON ONLY, THAT ORIGINATES FROM THE POWER OF THE FIRE WHICH IS IN THE EARTH, as is written: "There is the crystal and the onyx stone" (Ibid. 12). And these precious stones are twelve in number, to the four directions of the world, THREE TO EVERY SIDE. FOR WHEN THEY ARE INCLUDED WITHIN EACH OTHER THERE ARE ONLY THREE TO EACH OF FIRE, WATER, AIR AND EARTH, INSTEAD OF FOUR TO EACH SIDE, SINCE EARTH HAS NO ILLUMINATION OF ITS OWN, BEING JUST THE RECIPIENT. And they correspond to the twelve tribes, as is written: "And the stones shall be with the names of the children of Yisrael, twelve, according to their names" (Shemot 28:21). And these are the twelve oxen that stood under the sea THAT SOLOMON MADE, MENTIONED IN I MELACHIM 7:25.

48. תָּא חֲזֵי, כָּל אַרְבְּעָה סִטְרִין עִלָּאִין דְּקָאמְרָן, אַף עַל גַּב דְּמִתְקַשְּׁרָן דָּא בְּדָא, וְאִינּוּן קִיּוּמָא דִּלְעֵילָא וְתַתָּא, קִיּוּמָא דְּעָלְמָא יַתִּיר רוּחַ, בְּגִין דְּכֹלָּא קַיְּימָא בְּגִינֵיהּ, וְנַפְשָׁא לָא קַיְּימָא אֶלָּא בְּרוּחָא, דְּאִי גָּרַע רוּחָא אֲפִילּוּ רִגְעָא חֲדָא, נַפְשָׁא לָא יָכִילַת לְאִתְקַיְּימָא, וְרָזָא דָּא כְּתִיב, גַּם בְּלֹא דַעַת נֶפֶשׁ לֹא טוֹב. נַפְשָׁא בְּלֹא רוּחָא לָאו אִיהוּ טוֹב, וְלָא יָכְלָא לְאִתְקַיְּימָא.

48. Come and see: Even though the four aspects that we mentioned are interconnected and sustain the world, it is mostly sustained on air. Everything exists because of it. The Nefesh exists only with air (Ruach), for

if air would be missing FROM IT even for one moment, the Nefesh could not exist. This is the secret of what is written: "Also, that the soul (Nefesh) be without knowledge is not good" (Mishlei 19:2). DA'AT (KNOWLEDGE) IS THE CENTRAL COLUMN THAT IS CALLED AIR. A Nefesh without Ruach is no good and cannot exist.

49. וְתָא חֲזֵי, אִינּוּן תְּרֵיסַר דְּקָאמְרָן, דְּאִינּוּן תְּרֵיסַר אַבְנִין, אִינּוּן תְּרֵיסַר בָּקָר, דִּתְחוֹת יַמָּא. בְּגִין כַּךְ, נָטְלוּ אִינּוּן תְּרֵיסַר נְשִׂיאִים, כָּל הַבָּקָר לָעֹלָה שְׁנֵים עָשָׂר פָּרִים וְגוֹ'. וְכֹלָּא רָזָא עִלָּאָה הוּא, וּמַאן דְּיִשְׁגַּח בְּמִלִּין אִלֵּין, יַשְׁגַּח בְּרָזָא דְּחָכְמְתָא עִלָּאָה, דְּעִקָּר דְּכֹלָּא בֵּיהּ.

49. Come and see: These twelve stones we mentioned are the twelve oxen that are under the sea THAT SOLOMON MADE. FOR THE NUKVA IS CALLED SEA, AND IT STANDS UPON TWELVE OXEN, WHICH ARE FOUR OXEN EACH ONE COMPOSED OF THREE IN THE WORLD OF BRIYAH. THEY ARE CALLED OXEN BECAUSE THEY ARE MOSTLY UNDER THE DOMINATION OF THE LEFT, AS IT IS SAID: "THE FACE OF AN OX ON THE LEFT SIDE" (YECHEZKEL 1:10). Therefore, the twelve tribal princes took, AS IS SAID: "All the oxen for burnt offering were twelve bullocks..." (Bemidbar 7:87). It is all a lofty secret, and one who will observe these things will understand the secret of Supernal Wisdom wherein lies the essence of everything.

50. אָמַר ר' שִׁמְעוֹן, הָא דְּאָמַר ר' חִזְקִיָּה, דְּכַד בָּרָא קוּדְשָׁא בְּרִיךְ הוּא לְאָדָם, מֵעַפְרָא דְּמַקְדְּשָׁא דִּלְתַתָּא אִתְבְּרֵי, מֵעַפְרָא דְּמַקְדְּשָׁא דִּלְעֵילָּא אִתְיְיהִיב בֵּיהּ נִשְׁמָתָא. כְּמָה דְּכַד אִתְבְּרֵי מֵעַפְרָא דִּלְתַתָּא, אִתְחַבְּרוּ בֵּיהּ תְּלַת סִטְרָא יְסוֹדֵי עָלְמָא. הָכִי נָמֵי כַּד אִתְבְּרֵי מֵעַפְרָא דִּלְעֵילָּא, אִתְחַבְּרוּ בֵּיהּ תְּלַת סִטְרֵי יְסוֹדֵי עָלְמָא, וְאִשְׁתְּלִים אָדָם. וְהַיְינוּ דִּכְתִיב, אַשְׁרֵי אָדָם לֹא יַחְשֹׁב יְיָ' לוֹ עָוֹן וְאֵין בְּרוּחוֹ רְמִיָּה. אֵימָתַי לֹא יַחְשֹׁב יְיָ' לוֹ עָוֹן, בִּזְמַן דְּאֵין בְּרוּחוֹ רְמִיָּה.

50. Rabbi Shimon said, Rabbi Chizkiyah said that when the Holy One, blessed be He, created Adam, NAMELY HIS BODY, it was created from the earth of the terrestrial Temple, WHICH IS MALCHUT. Yet his soul was given to him from the earth of the celestial Temple, WHICH IS BINAH. As he was created from the lower earth, three aspects of the elements, WHICH ARE

LOWER FIRE, AIR, AND WATER were combined with it, WITH EARTH. So when he was created from the upper earth, three aspects of the elements, UPPER FIRE, AIR AND WATER, were combined WITH EARTH, and Adam was complete IN BODY AND IN SOUL. This is the meaning of: "Blessed is the man to whom Hashem imputes no iniquity, and in whose spirit there is no guile" (Tehilim 32:2). When will Hashem not impute iniquity to him? When there is no guile in his spirit, NAMELY, WHEN HE HAS A SOUL FROM BINAH.

51. תָּא חֲזֵי, מֹשֶׁה אִשְׁתְּלִים יַתִּיר מֵאֲבָהָן, בְּגִין דְּמַלִּיל עִמֵּיהּ קוּדְשָׁא בְּרִיךְ הוּא, מִדַּרְגָּא עִלָּאָה יַתִּיר מִכֻּלְּהוּ, וּמֹשֶׁה פְּנִימָאָה דְּבֵי מַלְכָּא עִלָּאָה הֲוָה, וְעַל דָּא כְּתִיב, וָאֵרָא אֶל אַבְרָהָם אֶל יִצְחָק וְאֶל יַעֲקֹב וְגוֹ', וְהָא אוֹקִימְנָא מִלֵּי.

51. Come and see: Moses was more perfect than the patriarchs because the Holy One, blessed be He, spoke to him from a higher grade than all of them, THAN THE GRADE OF THE PATRIARCHS. Moses frequented the inside of the King's house, WHICH IS ZEIR ANPIN, NAMELY THAT HE WAS OF THE ASPECT OF DA'AT, WHO IS INNER ASPECT OF ZEIR ANPIN. Therefore it is written: "And I appeared to Abraham, to Isaac, and to Jacob..." and we already explained this.

4. "And I will bring you out...and I will deliver you... and I will redeem you"

A Synopsis
Rabbi Yehuda tells us that the exodus from Egypt was the most important part of the events in the title verse; that is why it was mentioned first. But Rabbi Yosi thinks that the best parts are: "and I will deliver you" "and I will redeem you" because this meant the children of Yisrael would not be followed or harmed and they would be redeemed. Furthermore, Hashem promised to accept them as His people and bring them to the land of Yisrael.

The Relevance of the paragraph
For deeper understanding of this section it is essential to remember that it applies to each of us as individuals. Remembering God's promise to deliver us from *any kind* of servitude, to keep us safe, to bring us back to Himself and to give us a home, we can go through our days with renewed faith and hope in our own futures.

52. לָכֵן אֱמֹר לִבְנֵי יִשְׂרָאֵל אֲנִי יְיָ' וְהוֹצֵאתִי אֶתְכֶם. רִבִּי יְהוּדָה אָמַר, הַאי קְרָא אִפְּכָא הוּא, דִּכְתִּיב וְהוֹצֵאתִי אֶתְכֶם מִתַּחַת סִבְלוֹת מִצְרַיִם בְּקַדְמֵיתָא, וּלְבָתַר וְהִצַּלְתִּי אֶתְכֶם מֵעֲבוֹדָתָם, וּלְבָתַר וְגָאַלְתִּי אֶתְכֶם, הֲוָה לֵיה לְמֵימַר מֵעִיקָּרָא וְגָאַלְתִּי אֶתְכֶם, וּלְבָתַר וְהוֹצֵאתִי אֶתְכֶם. אֶלָּא, עִקָּרָא דְכֹלָּא בְּקַדְמֵיתָא, דְּבָעָא קוּדְשָׁא בְּרִיךְ הוּא לְבַשְּׂרָא לוֹן בְּשְׂבָחָא דְכֹלָּא בְּקַדְמֵיתָא.

52. "Therefore say to the children of Yisrael, 'I am Hashem and I will bring you out'" (Shemot 6:6). Rabbi Yehuda said this passage is in reverse order, for it is first written: "And I will bring you out from under the burdens of Egypt" and then: "And I will deliver you out of their bondage" and then: "And I will redeem you." Should it not have first said, 'I will redeem you' and then: 'And I will bring you out.' AND HE ANSWERS, The most important point of all HE MENTIONED first. Because the Holy One, blessed be He, wanted to herald to them first the best of all, WHICH IS THE EXODUS FROM EGYPT.

53. אָמַר רִבִּי יוֹסֵי, וְהָא שְׁבָחָא דְכֹלָּא, וְלָקַחְתִּי אֶתְכֶם לִי לְעָם וְהָיִיתִי לָכֶם לֵאלֹהִים, וְאָמַר לֵיה לְבָתַר. א"ל, בְּהַהוּא זִמְנָא, לֵית לְהוּ שְׁבָחָא

אֶלָּא יְצִיאָה. דְּחָשִׁיבֵי דְּלָא יִפְּקוּן מֵעַבְדּוּתְהוֹן לְעָלְמִין, בְּגִין דַּהֲווֹ
חָמָאן תַּמָּן דְּכָל אֲסִירֵי דַּהֲווֹ בֵּינַיְיהוּ מְקַשְּׁרוּ לוֹן בְּקִשְׁרָא דְּחָרָשֵׁי, וְלָא
יַכְלִין לְנָפְקָא מִבֵּינַיְיהוּ לְעָלְמִין. וּבְגִין כַּךְ, מַה דְּחָבִיב עֲלַיְיהוּ מִכֹּלָּא,
אִתְבַּשָּׂרוּ בֵּיהּ.

53. Rabbi Yosi said, But the best of all is: "And I will take you to Me for a people, and I will be to you as an Elohim" (Ibid. 7). YET He told them this afterwards. He said to him that there was nothing better for them than an exodus at that time, because they thought they would never leave their bondage. For they saw that all the prisoners among them were tied with knots of sorcery, and that they would be forever prevented to go free from them. Therefore, they were announced FIRST of that which was more dear to them than anything else.

54. וְאִי תֵּימָא אע"ג דְּנָפְקוּ, הָא דִּילְמָא יִזְלוּן בַּתְרַיְיהוּ לְאַבְאָשָׁא לוֹן,
כְּתִיב וְהִצַּלְתִּי אֶתְכֶם מֵעֲבוֹדָתָם. וְאִי תֵּימָא הָא יִפְּקוּן וְיִשְׁתֵּזְבוּן, וְלָא
יְהֵא לוֹן פְּרִיקָא, ת"ל וְגָאַלְתִּי אֶתְכֶם בִּזְרוֹעַ נְטוּיָה. וְאִי תֵּימָא לֹא
יְקַבְּלֵם, הָא כְּתִיב וְלָקַחְתִּי. וְאִי תֵּימָא כְּשֶׁיְּקַבְּלֵם לֹא יְבִיאֵם לָאָרֶץ, הָא
כְּתִיב וְהֵבֵאתִי אֶתְכֶם וְגוֹ'.

54. And if you argue that even though they left EGYPT, the Egyptians might follow them to harm them, THEREFORE it is written: "And I will deliver you out of their bondage." If you say it is possible that they would go out and be saved BUT they would not be redeemed, the Torah says, "And I will redeem you with an outstretched arm." If you say that He would not accept them AS HIS PEOPLE, it is written: "And I will take". And if you say that when He accepts them AS A PEOPLE, He will not bring them to the land of Yisrael, of this is written: "And I will bring you into the land..." (Shemot 6:8).

5. General and particular

A Synopsis

Rabbi Yosi opens with: "And I shall take you to me as a people and I will be to you as a Elohim and you will know that I am Hashem your Elohim." Rabbi Shimon tells us that the first and most important precept is to know God in the general sense – to know that there is a supernal ruler who is the master of the world and who created all the worlds, heaven and earth, and all their beings. Just as this is the beginning of the precepts, the end of them is to know Him particularly: General and Particular are Beginning and End. They are also the secret of male and female as in Zeir Anpin and Nukva. At the end of 40 years of wandering after leaving Egypt, Moses told the children of Yisrael: "Know therefore this day, and consider it in your heart that Yud hei vav hei is the Elohim." This then is the particular. Rabbi Shimon says that the fear of Hashem is the beginning of knowing Him in particular. We are told next that a person should perfect the 248 limbs of the soul of the soul of man – the 248 positive precepts. After he has been perfected in general he will know in particular. Rabbi Shimon turns to a discussion of the limbs, the days of the year, the Sfirot and their cures. Blessings, life and cures come down to a person only after he completes all 248 precepts. The first word of the Torah when it was given on Mount Sinai was "Anochi (I am)" which is the secret of the first precept of knowing Him in general. "For Hashem your Elohim is a consuming fire" is an allusion to the particular.

The Relevance of the paragraph

It seems that we can in no way learn to know God until we acknowledge that He exists and that He created all the worlds, heaven and earth, and all their inhabitants. If we find it difficult to 'know' God, to encounter Him in a particular and personal way, a reading of this passage can encourage us by bringing us back to encounter Him in general. We may softly think to ourselves about what we know of the world and its people, and what we imagine of heaven and the angels, and then remember that God made them all. This understanding will lead us to the wisdom which enables us to encounter God in the particular.

רעיא מהימנא

55. וְלָקַחְתִּי אֶתְכֶם לִי לְעָם וְהָיִיתִי לָכֶם לֵאלֹהִים וִידַעְתֶּם כִּי אֲנִי יְיָ'

אֱלֹהֵיכֶם וְגוֹ' פִּקּוּדָא דָא קַדְמָאָה דְּכָל פִּקּוּדִין. רֵאשִׁיתָא קַדְמָאָה דְּכָל פִּקּוּדִין, לְמִנְדַּע לֵיהּ לְקוּדְשָׁא בְּרִיךְ הוּא בִּכְלָלָא. מַאי בִּכְלָלָא. לְמִנְדַּע דְּאִית שַׁלִּיטָא עִלָּאָה, דְּאִיהוּ רִבּוֹן עָלְמָא, וּבָרָא עָלְמִין כֻּלְּהוּ, שְׁמַיָּא וְאַרְעָא וְכָל חֵילֵיהוֹן. וְדָא אִיהוּ בִּכְלָלָא. וְסוֹפָא דְכֹלָּא בִּפְרָט, לְמִנְדַּע לֵיהּ בִּפְרָט.

Ra'aya Meheimna (The Faithful Shepherd)

55. "And I will take you to Me for a people, and I will be to you as an Elohim; and you shall know that I am Hashem your Elohim..." (Shemot 6:7). This commandment is the first of all the precepts BECAUSE the very beginning of all the precepts IS to know the Holy One, blessed be He, in the general ASPECT. HE ASKS, What is meant by general? HE ANSWERS, IT IS to know that there is a Supernal Ruler, who is the Master of the world, and who created all the worlds, heaven and earth, and all their hosts. This is in general. And everything ends in the particular, NAMELY to know Him in the details.

56. וּכְלָל וּפְרָט אִיהוּ רֵישָׁא וְסוֹפָא רָזָא דְּכַר וְנוּקְבָּא כַּחֲדָא, וְאִשְׁתְּכַח בַּר נָשׁ בְּהַאי עָלְמָא, דְּאִתְעַסַּק בִּכְלָל וּפְרָט, בַּר נָשׁ בְּהַאי עָלְמָא אִיהוּ כְּלָל וּפְרָט. תִּקּוּנָא דְּהַאי עָלְמָא, אִיהוּ כְּלָל וּפְרָט. בְּג"כ, רֵאשִׁיתָא דְּכֹלָּא, לְמִנְדַּע דְּאִית שַׁלִּיט וְדַיָּין עַל עָלְמָא, וְאִיהוּ רִבּוֹן כָּל עָלְמִין. וּבָרָא לֵיהּ לְבַר נָשׁ מֵעַפְרָא, וְנָפַח בְּאַפּוֹי נִשְׁמָתָא דְּחַיֵּי, וְדָא אִיהוּ בְּאוֹרַח כְּלָל.

56. General and particular is beginning and end. THEY ARE the secret of male and female as one BECAUSE ZEIR ANPIN IS CALLED GENERAL AND THE NUKVA IS CALLED PARTICULAR. Thus man in this world WHO IS OCCUPIED WITH PRECEPTS is occupied with the general and particular, WHICH ARE THE BEGINNING AND THE END OF THE PRECEPTS. AND WE FIND man in this world to be general and particular MEANING THAT HE HAS TO BE PERFECTED BY BOTH. And the perfection of this world is general and particular, SO THE GENERAL, WHICH IS ZEIR ANPIN, WOULD BE UNITED WITH THE NUKVA, WHICH IS PARTICULAR. Therefore, it is first of all necessary to know that there is a ruler and judge in the world, who is the

master of all the worlds, who created man from dust and blew into his nostrils the breath of life. This is general.

57. כַּד נָפְקוּ יִשְׂרָאֵל מִמִּצְרַיִם, לָא הֲווֹ יַדְעֵי לֵיהּ לְקוּדְשָׁא בְּרִיךְ הוּא כֵּיוָן דְּאָתָא מֹשֶׁה לְגַבַּיְיהוּ, פִּקוּדָא קַדְמָאָה דָּא אוֹלִיף לוֹן, דִּכְתִּיב, וִידַעְתֶּם כִּי אֲנִי יְיָ' אֱלֹהֵיכֶם הַמּוֹצִיא אֶתְכֶם וְגוֹ'. וְאִלְמָלֵא פִּקוּדָא דָּא, לָא הֲווֹ יִשְׂרָאֵל מְהֵימְנִין, בְּכָל אִינוּן נִיסִין וּגְבוּרָן דְּעָבֵד לוֹן בְּמִצְרַיִם. כֵּיוָן דְּיָדְעוּ פִּקוּדָא דָּא בְּאוֹרַח כְּלָל, אִתְעֲבֵידוּ לְהוֹן נִסִין וּגְבוּרָן.

57. When Yisrael left Egypt, they did not know the Holy One, blessed be He. When Moses came to them, he taught them this first precept, as written: "And you shall know that I am Hashem your Elohim, who brings you out…" Were it not for this commandment, Yisrael would not be faithful TO HASHEM, EVEN AFTER all these miracles and mighty acts that THE HOLY ONE, BLESSED BE HE, performed for them in Egypt. After they knew this commandment in general, miracles and mighty deeds were performed for them, FOR THEY WERE ALREADY CERTAIN THAT THEY WOULD BELIEVE IN HASHEM THROUGH THEM, AS IS WRITTEN: "AND YISRAEL SAW…AND BELIEVED IN HASHEM, AND IN MOSES HIS SERVANT" (SHEMOT 14:31).

58. וּלְסוֹף מ' שְׁנִין, דְּקָא אִשְׁתַּדְּלוּ בְּכָל אִינוּן פִּקוּדִין דְּאוֹרַיְיתָא, דְּאוֹלִיף לוֹן מֹשֶׁה, בֵּין אִינוּן דְּמִתְנַהֲגֵי בְּאַרְעָא בֵּין אִינוּן דְּמִתְנַהֲגֵי לְבַר מֵאַרְעָא כְּדֵין, אוֹלִיף לוֹן בְּאוֹרַח פְּרָט, הה"ד וְיָדַעְתָּ הַיּוֹם וַהֲשֵׁבֹתָ אֶל לְבָבֶךָ, הַיּוֹם דַּיְיקָא, מַה דְּלָא הֲוָה רְשׁוּ מִקַּדְמַת דְּנָא. כִּי יְיָ' הוּא הָאֱלֹהִים, דָּא בְּאוֹרַח פְּרָט, בְּמִלָּה דָּא, כַּמָּה רָזִין וְסִתְרִין אִית בָּהּ. וְדָא, וְהַהוּא דְּקַדְמֵיתָא, כֹּלָּא מִלָּה חֲדָא, דָּא בִּכְלָל, וְדָא בִּפְרָט.

58. At the end of forty years, they endeavored in all the precepts of the Torah that Moses taught them, both those that apply in the Holy Land and those that are also applicable outside the Holy Land. Then he taught them the particular, as is written: "Know therefore this day, and consider it in your heart", "this day" is precise, that which they had no permission TO KNOW beforehand-"that Hashem is the Elohim" (Devarim 4:39). This is KNOWING by the way of particulars. In this word, PARTICULAR, there are many secrets and mysteries. This PASSAGE: "HASHEM IS THE ELOHIM" and the previous PASSAGE: "AND YOU SHALL KNOW THAT I AM HASHEM YOUR ELOHIM" all pertain to the same thing, only one is in general and the other is in particular.

59. וְאִי תֵּימָא, הָא כְּתִיב, יִרְאַת יְיָ' רֵאשִׁית דָּעַת. תֵּירוּצָא, דָּא בְּאוֹרַח פְּרָט, לְמִנְדַע מַאן אִיהוּ יִרְאַת יְיָ'. וְאע"ג דְּאִית לֵיהּ לְבַר נָשׁ לְדַחֲלָא מִנֵּיהּ, עַד לָא יִנְדַּע, אֲבָל הָכָא כְּתִיב רֵאשִׁית דַּעַת, לְמִנְדַע לֵיהּ דְּהָא אִיהוּ רֵאשִׁיתָא, לְמִנְדַע לֵיהּ בְּאוֹרַח פְּרָט.

59. And if you ask, Is it not written: "The fear of Hashem is the beginning of knowledge" (Mishlei 1:7) AND MALCHUT, WHICH IS THE SECRET OF PARTICULAR, IS CALLED THE FEAR OF HASHEM, YET STILL IN ALL, IT IS REFERRED TO AS "THE BEGINNING." SO WE SEE THAT THE PARTICULAR IS THE BEGINNING AND NOT THE GENERAL. The explanation is that we are here discussing the particular itself, MEANING THE BEGINNING OF THE PARTICULAR IS THAT IT IS NECESSARY to know FIRST what the fear of Hashem is. BUT THE BEGINNING OF EVERYTHING IS THE GENERAL AND NOT THE PARTICULAR. And one should fear Him, before knowing AND COCEIVING THE FEAR OF HASHEM, SO WHY IT IS WRITTEN: "THE FEAR OF HASHEM IS THE BEGINNING OF KNOWLEDGE" WHICH SEEMS TO MEAN IT IS FIRST NECESSARY TO KNOW HIM? HE ANSWERS, Yet here it is written: "the beginning of knowledge," MEANING THAT FIRST IT IS NECESSARY TO FEAR HIM AND THROUGH FEAR WE COME TO THE BEGINNING OF KNOWLEDGE AND TO KNOW HIM, SINCE THE FEAR OF HASHEM IS the beginning of knowing Him in particular, AS MENTIONED.

60. בְּגִין כָּךְ, פְּקוּדָא קַדְמָאָה לְמִנְדַּע לֵיהּ לְקוּדְשָׁא בְּרִיךְ הוּא בִּכְלָל וּפְרָט, בְּרֵישָׁא וּבְסוֹפָא. וְרָזָא דָּא אֲנִי רִאשׁוֹן וַאֲנִי אַחֲרוֹן. אֲנִי רִאשׁוֹן בִּכְלָל, וַאֲנִי אַחֲרוֹן בִּפְרָט. וְכֹלָּא בִּכְלָלָא חֲדָא, וְרָזָא חֲדָא. כֵּיוָן דְּיִנְדַּע דָּא בִּכְלָל, יַשְׁלִים כָּל שַׁיְיפוֹי. וּמַאן אִינּוּן. רמ"ח פְּקוּדִין, דְּאִינּוּן רמ"ח שַׁיְיפִין דְּבַר נָשׁ. כֵּיוָן דְּאִשְׁתְּלִים בְּהוּ עַל הַאי בִּכְלָל, כְּדֵין יִנְדַּע בְּאוֹרַח פְּרָט, דְּדָא אִיהוּ אַסְוָותָא לְכֻלְּהוּ, וְיִנְדַּע כָּל יוֹמֵי שַׁתָּא, דְּמִתְחַבְּרָן לְמֵיהַב אַסְוָותָא לְכָל שַׁיְיפִין.

60. Therefore, the first commandment is to know the Holy One, blessed be

He, in general and in particular, in the beginning and in the end, AS IS WRITTEN IN EGYPT: "AND YOU SHALL KNOW THAT I AM HASHEM YOUR ELOHIM...", WHICH IS IN THE FUTURE TENSE THAT CULMINATES AT THE END OF FORTY YEARS IN PARTICULAR. And this is the secret meaning of: "I am first and I am last" (Yeshayah 44:6). "I am first" in general, "and I am last" in particular. It is all spoken with the same principle and secret meaning. After knowing this in general, one should perfect all his limbs. And what are THE LIMBS? THEY ARE the 248 positive precepts, which are the 248 limbs of THE SOUL of man. BECAUSE EVERY POSITIVE PRECEPT PERFECTS A LIMB WHICH CORRESPONDS TO IT IN THE SOUL OF THE PERSON. After being perfected in them in general, one should know in particular, because this, MEANING PARTICULAR, is healing for everything, and one will know how all the days of the year, MEANING ALL THE SFIROT OF MALCHUT THAT IS CALLED YEAR, join to give healing to all the limbs THAT ARE THE PRECEPTS, THAT IS, THEY MAKE THEM WHOLE.

61. וְאִי תֵּימָא, כָּל יוֹמֵי שַׁתָּא, הֵיךְ יַהֲבִין אַסְוָותָא לְכָל שַׁיְיפִין. וַדַּאי הָכִי הוּא עֵילָא וְתַתָּא, שַׁתָּא וְיוֹמֵי דִילֵיהּ, יַהֲבִין אַסְוָותָא לְכָל שַׁיְיפִין עֵילָא וְתַתָּא, דְּשַׁיְיפִין אֲרִיקוּ בִּרְכָאן לְיוֹמֵי שַׁתָּא כְּדֵין אַסְוָותָא וְחַיִּין תַּלְיָין עֲלָן מִלְּעֵילָא, וְאִתְמַלְיָין מִכֹּלָּא. מַאן גָּרִים לוֹן. יוֹמֵי שַׁתָּא.

61. And if you ask, How do all the days of the year cure all the limbs, SEEING THAT MALCHUT, WHICH IS THE SECRET OF THE YEAR, HAS NOTHING OF HER OWN. ON THE CONTRARY, THE LIMBS, WHICH ARE THE SECRET OF THE GENERAL, NAMELY THE 248 CHANNELS OF ABUNDANCE OF ZEIR ANPIN, ARE THOSE THAT POUR EVERYTHING TO MALCHUT. HE ANSWERS, Certainly it is so above and below, NAMELY IN MALE AND FEMALE AND IN LOWER MAN, that the year and its days, THAT ARE ITS SFIROT, supply cure for all the limbs above IN ZEIR ANPIN, and below IN MAN. The limbs supply a flow of blessings for the days of the year, WHICH ARE THE SFIROT OF MALCHUT, WHICH IS THE PARTICULAR. FOR BY THE POSITIVE PRECEPTS A PERSON PERFORMS, HE DRAWS A FLOW OF BLESSINGS FROM A LIMB, WHICH IS THE SECRET OF ONE CHANNEL OF ZEIR ANPIN, TO ONE OF THE DAYS OF THE YEAR, WHICH IS THE MEANING OF PARTICULAR. Then, healing and life are suspended over us from above UNTIL THE LIMBS become filled with all PERFECTION, AND SUPPLY THEM TO THE PARTICULAR, WHICH IS THE YEAR. THEN THE MOCHIN OF THE PARTICULAR ARE REVEALED. Who caused THE LIMBS TO

BE FILLED WITH ALL PERFECTION-the days of the year ARE THOSE THAT
CAUSED THIS BECAUSE THE LIMBS WERE TO PERFECT IT. AND IF THE
YEAR DID NOT NEED IMPROVEMENT, THE LIMBS, WHICH ARE THE
CHANNELS OF THE FLOW FROM ZEIR ANPIN, WOULD NOT BECOME
FILLED WITH ABUNDANCE. THEREFORE, IT IS CONSIDERED AS THOUGH
THE DAYS OF THE YEAR GAVE HEALING AND LIFE TO THE LIMBS.

62. אוּף הָכִי נָמֵי לְתַתָּא, כַּד בַּר נָשׁ יַשְׁלִים גּוּפֵיהּ בְּאִינּוּן פְּקוּדִין
דְּאוֹרַיְיתָא לֵית לָךְ כָּל יוֹמָא דְּלָא אַתְיָיא לְאִתְבָּרְכָא מִנֵּיהּ, וְכַד אִינּוּן
אִתְבָּרְכָאן מִנֵּיהּ, כְּדֵין חַיִּין וְאַסְוָותָא תַּלְיָין עָלֵיהּ מִלְעֵילָּא. מַאן גָּרִים
לֵיהּ. אִינּוּן יוֹמֵי שַׁתָּא. יוֹמֵי שַׁתָּא, כְּמָה דְּאִתְבָּרְכָאן מִלְעֵילָּא מֵרָזָא
דְּאָדָם. הָכִי נָמֵי אִתְבָּרְכָאן מִתַּתָּא מֵרָזָא דְּאָדָם.

62. And so it is below. When a person perfects himself with these 248
POSITIVE precepts in the Torah, there is no day that will not be blessed by
him, BY THAT MAN, and when they are blessed from him, life and healing
are suspended over him from above. THIS MEANS THAT THEY ARE NOT
DRAWN TO MALCHUT BEFORE MAN COMPLETES ALL THE 248 POSITIVE
PRECEPTS IN THEIR ENTIRETY, AND THEY ARE SUSPENDED OVER HIM
FROM ABOVE UNTIL THEN. What caused THE SUPERNAL CHANNELS TO BE
FILLED WITH HEALING AND LIFE - the days of the year, AS MENTIONED
BEFORE. THEREFORE, IT IS CONSIDERED AS THOUGH THE DAYS OF THE
YEAR GAVE THEM HEALING AND LIFE, AS MENTIONED. Just as the days of
the year are blessed from above from the secret of man, WHICH IS ZEIR
ANPIN, they are also blessed below from the secret of THE LOWER man,
THROUGH THE PRECEPTS THAT HE FULFILLS.

63. זַכָּאִין אִינּוּן יִשְׂרָאֵל בְּהַאי עָלְמָא, בְּאִלֵּין פְּקוּדִין דְּאוֹרַיְיתָא,
דְּאִקְרוּן אָדָם, דִּכְתִיב. אָדָם אַתֶּם. אַתֶּם קְרוּיִים אָדָם, וְעכו"ם לָא
אִקְרוּן אָדָם. וּבְגִין דְּיִשְׂרָאֵל אִקְרֵי אָדָם, אִית לוֹן לְאִשְׁתַּדְּלָא בְּאִינּוּן
פְּקוּדִין דְּאוֹרַיְיתָא, לְמֶהֱוֵי כֹּלָּא חַד, בְּרָזָא דְּאָדָם.

63. Fortunate are Yisrael in this world with those precepts THAT THEY
OBSERVE, for they are called men BECAUSE OF THIS, as is written: "are
men" (Yechezkel 34:31). THIS MEANS you are called men and idol
worshippers are not called men. Since Yisrael are called men, they should

strive in the precepts of the Torah, WHICH ARE 613 CORRESPONDING TO THE 248 LIMBS AND 365 SINEWS THAT ARE IN THE HUMAN BODY, so they would all form one body in accordance with the secret meaning of man.

64. כַּד יָהַב קוּדְשָׁא בְּרִיךְ הוּא אוֹרַיְיתָא לְיִשְׂרָאֵל עַל טוּרָא דְּסִינַי, מִלָּה קַדְמָאָה אִיהוּ אָנֹכִי, אָנֹכִי סַלְּקָא לְרָזִין סַגִּיאִין. וְהָכָא אִיהוּ רָזָא דְּפִקוּדָא קַדְמָאָה, לְמִנְדַּע לֵיהּ בִּכְלָלָא. בְּגִין דִּכְתִיב אָנֹכִי, הָא קָא רָמִיז, דְּאִית אֱלָהָא שַׁלִּיטָא עִלָּאָה עַל עָלְמָא, כד"א כִּי יְיָ' אֱלֹהֶיךָ אֵשׁ אוֹכְלָה הוּא, פִּקוּדָא קַדְמָאָה בִּכְלָל. בִּפְרָט: בְּגִין דִּכְתִיב, ה' אֱלֹהֶיךָ דָּא פְּרָט, וְדָא כְּלָל וּפְרָט, פִּקוּדָא קַדְמָאָה, דְּאִצְטְרִיךְ לְמִנְדַּע בְּרֵישָׁא וּבְסוֹפָא, כְּמָה דְּאוֹקִימְנָא.

ע"כ רעיא מהימנא

64. When the Holy One, blessed be He, gave the Torah to Yisrael on Mount Sinai, the first word was: "I (Heb. *anochi*)." 'I' contains many secrets, and here is the secret of the first precept of knowing Him in general. For it is written: "I", which alludes to the existence of an Elohim, a Supernal Ruler over the world, WHICH IS THE SECRET OF ZEIR ANPIN, WHICH IS GENERAL, as written: "For Hashem your Elohim is a consuming fire" (Devarim 4:24), WHICH IS THE SECRET OF ZEIR ANPIN and is the first precept of the aspect of general. SO THERE IS HERE AN ALLUSION to the particular, for it is written: "Hashem your Elohim" which is a particular. And this general and particular is the first precept of the need to know in the beginning and in the end as we explained.

End of Ra'aya Meheimna (the Faithful Shepherd)

6. "But they hearkened not to Moses for anguish of spirit"

A Synopsis

Rabbi Yehuda says "anguish of spirit" means the people did not have enough rest or enough breath. But Rabbi Shimon answers that it means two things: that Binah had not yet released joy so rest and freedom were not yet available; and that Malchut had not yet ruled in the world to institute just laws.

65. וַיְדַבֵּר מֹשֶׁה כֵּן אֶל בְּנֵי יִשְׂרָאֵל וְלֹא שָׁמְעוּ אֶל מֹשֶׁה מִקֹּצֶר רוּחַ. מַאי מִקֹּצֶר רוּחַ. א"ר יְהוּדָה, דְּלָא הֲווֹ נְפִישֵׁי, וְלָא הֲווֹ לְקִיטֵי רוּחָא. א"ר שִׁמְעוֹן, מִקֹּצֶר רוּחַ: דְּעַד לָא נָפַק יוֹבְלָא, לְמֵיהַב לוֹן נְפִישׁוּ. וְרוּחַ בַּתְרָאָה, עַד לָא שַׁלְטָא לְמֶעְבַּד נִימוּסֵי, וּכְדֵין הֲוָה עָאקוּ דְּרוּחָא. מַאן אִיהוּ. רוּחַ בַּתְרָאָה דְּקַאמְרָן.

65. "And Moses spoke so to the children of Yisrael, but they hearkened not to Moses for anguish of spirit" (Shemot 6:9). HE ASKS, What is "anguish of spirit"? Rabbi Yehuda said, They did not rest FROM THEIR LABOR and they did not gather into themselves SUFFICIENT breath. Rabbi Shimon said, Anguish of spirit MEANS the Jubilee was still not released, WHICH IS BINAH, to give them rest AND FREEDOM, and the last spirit, WHICH IS MALCHUT, had not yet ruled IN THE WORLD to institute JUST laws IN THE WORLD. Therefore, there was anguish of spirit. Which spirit is it? It is the last spirit that we mentioned, WHICH IS MALCHUT, WHO WAS TOO HELPLESS TO SAVE YISRAEL, WHICH IS THE MEANING OF "ANGUISH OF SPIRIT."

7. Voice and speech

A Synopsis

Rabbi Shimon begins with: "Behold the children of Yisrael did not listen to me and how will Pharaoh hearken to me and I have impeded lips?" He says that Zeir Anpin is voice and Malchut is speech or words. Moses was voice but while the people were in exile he had no speech until he reached Mount Sinai and was given the Torah. Then voice combined with speech and he spoke words. We hear that 'said' in "For Elohim has said lest the people regret" does not mean speaking by mouth but is rather the silent wish of the heart. Rabbi Shimon turns to the verse: "And I appeared to Abraham, to Isaac and to Jacob." He tells us that Jacob was a vehicle for Tiferet, the central column, while Abraham and Isaac are the right and left columns, their perfection depending on the central one. Lastly he says that whoever has earned a covenant has earned the land, because the two are combined.

66. תָּא חֲזֵי, כְּתִיב הֵן בְּנֵי יִשְׂרָאֵל לֹא שָׁמְעוּ אֵלַי וְאֵיךְ יִשְׁמָעֵנִי פַרְעֹה וַאֲנִי עֲרַל שְׂפָתָיִם, מַאי וַאֲנִי עֲרַל שְׂפָתָיִם. וְהָא בְּקַדְמֵיתָא כְּתִיב לֹא אִישׁ דְּבָרִים אָנֹכִי וְגוֹ' כִּי כְבַד פֶּה וּכְבַד לָשׁוֹן אָנֹכִי, וְקוּדְשָׁא בְּרִיךְ הוּא הֲוָה אוֹתִיב לֵיהּ, מִי שָׂם פֶּה לָאָדָם וְגוֹ', וְהוּא אָמַר וְאָנֹכִי אֶהְיֶה עִם פִּיךְ, ס"ד דְּלָא הֲוָה כֵּן, וְהַשְׁתָּא אָמַר וַאֲנִי עֲרַל שְׂפָתָיִם, אִי הָכִי, אָן הוּא מִלָּה דְּאַבְטַח לֵיהּ קוּדְשָׁא בְּרִיךְ הוּא בְּקַדְמֵיתָא.

66. Come and see: It is written: "Behold, the children of Yisrael did not listen to me; how than shall Pharaoh hear me, who am of uncircumcised lips" (Shemot 6:12). HE ASKS, What is "who am of uncircumcised lips"? At first it was written: "I am not an eloquent man... but I am slow of speech, and of a slow tongue" to which the Holy One, blessed be He, replied, "Who gave man a mouth" and He said, "And I will be with your mouth" (Shemot 4:10-12). Can you imagine that it was not so? Yet now he says, I "am of uncircumcised lips." If so, where is the previous assurance of the Holy One, blessed be He, to him, NAMELY THE ASSURANCE, "AND I WILL BE WITH YOUR MOUTH..."

67. אֶלָּא רָזָא אִיהוּ, מֹשֶׁה קָלָא, וְדִבּוּר דְּאִיהוּ מִלָּה דִילֵיהּ, הֲוָה בְּגָלוּתָא, וַהֲוָה אִיהוּ אָטִים לְפָרְשָׁא מִלִּין, וּבְגִין דָּא אָמַר, וְאֵיךְ

יִשְׁמָעֵנִי פַרְעֹה, בְּעוֹד דְּמִלָּה דִּילִי אִיהִי בְּגָלוּתָא דִּילֵיהּ, דְּהָא לֵית לִי מִלָּה. הָא אֲנָא קָלָא מִלָּה גָּרַע, דְּאִיהִי בְּגָלוּתָא, וע"ד, שָׁתַּף קוּדְשָׁא בְּרִיךְ הוּא לְאַהֲרֹן בַּהֲדֵיהּ.

67. AND HE ANSWERS: It is a secret. Moses IS voice, NAMELY ZEIR ANPIN THAT IS CALLED VOICE, and speech, which is his words, NAMELY MALCHUT, was in exile. THEREFORE, Moses was impeded IN MOUTH from explaining things, and therefore he said, "how then shall Pharaoh hear me" when my speech, WHICH IS MALCHUT, is still in exile, and I am speechless, a speechless voice, for it is in exile. Therefore the Holy One, blessed be He, made Aaron a partner to him, INSTEAD OF MALCHUT, AS HE IS THE QUEEN'S BEST MAN.

68. תָּא חֲזֵי, כָּל זִמְנָא דְּדִבּוּר הֲוָה בְּגָלוּתָא, קָלָא אִסְתְּלַק מִנֵּיהּ, וּמִלָּה הֲוָה אָטִים בְּלָא קוֹל, כַּד אָתָא מֹשֶׁה, אָתָא קוֹל. וּמֹשֶׁה הֲוָה קוֹל בְּלָא מִלָּה, בְּגִין דַּהֲוָה בְּגָלוּתָא, וְכָל זִמְנָא דְּדִבּוּר הֲוָה בְּגָלוּתָא, מֹשֶׁה אָזִיל קָלָא בְּלָא דִבּוּר, וְהָכִי אָזִיל עַד דְּקָרִיבוּ לְטוּרָא דְּסִינַי, וְאִתְיְהִיבַת אוֹרַיְיתָא, וּבְהַהוּא זִמְנָא, אִתְחַבַּר קָלָא בְּדִבּוּר, וּכְדֵין מִלָּה מַלִיל, הה"ד, וַיְדַבֵּר אֱלֹהִים אֵת כָּל הַדְּבָרִים הָאֵלֶּה. וּכְדֵין, מֹשֶׁה אִשְׁתְּכַח שְׁלִים בְּמִלָּה כַּדְקָא יֵאוֹת, קוֹל וְדִבּוּר כַּחֲדָא בִּשְׁלִימוּ.

68. Come and see, as long as speech, WHICH IS MALCHUT, was in exile, voice, WHICH IS ZEIR ANPIN, was gone FROM SPEECH, and speech was uncircumcised, voiceless. When Moses came, the voice came BECAUSE HE WAS A CHARIOT TO ZEIR ANPIN, WHICH IS CALLED VOICE. Moses was voice without speech because SPEECH was in exile. And Moses went while speech was in exile to Mount Sinai and the Torah was given. At that time, voice joined with speech, NAMELY ZEIR ANPIN WITH MALCHUT, and then he spoke words. This is the meaning of: "And Elohim spoke all these words" (Shemot 20:1) IN THE ASPECT OF VOICE WITHOUT SPEECH, AND SO HE WENT UNTIL THESE BECAME CLOSE. Then Moses became properly whole with speech, BECAUSE voice and speech were whole together.

69. וְעַל דָּא מֹשֶׁה אִתְרְעִים, דְּמִלָּה גָּרַע מִנֵּיהּ, בַּר הַהוּא זִמְנָא דְּמַלִּילַת לְאִתְרַעֲמָא עֲלוֹי, בְּזִמְנָא דִּכְתִיב, וּמֵאָז בָּאתִי אֶל פַּרְעֹה לְדַבֵּר

בְּשִׁמְךָ, מִיַּד וַיְדַבֵּר אֱלֹהִים אֶל מֹשֶׁה. תָּא חֲזֵי דְּהָכִי הוּא דִּשְׁרָא מִלָּה לְמַלְּלָא וּפָסַק לָה, בְּגִין דְּעַד לָא מָטָא זִמְנָא דִּכְתִיב וַיְדַבֵּר אֱלֹהִים וְגוֹ׳. וּפָסַק וְאַשְׁלִים קָלָא, הה״ד וַיֹּאמֶר אֵלָיו אֲנִי ה׳. בְּגִין דְּדִבּוּר הֲוָה בְּגָלוּתָא, וְלָא מָטָא זִמְנָא לְמַלְּלָא.

69. And Moses complained that he lacked speech, except for the time when MALCHUT spoke to reproach him, NAMELY at the time that is written: "for since I came to Pharaoh to speak in Your name, HE HAD DONE EVIL TO THIS PEOPLE..." (Shemot 5:23). Immediately, "And Elohim spoke to Moses," SINCE MALCHUT, THE SECRET OF WORD, WHICH IS CALLED ELOHIM, SPOKE TO HIM STERNLY, AS THE WORD 'SPEAK' IMPLIES A STERN LANGUAGE. SHE REPROACHED HIM FOR SAYING, "FOR SINCE I CAME TO PHARAOH..." MALCHUT STARTED TO SPEAK TO HIM, EVEN THOUGH SHE WAS IN EXILE, THE REASON BEING THAT THE SPEECH WAS ONLY TO SHOW ANGER. Come and see that it was so, because speech started speaking and then stopped, and the voice, WHICH IS ZEIR ANPIN, completed it. Hence the passage ENDS: "And said to him, I am Hashem" BECAUSE HASHEM IS ZEIR ANPIN. That is because speech was still in exile, and its time to speak had not yet come. THEREFORE ZEIR ANPIN SPOKE WITH HIM.

70. בְּגִינֵי כַּךְ, מֹשֶׁה לָא הֲוָה שְׁלִים מִלָּה בְּקַדְמֵיתָא, דְּאִיהוּ קוֹל, וְאָתֵי בְּגִין דִּבּוּר, לְאַפָּקָא לֵיהּ מִן גָּלוּתָא. כֵּיוָן דְּנָפַק מִן גָּלוּתָא, וְאִתְחַבְּרוּ קוֹל וְדִבּוּר כַּחֲדָא בְּטוּרָא דְסִינַי, אִשְׁתְּלִים מֹשֶׁה וְאִתְּסֵי, וְאִשְׁתְּכַח כְּדֵין קוֹל וְדִבּוּר כַּחֲדָא בִּשְׁלִימוּ.

70. Because of this, Moses was not whole in the beginning, NOT HAVING THE WORD, THAT IS MALCHUT. For he was voice THAT NEEDS THE WORD, and came for speech to take it out of the exile. As soon as it emerged from the exile, and voice and speech united at Mount Sinai AS MENTIONED, Moses was perfected and was cured OF HIS SPEECH IMPEDIMENT. And then we find voice and word together wholly.

71. תָּא חֲזֵי, כָּל יוֹמִין דַּהֲוָה מֹשֶׁה בְּמִצְרַיִם, דְּבָעָא לְאַפָּקָא מִלָּה מִן גָּלוּתָא, לָא מַלִּיל מִלָּה, דְּאִיהוּ דִּבּוּר. כֵּיוָן דְּנָפַק מִן גָּלוּתָא, וְאִתְחַבַּר

קוֹל בְּדִבּוּר, הַהוּא מִלָּה דְּאִיהוּ דִּבּוּר, אַנְהִיג וְדִבֵּר לוֹן לְיִשְׂרָאֵל, אֲבָל לָא מַלִּיל, עַד דְּקָרִיבוּ לְטוּרָא דְּסִינַי, וּפָתַח בְּאוֹרַיְיתָא, דְּהָכִי אִתְחֲזֵי. וְאִי תֵּימָא, כִּי אָמַר אֱלֹקִים פֶּן יִנָּחֵם הָעָם, לָא כְּתִיב כִּי דִּבֵּר, אֶלָּא כִּי אָמַר, דְּאִיהוּ רְעוּתָא דְּלִבָּא בַּחֲשַׁאי, וְהָא אוֹקִימְנָא.

71. Come and see: All the days that Moses was in Egypt and wanted to take out the word from exile, the word, which is speech, did not speak. As soon as it emerged from the exile, and voice and speech combined, that word which is speech, NAMELY MALCHUT, led and guided Yisrael, but did not speak until YISRAEL approached Mount Sinai. It opened with the Torah, which is the proper way. And if you claim IT IS WRITTEN: "For Elohim said, lest the people repent" (Shemot 13:17). AND THE NAME ELOHIM DENOTES MALCHUT, SO IT SPOKE BEFORE TORAH WAS GIVEN. HE ANSWERS, It says "said," which is NOT SPEAKING BY MOUTH, BUT RATHER the silent wish of the heart, WHICH IS CALLED "SAYING" AS IN "HAMAN THOUGHT (LIT. 'SAID') IN HIS HEART" (ESTER 6:6), as we have already explained.

72. וַיְדַבֵּר אֱלֹהִים אֶל מֹשֶׁה וַיֹּאמֶר אֵלָיו אֲנִי ה'. ר' יְהוּדָה פָּתַח, קַמְתִּי אֲנִי לִפְתּוֹחַ לְדוֹדִי וְדוֹדִי חָמַק עָבָר וְגוֹ'. קַמְתִּי אֲנִי לִפְתּוֹחַ לְדוֹדִי, דָּא קָלָא. תָּא חֲזֵי, כְּנֶסֶת יִשְׂרָאֵל כַּד אִיהִי בְּגָלוּתָא, קָלָא אִסְתְּלַק מִינָּהּ, וּמִלָּה אִשְׁתְּכַךְ מִינָּהּ, כמד"א נֶאֱלַמְתִּי דוּמִיָּה. וְאִי אִתְּעַר מִלְּתָא, מַה כְּתִיב, וְדוֹדִי חָמַק עָבָר, דְּהָא קָלָא אִסְתְּלַק מִינָּהּ, וּפָסְקָא מִלָּה. וְעַל דָּא וַיְדַבֵּר אֱלֹהִים אֶל מֹשֶׁה, שָׁרִיאַת לְמַלְּלָא, וּפָסַק וְשָׁתִיק. לְבָתַר אַשְׁלִים קָלָא וְאָמַר וַיֹּאמֶר אֵלָיו אֲנִי ה'.

72. "And Elohim spoke to Moses, and said to him, 'I am Hashem'" (Shemot 6:2). Rabbi Yehuda opened the discussion saying, "I rose to open to my beloved; but my beloved has turned away, and was gone..." (Shir Hashirim 5:6). "I rose to open to my beloved": This is voice, WHICH IS ZEIR ANPIN, WHICH IS THE BELOVED OF MALCHUT. Come and see: When the Congregation of Yisrael, WHICH IS MALCHUT, is in exile, the voice was gone from it, and the words subsided from it, as is written: "I was dumb with silence" (Tehilim 39:3). And if the word awakened, MEANING THAT IT WAS STIMULATED TO SPEAK, it is written, "But my beloved has turned away, and was gone," since the voice was gone from it and the word discontinued. Hence, "And Elohim spoke to Moses." It started to speak and then stopped and remained silent. And afterwards the voice finished the sentence, WHICH IS ZEIR ANPIN, and said, "And said to him, 'I am Hashem.'"

73. וָאֵרָא אֶל אַבְרָהָם אֶל יִצְחָק וְאֶל יַעֲקֹב, בְּיַעֲקֹב תּוֹסֶפֶת וָא"ו, דְּאִיהוּ שְׁלִימוּ דַּאֲבָהָן, כְּמָה דְּאַתְּ אָמַר, אֱלֹהֵי אַבְרָהָם אֱלֹהֵי יִצְחָק וֵאלֹהֵי יַעֲקֹב, בְּיַעֲקֹב תּוֹסֶפֶת וָא"ו. אָמַר רִבִּי יוֹסֵי, אִי הָכִי, הָא כְּתִיב אֲנִי ה' אֱלֹהֵי אַבְרָהָם אָבִיךָ וֵאלֹהֵי יִצְחָק, הָא בְּיִצְחָק תּוֹסֶפֶת וָא"ו.

73. "And I appeared to Abraham, to Isaac, and to Jacob." By Jacob, there is an additional Vav (= and) AS IS SAID, "AND TO JACOB" TO SHOW that he is the selected of the patriarchs. VAV DENOTES TIFERET, WHICH IS THE CENTRAL COLUMN OF ZEIR ANPIN, AND JACOB WAS A CHARIOT FOR IT, AND ABRAHAM AND ISAAC ARE THE TWO COLUMNS, RIGHT AND LEFT OF ZEIR ANPIN, AND THEIR PERFECTION IS DEPENDENT ON THE CENTRAL COLUMN, WHICH IS JACOB. The same way, it is said, "The Elohim of Abraham, the Elohim of Isaac and the Elohim of Jacob" (Shemot 3:6). By Jacob there is an additional Vav (= and). Rabbi Yosi said, If so, it is written: "I am Hashem, Elohim of Abraham your father, and Elohim of Isaac" (Beresheet 28:13). Here Isaac is written with an additional Vav. BUT SURELY IT IS THE CONJUNCTIVE VAV. IT DOES NOT CARRY A HOMILETICAL REASON.

74. אָמַר לֵיהּ, שַׁפִּיר הֲוָה, בְּגִין דְּיַעֲקֹב הֲוָה קַיָּים, וְאַכְלִיל לֵיהּ לְיַעֲקֹב בְּיִצְחָק, דְּאִתְחַשְּׁכוּ עֵינוֹי, וַהֲוָה כַּמֵּת, דְּהָא בְּעוֹד דב"נ אִיהוּ קַיָּים בְּהַאי עָלְמָא, לָא אִדְכַּר עֲלוֹי שְׁמָא קַדִּישָׁא, וְעַל דָּא אַכְלִיל לֵיהּ בְּיִצְחָק. הַשְׁתָּא דְּמִית יַעֲקֹב, אָתָא מִלָּה בְּאַתְרֵיהּ. הה"ד וָאֵרָא אֶל אַבְרָהָם אֶל יִצְחָק וְאֶל יַעֲקֹב, בְּתוֹסֶפֶת ו'.

74. He said to him, It is well, AND THERE IS NO DIFFICULTY because Jacob was alive, and THE VERSE included Jacob in Isaac, whose eyes were dim, and who was as one who is dead. Because as long as a person lives in this world, the Holy Name is not mentioned in relation to him. Therefore, he was included in Isaac. THEREFORE THERE IS AN ADDITIONAL VAV BY

ISAAC, but now that Jacob has died, the matter has returned to its place. This is the meaning of: "And I appeared to Abraham, to Isaac, and to Jacob" with an additional Vav.

75. בְּאֵל שַׁדָּי: אִתְחֲזֵינָא לְהוּ, מִגּוֹ אַסְפָּקְלַרְיָא דְּלָא נָהֲרָא. וְלָא אִתְחֲזֵינָא מִגּוֹ אַסְפָּקְלַרְיָא דְּנָהֲרָא. וְאִי תֵּימָא דְּהָא אִשְׁתַּמְּשׁוּ בְּנוּקְבָא בִּלְחוֹד וְלָא יַתִּיר. תָּא חֲזֵי, דְּלָא אִתְפָּרְשָׁן לְעָלְמִין, הה״ד וְגַם הֲקִימוֹתִי אֶת בְּרִיתִי אִתָּם, דְּהָא בְּרִית אִתְחַבַּר עִמָּה.

75. "By the name of El Shadai" means I appeared to them from within the mirror that does not illuminate, WHICH IS MALCHUT THAT IS CALLED EL SHADAI, but did not appear through the illuminating mirror, WHICH IS ZEIR ANPIN CALLED YUD HEI VAV HEI. And if you say THE PATRIARCHS united with the Nukva only, NAMELY MALCHUT, and not more, come and see that ZEIR ANPIN never separated FROM THE NUKVA IN RELATION TO THE PATRIARCHS. This is the meaning of: "And I have also established my covenant with them" (Shemot 6:4), because the covenant THAT IS THE YESOD OF ZEIR ANPIN joined with MALCHUT.

76. מְקוּדְשָׁא בְּרִיךְ הוּא אִית לֵיהּ לְבַר נָשׁ לְמֵילַף, דְּהָא אִיהוּ קָאָמַר דְּלָא פָּרִישׁ לוֹן, דִּכְתִּיב בְּאֵל שַׁדָּי, וּכְתִיב וְגַם הֲקִימוֹתִי אֶת בְּרִיתִי אִתָּם, בְּגִין לְקַיְּימָא קַיּוּמָא בְּיִחוּדָא חַד, וְגַם הֲקִימוֹתִי אֶת בְּרִיתִי אִתָּם וְגוֹ'. הָא אִתְּמַר, מַאן דְּזָכֵי לִבְרִית, יָרִית לְאַרְעָא.

76. One should learn from the Holy One, blessed be He, NOT TO SEPARATE BETWEEN ZEIR ANPIN AND THE NUKVA because He did not separate them, as is written: "El Shadai", WHICH IS THE NUKVA, and also, "And also I have sustained My covenant with them", WHICH IS YESOD OF ZEIR ANPIN THAT HAS JOINED WITH HER. And we learned that whoever has merited to a covenant, TO YESOD OF ZEIR ANPIN, merited the land, WHICH IS THE NUKVA, SINCE THEY ARE JOINED TOGETHER, AS MENTIONED.

8. "Be afraid of the sword"

A Synopsis

Rabbi Shimon speaks to Rabbi Chiya and Rabbi Yosi about the verse: "Be afraid of the sword. For wrath brings the punishment of the sword, that you may know that there is a judgment." He says 'the sword' is "the sword that avenges the revenge of the covenant," in other words, that punishes anyone who cheats the covenant or is perverse. "For wrath brings the punishments of the sword" because all who falsify the covenant decrease the desire of Malchut to take sustenance from Zeir Anpin. On the other hand, everyone who observes the covenant stimulates it properly, thereby blessing those above and those below. The covenant is stimulated whenever righteous people are found in the world. As evidence for this Rabbi Shimon offers: "And also I have sustained my covenant with them to give them the Land of Canaan, the land of their sojourns (Heb. *megureihem*)." When the covenant was still remembered and kept by the children of Yisrael all the Sfirot combined in one to liberate them from Egypt.

77. רִבִּי חִיָּיא וְרִבִּי יוֹסֵי, הֲווֹ שְׁכִיחֵי יוֹמָא חַד קַמֵּיהּ דְּרִבִּי שִׁמְעוֹן, פָּתַח רִבִּי שִׁמְעוֹן וְאָמַר, גּוּרוּ לָכֶם מִפְּנֵי חֶרֶב כִּי חֵמָה עֲוֹנוֹת חֶרֶב לְמַעַן תֵּדְעוּן שַׁדּוּן. שַׁדִּין כְּתִיב. גּוּרוּ לָכֶם מִפְּנֵי חֶרֶב, מַאן חֶרֶב. דָּא חֶרֶב נוֹקֶמֶת נְקַם בְּרִית, דְּהָא הַאי חֶרֶב קָאִים לְאִסְתַּכְּלָא מַאן דִּמְשַׁקֵּר בִּבְרִית, דְּכָל מַאן דִּמְשַׁקֵּר בִּבְרִית, נוּקְמָא דְּנַקְמִין מִנֵּיהּ, הַאי חֶרֶב הוּא.

77. One day, Rabbi Chiya and Rabbi Yosi were before Rabbi Shimon. Rabbi Shimon opened the discussion saying, "Be afraid of the sword. For wrath brings the punishments of the sword, that you may know that there is a judgment" (Iyov 19:29). HE ASKS, It is written: "Be afraid of the sword." What sword? HE ANSWERS, This is "a sword…that shall avenge My covenant" (Vayikra 26:25). This sword, WHICH IS MALCHUT, stands to observe who is false to the covenant, WHICH IS YESOD, because anyone who is false to the covenant BLEMISHES IT WITH SEXUAL MISCONDUCT OR SPILLING SEMEN IN VAIN, it is this sword that takes vengeance on him.

78. הֲדָא הוּא דִּכְתִיב, כִּי חֵמָה עֲוֹנוֹת חָרֶב. מַאי טַעְמָא. בְּגִין דְּמַאן דִּמְשַׁקֵּר בִּבְרִית, פָּרִישׁ תִּיאוּבְתָּא, וְלָא נָטִיל מַאן דְּנָטִיל, וְלָא יָהִיב

לְאַתְרֵיה, דְּהָא לָא אִתְּעַר לְגַבֵּיה אַתְרֵיה. וְכָל מַאן דִּנְטִיר לֵיה לְהַאי בְּרִית, אִיהוּ גָּרִים לְאִתְעֲרָא לְהַאי בְּרִית לְאַתְרֵיה. וְאִתְבָּרְכָאן עֶלָּאִין וְתַתָּאִין.

78. This is the meaning of: "For wrath brings the punishments of the sword." What is the reason? IT IS that anyone who is false to the covenant distances the desire OF MALCHUT TO RECEIVE SUSTENANCE FROM ZEIR ANPIN, and thus whoever should receive SUSTENANCE, NAMELY YESOD does not receive it, and does not give to his place, since his place, WHICH IS MALCHUT, is not awakened toward him. BECAUSE OF THE BLEMISH IN THE COVENANT THE DESIRE TO RECEIVE SUSTENANCE WAS TAKEN FROM HER. Everyone who observes this covenant arouses the covenant towards its place, WHICH IS MALCHUT, and the upper and lower beings are blessed.

79. מַאן אִתְּעַר הַאי בְּרִית לְאַתְרֵיה. כַּד אִשְׁתְּכָחוּ זַכָּאִין בְּעָלְמָא. מְנָא לָן, מֵהָכָא, דִּכְתִּיב וְגַם הֲקִימוֹתִי אֶת בְּרִיתִי אִתָּם לָתֵת לָהֶם אֶת אֶרֶץ כְּנַעַן אֶת אֶרֶץ מְגוּרֵיהֶם. מַאי מְגוּרֵיהֶם. כְּמָה דְּאַתְּ אָמֵר גּוּרוּ לָכֶם מִפְּנֵי חָרֶב. בְּגִין דְּאִיהוּ אֲתָר, דְּאַשְׁדֵי מָגוֹר בְּעָלְמָא, וְעַל דָּא גּוּרוּ לָכֶם מִפְּנֵי חָרֶב.

79. Who awakens this covenant to its place? When there are righteous people in the world, THEY AWAKEN IT. How do we know this? From the words: "And I have also established My covenant with them, to give them the land of Canaan, the land of their sojourns (Heb. *megureihem*)" (Shemot 6:4). What is 'megureihem'? IT IS as written: "Be afraid (Heb. *guru*) of the sword", WHICH IS MALCHUT AS MENTIONED. Because it is a place that causes fear in the world. Therefore IT SAYS: "Be afraid of the sword." SO THE PATRIARCHS STIMULATED THE COVENANT TO ITS PLACE, WHICH IS MALCHUT, OF WHICH IT SAYS, "TO GIVE TO THEM THE LAND OF THEIR SOJOURNS," AS EXPLAINED.

80. אֲשֶׁר גָּרוּ בָהּ, מִיּוֹמָא דְּאִתְקְרִיבוּ לְגַבֵּי קוּדְשָׁא בְּרִיךְ הוּא, דְּחִילוּ בָּהּ דְּחִילוּ, וּדְחִילוּ עֶלָּאָה בָּהּ לְמֵיטַר פְּקוּדוֹי. דְּאִי בְּהַאי לָא יִשְׁדֵי דְחִילוּ עַל רֵישֵׁיהּ דְּבַר נָשׁ, לָא דָּחִיל לֵיה לְקוּדְשָׁא בְּרִיךְ הוּא לְעָלְמִין בִּשְׁאָר פְּקוּדוֹי.

80. "in which they sojourned (Heb. *garu*)" (Ibid.). 'GARU' MEANS THAT from the day that they approached the Holy One, blessed be He, they had feared in it FROM HASHEM and it consisted of a supernal fear in observing His commandments. BECAUSE MALCHUT IS THE ASPECT OF FEAR, and if a person will not place fear over his head IN OBSERVING THE COVENANT, he will never fear of the Holy One, blessed be He, in the other precepts.

81. תָּא חֲזֵי, בְּאִתְעָרוּתָא דִּלְתַתָּא, כַּד אִתְּעָרוּ יִשְׂרָאֵל לְגַבֵּי קוּדְשָׁא בְּרִיךְ הוּא, וְצַוְוחוּ לָקֳבְלֵיה, מַה כְּתִיב, וָאֶזְכֹּר אֶת בְּרִיתִי, דְּהָא בִּבְרִית הֲוֵי זָכוֹר. וּכְדֵין אִתְּעַר תִּיאוּבְתָּא, לְאִתְקַשְׁרָא כֹּלָּא בְּקִשּׁוּרָא חַד. כֵּיוָן דְּהַאי בְּרִית אִתְּעַר, הָא קְשּׁוּרָא דְּכֹלָּא אִתְּעַר. וָאֶזְכֹּר אֶת בְּרִיתִי, לְאִזְדַּוְּוגָא לֵיהּ בְּאַתְרֵיה. וְעַל דָּא, לָכֵן אֱמוֹר לִבְנֵי יִשְׂרָאֵל אֲנִי ה'.

81. Come and see, of the awakening from below, when Yisrael were awakened towards the Holy One, blessed be He, and cried before Him, it is written: "And I have remembered My covenant" (Shemot 6:5), because He remembered the covenant. Then the desire arose to connect everything in one bond, as since the covenant was awakened, WHICH IS YESOD OF ZEIR ANPIN, the bond of all THE SFIROT OF ZEIR ANPIN became awakened. "And I have remembered My covenant" MEANS to attach it to its place, WHICH IS MALCHUT. Therefore it is written, "Therefore say to the children of Yisrael, I am Hashem" (Ibid. 6) FOR ALL THE SFIROT JOINED INTO ONE BOND TO REDEEM YISRAEL FROM EGYPT.

9. "These are the heads of their fathers' houses"

A Synopsis

This section opens with the verse: "And Hashem spoke to Moses and Aaron and commanded them about the children of Yisrael and about Pharaoh the king of Egypt." Rabbi Yosi explains that this means the children of Yisrael were to be led with gentleness and the Pharaoh was to be treated with honor and respect. Rabbi Yisa wonders why it says: "These are the leaders of their fathers' house," and Rabbi Shimon answers that they were kings and the children of kings, leaders of their clans who did not deny their customs or mingle with other nations. Moses and Aaron were without equal among the princes of Yisrael because of their lineage, especially because of Pinchas who saved so many thousands when he killed Zimri and Kozbi and halted the plague. God saw that two of Aaron's sons would eventually blemish the covenant, so he did not want to send Aaron on the mission, but when he saw Pinchas repairing the blemish – sustaining the covenant – he reinstated Aaron with Moses. Rabbi Shimon adds that Moses is air or spirit and Aaron is water, and together they combine Tiferet and Chesed.

The Relevance of the paragraph

When people are chosen to be leaders it is because they have some quality or qualities that make them fit for leadership. As we think about this section we can study the ways in which Moses and Aaron exhibited these qualities by showing gentleness, honor and respect to both their own people and their adversary. This ability in a man to transcend his own nature and honor his enemies – for even criminals treat their friends with respect – is the sign of a great soul, one who has overcome his lower nature and thereby rules his inner kingdom. This is the true 'royal man', who is also the natural choice for a temporal leader. Reading this section will make us more fit for leadership ourselves, and help us guide others to their own freedom.

82. וַיְדַבֵּר ה' אֶל מֹשֶׁה וְאֶל אַהֲרֹן וַיְצַוֵּם אֶל בְּנֵי יִשְׂרָאֵל וְאֶל פַּרְעֹה מֶלֶךְ מִצְרָיִם. ר' יוֹסֵי אָמַר, אֶל בְּנֵי יִשְׂרָאֵל לְדַבְּרָא לוֹן בְּנַחַת כִּדְקָא חֲזֵי, וְאֶל פַּרְעֹה: לְאַנְהָגָא בֵּיהּ יְקָר, וְאוּקְמוּהָ.

82. "And Hashem spoke to Moses and to Aaron, and gave them a charge to the children of Yisrael, and to Pharaoh king of Egypt" (Shemot 6:13). Rabbi

Yosi said, THE REASON IT SAYS, "AND GAVE THEM A CHARGE to the children of Yisrael," is that He commanded to lead them with gentleness as necessary. "And to Pharaoh" MEANS treating him with honor. This has already been explained.

83. אָמַר רִבִּי יֵיסָא, אֲמַאי סָמִיךְ הָכָא אֵלֶּה רָאשֵׁי בֵית אֲבוֹתָם. אֶלָּא, אֲמַר לֵיהּ קוּדְשָׁא בְּרִיךְ הוּא, דַּבְּרוּ לוֹן לִבְנֵי יִשְׂרָאֵל בְּנַחַת, דְּאַע"ג דְּאִינּוּן יַתְבֵי בְּפוּלְחָנָא קַשְׁיָא, מַלְכִין בְּנֵי מַלְכִין אִינּוּן. וּבְגִין כַּךְ, כְּתִיב, אֵלֶּה רָאשֵׁי בֵית אֲבוֹתָם אִלֵּין דְּאַתְּ חָמֵי, רֵישֵׁי בֵית אֲבָהָן אִינּוּן.

83. Rabbi Yisa said, Why did THE TORAH place close to the verse THE PARAGRAPH OF: "These are the heads of their fathers' houses" (Ibid. 14)? HE ANSWERS, The Holy One, blessed be He, said to him, Speak to the children of Yisrael gently, because even though they are in hard labor, they are kings, the children of kings. Therefore it is written, "These are the heads of their fathers' houses," AS HE SAID TO HIM, These that you see are the heads of fathers' houses.

84. א"ר חִיָּיא, דְּכֻלְּהוּ לָא שַׁקְרוּ נִימוּסֵיהוֹן, וְלָא אִתְעָרְבוּ בְּעַמָּא אַחֲרָא אִלֵּין אִינּוּן דְּקַיְימוּ בְּדוּכְתַּיְיהוּ קַדִּישָׁא, וְלָא שַׁקְרוּ לְאִתְעָרְבָא בְּהוּ בְּמִצְרָאֵי. אָמַר רִבִּי אַחָא, בְּגִין לְאַיְיתָאָה לְמֹשֶׁה וּלְאַהֲרֹן, דְּאִינּוּן אִתְחֲזוּן לְאַפָּקָא לְהוּ לְיִשְׂרָאֵל, וּלְמַלְּלָא לְפַרְעֹה, וּלְרַדְּאָה לֵיהּ בְּחוּטְרָא, בְּגִין דִּבְכָל רֵישֵׁיהוֹן דְּיִשְׂרָאֵל, לָא אִשְׁתְּכַח כְּוָותַיְיהוּ.

84. Rabbi Chiya said, THIS IS WHY, "THESE ARE THE HEADS OF THEIR FATHERS' HOUSES" IS THE ADJACENT VERSE, TO TEACH that they all did not deny their customs, did not mingle with any other nation. There are those who stood on their holy ground and were not false by mingling with the Egyptians. Rabbi Acha said, THE REASON "THESE ARE THE HEADS OF THEIR FATHERS' HOUSES...," IS ADJACENT IS in order to express THE LINEAGE of Moses and Aaron, that they were suitable to take out Yisrael, to speak to Pharaoh, and to chastise him with the rod. Their equal was not to be found among all the princes of Yisrael.

85. תָּא חֲזֵי, וְאֶלְעָזָר בֶּן אַהֲרֹן לָקַח לוֹ מִבְּנוֹת פּוּטִיאֵל לוֹ לְאִשָּׁה וַתֵּלֶד

לוֹ אֶת פִּינְחָס אֵלֶּה רָאשֵׁי אֲבוֹת הַלְוִיִּם. וְכִי אֵלֶּה רָאשֵׁי, וְהָא הוּא בִּלְחוֹדוֹי הֲוָה. אֶלָּא, בְּגִין דְּפִינְחָס קַיֵּים כַּמָּה אַלְפִין וְרִבְּוָון מִיִּשְׂרָאֵל, וְהוּא קַיֵּים לְרָאשֵׁי אֲבָהָן, כְּתִיב בֵּיהּ אֵלֶּה.

85. Come and see, IT IS WRITTEN: "And Elazar the son of Aaron took him one of the daughters of Putiel to wife; and she bore him Pinchas. These are the heads of the fathers of the Levites" (Shemot 6:25). HE ASKS, WHY DOES IT SAY, "These are the heads," IN PLURAL? PINCHAS was only one. HE ANSWERS, Because Pinchas saved so many thousands and tens of thousands of Yisrael, and saved many heads of fathers WHEN HE KILLED ZIMRI AND KOZBI, SO THE PLAGUE WAS STAYED FROM YISRAEL. Therefore, it is written of him: "These" IN PLURAL.

86. תּוּ, וַתֵּלֶד לוֹ אֶת פִּינְחָס אֵלֶּה רָאשֵׁי, אוֹבָדָא דְּרֵישֵׁי דִלְוָואֵי אִשְׁתְּכַח בֵּיהּ, וּמַה דְּאִינּוּן גָּרְעוּ וְאִתּוֹקְדוּ, הוּא אַשְׁלִים, וְרָוַוח כְּהוּנָתָא דִּילְהוֹן, וְשַׁרְיָא בֵּיהּ טַסְטוּקָא דְּתַרְוַויְיהוּ. אוֹבָדָא דְּרֵישֵׁי דִלְוָואֵי אִשְׁתְּכַח בֵּיהּ, וּמַאן נִינְהוּ. נָדָב וַאֲבִיהוּא. אִינּוּן פְּרִישׁוּ אֶת קַיְימָא מֵאַתְרֵיהּ, וְהוּא אָתָא וְחַבֵּר לוֹן. בְּגִין כָּךְ, אִתְיְיהִיב לֵיהּ יָרוּתָא, וְרוּחָא דְּתַרְוַויְיהוּ. וְאַדְכַּר הָכָא עַל מַה דִּלְהֱוֵי לְבָתַר.

86. Another EXPLANATION OF THE PASSAGE THAT SAYS, "And she bore Pinchas. These are the heads" IN PLURAL: Because the loss of the heads of the Levites was recovered in him, and he restored whatever they missed and was burned. He earned their priesthood and the form of both of them dwelt IN PINCHAS. HE ASKS, You say that the loss of the heads of Levites is found in him. Who are they? HE ANSWERS, They are Nadab and Abihu. They separated the sign of the covenant from its place, WHICH IS MALCHUT, BECAUSE THEY OFFERED A STRANGE FIRE, and he came and connected them. Therefore the inheritance and the spirit of both of them was given to him. And it is mentioned here IN THE PASSAGE what will occur later on. THEREFORE IT IS WRITTEN BY HIM: "THESE ARE THE HEADS," IN PLURAL.

87. וְאִי תֵּימָא, אֲמַאי אַדְכַּר הָכָא פִּינְחָס. אֶלָּא חָמָא קוּדְשָׁא בְּרִיךְ הוּא לְאַהֲרֹן, בְּשַׁעֲתָא דְּאָמַר וְאָזְכּוֹר אֶת בְּרִיתִי, דִּזְמִינִין תְּרֵין בְּנוֹהִי

דְּאַהֲרֹן לְאַפְגְּמָא לֵיהּ לְהַאי בְּרִית, וְהַשְׁתָּא דְּקָא מְשַׁדֵּר לֵיהּ לְמִצְרַיִם, בָּעָא לְאַעְבְּרָא לֵיהּ לְאַהֲרֹן, דְּלָא לְמֵיהַךְ בִּשְׁלִיחוּתָא דָּא. כֵּיוָן דְּחָמָא קוּדְשָׁא בְּרִיךְ הוּא, דְּקָאֵים פִּינְחָס וְקַיֵּים לֵיהּ לְהַאי בְּרִית בְּאַתְרֵיהּ, וְאַתְקִין עֲקִימָא דִּילְהוֹן, מִיָּד הוּא אַהֲרֹן וּמֹשֶׁה. אָמַר קוּדְשָׁא בְּרִיךְ הוּא, הַשְׁתָּא הוּא אַהֲרֹן, אִיהוּ אַהֲרֹן דְּקַדְמֵיתָא.

87. And if you ask, Why is Pinchas mentioned here; AFTER ALL, THE PASSAGE CAME ONLY TO IMPRESS THE LINEAGE OF MOSES AND AARON AS MENTIONED. HE ANSWERS, Because the Holy One, blessed be He, saw Aaron, when He said, "And I remembered My covenant," that his two sons would eventually blemish this covenant. Now that He was sending him to Egypt TO TAKE OUT YISRAEL, He wanted to remove Aaron, not allowing him to go on this mission. BUT as soon as the Holy One, blessed be He, saw Pinchas standing and sustaining this covenant in its place, and repairing the blemish OF NADAB AND ABIHU, immediately THE PASSAGE SAYS, "These are that Aaron and Moses" (Shemot 6:26). The Holy One, blessed be He, said, Now he is Aaron, the original Aaron, AS BEFORE NADAB AND ABIHU BLEMISHED THE COVENANT, BECAUSE PINCHAS REPAIRED THE BLEMISH.

88. הוּא אַהֲרֹן וּמֹשֶׁה אֲשֶׁר אָמַר ה' לָהֶם הוֹצִיאוּ אֶת בְּנֵי יִשְׂרָאֵל מֵאֶרֶץ מִצְרַיִם וְגוֹ'. הוּא אַהֲרֹן וּמֹשֶׁה. הֵם אַהֲרֹן וּמֹשֶׁה מִבָּעֵי לֵיהּ. אֶלָּא, לְאַכְלָלָא דָּא בְּדָא, רוּחָא בְּמַיָּא. הוּא מֹשֶׁה וְאַהֲרֹן: לְאַכְלָלָא מַיָּא בְּרוּחָא, וְעַל דָּא כְּתִיב הוּא, וְלֹא הֵם.

88. "These are that Aaron and Moses, to whom Hashem said 'Take out the children of Yisrael from the Land of Egypt...'" HE ASKS, THE PASSAGE SAYS, "These are that (lit. 'he is') Aaron and Moses", but it should say, 'These are Aaron and Moses.' HE ANSWERS, it is to combine the air, WHICH IS MOSES, with water, WHICH IS AARON. AND WHEN IT SAYS, "He is Moses and Aaron" (Ibid. 27), it is to combine water, WHICH IS AARON, with air, WHICH IS MOSES. MOSES IS THE ASPECT OF AIR, WHICH IS TIFERET OF ZEIR ANPIN, AND AARON IS THE ASPECT OF WATER, WHICH IS CHESED OF ZEIR ANPIN. Therefore, it is written: "He is AARON AND MOSES" instead of "These are" BECAUSE THEY ARE COMBINED ONE WITH THE OTHER, AS EXPLAINED.

10. "Know therefore this day, and consider it in your heart"

A Synopsis

Rabbi Elazar opens the discussion, saying: "And you should know today and lay it to your heart (Heb. *levavecha*) that Hashem is Elohim." Rabbi Shimon says if you really want to understand this and know that Hashem is Elohim, you need to know that the good and evil inclinations dwell in the heart together, and that you must love Him with both. One should convert the evil attributes so that instead of sinning they serve Hashem. Then the evil inclination and the good inclination will be one, and you will find that Hashem is Elohim. In this way judgment and mercy are included together. We are told that the wicked prevent the blessings from above from being drawn down to them, as in: "And He will hold up the heaven so that there shall be no rain." This is because they separate the evil inclination from the good one, using the evil one. Rabbi Shimon speaks about the left and right, and how they relate to Judgment. He next returns to a discussion in the previous section, reiterating that the element of air combined with that of water in Moses and Aaron – thus combining Tiferet with Chesed. He also repeats the admonition to unify the Holy Name properly by worshipping with one's whole heart and with one's whole soul.

89. רִבִּי אֶלְעָזָר וְרִבִּי אַבָּא, הֲווֹ שְׁכִיחֵי לֵילְיָא חַד בְּבֵי אוֹשְׁפִּיזַיְיהוּ בְּלוֹד, קָמוּ לְאִשְׁתַּדְּלָא בְּאוֹרַיְיתָא. פָּתַח רִבִּי אֶלְעָזָר וְאָמַר, וְיָדַעְתָּ הַיּוֹם וַהֲשֵׁבֹתָ אֶל לְבָבֶךָ כִּי ה' הוּא הָאֱלֹהִים. הַאי קְרָא הָכִי מִבָּעֵי לֵיהּ. וְיָדַעְתָּ הַיּוֹם כִּי ה' הוּא הָאֱלֹהִים וַהֲשֵׁבֹתָ אֶל לְבָבֶךָ. תּוּ, וַהֲשֵׁבֹתָ אֶל לִבְּךָ מִבָּעֵי לֵיהּ.

89. One night, Rabbi Elazar and Rabbi Aba were in their lodgings in Lod. They awoke to study Torah. Rabbi Elazar opened the discussion saying, "Know therefore this day, and consider it in your heart (Heb. *levavecha*), that Hashem He is Elohim" (Devarim 4:39). HE ASKS, This passage should have said, 'Know therefore this day, that Hashem He is Elohim' AND AT THE END, 'and consider it in your heart.' BECAUSE THE KNOWLEDGE THAT HASHEM IS ELOHIM PREPARES ONE TO CONSIDER IT IN THE HEART SO, AND IF HE HAS ALREADY CONSIDERED IT IN HIS HEART ONE MOST CERTAINLY HAS THE KNOWLEDGE. Also, it should have said 'libecha (heart, with one Bet)' NOT "LEVAVECHA (WITH TWO BET'S)."

‏90. אֶלָּא, אָמַר מֹשֶׁה, אִי אַתְּ בָּעֵי לְמֵיקַם עַל דָּא, וּלְמִנְדַּע כִּי ה' הוּא הָאֱלֹהִים, וְהָשִׁבוֹתָ אֶל לְבָבֶךָ וּכְדֵין תִּנְדַּע לֵיהּ. לְבָבֶךָ: יֵצֶר טוֹב וְיֵצֶר רַע, דְּאִתְכְּלִיל דָּא בְּדָא, וְאִיהוּ חַד, כְּדֵין תִּשְׁכַּח כִּי ה' הוּא הָאֱלֹהִים, דְּהָא אִתְכְּלִיל דָּא בְּדָא, וְאִיהוּ חַד. וְעַל דָּא וְהָשִׁבוֹתָ אֶל לְבָבֶךָ, לְמִנְדַּע מִלָּה.

90. HE ANSWERS, But Moses said, If you really want to understand this and know that Hashem is Elohim, then "consider it in your heart (Heb. *levavcha*)," and thus know it. For "levavcha" MEANS the Good Inclination and the Evil Inclination THAT DWELL IN THE HEART are included within one another and are one. "AND YOU SHALL LOVE HASHEM YOUR ELOHIM WITH ALL YOUR HEART (HEB. *LEVAVCHA*)" (DEVARIM 6:5), MEANING WITH BOTH YOUR INCLINATIONS, THE GOOD INCLINATION AND THE EVIL INCLINATION. THUS HE SHOULD CONVERT THE EVIL ATTRIBUTES OF THE EVIL INCLINATION TO BE GOOD, NAMELY TO SERVE HASHEM WITH THEM AND NOT SIN THROUGH THEM. THEN, CERTAINLY THERE IS NO MORE DIFFERENCE BETWEEN THE GOOD INCLINATION AND THE EVIL INCLINATION, AND THEY ARE ONE. Then you will find that Hashem is Elohim. THE ATTRIBUTE OF JUDGMENT, WHICH IS CALLED ELOHIM, IS INCLUDED IN YUD HEI VAV HEI, WHICH IS THE ATTRIBUTE OF MERCY because they are included the one within the other, AS THE EVIL INCLINATION AND THE GOOD INCLINATION ARE COMBINED IN THE HEART, and they are one. SO IT CAN NOT BE KNOWN THAT HASHEM IS ELOHIM EXCEPT THROUGH CONSIDERING IT IN THE HEART. Therefore, THE PASSAGE MENTIONED FIRST, "and consider it in your heart" to know THROUGH IT that HASHEM HE IS ELOHIM.

‏91. תּוּ אָמַר רִבִּי אֶלְעָזָר, חַיָּיבִין עַבְדִּין פְּגִימוּתָא לְעֵילָא, מַאי פְּגִימוּתָא. דִּשְׂמָאלָא לָא אִתְכְּלִיל בִּימִינָא. דְּיֵצֶר רַע לָא אִתְכְּלִיל בְּיֵצֶר טוֹב, בְּגִין חוֹבַיְיהוּ דִּבְנֵי נָשָׁא. וּפְגִימוּ לָא עַבְדֵי, אֶלָּא לוֹן מַמָּשׁ, הֲדָא הוּא דִּכְתִיב, שִׁחֵת לוֹ לֹא בָּנָיו מוּמָם. כִּבְיָכוֹל עַבְדֵי וְלָא עַבְדֵי: עַבְדֵי: דְּלָא יִתְמְשֵׁךְ עֲלַיְיהוּ בִּרְכָּאן דִּלְעֵילָא, כְּמָה דְּאַתְּ אָמַר וְעָצַר אֶת הַשָּׁמַיִם וְלֹא יִהְיֶה מָטָר. וְלָא עַבְדֵי: דְּהָא שְׁמַיָּא נַטְלֵי לוֹן לְגַרְמַיְיהוּ בִּרְכָּאן מַאי דְּאִצְטְרִיךְ. וְלָא נַטְלֵי לְאַמְשָׁכָא לְתַתָּא וְדַאי מוּמָם דְּאִינוּן חַיָּיבִין אִיהוּ.

91. Rabbi Elazar also said, The wicked cause a blemish above WITH THEIR EVIL ACTIONS. What is the blemish? IT IS THAT the left is not included within the right ABOVE, IT RATHER DOMINATES BY MEANS OF JUDGMENT BY ITSELF. THIS IS BECAUSE the Evil Inclination BELOW is not included in the Good Inclination, TO WORK WITH IT TO DRAW GOOD AS MENTIONED because of the sins of people WHO SIN, THROUGH THE EVIL INCLINATION, AND ATTRACT BY IT THE DOMINATION OF JUDGMENT. And they do not cause a blemish ABOVE, but actually to themselves. This is the meaning of: "Not His the corruption, but the blemish of His sons (or: His (Heb. *lo*, with *Vav*) the corruption, not (Heb. *lo*, with *Aleph*) the blemish...)" (Devarim 32:5). FIRST IT IS SAID "HIS THE CORRUPTION", SEEMINGLY INDICATING THAT THEY BLEMISH ABOVE AND THEN, "NOT THE BLEMISH OF HIS SONS" SEEMINGLY, THAT THEY DO NOT CAUSE BLEMISH ABOVE. It is as if they cause A BLEMISH yet do not cause A BLEMISH. They cause, THAT IS, THEY BRING ABOUT that blessings from above do not flow to them, as is written: "And shut up the heavens, that there be no rain" (Devarim 11:17). THEY DAMAGE THE CHANNELS OF SUSTENANCE ABOVE yet they do not cause, because the heavens, NAMELY THE CHANNELS OF ABOVE, receive for themselves as much blessings AND SUSTENANCE as they need, but they do not receive SUSTENANCE to pour downward. Certainly THIS IS NOT A BLEMISH AND FLAW OF THE ABOVE, BUT RATHER, it is the blemish of these wicked, AND IT IS UPON THEM THAT THIS FLAW RESTS AND NOT ABOVE.

92. תּוּ, לוֹ בּוֹ׳, דְּלָא אִתְכְּלִיל יְמִינָא בִּשְׂמָאלָא, בְּגִין דְּלָא יִתְמַשְׁכוּן בִּרְכָאן לְתַתָּא. לֹא בְּאָלֶ״ף, דְּהָא לָא נַטְלֵי לְאִתְמַשְׁכָא לְתַתָּאֵי. מַאן גָּרִים דָּא. בְּגִין דְּחַיָּיבִין מַפְרִישִׁין יֵצֶר רָע מִיֵּצֶר טוֹב, וּמִתְדַּבְּקִין בְּיֵצֶר רָע.

92. Also, IT CAN BE EXPLAINED, "His" (Heb. *lo,* with *Vav*) MEANS that the right is not included in the left ABOVE, so that blessings are not drawn downwards AND TO THIS IS SAID 'HIS' WITH *VAV*. "not (Heb. *lo*) is spelled with *Aleph*," since they do not receive BLESSINGS to draw to those below. THEREFORE THEY REST BLEMISHED. Who caused this? IT IS because the wicked separate the Evil Inclination from the Good Inclination and cleave to the Evil Inclination.

93. תָּא חֲזֵי יְהוּדָה אָתֵי מִסְּטְרָא דִּשְׂמָאלָא, וְאִתְדְּבַק בִּימִינָא, בְּגִין

לְנַצְחָא עַמִין, וּלְתַבְרָא חֵילֵיהוֹן. דְּאִי לָא אִתְדְּבַק בִּימִינָא, לָא יִתְבַּר
חֵילֵיהוֹן. וְאִי תֵּימָא אַמַּאי בִּימִינָא. וְהָא שְׂמָאלָא אִתְעַר דִּינִין בְּעָלְמָא.

93. Come and see: Judah is come from the left side BECAUSE JUDAH IS
THE SECRET OF MALCHUT AND MALCHUT ORGINATES IN THE LEFT SIDE,
and he cleft to the right in order to overpower nations and break their power.
For had he not cleft to the right he would not break their power. And if you
ask, Why DID HE CLEAVE to the right, seeing that it is the left that provokes
judgments in the world. AND WHY WAS NOT THE LEFT SUFFICIENT FOR
HIM TO BREAK THE POWER OF THE NATIONS?

94. אֶלָּא רָזָא דָא, בְּשַׁעֲתָא דְּקוּדְשָׁא בְּרִיךְ הוּא דָן לְהוּ לְיִשְׂרָאֵל, לָא
דָן לְהוּ אֶלָּא מִסִּטְרָא דִּשְׂמָאלָא, בְּגִין דְּיֶהֱא דָּחֵי לוֹן בִּשְׂמָאלָא, וּמְקָרֵב
בִּימִינָא. אֲבָל לִשְׁאָר עַמִּין, דָּחֵי לוֹן בִּימִינָא, וּמְקָרֵב לוֹן בִּשְׂמָאלָא.
וְסִימָנִיךְ גֵּר צֶדֶק, דָּחֵי לוֹן בִּימִינָא, כְּמָה דִּכְתִיב, יְמִינְךָ ה' נֶאְדָּרִי בַּכֹּחַ
יְמִינְךָ ה' תִּרְעַץ אוֹיֵב. מְקָרֵב לוֹן בִּשְׂמָאלָא כְּמָה דְּאַמְרָן.

94. HE ANSWERS, But this is a secret. When the Holy One, blessed be He,
judges Yisrael, He judges them only from the left side, in order to reject
them with the left and beckon them with the right. But with the other
nations, He fends them off with the right, and draws them with the left. And
this may be deduced from the proselyte by conviction, NAMELY BECAUSE
WHEN ONE OF THEM BECOMES ATTRACTED TO HOLINESS AND HE
CONVERTS, HE IS CALLED A PROSELYTE BY CONVICTION (LIT. 'A CONVERT
OF RIGHTEOUSNESS'). RIGHTEOUSNESS IS THE NAME OF THE LEFT
ASPECT OF MALCHUT. SO WE SEE THAT HE ATTRACTS THEM WITH THE
LEFT. AND HE EXPLAINS, He fends them off with the right, as it is written:
"Your right hand, Hashem, is glorious in power; Your right hand, Hashem,
has dashed the enemy in pieces" (Shemot 15:6). He attracts them with the
left, as we already said, THAT THE ONE FROM AMONG THEM, WHO HAS
COME CLOSER TO JUDAISM IS CALLED A CONVERT OF RIGHTEOUSNESS,
WHICH IS LEFT.

95. בְּגִינֵי כַּךְ, יְהוּדָה דְּאִיהוּ מִסְטַר שְׂמָאלָא, אִתְדְּבַּק בִּימִינָא, וּמְטַלְנוֹי
לִימִינָא. וְאִינוּן דְּעִמֵּיהּ אִתְחַבְּרוּ כֻּלְּהוּ לִימִינָא. יִשָּׂשכָר דְּלָעֵי

בְּאוֹרַיְיתָא, דְּאִיהִי יְמִינָא, דִּכְתִּיב, מִימִינוֹ אֵשׁ דָּת לָמוֹ. זְבוּלוּן דְּאִיהוּ תָּמִיךְ אוֹרַיְיתָא יְמִינָא, כד"א שׁוֹק הַיָּמִין. וע"ד יְהוּדָה אִתְקְשַׁר מִסִּטְרָא דָּא וְדָא. צָפוֹן בַּמַּיִם, שְׂמָאלָא בִּימִינָא.

95. Therefore, Judah, who is from the left side, combined with the right IN ORDER TO SUBDUE THE NATIONS, and his journeys were to the right OF THE STANDARDS. Those TRIBES that were with him all joined to the right. Yisaschar toiled in Torah, which is right, as is written, "From His right hand a fiery law unto them" (Devarim 33:2). And so Zebulun who supported the Torah which is right. It is written: "the right thigh" (Vayikra 7:32) BECAUSE THE RIGHT LEG SUPPORTS THE RIGHT SIDE OF THE BODY. Therefore, Judah was attached to this side and that side, NAMELY TO THE LEFT AND THE RIGHT, north, which is left, to water, which is right.

96. רְאוּבֵן דְּחָטָא לְגַבֵּי אֲבוֹי, שָׁרָא בִּימִינָא, וְאִתְקְשַׁר בִּשְׂמָאלָא, וְאִתְדַּבַּק בֵּיהּ. וע"ד, אִינוּן דְּאִשְׁתְּכָחוּ עִמֵּיהּ, אִינוּן שְׂמָאלָא. שִׁמְעוֹן דְּאִיהוּ שְׂמָאלָא מִסִּטְרָא דְּשׁוֹר, דִּכְתִּיב, וּפְנֵי שׁוֹר מֵהַשְּׂמֹאל. גָּד שׁוֹקָא שְׂמָאלָא, כְּתִיב גָּד גְּדוּד יְגוּדֶנּוּ וְהוּא יָגוּד עָקֵב. הָכָא, אִתְדַּבַּק דָּרוֹם בְּאֶשָּׁא, יְמִינָא בִּשְׂמָאלָא.

96. Reuben, who sinned against his father, dwelt in the right, WHICH IS CHESED. BECAUSE OF THE SIN, he connected with the left and clove to it. Therefore those who are with him IN HIS STANDARD are left. Shimon is left because OF THE LIVING CREATURE THAT HAS THE FACE of the ox, WHICH IS GVURAH, as is written: "The face of an ox on the left side" (Yechezkel 1:10). Gad is the left leg, NAMELY HOD, as is written: "Gad, raiders shall maraud him, but he shall overcome at last (lit. 'heel')" (Beresheet 49:19). OVERCOMING IS THE ACTION OF THE LEFT, AND HEEL IS THE LEG. Thus, south clove to fire, right with the left.

97. וע"ד הָא דְּאָמְרָן וַהֲשֵׁבֹתָ אֶל לְבָבֶךָ, לְאַכְלְלָא לוֹן כַּחֲדָא, שְׂמָאלָא בִּימִינָא. כְּדֵין תֵּדַע כִּי ה' הוּא הָאֱלֹהִים. א"ר אַבָּא וַדַּאי הָכִי הוּא, וְהַשְׁתָּא יְדִיעָא, הוּא אַהֲרֹן וּמֹשֶׁה, הוּא מֹשֶׁה וְאַהֲרֹן, רוּחָא בְּמַיָּא, וּמַיָּא בְּרוּחָא, לְמֶהֱוֵי חַד. וע"ד כְּתִיב הוּא.

97. And similarly the purpose of what we said: "and consider it in your heart (Heb. *levavecha*, spelled with two *Bet's*)" is to include them together, the left and the right, and then you will know that "Hashem He is Elohim." Rabbi Aba said, Definitely it is so. And now it is understandable, WHAT IS SAID, "He is Aaron and Moses" (Shemot 6:26), "he is Moses and Aaron" (Ibid. 27). IT IS TO TEACH THAT air, WHICH IS TIFERET, COMBINED with water, WHICH IS CHESED, and water, WHICH IS CHESED, COMBINED with air, WHICH IS TIFERET, to be one. Therefore, it is written "he."

98. ר' אַבָּא פָּתַח וְאָמַר, וְאָהַבְתָּ אֵת ה' אֱלֹהֶיךָ בְּכָל לְבָבְךָ וּבְכָל נַפְשְׁךָ וּבְכָל מְאֹדֶךָ. כְּהַאי גַּוְונָא הָכָא אִתְרְמִיז יִחוּדָא קַדִּישָׁא, וְאַזְהָרָה הוּא לְבַר נָשׁ, לְיַחֲדָא שְׁמָא קַדִּישָׁא כַּדְקָא יֵאוֹת, בִּרְחִימוּ עִלָּאָה. בְּכָל לְבָבְךָ: דָּא יְמִינָא וּשְׂמָאלָא דְּאִקְרֵי יֵצֶר טוֹב וְיֵצֶר רָע. וּבְכָל נַפְשְׁךָ: דָּא נֶפֶשׁ דָּוִד, דְּאִתְיְהִיבַת בֵּינַיְיהוּ. וּבְכָל מְאֹדֶךָ לְאַכְלְלָא לוֹן לְעֵילָּא בַּאֲתַר דְּלֵית בֵּיהּ שִׁעוּרָא. הָכָא הוּא יִחוּדָא שְׁלִים לְמִרְחַם לֵיהּ לְקוּדְשָׁא בְּרִיךְ הוּא כַּדְקָא יֵאוֹת.

98. Rabbi Aba opened the discussion saying, "And you shall love Hashem your Elohim with all your heart, and with all your soul, and with all your might" (Devarim 6:5). Similarly, WHAT WE SAID ABOUT THE UNIFICATION OF RIGHT AND LEFT, the holy unification is also alluded to here, and it serves as an admonition to man to profess the unity the Holy Name properly with supernal love. "With all your heart": NAMELY WITH BOTH YOUR INCLINATIONS, WHICH ARE right and left and are called Good Inclination and Evil Inclination. "And with all your soul": This is the soul of David that is placed between them, "and with all your might" MEANING to join them, THE RIGHT AND THE LEFT, above in the place where there is no limit.

99. תּוּ, וּבְכָל מְאֹדֶךָ: דָּא יַעֲקֹב, דְּאִיהוּ אָחִיד לְכָל סִטְרִין, וְכֹלָּא הוּא יִחוּדָא שְׁלִים כַּדְקָא יֵאוֹת, בְּגִינֵי כָּךְ, הוּא אַהֲרֹן וּמֹשֶׁה הוּא מֹשֶׁה וְאַהֲרֹן, כֹּלָּא הוּא חַד בְּלָא פֵּרוּדָא.

99. Another explanation of: "And with all your might": This is Jacob, NAMELY ZEIR ANPIN, who is attached to all sides TO THE RIGHT AND TO THE LEFT, BEING THE CENTRAL COLUMN. And it all is the complete unity as it should be. Therefore, THE PASSAGE SAYS, "He is Aaron and Moses," "he is Moses and Aaron." It is all one, FOR THEY HAVE UNITED ONE WITH THE OTHER without division BETWEEN THEM.

11. "Take your rod...and it shall turn into a snake"

A Synopsis
Rabbi Yehuda talks about how much he loves studying and talking about the Torah and praising God for his righteous laws. He says that David as the King of Yisrael had to judge and lead his people to keep them on the way of truth.

The Relevance of the paragraph
Again we have the recurring themes of the law, or the Word as expressed in the Torah, and judgment and leadership. The title verse talks about the rod that turned into a snake in front of the Pharaoh. Imagining the snake/rod as the symbol of stewardship will help us pull these themes together for our meditation. When the power was given to Aaron to do this miracle he enabled himself and Moses to assume leadership over the people, and therefore also the right to judge them. The rod was the symbol of authority. Remembering that the snake was symbolic of man's original fall, we can see that assuming leadership at a high level gives one power over even original sin. Thus when we pray we may use the lesson in this text to pray for our own accession to a level where God may use us as leaders in His battle against sin.

100. כִּי יְדַבֵּר אֲלֵיכֶם פַּרְעֹה לֵאמֹר. רַבִּי יְהוּדָה פָּתַח וְאָמַר, מָה אָהַבְתִּי תוֹרָתֶךָ כָּל הַיּוֹם הִיא שִׂיחָתִי. וּכְתִיב, חֲצוֹת לַיְלָה אָקוּם לְהוֹדוֹת לָךְ עַל מִשְׁפְּטֵי צִדְקֶךָ. תָּא חֲזֵי, דָּוִד אִיהוּ מַלְכָּא דְּיִשְׂרָאֵל, וְאִצְטְרִיךְ לְמֵידָן עַמָּא, לְדַבְּרָא לוֹן לְיִשְׂרָאֵל, כְּרַעְיָא דִּמְדַבֵּר עָאנֵיהּ דְּלָא יִסְטוּן מֵאוֹרְחָא דִּקְשׁוֹט. הָא בַּלַּיְלָה כְּתִיב, חֲצוֹת לַיְלָה אָקוּם לְהוֹדוֹת לָךְ עַל מִשְׁפְּטֵי צִדְקֶךָ. וְאִיהוּ אִתְעֲסַק בְּאוֹרַיְיתָא וּבְתוּשְׁבְּחָן דְּקוּדְשָׁא בְּרִיךְ הוּא, עַד דְּאָתֵי צַפְרָא.

100. "When Pharaoh shall speak to you" (Shemot 7:9). Rabbi Yehuda opened the discussion saying, "How I love Your Torah! it is my meditation all the day" (Tehilim 119:97) and it is written: "At midnight I will rise to give thanks to You because of Your righteous laws" (Ibid. 62). Come and see, David is the King of Yisrael and he has to judge the people, to lead Yisrael as a shepherd leads his sheep, so that they will not turn off the way of truth. And at night it is written, "At midnight I will rise to give thanks to

You because of Your righteous laws." And he occupied himself with the Torah and praised the Holy One, blessed be He, until morning came.

12. Midnight and day

101. וְאִיהוּ אִתְּעַר צַפְרָא, כְּמָה דִּכְתִּיב, עוּרָה כְבוֹדִי עוּרָה הַנֵּבֶל וְכִנּוֹר
אָעִירָה שָּׁחַר. כַּד אָתֵי יְמָמָא, אָמַר הַאי קְרָא, מָה אָהַבְתִּי תוֹרָתֶךָ כָּל
הַיּוֹם הִיא שִׂיחָתִי. מַאי כָּל הַיּוֹם הִיא שִׂיחָתִי. אֶלָּא, מִכָּאן אוֹלִיפְנָא,
דְּכָל מַאן דְּיִשְׁתְּדַל בְּאוֹרַיְיתָא, לְאַשְׁלְמָא דִּינָא עַל בּוּרְיֵיהּ, כְּאִילוּ
קַיֵּים אוֹרַיְיתָא כֹּלָּא. בְּג"כ, כָּל הַיּוֹם הִיא שִׂיחָתִי.

101. He wakened the dawn, as is written: "Wake up, my glory; awake, the
harp and the lyre; I will awake the dawn" (Tehilim 57:9). And when day
came, he said this passage: "How I love Your Torah! it is my meditation all
the day." HE ASKS, What is the meaning of: "it is my meditation all the
day"? HE ANSWERS, From here we learn that all who study the Torah to
complete and clarify the law with lucidity, it is as though they fulfilled the
entire Torah. Therefore, THE VERSE SAYS, "it is my meditation all the day"
BECAUSE HE WAS OCCUPIED WITH ELUCIDATING THE LAW.

102. תָּא חֲזֵי, בְּיוֹמָא אִשְׁתַּדַּל בְּאוֹרַיְיתָא, לְאַשְׁלְמָא דִּינִין. בְּלֵילְיָא,
אִשְׁתַּדַּל בְּשִׁירִין וְתוּשְׁבְּחָן, עַד דְּאָתֵי יְמָמָא. מ"ט. כָּל יוֹמָא אִתְעַסַּק
לְאַשְׁלְמָא דִּינִין, בְּגִין לְאַכְלְלָא שְׂמָאלָא בִּימִינָא. בְּלֵילְיָא, בְּגִין
לְאַכְלְלָא דַּרְגָּא דְּלֵילְיָא בִּימָמָא.

102. Come and see: By day, he was occupied with the Torah to carry out
justice. And at night, he was occupied with songs and praises until day
came. What was the reason? IT WAS because he was occupied all day to
complete and clarify the laws, WHICH ARE THE ASPECT OF THE LEFT, in
order to include the left in the right, BECAUSE DAY IS THE ASPECT OF THE
RIGHT, WHICH IS CHESED. By night, HE WAS OCCUPIED WITH PRAISES
WHICH ARE CHASSADIM in order to include the grade of the night, WHICH
IS JUDGMENT, with day, WHICH IS CHESED.

103. וְתָא חֲזֵי, בְּיוֹמֵי דְּדָוִד מַלְכָּא, הֲוָה מְקָרֵב כָּל אִינּוּן חַיְותוּ שָׂדַי,
לְגַבֵּי יַמָּא. כֵּיוָן דְּאָתָא שְׁלֹמֹה, נָפַק יַמָּא וְאִתְמְלֵי, וְאַשְׁקֵי לְהוּ. הֵי
מִנַּיְיהוּ אִתְשַׁקְיָין בְּקַדְמֵיתָא. הָא אוּקְמוּהָ. אִלֵּין תַּנִּינַיָּא רַבְרְבִין

עֶלָּאִין, דִּכְתִּיב בְּהוּ, וּמִלְאוּ אֶת הַמַּיִם בַּיַּמִּים.

103. And come and see: In the days of King David, he brought close all the beasts in the field, WHO INHABITED THE THREE WORLDS — BRIYAH, YETZIRAH AND ASIYAH — to the sea, WHICH IS MALCHUT. When Solomon arrived AND THE NUKVA WAS IN HER FULLNESS IN HIS DAYS, the sea, WHICH IS THE NUKVA, flowed and became full, MEANING THAT IT ASCENDED TO SUPERNAL ABA AND IMA, and watered them, FOR THERE IS ITS ABSOLUTE FULFILLMENT. THEN ALL THE INHABITANTS OF BRIYAH, YETZIRAH AND ASIYAH ASCENDED TO ATZILUT AND RECEIVED THEIR SUSTENANCE FROM THE SEA. HE ASKS, Which was watered first? HE ANSWERS, It was already explained that they are the supernal great crocodiles about which it is written: "And fill the waters in the seas" (Beresheet 1:22). THEY ARE METATRON AND SANDALPHON OF BRIYAH WHO ARE SUPERIOR TO ALL THE INHABITANTS OF BRIYAH, YETZIRAH AND ASIYAH.

13. The serpent couches in the midst of the streams

104. א״ר אֶלְעָזָר, בְּסִטְרָא יְמִינָא עִלָּאָה, נָפְקִין תְּלֵיסָר מַבּוּעִין עִלָּאִין, נַהֲרִין עֲמִיקִין, אִלֵּין סַלְקִין, וְאִלֵּין נַחְתִּין, עַיֵּיל כָּל חַד בְּחַבְרֵיהּ. חַד אַפִּיק רֵישֵׁיהּ, וְאָעִיל לֵיהּ בִּתְרֵין גּוּפִין, חַד גּוּפָא דְּנַהֲרָא נָטִיל מִיָּמִין לְעֵילָא, אַפְרִישׁ לְתַתָּא אֶלֶף יְאוֹרִין, נָפְקִין לְאַרְבַּע סִטְרִין.

104. RABBI YEHUDA BRINGS HERE THE WORDS OF RABBI ELAZAR, TO DIFFERENTIATE BETWEEN THE GREAT CROCODILES (HEB. *TANINIM*) OF HOLINESS AND THE GREAT CROCODILE OF THE KLIPAH. FOR THE PREVIOUSLY MENTIONED PASSAGE OPENED WITH THE PHRASE: "WHEN PHARAOH SHALL SPEAK TO YOU...THEN YOU SHALL SAY TO AARON, TAKE YOUR ROD, AND CAST IT BEFORE PHARAOH, AND IT SHALL TURN INTO A SNAKE" (SHEMOT 7:9). AFTERWARDS, IT IS WRITTEN: "AND THE MAGICIANS OF EGYPT, THEY ALSO DID IN LIKE MANNER WITH THEIR SECRET ARTS. FOR THEY CAST DOWN EVERY MAN HIS ROD, AND THEY TURNED TO SNAKES (HEB. *TANINIM*)" (IBID. 11-12). AND THE DIFFERENCE BETWEEN THE SERPENT OF HOLINESS OF AARON'S ROD AND THE SERPENT OF THE SORCERERS IS EXPLAINED IN THE WORDS OF RABBI ELAZAR. Rabbi Elazar said, On the supernal right side, NAMELY FROM THE RIGHT COLUMN OF BINAH, emerge thirteen supernal springs and deep rivers. THIS IS THE SECRET OF THE SUPERNAL THRONE WHICH IS BINAH. AND THERE ARE FOUR LEGS OF THE THRONE WHICH ARE CHESED, GVURAH, TIFERET AND MALCHUT OF ZEIR ANPIN, EACH CONTAINING CHESED, GVURAH AND TIFERET, SO THEY ARE TWELVE, AND BINAH ITSELF WHICH IS OVER THEM, WHICH IS THE SECRET OF THE THRONE, IS THIRTEENTH. THEY ARE DIVIDED INTO TWO COLUMNS, RIGHT AND LEFT, BECAUSE TIFERET IS ALSO DIVIDED INTO RIGHT AND LEFT, WHICH ARE CHESED AND GVURAH. THOSE ON THE RIGHT SIDE ARE CALLED SPRINGS, AND THOSE ON THE LEFT, RIVERS. The ones ascend, NAMELY THOSE THAT BELONG TO THE LEFT, WHICH ILLUMINATE FROM BELOW UPWARDS. And the others descend, NAMELY THOSE THAT BELONG TO THE RIGHT, ILLUMINATING FROM ABOVE DOWNWARDS. They interpenetrate each other, MEANING THAT THEY COMBINE ONE WITH THE OTHER, because one, WHICH IS THE CENTRAL COLUMN, withdraws, THAT IS, IT LESSENS its head OF THE LEFT COLUMN THAT IS CALLED RIVER, and brings it in two bodies CALLED STREAM AND RIVER. One body FROM THE ASPECT of river, WHICH IS LEFT AND CHOCHMAH, receives FROM

THE CHASSADIM of the right above and brings forth TO THE LOWER BEINGS a thousand streams that emerge to four sides, WHICH ARE CHESED, GVURAH, TIFERET AND MALCHUT, EACH CONTAINING 250 STREAMS.

105. מֵאִינּוּן נַהֲרִין מַבּוּעִין תְּלֵיסָר, מִתְפָּרְשָׁן תְּלֵיסַר יְאוֹרִין, עָאלִין וְנַטְלֵי מַיָּא, אַרְבַּע מֵאָה וְתִשְׁעִין וְתִשְׁעָה יְאוֹרִין וּפַלְגָּא, מִסְּטְרָא דָא. וְאַרְבַּע מֵאָה וְתִשְׁעִין וְתִשְׁעָה יְאוֹרִין וּפַלְגָּא, מִסְּטְרָא דָא בִּשְׂמָאלָא. אִשְׁתְּאַר פַּלְגָּא מִכָּאן, וּפַלְגָּא מִכָּאן, וְאִתְעֲבֵיד חַד. דָא עָאִיל בֵּין יְאוֹרִין, וְאִתְעֲבֵיד חִוְיָא.

105. From these thirteen rivers OF THE LEFT, and the springs ON THE RIGHT AS MENTIONED, emerge thirteen streams, WHICH ARE LIGHTS OF THE LEFT. Entering into them, 499 and one half FROM THE RIGHT and 499 and one half from the left, take water. One half on this side and one half from this side remain, and the two halves become one. This enters between the streams and turns into a serpent.

106. רֵישָׁא: סוּמָקָא כְּוַרְדָּא. קַשְׂקְשׂוֹי: תַּקִּיפִין כְּפַרְזְלָא. גַּדְפוֹי: גַּדְפִּין שָׁטָאן וְאִתְפָּרְשָׁן לְכָל אִינּוּן יְאוֹרִין. כַּד סָלִיק זַנְבֵיה, מָחֵי וּבָטַשׁ לִשְׁאַר נוּנִין, לֵית מַאן דְּיֵקוּם קָמֵיה.

106. The head OF THE SERPENT (HEB. TANIN) is red like a rose. THE COLOR RED DENOTES JUDGMENTS THAT ARE DRAWN FROM BINAH. His scales are hard as iron, FOR THE ASPECT OF MALCHUT IS ESSENTIALLY CALLED IRON, WHICH IS THE SECRET OF THE ATTRIBUTE OF JUDGMENT. His wings are swimming wings, NAMELY FINS, and they go into all these streams THAT WERE MENTIONED. When he raises his tail, he smites and kicks the other fish, and no one can withstand him.

107. פּוּמֵיה: מְלַהֲטָא אֶשָּׁא. כַּד נָטִיל בְּכָל אִינּוּן יְאוֹרִין, מִזְדַּעְזְעָן שְׁאַר תַּנִּינַיָּא, וְעָרְקִין וְעָאלִין בְּיַמָּא. חַד לְשַׁבְעִין שְׁנִין רָבִיץ לְסִטְרָא דָא. וְחַד לְשַׁבְעִין שְׁנִין רָבִיץ לְסִטְרָא דָא. אֶלֶף יְאוֹרִין חָסֵר חַד אִתְמַלְּיָין מִנֵּיה. דָּא תַּנִּינָא, רָבִיץ בֵּין אִינּוּן יְאוֹרִין.

107. The mouth OF THE SERPENT is a flaming fire. When he swims in all these streams, NAMELY, WHEN HE DRAWS CHOCHMAH FROM ABOVE DOWNWARDS LIKE THE STREAMS, the other fish there, MEANING THE GRADES, tremble and flee from there to the sea, WHICH IS MALCHUT OF HOLINESS. Once in seventy years, he couches this way, NAMELY IN 499 AND ONE HALF STREAMS ON THE RIGHT AND COMPLETES THE HALF THAT IS MISSING ON THE RIGHT. And once in seventy years, he couches that way, NAMELY IN 499 AND ONE HALF STREAMS ON THE LEFT, AND COMPLETES THE HALF THAT IS MISSING ON THE LEFT, SINCE THE SERPENT IS CONSTRUCTED FROM THESE TWO HALVES THAT ARE MISSING IN THEM. THUS the thousand streams less one were filled by him, THAT IS, BECOME COMPLETED BY HIM. The serpent couches in the midst of the streams, BUT DOES NOT SWIM IN THEM. FOR CROUCHING DOES NO ACTION AND DOES NOT DRAW CHOCHMAH FROM ABOVE DOWNWARDS, UNLIKE SWIMING, WHICH ACTS AND DRAWS FROM ABOVE DOWNWARDS, AND THEREFORE HIS ASPECT OF JUDGMENT IS REVEALED, AS IS MENTIONED AND WRITTEN BEFORE US.

108. כַּד נָטִיל נָפַק חַד פְּסוּתָא דְּאֶשָׁא בְּקְלִיפִין, כֻּלְהוּ קַיְימִין וְזַעֲפִין בְּזַעֲפוֹי, מִתְעָרְבִין אִינּוּן יְאוֹרִין לְעֵין תְּכֶלָּא אוּכְמָא. וְגַלְגְּלִין נַטְלִין לְאַרְבַּע סִטְרֵי דְּעָלְמָא. זָקִיף זַנְבֵיה, מָחֵי לְעֵילָא, מָחֵי לְתַתָּא, כֹּלָּא עַרְקִין קַמֵיה.

108. BUT when he swims IN THEM, a flame of fire emerges among the Klipot. And THEN THE STREAMS all rise and storm, MEANING THAT THEY RAISE THEIR WAVES ABOVE AND BRING THEM DOWN, WHICH IS CALLED STORM IN RHETORICAL LANGUAGE. These streams mix ONE WITH THE OTHER, and receive the blue color that tends to black, WHICH IS THE COLOR OF MALCHUT. And wheels move ABOVE to the four directions, NAMELY THE WHEELS OF THE CHARIOT OF HOLINESS DRAW THE TOP THREE SFIROT BY THEIR TRAVELS, and the serpent straightens up his tail and smites upward THE WHEELS, THUS DAMAGING THEM, and smites below THE RIVERS. They all flee him.

109. עַד דְּלִסְטַר צָפוֹן, קָם חַד שַׁלְהוֹבָא דְּאֶשָׁא, וְכָרוֹזָא קָרֵי, אִזְדְּקָפוּ סַבְתִּין אִתְבַּדָּרוּ לְד' זַוְויָין, הָא אִתְּעַר מַאן דְּשַׁוֵּי קוֹלָא, עַל אַנְפּוֹי דְּתַנִּינָא, כְּמָה דְּאִתְּמַר, וְנָתַתִּי חַחִים בִּלְחָיֶיךָ וְגוֹ'. כְּדֵין כֻּלְהוּ

אִתְבַּדְרוּן. וְנַקְטִין לֵיהּ לְתַנִינָא, וְנַקְבֵי אַנְפּוֹי בְּסְטַר עִלָּעוֹי, וְעָאלִין לֵיהּ לְנוּקְבָּא דִּתְהוֹמָא רַבָּא, עַד דְּאִתְבַּר חֵילֵיהּ, כְּדֵין אַהַדְרוּ לֵיהּ לְנַהֲרוֹי.

109. Until a certain flame of fire arises in the north side, and a proclamation resounds, 'Stand in groups and disperse to four sides, for he who will put a snare upon the face of the serpent has awoken,' as written, "And I will put hooks in your jaws..." (Yechezkel 29:4). THIS REFERS TO THE SERPENT THAT COUCHES IN THE MIDST OF HIS STREAMS. Then all THE GROUPS scatter, take the serpent and puncture his face by the side of his jaws, and bring him into a hole in the great abyss, WHICH IS BINAH OF THE KLIPOT until his power is broken. Then he is returned to his rivers.

110. חַד לְשַׁבְעִין שְׁנִין עַבְדִין לֵיהּ כְּדֵין, בְּגִין דְּלָא יְטַשְׁטֵשׁ אַתְרִין דִּרְקִיעִין וְסָמְכַיְיהוּ. וְעָלַיְיהוּ כֻּלָּא אוֹדָן, וּמְבָרְכָאן וְאַמְרִין, בּוֹאוּ נִשְׁתַּחֲוֶה וְנִכְרָעָה נִבְרְכָה לִפְנֵי ה' עוֹשֵׂנוּ.

110. This is done to him once in seventy years, BECAUSE WHEN HE REACHES THE END OF SEVENTY YEARS WHICH IS HIS MALCHUT OF MALCHUT, THE POWER OF JUDGMENT IN HIS TAIL IS AGAIN STIMULATED, so that he would not ruin the places of the firmaments and their pillars. For this they all praise and laud: "Come, let us prostrate and bow down, let us kneel before Hashem our maker" (Tehilim 95:6).

111. תַּנִינַיָּיא עִלָּאִין לְעֵילָא קַיְימִין אִינּוּן דְּמִתְבָּרְכָאן, כמד"א וַיְבָרֶךְ אוֹתָם אֱלֹהִים. אִלֵּין שַׁלְטִין עַל כָּל שְׁאַר נוּנִין, דִּכְתִיב וּמִלְאוּ אֶת הַמַּיִם בַּיַּמִּים. וְעַל דָּא כְּתִיב, מָה רַבּוּ מַעֲשֶׂיךָ ה' כֻּלָּם בְּחָכְמָה עָשִׂיתָ.

111. BUT the supernal serpents that stand above IN HOLINESS, WHO ARE LEVIATHAN AND HIS SPOUSE, are the ones who were blessed as written: "And Elohim blessed them" (Beresheet 1:22). These rule over all the other fish, WHICH ARE THE VARIED LEVEL GRADES IN THE STREAMS, as is written: "And fill the waters in the seas." And of this, it is written, "Hashem, how manifold are Your works! In wisdom have You made them all." (Tehilim 104:24).

14. "The bright blade of a revolving sword"

‏112. אֶשְׁכּוֹל הַכּוֹפֶר דּוֹדִי לִי. אֶשְׁכּוֹל: דָּא אִימָא עִלָּאָה. מַה אֶשְׁכּוֹל מִתְקַשֵּׁט בְּכַמָּה עָלִין בְּכַמָּה זְמוֹרוֹת לְיִשְׂרָאֵל דְּאַכְלִין לֵיהּ, הָכִי שְׁכִינְתָּא עִלָּאָה, מִתְקַשְּׁטַת בְּכַמָּה קִשּׁוּטִין דִּשְׁמָנָה כֵּלִים, מִכַּמָּה קָרְבָּנִין, מִכַּמָּה מִינֵי תַּכְשִׁיטִין דְּכַפָּרָה לִבְנָהָא, וְאִיהִי קָמַת בְּהוֹן קָמֵי מַלְכָּא, וּמִיַּד וּרְאִיתִיהָ לִזְכּוֹר בְּרִית עוֹלָם. וְיָהֲבַת לָן שְׁאִילְתִּין דִּילָהּ, בְּאִלֵּין בִּרְכָּאן דְּתַקִּינוּ רַבָּנָן בִּצְלוֹתָא, לְמִשְׁאַל קָמֵי מַלְכָּא.

Tosefta (addendum)

112. "My beloved is to me a cluster of henna" (Shir Hashirim 1:14). A cluster refers to Supernal Ima, NAMELY BINAH. As a cluster is decorated with so many leaves and so many branches to Yisrael who eat it, so the Supernal Shechinah, WHICH IS BINAH, is decorated. SHE ELEVATES MAYIN NUKVIN (FEMALE WATERS) TO CHOCHMAH, with many jewels of eight vessels, NAMELY THE FOUR LETTERS OF YUD HEI VAV HEI AND THE FOUR LETTERS OF ADONAI, WHICH ARE MALE AND FEMALE, many offerings THAT YISRAEL OFFER, and many kinds of ornaments of atonement for Her children. She stands in them before the King, WHICH IS CHOCHMAH, and immediately, "And I will look upon it, that I may remember the everlasting covenant" (Beresheet 9:16), MEANING THAT HE UNITES WITH HER. AND BINAH gives us from her petitions SHE ASKED FROM CHOCHMAH FOR OUR SAKES, THROUGH those blessings that the sages composed to request before the King in the prayer service.

‏113. בְּהַהוּא זִמְנָא, כָּל דִּינִין דִּשְׁכִינְתָּא תַּתָּאָה, דְּאִיהִי הוֹה״י אֲדֹנָ״י, מִתְהַפְּכָן לְרַחֲמֵי, כְּגַוְונָא דָּא יְדוּ״ד, לְקַיֵּים אִם יִהְיוּ חֲטָאֵיכֶם כַּשָּׁנִים כַּשֶּׁלֶג יַלְבִּינוּ, יְדוּ״ד. אִם יַאְדִּימוּ כַתּוֹלָע. דּוֹד״י. כַּצֶּמֶר יִהְיוּ, יְדוּ״ד. כָּל דִּינִין דְּדָא, מִתְלַבְּנִין מִשְּׁכִינְתָּא עִלָּאָה.

113. At the time OF THE AFOREMENTIONED UNION OF CHOCHMAH AND BINAH, all the Judgments of the Lower Shechinah, WHICH IS MALCHUT

which is Hei Vav Hei Yud Adonai, convert into Mercy such as Yud Hei
Vav Hei, to fulfill the verse: "though your sins be like scarlet, they shall be
as white as snow" (Yeshayah 1:18), NAMELY Yud Hei Vav Hei. "Though
they be like red crimson," which is Hei-Vav-Hei-Yud "they shall be as
white as wool," WHICH IS Yud Hei Vav Hei. All the Judgments of this,
NAMELY OF MALCHUT, become whitened by the supernal Shechinah,
WHICH IS BINAH.

114. וְאִיהִי שְׁכִינְתָּא דוד"י, לַהַט הַחֶרֶב הַמִּתְהַפֶּכֶת לִשְׁמוֹר אֶת דֶּרֶךְ
עֵץ הַחַיִּים. וְאוּקְמוּהָ רַבָּנָן, דְּמִתְהַפְּכָא זִמְנִין רַחֲמֵי, זִמְנִין דִּינָא פְּעָמִים
אֲנָשִׁים, פְּעָמִים נָשִׁים. זִמְנִין דִּינָא, כְּגַוְונָא דָּא דוד"י. זִמְנִין רַחֲמֵי,
כְּגַוְונָא דָּא ידו"ד. דְּהָא אִיהוּ מִסִּטְרָא דְּאִילָנָא דְּחַיֵּי, כָּל דִּינִין
מִתְהַפְּכִין לְרַחֲמֵי. וּמִסִּטְרָא דְּעֵץ הַדַּעַת טוֹב וָרָע, כָּל רַחֲמֵי מִתְהַפְּכָן
לְדִינָא, לְמֵידָן בְּהוּ לְאִינוּן דְּעַבְרֵי עַל פִּתְגָּמֵי אוֹרַיְיתָא.

114. And the Shechinah, which is Hei Vav Hei Yud, is "the bright blade of a
revolving sword to guard the way to the Tree of Life" (Beresheet 3:24). The
sages explained THAT THE REASON IT IS CALLED THE BLADE OF A
REVOLVING SWORD IS BECAUSE it revolves sometimes to Mercy and
sometimes to Judgment, sometimes to men and sometimes to women;
sometimes to Judgment as in Hei Vav Hei Yud, sometimes to Mercy, as in
Yud Hei Vav Hei. It is from the side of the Tree of Life, MEANING THAT IF
THE SHECHINAH JOINS WITH THE TREE OF LIFE, WHICH IS ZEIR ANPIN
THAT ASCENDED TO BINAH, all the Judgments that She contains turn to
Mercy. And from the side of the Tree of Knowledge of Good and Evil,
MEANING THE SHECHINAH THAT IS NOT ATTACHED TO THE TREE OF
LIFE, all the Mercy contained in Her turns to Judgment, to judge all those
who transgress the words of Torah.

115. וְעֵץ דָּא בְּעָלְמָא דְּאָתֵי, דְּאִיהוּ בִּינָה, כָּל שְׁמָהָן דְּדִינָא מִתְהַפְּכִין
בֵּהּ רַחֲמֵי, בְּגִין דָּא אוּקְמוּהָ רַבָּנָן, לֹא כְּהָעוֹלָם הַזֶּה הָעוֹלָם הַבָּא.
וּבְגִין דָּא, אִיהִי לַהַט הַחֶרֶב הַמִּתְהַפֶּכֶת, דְּמִתְהַפֶּכֶת מִדִּינָא
לְרַחֲמֵי לַצַּדִּיקִים, לְמֵיהַב לוֹן אַגְרָא בְּעָלְמָא דְּאָתֵי. מַלְכוּת, לַהַט
הַחֶרֶב הַמִּתְהַפֶּכֶת, מֵרַחֲמֵי לְדִינָא, לְמֵידָן בָּהּ לְרַשִׁיעַיָּיא בְּעָלְמָא דֵּין.

115. And this Tree OF LIFE is in the World to Come, which is Binah, in which all the names of Judgment turn into Mercy, and the sages therefore explained that the World to Come, WHICH IS BINAH, is not like this world, WHICH IS MALCHUT. FOR GOOD TIDINGS IN THIS WORLD, WE SAY 'BLESSED IS HE WHO IS GOOD AND DOES GOOD'. AND FOR BAD TIDINGS WE SAY, 'BLESSED IS THE TRUE JUDGE'. BUT IN THE WORLD TO COME, HE IS COMPLETELY GOOD AND DOES GOOD, AS THERE IS NO JUDGMENT THERE. Therefore, Binah is the blade of a revolving sword that revolves from Judgment to Mercy for the righteous, to give them reward in the World to Come. Malchut is the blade of a revolving sword that revolves from Mercy to Judgment to judge the wicked in this world

116. אֲבָל מֵעֵץ הַדַּעַת טוֹב וָרָע, דְּאִיהוּ כְּגַוְונָא דְּמַטֶּה, זְמְנִין דְּמִתְהַפְּכִין הַנָּשִׁים לְשֵׁדוֹת, אֲנָשִׁים לְשֵׁדִים. וּבְגִין דָּא, וַיַּגֵּד יַעֲקֹב לְרָחֵל. וּבְגִין דָּא, אוּקְמוּהָ רַבָּנָן, דְּלֵית לֵיהּ לְבַר נָשׁ לְשַׁמְשָׁא עִם אִתְּתֵיהּ, עַד דְּמְסַפֵּר עִמָּהּ, שֶׁמָּא נִתְחַלְּפָה לוֹ בְּשֵׁידָה. בְּגִין דְּלָהַט בְּעֵץ הַדַּעַת טוֹב וָרָע, מִתְהַפֶּכֶת מִטּוֹב לְרָע, וְאִי תֵּימָא דִּמְכַשְׁפֵי פַרְעֹה, דִּכְתִּיב וַיַּעֲשׂוּ כֵן הַחַרְטֻמִּים בְּלָטֵיהֶם. הֲווֹ מְהַפְּכִין אִינּוּן מַטּוֹת דִּלְהוֹן לִנְחָשִׁין. וּמִסִּטְרָא דְּאִלֵּין הַפּוּכָן יַכְלִין לְאִתְהַפְּכָא.

ע"כ תּוֹסֶפְתָּא

116. But from the Tree of Knowledge of Good and Evil, which is similar to the rod THAT TURNED INTO A SERPENT, MEANING IT IS TURNED TO REAL EVIL AND NOT FROM MERCY INTO JUDGMENT AS MENTIONED, sometimes women turn into female demons and men to male demons. Hence "And Jacob told Rachel" (Beresheet 29:12). Therefore, our sages explained that a man should not have intercourse with his wife before he converses with her, since his wife might has been exchanged with a demon, because the blade in the Tree of Knowledge of Good and Evil revolves from good to REAL evil. And if you ask about the sorcerers of Pharaoh, of whom it is written: "And the magicians did so with their secret arts (lit. 'rods')" (Shemot 8:3), who turned their rods into serpents through their blades, HOW THEY COULD DO THIS? HE ANSWERS, Because of these rotations IN THE TREE OF KNOWLEDGE OF GOOD AND EVIL, they could do it.

End of Tosefta

15. "Take your rod"

117. וְאָמַרְתָּ אֶל אַהֲרֹן קַח אֶת מַטְּךָ. מַאי טַעֲמָא מַטֵּה אַהֲרֹן, וְלֹא מַטֵּה מֹשֶׁה. אֶלָּא, הַהוּא דְּמֹשֶׁה אִיהוּ קַדִּישָׁא יַתִּיר, דְּאִתְגְּלִיף בִּגְנְתָּא עִלָּאָה בִּשְׁמָא קַדִּישָׁא, וְלָא בָּעֵי קוּדְשָׁא בְּרִיךְ הוּא לְסָאֲבָא לֵיהּ בְּאִינוּן חוּטְרִין דְּחַרְשַׁיָּא. וְלָא עוֹד, אֶלָּא לְאַכְפְּיָיא לוֹן לְכָל אִינוּן דְּאַתְיָין מִסִּטְרָא דִּשְׂמָאלָא, בְּגִין דְּאַהֲרֹן אָתָא מִימִינָא, וּשְׂמָאלָא אִתְכַּפְיָיא בִּימִינָא.

117. "Then you shall say to Aaron, 'Take your rod'" (Shemot 7:9). HE ASKS, What is the reason the rod of Aaron and not the rod of Moses WAS SELECTED FOR THIS? HE ANSWERS, The rod of Moses was especially holy because the Holy Name was carved into it in the Supernal Garden of Eden, and the Holy One, blessed be He, did not want to defile it with the rods of the sorcerers, BECAUSE IT HAD TO SWALLOW THEM, AS WRITTEN: "AND THE ROD OF AARON SWALLOWED THEIR RODS." Moreover, in order to subdue all that comes from the left side, THE ROD OF AARON IS NECESSARY, because Aaron, a priest, came from the right, and the left is subjected to the right.

118. רִבִּי חִיָּיא שָׁאִיל לְרִבִּי יוֹסִי, הָא גַּלֵּי קָמֵי קוּדְשָׁא בְּרִיךְ הוּא, דְּאִינוּן חַרְשִׁין יַעַבְדוּן תַּנִּינַיָּיא, מַאי גְּבוּרְתָּא אִיהוּ לְמֶעְבַּד קָמֵי פַּרְעֹה תַּנִּינַיָּיא. א"ל, בְּגִין דְּמִתַּמָּן הוּא שֵׁירוּתָא לְאַלְקָאָה, וּמְשִׁירוּתָא דְּתַנִּינָא שָׁאֵרִי שׁוּלְטָנֵיהּ, כְּדֵין, חַדוּ כּוּלְּהוּ חַרְשֵׁי, דְּהָא רֵישׁ חָכְמְתָא דְּנָחָשׁ דִּילְהוֹן הָכִי הֲוָה. מִיָּד אִתְהַדַּר הַהוּא תַּנִּינָא דְּאַהֲרֹן לְאָעָא יְבֵישָׁא, וּבָלַע לוֹן.

118. Rabbi Chiya asked Rabbi Yosi, It was revealed before the Holy One, blessed be He, that these sorcerers will make serpents AND, IF SO, what is the significance of making serpents before Pharaoh? He said to him, It is because the origin of the punishments is in there, MEANING THE PRIMORDIAL SERPENT THAT CAUSED ADAM AND EVE TO FAIL. The reign OF PHARAOH starts at the origin of the serpent, NAMELY FROM THE LEFT SIDE. Then WHEN THEY SAW THE TRANSITION OF AARON'S ROD TO A SERPENT, all

the sorcerers rejoiced, because the beginning of the wisdom of their serpent was such. Immediately Aaron's rod turned back into a dry piece of wood and swallowed them.

119. וע״ד תַּוְוהוּ, וְיָדְעוּ דְשׁוּלְטָנָא עִלָּאָה אִית בְּאַרְעָא, דְּאִינוּן חֲשִׁיבוּ, דְּהָא לְתַתָּא, בַּר מִנַּיְיהוּ לָא אִית שָׁלְטָנָא לְמֶעְבַּד מִידִי, כְּדֵין, וַיִּבְלַע מַטֵּה אַהֲרֹן, מַטֵּה אַהֲרֹן דַּיְיקָא, דְּאִתְהַדָּר לְאָעָא וּבָלַע לוֹן.

119. Because of this, they were amazed and knew that there was a higher dominion on earth, for they thought that below, ON EARTH, there is no dominion aside from them to do anything. Then, "And the rod of Aaron swallowed their rods." It is precisely "the rod of Aaron," as THE SERPENT reverted into wood, and swallowed them.

120. וע״ד עָבַד אַהֲרֹן תְּרֵין אָתִין, חַד לְעֵילָא, וְחַד לְתַתָּא. חַד לְעֵילָא, תַּנִּינָא עִלָּאָה דְּשַׁלְטָא עַל אִינוּן דִּלְהוֹן. חַד לְתַתָּא, דְּשָׁלִיט אָעָא עַל תַּנִּינָא דִּילְהוֹן. וּפַרְעֹה חַכִּים הֲוָה מִכָּל חֲרָשׁוֹי, וְאִסְתַּכַּל דְּשָׁלְטָנָא עִלָּאָה שָׁלִיט עַל אַרְעָא, שָׁלִיט לְעֵילָא שָׁלִיט לְתַתָּא.

120. Therefore Aaron made two signs, one above and one below. The one above, NAMELY that the supernal serpent of Holiness overpowered their serpents, and the one below, namely that the wood dominated their serpents, BY SWALLOWING THEM. And Pharaoh was wiser than all his sorcerers, and he perceived that the supernal dominion ruled over the earth, ruling above and below.

121. אָמַר רַבִּי יוֹסֵי, אִי תֵּימָא כָּל מַה דְּעַבְדִין לָאו אִיהוּ אֶלָּא בְּחֵיזוּ דְּעֵינָא, דְּהָכִי אִתְחֲזֵי, וְלָא יַתִּיר, קָא מַשְׁמַע לָן וַיִּהְיוּ דַּיְיקָא, דִּכְתִיב וַיִּהְיוּ לְתַנִּינִם. וְאָמַר רַבִּי יוֹסֵי, אֲפִילוּ אִינוּן תַּנִּינַיָּא דִּילְהוֹן אַהֲדְרוּ לְמֶהֱוֵי אָעָיו, וְאָעָא דְּאַהֲרֹן בָּלַע לוֹן.

121. Rabbi Yosi said, Lest you say that everything the sorcerers do, they do only with optical illusions, that it only appears so, but not more, the Torah tells us: "And they turned" precisely, as written: "And they turned snakes"

(Shemot 7:12), AS THEY ACTUALLY MADE THE SERPENTS. And Rabbi Yosi said, Even when their serpents returned to be wood, the wood of Aaron swallowed them. BECAUSE IT IS SAID, "AND THE ROD OF AARON SWALLOWED THEIR RODS."

122. כְּתִיב, הִנְנִי עָלֶיךָ פַּרְעֹה מֶלֶךְ מִצְרַיִם הַתַּנִּים הַגָּדוֹל הָרֹבֵץ בְּתוֹךְ יְאֹרָיו. מִתַּמָּן שֵׁרוּתָא לְתַתָּא בְּשׁוּלְטָנָא דִּילְהוֹן. אֲבָל חָכְמְתָא דִּילְהוֹן, לְתַתָּא מִכֻּלְּהוּ דַּרְגִּין אִיהוּ.

122. It is written: "Behold I am against you, Pharaoh King of Egypt, the great crocodile that couches in the midst of his streams" (Yechezkel 29:3). HE IS CALLED SO, BECAUSE from THE GREAT SERPENT starts their dominion below, but their wisdom is drawn from under all the levels OF THE SERPENT AND HIS STREAMS.

123. תָּא חֲזֵי, חָכְמְתָא דִּילְהוֹן בְּדַרְגִּין תַּתָּאִין, לְאַכְפְּיָין לוֹן לְאִלֵּין דַּרְגִּין בְּדַרְגִּין עִלָּאִין, רֵישֵׁי שׁוּלְטָנוּתְהוֹן וְעִקָּרָא דִּילְהוֹן, לְתַתָּא מֵהַהוּא תַּנִּינָא, וּמִשְׁתַּלְשְׁלָן בְּתַנִּינָא, דְּהָא מִתַּמָּן נָטִיל חֵילָא דַּרְגָּא עִלָּאָה דִּילְהוֹן. מַשְׁמַע דִּכְתִיב, אֲשֶׁר אַחַר הָרֵחָיִם.

123. Come and see, their wisdom abides in the lowest levels in order to subdue and subjugate these levels to the upper levels, WHICH ARE THE GREAT SERPENT AND HIS STREAMS, TO BE INCLUDED IN THEM, AND THEN THEY CAN DRAW LIGHT TO THE LOWER LEVELS. The tops of their dominion and their sources are under the serpent. They hold to the serpent, because their highest level, WHICH IS THE KING, receives power from there. THEREFORE THEIR KING IS LIKENED TO A GREAT SERPENT WHO COUCHES IN THE MIDST OF HIS STREAMS. This is understood from the verse: "That is behind the mill" (Shemot 11:5), MEANING BEHIND THE HIGHEST LEVELS THAT ARE CALLED MILL, SINCE THEY ARE NOT CAPABLE OF RECEIVING THE LIGHT OF CHOCHMAH, WHICH IS CALLED FIRSTBORN, EXCEPT BY SUBDUING AND SUBJUGATING IT TO THE HIGHER LEVELS AS MENTIONED. THEREFORE, IT IS CALLED THE FIRSTBORN OF THE MAIDSERVANT.

124. רִבִּי חִיָּיא, הֲוָה יָתִיב יוֹמָא חַדָא, אַבָּבָא דְּתַרְעָא דְּאוּשָׁא. חָמָא

לֵיהּ לְרִבִּי אֶלְעָזָר חַד קַטְפִּירָא טָאסָא גַּבֵּיהּ, אָמַר לֵיהּ לְרִבִּי אֶלְעָזָר, מַשְׁמַע, דַּאֲפִילוּ בְּאוֹרְחָךְ כֹּלָּא תְּאִיבִין לְמֵהַךְ אֲבַתְרָךְ. אַהֲדָר רֵישָׁא וְחָמָא לֵיהּ. אָמַר, וַדַּאי שְׁלִיחוּתָא אִית גַּבֵּיהּ. דְּהָא קוּדְשָׁא בְּרִיךְ הוּא בְּכֹלָּא עָבֵיד שְׁלִיחוּתֵיהּ, וְכַמָּה שְׁלִיחִין אִית לֵיהּ לְקוּדְשָׁא בְּרִיךְ הוּא, דְּלָא תֵּימָא מִלִּין דְּאִית בְּהוּ רוּחָא בִּלְחוֹדַיְיהוּ, אֶלָּא אֲפִילוּ אִינּוּן מִלִּין דְּלֵית בְּהוּ רוּחָא.

124. Rabbi Chiya was sitting one day at the gate of Usha. He saw Rabbi Elazar and A BIRD THAT IS NAMED Katfira flying by him. He said to Rabbi Elazar, It seems that even when you are going on the road everyone desires to follow you. RABBI ELAZAR turned his head and saw it. He said, Certainly THE BIRD has a mission since the Holy One, blessed be He, accomplishes His missions through everyone, and the Holy One, blessed be He, has many messengers. Do not say THAT HE DOES HIS MISSION only with living things, but also with inanimate things.

125. פָּתַח וְאָמַר, כִּי אֶבֶן מִקִּיר תִּזְעָק וְכָפִיס מֵעֵץ יַעֲנֶנָּה. כַּמָּה אִית לֵיהּ לְבַר נָשׁ לְאִזְדַּהֲרָא מֵחוֹבוֹי, דְּלָא יֶחֱטָא קָמֵי קוּדְשָׁא בְּרִיךְ הוּא. וְאִי יֵימָא מַאן יַסְהִיד בֵּיהּ. הָא אַבְנֵי בֵּיתֵיהּ וְאָעֵי בֵּיתֵיהּ יַסְהִידוּ בֵּיהּ. וּלְזִמְנִין דְּקוּדְשָׁא בְּרִיךְ הוּא הוּא עָבֵיד בְּהוּ שְׁלִיחוּתָא. תָּא חֲזֵי חוּטְרָא דְּאַהֲרֹן, דְּאִיהוּ אָעָא יְבֵישָׁא, קֻדְשָׁא בְּרִיךְ הוּא שֵׁירוּתָא דְּנִסִּין עָבֵד בֵּיהּ, וּתְרֵי שְׁלִיחוּתֵי בֵּיהּ אִתְעֲבִידוּ. חַד דְּאִיהוּ אָעָא יְבֵישָׁא וּבָלַע לְאִינּוּן תַּנִּינַיָּיא דִּילְהוֹן. וְחַד דְּהָא לְשַׁעֲתָא אִתְהַדָּר בְּרוּחָא וְאִתְעֲבֵיד בְּרִיָּה.

125. He opened the discussion saying, "For the stone will cry out of the wall and the beam out of the timber shall answer it" (Chavakuk 2:11). How careful a person must be not to sin before the Holy One, blessed be He. And if you ask who will bear testimony against him, lo and behold the stones of his house and the beams of his house will bear testimony against him. And sometimes the Holy One, blessed be He, carries out His missions through them. Come and see the rod of Aaron, which was a dry piece of wood, the Holy One, blessed be He, performed with it the first of the miracles. Two missions were accomplished with it: One is though it was a dry piece of wood yet it swallowed their serpents; the second is that it temporarily received the spirit OF LIFE and became a creature.

‎126. אָמַר רִבִּי אֶלְעָזָר, תִּפַּח רוּחֵיהוֹן, דְּאִינּוּן דְּאַמְרִין, דְּלָא זַמִין קוּדְשָׁא בְּרִיךְ הוּא לְאַחֲיָיא מֵתַיָּיא, וְהֵיךְ יִתְעֲבִיד מִנַּיְיהוּ בְּרִיָּה חַדְתָּא. יֵיתוּן וְיֶחֱמוּן אִינּוּן טִפְּשָׁאִין חַיָּיבַיָא, רְחִיקִין מֵאוֹרַיְיתָא, רְחִיקִין מִנֵּיהּ, בִּידֵיהּ דְּאַהֲרֹן הֲוָה חוּטְרָא, אָעָא יְבֵישָׁא, וְקוּדְשָׁא בְּרִיךְ הוּא לְפוּם שַׁעֲתָא אַהֲדַר לֵיהּ בְּרִיָּה, מְשַׁנְיָא בְּרוּחָא וְגוּפָא. אִינּוּן גּוּפִין, דַּהֲווֹ בְּהוּ רוּחִין וְנִשְׁמָתִין קַדִּישִׁין, וְנָטְרוּ פִּקּוּדֵי אוֹרַיְיתָא, וְאִשְׁתַּדְּלוּ בְּאוֹרַיְיתָא יְמָמָא וְלֵילֵי, וְקוּדְשָׁא בְּרִיךְ הוּא טָמִיר לוֹן בְּעַפְרָא. לְבָתַר, בְּזִמְנָא דְּיֶחֱדֵי עָלְמָא, עַל אַחַת כַּמָּה וְכַמָּה דְּיִעֲבַד לְהוּ בְּרִיָּה חַדְתָּא.

126. Rabbi Elazar said, May the spirit expire of those who say that the Holy One, blessed be He, will not resurrect the dead, because it is not possible that He could make a new creature of them. Let these wicked, foolish people, who are far from Torah and far from THE HOLY ONE, BLESSED BE HE, see that Aaron had in his hands a rod, dry wood, which the Holy One, blessed be He, turned temporarily into a creature. That is, it changed in spirit and body. The Holy One, blessed be He, concealed in the dust those bodies that already had holy spirits and souls, observed the precepts of the Torah, and were occupied with Torah days and nights. At the time when the world will rejoice, MEANING AFTER THE END OF CORRECTION, how much more so will the Holy One, blessed be He, make them new creatures.

‎127. אָמַר רִבִּי חִיָּיא, וְלֹא עוֹד, אֶלָּא דְּהַהוּא גּוּפָא דַּהֲוָה, יָקוּם. מַשְׁמַע דִּכְתִיב, יִחְיוּ מֵתֶיךָ, וְלָא כְּתִיב יִבְרָא, מַשְׁמַע דְּבִרְיָין אִינּוּן אֲבָל יִחְיוּ. דְּהָא גַּרְמָא חַד, יִשְׁתְּאַר מִן גּוּפָא תְּחוֹת אַרְעָא, וְהַהוּא לָא אִתְרְקַב וְלָא אִתְבְּלֵי בְּעַפְרָא לְעָלְמִין, וּבְהַהוּא זִמְנָא, קוּדְשָׁא בְּרִיךְ הוּא יְרַכֵּךְ לֵיהּ, וְיַעֲבִיד לֵיהּ כַּחֲמִירָא בְּעִיסָה, וְיִסְתַּלַּק וְיִתְפַּשַּׁט לְאַרְבַּע זָוְיָין וּמִנֵּיהּ יִשְׁתַּכְלַל גּוּפָא וְכָל שַׁיְיפוֹי. וְקוּדְשָׁא בְּרִיךְ הוּא יָהִיב בֵּיהּ רוּחָא לְבָתַר. אָמַר לֵיהּ רִבִּי אֶלְעָזָר הָכִי הוּא. וְתָא חֲזֵי, הַהוּא גַּרְמָא בְּמָה אִתְרְכַךְ. בַּטַל. דִּכְתִיב, כִּי טַל אוֹרוֹת טַלֶּךָ וְגוֹ'.

127. Rabbi Chiya said, not only this but that body that previously existed will rise. This is understood from the words: "Your dead will again live" (Yeshayah 26:19). It is not written: '…will He create', so it means that they were already created before, but THEY ONLY NEED to come alive again. One bone will remain from the body under the earth, and that bone never rots or disappears in the dust. At that time, the Holy One, blessed be He, will soften it and make it like leaven in the dough, and it will rise and spread to four corners, and the body and all its limbs will be completed from it. Afterwards, the Holy One, blessed be He, will put the spirit into it. Rabbi Elazar said to him, It is so. Come and see, this bone is softened with dew, as written: "For the dew of lights is your dew…" (Ibid.).

16. "That they may become blood"

128. וַיֹּאמֶר ה' אֶל מֹשֶׁה אֱמוֹר אֶל אַהֲרֹן קַח מַטְּךָ וּנְטֵה יָדְךָ עַל מֵימֵי מִצְרַיִם עַל נַהֲרוֹתָם עַל יְאוֹרֵיהֶם וְעַל אַגְמֵיהֶם וְעַל כָּל מִקְוֵה מֵימֵיהֶם וְיִהְיוּ דָם וְגוֹ'. אָמַר רִבִּי יְהוּדָה, הַאי קְרָא אִית לְאִסְתַּכְּלָא בֵּיהּ, וְהֵיךְ יָכִיל לְמֵהַךְ לְכָל הֲנֵי אַתְרֵי. וְתוּ, דְּהָא כְּתִיב וַיִּמָּלֵא שִׁבְעַת יָמִים אַחֲרֵי הַכּוֹת ה' אֶת הַיְאוֹר. אֶת הַיְאוֹר כְּתִיב, וְאַתְּ אָמַרְתְּ עַל מֵימֵי מִצְרַיִם עַל נַהֲרוֹתָם עַל יְאוֹרֵיהֶם וְעַל אַגְמֵיהֶם.

128. "And Hashem said to Moses, 'Say to Aaron, take your rod and stretch your hand on the waters of Egypt on their streams, on their canals, and on their ponds, and on all their pools of water, that they may become blood...'" (Shemot 7:19). Rabbi Yehuda said, We must concentrate on this passage. How could he have gone to all these places, NAMELY TO ALL THE WATERS OF EGYPT AND ALL THEIR PONDS THROUGHOUT THE LAND OF EGYPT? It is also written, "And seven days were completed, after Hashem had smitten the River" (Ibid. 25). It is written: "The River," yet you say: "on the waters of Egypt, on their streams, on their canals, and on their ponds."

129. אֶלָּא, מֵימֵי מִצְרַיִם נִילוּס הֲוָה. וּמִתַּמָּן אִתְמַלְיָין כָּל אִינוּן שְׁאָר אֲגַמִּין וְיָאוֹרִין וּמַבּוּעִין וְכָל מֵימִין דִּילְהוֹן. וְעַל דָּא, אַהֲרֹן לֹא נָטָה לְמַחֲאָה אֶלָּא לְנִילוּס בִּלְחוֹדוֹי. וְתָא חֲזֵי דְּהָכִי הוּא, דִּכְתִיב וְלֹא יָכְלוּ מִצְרַיִם לִשְׁתּוֹת מַיִם מִן הַיְאוֹר.

129. HE ANSWERS, "The waters of Egypt" is the Nile. All the other ponds and streams and wellsprings and all their waters were filled from there. Therefore, Aaron raised his hand only to smite the Nile. Come and see that it is so, for it is written, "And Egypt could not drink of the water of the River" (Ibid. 21). SO WE SEE THAT THE RIVER INCLUDES ALL THE WATERS OF EGYPT.

130. אָמַר רִבִּי אַבָּא, תָּא חֲזֵי, מַיִין תַּתָּאִין מִתְפָּרְשָׁאן לְכַמָּה סִטְרִין, וּמַיִין עִלָּאִין מִתְכַּנְּשֵׁי בְּבֵי כְּנִישׁוּ מַיָּא, דִּכְתִיב, וַיֹּאמֶר אֱלֹהִים יִקָּווּ הַמַּיִם מִתַּחַת הַשָּׁמַיִם אֶל מָקוֹם אֶחָד. וּכְתִיב וּלְמִקְוֵה הַמַּיִם קָרָא יַמִּים.

הַאי קְרָא אוּקְמוּהָ. וְתָא חֲזֵי, הַהוּא רְקִיעָא דְּאִית בֵּיהּ שִׁמְשָׁא וְסִיהֲרָא כּוֹכְבַיָּיא וּמַזָּלֵי, דָּא אִיהוּ בֵּי כְּנִישׁוּת מַיָּא רַבָּא, דְּהוּא נָטִיל כָּל מַיִּין, וְאַשְׁקֵי לְאַרְעָא, דְּהִיא עָלְמָא תַּתָּאָה, כֵּיוָן, דְּנָטַל מַיָּא בָּדַר לוֹן, וּפָלִיג לוֹן לְכָל עִיבָר, וּמִתַּמָּן אִתְשַׁקְיָין כֹּלָּא.

130. Rabbi Aba said, Come and see, the lower waters spread in many directions, NAMELY RIGHT AND TO LEFT, and the upper waters gather in the gathering place of the water, WHICH IS YESOD OF ZEIR ANPIN, as written: "And Elohim said, 'Let the waters under the heaven be gathered together to one place'...and the gathering together of the waters He called seas" (Beresheet 1:9-11). This passage was explained. Come and see, the firmament that contains the sun and moon and stars and constellations, WHICH IS YESOD OF ZEIR ANPIN, THAT INCLUDES WITHIN IT ALL THE LIGHTS OF ZEIR ANPIN, is the gathering place of the water, for it receives all the water, NAMELY ALL THE LIGHTS, and waters the earth which is the lower world, NAMELY MALCHUT. As soon as THE EARTH receives the waters, it spreads them and divides them to every side, and from there everything is watered.

131. וּבְזִמְנָא דְּדִינָא שַׁרְיָא, עָלְמָא תַּתָּאָה לָא יַנְקָא מִן הַהוּא רְקִיעָא, וְיַנְקָא מִסְטַר שְׂמָאלָא, וּכְדֵין אִקְרֵי חֶרֶב לַה' מָלְאָה דָם. וַוי לְאִינּוּן דְּיַנְקִין כְּדֵין מִינָהּ, וְאִתְשַׁקְיָין מִינָהּ, דִּבְהַהוּא זִמְנָא יַמָּא יַנְקָא מִתְּרֵין סִטְרִין, הֲוָה אִתְפְּלַג לִתְרֵין חוּלָקִין, חִוָּור וְסוּמָק. וּכְדֵין שָׁדֵי לִיאוֹרָא חוּלָקָא דְּמִצְרַיִם, וְאַלְקֵי לְעֵילָא וְאַלְקֵי לְתַתָּא. וְעַל דָּא שָׁתָאן יִשְׂרָאֵל מַיָּא. וּמִצְרָאֵי דָּמָא.

131. During the time when Judgment dwells, the lower world, WHICH IS MALCHUT, does not nurture from that firmament, but nurtures from the left side THAT IS NOT INCLUDED IN THE RIGHT. Then MALCHUT is called: "The sword of Hashem is filled with blood" (Yeshayah 34:6). Woe to those who then nurture from her and are sustained by her, because at that time the sea, WHICH IS MALCHUT, was nurturing from two sides, FROM YESOD OF ZEIR ANPIN AND FROM THE LEFT SIDE. THEREFORE, it is divided into two parts, white FROM THE SIDE OF YESOD, and red FROM THE LEFT SIDE. Then it casts into the River the portion of Egypt, NAMELY THE RED, smites THEIR SOURCE above, and smites below. Therefore, Yisrael drink water BECAUSE THEY ARE ATTACHED TO YESOD OF ZEIR ANPIN, WHICH IS THE WHITE PART OF MALCHUT, and the Egyptians drink blood, WHICH IS THE RED PART OF MALCHUT.

132. אִי תֵּימָא בְּגִין גִּיעוּלָא הֲוָה וְלָא יַתִּיר. תָּא חֲזֵי, שָׁתָאן דְּמָא וְעָאל לִמְעַיְיהוּ, וְאִסְתַּלָּק וּבָקַע, עַד דַּהֲווֹ מְזַבְּנִין לוֹן יִשְׂרָאֵל מַיָּא בְּמָמוֹנָא, וּכְדֵין שָׁתָאן מַיָּא בְּגִינֵי כַּךְ שֵׁירוּתָא לְאַלְקָאָה לוֹן הֲוָה דְּמָא.

132. So if you say that THE PLAGUE OF BLOOD was only to repel them, come and see. They drank the blood, which entered their intestines, broke through and rose. So Yisrael sold them water for money. Then they drank water. Therefore, the first plague that smote them was blood.

133. רִבִּי יִצְחָק פָּתַח הַאי קְרָא, אֲרוֹמִמְךָ אֱלֹהַי הַמֶּלֶךְ וַאֲבָרְכָה שִׁמְךָ לְעוֹלָם וָעֶד. תָּא חֲזֵי, דָּוִד לָקֳבֵיל דַּרְגָּא דִּילֵיה קָאמַר, דִּכְתִיב אֱלֹהַי דִּידִי. בְּגִין דְּבָעָא לְסַלְּקָא שְׁבָחֵיה, וּלְאַעֲלָא לֵיה לִנְהוֹרָא עִלָּאָה, לְאִתְעָרְבָא דָּא בְּדָא, לְמֶהֱוֵי כֹּלָּא חַד. בְּגִינֵי כַּךְ, אֲרוֹמִמְךָ אֱלֹהַי הַמֶּלֶךְ וְגוֹ'.

133. Rabbi Yitzchak opened the discussion with this passage: "I will extol You, my Elohim, O King; and I will bless Your name forever and ever" (Tehilim 145:1). Come and see that David spoke of his level, "I WILL EXTOL YOU," for he wrote "my Elohim," MEANING my own ELOHIM, NAMELY MALCHUT, WHICH IS HIS LEVEL. For he wanted to raise the praise OF MALCHUT, and to bring it to the supernal light, NAMELY BINAH, to mix them one with the other, so THAT MALCHUT AND BINAH should be one. Therefore he said, "I will extol You, my Elohim, O King..."

134. דְּתָנֵינָן, כָּל יוֹמוֹי דְּדָוִד, אִשְׁתַּדַּל לְאַתְקָנָא כּוּרְסְיָה, וּלְאַנְהָרָא אַנְפָּהָא, בְּגִין דְּיָגִין עֲלֵיה וְאִתְנְהִיר תָּדִיר נְהוֹרָא תַּתָּאָה בִּנְהוֹרָא עִלָּאָה, לְמֶהֱוֵי כֹּלָּא חַד. וְכַד אָתָא שְׁלֹמֹה, אַשְׁכַּח עָלְמָא שְׁלִים, וְסִיהֲרָא דְּאִתְמַלְיָא, וְלָא אִצְטְרִיךְ לְאַטְרָחָא עֲלָה לְאַנְהָרָא.

134. For we learned that David endeavored all the days of his life to restore the Throne, WHICH IS MALCHUT, and to illuminate its face WITH THE LIGHT OF BINAH so it would protect it, and constantly illuminate the lower light, WHICH IS MALCHUT, with the upper light, WHICH IS BINAH, so that they would be one. MEANING THAT MALCHUT WOULD ASCEND TO BINAH, WHEN THEY ARE ONE. And when Solomon came, he found a world, WHICH IS MALCHUT, whole, and the moon, WHICH IS MALCHUT, full. MALCHUT HAD ALREADY ASCENDED TO BINAH, AND WAS COMPLETED AND FILLED WITH ALL ITS LIGHTS and he no longer had to toil at illuminating it.

135. תָּא חֲזֵי, בְּשַׁעֲתָא דְּבָעֵי קוּדְשָׁא בְּרִיךְ הוּא לְמֶיסָב נוּקְמִין מֵעַמִּין עוֹבְדֵי ע״ז, אִתְּעַר שְׂמָאלָא, וְאִתְמַלְיָא סִיהֲרָא מֵהַהוּא סִטְרָא דָּמָא. וּכְדֵין, נַבְעִין מַבּוּעִין וּנְחָלִין דִּלְתַתָּא, כָּל אִינּוּן דִּלְסְטַר שְׂמָאלָא דָּמָא. וע״ד, דִּינָא דִּילְהוֹן דָּמָא.

135. Come and see, when the Holy One, blessed be He, wishes to do vengeance upon the idol-worshipping nations, the left SIDE is stimulated and the moon becomes full, FOR IT IS MALCHUT with blood from that side. Then the springs and rivers of below and all that are on the left side flow with blood. Therefore their punishment is blood.

136. תָּא חֲזֵי, כַּד הַאי דָּמָא אִתְּעַר עַל עַמָּא, הַהוּא דָּמָא דְּקַטּוֹלִין אִיהוּ דְּיִתְּעַר עָלַיְיהוּ עַמָּא אַחֲרָא וְקָטִיל לוֹן. אֲבָל בְּמִצְרַיִם, לָא בָּעָא קוּדְשָׁא בְּרִיךְ הוּא לְאַיְיתָאָה עָלַיְיהוּ עַמָּא אַחֲרָא לְאַתְעָרָא עָלַיְיהוּ דָּמָא בְּגִין דְּיִשְׂרָאֵל הֲווֹ בֵּינַיְיהוּ, וְלָא יִצְטַעֲרוּן בְּגִין דְּדַיְירִין בְּאַרְעָא דִּילְהוֹן, אֲבָל קוּדְשָׁא בְּרִיךְ הוּא מָחָא לוֹן בְּדָמָא, בְּנַהֲרִין דִּלְהוֹן, דְּלָא הֲווֹ יַכְלִין לְמִשְׁתֵּי.

136. Come and see: When this blood is aroused against any nation, it is the blood of killed people, because another nation is provoked to come and kill them. But in Egypt, the Holy One, blessed be He, did not want to bring another nation to arouse blood against them, NAMELY TO KILL THEM, because of Yisrael that were living among them, so that YISRAEL who dwelt in their country would not be distressed. The Holy One, blessed be He, smote them with blood in their streams instead, so they were not able to drink.

137. וּבְגִין דְּשׁוּלְטָנוּתָא דִּלְהוֹן, שַׁלְטָא בְּהַהוּא נַהֲרָא, פָּקִיד קוּדְשָׁא בְּרִיךְ הוּא לְשׁוּלְטָנוּתָא דִּלְהוֹן בְּקַדְמֵיתָא, בְּגִין דְּיַלְקֵי דַּחֲלָא דִּלְהוֹן בְּקַדְמֵיתָא, בְּגִין דְּנִילוּס חַד דַּחֲלָא דִּלְהוֹן הֲוָה, וְכֵן שְׁאָר דַּחֲלִין דִּלְהוֹן נַבְעִין דָּמָא. הה"ד וְהָיָה דָם בְּכָל אֶרֶץ מִצְרַיִם וּבָעֵצִים וּבָאֲבָנִים.

137. Since their dominion rules over that river, the Holy One, blessed be He, punished their dominion first, in order that their deity would be smitten first, because the Nile was one of their deities. Similarly their other deities were gushing with blood. This is the meaning of: "And that there may be blood throughout all the land of Egypt both in vessels of wood, and in vessels of stone" (Shemot 7:19).

138. ר' חִיָּיא קָם לֵילְיָא חַד לְמִלְעֵי בְּאוֹרַיְיתָא, וַהֲוָה עִמֵּיהּ ר' יוֹסֵי זוּטָא, דַּהֲוָה רַבְיָא. פָּתַח ר' חִיָּיא וְאָמַר, לֵךְ אֱכֹל בְּשִׂמְחָה לַחְמֶךְ וּשְׁתֵה בְלֶב טוֹב יֵינֶךָ כִּי כְבָר רָצָה הָאֱלֹהִים אֶת מַעֲשֶׂיךָ. מַאי קָא חָמָא שְׁלֹמֹה דְּאָמַר הַאי קְרָא.

138. Rabbi Chiya arose one night to study Torah. The young Rabbi Yosi, who was still a child, was with him. Rabbi Chiya opened the discussion saying, "Go your way, eat your bread with joy, and drink your wine with a merry heart; for the Elohim has already accepted your works" (Kohelet 9:7). HE ASKS, What did Solomon see that caused him to say this passage.

139. אֶלָּא שְׁלֹמֹה כָּל מִלּוֹי בְּחָכְמָה הֲווֹ, וְהַאי דְּאָמַר לֵךְ אֱכֹל בְּשִׂמְחָה לַחְמֶךְ, בְּשַׁעֲתָא דְּבַר נָשׁ אָזִיל בְּאוֹרְחוֹי דְּקוּדְשָׁא בְּרִיךְ הוּא, קוּדְשָׁא בְּרִיךְ הוּא מְקָרֵב לֵיהּ לְגַבֵּיהּ, וְיָהִיב לֵיהּ שַׁלְוָה וְנַיְיחָא, כְּדֵין נַהֲמָא וְחַמְרָא דְּאָכִיל וְשָׁתֵי, בְּחֶדְוָה דְּלִבָּא, בְּגִין דְּקוּדְשָׁא בְּרִיךְ הוּא אִתְרְעֵי בְּעוֹבָדוֹי.

139. AND HE ANSWERS, All the words of Solomon were said with wisdom. "Go your way, eat your bread with joy" MEANS that the Holy One, blessed be He, brings a person who goes in the ways of the Holy One, blessed be He, close to Him, and gives him tranquillity and repose. Then, he eats and drinks the bread and wine with a joyful heart because the Holy One, blessed be He, has accepted his actions.

140. א"ל הַהוּא רַבְיָא, אִי הָכִי, הָא אֲמַרְתְּ דְּכָל מִלּוֹי דִּשְׁלֹמֹה
בְּחָכְמְתָא הֲווֹ, אָן הוּא חָכְמְתָא הָכָא. א"ל בְּרִי תְּבַשֵּׁל בְּשׁוּלָךְ, וְתֶחֱמֵי
הַאי קְרָא. א"ל עַד לָא בָּשִׁילְנָא יְדַעְנָא. א"ל מנ"ל.

140. That boy said to him, If so, then you have said that all the words of Solomon were with wisdom, so where is the wisdom here IN THIS PASSAGE. RABBI CHIYA said to him, My son, cook your food, MEANING CONCENTRATE WELL, and you will understand this passage. The boy said to him, Before I have cooked, I already know. RABBI CHIYA said to him, How do you know?

141. א"ל קָלָא חַד שְׁמַעְנָא מֵאַבָּא, דַּהֲוָה אָמַר בְּהַאי קְרָא, דִּשְׁלֹמֹה
קָא אַזְהַר לֵיהּ לב"נ, לְאַעְטְרָא לָהּ לכנ"י בְּשִׂמְחָה, דְּאִיהוּ סְטְרָא
דִּימִינָא, וְאִיהוּ נָהֲמָא, דְּיִתְעֲטַּר בְּחֶדְוָה. וּלְבָתַר, יִתְעֲטַּר בְּחַמְרָא,
דְּאִיהוּ שְׂמָאלָא, בְּגִין דְּתִשְׁתְּכַח בִּמְהֵימְנוּתָא דְּכֹלָּא, חֶדְוָותָא
שְׁלֵימָתָא, בִּימִינָא וּשְׂמָאלָא, וְכַד תֶּהֱוֵי בֵּין תַּרְוַויְיהוּ כְּדֵין כָּל בִּרְכָּאן
שָׁרָאן בְּעָלְמָא. וְכָל דָּא, כַּד אִתְרָעֵי קוּדְשָׁא בְּרִיךְ הוּא בְּעוֹבָדֵיהוֹן דִּבְנֵי
נָשָׁא, הה"ד כִּי כְבָר רָצָה הָאֱלֹהִים אֶת מַעֲשֶׂיךָ. אָתָא ר' חִיָּיא וּנְשָׁקֵיהּ,
אָמַר, חַיֶּיךָ בְּרִי הַאי מִלָּה שָׁבַקְנָא בְּגִינָךְ, וְהַשְׁתָּא יְדַעְנָא, דְּקוּדְשָׁא
בְּרִיךְ הוּא בָּעֵי לְאַעְטְרָא לָךְ בְּאוֹרַיְיתָא.

141. The boy said to him, I heard one voice, MEANING ONE THING my father used to say about this passage. Solomon cautioned people to crown the Congregation of Yisrael, WHICH IS MALCHUT, with joy, which is the right side, NAMELY THE LIGHT OF CHASSADIM, which is bread, so it would be crowned with joy. BREAD ALLUDES TO THE LIGHT OF CHASSADIM. Then it should be crowned with wine, which is the left side, NAMELY THE ILLUMINATION OF CHOCHMAH, WHICH IS THE LEFT OF BINAH, so that the Faith of all, NAMELY MALCHUT, will be in complete joy in the right and left. When it will be between both, all the blessings will dwell in the world. THIS IS THE UTMOST PERFECTION OF MALCHUT, THAT THE ILLUMINATION OF THE LEFT, WHICH IS CHOCHMAH, WOULD BE ENVELOPED IN THE LIGHT OF CHASSADIM THAT IS ON THE RIGHT, FOR THEN BOTH ILLUMINATE IN HER. FOR THIS IS THE SECRET OF BREAD

AND WINE. All this occurs when the Holy One, blessed be He, accepts the deeds of people as written: "For the Elohim has already accepted your works." Rabbi Chiya approached and kissed him. He said, I swear my son that I left this for you, MEANING THAT EVEN THOUGH I ALSO KNEW IT, I DID NOT SAY IT, AND I LEFT IT FOR YOU TO SAY. And now I know that the Holy One, blessed be He, wishes to crown you with Torah.

142. תּוּ פָּתַח ר' חִיָּיא וְאָמַר, אֱמוֹר אֶל אַהֲרֹן קַח מַטְּךָ וּנְטֵה יָדְךָ עַל מֵימֵי מִצְרַיִם. מ"ט אַהֲרֹן וְלֹא מֹשֶׁה. אֶלָּא, אָמַר קוּדְשָׁא בְּרִיךְ הוּא, אַהֲרֹן מַיִין קַיְימִין בְּדוּכְתֵּיה, וּשְׂמָאלָא בָּעֵי לְנַגְדָּא מַיִין מִתַּמָּן, אַהֲרֹן דְּאָתֵי מֵהַהוּא סִטְרָא יִתְּעַר לֵיה, וְכַד שְׂמָאלָא נָקִיט לוֹן, אִינוּן יִתְהַדְרוּן דָּמָא.

142. Rabbi Chiya again opened the discussion saying, "Say to Aaron, 'Take your rod, and stretch your hand on the waters of Egypt'..." (Shemot 7:19). HE ASKS, Why Aaron and not Moses, AND ANSWERS, For the Holy One, blessed be He, said, water remains in the place where Aaron is, BECAUSE WATER IS IN THE RIGHT, and the left wants to draw water from there. Aaron, who comes from that side, will stimulate A FLOW OF WATER, and when the left, WHICH IS EGYPT, receives it, it will be transformed into blood.

143. תָּא חֲזֵי תַּתָּאָה דְּכָל דַּרְגִּין מָחָא בְּקַדְמֵיתָא. אר"ש מִתַּתָּאָה שָׁרָא קוּדְשָׁא בְּרִיךְ הוּא. וִידָא דִילֵיה, מָחָא בְּכָל אֶצְבְּעָא וְאֶצְבְּעָא. וְכַד מָטָא לְדַרְגָּא עִלָּאָה דְּכָל דַּרְגִּין, עֲבֵד אִיהוּ דִילֵיה, וְעָבַר בְּאַרְעָא דְמִצְרַיִם, וְקָטַל כֹּלָּא. וּבְגִינֵי כַּךְ קָטַל כָּל בּוּכְרִין בְּאַרְעָא דְמִצְרַיִם, בְּגִין דְּאִיהוּ דַּרְגָּא עִלָּאָה וּבוּכְרָא דְּכֹלָּא.

143. Come and see, the lowest of all levels, WHICH IS MALCHUT, WHICH IS CALLED "THE SWORD OF HASHEM IS FILLED WITH BLOOD," smote first, AND THEIR WATERS TURNED INTO BLOOD. Rabbi Shimon said, The Holy One, blessed be He, started to smite from the lowest, WHICH IS MALCHUT. His hand THAT CONTAINS TEN FINGERS, WHICH IS THE SECRET OF THE TEN SFIROT smote with each finger, FROM MALCHUT UNTIL KETER. And when He reached their highest level, WHICH IS THE FIRSTBORN OF ALL

THE LEVELS, NAMELY CORRESPONDING TO KETER, He acted and passed over the land of Egypt and killed them all. Therefore, He killed all the firstborn in the land of Egypt, because this is their highest level and the firstborn to everything.

17. "And the River shall bring forth frogs in swarms"

144. וְתָא חֲזֵי, פַּרְעֹה הֲוָה שׁוּלְטָנֵיהּ בְּמַיָּא, דִּכְתִיב הַתַּנִּים הַגָּדוֹל הָרוֹבֵץ בְּתוֹךְ יְאוֹרָיו, בג"כ אִתְהַפַּךְ נַהֲרֵיהּ בְּדָמָא בְּקַדְמֵיתָא. לְבָתַר צְפַרְדְּעִים דְּמְשַׁמְּטֵי לוֹן בְּקָלִין טְסִירִין מְקַרְקְרִין בְּגוֹ מֵעַיְיהוּ, וְנָפְקֵי מִגּוֹ יְאוֹרָא, וְסַלְקֵי בְּיַבֶּשְׁתָּא וְרָאמִין קָלִין בְּכָל סִטְרִין, עַד דְּאִינּוּן נַפְלִין כְּמֵתִין בְּגוֹ בֵּיתָא.

144. Come and see, Pharaoh ruled with THE POWER OF water, as written: "The great crocodile that couches in the midst of his streams" (Yechezkel 29:3). Therefore, first his river was turned into blood. Afterward, frogs CAME OUT OF IT that plagued EGYPT with sounds that shook within their bowels. They came out of the River and onto the ground with high pitched voices in all directions until the Egyptians fell as if dead in their homes.

145. וְרָזָא דְּמִלָּה, כָּל אִינּוּן עֶשֶׂר אָתִין דְּעָבֵד קוּדְשָׁא בְּרִיךְ הוּא, כֻּלְּהוּ הֲווֹ מִגּוֹ יָדָא תַּקִּיפָא, וְהַהוּא יָדָא אִתְתַּקַּף עַל אִינּוּן דַּרְגִּין כּוּלְּהוּ שֻׁלְטָנוּתָא דִּלְהוֹן, בְּגִין לְבַלְבְּלָא דַּעְתַּיְיהוּ, וְלָא הֲווֹ יַדְעֵי לְמֶעְבַּד מִידִי. תָּא חֲזֵי, כָּל אִינּוּן דַּרְגִּין דִּלְהוֹן, כֵּיוָן דְּנַפְקֵי לְמֶעְבַּד מִידִי, דְּאִתְחֲזֵי לְכֹלָּא לָא יַכְלִין לְמֶעְבַּד מִידִי. בְּגִין הַהוּא יָדָא תַּקִּיפָא דְּשַׁרְיָא עֲלַיְיהוּ.

145. And the secret of the matter is that all the ten signs the Holy One, blessed be He, performed originated from the strong hand, WHICH IS GVURAH, and this hand overpowered all the levels of their dominion in order to confuse them. They did not know what to do TO BE SAVED. COME AND SEE, When the grades tried to do something, it became apparent to all that they could do nothing TO BE SAVED FROM THE PLAGUES because of the strong hand that rested upon them.

146. וְשָׁרַץ הַיְאֹר צְפַרְדְּעִים וְעָלוּ וּבָאוּ בְּבֵיתֶךָ. ר' שִׁמְעוֹן פָּתַח וְאָמַר, קוֹל בְּרָמָה נִשְׁמָע נְהִי בְּכִי תַמְרוּרִים רָחֵל מְבַכָּה עַל בָּנֶיהָ וְגוֹ'. תָּא חֲזֵי, הַאי קְרָא אוּקְמוּהָ בְּכַמָּה אַתְרֵי. וְהַאי קְרָא קַשְׁיָא, רָחֵל מְבַכָּה עַל

בָּנֶיהָ, בְּנָהָא דְרָחֵל יוֹסֵף וּבִנְיָמִין הֲווֹ וְלָא יַתִּיר, וְלֵאָה שִׁית שְׁבָטִין הֲווֹ
דִילָהּ, אֲמַאי בָּכַת רָחֵל וְלָא לֵאָה.

146. "And the River shall bring forth frogs in swarms, and these will go up and come into your house" (Shemot 7:28). Rabbi Shimon opened the discussion saying, "A voice was heard in Ramah, lamentation, and bitter weeping; Rachel weeping for her children..." (Yirmeyah 31:14). Come and see: This passage has been explained in many places. But this passage is difficult, for it says, "Rachel weeping for her children," yet only Joseph and Benjamin were the children of Rachel and no more, while Leah had her six tribes, so why did Rachel weep and not Leah?

147. אֶלָּא הָכִי אָמְרוּ כְּתִיב. וְעֵינֵי לֵאָה רַכּוֹת. אֲמַאי רַכּוֹת. בְּגִין דְּכָל
יוֹמָא נַפְקַת לְפָרָשַׁת אָרְחִין, וְשָׁאֲלַת עַל עֵשָׂו, וַהֲווֹ אַמְרִין לָהּ עוֹבָדוֹי
דְּהַהוּא רָשָׁע, וְדָחִילַת לְמִנְפַּל בְּגוֹ עַדְבֵיהּ, וַהֲוַת בָּכַת כָּל יוֹמָא, עַד
דְּאִתְרְכִיכוּ עֵינָהָא.

147. HE ANSWERS, But it has been said, it is written: "And Leah's eyes were weak" (Beresheet 29:17). Why were they weak? Because everyday she would go out to the crossroads and ask about Esau. They would tell her about the actions of that wicked man, and she feared she would fall into his lot, so she wept daily until her eyes became weak.

148. וְקוּדְשָׁא בְּרִיךְ הוּא אָמַר, אַנְתְּ בָּכַת בְּגִין הַהוּא צַדִּיקָא, דְּלָא
תֶּהֱוֵי בְּעַדְבֵיהּ דְּהַהוּא רָשָׁע. חַיָּיךְ, אֲחָתָךְ תָּקוּם בְּפָרָשַׁת אָרְחִין, וְתִבְכֵּי
עַל גָּלוּתְהוֹן דְּיִשְׂרָאֵל, וְאַתְּ תָּקוּם לְגוֹ וְלָא תִּבְכֵּי עֲלַיְיהוּ וְרָחֵל אִיהִי
בָּכַת עַל גָּלוּתְהוֹן דְּיִשְׂרָאֵל.

148. The Holy One, blessed be He, said, You are weeping to merit that righteous man, Jacob, and not be the lot of that wicked man. Upon your life, your sister will rise at the crossroads and weep over the exile of Yisrael. But you will be inside, NAMELY IN THE CAVE OF MACHPELAH, and will not weep over them. Rachel will weep over the exile of Yisrael.

149. אֲבָל הַאי קְרָא, אִיהוּ עַל מַה דְּאַמְרָן. אֲבָל רָזָא דְמִלָּה, דְּרָחֵל

וְלָאָה תְּרֵי עָלְמִין נִינְהוּ. חַד עָלְמָא דְּאִתְכַּסְיָא, וְחַד עָלְמָא דְּאִתְגַּלְיָא.
וע״ד, דָּא אִתְקַבְּרַת וְאִתְחַפְיַאת לְגוֹ בִּמְעַרְתָּא וְאִתְכַּסְיַאת. וְדָא קַיְּימָא
בְּפָרָשַׁת אָרְחִין בְּאִתְגַּלְיָא. וְכֹלָּא כְּגַוְונָא עִלָּאָה. וּבְגִין כָּךְ לָא עָאִיל לָהּ
יַעֲקֹב בִּמְעַרְתָּא, וְלָא בַּאֲתָר אַחֲרָא, דְּהָא כְּתִיב בְּעוֹד כִּבְרַת אֶרֶץ לָבוֹא
אֶפְרָתָה, וְלָא עָאִיל לָהּ לְמָתָא. בְּגִין דַּהֲוָה יָדַע דְּאַתְרָהּ הֲוָה בְּאַתְרָא
דְּאִתְגַּלְיָא.

149. However, this passage really refers to what we said, MEANING THAT ACCORDING TO THE LITERAL MEANING IT IS INTERPRETED THIS WAY, but the secret meaning of the matter is that Rachel and Leah are two worlds. THE NUKVA FROM THE CHEST UP OF ZEIR ANPIN IS CALLED LEAH, AND THE NUKVA THAT IS FROM THE CHEST DOWN OF ZEIR ANPIN IS CALLED RACHEL. One is the world of concealment, NAMELY LEAH, and one is the world of revelation, NAMELY RACHEL. Therefore, the one, LEAH, was buried and concealed within the cave and was covered, while the other, RACHEL, remains at the crossroads, FOR SHE WAS BURIED ON THE WAY TO EFRAT, in the open. And everything is in the likeness of above. Therefore, Jacob did not bring RACHEL into the cave or to any other place, as it is written: "yet there was but a little way to come to Efrat" (Beresheet 48:7). He did not bring her to the city, because he knew that her place was in an open spot.

150. תָּא חֲזֵי, כְּנֶסֶת יִשְׂרָאֵל הָכִי אִקְרֵי, רָחֵל. כְּמָה דְאַתְּ אָמַר, וּכְרָחֵל
לִפְנֵי גּוֹזְזֶיהָ נֶאֱלָמָה. אֲמַאי נֶאֱלָמָה. דְּכַד שַׁלְטִין שְׁאָר עַמִּין, קָלָא
אִתְפְּסַק מִינָהּ, וְהִיא אִתְאַלְּמַת.

150. Come and see, the Congregation of Yisrael, WHICH IS MALCHUT, is called Rachel, as written: "And as a sheep (Heb. rachel) before her shearers is dumb" (Yeshayah 53:7). Why is she dumb? IT IS because her voice, WHICH IS ZEIR ANPIN, is stopped when other nations rule, and she becomes dumb.

151. וְדָא הוּא דִּכְתִיב, קוֹל בְּרָמָה נִשְׁמָע נְהִי בְּכִי תַמְרוּרִים. קוֹל
בְּרָמָה נִשְׁמָע דָּא יְרוּשָׁלַיִם לְעֵילָא. רָחֵל מְבַכָּה עַל בָּנֶיהָ, כָּל זִמְנָא

דְּיִשְׂרָאֵל אִינּוּן בְּגָלוּתָא, אִיהִי מְבַכָּה עֲלַיְיהוּ דְּאִיהִי אִימָּא דִּלְהוֹן.
מֵאֲנָה לְהִנָּחֵם עַל בָּנֶיהָ. מ״ט. כִּי אֵינֶנּוּ. כִּי אֵינָם מִבָּעֵי לֵיהּ. אֶלָּא,
בְּגִין דְּבַעְלָהּ דְּאִיהוּ קוֹל, אִסְתַּלָּק מִינָהּ, וְלָא אִתְחַבָּר בַּהֲדָהּ.

151. This is the meaning of: "A voice was heard in Ramah, lamentation, and bitter weeping..." "A voice was heard in Ramah" refers to celestial Jerusalem, NAMELY BINAH. "Rachel weeping for her children": As long as Yisrael are in exile, she weeps for them because she is their mother. "She refused to be comforted for her children." What is the reason? "Because he is not." HE ASKS, It should have said, 'Because they are not', AND ANSWERS it is because her husband, WHO IS ZEIR ANPIN called voice, is gone from her and is not joined to her.

152. וְתָא חֲזֵי, לָאו שַׁעֲתָא חֲדָא, אִיהִי דְּבָכַת עֲלַיְיהוּ דְּיִשְׂרָאֵל, אֶלָּא
בְּכָל זִמְנָא וְזִמְנָא דְּאִינּוּן בְּגָלוּתָא. וּבְגִינֵי כַּךְ, קוּדְשָׁא בְּרִיךְ הוּא גָּרַם
לוֹן קָלָא לְמִצְרָאֵי, דִּכְתִּיב וְהָיְתָה צְעָקָה גְדוֹלָה בְּכָל אֶרֶץ מִצְרַיִם אֲשֶׁר
כָּמוֹהוּ לֹא נִהְיָתָה וְגוֹ'. וְזַמִּין לוֹן קָלִין אַחֲרָנִין, בְּאִינּוּן עוּרְדְּעָנִין,
דְּרָמָאן קָלִין בְּמֵעַיְיהוּ, וַהֲווֹ נָפְלֵי בְּשׁוּקֵי כְּמֵתִים.

152. Come and see: She did not just weep over Yisrael just once, but rather every moment they were in exile. For the reason THEY BLEMISHED THE VOICE, WHICH WAS GONE FROM RACHEL, the Holy One, blessed be He, brought about a voice to the Egyptians TO PUNISH THEM, as written: "And there shall be a great cry throughout all the land of Egypt, such as there was none like it..." (Shemot 11:6). He also arranged for them other voices in these frogs that raised their voices in their intestines, so they fell dead in the marketplaces.

153. וַתַּעַל הַצְפַרְדֵּעַ, חֲדָא הֲוַת, וְאוֹלִידַת, וְאִתְמַלְיַית אַרְעָא מִינַיְיהוּ.
וַהֲווֹ כֻּלְּהוּ מַסְרִין גַּרְמַיְיהוּ לְאֶשָּׁא, דִּכְתִּיב וּבְתַנּוּרֶיךָ וּבְמִשְׁאֲרוֹתֶיךָ,
וּמַאי הֲווֹ אָמְרוּ. בָּאנוּ בְּאֵשׁ וּבַמַּיִם וַתּוֹצִיאֵנוּ לָרְוָיָה. וְאִי תֵּימָא, אִי
הָכִי, מַאי אִכְפַּת לְהוּ לְמִצְרָאֵי, דְּעָאלִין לְאֶשָּׁא כָּל אִינּוּן עוּרְדְּעָנִין.
אֶלָּא, כֻּלְּהוּ עָאלִין לְאֶשָּׁא, וְאַזְלִין בְּתַנּוּרָא וְלָא מֵתִים. וְאִינּוּן דְּמֵתִים
מַאי קָא עַבְדֵי, נָהֲמָא הֲוָה בְּתַנּוּרָא, וְעָאלִין בְּגוֹ נָהֲמָא, וּמִתְבַּקְעִין,

וְנַפְקֵי מִנַּיְיהוּ אַחֲרָנִין, וְאִשְׁתְּאָבִין בְּנַהֲמָא. אָתוּ לְמֵיכַל מִינָה, הַהוּא
פִּתָּא אִתְהַדָּר עוּרְדְּעָנַיָּא בִּמְעַיְיהוּ, וְרַקְדָן, וְרָמָאן קָלִין, עַד דַּהֲווֹ
מֵתִים. וְדָא קַשְׁיָא לוֹן מִכֹּלָּא. תָּא חֲזֵי, כְּתִיב וְשָׁרַץ הַיְאוֹר צְפַרְדְּעִים
וְעָלוּ וּבָאוּ בְּבֵיתֶךָ וּבַחֲדַר מִשְׁכָּבְךָ וְעַל מִטָּתֶךָ. פַּרְעֹה אִיהוּ אַלְקֵי
קַדְמָאָה מִכֻּלְּהוּ, וְיַתִּיר מִכֻּלְּהוּ. לֶהֱוֵי שְׁמֵיהּ דִּי אֱלָהָא מְבָרַךְ מִן עָלְמָא
וְעַד עָלְמָא, דְּהוּא פָּקִיד עוֹבָדִין דִּבְנֵי נָשָׁא, בְּכָל מַה דְּעַבְדֵי.

153. "And the frog came up" (Shemot 8:2). IT SHOULD HAVE SAID 'FROGS' IN THE PLURAL. HE ANSWERS, It was one frog, but it bred and the land became filled with them. And they all gave themselves over to the fire, as written: "And into your ovens, and into your kneading troughs" (Shemot 7:28). What did they say: "We went through fire and through water; but You did bring us out into abundance" (Tehilim 66:12). And if you ask, how does this concern the Egyptians that all these frogs went into the fire? HE ANSWERS, they all came into the fire and went into the ovens yet did not die. Those that did die, what did they do? There was bread in the oven, and they came into the bread and burst, and others came out of them and were swallowed in the bread. And when they wanted to eat of the bread, the bread in their bowels turned back into frogs that danced and raised their voices until THE EGYPTIANS died. This PLAGUE was harder on them than all the others. Come and see, it is written: "And the River shall bring forth frogs in swarms, and these will go up and come into your house, and on your bedchamber, and upon your bed...AND THE FROGS SHALL COME UP BOTH ON (LIT. 'IN') YOU, AND ON (IN) YOUR PEOPLE, AND ON (IN) ALL YOUR SERVANTS" (Shemot 7:28-29). SO THEY CAME INSIDE THEIR BODIES. Pharaoh was smitten first and more than everyone else, FOR IT SAYS, "ON YOU, AND ON YOUR PEOPLE, AND ON ALL YOUR SERVANTS." May the name of Hashem be blessed from everlasting to everlasting, for He examines the actions of people in everything they do.

154. כְּתִיב וַיִּרְאוּ אֹתָהּ שָׂרֵי פַרְעֹה וַיְהַלְלוּ אֹתָהּ אֶל פַּרְעֹה וַתֻּקַּח
הָאִשָּׁה בֵּית פַּרְעֹה. הַאי קְרָא לִדְרְשָׁא הוּא דְּאָתָא. תְּלַת פַּרְעֹה הָכָא.
חַד, בְּהַהוּא זִמְנָא. וְחַד, בְּיוֹמוֹי דְּיוֹסֵף. וְחַד, בְּיוֹמוֹי דְּמֹשֶׁה דְּאַלְקֵי
בְּקוֹלְפוֹי.

154. It is written: "And the princes also of Pharaoh saw her, and commended her before Pharaoh; and the woman was taken into the house of Pharaoh" (Beresheet 12:15). This passage is to be interpreted as Pharaoh is mentioned three times. One Pharaoh refers to Pharaoh of that time, one ALLUDES to Pharaoh during the time of Joseph, and one ALLUDES to Pharaoh in the days of Moses, who was smitten with his rod.

155. פַּרְעֹה קַדְמָאָה, בְּשַׁעֲתָא דְּאִתְנְסִיבַת שָׂרָה לְגַבֵּיה, רָמַז לְאוּמָנִין, וְצִיְּירוּ הַהוּא דְּיוּקְנָא בְּאַדְרֵיה, עַל עַרְסֵיה בְּכוֹתָלָא, לָא נָח דַּעְתֵּיה, עַד דְּעָבְדוּ דְּיוּקְנָא דְּשָׂרָה בִּנְסִירוּ, וְכַד סָלִיק לְעַרְסֵיה, סָלִיק לָה עִמֵּיה. כָּל מַלְכָּא דְּאָתָא אֲבַתְרֵיה, הֲוָה חָמֵי הַהוּא דְּיוּקְנָא מְצַיְּירָא צִיּוּרָא, וְהֲווֹ עָאלִין קַמֵּיה בְּדִיחִין, כַּד סָלִיק לְעַרְסֵיה הֲוָה אִתְהֲנֵי בְּהַהוּא צִיּוּר. בְּגִין כָּךְ, מַלְכָּא אַלְקֵי הָכָא יַתִּיר מִכֹּלָּא. הַיְינוּ דִכְתִּיב, וּבַחֲדַר מִשְׁכָּבְךָ וְעַל מִטָּתֶךָ. וּלְבָתַר, וּבְבֵית עֲבָדֶיךָ וּבְעַמֶּךָ. וּבְכֻלְּהוּ לָא כְּתִיב עַל מִטָּתָם, אֶלָּא לֵיה בִּלְחוֹדֵיה.

155. The first Pharaoh, when Sarah was taken to him, hinted to his artists and they drew her picture in his room on the wall over his bed. He had no peace until they made a picture of Sarah on a panel and when he entered his bed, he brought the panel with him. Every king who succeeded him saw the painted image, and jesters came before him, so when he got into his bed he enjoyed that picture. Therefore the king was smitten here more than everyone else. This is the meaning of: "And into your bedchamber, and on your bed," and afterwards "and into the house of your servants, and on your people." The expression "on your bed," appears in relation to none except him alone.

156. ר' אַבָּא פָּתַח, כָּל הַנְּחָלִים הוֹלְכִים אֶל הַיָּם וְהַיָּם אֵינֶנּוּ מָלֵא אֶל מָקוֹם שֶׁהַנְּחָלִים הוֹלְכִים שָׁם הֵם שָׁבִים לָלָכֶת. הַאי קְרָא אִתְּמַר, וְאָמְרֵי לֵיה חַבְרַיָּיא. אֲבָל תָּא חֲזֵי, כַּד אִינּוּן נָחֲלִין עָאלִין לְגוֹ יַמָּא, וְיַמָּא נָקִיט לוֹן, וְשָׁאִיב לוֹן בְּגַוֵּיה, בְּגִין דְּקָפְאָן מַיָּא בְּגוֹ יַמָּא, וְהַהוּא גְּלִידִי שָׁאִיב כָּל מַיָּא דְּעָאלִין בֵּיה, וּלְבָתַר נָפְקִין מַיָּא בְּתוּקְפָּא דְּדָרוֹם, וְאַשְׁקֵי יַת כָּל חֵיוַת בָּרָא, כמד"א יַשְׁקוּ כָּל חַיְתוֹ שָׂדָי.

156. Rabbi Aba opened the discussion saying, "All the rivers run into the sea, yet the sea is not full. To the place where the rivers flow, thither they return" (Kohelet 1:7). This passage is explained and the sages have spoke of it. Yet come and see, when these rivers, WHICH ARE THE LIGHTS OF ZEIR ANPIN, run to the sea, WHICH IS MALCHUT, the sea receives them and absorbs them in itself because the water freezes in the sea, and the ice draws to itself all the water that flows to it. Afterwards, the water emerges with the power of the south, NAMELY CHASSADIM ON THE RIGHT SIDE, and waters all the wild animals, as written: "they give drink to every wild beast" (Tehilim, 104:11).

157. וְתָא חֲזֵי, יַמָּא דְקָפָא שָׁאִיב כָּל מַיָּא, וְאִשְׁתְּרֵי בְּתוּקְפָּא דְדָרוֹם, כְּמָה דְּאִתְּמַר, וּבְגִין כָּךְ אֵינֶנּוּ מָלֵא, וְאִתְּמַר.

157. Come and see, the frozen sea draws in all the water and melts by the power of the south, as we have learned. This is why it "is not full." This has already been explained

158. וְהָא אִתְעָרוּ בֵּיהּ חַבְרַיָּיא. אֶל מָקוֹם שֶׁהַנְּחָלִים הוֹלְכִים שָׁם הֵם שָׁבִים לָלֶכֶת. מַאי טַעֲמָא הֵם שָׁבִים. בְּגִין דְּהַהוּא נָהָר דְּנָגִיד וְנָפִיק מֵעֵדֶן לָא פָּסִיק לְעָלְמִין, וְהוּא אַפִּיק תָּדִיר מַיָּא לְיַמָּא, וְעַל דָּא, מַיִין שָׁבִין לָלֶכֶת, וְתָבִין, וְאַזְלִין וְתָבִין, וְלָא פָּסְקִין לְעָלְמִין. וְכַד אִיהוּ תָּב לָלֶכֶת, בְּגִין לְמֶהַךְ לְאַשְׁקָאָה לְכֹלָּא, וְאָתֵי רוּחַ צָפוֹן וְקָפֵי מַיָּא, וְרוּחָא דְּדָרוֹם דְּאִיהוּ חֲמִימָא, שָׁרֵי לוֹן לְמֶהַךְ לְכָל סְטָר. וְעַל דָּא, הַאי יַמָּא יָתִיב בֵּין תְּרֵי סִטְרֵי אִלֵּין, וּבְגִינַיְיהוּ קַיְימָא, וְאַרְבִּין אַזְלִין וְנַטְלִין לְכָל סְטָר.

158. Here, the friends remarked ABOUT THE PASSAGE: "To the place where the rivers flow, thither they return." Wherefore do they return? HE ANSWERS, Because the river that flows and comes out of Eden, WHICH IS YESOD OF ZEIR ANPIN, never interrupts its flow FROM MALCHUT, and always supplies water to the sea. Therefore, the waters return, flow and again return, never stopping. When it again flows to water everything, NAMELY TO DRAW CHOCHMAH THAT SUBDUES ALL THE KLIPOT, a northern wind arrives and the water freezes. And the southern wind, which is warm, thaws it so it can flow in every direction. Therefore, that sea abides between the two sides, NORTH AND SOUTH, and through them THE SEA

perseveres. Ships, WHICH ARE THE GRADES THAT RECEIVE FROM MALCHUT, travel in it in every direction, NAMELY, AFTER ALL THE DIRECTIONS-SOUTH, NORTH, EAST AND WEST-ARE INCLUDED WITHIN EACH OTHER.

159. תָּא חֲזֵי, כַּד מַלְכָּא, אָתֵי לְעַרְסֵיה, בְּשַׁעֲתָא דְּאִתְפְּלִיג לֵילְיָא, רוּחָא דְּצָפוֹן אִתְּעַר, דְּאִיהוּ אִתְּעַר חֲבִיבוּתָא לְגַבֵּי מַטְרוֹנִיתָא, דְּאִלְמָלֵא אִתְעָרוּתָא דְּצָפוֹן, לָא אִתְחַבַּר מַלְכָּא בַּהֲדָהּ, בְּגִין דְּצָפוֹן שָׁארֵי חֲבִיבוּתָא, כְּמָה דְּאִתְּמַר, שְׂמֹאלוֹ תַּחַת לְרֹאשִׁי. וְדָרוֹם חָבִיק בִּרְחִימוּ דִּכְתִיב וִימִינוֹ תְּחַבְּקֵנִי, כְּדֵין כַּמָּה בְּדִיחִין מִתְעָרִין שִׁירָתָא, עַד דְּאָתֵי צַפְרָא, דִּכְתִיב, בְּרָן יַחַד כּוֹכְבֵי בֹקֶר וַיָּרִיעוּ כָּל בְּנֵי אֱלֹהִים.

159. Come and see: when the King, WHO IS ZEIR ANPIN, comes to His bed, WHICH IS MALCHUT, at midnight, the northern wind awakens, WHICH IS THE LEFT SIDE, which arouses love towards the Queen, NAMELY TO MALCHUT. Without the stimulation of the north, the King would not join with her, because love starts at the north, as is said, "His left hand is under my head" (Shir Hashirim 2:6). The south, WHICH IS THE RIGHT COLUMN, embraces with love, as written: "And his right hand embraces me" (Ibid.). Then many jesters call forth songs until the morning comes, as written: "When the morning stars sang together and all the sons of Elohim shouted for joy" (Iyov 38:7).

160. וְכַד אָתֵי צַפְרָא, כֻּלְּהוּ עִלָּאֵי וְתַתָּאֵי אַמְרֵי שִׁירָתָא, וְיִשְׂרָאֵל כְּגַוְונָא דָּא לְתַתָּא, דִּכְתִיב, הַמַּזְכִּירִים אֶת יְיָ' אַל דֳּמִי לָכֶם. אַל דֳּמִי לָכֶם לְתַתָּא דַּיְיקָא.

160. When morning comes, all the upper and lower beings recite songs. BECAUSE AT NIGHT, ONLY THE ANGELS THAT ARE DRAWN FROM THE LEFT COLUMN RECITE POETRY, BUT IN THE MORNING THEY ALL RECITE SONGS, MEANING EVEN THOSE THAT ARE DRAWN FROM THE RIGHT. THEN ALL THE COLUMNS ARE COMBINED ONE WITH THE OTHER UNDER THE DOMINION OF THE RIGHT, and similarly YISRAEL RECITE POEMS below, as written: "You that make mention of Hashem, take no rest" (Yeshayah 62:6). THIS IS ADDRESSED specifically to the lower beings,

NAMELY TO YISRAEL.

161. כַּד אִתְפְּלִיג לֵילְיָא, אִינּוּן דְּתִיאוּבְתָּא דִּילְהוֹן לְאַדְכְּרָא תָּדִיר לְקוּדְשָׁא בְּרִיךְ הוּא, לָא יָהֲבֵי שְׁכִיבוּ לְלִבָּא, וְקַיְימִין לְאַדְכְּרָא לֵיהּ לְקוּדְשָׁא בְּרִיךְ הוּא. כַּד סָלִיק צַפְרָא מַקְדִּימִין לְבֵי כְּנִישְׁתָּא, וּמְשַׁבְּחָאן לֵיהּ לְקוּדְשָׁא בְּרִיךְ הוּא. וְכֵן בָּתַר פַּלְגּוּת יוֹמָא. וְכֵן בְּלֵילְיָא, כַּד אִתְחֲשָׁךְ וְאִתְדְּבַק לֵילְיָא בַּחֲשׁוֹכָא, וּבַת שִׁמְשָׁא. עַל אִלֵּין כְּתִיב הַמַּזְכִּירִים אֶת יְיָ׳ אַל דֳּמִי לָכֶם. וְדָא עַמָּא קַדִּישָׁא דְּיִשְׂרָאֵל.

161. At midnight, those who desire to constantly mention the Holy One, blessed be He, do not allow their hearts to be silent and rise FROM THEIR BEDS to make mention of the Holy One, blessed be He. With the light of morning, they hasten to the synagogue to praise the Holy One, blessed be He, and again after midday, MEANING AT MINCHAH (THE AFTERNOON PRAYER), and also at night, when darkness falls, and night is enveloped in darkness and the sun has rest. About these is written: "You that make mention of Hashem, take no rest." This refers to Yisrael, the holy nation.

162. וְעַל דָּא, אַדְכַּר לוֹן קוּדְשָׁא בְּרִיךְ הוּא בְּמִצְרַיִם, וְסָלִיק עַל פַּרְעֹה, אִלֵּין דְּלָא מִשְׁתַּכְּחֵי יְמָמָא וְלֵילְיָא, וּמַאן אִינּוּן. אוּרְדְּעָנַיָּא, דְּקָלְהוֹן לָא מִשְׁתַּכַּךְ תָּדִיר, בְּגִין דְּאִתְתְּקַף בְּעַמָּא קַדִּישָׁא, דְּלָא מִשְׁתַּכְּחֵי יְמָמָא וְלֵילֵי, לְשַׁבְּחָא לֵיהּ לְקוּדְשָׁא בְּרִיךְ הוּא. וְלָא הֲוָה ב״נ בְּמִצְרַיִם, דְּיָכִיל לְמִשְׁתָּעֵי בַּהֲדֵי הֲדָדֵי. וּמִנַּיְיהוּ אִתְחַבְּלַת אַרְעָא. וּמִקָּלְהוֹן הֲווֹ יְנוֹקִין וְרַבְיָין מֵתִין.

162. The Holy One, blessed be He, remembered them for that in Egypt, and those that take no rest day or night rose against Pharaoh. And who are they? They are the frogs whose voices are never still. It is because He strengthened the holy people that are not silent day or night from praising the Holy One, blessed be He. And there was no one in Egypt who could speak with another. The land became devastated because of them, and babies and children died because of their sound.

163. וְאִי תֵּימָא הֵיךְ לָא יַכְלִין לְקַטְלָא לוֹן. אֶלָּא, אִי אָרִים בַּר נָשׁ

חוּטְרָא, אוֹ אֲבָנָא, לְקַטְלָא חֲדָא, אִתְבַּקְעַת, וְנָפְקִין שִׁית מִינָהּ, מִגּוֹ
מֵעָהָא, וְאַזְלֵי וְטַרְטָשֵׁי בְּאַרְעָא, עַד דַּהֲוֵי, מִתְמַנְּעֵ לְמִקְרַב בְּהוּ.

163. And if you ask, Why were they not able to kill THE FROGS? HE ANSWERS, For when one raised a stick or a stone to kill one, it would burst and six frogs emerged from its bowels, which went and kicked about the land so eventually they refrained from approaching them.

164. תָּא חֲזֵי, כַּמָּה נַהֲרִין, כַּמָּה יְאוֹרִין, נַפְקָא מִגּוֹ יַמָּא עִלָּאָה, כַּד אִתְמַשְׁכָן וּמִשְׁתַּרְיָן מַיָּא, וּמִתְפַּלְּגִין כַּמָּה נַחֲלִין, לְכַמָּה סִטְרִין, לְכַמָּה יְאוֹרִין, לְכַמָּה נַהֲרִין. וְחוּלָקָא דִּמְמַנָּא דְּסִטְרָא דְּמִצְרַיִם אִינּוּן מַיִין מְרַחֲשָׁן אִלֵּין, דְּלֵית לָךְ מַיִין דְּנַפְקִין מִגּוֹ יַמָּא, דְּלָא מַפְקֵי נוּנִין לְזִינִין.

164. Come and see how many rivers and how many streams emerged from the supernal sea, WHICH IS MALCHUT, at the time the water was thawed and flowed. Many rivers divide in many directions into many streams and many brooks. They belong to the minister appointed over the aspect of Egypt. These are swarming waters, for there are no waters that come from the sea, that do not bring forth fishes after their kind.

165. מַאן אִינּוּן נוּנִין. אִינּוּן שְׁלִיחָן בְּעָלְמָא, מְמַנָּן לְמֶעְבַּד רְעוּתָא דְּמָארֵיהוֹן, מְמַנָּן בְּרוּחָא דְּחָכְמְתָא. וע"ד תְּנֵינָן, אִית מַיִין מְגַדְּלִין חַכִּימִין. וְאִית מַיִין מְגַדְּלִין טִפְּשִׁין. לְפוּם אִינּוּן נַהֲרִין דְּמִתְחַלְּקִין לְכָל סִטְרִין.

165. HE ASKS, IF THE RIVERS AND STREAMS ARE HIGH LEVELS THAT ARE DRAWN FROM MALCHUT, then who are the fishes? HE ANSWERS, They are messengers in the world who are appointed to do the bidding of their Master. And they are appointed with the spirit of wisdom. Therefore we have learned, there is water that raises wise people and there is water that raises fools, according to these rivers that split to all the aspects.

166. וְהָכָא נַהֲרֵי דְּמִצְרָאֵי, מְגַדְּלִין מָארֵי דְּחָרָשִׁין, נוּנִין בְּסִיטִין, קָפִיטִין בְּעֶשֶׂר דַּרְגִּין דְּחָרָשִׁין, דִּכְתִיב, קוֹסֵם, קְסָמִים, מְעוֹנֵן, וּמְנַחֵשׁ,

וּמְכַשֵּׁף, וְחוֹבֵר חָבֶר, וְשׁוֹאֵל אוֹב, וְיִדְּעוֹנִי, וְדוֹרֵשׁ אֶל הַמֵּתִים. הָא עֶשֶׂר זִינִין דְּחָכְמְתָא דְּחָרָשַׁיָּא.

166. The rivers of Egypt raise sorcerers, WHICH ARE strong fish, bound in the ten levels of sorcery, as written: "…that uses, divinations, soothsayer, or an enchanter, or a witch, or a charmer, or a medium, or a wizard, or a necromancer" (Devarim 18:11-12). "THAT USES" IS ONE, AND "DIVINATIONS" IS TWO, SO WE HAVE THREE, AND WITH THE OTHER SEVEN THERE ARE TEN. These are ten kinds in the art of sorcery.

167. וּבְהַהוּא זִמְנָא, אוֹשִׁיט קוּדְשָׁא בְּרִיךְ הוּא אֶצְבְּעָא דִּידֵיהּ, וּבַלְבֵּל אִינּוּן נְחָלִין נַהֲרִין דְּמִצְרָאֵי, וְאִתְמְנָעוּ אִינּוּן נוּנֵי דְּחָכְמְתָא דִּילְהוֹן. חַד אִתְהַפַּךְ לְדָמָא, וְחַד דְּסָלִיקוּ נוּנֵי קָלִין, בְּלָא תּוֹעַלְתָּא, וְלָא אָתֵי עֲלַיְיהוּ רוּחָא דְּאִינּוּן חָכְמְתָן.

167. At the time OF THE EXODUS FROM EGYPT, the Holy One, blessed be He, extended His finger and mixed these streams and rivers of Egypt, WHICH ARE THE HIGH LEVELS FROM WHICH EGYPT ARE NURTURED. Their fish of wisdom were prevented FROM ISSUING TO THEM WISDOM. One reason was that it changed into blood, and another is that the fish, NAMELY THE FROGS, raised their voices, TO DRAW THE SPIRIT OF WISDOM, in vain; the spirit of their arts did not rest on them.

168. עָרוֹב: כִּי הַאי גַּוְונָא, דְּעִרְבֵּב לוֹן זִינֵי דְּחָכְמְתָא דִּילְהוֹן, וְלָא יַכְלִין לְאִתְדַבְּקָא, וְלָא עוֹד, אֶלָּא אֲפִילוּ דְּהָנֵי דְּאִשְׁתְּכָחוּ בְּאַרְעָא, מְחַבְּלָן לוֹן בְּאַרְעָא, וּמְחַבְּלָן אוֹרְחַיְיהוּ. עָרוֹב, מַאי עָרוֹב. עִרְבּוּבְיָא. כמד"א וּבֶגֶד כִּלְאַיִם. עֵרוּבִין: שָׂדְךָ לֹא תִזְרַע כִּלְאָיִם: זִינִין סַגִּיאִין בְּאַרְמוּת יְדָא.

168. The swarm of gnats (lit. 'mixture') is ALSO like that, in that He mixed the various kinds OF LEVELS of their wisdom so they could not attain them. Even those LEVELS OF THEIR WISDOM that were already available in the land were bringing destruction upon the land, NAMELY THEY BECAME DEMONS and turned their ways evil. What is mixture? HE ANSWERS, It is a medley, as written: "A garment mingled of linen and wool" (Vayikra 19:19), and: "You shall not sow your field with mingled seed" (Ibid.), WHICH MEANS TO SOW many species by throwing by hand. SIMILARLY, MIXTURE THAT IS MENTIONED HERE MEANS A MEDLEY.

169. תָּא חֲזֵי, כַּמָּה חֵילִין אִתְעָרוּ לְעֵילָּא כְּחַד, וּבַלְבֵּל לוֹן קוּדְשָׁא בְּרִיךְ הוּא כַּחֲדָא, בְּגִין לְבַלְבְּלָא חֵיילַיְיהוּ תַּקִּיפָא לְעֵילָּא. וְכָל אִינוּן גְּבוּרָן דְּעָבֵד קוּדְשָׁא בְּרִיךְ הוּא בְּמִצְרַיִם, בִּידָא חֲדָא הֲוָה, דְּאָרִים יְדֵיהּ עָלַיְיהוּ, לְעֵילָּא וְתַתָּא, וּמִתַּמָּן אִתְאֲבִידַת חָכְמְתָא דְּמִצְרַיִם, דִּכְתִּיב, וְאָבְדָה חָכְמַת חֲכָמָיו וּבִינַת נְבוֹנָיו תִּסְתַּתָּר.

169. Come and see how many powers were aroused above as one. The Holy One, blessed be He, mixed them together in order to confuse their strong powers above. All these mighty deeds that the Holy One, blessed be He, performed in Egypt were with one hand, WHICH IS THE STRONG HAND AS MENTIONED, for He raised His hand upon them above and below. Hence, the wisdom of Egypt was lost, as written: "for the wisdom of their wise men shall perish, and the understanding of their prudent men shall be hid" (Yeshayah 29:14).

170. וְתָא חֲזֵי, כְּתִיב, וְסִכְסַכְתִּי מִצְרַיִם בְּמִצְרַיִם. מִצְרַיִם לְעֵילָּא, בְּמִצְרַיִם לְתַתָּא. בְּגִין דְּאִינּוּן חֵילִין לְעֵילָּא, מְמָנָן עַל חֵילִין דִּלְתַתָּא, וְאִתְעָרְבוּ כֻּלְּהוּ. אִתְעָרְבוּ לְעֵילָּא, דְּלָא הֲווֹ מִצְרָאֵי יַכְלֵי לְאִתְקַשְּׁרָא בְּחַרְשַׁיְיהוּ, בְּאִינּוּן דּוּכְתֵּי דַּהֲווֹ מִתְקַשְּׁרֵי בְּקַדְמֵיתָא, דְּהָא אִתְבַּלְבָּלוּ. וְעַל דָּא אַיְיתֵי עָלַיְיהוּ עָרוֹב, חִיוָון דַּהֲווֹ מִתְעָרְבֵי דָּא בְּדָא.

170. Come and see: it is written: "And I will set Egypt against Egypt" (Yeshayah 19:2), MEANING THAT HE WILL INCITE Egypt of above, WHICH ARE THEIR MINISTERS, against Egypt on earth. These hosts of above, appointed over the hosts of below, were mixed; THEIR ARRAYS were confused above, and the Egyptians were not able to attain through their sorcery these places OF THEIR MINISTERS ABOVE, that they were able to attain before, because they were confused. Therefore, He brought upon them the plague of mixture, THAT IS, a mixture of animals.

171. כִּנִּים, דְּסַלְקָא עַפְרָא דְּאַרְעָא. וְתָא חֲזֵי, כָּל אִיבָּא דְּאִתְיְלִידַת

בְּאַרְעָא, מֵחֵילָא דִּלְעֵילָא מְמָנָא דְּאִזְדְּרַע עָלָה אִיהוּ, וְכֹלָּא הֲוָה כְּגַוְונָא דִּלְעֵילָא.

171. WHAT IS THE MEANING OF the lice that the dust of the land raised. Come and see: every creature that is produced on earth IS DRAWN from the power of a minister above that was sown on it, and everything is based on supernal pattern.

172. וְתָא חֲזֵי, שִׁבְעָה רְקִיעִין עָבֵד קוּדְשָׁא בְּרִיךְ הוּא, כְּגַוְונָא דָּא שִׁבְעָה אַרְעָאן. וְאִינּוּן תְּחוּמִין דְּמִתְפָּרְשָׁן בְּדוּכְתַּיְיהוּ. ז' רְקִיעִין לְעֵילָא, שִׁבְעָה תְּחוּמֵי אַרְעָא לְעֵילָא, כְּהַאי גַּוְונָא לְתַתָּא מִתְפָּרְשָׁן דַּרְגִּין, ז' רְקִיעִין, וְז' תְּחוּמֵי אַרְעָא. וְהָא אוּקְמוּהוּ חַבְרַיָּיא, בְּז' אַרְעִין כְּסוּפְטָא דָּא עַל דָּא.

172. Come and see that the Holy One, blessed be He, made seven firmaments and similarly seven lands. They are the boundaries that are explained in their place, NAMELY THAT THEY CORRESPOND TO THE SEVEN SFIROT: CHESED, GVURAH, TIFERET, NETZACH, HOD, YESOD AND MALCHUT. There are seven firmaments above and seven peripheries of the earth above. Similarly, the grades spread below, seven firmaments and seven peripheries of the earth. And the friends explained that the seven lands are like boxes one over the other.

173. וְאִינּוּן ז' תְּחוּמֵי אַרְעָא לְעֵילָא, כָּל חַד וְחַד מִתְפָּרְשָׁן לְעֶשֶׂר, וְאִינּוּן מִתְפַּלְּגָאן לְע' מְמָנָן, דִּמְמָנָן עַל שַׁבְעִין עַמִּין. וְהַהוּא אַרְעָא, תְּחוּמָא דְּכָל עַמָּא וְעַמָּא, סַחֲרָא לְאַרְעָא קַדִּישָׁא דְּיִשְׂרָאֵל. כד"א הִנֵּה מִטָּתוֹ שֶׁלִּשְׁלֹמֹה שִׁשִּׁים גִּבּוֹרִים סָבִיב לָהּ מִגִּבּוֹרֵי יִשְׂרָאֵל וַעֲשָׂרָה בְּגַוְונַיְיהוּ טְמִירִין, וְאִינּוּן ע' דְּסַחֲרָן אַרְעָא קַדִּישָׁא. וְדָא הוּא לְעֵילָא, כְּגַוְונָא דָּא לְתַתָּא.

173. These seven peripheries of the earth above, WHICH CORRESPOND TO CHESED, GVURAH, TIFERET, NETZACH, HOD, YESOD AND MALCHUT, each expands into ten, BECAUSE EACH ONE OF CHESED, GVURAH, TIFERET, NETZACH, HOD, YESOD AND MALCHUT IS COMPOSED OF TEN

SFIROT. Therefore, they divide to seventy princes who were appointed over the 70 nations, and those lands, which are the boundaries of every nation, WHICH ARE SEVENTY LANDS, surround the Holy Land of Yisrael, as written: "Behold it is his litter, that of Solomon! Sixty valiant men are round about it, of the mighty men of Yisrael" (Shir Hashirim 3:7). There are ten concealed in them, WITH WHICH THEY ARE SEVENTY, and they are the seventy that surround the Holy Land. This is above and is also so below.

174. וְתָא חֲזֵי, הַהוּא אַרְעָא, תְּחוּמָא דְּחוּלָקָא דְּמִצְרָאֵי, בְּהַהוּא זִמְנָא, אוֹשִׁיט קוּדְשָׁא בְּרִיךְ הוּא אֶצְבְּעָא דִּילֵיהּ, וְאִתְיְלִידוּ טַפְסִירִין בְּהַהוּא תְּחוּמָא, וְאִתְיַבָּשׁוּ כָּל אִינּוּן תְּחוּמִין דְּרַכִּיכוּ מַיָּא. וְכָל יְרוֹקָא דְּמַיִין דְּנַבְעִין, כְּדֵין לְתַתָּא, אִתְחֲזִיאוּ קַלְמִין מֵעַפְרָא דְּאַרְעָא.

174. Come and see that land, the boundary of the portion of Egypt. The Holy One, blessed be He, stretched out His finger at that time, and flames of fire were produced in that periphery. All these boundaries that were moist with water were dried out, as was every drop of spring water. Then, below, IN THE LAND OF EGYPT, the lice appeared from the dust of the earth.

175. וְהָא אִתְּמַר דְּאַהֲרֹן הֲוָה מָחֵי. אֲבָל בְּגִין דָּא אַהֲרֹן הֲוָה מָחֵי, לְאַחֲזָאָה דִּימִינָא דְּקוּדְשָׁא ב״ה תָּבַר לְשַׂנְאָין, כד״א, יְמִינְךָ יְיָ׳ תִּרְעַץ אוֹיֵב. כְּגַוְונָא דָּא, זַמִּין קוּדְשָׁא בְּרִיךְ הוּא לְאַיְיתָאָה עַל קַרְתָּא דְּרוֹמִי רַבְּתָא, דִּכְתִיב וְנֶהֶפְכוּ נְחָלֶיהָ לְזֶפֶת וַעֲפָרָה לְגָפְרִית. וְעַל דָּא, כָּל עֲפַר הָאָרֶץ הָיָה כִנִּים בְּכָל אֶרֶץ מִצְרָיִם.

175. HE ASKS, It says that Aaron was smiting THE DUST OF THE EARTH WITH LICE, YET YOU SAY THAT THE HOLY ONE, BLESSED BE HE, EXTENDED HIS FINGER, ETC. HE ANSWERS, For this reason, Aaron was smiting, to show that the right hand of the Holy One, blessed be He, broke the enemies, as written: "Your right hand, Hashem, has dashed the enemy in pieces" (Shemot 15:6). BECAUSE AARON IS A PRIEST, WHO IS A CHARIOT FOR THE RIGHT HAND OF THE HOLY ONE, BLESSED BE HE. The Holy One, blessed be He, is going to bring the like upon the great city of Rome, as is written: "And its streams shall be turned into pitch, and its dust into brimstone" (Yeshayah 34:9). And because HE DRIED THE WATER FROM THE DUST OF EGYPT AS MENTIONED, all the dust of the land became lice in the whole land of Egypt.

18. "And he built it seven years"

176. רְבִּי יְהוּדָה וְרִבִּי חִיָּיא, הֲווֹ אַזְלֵי בְּאוֹרְחָא. אָמַר רְבִּי חִיָּיא,
חַבְרַיָּיא כַּד אִינּוּן בְּאוֹרְחָא, בַּעְיָין לְמֵהַךְ בְּלִבָּא חַד. וְאִי אִיעָרְעוּ, אוֹ
אַזְלֵי בְּגַוְויְיהוּ חַיָּיבֵי עָלְמָא, אוֹ בְּנֵי נָשָׁא דְּלָאו אִינּוּן מֵהֵיכְלָא
דְּמַלְכָּא, בָּעוּ לְאִתְפָּרְשָׁא מִנַּיְיהוּ. מְנָא לָן. מִכָּלֵב, דִּכְתִּיב, וְעַבְדִּי כָלֵב
עֵקֶב הָיְתָה רוּחַ אַחֶרֶת עִמּוֹ וַיְמַלֵּא אַחֲרָי. מַאי רוּחַ אַחֶרֶת. דְּאִתְפְּרַשׁ
מֵאִינּוּן מְאַלְּלִין, דִּכְתִּיב, וַיַּעֲלוּ בַנֶּגֶב וַיָּבֹא עַד חֶבְרוֹן. דְּאִתְפְּרַשׁ
מֵאִינּוּן מְאַלְּלִין וְאָתָא אִיהוּ בִּלְחוֹדוֹי לְחֶבְרוֹן, לְאִשְׁתַּטְחָא עַל קִבְרֵי
אֲבָהָן.

176. Rabbi Yehuda and Rabbi Chiya were traveling on the road. Rabbi Chiya said, When they are on the road, the friends have to travel with one heart. And if it happens that either wicked of the world or people who are not of the King's palace should walk among them, they must separate from them. Whence do we know this? From Kalev, for it is written: "but My servant Kalev, because he had another spirit with him, and followed Me fully" (Bemidbar 14:24). What is "another spirit"? It is that he separated from the spies as is written: "And they ascended to the Negev and he came to Hebron" (Bemidbar 13:22). IT SHOULD HAVE SAID, 'AND THEY CAME' IN PLURAL, but he separated from the spies and he alone came to Hebron to prostrate himself on the graves of the Patriarchs. THEREFORE IT IS SAID ABOUT HIM, "AND HE CAME TO HEBRON" IN THE SINGULAR.

177. וְחֶבְרוֹן, אִתְיְהִיב לֵיהּ חוּלָק אַחֲסָנָא לְאִתַּתְקְפָא בֵּיהּ, כְּמָה דְּאַתְּ
אָמֵר, וְלוֹ אֶתֵּן אֶת הָאָרֶץ אֲשֶׁר דָּרַךְ בָּהּ. אֲמַאי יָהִיבוּ לֵיהּ חֶבְרוֹן. אִי
בְּגִין דְּאִשְׁתַּטַּח בְּקִבְרֵי אֲבָהָן לְאִשְׁתְּזָבָא מֵהַהוּא עֵיטָא דִּילְהוֹן
דְּאִשְׁתְּזִיב. לָא.

177. Hebron was given to him as a portion and inheritance to strengthen himself with, as is written: "And to him shall I give the land that he has trodden upon" (Devarim 1:36). HE ASKS, Why was Hebron given to him? If it is because he prostrated himself there on the graves of the Patriarchs to be delivered from the plans OF THE SPIES and he was delivered, it is not so.

178. אֶלָּא, רָזָא דְמִלָּה שְׁמַעְנָא. כְּגַוְונָא דָא כְּתִיב, וַיִּשְׁאַל דָוִד בַּיְיָ׳ לֵאמֹר הַאֶעֱלֶה בְּאַחַת עָרֵי יְהוּדָה וַיֹּאמֶר יְיָ׳ אֵלָיו עֲלֵה וַיֹּאמֶר דָוִד אָנָא אֶעֱלֶה וַיֹּאמֶר חֶבְרוֹנָה. הָכָא אִית לְאִסְתַּכְּלָא, כֵּיוָן דְהָא מִית שָׁאוּל, וְדָוִד בְּיוֹמֵי דְשָׁאוּל אִתְמְשַׁח לְקַבְּלָא מַלְכוּ. כֵּיוָן דְמִית שָׁאוּל אַמַּאי לָא אַמְלִיכוּ לֵיה לְדָוִד, וְלָא קַבִּיל מַלְכוּ עַל כָּל יִשְׂרָאֵל, וְאָתָא לְחֶבְרוֹן, וּמַלְכוּ קַבִּיל עַל יְהוּדָה בִּלְחוֹדוֹי שֶׁבַע שָׁנִים, וְאִתְעַכַּב תַּמָּן כָּל הָנֵי שֶׁבַע שָׁנִים. וּלְבָתַר דְמִית אִישׁ בּוֹשֶׁת, קַבִּיל מָלְכוּ עַל כָּל יִשְׂרָאֵל בִּירוּשָׁלַיִם.

178. HE ANSWERS, I heard the secret meaning of this matter IS similar to the words: "David inquired of Hashem saying, 'Shall I go up into any of the cities of Judah?' And Hashem said to him, 'Go up.' And David said, 'Where shall I go up?' And He said, 'To Hebron'" (II Shmuel 2:1). Here we have to reflect. Since Saul was already dead and David was anointed to receive the kingship even during the days of Saul, IF SO, why was David not made king if Saul had died? And why did not he receive the reign over all the children of Yisrael, BUT came to Hebron and received the reign over Judah alone for seven years, and he tarried there all those seven years. Only after the death of Ish Boshet did he receive the reign over Yisrael in Jerusalem.

179. אֶלָּא, כֹּלָּא הוּא רָזָא קַמֵּי קוּדְשָׁא בְּרִיךְ הוּא. תָּא חֲזֵי, מַלְכוּתָא קַדִּישָׁא לָא קַבִּיל מַלְכוּ שְׁלֵימָתָא, עַד דְאִתְחַבַּר בַּאֲבָהָן. וְכַד אִתְחַבַּר בְּהוּ, אִתְבְּנֵי בְּבִנְיָינָא שְׁלִימוּ, מֵעַלְמָא עִלָּאָה, וְעַלְמָא עִלָּאָה אִקְרֵי שֶׁבַע שָׁנִים, בְּגִין דְכֻלְּהוּ בֵּיה.

179. HE ANSWERS, But it is all a secret before the Holy One, blessed be He. Come and see: The Holy Malchut OF ABOVE did not receive THE LIGHT OF Malchut completely until she joined with the Patriarchs, WHO ARE CHESED, GVURAH AND TIFERET THAT ARE FROM THE CHEST UP OF ZEIR ANPIN. When she joined with them, she was built a complete edifice from the higher world, WHICH IS BINAH. And the upper world is called seven years, because all THE SEVEN SFIROT: CHESED, GVURAH, TIFERET, NETZACH, HOD, YESOD AND MALCHUT-are INCLUDED in it.

180. וְסִימָנִיךְ וַיִּבְנֵהוּ שֶׁבַע שָׁנִים, דָא עָלְמָא עִלָּאָה, וְלָא כְּתִיב וַיִּבְנֵהוּ

בְּשֶׁבַע שָׁנִים. כְּמָה דְאַתְּ אָמֵר, כִּי שֵׁשֶׁת יָמִים עָשָׂה ה' אֶת הַשָּׁמַיִם
וְאֶת הָאָרֶץ. מַאן שֵׁשֶׁת יָמִים, דָּא אַבְרָהָם. דִּכְתִּיב, אֵלֶּה תוֹלְדוֹת
הַשָּׁמַיִם וְהָאָרֶץ בְּהִבָּרְאָם בְּאַבְרָהָם. וְאַבְרָהָם שֵׁשֶׁת יָמִים אִקְרֵי. וּבְגִין
דְּאִיהוּ שֵׁשֶׁת יָמִים, אִתְבְּנֵי עָלְמָא. בְּהַהוּא גַּוְונָא וַיִּבְנֵהוּ שֶׁבַע שָׁנִים.

180. This is understood from: "And he built it seven years" (I Melachim 6:38). This is the upper world, and THEREFORE it is not written: 'In seven years' BECAUSE IT REFERS TO THE UPPER WORLD WHICH IS CALLED SEVEN YEARS, as is written: "For six days Hashem made the heavens and the earth" (Shemot 31:17). Who are the six days – namely Abraham, as written: "These are the generations of the heaven and of the earth (Heb. *behibar'am*) when they were created" (Beresheet 2:4) WHICH IS SPELLED WITH THE SAME LETTERS AS 'beAbraham' (with Abraham). Abraham is called six days, FOR HE IS CHESED OF ZEIR ANPIN, WHICH INCLUDES CHESED, GVURAH, TIFERET, NETZACH, HOD AND YESOD. The world was built with him, because he is six days. Similarly, "he built it seven years", WHICH ENCOMPASSES THE UPPER WORLD, WHICH IS BINAH, CALLED SEVEN YEARS.

181. וְתָא חֲזֵי, דָּוִד בָּעָא לְאִתְבַּנָאָה בְּמַלְכוּ שְׁלֵימָתָא לְתַתָּא, בְּגַוְונָא
דִּלְעֵילָא, וְלָא אִתְבְּנֵי, עַד דְּאָתָא וְאִתְחַבַּר בַּאֲבָהָן. וְקָאִים שֶׁבַע שָׁנִים
לְאִתְבַּנָאָה בְּגַוַוְיְיהוּ. לְבָתַר שֶׁבַע שָׁנִים, אִתְבְּנֵי בְּכֹלָּא, אִתְמַשְׁכָא
מַלְכוּתֵיהּ דִּי לָא תַּעְדֵי לְעָלְמִין. וְאִי לָאו דְּאִתְעֲבַד בְּחֶבְרוֹן לְאִתְחַבְּרָא
בְּדוּכְתֵּיהּ, לָא אִתְבְּנֵי מַלְכוּתֵיהּ לְאִתְמַשְׁכָא כַּדְקָא יָאוֹת. כְּהַאי גַּוְונָא
כָּלֵב, אִתְנְהִיר בֵּיהּ רוּחָא דְחָכְמְתָא, וְאָתָא לְחֶבְרוֹן, לְאִתְחַבְּרָא
בַּאֲבָהָן, וּלְדוּכְתֵּיהּ אָזַל, וּלְבָתַר, דּוּכְתֵּיהּ הֲוָה, וְיָרִית לֵיהּ.

181. Come and see: David wished to be built in the complete lower Malchut (kingdom), in the likeness of the upper MALCHUT. Yet he was not built until he came to join with the Patriarchs IN HEBRON. He stayed there seven years to be built among them. After seven years, he was built in everything NECESSARY and his reign was formed so that it would never be removed from him. Were he not made ready in Hebron to join his place WITH THE PATRIARCHS, his reign would not have been constructed ENABLING IT to persevere properly. Similarly, Kalev, within whom the spirit of Chochmah shone, came to Hebron to join with the Patriarchs, and to his own place did he go, BECAUSE THE ASPECT OF THE SPIRIT OF CHOCHMAH IS ACQUIRED ONLY THROUGH LINKING WITH THE PATRIARCHS, AS ALL THIS SAID. Afterwards it became his place, SINCE IT WAS GIVEN TO HIM, AS MENTIONED, and he inherited it.

19. Ways, paths, pleasantness and peace

182. רִבִּי יֵיסָא וְרִבִּי חִזְקִיָּה, הֲווֹ אַזְלֵי מִקַּפּוֹטְקִיָּא לְלוּד, וַהֲוָה עִמְהוֹן חַד יוּדָאי בְּמָטוּל דְּקַטְפִירָא דַּחֲמָרָא. עַד דַּהֲווֹ אַזְלֵי, א"ר יֵיסָא לְרִבִּי חִזְקִיָּה, אַפְתַּח פּוּמָךְ, וְאֵימָא חַד מִלָּה, מֵאִינּוּן מִלֵּי מְעַלְיָיתָא דְּאוֹרַיְיתָא, דְּאַתְּ אֲמָרְתְּ בְּכָל יוֹמָא, קָמֵי בּוּצִינָא קַדִּישָׁא.

182. Rabbi Yisa and Rabbi Chizkiyah were traveling from Cappadocia to Lod. A Jew who had a load of BIRDS CALLED Katfira was with them on a donkey. While they were traveling, Rabbi Yisa said to Rabbi Chizkiyah, Open your mouth and say something of those good words of Torah that you speak everyday before the holy luminary, RABBI SHIMON.

183. פָּתַח וְאָמַר, דְּרָכֶיהָ דַרְכֵי נֹעַם וְכָל נְתִיבוֹתֶיהָ שָׁלוֹם. דְּרָכֶיהָ דַּרְכֵי נֹעַם, אִלֵּין אוֹרְחִין דְּאוֹרַיְיתָא, דְּמַאן דְּאָזִיל בְּאוֹרְחֵי דְּאוֹרַיְיתָא, קוּדְשָׁא בְּרִיךְ הוּא, אַשְׁרֵי עֲלֵיהּ נְעִימוּתָא דִּשְׁכִינְתָּא, דְּלָא תַּעְדֵּי מִנֵּיהּ לְעָלְמִין. וְכָל נְתִיבוֹתֶיהָ שָׁלוֹם, דְּכָל שְׁבִילִין דְּאוֹרַיְיתָא, כּוּלְּהוֹן שְׁלָם. שְׁלָם לֵיהּ לְעֵילָא, שְׁלָם לֵיהּ לְתַתָּא, שְׁלָם לֵיהּ בְּעָלְמָא דֵין, שְׁלָם לֵיהּ בְּעָלְמָא דְּאָתֵי.

183. He opened the discussion saying, "Her ways are ways of pleasantness, and all her paths are peace" (Mishlei 3:17). "Her ways are ways of pleasantness" refers to roads of Torah, because whoever goes in the way of the Torah, the Holy One, blessed be He, causes the pleasantness of the Shechinah to dwell upon him to never be removed from him. "And all her paths are peace" ARE THE PATHS OF THE TORAH, because all the paths of the Torah are peace. He has peace above, peace below, he has peace in this world, peace in the World to Come.

184. אָמַר הַהוּא יוּדָאי אִיסוּרָא בְּקִיסְטְרָא, בְּהַאי קְרָא אִשְׁתְּכַח. א"ל מִנַּיִן לָךְ. אָמַר לֵיהּ, מֵאַבָּא שְׁמַעְנָא, וְאוֹלִיפְנָא הָכָא בְּהַאי קְרָא מִלָּה טָבָא.

184. The Yisrael said, There is a coin in the box, MEANING THERE IS AN INNER MEANING TO THIS PASSAGE. He said to him, How do you know this? He said to him, I heard it from my father and I learned here in this passage a good thing.

185. פָּתַח וְאָמַר, הַאי קְרָא בִּתְרֵין גְּווֹנִין אִיהִי, וּבִתְרֵין סִטְרִין. קָרֵי בֵּיהּ דְּרָכִים, וְקָרֵי בֵּיהּ נְתִיבוֹת. קָרֵי בֵּיהּ נוֹעַם, וְקָרֵי בֵּיהּ שָׁלוֹם. מַאן דְּרָכִים. וּמַאן נְתִיבוֹת. מַאן נֹעַם. וּמַאן שָׁלוֹם.

185. He opened the discussion saying, This passage has two manners and two aspects. You read in it of ways, and read of paths. You read in it of pleasantness and read of peace. What is ways and what is paths? What is pleasantness and what is peace?

186. אֶלָּא, דְּרָכֶיהָ דַּרְכֵי נֹעַם, הַיְינוּ דִכְתִיב, הַנּוֹתֵן בַּיָּם דָּרֶךְ. דְּהָא כָּל אֲתָר דְּאִקְרֵי בְּאוֹרַיְיתָא דֶּרֶךְ, הוּא אוֹרְחָא פְּתִיחָא לְכֹלָּא. כְּהַאי אוֹרְחָא דְּהוּא פָּתִיחַ לְכָל ב"נ. כַּךְ דְּרָכֶיהָ, אִלֵּין דְּרָכִים דְּאִינּוּן פְּתִיחָן מֵאֲבָהָן, דְּכָרָאן בְּיַמָּא רַבָּא, וְעָאלִין בְּגַוֵּיהּ. וְאִינּוּן אוֹרְחִין מִתְפַּתְּחִין לְכָל עִיבָר, וּלְכָל סִטְרֵי עָלְמָא.

186. HE ANSWERS, "Her ways are ways of pleasantness" resembles the words: "Who places a way in the sea" (Yeshayah 43:16), for any "way" in the Torah is a road open to all, like a way that is open to everyone. Similarly, her ways are the ways that are open by MEANS OF the Patriarchs, WHO ARE CHESED, GVURAH AND TIFERET, who carved in the great sea, WHICH IS MALCHUT, and entered it. These are the roads that open to all sides and all directions in the world.

187. וְהַאי נֹעַם, הוּא נְעִימוּ דְּנָפִיק מֵעָלְמָא דְּאָתֵי, וְנָהִיר לְכָל בּוּצִינִין, וּמִתְפָּרְשִׁין לְכָל עִיבָר, וְהַהוּא טִיבוּ, וּנְהוֹרָא דְּעָלְמָא דְּאָתֵי, דְּיַנְקִין אֲבָהָן, אִקְרֵי נֹעַם. דָּבָר אַחֵר, עָלְמָא דְּאָתֵי, אִקְרֵי נֹעַם. וְכַד אִתְּעַר עָלְמָא דְּאָתֵי, כָּל טִיבוּ, וְכָל חֵידוּ, וְכָל נְהוֹרִין, וְכָל חֵירוּ דְּעָלְמָא אִתְּעַר. וּבְגִינֵי כַּךְ, אִקְרֵי נֹעַם.

187. And this pleasantness THE VERSE SPEAKS OF is the pleasantness that emanates from the World to Come, WHICH IS BINAH, and illuminates on all

the lights, WHICH ARE MALE AND FEMALE, and they spread in every direction, NAMELY TO RIGHT AND LEFT. The Patriarchs, WHO ARE CHESED, GVURAH AND TIFERET OF ZEIR ANPIN, nourish on the goodness and the light of the World to Come that is called pleasantness. Another explanation is that the World to Come is called pleasantness because when the World to Come is roused TO BESTOW, all goodness, all joy, all the lights and all the freedom of the world are awakened. Therefore THE WORLD TO COME, WHICH IS BINAH, is called pleasantness.

188. וְעַל דָּא תָּנֵינָן, חַיָּיבִין דְּגֵיהִנָּם, בְּשַׁעֲתָא דְּעָאל שַׁבְּתָא, כֻּלְּהוּ נַיְיחִין, וְאִית לְהוּ חֵידוּ, וְנַיְיחָא בְּשַׁבְּתָא. כֵּיוָן דְּנָפִיק שַׁבְּתָא, אִית לָן לְאִתְעֲרָא חֵידוּ עִלָּאָה עֲלָנָא, דְּנִשְׁתְּזִיב מֵהַהוּא עוֹנָשָׁא דְּחַיָּיבַיָּא, דְּאִתְדָּנוּ מֵהַהִיא שַׁעֲתָא וּלְהָלְאָה. וְאִית לָן לְאִתְעֲרָא וְלֵימָא, וִיהִי נֹעַם יְיָ' אֱלֹהֵינוּ עָלֵינוּ. דָּא הוּא נֹעַם עִלָּאָה, חֵידוּ דְּכֹלָּא. וְעַל דָּא, דְּרָכֶיהָ דַרְכֵי נֹעַם וְכָל נְתִיבוֹתֶיהָ שָׁלוֹם.

188. Therefore we have learned, the wicked who are in Gehenom all have joy and rest on Shabbat, once Shabbat enters. As the end of Shabbat, we have to arouse the supernal joy over us in order to be delivered from the punishment of the wicked, who, from that moment onwards, are punished. We have to awaken, saying: "And let the pleasantness of Hashem our Elohim be upon us" (Tehilim 90:17), for this DRAWS AGAIN the supernal pleasantness, WHICH IS THE MOCHIN OF BINAH, which is general joy. Therefore, "Her ways are ways of pleasantness and all her paths are peace."

189. מַאן נְתִיבוֹתֶיהָ. אֵלֵּין אִינּוּן נְתִיבוֹת וּשְׁבִילִין, דְּנַפְקֵי מִלְּעֵילָא, וְכֻלְּהוּ נָקִיט לוֹן בְּרִית יְחִידָאִי, דְּאִיהוּ אִקְרֵי שָׁלוֹם, שְׁלָמָא דְּבֵיתָא, וְעָאִיל לוֹן לְיַמָּא רַבָּא, כַּד אִיהוּ בְּתוּקְפֵּיהּ. וּכְדֵין יָהִיב לֵיהּ שְׁלָם. הה"ד וְכָל נְתִיבוֹתֶיהָ שָׁלוֹם. אָתוּ רִבִּי יֵיסָא וְר' חִזְקִיָּה, וְנָשְׁקוּ לֵיהּ, אָמְרוּ וּמַה כָּל הָנֵי מִלִּין עִלָּאִין טְמִירִין גַּבָּךְ, וְלָא יָדַעֲנָא. אֲזְלוּ. כַּד מָטוּ חַד בֵּי חֲקָל, חָמוּ בְּעִירֵי דְּבֵי חֲקָל מֵתִין, אָמְרוּ וַדַּאי הֶבֶר דִּבְעִירֵי אִית בַּאֲתַר דָּא.

189. HE ASKS, What is "her paths"? HE ANSWERS, These are the paths and courses that emerge from above, FROM ABA AND IMA. A single covenant

called peace receives them, WHICH IS YESOD OF ZEIR ANPIN, household peace, and brings them to the great sea, WHICH IS MALCHUT, when in full strength, and thus it grants it peace. Hence it says: "And all her paths are peace." AND THIS EXPLAINS THE MEANING OF PATHS AND PEACE. Rabbi Yisa and Rabbi Chizkiyah came and kissed him. They said, All these lofty words were hidden by you, yet we were not aware of it. They went. When they reached a field and saw that the wild animals were dead, they said, most certainly there is an animal pestilence in this place.

20. "Behold, the hand of Hashem is"

190. אָמַר הַהוּא יוּדָאי, הָא דְּאֲמָרִיתוּ דְקוּדְשָׁא בְּ"ה קָטַל בְּמִצְרַיִם, כָּל אִינּוּן עָאנֵי, כָּל אִינּוּן בְּעִירֵי. תְּלַת מוֹתָנֵי הֲווֹ בִּבְעִירֵי. חַד, דֶּבֶר. וְחַד, אִינּוּן דְּקַטִיל בָּרָד. וְחַד, אִינּוּן בּוּכְרֵי דִּבְעִירֵי.

190. The Jew said, You said that the Holy One, blessed be He, had killed in Egypt all those cattle and all those sheep. There were three types of deaths among the animals: 1) Pestilence; 2) those killed by hail; and 3) the firstborn of the animals THAT DIED DURING THE PLAGUE OF THE FIRSTBORN.

191. וּמַה הֲוָה מוֹתָנָא דִּילְהוֹן. אֶלָּא, הָא, כְּתִיב בְּקַדְמֵיתָא, הִנֵּה יַד יְיָ׳ הוֹיָה בְּמִקְנָךָ אֲשֶׁר בַּשָׂדֶה, אֲמַאי בְּכֻלְּהוּ לָא כְּתִיב יַד יְיָ׳. אֶלָּא, הָכָא אִיהוּ יָדָא בַּחֲמִשָׁה אֶצְבְּעָאן. דְּהָא בְּקַדְמֵיתָא כְּתִיב, אֶצְבַּע אֱלֹהִים הִיא. וְהָכָא כֻּלְּהוּ חָמֵשׁ אֶצְבְּעָאן, וְכָל אֶצְבְּעָא וְאֶצְבְּעָא, קָטַל זִינָא חֲדָא. וַחֲמִשָׁה זִינִין הֲווֹ, דִּכְתִּיב, בַּסּוּסִים, בַּחֲמוֹרִים, בַּגְּמַלִּים, בַּבָּקָר, וּבַצֹּאן. הָא חֲמִשָׁה זִינִין, לַחֲמִשָׁה אֶצְבְּעָאן, דְּאִקְרוּן יַד. בְּגִינֵי כָּךְ, הִנֵּה יַד יְיָ׳ הוֹיָה וְגוֹ׳ דֶּבֶר כָּבֵד מְאֹד. דַּהֲווֹ מֵתִים מִגַּרְמַיְיהוּ, וְאִשְׁתְּכָחוּ מֵתִים.

191. HE ASKS, What was their type of death? HE ANSWERS, it is first written: "Behold the hand of Hashem is on your cattle which is in the field" (Shemot 9:3). Why is it that it is not written: "The hand of Hashem" of all the plagues? Here a hand with five fingers is concerned, because at first, BY THE PLAGUE OF LICE, it is written: "This is the finger of Elohim" (Shemot 8:15). Here all five fingers participate, each finger killing one species. And there were five species as written: "On the horses, on the asses, on the camels, on the oxen, and on the sheep" (Shemot 9:3). We see five kinds for the five fingers, which are considered a hand. Therefore, "Behold, the hand of Hashem...there shall be a very grievous plague." They died of themselves, for they were found dead.

192. בָּתַר דְּלָא אֲהַדְרוּ מִצְרָאֵי, אִינּוּן אַתְוָון מַמָּשׁ, אֲהַדְרוּ וְקָטִילוּ כָּל

אִינּוּן דְּאִשְׁתְּאָרוּ. וְדֶבֶר, אַהֲדָר בָּרָד. מַה בֵּין הַאי לְהַאי. אֶלָּא דָא
בְּנִיחוּתָא, וְדָא בִּתְקִיפוּ דְּרוּגְזָא. וּתְרֵין אִלֵּין, הֲווֹ בַּאֲתַר חַד, בְּחָמֵשׁ
אֶצְבְּעָאן.

192. Since Egypt did not return IN REPENTANCE, the very letters OF 'PESTILENCE (HEB. *DEVER, DALET BET RESH*)' returned and killed all those that survived, AND THE LETTERS Dalet Bet Resh turned into hail (Heb. *barad, Bet Resh Dalet*). What is the difference between them? PESTILENCE is affected quietly while HAIL with the strength of anger. Both of these were in one place, namely in five fingers.

193. תָּא חֲזֵי, דֶּבֶר אַתְוָון דַּהֲווֹ בְּנִיחוּתָא, מוֹתָנָא בְּנַיְיחָא, דַּהֲווֹ מֵתִין
מִגַּרְמַיְיהוּ. בָּרָד, דְּאִתְהַדָּרוּ אַתְוָון בִּתְקוֹף רוּגְזָא, וְקָטַל כֹּלָּא. יָתְבוּ
בְּהַהוּא חֲקַל, חָמוּ עָאנֵי דְּאַתְיָין לַאֲתַר חַד, וּמֵתִין תַּמָּן, קָם הַהוּא
יוּדָאי לְגַבֵּי הַהוּא אֲתַר, וְחָמָא תְּרֵין קַטְפִירֵי, דְּמַלְיָין אֲקוּסְטְרָא.

193. Come and see, pestilence (*Dalet Bet Resh*): These are letters that are quiet, a quiet death, for they died of themselves. There was hail (*Bet Resh Dalet*) since the letters changed to be with the strength of anger, and killed everything. They remained sitting in that field. They saw sheep coming to a certain place and die there. That Jew rose AND WENT to that place, and saw two dead birds called Katfiri full of worms AND POISON THAT CAUSED THE SHEEP TO DIE.

21. "And I will make of you a great nation"

194. פָּתַח וְאָמַר, כְּתִיב וְאֶעֶשְׂךָ לְגוֹי גָּדוֹל וַאֲבָרֶכְךָ וַאֲגַדְּלָה שְׁמֶךָ וֶהְיֵה בְּרָכָה, הַאי מִלָּה דְּרִבִּי אֶלְעָזָר, דְּאָמַר, וְאֶעֶשְׂךָ לְגוֹי גָּדוֹל, לָקֳבֵל לֶךְ לְךָ. וַאֲבָרֶכְךָ, לָקֳבֵל מֵאַרְצֶךָ. וַאֲגַדְּלָה שְׁמֶךָ, לָקֳבֵל וּמִמּוֹלַדְתְּךָ. וֶהְיֵה בְּרָכָה, לָקֳבֵל וּמִבֵּית אָבִיךָ. וְדָא לָקֳבֵל דָּא.

194. He opened the discussion saying, "And I will make of you a great nation, and I will bless you, and make your name great; and you shall be a blessing" (Beresheet 12:2). This matter is of Rabbi Elazar, who said, "And I will make of you a great nation" corresponds to THE WORDS "Get you out." "And I will bless you" corresponds to THE WORDS: "of your country," "and make your name great" corresponds to "and from your kindred." "And you shall be a blessing" corresponds to "and from your father's house" (Ibid. 1). One corresponds to the other.

195. ר׳ שִׁמְעוֹן אָמַר, רָזָא דְּחָכְמְתָא הָכָא. וְאֶעֶשְׂךָ לְגוֹי גָּדוֹל, לָקֳבֵל סְטַר יְמִינָא. וַאֲבָרֶכְךָ, לָקֳבֵל סְטַר שְׂמָאלָא. וַאֲגַדְּלָה שְׁמֶךָ, לָקֳבֵל סְטַר אֶמְצָעִיתָא. וֶהְיֵה בְּרָכָה, לָקֳבֵל סְטַר אַרְעָא דְּיִשְׂרָאֵל. וְכֹלָּא רָזָא דִּרְתִיכָא קַדִּישָׁא.

195. Rabbi Shimon said, There is a secret of wisdom here. "And I will make of you a great nation" corresponds to the right aspect, WHICH IS CHESED. "And I will bless you" corresponds to the left aspect, WHICH IS GVURAH. "And make your name great" corresponds to central aspect, WHICH IS TIFERET and "And you shall be a blessing" corresponds to the aspect of the Land of Yisrael, WHICH IS MALCHUT. This is all the secret of the Holy Chariot, BECAUSE CHESED, GVURAH AND TIFERET AND MALCHUT ARE THE FOUR LEGS OF THE CHARIOT.

196. תָּא חֲזֵי, בְּאִתְעֲרוּתָא דִּלְתַתָּא, אִתְעַר לְעֵילָּא. וְעַד לָא יִתְעַר לְתַתָּא, לָא יִתְעַר לְעֵילָּא, לְאַשְׁרָאָה עֲלֵיהּ. מַה כְּתִיב בְּאַבְרָהָם, וַיֵּצְאוּ אִתָּם מֵאוּר כַּשְׂדִּים. וַיֵּצְאוּ אִתָּם, וַיֵּצְאוּ אָתוּ מִבָּעֵי לֵיהּ. דְּהָא כְּתִיב וַיִּקַּח תֶּרַח אֶת אַבְרָם בְּנוֹ וְגו׳. מַהוּ וַיֵּצְאוּ אִתָּם. אֶלָּא, תֶּרַח וְלוֹט נָפְקוּ

עִם אַבְרָהָם וְשָׂרָה, דְּכֵיוָן דְּאִשְׁתְּזִיב אַבְרָהָם מִן נוּרָא, אִתְהַדָּר תֶּרַח
לְמֶעְבַּד רְעוּתֵיהּ. וּבְגִין כָּךְ, וַיֵּצְאוּ אִתָּם. כֵּיוָן דְּאִינּוּן אִתְעָרוּ
בְּקַדְמֵיתָא, א"ל קוּדְשָׁא בְּרִיךְ הוּא לֶךְ לְךָ.

196. Come and see, through the awakening below there is an awakening above. There will be no awakening above to dwell on one before the awakening below. It is written of Abraham: "And they went out with them from Ur of the Chaldeans" (Beresheet 11:31). HE ASKS, "They went out with them" should have been 'And they went out with him' since it says, "And Terwh took Abram his son..." (Ibid.). Why then does it say, "They went out with them"? HE ANSWERS, Rather Terah and Lot went out with Abraham and Sarah. For after Abraham was saved from the fire, Terah again reverted to doing his bidding. Therefore it is written: "They went out with them," BECAUSE TERAH AND LOT WENT OUT WITH ABRAHAM AND SARAH. And since they were awakened below first TO GO TO THE LAND OF CANAAN, IMMEDIATELY THERE WAS AN AWAKENING TOWARDS HIM ABOVE AND the Holy One, blessed be He, said to him "Get you out" (Beresheet 12:1).

197. רִבִּי שִׁמְעוֹן אָמַר, לֶךְ לְךָ. לְתִקּוּנָךְ לְגַרְמָךְ. מֵאַרְצְךָ, מֵהַהוּא
סִטְרָא דְּיִשׁוּבָא דְּאַתְּ תָּקִיל, דְּאִתְיְלִידַת בֵּיהּ. וּמִמוֹלַדְתְּךָ, מֵהַהוּא
תוֹלָדָה דִּילָךְ. וּמִבֵּית אָבִיךָ, דְּאַתְּ אַשְׁגַּח בְּשָׁרְשָׁא דִּלְהוֹן. אֶל הָאָרֶץ
אֲשֶׁר אַרְאֶךָּ, תַּמָּן אִתְגְּלֵי לָךְ, מַה דְּאַתְּ בָּעֵי, הַהוּא חֵילָא דִּמְמַנָּא עָלָהּ,
דְּאִיהוּ עָמִיק וְסָתִים. מִיָּד, וַיֵּלֶךְ אַבְרָם כַּאֲשֶׁר דִּבֶּר אֵלָיו יְיָ'. וַאֲנָן קָא
בָּעֵינָן לְמֵהַךְ מֵהָכָא לְמִנְדַּע רָזָא דְּחָכְמְתָא.

197. Rabbi Shimon said, "Get you out (or: for yourself)", namely, to better yourself; "from your land," from that aspect of habitation that you weigh, where you were born, NAMELY FROM THE RIGHT SIDE BEFORE IT WAS INCLUDED IN THE LEFT. AND THE HOLY ONE, BLESSED BE HE, TOLD HIM TO GO FROM THERE, "and from your kindred," from your own generations, NAMELY FROM THE LEFT SIDE BEFORE IT WAS INCLUDED IN THE RIGHT, FOR THE LEFT IS THE PRODUCT OF THE RIGHT. "And from your father's house" that you regard their source. AND THE HOLY ONE, BLESSED BE HE, SAID TO HIM THAT HE MUST NO LONGER HEED THEM. "To the land that I will show you," for there that which you desire will be revealed to you, namely the power that is appointed over it, which is deep and hidden. Immediately, "So Abram departed, as Hashem has spoken to him" (Ibid. 4). We wish to go from here in order to acquire the secret of wisdom. (THE END IS MISSING)

22. "But Sarai was barren"

198. רִבִּי יוֹסֵי וְרִבִּי חִיָּיא הֲווֹ אַזְלֵי בְּאוֹרְחָא. א״ר יוֹסֵי לְרִבִּי חִיָּיא, אֲמַאי אַתְּ שָׁתִיק, הָא אוֹרְחָא לָא אִתְּתְּקַן, אֶלָּא בְּמִלֵּי דְאוֹרַיְיתָא. אִתְנְגִיד רִבִּי חִיָּיא, וּבָכָה, פָּתַח וְאָמַר, וַתְּהִי שָׂרַי עֲקָרָה אֵין לָה וָלָד וַוי עַל דָּא, וַוי עַל הַהוּא זִמְנָא דְאוֹלִידַת הָגָר לְיִשְׁמָעֵאל.

198. Rabbi Yosi and Rabbi Chiya were traveling on the road. Rabbi Yosi said to Rabbi Chiya, Why are you silent? The road is not improved save with words of Torah. Rabbi Chiya sighed and wept. He opened the discussion saying, "But Sarai was barren; she had no child" (Beresheet 11:30). Woe unto this, woe unto the time that Hagar bore Ishmael.

199. א״ל רִבִּי יוֹסֵי, אֲמַאי. וְהָא אוֹלִידַת לְבָתַר, וַהֲוָה לָה בְּרָא גִּזְעָא קַדִּישָׁא. א״ל, אַתְּ חָמֵי, וַאֲנָא חֲמֵינָא, וְהָכִי שְׁמַעֲנָא מִפּוּמוֹי דר״ש מִלָּה, וּבָכֵינָא וַוי עַל הַהוּא זִמְנָא, דִּבְגִין דְּשָׂרָה אִתְעַכְּבַת, כְּתִיב, וַתֹּאמֶר שָׂרַי אֶל אַבְרָם וְגוֹ׳ בֹּא נָא אֶל שִׁפְחָתִי וְגוֹ׳. וְעַל דָּא, קַיְימָא שַׁעְתָּא לְהָגָר, לְמֵירַת לְשָׂרָה גְּבִירְתָּהּ, וַהֲוָה לָה בְּרָא מֵאַבְרָהָם.

199. Rabbi Yosi said to him, Why? SARAH gave birth after ISHMAEL WAS BORN, and had a son of a holy stock. WHY DO YOU SAY WOE? He said to him, You see, and I see, and so I heard the matter from the mouth of Rabbi Shimon, and I wept. FOR HE SAID, Woe for that time, because since Sarah was tardy, it is written: "And Sarai said to Abram...I pray you, go in to my maid" (Beresheet 16:2). Therefore, the moment was propitious for Hagar to inherit Sarah her mistress, and HAGAR bore a son from Abraham.

200. וְאַבְרָהָם אָמַר, לוּ יִשְׁמָעֵאל יִחְיֶה לְפָנֶיךָ, ואע״ג דְּקוּדְשָׁא בְּרִיךְ הוּא הֲוָה מְבַשֵּׂר לֵיהּ עַל יִצְחָק, אִתְדְּבַק אַבְרָהָם בְּיִשְׁמָעֵאל, עַד דְּקוּדְשָׁא בְּרִיךְ הוּא אֲתִיב לֵיהּ, וּלְיִשְׁמָעֵאל שְׁמַעְתִּיךָ וְגוֹ׳. לְבָתַר אִתְגְּזַר, וְעָאל בְּקַיְימָא קַדִּישָׁא, עַד לָא יִפּוּק יִצְחָק לְעָלְמָא.

200. And Abraham said, "O that Ishmael might live before you" (Beresheet 17:18). Even though the Holy One, blessed be He, gave him the news about

Isaac, Abraham cleaved to Ishmael, until the Holy One, blessed be He, answered him, "And as for Ishmael, I have heard you..." (Ibid. 20). He was later circumcised and entered the Holy Covenant before Isaac came into the world.

201. וְתָא חֲזֵי, אַרְבַּע מְאָה שְׁנִין, קַיְימָא הַהוּא מְמָנָא דִּבְנֵי יִשְׁמָעֵאל, וּבָעָא קָמֵי קוּדְשָׁא בְּרִיךְ הוּא, א"ל, מַאן דְּאִתְגְּזַר אִית לֵיהּ חוּלָקָא בִּשְׁמָךְ. א"ל אִין. א"ל וְהָא יִשְׁמָעֵאל דְּאִתְגְּזַר, אֲמַאי לֵית לֵיהּ חוּלָקָא בָּךְ כְּמוֹ יִצְחָק. א"ל, דָּא אִתְגְּזַר כַּדְקָא יֵאוֹת וּכְתִיקּוּנוֹי, וְדָא לָאו הָכִי. וְלֹא עוֹד, אֶלָּא דְּאִלֵּין מִתְדַּבְּקִין בִּי כַּדְקָא יֵאוֹת, לִתְמַנְיָא יוֹמִין וְאִלֵּין רְחִיקִין מִנִּי עַד כַּמָּה יָמִים. א"ל, וְעִם כָּל דָּא, כֵּיוָן דְּאִתְגְּזַר לָא יְהֵא לֵיהּ אֲגַר טַב בְּגִינֵיהּ.

201. Come and see, for four hundred years, the minister of the children of Ishmael stood and begged before the Holy One, blessed be He. He said to Him, Whoever is circumcised has a portion in Your name. THE HOLY ONE, BLESSED BE HE, said to him, it is so. He said to Him, Behold Ishmael who is circumcised. Why does he not have a portion in You like Isaac? He said to him, It is not so, the one was circumcised well and properly, while the other was not so. Moreover, the ones cleave to Me properly at the eighth day, while the others are distanced from me for many days. THE APPOINTED MINISTER said to Him, But still in all, since he is circumcised, would not he have a good reward for this?

202. וַוי עַל הַהוּא זִמְנָא, דְּאִתְיְלִיד יִשְׁמָעֵאל בְּעָלְמָא, וְאִתְגְּזַר. מַה עָבֵד קוּדְשָׁא בְּרִיךְ הוּא, אַרְחִיק לְהוּ לִבְנֵי יִשְׁמָעֵאל, מִדְּבֵקוּתָא דִּלְעֵילָּא, וְיָהַב לְהוּ חוּלָקָא לְתַתָּא בְּאַרְעָא קַדִּישָׁא, בְּגִין הַהוּא גְּזִירוּ דִּבְהוֹן.

202. Woe is to the time that Ishmael was born into the world and was circumcised. What did the Holy One, blessed be He, do PERTAINING TO THE COMPLAINT OF THE MINISTER OF ISHMAEL? He distanced the children of Ishmael from supernal cleaving and gave them a portion below in the Holy Land, because of their circumcision.

203. וּזְמִינִין בְּנֵי יִשְׁמָעֵאל, לְמִשְׁלָט בְּאַרְעָא קַדִּישָׁא, כַּד אִיהִי רֵיקַנְיָא
מִכֹּלָּא, זִמְנָא סַגִּי, כְּמָה דִּגְזִירוּ דִּלְהוֹן בְּרֵיקַנְיָא בְּלָא שְׁלִימוּ. וְאִינּוּן
יְעַכְּבוּן לְהוֹן לבנ"י לְאָתָבָא לְדוּכְתַּיְיהוּ, עַד דְּאִשְׁתְּלִים הַהוּא זְכוּתָא
דִּבְנֵי יִשְׁמָעֵאל.

203. The children of Ishmael are destined to rule over the Holy Land for a
long time when it is empty from anything, like their circumcision, which is
empty and imperfect. And they will prevent the children of Yisrael from
returning to their place until the reward for the merit of the children of
Ishmael reaches completion.

204. וּזְמִינִין בְּנֵי יִשְׁמָעֵאל, לְאִתְּעָרָא קְרָבִין תַּקִּיפִין בְּעָלְמָא,
וּלְאִתְכַּנְּשָׁא בְּנֵי אֱדוֹם עֲלַיְיהוּ, וְיִתְעָרוּן קְרָבָא בְּהוֹ, חַד עַל יַמָּא, וְחַד
עַל יַבֶּשְׁתָּא וְחַד סָמוּךְ לִירוּשְׁלֵים, וְיִשְׁלְטוּן אִלֵּין בְּאִלֵּין, וְאַרְעָא
קַדִּישָׁא לָא יִתְמְסַר לִבְנֵי אֱדוֹם.

204. The children of Ishmael will cause great wars in the world and the
children of Edom will gather against them, and wage war against them, one
on the sea, one on the dry land, and one near Jerusalem. And they will rule
over each other, but the Holy Land will not be given over to the children of
Edom.

205. בְּהַהוּא זִמְנָא, יִתְּעַר עַמָּא חַד מִסַּיְיפֵי עָלְמָא, עַל רוֹמִי חַיָּיבָא,
וְיִגַּח בָּהּ קְרָבָא תְּלַת יַרְחִין, וְיִתְכַּנְּשׁוּן תַּמָּן עַמְמַיָּא, וְיִפְּלוּן בִּידַיְיהוּ,
עַד דְּיִתְכַּנְּשׁוּן כָּל בְּנֵי אֱדוֹם עֲלָהּ, מִכָּל סַיְיפֵי עָלְמָא. וּכְדֵין יִתְּעַר
קוּדְשָׁא בְּרִיךְ הוּא עֲלַיְיהוּ, הה"ד כִּי זֶבַח לַיְיָ' בְּבָצְרָה וְגוֹ'. וּלְבָתַר דָּא
מַה כְּתִיב, לֶאֱחוֹז בְּכַנְפוֹת הָאָרֶץ וְגוֹ' וְיִשֵׁיצֵי לִבְנֵי יִשְׁמָעֵאל מִינָּהּ,
וְיִתְבַּר כָּל חֵילִין דִּלְעֵילָּא וְלָא יִשְׁתְּאַר חֵילָא לְעֵילָּא עַל עַמָּא דְּעָלְמָא,
אֶלָּא חֵילָא דְּיִשְׂרָאֵל בִּלְחוֹדוֹי. הה"ד, יְיָ' צִלְּךָ עַל יַד יְמִינֶךָ.

205. At that time, a nation from the end of the earth will be roused against
evil Rome and wage war against it for three months. Nations will gather
there, and will fall into their hands until all the children of Edom will gather

against it from all the corners of the world. Then the Holy One, blessed be He, will be roused against them. This is the meaning of: "For Hashem has a sacrifice in Botzrah" (Yeshayah 34:6). And afterwards, it is written: "That it might take hold of the ends of the earth…" (Iyov 38:13). He will destroy the descendants of Ishmael from the land, and break all the powers of above. There will not remain any power above over the eternal people, MEANING YISRAEL, except the power of Yisrael alone. This is the meaning of: "Hashem is your shade upon your right hand" (Tehilim 121:5).

206. בְּגִין דִּשְׁמָא קַדִּישָׁא בִּימִינָא, וְאוֹרַיְיתָא בִּימִינָא, וְעַל דָּא בִּימִינָא תַּלְיָא כֹּלָּא וְתָנֵינָן, דְּבָעֵי לְזַקְפָּא יְמִינָא עַל שְׂמָאלָא, כְּמָה דְּאוּקְמוּהָ. דִּכְתִּיב, מִימִינוֹ אֵשׁ דָּת לָמוֹ. וּבְזִמְנָא דְּאָתֵי, הוֹשִׁיעָה יְמִינְךָ וַעֲנֵנִי. וּבְהַהוּא זִמְנָא כְּתִיב, כִּי אָז אֶהְפֹּךְ אֶל עַמִּים שָׂפָה בְרוּרָה לִקְרֹא כֻלָּם בְּשֵׁם יְיָ' לְעָבְדוֹ שְׁכֶם אֶחָד. וּכְתִיב, בַּיּוֹם הַהוּא יִהְיֶה ה' אֶחָד וּשְׁמוֹ אֶחָד.

206. For the Holy Name is on the right, and the Torah is on the right. Therefore, everything stems from the right. We learned that we should raise the right over the left, as it is written: "At His right hand was a fiery law unto them" (Devarim 33:2). In the future to come, IT IS WRITTEN: "Save with Your right hand and answer me" (Tehilim 60:7). And of that time, it is written: "For then I will convert the peoples to a purer language, that they may all call upon the name of Hashem, to serve Him with one consent" (Tzefanyah 3:9), and: "On that day Hashem shall be one, and His Name One" (Zecharyah 14:9).

בָּרוּךְ יְיָ' לְעוֹלָם אָמֵן וְאָמֵן:

Blessed is Hashem forever, amen and amen.

NOTES

NOTES

NOTES

NOTES

NOTES

NOTES

NOTES

NOTES